Innovation, Evolution of Industry and Economic Growth
Volume III

The International Library of Critical Writings in Economics

Series Editor: Mark Blaug

Professor Emeritus, University of London, UK
Professor Emeritus, University of Buckingham, UK
Visiting Professor, University of Amsterdam, The Netherlands

This series is an essential reference source for students, researchers and lecturers in economics. It presents by theme a selection of the most important articles across the entire spectrum of economics. Each volume has been prepared by a leading specialist who has written an authoritative introduction to the literature included.

A full list of published and future titles in this series is printed at the end of this volume.

Wherever possible, the articles in these volumes have been reproduced as originally published using facsimile reproduction, inclusive of footnotes and pagination to facilitate ease of reference.

For a list of all Edward Elgar published titles visit our site on the World Wide Web at
http://www.e-elgar.co.uk

Innovation, Evolution of Industry and Economic Growth
Volume III

Edited by

David B. Audretsch

*Ameritech Chair of Economic Development and
Director, Institute for Development Strategies,
Indiana University, USA*

and

Steven Klepper

*Professor of Economics and Social Science,
Carnegie Mellon University, USA*

THE INTERNATIONAL LIBRARY OF CRITICAL WRITINGS IN ECONOMICS

An Elgar Reference Collection
Cheltenham, UK • Northampton, MA, USA

© David B. Audretsch and Steven Klepper 2000. For copyright of individual articles, please refer to the Acknowledgements.

Published by
Edward Elgar Publishing Limited
Glensanda House
Montpellier Parade
Cheltenham
Glos GL50 1UA
UK

Edward Elgar Publishing, Inc.
136 West Street, Suite 202
Northampton
Massachusetts 01060
USA

A catalogue record for this book
is available from the British Library

Library of Congress Cataloguing in Publication Data

Innovation, evolution of industry and economic growth / edited by David B. Audretsch
and Steven Klepper.
        — (The International library of critical writings in economics)
        1. Technological innovations—Economic aspects. 2. Industries—Size. 3. Economic
development. I. Audretsch, David B. II. Klepper, Steven. III. Series.

HC79.T4 I54654 2000
338.9—dc21   00–028822
                                                                                                              CIP

ISBN   1 84064 175 4 (3 volume set)

Printed and bound in Great Britain by MPG Books Ltd, Bodmin, Cornwall

Contents

Acknowledgements

The editors and publishers wish to thank the authors and the following publishers who have kindly given permission for the use of copyright material.

American Economic Association for articles: Richard J. Gilbert and David M.G. Newbery (1982), 'Preemptive Patenting and the Persistence of Monopoly', *American Economic Review*, **72** (3), June, 514–26; Jennifer F. Reinganum (1983), 'Uncertain Innovation and the Persistence of Monopoly', *American Economic Review*, **73** (4), September, 741–48; Richard J. Gilbert and David M.G. Newbery (1984), 'Uncertain Innovation and the Persistence of Monopoly: Comment', *American Economic Review*, **74** (1), March, 238–42; Jennifer F. Reinganum (1984), 'Uncertain Innovation and the Persistence of Monopoly: Reply', *American Economic Review*, **74** (1), March, 243–46; Richard J. Gilbert and David M.G. Newbery (1984), 'Preemptive Patenting and the Persistence of Monopoly: Reply', *American Economic Review*, **74** (1), March, 251–53; Richard E. Caves (1998), 'Industrial Organization and New Findings on the Turnover and Mobility of Firms', *Journal of Economic Literature*, **XXXVI** (4), December, 1947–82.

Cambridge University Press for excerpt: Dennis C. Mueller (1986), 'The Persistence of Profits above the Norm', and 'Profitability and Market Structure', in *Profits in the Long Run*, Chapter 2 and Chapter 4, 8–32 and notes, 50–84 and notes, references and appendix, 234–58.

Econometric Society for article: Robert E. Lucas, Jr. (1993), 'Making a Miracle', *Econometrica*, **61** (2), March, 251–72.

Elsevier Science Ltd for articles: Clayton M. Christensen and Richard S. Rosenbloom (1995), 'Explaining the Attacker's Advantage: Technological Paradigms, Organizational Dynamics, and the Value Network', *Research Policy*, **24** (2), March, 233–57; B.-Y. Aw and A.R. Hwang (1995), 'Productivity and the Export Market: A Firm-Level Analysis', *Journal of Development Economics*, **47**, 313–32; John Sutton (1996), 'Technology and Market Structure', *European Economic Review*, **40**, 511–30; Maryann P. Feldman and David B. Audretsch (1999), 'Innovation in Cities: Science-Based Diversity, Specialization and Localized Competition', *European Economic Review*, **43**, 409–29.

Harvard University Press for excerpt: Alfred D. Chandler, Jr. with the assistance of Takashi Hikino (1990), 'Scale, Scope, and Organizational Capabilities', in *Scale and Scope: The Dynamics of Industrial Capitalism*, Chapter 2, 14–46 and notes.

Kluwer Academic Publishers B.V. for article: Wesley M. Cohen and Steven Klepper (1992), 'The Tradeoff Between Firm Size and Diversity in the Pursuit of Technological Progress', *Small Business Economics*, **4** (1), March, 1–14.

MIT Press for excerpts: John Sutton (1991), 'From Theory to Measurement' and 'Econometric Evidence', in *Sunk Costs and Market Structure: Price Competition, Advertising, and the Evolution of Concentration*, Chapter 4 and Chapter 5, 83–109, 111–23 and references.

Oxford University Press for article: Richard R. Nelson (1992), 'National Innovation Systems: A Retrospective on a Study', *Industrial and Corporate Change*, **1** (2), 347–74.

Rand Corporation for article: Steven Klepper and Elizabeth Graddy (1990), 'The Evolution of New Industries and the Determinants of Market Structure', *Rand Journal of Economics*, **21** (1), Spring, 27–44.

University of Chicago Press for articles: Edward L. Glaeser, Hedi D. Kallal, José A. Scheinkman and Andrei Shleifer (1992), 'Growth in Cities', *Journal of Political Economy*, **100** (6), December, 1126–52; Glenn Ellison and Edward L. Glaeser (1997), 'Geographic Concentration in U.S. Manufacturing Industries: A Dartboard Approach', *Journal of Political Economy*, **105** (5), October, 889–927.

World Bank for article: Joseph E. Stiglitz (1996), 'Some Lessons from the East Asian Miracle', *World Bank Research Observer*, **11** (2), August, 151–77.

Every effort has been made to trace all the copyright holders but if any have been inadvertently overlooked the publishers will be pleased to make the necessary arrangement at the first opportunity.

In addition the publishers wish to thank the Library of the London School of Economics and Political Science, B&N Microfilm, London, and the Library of Indiana University at Bloomington, USA, for their assistance in obtaining these articles.

Introduction

David B. Audretsch and Steven Klepper

Some of the most compelling developments in the economic landscape of the past quarter century have greatly challenged traditional economic thinking. How do traditional models, for example, measure up to explaining phenomena such as the economic miracles that enabled Japan and Germany to rise out of the ashes of World War II, only to be besieged by slumps in the last decade of the twentieth century? How do traditional models explain the sustained growth and employment creation in the USA in the 1990s while Europe and Asia stagnated, which only a decade earlier would have been dismissed as a quixotic dream? How can traditional models account for IBM, the giant which dominated the computer industry for a quarter of a century, suddenly stumbling and giving way to two upstarts, Microsoft and Intel, that now rank among the most profitable companies in the world? More fundamentally, how can traditional models account for the precipitous decline of the leading US automobile, steel and consumer electronics firms that not long ago dominated their world markets, and for the equally impressive rise of US software and biotechnology companies?

Traditional economics has been remarkably silent on pressing questions such as these. The most obvious explanation for this reticence is the inherently static nature of the discipline. The intellectual heritage of economics is rooted in equilibrium thinking, yet the common denominator among the questions posed above is change. Traditional static analyses have proven to be more of a burden than an instrument of enlightenment in making sense of many of these important issues. The growing gap between the methods of the economics discipline and their ability to explain, understand and predict the most compelling economic events of our time is alarming. The validity of the discipline lies in its ability to make sense of real-world phenomena.

Perhaps in response to this gap, scholars in the past quarter century have begun developing alternative frameworks and methodologies for analysing economic phenomena involving change. They seek to explain how and why firms are diverse, and how firms, industries and regions change over time. They build on a rich intellectual heritage dating back to an earlier tradition represented by scholars such as Josef Schumpeter and Frank Knight.

The purpose of these volumes is to bring together the seminal contributions of this emerging new literature. At first glance, these new approaches may seem disparate in that they cover different subjects using different approaches and methodologies. However, what links this new generation of scholarship is the focus on change as a central phenomenon. Innovative activity, one of the central manifestations of change, is at the heart of much of this work. Entry, growth, survival, and the way firms and entire industries change over time are linked to innovation. The dynamic performance of regions, and even entire economies, is linked to how well the potential from innovation is tapped.

The contributions included in the volumes can be grouped based on a number of perspectives and lines of research. These perspectives span the firm, the industry, the region and the country, as well as the interactions among all of these. Our starting point is with a core theory that has been applied to each of these units of observation – the model of the life cycle.

The Product Life Cycle and Industry Evolution

One of the earliest acknowledgements that firms and entire industries may not be well described by equilibrium models comes from investigations of how new product industries evolve. Such industries commonly experience high initial rates of entry and innovation, with the number of producers rising over time. In many instances, though, entry eventually dries up and a shakeout occurs in which the number of producers declines sharply for a prolonged period despite continued growth in the industry's output. Innovation also tends to become more incremental and oriented towards improving the production process over time. Various models have been proposed to explain these patterns, which collectively have come to be known as the 'product life cycle'. We begin the volumes with various selections from the literature on the product life cycle. This provides a broad overview of the forces governing industries as they evolve from birth to maturity.

In 'Research and Development Costs as a Barrier to Entry', Dennis Mueller and John Tilton use case study evidence to reflect on the forces contributing to the product life cycle. They argue that when new products are introduced, customer wants are not well known and the returns to research and development (R&D) are uncertain. These circumstances favour small firms and many new firms enter. Over time, uncertainty abates and R&D becomes more ordered and structured, giving rise to scale economies in R&D, which favours larger firms. Incumbents also acquire tacit knowledge and competition compresses price–cost margins. This discourages entry and forces less able firms from the market, causing the number of firms to decline. Price competition also becomes more intense, and firms increasingly devote their innovative efforts to lowering the cost of production.

In the second paper of this section, 'The Life Cycle of a Competitive Industry' by Boyan Jovanovic and Glenn MacDonald, a shakeout in the number of firms is brought about by a major innovation which increases the minimum efficient scale of production. Experienced firms are more able to develop the new innovation, and firms that fail to develop it sufficiently quickly are forced out of the industry as expansion by successful innovators forces down the industry's price. The model is shown to account for the sharp shakeout that occurred in the US tyre industry and also the time paths in tyre prices, output and stock market valuations of publicly traded producers.

In 'Entry, Exit, Growth, and Innovation over the Product Life Cycle', Steven Klepper develops a model in which firm size conditions the returns to innovation to explain a number of regularities in the way new product industries evolve. Firms incur costs of growth which limit their size, but over time successful firms expand. This causes price to decline, which eventually renders entry unprofitable, and the number of firms declines as the earliest entrants with the greatest capabilities take over an increasing share of the industry's output. Firm size conditions the returns to process more than product innovation, and thus as the industry evolves firms devote an increasing share of their innovative activity to improving the production process. The decline in the number of producers also compromises industry diversity, which in turn retards the rate at which the product is improved over time. The theory also explains various cross-sectional regularities involving firm size and R&D and average cost.

In the final selection of this section, 'Technological Extinctions of Industrial Firms: An Inquiry into their Nature and Causes', Steven Klepper and Kenneth Simons examine the ability of alternative models of industry shakeouts, including the Jovanovic–MacDonald and Klepper models and a third based on the concept of a 'dominant design', to explain the technological and market evolution of four major new products that experienced sharp shakeouts: automobiles, tyres, televisions and penicillin. Their findings suggest that shake-outs are not triggered by particular technological developments but by an evolutionary process in which technological innovation contributes to a mounting dominance by early entrants in the industry.

The Start-Up of New Firms

Why are new firms started? The traditional, equilibrium-based view is that new firms to an industry, whether they be start-ups or firms diversifying from other industries, enter when incumbent firms in the industry earn supranormal profits. By expanding industry supply, entry depresses price and restores profits to their long-run equilibrium level. Thus in equilibrium-based theories entry serves as a mechanism to discipline incumbent firms. The papers in this section probe empirically this characterization of entry. They also develop and evaluate alternative characterizations of entry based on innovation and costs of firm growth.

In 'What Do We Know About Entry?', Paul Geroski distils a series of 'stylized facts and results' from the empirical literature on entry. Four-digit SIC industries regularly experience substantial entry by small start-up firms. These firms have high failure rates, and survivors often take more than a decade to reach the size of incumbents. Entry within industries tends to occur in bursts that are related to innovation but are not closely tied to the profitability of incumbents, and entry has limited effects on industry price–cost margins and incumbent behaviour. Geroski concludes that entry is less a mechanism for keeping prices down and more a mechanism for bringing about change associated with innovation.

The other three papers in this section analyse the factors that stimulate entry. In 'Spin-Offs and the New Firm Formation Process', David Garvin analyses the circumstances that lead employees of incumbent firms to start their own firms in an industry. In reviewing evidence from a large number of industries, he finds such 'spin-offs' are more likely in younger industries whose technology is more embodied in human rather than physical capital and which are composed of more specialized market niches.

In chapter 3 of his book, *Innovation and Industry Evolution*, published by MIT Press, David Audretsch analyses the factors that influence the rate of new firm start-ups. He finds that such start-ups are more likely in industries in which small firms account for a greater percentage of the industry's innovations. This suggests that firms are started to capitalize on distinctive knowledge about innovation that originates from sources outside an industry's leaders.

In 'Entry, Industry Growth, and the Microdynamics of Industry Supply', John Hause and Gunnar Du Rietz develop a theory of entry based on firm costs of adjustment to growth. Consistent with their model, they find that entry is greater in industries subject to greater growth in employment.

Sources and Implications of Diversity

Market competition is generally thought to pressure less efficient firms either to copy their more successful rivals or to exit. Thus strong selection forces exist to reduce diversity among firms in the same industry. Nevertheless, considerable diversity exists within industries. The papers in this section explore the nature, sources and implications of this diversity.

In 'Heterogeneous Firms and the Organization of Production', Walter Oi asks why firms vary in size within industries and why larger firms are more capital intensive, have higher capital utilization rates, invest more in new equipment, and employ more educated, salaried and full-time workers who receive more training and greater wages and fringe benefits. Size differences are related to the types of need which firms service. Differences in internal structure are related to differential abilities of entrepreneurs and the need for entrepreneurs to monitor workers. More able entrepreneurs head larger firms and have a higher opportunity cost to monitor workers and thus engage in various practices to economize on monitoring costs, which include using more capital-intensive methods of production and employing better quality, and thus more highly compensated, workers.

Another source of industry diversity arises from differential firm experiences in related industries. In 'The Fates of *De Novo* and *De Alio* Producers in the American Automobile Industry 1885–1981', Glenn Carroll, Lyda Bigelow, Marc-David Seidel and Lucia Tsai examine the relationship between the pre-entry background of entrants to the automobile industry and the length of their survival. They show that among all firms that ever entered the automobile industry, those that produced technologically related products prior to automobiles, especially bicycles, engines and carriages, had a lower hazard of exit for many years after entry.

In the last paper in this section, 'The Anatomy of Industry R&D Intensity Distributions', Wesley Cohen and Steven Klepper explore the sources of variation within industries in the intensity of firm R&D efforts, defined as the ratio of R&D expenditures to size. They conjecture that variations in R&D intensity reflect differences in the expertise possessed by firms and the effect of firm size on the returns from R&D. Modelling the acquisition of expertise as a random process, they show how their theory can explain a number of features of the distributions of firm R&D intensities within industries. The theory also provides a noncausal explanation for long-observed relationships across industries in mean R&D intensity, market concentration and the coefficient of variation of R&D intensity, and for the inverse relationship across firms between R&D productivity and size.

The Size Distribution of Firms

While in most industries firms periodically change rank in terms of their size, the size distribution of firms within industries, and even whole economies, almost always assumes a predictable form, which is highly positively skewed. The papers in this section explore the dynamic process that could give rise to such a distribution.

In 'The Size Distribution of Business Firms', Herbert Simon and Charles Bonini continue a tradition initiated by Robert Gibrat in which the growth of firms is conceptualized as a random process. They show that if in each period the distribution of firm growth rates is the same for all firms above a minimum size, and the birth rate of new firms is constant over time, then a positively skewed steady-state size distribution emerges that conforms closely with industry and economy firm-size distributions. The parameters of the distribution for each industry provide a natural way to measure industry market structure, and departures from the predicted size distribution at small firm (or plant) sizes provide a way of inferring the minimum efficient size firm (or plant).

Using data for the steel, petroleum, rubber tyre and automobile industries for various periods, in 'Entry, Gibrat's Law, Innovation and the Growth of Firms', Edwin Mansfield probes the stochastic framework used by Simon and Bonini. He shows that allowing the probability of failure and the variability of firm growth rates to decline with firm size can accommodate his findings that the mean and variance of firm growth rates among surviving firms declined with size. Successful innovators grew by higher rates, especially among smaller firms, which may account for the greater variability of growth rates of smaller firms. Mansfield also finds support for a model in which the probability of firms changing rank in an industry's size distribution declines with the age of the industry and the degree of inequality of the industry's size distribution.

In the last paper of this section, 'Selection and the Evolution of Industry', Boyan Jovanovic develops a model in which the stochastic factor underlying firm growth rates is noisy signals about relative firm efficiencies. Young firms have less experience and respond more sensitively to signals, which Jovanovic shows can account for smaller firms having higher probabilities of failure and higher and more variable growth rates. The theory can also explain other patterns, including why more concentrated industries tend to have more stability over time in firm rates of return, greater variability in firm rates of return at a moment in time, and higher rates of return enjoyed by larger firms.

Growth

As the selections in the prior section indicate, firm growth patterns can provide discriminating evidence regarding the forces shaping industry market structure. The papers in this section dig deeper empirically into the firm growth process in order to develop a greater understanding of the forces governing the firm-size distribution and industry market structure.

In 'The Relationship between Firm Size and Firm Growth in the US Manufacturing Sector,' Bronwyn Hall explores growth patterns among publicly traded manufacturing firms. She demonstrates that the tendency for mean firm growth rates to decline with size is robust to two econometric problems that could spuriously contribute to this pattern of errors in measuring firm size and sample selection due to small firms having higher failure rates.

In 'The Growth and Failure of U. S. Manufacturing Plants', Timothy Dunne, Mark Roberts and Larry Samuelson investigate further the size–growth relationship as well as other influences on the mean and variance of growth rates using Census data on all US manufacturing plants. They find that the failure rate and the mean and variance of the growth rate for nonfailing plants decline with size and age for both plants owned by single and multi-plant firms. When all plants, including failing plants which are assigned a growth rate of 100 per cent, are considered, however, the patterns change. Their most striking finding is that for plants owned by single-plant firms mean firm growth rates continue to decline with size, but for plants owned by multi-plant firms the decrease of failure with size overwhelms the decline in growth rates with size for nonfailing plants, leading the mean growth rate for all plants to increase with size for larger and older plants. These older and larger plants of multi-plant firms have distinctively low failure and high growth rates.

In the final paper of this section, 'Gibrat's Legacy', John Sutton reviews theoretical and empirical work on firm growth and failure rates and on the firm-size distribution and develops a stochastic model for the firm-size distribution that can accommodate the most distinctive patterns. His model is similar to Simon and Bonini's but relaxes their growth assumption by assuming only that firm growth in absolute terms (not the rate of growth) is a nondecreasing function of firm size. Sutton's model yields a lower bound relationship for the firm-size distribution that is well satisfied by industries in the UK, USA and Germany. The model implies a positively skewed firm-size distribution, with industry concentration dependent on the extent to which absolute firm growth increases with firm size.

Survival

Growth is one aspect of the performance of firms. Another that is closely linked to growth is survival. The papers in this section explore empirically how the characteristics of entrants and the industries they enter influence survival.

In 'New Firm Survival: New Results Using a Hazard Function', David Audretsch and Talat Mahmood find that the survival of new establishments in the manufacturing sector depends on establishment and industry conditions. The hazard of exit appears to be related to the degree of scale economies in an industry, with the hazard greater the more capital intensive the industry entered and the smaller the establishment at entry relative to an estimate of the industry's minimum efficient size plant. The hazard of exit is also greater in more innovative industries and when unemployment is high. These relationships hold principally for new start-ups rather than diversifying entrants, suggesting that environmental conditions are most determinative of performance of new firms.

In 'Life Duration of New Firms', José Mata and Pedro Portugal find that for Portuguese entrants, the length of survival is a function of entrant and industry characteristics. Similarly to Audretsch and Mahmood, they find that larger entrants survive longer, but that the (estimated) size of the minimum efficient firm in the entrant's industry does not affect survival. They also find that the growth rate of the entrant's industry positively affects the length of survival.

In 'On the Turnover of Business Firms and Business Managers', Thomas Holmes and James Schmitz analyse the determinants of the length of survival and the likelihood of ownership transfers among US small businesses mainly organized as sole proprietorships. They develop a model in which businesses are heterogeneous on two dimensions: the quality of the business and the quality of the match between the skills of the owner/manager of the business and the needs of the business, with both subject to temporary random shocks. They show that the model can explain detailed aspects of how the age of the business, the tenure of the current owner and whether the owner was the founder affect the hazard of discontinuance of the business and the hazard of an ownership change in the business, suggesting that heterogeneity among small businesses plays a key role in shaping their fates.

In the last paper of this section, 'The Role of Technology Use in the Survival and Growth of Manufacturing Plants', Mark Doms, Timothy Dunne and Mark Roberts exploit data on 17 advanced production technologies to analyse how technology usage affects survival and growth among manufacturing plants in five two-digit SIC manufacturing industries in which the technologies are used. Similarly to other studies, older and larger firms have higher survival rates and lower growth rates, and this persists even after controlling for differences across plants in their capital intensity, productivity and technology usage. Larger firms tend to be more advanced technologically, more capital intensive and more productive, all of which independently contribute to longer survival and greater growth. A possible explanation for all these findings, which is reminiscent of Walter Oi's model, is that firms differ in terms of managerial efficiency, which conditions their size, productivity and technology choices, and in turn their survival and growth.

Learning and Adaptation

The performance of firms can improve over time as firms learn about how to perform better and also as the mix of firms changes. The former type of improvement has been dubbed 'active learning'. It can result from 'learning by doing', in which firms discover how to do things better through experience in production. It can also result from firms exploring how to improve their performance through activities such as R&D. The latter type of improvement has been dubbed 'passive learning'. As modelled by Jovanovic, it can occur through a process of selection in which less efficient firms exit as they learn through experience about their relative efficiency. The papers in this section explore these two types of learning.

The first article is a seminal contribution by Michael Spence on 'The Learning Curve and Competition'. Spence considers the nature of firm and industry evolution when firms learn by doing, which causes a firm's unit costs to fall over time as a function of its cumulative output. Spence shows that the true marginal cost of production in each period for a monopolist with a limited horizon and a zero discount rate is its marginal cost of production at the end of its lifetime, which it should equate with its marginal revenue in each period to maximize its profits. He considers the evolution of the number of producers when there are multiple potential entrants with exogenously determined entry times and bounded learning. Using different equilibrium concepts, Spence shows that a moderate rate of learning yields the most concentrated industry structure.

In 'The Learning Curve, Technology Barriers to Entry, and Competitive Survival in the Chemical Processing Industries', Marvin Lieberman considers the importance of learning by doing in the entry and survival of producers in 39 chemical product industries. If costs decline with experience, then potential entrants should be at a greater disadvantage the larger the cumulative output of incumbent firms. The likelihood of entry, however, was not related to the cumulative output of incumbents, which Lieberman attributes to widespread technology licensing in most of the products. The hazard of firm exit was greater the larger the cumulative output of the leading producer, though, suggesting that learning did affect firm performance.

In 'Selection versus Evolutionary Adaptation: Learning and Post-Entry Performance,' John Baldwin and Mohammed Rafiquzzaman consider how learning affected the survival and growth of *de novo* entrants in the Canadian manufacturing sector. They find that the performance of entrants improved through the greater exit of less efficient entrants and, to a limited extent, through the improvement in the performance of surviving entrants. The latter type of learning was greater in industries in which the initial performance of entrants relative to incumbents was worse.

In 'New-Firm Survival and the Technological Regime', David Audretsch also considers the survival of *de novo* entrants into the US manufacturing sector. He finds that over a ten-year period the survival rate of entrants was lower in industries which were more capital intensive and in which the leading firms were larger (a proxy for the degree of production scale economies). Alternatively, survival rates were greater in industries in which smaller firms had higher innovation rates relative to larger firms, suggesting that technological opportunities play an important role in enabling entrants to compete with incumbent firms. These effects were not apparent for shorter periods, suggesting that it takes some time before entrants can assess their competitive standing.

In the last paper of this section, 'Empirical Implications of Alternative Models of Firm Dynamics', Ariel Pakes and Richard Ericson consider the importance of active and passive learning. They distinguish between the two types of learning according to whether cross-sectional variations in firm size are related to initial firm size after controlling for variations in firm size in the immediate past. Using data for Wisconsin firms in the manufacturing and retail sectors for the period 1978–86, they find support for passive learning in retailing and active learning in manufacturing, which suggests greater volatility in relative firm profitability over time in manufacturing than in retailing.

Productivity

Improvements in productivity drive economic growth. At the aggregate level, growth results from active learning, which contributes to productivity improvements within firms, and from market selection or passive learning, which leads to reallocation of output across firms. The papers in this section explore these two mechanisms. They analyse the effects of entry, exit and differential firm growth rates on aggregate productivity growth. They also probe the factors that influence productivity growth within firms, including industry conditions and ownership changes.

In 'Productivity Dynamics in Manufacturing Plants', Martin Baily, Charles Hulten and David Campbell decompose total factor productivity growth in manufacturing industries into productivity growth of continuing plants, entrants and exits. Although surviving entrants eventually have greater productivity than exiters, initially their productivity is comparable with exiters. Combined with the relatively small outputs of both groups, exit and entry contribute little to aggregate productivity growth. Among continuing plants, they find that the productivity rankings of plants persist over time, which is consistent with plants differing in terms of management quality, as discussed in the papers by Oi, and Doms, Dunne and Roberts. Over time, continuing plants with higher productivity gain market share, which is an important contributor to aggregate productivity growth along with improvements in productivity within plants.

In 'Productivity Growth in Chile and Colombia: The Role of Entry, Exit, and Learning', Lili Liu and James Tybout examine total factor productivity growth in manufacturing industries in Chile and Colombia in the late 1970s and early 1980s. During this period, Chile experienced a severe recession and a financial crisis whereas Colombia experienced more mild cyclical swings.

Liu and Tybout's findings are similar to Baily, Hulten and Campbell in that continuing plants differed considerably in productivity, output was allocated over time to higher productivity plants, and entry and exit did not contribute much to growth in aggregate productivity. In contrast to Baily, Hulten and Campbell, however, they find some periods in which higher productivity firms were more likely to exit. This may reflect that financial factors such as liquidity were more determinative of survival than productivity during business cycles and financial crises. They also find that reallocations of output among continuing plants contributed less to aggregate productivity growth than in the USA.

In 'Entry, Innovation and Productivity Growth', Paul Geroski explores the factors that account for differences in total factor productivity growth across UK manufacturing industries over the period 1970–79. He finds that total factor productivity growth varied greatly within industries over time, suggesting that high industry productivity growth did not persist over time. Industries that introduced more innovations and secondarily experienced greater domestic entry on average sustained higher productivity growth, whereas industries subject to greater international entry sustained lower productivity growth. Entry is interpreted as a measure of competition, and the effects of domestic entry are interpreted as indicating that greater competition spurs productivity growth. Various explanations are offered to reconcile why international entry was associated with lower productivity growth if entry in general spurs innovation.

In the final paper of the section, 'Productivity and Changes in Ownership of Manufacturing Plants', Frank Lichtenberg and Donald Siegel analyse the relationship between total factor productivity and ownership change. Focusing on relatively large US manufacturing plants that continued producing over the period 1972–81, they find that the total factor productivity of acquired plants was below their industry average prior to acquisition and declined relative to the industry average for a number of years prior to acquisition. In contrast, after acquisition the total factor productivity of the acquired plants increased relative to their industry average for a number of years. Similarly to the matching model in Holmes and Schmitz's paper on small businesses, Lichtenberg and Siegel attribute these patterns to a process in which plants are transferred to new owners to improve the match between the skills needed to manage the plant and the skills of the owner of the plant.

Turbulence

While industry firm-size distributions exhibit remarkable stability over time, this masks considerable turbulence at the firm level. As noted in some of the earlier papers, most industries experience high entry rates and, while failure rates of entrants tend to be high relative to incumbents, some of the entrants grow and eventually displace the industry's leaders. The papers in this section explore the nature of this turbulence and the forces that underlie it.

In 'Information, Mobility and Profit', Dennis Mueller develops a theory of profit based on the costs of trading information and the mobility of factor owners to clarify where profit comes from, how it differs from rent and how it influences the allocation of resources. Profit flows as a residual to factor owners that possess distinctive information regarding an incumbent or prospective firm that is costly to trade. Consistent with Geroski's findings regarding entry, Mueller conjectures that entrepreneurs start firms to appropriate the value of information that is costly to trade. The residual profit they earn after making contractual payments to other factor owners provides a return on their information. This suggests that the importance of new knowledge combined with the cost of transferring the knowledge influences the rate of entry into an industry, which is a key element of industry turbulence.

In 'Small Firms' Seedbed Role and the Concept of Turbulence', Mark Beesley and Robert Hamilton explore the factors that influence the degree of industry turbulence, which they measure by the sum of firm entry and exit rates. Using data on Scottish manufacturers in the late 1970s, they find that industries with higher entry plus exit rates are characterized primarily by greater rates of entry and exit of independent versus diversified firms. They also find greater turbulence in industries defined as residual categories, which contain novel or unconventional products that may later spawn new industries. Consistent with Audretsch's findings on entry and Geroski's stylized facts and results regarding entry, these patterns suggest that turbulence is related to new product innovation and primarily involves the formation and death of new, independent firms, which tend to be smaller than diversified firms. The latter appear to account for the primary challenge to incumbent producers in more concentrated industries, which experience higher rates of entry and exit of diversified but not independent firms.

In 'Industry Evolution with Sunk Costs and Uncertain Market Conditions', Val Lambson develops a model to account for turbulent industries characterized by simultaneous entry and exit. He shows that when there are alternative production technologies based on different input combinations, each of which involves sunk costs, and input prices and demand fluctuate unpredictably over time, then industries can experience simultaneous entry and exit of firms employing different technologies. Firms with identical expectations may also find it profitable to invest in different technologies at the same moment in time, suggesting that the age of firm capital stocks cannot necessarily be associated with particular technology vintages.

In 'Markov-Perfect Industry Dynamics: A Framework for Empirical Work', Richard Ericson and Ariel Pakes develop a general model of industry evolution in which industry leaders are eventually overturned by (fortunate) entrants, but an industry's market structure reverts back to a limited set of possible states. Thus the model can account for turbulence as a regular feature of industrial competition while reconciling the tendency for industry structure, measured in terms of the firm-size distribution, to remain stable over time. The key force in their model that generates turbulence is uncertainty associated with R&D, in which firms invest to improve their productivity. By assuming that firm valuations are bounded, firms that grow largest by dint of their greater productivity eventually experience diminishing returns from R&D and decrease their R&D expenditures, causing them to decline. While entrants have high failure rates, the few that succeed at R&D increase their R&D expenditures and displace the industry's leaders, only to later decline.

In the final paper of the section, 'Entry, Exit, and Firm Dynamics in Long Run Equilibrium', Hugo Hopenhayn constructs a similar model to that of Ericson and Pakes in which firms are subject to random productivity shocks, but simplifies it by not linking the productivity shocks to firm R&D choices. If the cost of entry is sufficiently low, his model admits a unique equilibrium in which input and output prices, industry output and the number of firms are constant over time and entry and exit occur regularly, with the relative positions of firms changing over time. Thus, similarly to Ericson and Pakes, the model reconciles turbulence at the firm level with stability at the industry level, and it can accommodate a number of well-documented empirical patterns, including that older firms tend to be larger, more profitable and have lower hazard rates. The model can be used to assess how changes in certain industry conditions, such as the cost of entry and industry demand, affect such dynamic aspects of the steady-state equilibrium as the rate of firm turnover.

Persistence

Are industry leaders better able to retain their positions over time in certain types of industry and, if so, why? Are there particular circumstances that undermine the leaders? The selections in this section explore these questions, focusing particularly on how innovation affects the persistence of leadership.

In 'Preemptive Patenting and the Persistence of Monopoly', Richard Gilbert and David Newbery explore the circumstances under which a monopolist will pre-emptively patent an innovation to deter entry by a challenger. They consider innovations that are not drastic in that both the challenger and incumbent would compete if the challenger innovated first. For such innovations, they show that the incumbent will commit to an R&D strategy in which it develops and patents the innovation first, assuming that the incumbent earns greater profits from monopolizing the innovation than from competing with the challenger. To be credible, such a strategy may require the incumbent to commit to the R&D needed to develop the innovation even if it is profitable not to employ the innovation once produced.

In 'Uncertain Innovation and the Persistence of Monopoly', Jennifer Reinganum introduces uncertainty regarding when the incumbent's and challenger's efforts to develop the innovation will succeed, with greater spending expected to speed up the time of successful innovation. Prior to successful innovation, the incumbent enjoys monopoly profits and thus has a greater amount to lose than the challenger from earlier innovation. Consequently, for drastic and near-drastic innovations, the incumbent spends less than the challenger on R&D and therefore is less likely than the challenger to innovate first. Thus uncertainty in the innovation process can undermine the incentives for industry leaders to maintain their leadership over time.

In 'Uncertain Innovation and the Persistence of Monopoly: Comment', Richard Gilbert and David Newbery argue that in Reinganum's model it is not uncertainty *per se* that undermines the tendency for incumbents to maintain their leadership, but rather other assumptions that differ from theirs, especially regarding the timing of moves in the R&D game. Reinganum assumes simultaneous R&D choices by incumbent and challenger. They show that this renders entry deterrence unprofitable and consequently Reinganum's conclusions follow even with no R&D uncertainty.

In 'Uncertain Innovation and the Persistence of Monopoly: Reply', Jennifer Reinganum acknowledges that the order of play is the key distinction between her model and Gilbert and Newbery's, but questions the usefulness of modelling incumbents as having first mover advantages. Even if incumbents can make pre-emptive commitments, she argues, it is the mechanism underlying such commitments and not the patent system, as Gilbert and Newbery claim, that is responsible for the persistence of industry leadership.

Finally, in 'Preemptive Patenting and the Persistence of Monopoly: Reply', Richard Gilbert and David Newbery show that allowing the challenger to be more efficient at R&D than the incumbent will not necessarily undermine the incumbent's incentive to pre-empt the challenger. They assume that the incumbent can bargain with the challenger over monopoly rights to the product and also over the sources of the challenger's advantage. Assuming the transaction costs of the latter do not exceed the transaction costs of the former, the incumbent will secure the basis for the challenger's advantage and pre-empt the challenger as long as transaction costs do not exhaust the benefits of pre-emption.

In excerpts from his book, *Profits in the Long Run*, Dennis Mueller investigates empirically the extent to which industry leaders maintain their profitability over time. He finds considerable persistence in above and below average firm rates of return over the period 1950–72 among the largest firms in the US economy. Estimated long-run firm rates of return were regressed on industry concentration and estimated firm long-run market shares, entered both alone and interacted with industry advertising and R&D intensity, to explore the determinants of persistent profitability. The estimates indicate that firms with greater market share earned persistent above average returns in (only) advertising- and R&D-intensive industries. These findings suggest that R&D (and advertising) competition contributes to greater persistence in industry leadership.

In 'Explaining the Attacker's Advantage: Technological Paradigms, Organizational Dynamics, and the Value Network', Clayton Christensen and Richard Rosenbloom consider the kinds of innovation in disk drives that favoured entrants over industry leaders. In contrast to various theories, they find that nonincremental innovations that required new types of technical expertise or that altered the interrelationship of components did not consistently undermine the leaders. Industry leaders sometimes pioneered these innovations, and entrants and lesser incumbents later adopted them, suggesting that it was not the ability of the leaders to pre-empt challengers, as in Gilbert and Newbery's model, that enabled them to maintain their position. Innovations that were pioneered by entrants and undermined incumbents were ones that led to new types of disk drive that appealed primarily to new users. In contrast to Reinganum's model, these innovations were not drastic in that they did not challenge the sales of incumbent firms, and thus incumbents did not have less incentive than challengers to develop them. Christensen and Rosenbloom explain their findings as reflecting that the attention of firms tends to be captured by their customers, which makes incumbents slow to pursue innovations opening up new markets.

Evolution and Horizontal Market Structure

A number of the papers attest to the considerable turnover of firms that typically occurs in industries. They also indicate that in certain types of industry a few firms capture a large market share and maintain it over time. The papers in this section explore the factors which affect the number of firms in an industry and the market share of the leading firms.

In 'The Evolution of New Industries and the Determinants of Market Structure', Steven Klepper and Elizabeth Graddy analyse the evolution of the number of producers and industry output and price in 46 narrowly defined new product industries. Characteristic of the product life cycle, the products exhibit an initial rise and then shakeout in the number of producers and also a dampening over time in the percentage growth in output and fall in price. These patterns are explained using a model that features random, persistent firm cost differences, limited firm growth and imitation of more efficient rivals, and sunk entry costs. The share of output accounted for by the industry's leaders in the model is determined by the pace and severity of the evolutionary process, which is shaped by systematic factors governing firm growth and imitation, and stochastic factors conditioning the cost advantage of the early leaders.

In 'Industrial Organization and New Findings on the Turnover and Mobility of Firms', Richard Caves notes how the new findings on business turnover suggest, consistent with Klepper and Graddy, the importance of both stochastic and systematic factors in shaping an industry's market structure. Industries that are R&D and advertising intensive appear to be especially susceptible to becoming oligopolies. In Sutton's model of endogenous sunk costs the returns to both R&D and advertising depend on the size of the market, which is similar to Klepper's model of the industry life cycle in which the returns to R&D depend on the size of the firm. In both models, an escalation process occurs in which successful firms expand their R&D and/or advertising, enabling only the largest firms to survive and thus contributing to the evolution of an oligopolistic market structure. Both models are consistent with Mueller's findings on the persistence of firm profits.

As Sutton recounts in chapter 4 of his book, *Sunk Costs and Market Structure*, his model implies that, as the size of the market increases, the share of output accounted for by the leaders will decline to zero in industries characterized by production scale economies, but will be bounded away from zero in advertising-intensive industries. He tests this prediction by examining the market structure of 20 food and drink industries in six countries of varying size. Consistent with the theory, in the largest countries the lower bound of the share of output accounted for by the leading firms approached zero in the less advertising-intensive industries but remained well above zero in the advertising-intensive industries.

In chapter 2 of his book, *Scale and Scope*, Alfred Chandler recounts the emergence in the late nineteenth and early twentieth centuries of the large industrial enterprise. Such enterprises were concentrated in the food, chemicals, petroleum, primary metals, machinery and transportation equipment industries. They exploited economies of scale and scope made possible by new methods of production and integrated into marketing and distribution, the supply of inputs and R&D to exploit fully the potential of the new production technologies. Firms that were first to make the large capital investments and establish the necessary organizational structures to manage the new large-scale enterprises were difficult for latecomers to compete with because of the large investments needed to match their efficiencies and the uncertainty inherent in such investments. Their industries evolved to be oligopolies which they dominated for many years, pointing again to the role played by marketing/advertising and R&D in shaping industry market structure.

In the last selection of this section, 'Technology and Market Structure', John Sutton explores why all R&D-intensive industries do not experience an escalation process that leads to an oligopolistic market structure. He shows that such a process will not necessarily occur if, besides improving the quality of existing products, R&D can be also be used to develop new product varieties with distinctive markets. This is consistent with Christensen and Rosenbloom's findings that incumbent firms are slow to develop new product variants appealing to new users. Consistent with the theory, the four-firm concentration ratio among R&D-intensive manufacturing industries is consistently high when the leading product of the industry accounts for a large percentage of its sales, but can be quite low in industries in which no product commands a large share of the industry's sales.

Regional Evolution

The preceding sections provide both a theoretical framework and empirical evidence suggesting that the evolution of firms and industries plays an important role in generating and commercializing new knowledge. It is the drive to deviate from the existing products and processes – to innovate – that makes a stable industrial structure when viewed from a static framework actually remarkably turbulent when viewed through the dynamic lens described in the previous sections. In the new growth theory developed by Paul Romer and Paul Krugman, among others, an economy's capacity to generate and commercialize new knowledge is what determines its rate of growth. These theories feature the positive externalities associated with knowledge; knowledge spills over from the sources where it is produced and benefits those that acquire it. The papers in this section explore how geographic proximity mediates knowledge spillovers and how in turn knowledge spillovers shape the way industries and regions evolve.

In 'Growth in Cities', Edward Glaeser, Hedi Kallal, José Scheinkman and Andrei Shleifer examine whether employment growth in industries in different cities is related to the economic structure of the cities. They find that local competition and regional variety promote growth but that regional industry specialization does not. To the extent that their findings support the importance of knowledge spillovers, they suggest that such spillovers transcend individual industries.

In 'Innovation in Cities: Science-Based Diversity, Specialization and Localized Competition', Maryann Feldman and David Audretsch find complementary evidence that urban variety and local competition promote innovative activity. They find that the number of innovations developed in an industry in a city is larger the greater the share of employment in the city accounted for by related industries sharing the same science base, and the greater the number of firms per employee in the industry relative to the average city. In contrast, greater employment in the city within the same industry contributes to a lower rate of innovation in the industry. These findings suggest that innovation in a region is promoted by complementary skills and capabilities, and by competition rather than by industry specialization.

In the final paper of this section, 'Manufacturing Industries: A Dartboard Approach', Glenn Ellison and Edward Glaeser examine the extent to which activity within industries is geographically clustered. They develop and test a model in which localized industry-specific spillovers, natural advantages and chance all contribute to geographic concentration. The empirical evidence suggests that geographic clustering cannot be explained simply by chance, although most industries are not heavily concentrated geographically. While geographic clustering of firms within an industry may promote knowledge spillovers, as Ellison and Glaeser's results suggest, such spillovers may not persist and may later be offset by disadvantages of clustering, which could explain Glaeser *et al.* and Feldman and Audretsch's findings concerning the effect of industry specialization on city growth.

International Competitiveness of Industries

If knowledge spills over within and across industries, then economic growth is likely to be affected by the composition of a country's industrial activity. To the extent that specialization in certain industries requires a country to export, its export orientation will also affect its rate of growth. The two papers in this section explore the extent to which the sustained high growth rates experienced by the East Asian countries in the 1980s is related to industry specialization and to greater productivity of firms engaged in exporting.

In 'Making a Miracle', Robert Lucas inquires whether models exist that could explain the distinctive sustained high growth rates of the East Asian countries in recent years. His main inference is that learning by doing, as modelled by Spence, or something comparable that generates high productivity growth in particular industries, coupled with knowledge spillovers across technologies and possibly industries, is required to explain the East Asian growth miracles. In order for growth to be sustained at high rates, workers and managers must continually take on tasks that are new to them, and for it to be done on a large scale the economy must be export oriented. The limited number of economies that achieve sustained high growth are those that find a way to channel their activities towards industries with high growth and export potential.

In 'Productivity and the Export Market: A Firm-Level Analysis', Bee-Yaw Aw and Amy Hwang estimate separate production functions for Taiwanese firms exporting and servicing the domestic market in four electronics industries. They find that exporters generally had higher labour productivity. In three of the four industries, the estimates of the coefficients of the production functions indicated significantly greater productivity for the exporters. These findings are consistent with Lucas's speculation that an export orientation in higher productivity growth industries, such as electronics, is essential for an economy to experience sustained high growth rates.

Public Policy

The preceding sections have laid out the building blocks of a strikingly different view of the organization of firms and industries than is offered by conventional economics. At the heart of this new framework is the process of change in which the evolution of firms and industries is shaped by the drive to innovate. What emerges is a view of the organization of firms and industries in motion, where new firms are started to commercialize new ideas, many of those new firms fail, fewer of them survive and prosper, and even fewer rise to become dominant firms in new industries.

How does the role of public policy in this evolutionary framework differ from that suggested by the more conventional view of industrial economics? Under the traditional view, the role of public policy is to provide a mechanism for reaping the gains from large-scale production while mitigating abuses associated with market dominance. The policy debate in the literature has largely focused on antitrust (competition policy in Europe), regulation and public ownership. What these three instruments have in common is that they constrain the freedom of firms to contract.

The role of public policy towards business is strikingly different when viewed through the dynamic lens of an evolutionary framework. Rather than focusing on mechanisms to constrain firms, public policy is oriented towards creating institutions and linkages that promote the generation and commercialization of new knowledge. Thus in the evolutionary view the role of public policy is essentially enabling in nature. This very different view of public policy becomes clear in the papers in the final section of the volumes, which is devoted to the role of public policy.

In the first paper, 'The Tradeoff Between Firm Size and Diversity in the Pursuit of Technological Progress', Wesley Cohen and Steven Klepper identify a potential role for public policy in mediating the competing benefits of large-sized firms and a diversity of smaller firms. Consistent with a number of papers in the volumes, they suggest that firms have different perceptions about technological opportunities, so that a greater number of firms will make it less likely that good opportunities for innovation are overlooked. Alternatively, large firms have advantages in appropriating the returns from innovation that provide social as well as private benefits, but also compromise an industry's diversity. Public policy may be able to stimulate technological advance in some industries by encouraging the start up and survival of new firms while at the same time promoting cooperation among competing firms to exploit the advantage in innovation of large size.

In 'Some Lessons from the East Asian Miracle', Joseph Stiglitz explains how public policies in East Asia contributed to rapid growth and development. He points out that public policy in most East Asian countries had three essential goals: developing technological capabilities, promoting exports, and building the domestic capacity to manufacture a range of intermediate goods. Rather than constraining or replacing markets, as in the former Soviet Union, public policy was oriented towards creating markets where they did not exist and complementing existing markets. In addition, governments undertook targeted investments in education and in the production and commercialization of knowledge.

The final paper, by Richard Nelson, 'National Innovation Systems: A Retrospective on a Study', is a summary of studies of 15 countries of differing size and income concerning the impact of their national systems of innovation on their dynamic performance. Three important lessons emerge regarding the role that public policy can play in guiding the processes of innovation, industry evolution and economic development. First, the innovative capacity of a country is shaped not by a narrow technology policy but by a range of institutions and policies influencing a broad spectrum of the economy. Especially important in a number of industries is public support of education and research at universities and government labs, and the orientation of the universities and labs towards servicing industry. Second, the process by which firms and industries evolve over time is strongly influenced by the national system of innovation. Third, no single national system of innovation is superior. Rather, differences in size, natural resource endowments, income and national security concerns lead countries to develop different sets of institutions that support distinctive industries.

Together, the three papers in this section make a strong case that public policy can play an important role in shaping the direction of economic development, and that the appropriate role of public policy is very different in an evolutionary than in a static context. The papers stress that public policy needs to create the institutions and environment facilitating knowledge flows. Such policies generate the micro-linkages for the knowledge externalities driving economic growth.

Part I
Persistence

[1]

Preemptive Patenting and the Persistence of Monopoly

By RICHARD J. GILBERT AND DAVID M. G. NEWBERY*

The problem of dominant firms has received much attention in the antitrust literature. One strand of thought, exemplified by George Stigler, argues that the forces of natural selection are strong and that firms which stay dominant are firms with superior managerial or technological performance. Others, notably Oliver Williamson (1977a), have argued that market imperfections and chance events contribute to the persistence of dominant firms. This paper takes a different tack and inquires whether institutions such as the patent system create opportunities for firms with monopoly power to maintain their monopoly power. The results apply to other situations such as brand identification, spatial location, and capacity expansion, which share the characteristic that early, or preemptive, actions may lower the returns to potential competitors.

Preemptive invention is not without topical interest. In a recent antitrust case—the longest jury trial on record in the federal courts—the SCM Corporation sought more than $500 million in damages on its claim that the Xerox Corporation, among other alleged anticompetitive behavior, had maintained a "patent thicket" where some inventions were used while others were neither used nor licensed to others.[1]

This paper shows that, under certain conditions, a firm with monopoly power has

an incentive to maintain its monopoly power by patenting new technologies before potential competitors and that this activity can lead to patents that are neither used nor licensed to others (sometimes called "sleeping patents"). Section I examines the incentives for preemptive invention in an illustrative market model with an existing monopolist and a single patentable substitute technology. While highly simplified, the example serves to identify the incentives for preemptive patenting. The monopolist will preempt if the cost is less than the profits gained by preventing entry, which follows whenever entry brings about an anticipated reduction of total industry profits below the monopoly level.

Section II examines several questions that arise in the context of the simple example, such as threat credibility, the occurrence of sleeping patents, and limits to the span of control by the monopolistic firm. Section III develops a more general model that permits analysis of the interaction of patenting and strategic investment activity, the consequences of limited patent protection and many potentially patentable technologies, and the effects of uncertainty on the preemption decision. These considerations significantly affect attainable monopoly profits with and without patenting, but they do not necessarily destroy incentives for preemption.

Although patents serve to illustrate incentives for preemptive activity, the complexities of research and development limit preemptive patenting to exceptional circumstances. Patent protection is typically quite limited and even modest prospects for developing new products can make the cost of entry deterrence by preemptive patenting excessively costly.[2] In addition, complementarities

*University of California-Berkeley, and Churchill College, Cambridge University, respectively. We acknowledge helpful discussions with Ted Keeler, Robert Masson, John Panzar, Michael Riordan, Robert Reynolds, Joseph Stiglitz, and participants of the July 1978 seminar at the U.S. Department of Justice. This research was supported by the National Science Foundation (grant SOC77-08822), the Social Science Research Council of Great Britain, and Churchill College, Cambridge. We are grateful to an anonymous referee for providing constructive comments.

[1]*New York Times*, "Damages Denied in Xerox Case," December 30, 1978. The case reference is 463 F. Supp. 983 (1978). Other cases involving alleged anticompetitive research and development include the *U.S. v. IBM* and the *U.S. v. AT & T*.

[2]The survey by Chris T. Taylor and Z. Aubrey Silberston (1973) reveals the scope of patent protection in the United Kingdom.

between patentable product components encourage cross-licensing agreements and discourage restrictive patent enforcement. Preemptive patenting may be unnecessary if potential entrants can be deterred more cheaply by other behavior, such as capacity expansion. Preemption is too costly if an established firm has a sufficient comparative disadvantage in research or production; and uncertainty about the expectations and resulting investment activities of potential rivals may lead an established firm to choose a *R&D* strategy that allows entry by optimistic firms.

The existence of patent rights is neither necessary nor sufficient for preemptive activity. The crucial element is that the rewards from acting first must be sufficiently large relative to the gains to subsequent investors. Patents provide a vivid example where the award goes only to the first firm, although in practice the advantage offered by patent protection is typically small. The acquisition of technical know-how, with or without patent protection, provides the significant returns from accelerated investments in research and development.

Several examples of preemptive competition have appeared recently. Preemptive brand proliferation is discussed by Richard Schmalensee. One-dimensional spatial location models where preemption may occur are described by B. Curtis Eaton, Edward Prescott and Michael Visscher, and Robert Reynolds; these are similar in structure to the problem discussed by Nicholas Kaldor. Examples of preemption by accelerated investment in new plant capacity appear in Gilbert and Richard Harris, A. Michael Spence (1977, 1979), and Ram Rao and David Rutenberg.

I. The Elements of Preemptive Patenting

The incentives for preemptive patenting emerge most clearly in a simple model. Suppose an established firm has a monopoly position in the sale or manufacture of a product (labelled product 1). The monopoly may be the consequence of an earlier patent or unique access to factors of production or distribution. Entry into the monopolized industry can take place only through the invention and patenting of a single patentable substitute for the monopolist's product. The cost of inventing the substitute (labelled product 2) depends only on the expected lag before a patentable design can be produced. In its simplest representation the date of invention, T, is a deterministic function of the time path of expenditures. The present value of an optimal expenditure path defines a cost function $C(T)$, that is a decreasing function of the invention date.[3] The cost function is the same for all firms engaged in research and development for the substitute product.

The strategy space for each firm is restricted to the research and development expenditure on product 2 and the price(s) the firm charges for the product(s) it sells. Let P^j represent the product price ($j = 1, 2$). Product 1 is sold only by the established firm (i.e., the monopolist); either the monopolist (labelled $i = m$) or an entrant ($i = e$) can patent product 2. Demand is known with certainty and is unchanging over time.

Before patenting of the substitute product, the monopolist earns profits at the rate $\pi_m(P_m^1)$. If the monopolist patents the substitute, profits are $\pi_m(P_m^1, P_m^2)$. If an entrant patents the substitute, the former monopolist's profit is $\pi_m(P_m^1, P_e^2)$ and the entrant earns profits at the rate $\pi_e(P_m^1, P_e^2)$. Profits are written as independent of time, which implicitly assumes any capital expenditures are included as fully amortized costs. In all cases P_i^j ($j = 1, 2$; $i = m, e$) denotes firm i's maximizing choice of price for product j, given the prevailing market structure.

The monopolist has the option of patenting the substitute technology or allowing entry to occur. We allow the monopolist to

---

[3] Although studies by Edwin Mansfield (1968) and others suggest a positive relation between perceived profitability and the commitment of funds to research and development, the relation between *R&D* expenditures and the timing of product development and patenting is more difficult to substantiate. R. G. Richels and J. L. Plummer (1977) cite an example of the cost-time tradeoff in the development of the nuclear breeder reactor. The cost should be a strictly decreasing function of the invention date with any positive discount rate if it is possible to postpone expenditures.

choose a patent date under the assumption that competitors will patent at the date determined by free entry into the patent competition. Questions relating to the credibility of the preemption threat are deferred until Section II. The return to the monopolist from patenting is the difference between monopoly profits with the patent and profits when entry is allowed to occur. The firm should patent the substitute product and preempt potential entrants whenever this difference exceeds the cost of securing the patent. A simple comparison of profit streams shows that, under a general set of conditions, the monopolist will always gain by spending more on inventive activity than the present value of returns a rival can expect to earn from the new product. Specifically, the monopolist will spend more on $R \& D$ than rival firms *if entry results in any reduction of total profits below the joint-maximizing level.*

The demonstration of this result is straightforward. Let r represent the rate of interest (the same for all firms). The reward to any entrant depends on the price set by the former monopolist for product 1, P_m^1, and the price set by the entrant, P_e^2, as well as the entry date, T. Free entry into the patent race will dissipate profits so that

$$(1) \qquad C(T) = \int_T^\infty \pi_e(P_m^1, P_e^2) e^{-rt} dt.$$

If equation (1) is satisfied for more than one invention date T, competition for the patent will select the earliest date. When entry occurs at the competitive entry date, the former monopolist's profits are

$$(2) \qquad V_e = \int_0^T \pi_m(P_m^1) e^{-rt} dt$$

$$+ \int_T^\infty \pi_m(P_m^1, P_e^2) e^{-rt} dt.$$

Now suppose the monopolist takes the competitive invention date as determined by equation (1) and considers inventing before this date. If the cost of invention is continuous at date T, the monopolist can preempt rivals (i.e., invent at a date $T - \varepsilon$ for some arbitrarily small positive ε) by spending an

amount $C(T) + \delta(\varepsilon)$. The firm remains a monopolist and earns

$$(3) \qquad V_p = \int_0^{T-\varepsilon} \pi_m(P_m^1) e^{-rt} dt$$

$$+ \int_{T-\varepsilon}^\infty \pi_m(P_m^1, P_m^2) e^{-rt} dt - [C(T) + \delta].$$

The difference between profits with preemption and profits with entry is, in the limit as ε and δ approach zero,

$$(4) \qquad V_p - V_e = \int_T^\infty \pi_m(P_m^1, P_m^2) e^{-rt} dt$$

$$- \int_T^\infty \pi_m(P_m^1, P_e^2) e^{-rt} dt - C(T).$$

Note that the monopolist's price of product 1 with entry may differ from the price the monopolist sets when entry is preempted. Indeed, the monopolist need not even produce the patented substitute technology.

Substituting equation (1) for $C(T)$ gives an alternative expression for the relative benefits of preemptive patenting;

$$(5) \qquad V_p - V_e = \int_T^\infty \left\{ \pi_m(P_m^1, P_m^2) \right.$$

$$\left. - \left[\pi_m(P_m^1, P_e^2) + \pi_e(P_m^1, P_e^2) \right] \right\} e^{-rt} dt.$$

The monopoly profits from preemptive patenting strictly exceed the monopolist's profits with entry if

$$(6) \qquad \pi_m(P_m^1, P_m^2) > \pi_m(P_m^1, P_e^2) + \pi_e(P_m^1, P_e^2).$$

The left-hand side of equation (6) is the maximum monopoly profit attainable with both product 1 and product 2, while the right-hand side is the total industry profit earned when a rival patents. The former will exceed the latter whenever entry results in some reduction in total profits, provided the monopolist suffers no diseconomies in the production of the substitute relative to production by a rival firm.[4] Moreover, the same

---

[4] Clearly there is no incentive for preemption if production of product 2 has no effect on the profits from product 1. Also, if the entrant's profit-maximizing price for product 2 results in zero profits for the former monopolist, then $\pi_m(P_m^1, P_m^2) = \pi_e(P_m^1, P_e^2)$ and again there is no incentive for preemptive patenting.

VOL. 72 NO. 3   GILBERT AND NEWBERY: PREEMPTIVE PATENTING   517

argument holds if competition for the patent is less intense, so that the potential entrant anticipates positive profits instead of the zero profits implied by equation (1).[5]

Kenneth Arrow observed that, with patent protection, the incentive to invest in research and development is less under monopoly than under competitive conditions, which would suggest that monopolistic firms would be slower than competitors in developing new products or processes, *ceteris paribus*. This does not contradict the arguments in Section I because Arrow assumed that entry was blockaded in the monopoly case. This paper does show that allowing for the possibility of entry can have a marked effect on monopoly incentives for $R\&D$.

II. Comments on the Simple Model

The preceding example illustrates the source of incentives for preemptive patenting. The incentives are not the result of market failures which Williamson (1977a) describes as shielding dominant firms from the forces of competition. In the preemption example, markets operate efficiently except for the assumed prior existence of a firm with substantial monopoly power. The firm can sustain its monopoly if potential entrants rationally expect that rivalry will erode total industry profits. This does require some foresight on the part of potential entrants, and it implicitly assumes entrants are large enough to have some effect on total industry profits.

The example ignores several potentially significant complications. Those which can be addressed without a more general model are discussed below, while more involved issues are deferred to the next section.

A. *Monopoly Expenditure on R&D*

The monopolist prevents entry by patenting before the competitive date. If a potential competitor knows this strategy is rational for

the monopolist, entry through research and development will not occur. This raises the question of whether the monopolist actually has to carry out an $R\&D$ plan which produces a patent before the competitive date. The preemption threat would be credible if the monopolist could accelerate $R\&D$ activity in response to $R\&D$ spending by potential rivals without incurring significant additional costs or delays. In this case, the potential of entry does not alter the behavior of the monopolist, and the monopolist invests in research and development as if entry were blockaded. Potential competitors do not invest in $R\&D$ because they know it is rational for the monopolist to accelerate his research if any competitor enters the patent race.

Conversely, if the monopolist incurs substantial costs by speeding up $R\&D$ in response to the inventive activities of rivals, the monopolist may be forced to play the preemption threat. This would be rational if the cost of waiting for a competitor to begin a research and development program exceeded the return from preemption. In this circumstance, research is carried out at the intensity determined by competitive forces, but it is the monopolist who performs the research (as, indeed, Joseph Schumpeter argued).

The remainder of this paper assumes the monopolist must play the preemption threat. A formal model of the patent competition is that of an auction market. Each firm enters a bid which is the maximum present-value amount that the firm will spend on research and development. (Firms can be thought of as bidding for $R\&D$ services.) With free entry, competitors will bid up $R\&D$ expenditures to the level determined by equation (1). At this level of investment in $R\&D$, monopoly profits are strictly higher if the monopolist patents and if equation (6) is satisfied. Hence the established firm will enter a slightly higher bid which preempts the competitive patent date. Preemption is a Nash equilibrium of this bidding game.

B. *Preemption and "Sleeping Patents"*

A sleeping patent is an invention that is not put to commercial use. In a world of

---

[5] A potential competitor may patent with the expectation of bargaining with the monopolist for a share of the difference between monopoly profits with and without competition. This does not change the incentive to preempt provided the rival expects his share of monopoly profits to be less than unity.

certainty, a monopolist protected from entry would never invest resources to produce a sleeping patent, since the monopolist could postpone the patent date until the best moment for innovation and reduce present discounted costs.[6] Yet a sleeping patent may occur as the consequence of preemptive patenting by the monopolist. As an illustration, consider the case where the patented substitute product has the same production cost and the same demand characteristics as the product controlled by the monopolist, except that development of the substitute from the patented design to the production state is costly. This means that any revenue stream can be earned at lower cost by producing product 1 than by developing and producing the substitute product. In particular, when amortized development costs are deducted from profits,

$$(7) \qquad \pi_m\left(P_m^1, P_m^2\right) < \pi_m\left(P_m^1\right)$$

for any P_m^2 at which demand and production of the substitute is positive.[7]

With these assumptions a profit-maximizing monopolist will never choose to produce the substitute product, but might the monopolist patent the substitute and let it sleep? If entry of a rival is profitable, the argument developed in the simple model is still valid and the monopolist will preemptively patent the substitute whenever entry is expected to lower total industry profits.

The possibility of sleeping patents strengthens the argument for preemptive patenting by the monopolist. The monopolist's decision to let a patent sleep is effi-

cient given the monopolist's choice of output(s). If a rival uses the patent, the effect of entry is to lower industry profits by using an inefficient production technology as well as possibly lowering profits through price competition. Both effects serve as incentives for preemptive patenting.

The monopolist must patent before potential competitors to deter entry, and this determines the invention date. The date at which the monopolist actually uses the patent depends on the characteristics of the new technology and the characteristics of the monopolist's existing capital stock. In this illustration the monopolist will never use the patent, but more generally Yoram Barzel and Dasgupta et al. show that a monopolist's optimal date for use of a patented technology will be later than the date determined by competition (the preemption date).

C. *Managerial Diseconomies*

Managerial diseconomies exist if the monopolist cannot conduct a research program or production plan as efficiently as any rival. Formally, managerial diseconomies make no difference to the monopolist's decision problem. Preemption is a rational strategy if the cost of securing the patent is less than the difference between monopoly profits with the patent and the profits when entry is allowed to occur. Obviously if managerial diseconomies are significant, preemption is less likely to occur. What is more important is that in such cases the monopolist may dissipate much of the producers' surplus potentially available to the most efficient research group. For it may still pay the monopolist to preempt more efficient rivals, perhaps at the expense of almost all the potential profit.

III. Strategic Behavior, Uncertainty, and Multiple Competitive Threats

The illustrative example described in Section I was sufficient to introduce the monopolist's decision problem and show the incentives for preemptive patenting. The general problem is much more complex. The monopolist can pursue strategic activities that lower

---

[6]A monopolist protected from entry may hold a sleeping patent if the patent represents a step in the development of a more advanced technology or if the patent is a joint product from another line of research. Sleeping patents are not limited to monopoly since, as Partha Dasgupta, Gilbert, and Joseph Stiglitz show, free entry can lead to sleeping patents in a competitive *R&D* market.

[7]Peter Swan (1970) argued that a monopolist would use any new technology that a competitor would use, but his argument required the assumption of convex cost functions, which is ruled out by consideration of development costs.

the profitability of the patent to a potential competitor. The value of a patent and the process of invention are clouded by uncertainty. The assumption of a single patentable substitute for the monopolized product is clearly extreme, and in practice the protection afforded by a patent is limited by the ability to invent around and imitate the patent.

This section shows that these additional considerations do not destroy the incentives for preemptive patenting. The monopolist should take advantage of entry-deterring strategies, but these strategies should be used as complements to preemptive patenting, unless the strategies used alone efficiently impede entry. With uncertainty, preemption remains desirable if the expectations of potential entrants are known, but without this knowledge, optimistic competitors may succeed in patenting before the monopolist. The existence of more than one patentable substitute will generally have a large effect on the monopolist's maximum attainable profits, but these multiple potential patents need not alter the desirability of preemptive activity.

A. *Strategic Behavior*

In the simple example, firms' strategies were limited to setting a price and producing sufficient quantities to meet demand at that price. This ignores the possibility of strategic behavior by an incumbent firm with the objective of either deterring entry or reducing the losses from competition. This section shows that in the case of a single competitive threat, strategic behavior does not alter the incentive for preemption. Strategies that lower the expected profits to potential entrants make preemption more attractive by lowering the cost of an R&D program designed to patent before rivals. Strategic investments and preemption generally go hand-in-hand as components of the incumbent firm's business strategies, although investments can be so effective in preventing entry as to make preemptive patenting unnecessary.

We choose an illustrative example of strategic investment following the analysis in Avinash Dixit (1980) where a dominant firm acts as a Stackelberg leader in the choice of capacity. Investment in capacity may benefit the incumbent firm by increasing profits in the event of entry and by possibly delaying the date at which entry occurs. The latter follows in our patenting model because the date of entry (patenting) depends directly on anticipated profits through the cost of invention function. In particular, firms may abandon the patent race if the returns from entry are sufficiently small.

Industry capacity affects the profits of both the incumbent and entering firm directly through costs and indirectly through the selection of product prices. We assume strategic behavior takes place only in the selection of production capacity by the incumbent for the manufacture of product 1 and we amend the notation for profits to include this capacity choice, represented by K. For simplicity the choice of production capacities for product 2, which should be conditional on K, is suppressed in the notation.

One result emerges immediately. Suppose in the absence of preemptive patenting the incumbent firm chooses a strategy that results in entry at date T when capacity is K. If monopoly profits exceed total profits with entry, *the incumbent firm is at least as well off choosing the same investment strategy and patenting before date T.* The proof of this result is exactly the same as in Section I where only pricing decisions were considered. Note that the argument in Section I holds for any market environment described by demands, technology, and capacities, provided the environment is the same whether or not preemption occurs. What remains unanswered is the effect of preemption on the choice of strategic investment. Consider equation (5), the difference between incumbent profits with and without preemption, augmented to include capacity choice. Technically we should write profits as the time dependent flow of net revenues corresponding to a particular investment strategy, but we shall simply append the variable K to represent the actual capacity at the date of entry and omit time as an explicit argument of the profit functions. If capacity choice is the same with and without preemption, the difference in incumbent profits is

$$(8) \quad (V_p - V_e) = \int_T^\infty \left\{ \pi_m\left(P_m^1, P_m^2, K\right) \right.$$

$$\left. - \left[\pi_m\left(P_m^1, P_e^2, K\right) + \pi_e\left(P_m^1, P_e^2, K\right)\right]\right\} e^{-rt} dt.$$

The entry date T depends on the choice of K through the straightforward extension of equation (1) to include the effect of capacity on entrant profits.

Let P denote the price vector (P_m^1, P_m^2, P_e^2) and define

$$(9) \quad \Delta(P, K) = \pi_m\left(P_m^1, P_m^2, K\right)$$

$$- \left[\pi_m\left(P_m^1, P_e^2, K\right) + \pi_e\left(P_m^1, P_e^2, K\right)\right],$$

the difference between monopoly and competitive profits, or the loss from competition given capacity choice and prices at a particular (suppressed) date. Assuming continuity of the entry date and profits, differentiating equation (9) with respect to K gives the relative effect of a local change in capacity on incumbent profits with and without preemption.

$$(10) \quad \frac{d}{dK}(V_p - V_e)$$

$$= \int_T^\infty \frac{d\Delta(P, K)}{dK} e^{-rt} dt - \Delta(P, K) e^{-rT} \frac{dT}{dK}.$$

The first term in equation (10) is the change in the loss from competition due to a change in the level of capacity. Since the loss from competition is the incentive to preempt conditional on a capacity choice, if this increases (decreases) with capacity, it increases (decreases) the marginal value of capacity in the preemption decision. The second term represents the effect on the preemption decision of a change in the entry date due to a change in the capacity choice. This term is always nonpositive because T is a nondecreasing function of K and $\Delta(P, K)$ is nonnegative ($\Delta(P, K)$ is evaluated at date T in equation

(10)).[8] Hence a sufficient condition for

$$(11) \quad \frac{d}{dK}(V_p - V_e) < 0$$

is that the loss from competition decrease with an increase in capacity investment by the dominant firm. Simple models show that the loss from competition may increase or decrease with capacity, although it should be noted that a decrease is not necessary for the marginal value of capacity in the preemption decision to be less than the marginal value of capacity in strategic entry deterrence without preemption.

The opportunity to preempt competitors alters incentives for strategic investment in capacity. Preemption profits exceed profits without preemption whenever the loss from competition is positive. If the loss from competition does not increase with capacity, the marginal value of capacity is lower in the preemption decision. Then at least in the neighborhood of the capacity choice without preemption, allowing for preemption reduces the optimal capacity choice. If incumbent profits are a concave function of capacity, then the optimal capacity choice with preemption is less than the optimal choice without preemption when inequality (11) holds.

It could be the case that the capacity choice without preemption blockades entry, corresponding to $T \to \infty$. Preemption is unnecessary if entry never occurs, hence profits with and without preemption are identical. One can show that reducing capacity below the level that blockades entry and preemptively patenting is a preferred strategy if the entry date is a continuous function of the capacity choice. The intuition here is that the cost of preemption is negligible if the entry date is sufficiently distant, and at any finite entry date preemption is desirable. If a small change in the capacity choice leads to a

---

[8] Output is a nondecreasing function of capacity if capacity lowers, or does not increase, marginal production cost. Thus entrant profits are a nonincreasing function of incumbent firm capacity, and lower profits imply a later entry date.

discontinuous change in the entry date, the gain from avoiding rivalry may be offset by the nonnegligible cost of preemption. In this case blockading entry through strategic investment in capacity can prove superior to preemptive patenting.

B. *Uncertainty*

Several sources of uncertainty may affect the preemption decision. The invention process, the characteristics of the invention and the market, the competitive strategies of an entrant, and the appropriate response by the original monopolist are all more or less uncertain. Uncertainty in the invention process means that the patent date is not a deterministic function of the expenditure on $R\&D$. Uncertainty in the characteristics of the invention and in the strategies used by competitors after entry affect the value of the new technology after it is patented.

Consider first the implications of a patent with an uncertain value. If all agents are risk neutral, the analysis is essentially unchanged. The preceding results hold with the profit terms replaced by their expected values, conditional on those actions (price, capacity, etc.) under the control of the firm.

Preemption is desirable only if the expected loss from competition is positive for every potential entrant. Define the expectations of the monopolist and a potential entrant as consistent if the sum of the returns expected by each firm with entry are no greater than the monopolist's expected return without entry. The monopolist is better off preempting if expectations are consistent for the most optimistic entrant. If expectations are not consistent, either the monopolist or the entrant is unduly optimistic. In the former case, the monopolist's realized profits would be greater with preemption. The latter case is an example of the winner's curse; the entrant's realized profits fall short of expectations and may fail to cover the costs of product development.

Of course the monopolist need not know and may not be able to infer the expectations of potential rivals. Even if all expectations are consistent, uncertainty about competitors' expectations may lead the monopolist

to choose a strategy that allows entry with positive probability. For example, suppose profits expected by an entrant of $100 are consistent, but the monopolist thinks it is unlikely that any rival expects to earn more than $50. An investment program that preempts only those rivals with profit expectations of no more than $50 costs less than a program that preempts all rivals with consistent expectations, and it would have higher expected profits if the probability that any entrant expects to earn more than $50 is sufficiently small.

The presence of risk aversion alters incentives for preemptive activity, as suggested by the analysis of Spence and Michael Porter. Risk aversion has consequences similar to managerial diseconomies, in that both imply a lower expected return from a given level of effort.

Similar results are obtained when the assumption of a deterministic patent date is replaced by a more general stochastic function which describes the probability of invention at date T conditional on a particular $R\&D$ plan. Various authors have constructed models which suggest that the competitive equilibrium will be one in which several firms pursue research programs, each expecting to make sufficient profits if successful in the patent race to offset the risks of failure.[9] It might be thought that such models imply that the monopolist cannot guarantee successful preemption, but this is not so, at least on our present set of assumptions. If expectations are consistent, $R\&D$ inputs are observable, and there are no managerial diseconomies, the monopolist can guarantee negative expected profits to any potential entrant, and knowing this, firms would not invest in $R\&D$.

The argument is the same as before, except that the monopolist has to set up the correct number of rival research teams—the same number as the number of firms who would choose to enter under competitive conditions. If the monopolist is able to do so (the assumption of no managerial economies, that

---

[9]Stiglitz (1971), Glenn Loury (1979), and Dasgupta and Stiglitz (1978) characterize equilibrium research for patent rights with stochastic returns.

he is as good at research as anyone else) then no extra firms will be tempted to enter and compete.[10]

C. Multiple Competitive Threats

The assumption that entry can be blockaded by a single patent is a convenient simplification to emphasize the strategic value of patents as barriers to entry, but it remains to be seen whether the results in Sections I and II extend to more realistic situations. Typically, many different design routes lead to the development of products with similar market characteristics. Patents may not be effective in preventing potential competitors from making relatively minor design changes which avoid infringement. The cost of an infringement suit relative to the potential gains from patent enforcement may be so large as to discourage legal proceedings. In addition, potential competitors are often dependent on each other for the use of patented technology. This encourages cross licensing of patents and discourages attempts at restrictive patent enforcement. Finally, any monopoly power afforded by patent protection may be ephemeral or trivial if the firm does not continue to introduce improved technology and develop a range of products necessary to capture a substantial market.

This section examines the preemption decision in the situation where entry can occur over time by developing any of several technologies with or without patent protection. The problems of cross licensing and developing new and improved technology are ignored, and in order to focus on the questions of entry deterrence, all patentable technologies are assumed perfectly substitutable with each other and with the monopolist's existing technology. This removes any incentive for a monopolist to engage in $R\&D$ for reasons other than entry deterrence. Let t index discrete time periods ($t = 0, 1, \ldots, T$), and assume there exists a mapping from the time path of investments into a statistic $A(t)$, which provides all relevant information pertaining to cumulative $R\&D$ knowledge at date t. Given the current state of knowledge, the firm has an estimate of the number of new technologies that can be developed and patented. The estimate can change over time and may decrease as well as increase. For simplicity, assume the number of new $R\&D$ paths can only increase, and let $\sigma(n \mid A(t), t)$ denote the probability that n new paths will be discovered at date t given $A(t)$.[11]

Assume, as in Section I, that the monopolist has no strategic choices other than preemptive patenting. This permits specifying the monopoly return as conditional only on whether entry occurs. Since patentable designs are perfect substitutes, the value of a patent to a potential entrant should be the same for all patentable designs. (Alternatively, entrants might place different values on different designs, provided the highest valuation by any entrant is the same for all designs.) Let π_m represent the monopolist's amortized profit per period if no rival firm patents a new design, and let π_0 be the profit if a rival patents. The per period return to a rival who wins a patent is π_e. The present value of rival profits with an interest rate r and discount factor $\beta = 1/1 + r$ equals $\pi_e/(1-\beta)$, which determines the cost of preempting each patent, provided all firms have access to the same $R\&D$ technology.

An attempt to blockade entry by preemptive patenting may prove excessively costly. Even if a firm succeeds in patenting all product innovations, the patents may not seriously encumber potential competitors who

[10] The reason why these models predict more than one firm undertaking research is that there are essentially U-shaped costs curves to a particular research laboratory, and hence an optimum level at which to run a given program. Rather than putting more eggs into one basket, it is argued that it pays to pursue several parallel lines each at the optimum rate. Our argument is that, if this is a rational way to organize $R\&D$, the monopolist could replicate it, and perhaps improve on it by having more exchange of ideas between rival laboratories. If, on the other hand, monopolies are bad at optimally subdividing research tasks between competing teams and choose to have just one research team, they could be described as being relatively inefficient, and suffering from managerial diseconomies.

[11] This assumption, to the extent that it is significant, exaggerates the cost of preemptive patenting, and should lead to an underestimate of the value of a preemption strategy.

VOL. 72 NO. 3   *GILBERT AND NEWBERY: PREEMPTIVE PATENTING*   523

can invent around and imitate new designs.[12] Since patenting cannot prevent this activity, it is convenient to include the effect of imitators in the profit terms, π_m and π_0. This convention permits a distinction between competitors who invent around existing patents and competitors who develop new patented designs. A rival may patent a new design first if the monopolist overlooks a patentable design or fails to develop ideas which could lead to new patents. Let $\mu(A(t), t)$ represent the probability that a preemption strategy fails to prevent entry because the monopolist missed a patentable design and a rival succeeds in patenting. The probability depends on cumulative $R\&D$ experience and could decrease with $A(t)$ if the firm is able to cast a wider net with more experience, or could increase with $A(t)$ if the $R\&D$ experience spills over to potential competitors and generates opportunities for product innovation external to the firm.

If $C = \pi_e/(1-\beta)$ is the cost of preempting each patent, the expected returns from a preemption strategy in the current period is

$$(12) \quad (1-\mu(A(t), t))\pi_m + \mu(A(t), t)\pi_0$$

$$- \sum_{n=0}^{\infty} \sigma(n|A(t), t)nC \equiv \pi_p(A(t), t).$$

Let $V(A(t), t)$ represent the present value of profits when the monopolist chooses an optimal strategy. The strategy could call for preemption only up to some date, after which the firm no longer attempts to prevent entry. The general expression for $V(A(t), t)$ is

$$(13) \quad V(A(t), t) = max\{[\pi_p(A(t), t)$$

$$+ (1-\mu(A(t), t))\beta V(A(t+1), t+1)$$

$$+ \mu(A(t), t)\beta\pi_0/(1-\beta)]; \pi_0/(1-\beta)\}.$$

The term in the square brackets is the present value of a preemption strategy. The current return from preemption is $\pi_p(A(t), t)$; with probability $(1-\mu(A(t), t))$, no rival firm

[12]Milton Kamien and Nancy Schwartz (1978) construct a descriptive model of imitative research.

will patent and the monopolist can choose in the next period whether to continue preemption or allow entry to occur. This explains the term $(1-\mu(A(t), t))\beta V(A(t+1), t+1)$. With probability $\mu(A(t), t)$, a rival will patent and the former monopolist's profits next period, discounted to the present, are $\beta\pi_0/(1-\beta)$, which accounts for the third term in the square brackets. The last term is the present value of profits if entry occurs, and this equals the return if no attempt is made to preempt rivals.

A general solution for the monopolist's optimal policy is straightforward but cumbersome. Simplifying the dependence of the probabilities μ and σ offers insight into the determinants of the preemption decision without detailed computations. Assume the probability, μ, of a breakthrough by a competitor is constant and the expected number of new $R\&D$ paths in each period,

$$(14) \quad \bar{n}(A(t), t) = \sum_{n=0}^{\infty} \sigma(n|A(t), t)n$$

is also a constant. The present value of a preemption strategy for this case is

$$(15) \quad \bar{V} = \pi_p + (1-\mu)\beta\bar{V} + \mu\beta\pi_0/(1-\beta),$$

where $\pi_p = (1-\mu)\pi_m + \mu\pi_0 - \bar{n}\pi_e/(1-\beta)$. Rearranging terms gives

$$(16) \quad \bar{V} = \frac{\pi_0}{1-\beta} + \frac{1}{1-(1-\mu)\beta}$$

$$\times \left[(1-\mu)(\pi_m - \pi_0) - \frac{\bar{n}}{1-\beta}\pi_e\right].$$

Since $\pi_0/(1-\beta)$ is the present value of profits when the firm does not attempt a preemption strategy, the expected profits from preemption are positive only if

$$(17) \quad \pi_m - \pi_0 > \frac{\bar{n}}{(1-\beta)(1-\mu)}\pi_e.$$

This condition is much more restrictive than the requirement that monopoly profits exceed the industry profits if entry occurs, as determined in Section I. Entrant profits in equation (18) are multiplied by the factor $\bar{n}/(1-\beta)(1-\mu)$. The term $\bar{n}\pi_e/(1-\beta)$ is the present value cost of continued entry deterrence, and this is divided by $(1-\mu)$, the probability that deterrence is successful. Even modest prospects for new $R\&D$ opportunities cause a significant increase in the cost of entry deterrence. It is not difficult to see that a preemption strategy would be futile in a technologically progressive industry, where both $\bar{n}$ and μ are relatively large.

Furthermore, even if the factor $\bar{n}/(1-\beta)$ $\cdot(1-\mu)$ is close to one, inequality (17) is not equivalent to the condition that monopoly profits exceed profits with competition because the profit, π_m, is defined to include the impacts of imitating firms. This is less than pure monopoly profits by an amount equal to the sum of the profits of imitating firms plus the losses from imitative competition. Hence, even if the monopolist could succeed in preempting all patentable substitute technologies, this does not assure that a preemptive strategy would yield a higher net return.

Although these results imply that patenting may be an ineffective means to deter entry in most industries, other strategies may be used preemptively to erect barriers to entry. A monopolist may accelerate investment in new capacity in order to accumulate a capital stock large enough to serve as an entry deterrent. The effectiveness of preemptive capacity construction depends, as Dixit (1979, 1980) has argued, on the relation between a firm's capacity level (the threat level in game-theoretic terms) and the firm's production decision after entry occurs (i.e., the credibility of the threat). With free entry, a monopolist has an incentive to preemptively build capacity to deter entry, provided the capacity will be used if entry occurs (see Spence, 1977; Williamson, 1977b; and Gilbert and Harris, 1980).

IV. Concluding Remarks

While several conditions limit the efficacy of preemptive activity, the analysis in this paper shows that in some circumstances a firm can maintain a monopoly through preemptive activity despite the potential of entry. The conclusion is in agreement with that of Williamson (1977a), but for different reasons. Williamson attributes the persistence of dominant firms at least partly to market imperfections. We do not disagree with Williamson's arguments that market imperfections contribute to the persistence of dominant firms. We do disagree with the contrafactual statement that in the absence of market imperfections potential competition would eliminate dominant firms. Our results show that without market imperfections (except for an initial monopoly), incentives exist to maintain a monopoly position. Indeed, a perfect market for $R\&D$ inputs gives the monopolist a credible threat that it would overtake any rival undertaking a competitive research program, which reduces the cost of preemption to nil and makes the preservation of his monopoly position costless and hence doubly attractive.

The undesirable consequences of preemptive activity are evident. A firm may sustain its monopoly power through preemption. The firm may spend resources on the development of new technologies, and then deny society the use of these technologies. Resources are expended on research and development only to produce "sleeping patents" which are withheld from use, and the firm with monopoly power maintains its monopoly position. However, prohibiting preemptive activity need not lead to an increase in economic surplus even in those extreme situations where resources are expended primarily for entry deterrence rather than for product development.

The problem that may arise is implicit in the analysis of strategic behavior in Section III. Preemptive research and development is only one of many actions which, in the language of Joe Bain, may impede the entry of rivals or at least mitigate the profit loss from competition. In the absence of preemption, alternative entry-deterring behavior could incur private and social costs that exceed the social cost of monopoly sustained by preemptive activity. Section III showed conditions where strategic capital investment is lower when combined with preemptive research and development. If preemptive activity were prohibited, strategic capital investment, with its associated costs, would increase and the net cost in terms of economic surplus could be larger.

Preemption would be very hard to identify in any practical situation because it is difficult to distinguish product development that is the result of superior foresight and technological capabilities from development that is motivated by entry deterrence. This may be just as well since preemption need not have adverse consequences for economic welfare. Preemption requires investment in product development with only a probability of successful entry deterrence. Society gains from the development of new technology at a pace at least as rapid as would occur with more competition, and in all but rare instances the technology would be put to use. If entry deterrence is not successful, the burden of monopoly would be removed or reduced. Since entry at some date is inevitable, to the extent that preemption does occur it is a phase in the Schumpeterian process of creative destruction.

REFERENCES

Arrow, Kenneth J., "Economic Welfare and the Allocation of Resources for Invention," in *The Rate and Direction of Inventive Activity: Economic and Social Factors*, Conference No. 13, Universities–National Bureau of Economic Research, Princeton: Princeton University Press, 1962.

Bain, Joe, *Barriers to New Competition*, Cambridge, 1962.

Barzel, Yoram, "Optimal Timing of Innovation," *Review of Economic Statistics*, August 1968, *50*, 348–55.

Dasgupta, Partha, Gilbert, Richard J., and Stiglitz, Joseph E., "Invention and Innovation Under Alternative Market Structures: The Case of Natural Resources," *Review of Economic Studies*, forthcoming.

_____ and Stiglitz, Joseph E., "Market Structure and Research and Development," mimeo., Oxford University, 1978.

Dixit, Avinash K., "A Model of Duopoly Suggesting a Theory of Entry Barriers," *Bell Journal of Economics*, Spring 1979, *10*, 20–32.

_____, "The Role of Investment in Entry-Deterrence," *Economic Journal*,

March 1980, *90*, 95–106.

Eaton, B. Curtis, "The Theory of Spatial Preemption: Location as a Barrier to Entry," discussion paper no. 208, Queen's University, 1976.

Gilbert, Richard J. and Harris, Richard G., "Lumpy Investments and 'Destructive' Competition," presented at the NSF-NBER Conference on Industrial Organization and Public Policy, University of California-Berkeley, May 1980.

Kaldor, Nicholas, "Market Imperfections and Excess Capacity," *Economica*, February 1935, *2*, 35–50.

Kamien, Milton I., and Schwartz, Nancy L., "Potential Rivalry, Monopoly Profits and the Pace of Inventive Activity," *Review of Economic Studies*, October 1978, *45*, 547–58.

Loury, Glenn, "Market Structure and Innovation," *Quarterly Journal of Economics*, August 1979, *93*, 395–410.

Mansfield, Edwin, *Industrial Research and Technological Innovation*, New York: Norton, 1968.

Prescott, Edward C. and Visscher, Michael, "Sequential Location Among Firms with Foresight," *Bell Journal of Economics*, Autumn 1977, *8*, 378–93.

Rao, Ram and Rutenberg, David, "Preempting an Alert Rival: Strategic Timing of the First Plant by Analysis of Sophisticated Rivalry," *Bell Journal of Economics*, Autumn 1979, *10*, 412–28.

Reynolds, Robert, "Location and Entry Deterrence," discussion paper, U.S. Dept. of Justice, 1978.

Richels, Richard G. and Plummer, James L., "Optimal Timing of the US Breeder," *Energy Policy*, June 1977, *5*, 106–21.

Schmalensee, Richard, "Entry Deterrence in the Ready-to-Eat Breakfast Cereal Industry," *Bell Journal of Economics*, Autumn 1978, *9*, 305–27.

Schumpeter, Joseph, *Capitalism, Socialism, and Democracy*, 1942.

Spence, A. Michael, "Entry, Capacity, Investment and Oligopolistic Pricing," *Bell Journal of Economics*, Autumn 1977, *8*, 534–44.

_____, "Investment Strategy and Growth in a New Market," *Bell Journal of Economics*, Spring 1979, *10*, 1–19.

_____ and Porter, Michael, "The Capacity Expansion Process in a Growing Oligopoly: The Case of Corn Wet Milling," discussion paper no. 670, Harvard Institute of Economic Research, November 1978.

Stigler, George, *Industrial Organization*, Homewood: Richard D. Irwin, 1968.

Stiglitz, Joseph E., "Perfect and Imperfect Capital Markets," presented at the Econometric Society Meeting, New Orleans, 1971.

Swan, Peter L., "Market Structure and Technological Progress: The Influence of Monopoly on Product Innovation," *Quarterly Journal of Economics*, November 1970, *84*, 627–38.

Taylor, Chris T. and Silberston, Z. Aubrey, *The Economic Impact of the Patent System*, Cambridge, 1973.

Williamson, Oliver E., (1977a) *Markets and Hierarchies*, New York, 1977.

_____, (1977b) "Predatory Pricing—A Strategic and Welfare Analysis," *Yale Law Journal*, December 1977, *87*, 284–340.

New York Times, "Damages Denied in Xerox Case," December 30, 1978, pp. 25–26.

SCM Corp. v. Xerox Corp., 463 F. Supp. 983 (1978).

United States v. American Telephone & Telegraph Corp., Civil Action No. 74-1698 (District D.C.), dismissed January 8, 1982.

United States v. IBM Corp., 60 FRD 654, 658 (S.D. NY 1973), dismissed January 8, 1982.

[2]

Uncertain Innovation and the Persistence of Monopoly

By Jennifer F. Reinganum*

A topic of long-standing interest in industrial organization is the effect of monopoly power upon incentives to engage in innovative activity. More recently, the concept of monopoly has been replaced with incumbency, so that explicit account may be taken of the existence of potential (and actual) rivals. According to F. M. Scherer:

> There is abundant evidence from case studies to support the view that actual and potential new entrants play a crucial role in stimulating technical progress, both as direct sources of innovation and as spurs to existing industry members. ...new entrants contribute a disproportionately high share of all really revolutionary new industrial products and processes. [1980, pp. 437–38]

In a recent paper published in this *Review* (1982), Richard J. Gilbert and David M. G. Newbery show that, because an incumbent firm enjoys greater marginal incentives to engage in R&D (under their assumption of deterministic invention), the incumbent firm will engage in preemptive patenting. Thus the industry will tend to remain monopolized, and by the same firm.

In this paper, I present a model in which an incumbent firm and a challenger engage in a game of innovation in which the inventive process is stochastic. I show that when the first successful innovator captures a sufficiently high share of the post-innovation market (i.e., when the innovation is sufficiently revolutionary), then in a Nash equilibrium the incumbent firm invests less on a given project than the challenger. Under an alternative specification, in a Nash equilibrium an incumbent firm conducts fewer

*Associate Professor of Economics, Division of Humanities and Social Science, California Institute of Technology, Pasadena, CA 91125. I thank Ed Green, Roger Noll, John Roberts, and Louis Wilde for helpful comments. The financial support of the National Science Foundation is gratefully acknowledged.

parallel projects than would a challenger. In either case, the incumbent is less likely to patent the innovation than is the challenger.

The intuition for this result is relatively straightforward, at least in the case where the first successful innovator captures the entire post-innovation market. When the inventive process is stochastic, the incumbent firm continues to receive flow profits during the time preceding innovation. This period is of random length but is stochastically shorter the greater the firms' investments in R&D. Since a successful incumbent merely "replaces himself" (albeit with a more profitable product), the incumbent firm has a lower marginal incentive to invest in R&D than does the challenger.

Thus this paper provides a theoretical model that embodies Scherer's empirical observations: entrants stimulate progress both through their own innovative behavior and through their provocation of incumbent firms. Moreover, in equilibrium they contribute a disproportionate share of important innovations. I also attempt to isolate the causes of the discrepancy between my results and those of Gilbert and Newbery, and to integrate the two into a coherent theory consistent with the empirical observations.

I. Related Literature

For simplicity, consider a case of cost-reducing innovation in an industry with constant returns to scale. Let $\bar{c}$ denote the incumbent firm's initial unit cost, and let $c < \bar{c}$ be the unit cost associated with the new technology. Let the relevant profit rates be R = the current revenue flow to the incumbent firm; $\Pi(c)$ = the present value of monopoly profits using the new technology; also the present value of profits to the current incumbent if the incumbent receives a patent on the new technology; $\pi_i(c)$ = the present value of Nash-Cournot profits to the current incumbent firm if the challenger re-

742   THE AMERICAN ECONOMIC REVIEW   SEPTEMBER 1983

ceives a patent on the new technology; and $\pi_C(c)$ = the present value of Nash-Cournot profits to the challenger if the challenger receives a patent on the new technology.

ASSUMPTION 1: *The functions* $\Pi(c)$, $\pi_I(c)$, *and* $\pi_C(c)$ *are continuous, and piecewise continuously differentiable. Moreover,* $\Pi(c)$ *and* $\pi_C(c)$ *are nonincreasing in c while* $\pi_I(c)$ *is nondecreasing in c.*

That is, if the incumbent patents the new technology, its profits will be lower the higher is the unit cost associated with the new technology. On the other hand, if the challenger patents the new technology (and the incumbent continues to use the old one), then the challenger's profits will be lower and the incumbent's higher the higher is the unit cost associated with the new technology.

Definition 1: The innovation will be termed *drastic* if $c \leqslant c_0$, where c_0 is assumed to exist and to be uniquely defined as the maximum value of c such that $\pi_I(c) = 0$.

The important feature of the constant returns to scale assumption is that if profits are zero, so is output. Thus if $c \leqslant c_0$, then the current incumbent's output will be zero after the challenger patents the innovation. In this event, the challenger is a monopolist and $\pi_C(c) = \Pi(c)$. Note that $\Pi(c) \geqslant \pi_I(c) + \pi_C(c)$ with strict inequality whenever the innovation is not drastic.

Remark 1: Since $c < \bar{c}$, the present value of monopoly profits after innovation $\Pi(c)$ always exceeds the present value of monopoly profits without the innovation, R/r, where r is the discount rate. Furthermore, $R/r > \pi_I(c)$ for all $c < \bar{c}$. This is because $R/r = \Pi(\bar{c}) > \pi_I(\bar{c}) \geqslant \pi_I(c)$ for all $c < \bar{c}$ by Assumption 1.

The following example illustrates the preceding discussion and Assumption 1. If the demand curve is linear, $P = a - bQ$, then the functions above are $\Pi(c) = (a-c)^2/4rb$, $\pi_I(c) = (a - 2\bar{c} + c)^2/9rb$ and $\pi_C(c) = (a - 2c + \bar{c})^2/9rb$, whenever the expressions in parentheses are nonnegative; otherwise the

relevant value for the function is zero. Each of these functions is continuously differentiable except at the point at which the expression in parentheses becomes zero, and continuity is preserved at that point. The innovation is drastic whenever $c \leqslant c_0$, where $a - 2\bar{c} + c_0 = 0$. From this equality, it is easy to see that $\Pi(c_0) = \pi_C(c_0)$ and $\pi_I(c_0) = 0$.

Gilbert and Newbery argue as follows. If the inventive process is deterministic, then whoever is willing to bid most for the new technology receives the patent first with probability 1. The challenger will be willing to bid up to $\pi_C(c)$, while the incumbent will be willing to bid up to $\Pi(c) - \pi_I(c)$. Since $\Pi(c) \geqslant \pi_I(c) + \pi_C(c)$, with strict inequality for $c > c_0$, the incumbent preemptively patents the new technology. Only if the innovation is drastic will the incumbent and the challenger invest an equal amount. Consequently, preemption is the Nash equilibrium outcome in the bidding game. Thus the industry will remain monopolized and in the hands of the current incumbent.

This is clearly true when there is no uncertainty in the innovation process. The natural extension of this result to the case of uncertain innovation is that the incumbent is *more likely* to patent the innovation than is the challenger.[1] In the next section, a simple

---

[1] Gilbert subsequently argues; "Uncertainty in the invention process does not greatly change the deterministic analysis of preemption, provided R and D expenditures are sensitive to the expected returns and the established firm is no more averse to risk than rivals" (1981, p. 299). In a laudatory comment on the Gilbert paper, Richard Craswell continues: "Assuming any form of direct relationship between the amount spent on R and D and the likelihood of making the invention first, the incumbent will end up with the patent more often than not, and his monopoly will be maintained. In fact, the incumbent will usually end up with the patent even if he is less efficient at R and D than are his rivals, so long as his inefficiency does not completely negate the advantage due to his larger expenditure on R and D " (p. 272).

To summarize, Gilbert and Craswell evidently believe that the result that the incumbent invests more than the challenger extends straightforwardly to the case of uncertainty. A somewhat different argument is offered by Gilbert and Newbery in support of the same basic claim: "Similar results are obtained when the assumption of a deterministic patent date is replaced by a more general stochastic function which describes the probabil-

model is presented which incorporates uncertainty. It is found that, for drastic innovations, the incumbent always invests less than the challenger, so that the incumbency changes hands *more often than not*. Due to the continuity of the equilibrium investment rates in the unit cost associated with the new technology, there will be an open neighborhood of c_0, representing innovations which are not drastic, for which the incumbent still invests less than the challenger. In Section III, I briefly report results from a more general model in which firms are allowed to choose both the number of parallel projects to undertake, and the rate of investment on each project. Again there is a nontrivial set of innovations which the incumbent is less likely to patent than is the challenger.

II. A Model Incorporating Uncertainty

The model developed in this section is a generalization of that of Tom Lee and Louis Wilde (which is itself based upon a model by Glenn Loury). An incumbent and a challenger are simultaneously attempting to perfect a particular cost-reducing technology. Technological uncertainty takes the form of a stochastic relationship between the rate of investment and the eventual date of successful completion of the new technology. If x_I represents the rate of investment of the incumbent, and $\tau_I(x_I)$ the random success date of the incumbent, then $Pr\{\tau_I(x_I) \leqslant t\} = 1 - e^{-h(x_I)t}$, for $t \in [0, \infty)$. Similarly, if x_C and $\tau_C(x_C)$ represent the investment rate and the random success date for the challenger, then $Pr\{\tau_C(x_C) \leqslant t\} = 1 - e^{-h(x_C)t}$. The expected success date for firm i ($i = I, C$) is $1/h(x_i)$, where the function $h(.)$ is the hazard function used in much of the recent literature on patent races. In particular, following Loury, Lee and Wilde, and Partha Dasgupta and

Joseph Stiglitz, I assume:

ASSUMPTION 2: *The hazard function $h(.)$ is twice continuously differentiable, with $h'(x) > 0$ and $h''(x) < 0$ for all $x \in [0, \infty)$. Furthermore,*

$$h(0) = 0 = \lim_{x \to \infty} h'(x).$$

Thus the technology exhibits decreasing returns to scale.

Suppose that the new technology is patentable so that the race ends with the first success. The expected profit to the incumbent for any pair of investment rates (x_I, x_C) is

$$V^I(x_I, x_C) = \int_0^\infty e^{-rt} e^{-(h(x_I) + h(x_C))t}$$

$$\times \left[h(x_I)\Pi(c) + h(x_C)\pi_I(c) + R - x_I \right] dt$$

$$= \left[h(x_I)\Pi(c) + h(x_C)\pi_I(c) + R - x_I \right]$$

$$\Big/ \left[r + h(x_I) + h(x_C) \right].$$

That is, the incumbent receives $\Pi(c)$ at t if the challenger has not yet succeeded and the incumbent succeeds at t; this event has probability density $h(x_I)e^{-(h(x_I)+h(x_C))t}$. The incumbent receives $\pi_I(c)$ at t if the incumbent has not yet succeeded and the challenger succeeds at t; this event has probability density $h(x_C)e^{-(h(x_I)+h(x_C))t}$. Finally, the incumbent receives flow profits of R and pays flow costs of x_I so long as no firm has succeeded; this event has probability $e^{-(h(x_I)+h(x_C))t}$.

The challenger's payoff is analogous.

$$V^C(x_I, x_C) = \int_0^\infty e^{-rt} e^{-(h(x_I)+h(x_C))t}$$

$$\times \left[h(x_C)\pi_C(c) - x_C \right] dt$$

$$= \left[h(x_C)\pi_C(c) - x_C \right]$$

$$\Big/ \left[r + h(x_I) + h(x_C) \right].$$

The differences between these payoffs arise from the incumbent's current profit flow and

---

ity of invention at date T conditional on a particular R and D plan. ... The argument is the same as before, except that the monopolist has to set up the correct number of rival research teams..." (p. 521). Thus the implied claim is that, if allowed to select the number of parallel projects to be undertaken, an incumbent firm would choose a larger number than would a challenger.

744   THE AMERICAN ECONOMIC REVIEW   SEPTEMBER 1983

the fact that it shares the market in the event of successful innovation by the challenger.

Definition 2: A *strategy* for the incumbent (challenger) is an investment rate $x_I(x_C)$. The *payoff* to the incumbent (challenger) is $V^I(x_I, x_C)(V^C(x_I, x_C))$.

Definition 3: A *best response function for the incumbent* is a function $\phi_I : [0, \infty) \to [0, \infty)$ such that, for each x_C, $V^I(\phi_I(x_C), x_C) \geqslant V^I(x_I, x_C)$ for all $x_I \in [0, \infty)$. Similarly, a *best response function for the challenger* is a function $\phi_C : [0, \infty) \to [0, \infty)$ such that, for each $x_I, V^C(x_I, \phi_C(x_I)) \geqslant V^C(x_I, x_C)$ for all $x_C \in [0, \infty)$. The best response functions will also depend upon the parameters (c, R).

Definition 4: A strategy pair (x_I^*, x_C^*) is a *Nash equilibrium* if $x_I^* = \phi_I(x_C^*)$ and $x_C^* = \phi_C(x_I^*)$. That is, each firm's investment rate is a best response to the other's.

The proof of the following proposition can be found in the Appendix.

PROPOSITION 1: *If $h'(0) \geqslant \max\{1/[\Pi(c) - R/r], 1/\pi_C(c)\}$, then there exists a best response function[2] for the incumbent $\phi_I(x_C; c, R)$ which satisfies the first-order condition $\partial V^I(\phi_I, x_C)/\partial x_I = 0$ and the second-order condition $\partial^2 V^I(\phi_I, x_C)/\partial x_I^2 < 0$. The function ϕ_I is continuously differentiable in its argument x_C and continuous in the parameters c, R. Similarly, there exists a best response function for the challenger $\phi_C(x_I; c)$ which satisfies the analogous first- and second-order conditions, and is continuously differentiable in its argument x_I and continuous in the parameter c. Moreover, there exists a pair of Nash equilibrium strategies $x_I^*(c, R)$ and $x_C^*(c, R)$; each is continuous in the parameters c, R.*

---

[2] The hypothesis of this proposition ensures that each firm's payoff function is initially nondecreasing in that firm's investment level. Without this assumption, it is possible that the firm may have two (widely separated) best responses.

The first-order conditions which implicitly define the best response functions are

$$(1) \quad \partial V^I(\phi_I, x_C)/\partial x_I \propto [r + h(\phi_I)$$
$$+ h(x_C)][h'(\phi_I)\Pi(c) - 1]$$
$$- [h(\phi_I)\Pi(c) + h(x_C)\pi_I(c)$$
$$+ R - \phi_I]h'(\phi_I) = 0;$$

$$(2) \quad \partial V^C(x_I, \phi_C)/\partial x_C \propto [r + h(x_I)$$
$$+ h(\phi_C)][h'(\phi_C)\pi_C(c) - 1]$$
$$- [h(\phi_C)\pi_C(c) - \phi_C]h'(\phi_C) = 0.$$

Rearranging terms and noting the definitions of $V^I(\phi_I, x_C)$ and $V^C(x_I, \phi_C)$ yields

$$(3)$$
$$V^I(\phi_I, x_C) = [h'(\phi_I)\Pi(c) - 1]\big/ h'(\phi_I);$$

$$(4)$$
$$V^C(x_I, \phi_C) = [h'(\phi_C)\pi_C(c) - 1]\big/ h'(\phi_C).$$

Remark 2: Since the individual firm payoffs must be nonnegative, particularly when the firms play best responses, it follows that $h'(\phi_I)\Pi(c) - 1 \geqslant 0$ and $h'(\phi_C)\pi_C(c) - 1 \geqslant 0$.

LEMMA 1: $\partial \phi_I(x_C; c, R)/\partial x_C > 0$ *and* $\partial \phi_C(x_I; c)/\partial x_I \geqslant 0$. *Thus the existence of the challenger provokes the incumbent to invest more than it otherwise would on the innovation.*

PROOF:
By the implicit function theorem,

$$\partial \phi_I/\partial x_C = -[\partial^2 V^I(\phi_I, x_C)/\partial x_C \partial x_I]$$
$$\big/[\partial^2 V^I(\phi_I, x_C)/\partial x_I^2].$$

The denominator is negative by the second-order condition. The numerator is

$$- h'(x_C)[h'(\phi_I)(\Pi(c) - \pi_I(c)) - 1]$$
$$= - h'(x_C)h'(\phi_I)[V^I(\phi_I, x_C) - \pi_I(c)]$$

by equation (3). Since ϕ_I is a best response to x_C, $V^I(\phi_I, x_C) \geq V^I(0, x_C)$; but $V^I(0, x_C) - \pi_I(c) = [R - r\pi_I(c)]/[r + h(x_C)] > 0$ by Remark 1. Thus $V^I(\phi_I, x_C) - \pi_I(c) > 0$ for all x_C. It follows that $\partial\phi_I/\partial x_C > 0$ for all x_C.

By the implicit function theorem,

$$\partial\phi_C/\partial x_I = -[\partial^2 V^C(x_I, \phi_C)/\partial x_I \partial x_C]$$
$$/[\partial^2 V^C(x_I, \phi_C)/\partial x_C^2].$$

The denominator is negative by the second-order condition, while the numerator is $-h'(x_I)[h'(\phi_C)\pi_C(c) - 1]$, which is nonpositive by Remark 2.

LEMMA 2: *If the innovation is drastic and* $R > 0$, *then* $\phi_I(x; c, R) < \phi_C(x; c)$ *for all* x, c.

PROOF:

Recall that if the innovation is drastic, $\pi_C(c) = \Pi(c)$ and $\pi_I(c) = 0$. Then the only difference between equations (1) and (2), which implicitly define the best response functions ϕ_I and ϕ_C, is the term R, representing current profit flows to the incumbent firm. If $R = 0$, and the innovation is drastic, then $\phi_I(x; c, 0) = \phi_C(x; c)$ for all x, c. Again using the implicit function theorem, we see that

$$\partial\phi_I/\partial R = -[\partial^2 V^I(\phi_I, x)/\partial R \, \partial x_I]$$
$$/[\partial^2 V^I(\phi_I, x)/\partial x_I^2].$$

Since the denominator is negative and the numerator is $h'(\phi_I)$ which is positive, we have $\phi_I(x; c, R) < \phi_I(x; c, 0) = \phi_C(x; c)$ for all $R > 0$, and all x, c.

PROPOSITION 2: *If the innovation is drastic and* $R > 0$, *then in a Nash equilibrium, the incumbent invests less than the challenger; that is,* $x_I^*(c, R) < x_C^*(c, R)$.

PROOF:

Suppose, contrary to the proposition, that $x_I^*(c, R) \geq x_C^*(c, R)$. Then Lemmas 1 and 2 and the definition of a Nash equilibrium

imply that

$$x_C^*(c, R) = \phi_C(x_I^*(c, R); c)$$
$$\geq \phi_C(x_C^*(c, R); c)$$
$$> \phi_I^*(x_C^*(c, R); c, R) = x_I^*(c, R).$$

But this is a contradiction. Thus $x_I^*(c, R) < x_C^*(c, R)$.

COROLLARY 1: *If* $R > 0$, *then there exists an open neighborhood of* c_0 *(which may depend on* R*), denoted* $N(c_0; R)$, *such that if the technology is not drastic, but* $c \in N(c_0; R)$, *then* $x_I^*(c, R) < x_C^*(c, R)$.

PROOF:

This follows immediately from Proposition 2 and the continuity of the Nash equilibrium investment rates $x_I^*(c, R)$ and $x_C^*(c, R)$ in the parameter c.

Thus I have concluded that for sufficiently radical innovations (i.e., for technologies in the set $N(c_0; R)$), it is precisely the assumption of certainty vs. uncertainty which is responsible for the discrepancy between my results and those of Gilbert and Newbery. To see the economics of the issue, consider what happens in my model with drastic innovation if the incumbent were to consider investing a tiny bit less. It would suffer a slightly increased probability of losing the patent to the challenger and a slightly decreased chance of collecting the patent itself, but would spend a bit less and would receive the flow revenue R stochastically longer. The challenger, by investing a bit less, suffers a slightly increased probability of losing the patent to the incumbent and a slightly decreased probability of collecting the patent for itself; on the other hand, it spends a bit less. Since it *does not* collect any additional current revenue, its marginal benefits due to investing a bit less are lower than those of the incumbent, and hence in equilibrium the challenger invests more than the incumbent. Consider the same question under the assumption of certainty. What happens in the certainty model if the incumbent were to consider investing a tiny bit less? If the incumbent still invests more than the challenger, then the incumbent collects revenues R with probability 1 and suffers no threat of losing the patent to the challenger. If the incumbent was investing less than the challenger, then further reductions have no impact on their profits. The only important case is when the incumbent considers reducing its investment from above that of the challenger to below that of the challenger. This results in the incumbent receiving R for an infinitesimally short additional time, and losing the noninfinitesimal difference between the present values of monopoly profits and Nash-Cournot profits when the challenger patents the new technology. Consequently, the incumbent is always willing to invest more than the challenger when the innovation process is deterministic.

III. A Model with Parallel Projects

In this section, I report briefly on a model in which firms are allowed to select both the number of parallel projects to undertake, denoted n_I and n_C for incumbent and challenger, respectively, and the rate of investment on each project, x_I and x_C, respectively.[3] The conjecture is that the incumbent is more likely than the challenger to patent the innovation. However, it can be shown that both firms will select the same level of investment per project; that is, $x_I^* = x_C^*$. Thus each firm varies its "scale" by choosing the number of (statistically independent) projects. Moreover, it can be shown that if the innovation is drastic and $R > 0$, then $n_I^* < n_C^*$; that is, the incumbent invests in fewer parallel projects than does the challenger. Again by the continuity of these equilibrium strategies in the parameters R, c, there exists an open set of innovations which are not drastic, for which the incumbent still operates

---

[3]Since it would seem to add little to the essential intuition of the previous section, the analysis of this more general model is not included here; a technical appendix to this paper which contains the analysis of this more general model is available from the author upon request.

fewer parallel projects than does the challenger.

Thus the alternative form of the conjecture is also false for an open set of innovations—those which are sufficiently revolutionary. It fails for essentially the same reason as before; the incumbent has a lower marginal incentive to hasten the date of innovation, since it continues to receive the flow profit R until innovation, while the challenger does not.

IV. Conclusion

It seems clear that the assumption of certainty in the inventive process is not an innocuous one, particularly when one compares the policy implications of these two models. The Gilbert-Newbery model suggests that one ought to be very worried about the development of entrenched monopolies via preemptive patenting. This study suggests that one can reasonably worry far less on this score when the inventive process is stochastic.

It seems reasonable that the degree of cost reduction and the degree of associated uncertainty are related. That is, more drastic innovations may also be subject to greater uncertainty. Thus one can reconcile the Gilbert and Newbery paper with Scherer's observations by suggesting that the certainty model is most appropriate for incremental innovations.

Of course, the models discussed in this paper also rely upon simplifying assumptions. The assumption of constant returns to scale in the output production function is particularly useful, since it allows us to use simple parametric expressions for the post-innovation profit functions. Taken together, this paper and that of Gilbert and Newbery indicate that the influence of monopoly power on the persistence of monopoly is considerably more complicated than either paper taken alone might suggest.

APPENDIX: PROOF OF PROPOSITION 1

The method of proof is as follows. I first show that there is a finite investment level for each firm such that the firm's best re-

VOL. 73 NO. 4   *REINGANUM: PERSISTENCE OF MONOPOLY POWER*   747

sponse never exceeds this level, regardless of its rival's investment. Then we can restrict the firm to strategies within this interval without any loss of generality. Next it is shown that the firm's payoff function is single peaked in its own investment level, and reaches this peak on the aforementioned compact interval. Finally, we need to show that this peak is a stationary point and that the payoff function is locally concave at this point. This suffices to define the firm's best response function. A fixed-point argument completes the proof.

$$\partial V^I / \partial x_I = \left[h'(x_I)(\Pi(c)r - R + h(x_C) \right.$$

$$\left. \times (\Pi(c) - \pi_I(c)) + x_I) - B \right] / B^2,$$

where $B = r + h(x_I) + h(x_C)$. Let

$$f_I(x_I, x_C) = h'(x_I)\left[\Pi(c)r - R + h(x_C) \right.$$

$$\left. \times (\Pi(c) - \pi_I(c)) + x_I \right] - B.$$

Note that sgn $\partial V^I / \partial x_I =$ sgn f_I. Under the assumption that $h'(0) \geqslant \max\{1/(\Pi(c) - R/r), 1/\pi_C(c)\}$, it can be seen that $f_I(0, x_C) \geqslant 0$ for all x_C. Moreover, $f_I(\hat{x}_I(c, R), x_C) \leqslant 0$ for all x_C, where

$$\hat{x}_I(c, R) = \min\{x \in [0, \infty) | h'(x)$$

$$\leqslant \min\{1/(\Pi(c) - \pi_I(c)),$$

$$1/(\Pi(c) - R/r)\}\}.$$

This value exists and is finite since $\lim_{x \to \infty} h'(x) = 0$. Since

$$\partial f_I / \partial x_I = h''(x_I)\left[\Pi(c)r - R + h(x_C) \right.$$

$$\left. \times (\Pi(c) - \pi_I(c)) + x_I \right]$$

is strictly negative, the function V^I is first increasing, eventually peaks, and subsequently declines. Consequently, V^I is single peaked and reaches its peak at or before $\hat{x}_I(c, R)$ for all x_C.

The value of x_I which provides the peak is $\phi_I(x_C; c, R)$, the unique best response for the incumbent to x_C. Moreover, since V^I is

twice differentiable in (x_I, x_C) and continuous in (c, R), and since

$$\partial^2 V^I(\phi_I, x_C) / \partial x_I^2 = h''(\phi_I)\left[\Pi(c)r - R \right.$$

$$\left. + h(x_C)(\Pi(c) - \pi_I(c)) + \phi_I \right] / B^2 < 0,$$

ϕ_I is implicitly defined as a continuously differentiable function of x_C (and a continuous function of (c, R)) by the first-order condition $\partial V^I / \partial x_I = 0$. A similar argument establishes the analogous result for ϕ_C.

Define the composite function $\omega = \phi_I \circ \phi_C : [0, \hat{x}_I(c, R)] \to [0, \hat{x}_I(c, R)]$ (holding c and R fixed). The function $\omega(x; c, R)$ is continuously differentiable in x on a compact, convex and nonempty domain. Hence it has a fixed point $x_I^*(c, R)$ by Brouwer's theorem; that is, there is a point $x_I^*(c, R)$ such that $\omega(x_I^*(c, R); c, R) - x_I^*(c, R) = 0$. Under the assumption that $x_I^*(c, R)$ is not a critical point of $\omega(x; c, R) - x$ (i.e., $\partial \omega(x_I^*(c, R); c, R)/\partial x \neq 1$), there exists a neighborhood of c in which the implicit function $x_I^*(c, R)$ is continuous (see Magnus Hestenes, p. 22, Theorem 7.1). Let $x_C^*(c, R) = \phi_C(x_I^*(c, R); c)$. The strategies $x_I^*(c, R)$ and $x_C^*(c, R)$ constitute a Nash equilibrium, and they are continuous in the parameter c.

REFERENCES

Craswell, Richard, "Patents, Sleeping Patents and Entry Deterrence: Comments," in Steven C. Salop, ed., *Strategy, Predation and Antitrust Analysis*, Federal Trade Commission, September 1981, 271–85.

Dasgupta, Partha and Stiglitz, Joseph, "Uncertainty, Industrial Structure and the Speed of R and D," *Bell Journal of Economics*, Autumn 1980, *11*, 1–28.

Gilbert, Richard J., "Patents, Sleeping Patents and Entry Deterrence," in Steven C. Salop, ed., *Strategy, Predation and Antitrust Analysis*, Federal Trade Commission, September 1981, 205–69.

_____ **and Newbery, David M. G.,** "Preemptive Patenting and the Persistence of Monopoly," *American Economic Review*, June 1982, *72*, 514–26.

Hestenes, Magnus R., *Calculus of Variations*

and Optimal Control Theory, Huntington: Robert E. Krieger, 1980.

Lee, Tom **and** Wilde, Louis L., "Market Structure and Innovation: A Reformulation," *Quarterly Journal of Economics*, March 1980, *94*, 429–36.

Loury, Glenn C., "Market Structure and Innovation," *Quarterly Journal of Economics*, August 1979, *93*, 395–410.

Scherer, F. M., *Industrial Market Structure and Economic Performance*, 2d ed., Chicago: Rand McNally & Co. 1980.

[3]

Uncertain Innovation and the Persistence of Monopoly: Comment

By Richard J. Gilbert and David M. G. Newbery*

In her 1983 article, Jennifer Reinganum offers a counterexample to our earlier claim that preemptive patenting applies to situations where success in a patent race is uncertain. It is true that Reinganum's model includes uncertainty, and in her model an incumbent would not preempt competitors, but uncertainty is not the reason why her results differ from ours. Rather, the differences are the consequence of 1) a different assumption about timing of moves in the *R&D* game, 2) the absence of free entry, and 3) assumed diseconomies in the management of the firm. Although it is useful to call attention to the importance of these assumptions, it is equally important to understand why they lead to different conclusions.

In our 1982 article, we assumed that the incumbent had a first-mover advantage, and that he could credibly commit himself to a strategy that would make entry unprofitable. Potential entrants, observing this already chosen and committed strategy, would then choose to stay out, whether or not the subsequent race was deterministic or stochastic. In Reinganum's model, the entrant and the incumbent simultaneously choose their expenditure rates, and the incumbent has no first-mover advantage.

An alternative specification which has the properties of competition with a first mover is the bidding game described in our article (p. 517). In this game the firms bid for *R&D* services, and a firm can preempt by out-bidding its rivals. If competition among challengers establishes a certain bid, the incumbent can preempt by bidding slightly more than this amount. Preemption by the incumbent is a Nash equilibrium of this game, and the end result is similar to preemption by a firm with a first-mover advantage.

*Department of Economics, University of California, Berkeley, CA 94720, and Churchill College, Cambridge, England CB3 ODS, respectively.

Preemption by the incumbent firm is a Nash equilibrium of the bidding game. Preemption is also a Nash equilibrium of the extensive form model when the incumbent can move first and commit to an *R&D* expenditure. The first-mover model follows the sequential perfect Nash equilibrium structure in Avinash Dixit (1980), although we had assumed free entry whereas Dixit models a duopoly. (The same equilibrium notion might be termed a Stackelberg equilibrium, which implies the ability of the leader--the incumbent—to commit to an *R&D* expenditure.) Reinganum's model is a Nash game where preemption need not occur, but the specification differs in extensive form and in the strategies available to competitors. These differences, and not the assumption of certainty or uncertainty, are primarily responsible for the contrasting conclusions in our papers. We return to the question of which is the more appropriate specification at the end of this comment.

I

Uncertainty is neither a necessary nor sufficient condition for the results demonstrated by Reinganum. Preemption can occur with an uncertain *R&D* process, and preemption need not occur when *R&D* is deterministic. For an example of the latter, consider a deterministic patent race as a one-shot Nash game. There is an incumbent and a challenger, and we employ the same notation as Reinganum: Π is the present value (PV) of the monopoly profits to the incumbent from the patent, π_I is the PV to the incumbent if the challenger wins, π_C is the PV to the challenger if he patents, R is the current profit of the incumbent, and r is the discount rate. The *R&D* technology is particularly simple. A firm can patent at date T and with a cost X (with $X \leq \pi_C$), or a firm can choose to do no *R&D*. The incumbent and the challenger make their decisions simultaneously, as in Reinganum. Ties are resolved by flipping a fair coin. With this simple technology, pure-strategy Nash equilibria can exist where either or both firms engage in $R\&D$. In addition, mixed-strategy equilibria can occur which have properties identified by Reinganum in her model of a stochastic $R\&D$ contest.

Let f be the probability that the incumbent patents, and g the probability that the challenger patents. Assuming (for simplicity of notation and without loss of generality) that T is sufficiently small for the time interval between the start of $R\&D$ and the patent date to be ignored, the challenger's expected return from $R\&D$ is

$$(1) \quad V_C = (1 - f)\pi_C + f\pi_C/2 - X.$$

The incumbent's expected return from no $R\&D$ is

$$(2) \quad V_I^0 = (1 - g)R/r + g\pi_I,$$

and the expected return from $R\&D$ is

$$(3) \quad V_I^1 = (1 - g)\Pi + g(\Pi + \pi_I)/2 - X.$$

In a mixed-strategy equilibrium, each competitor must be indifferent among the available alternatives. This requires $V_C = 0$ and $V_I^0 = V_I^1$, with the result that

$$(4) \quad f = 2(1 - X/\pi_C);$$

$$(5)\ g = 2[\Pi - X - R/r]/[\Pi + \pi_I - 2R/r].$$

Both f and g are between 0 and 1 if $\pi_C > X > (\Pi - \pi_I)/2$. If the innovation is drastic so that $\pi_I = 0$, $\Pi = \pi_C$, then $g > f$ and the challenger patents with higher probability. By the same continuity arguments set out in Reinganum, this will continue to hold for a range of less drastic innovations.

Although the strategies in this game are stochastic, the $R\&D$ process is not. Thus uncertainty in the $R\&D$ process is not necessary for the results reported by Reinganum. (See Drew Fudenberg et al., 1983, for a more detailed analysis of competition with a deterministic $R\&D$ technology.)

In our article (Section IIIB, p. 520), we argued that provided the incumbent was risk neutral and that players held consistent expectations, our results continued to hold with stochastic innovation, of which Reinganum's formulation is a special case. Again, we stress that this is true given our assumptions about the specification of the game, free entry, and the absence of managerial diseconomies. Uncertainty is not sufficient to undermine the ability of the incumbent to preempt.

The second major difference between our earlier paper and Reinganum's is that we assumed free entry while Reinganum considers only the case of an incumbent faced by a single challenger. Free entry is important for several reasons. First, in the bidding model analog set out above, it ensures that the required size of the winning bid is well-defined. If the incumbent is to retain the market, it is not sufficient for him to probably deter a particular entrant, since there are many others, one of whom would be bound to enter. Instead he must outbid the most any entrant would be willing to pay. Free entry is not a necessary condition for preemption in the deterministic patent race of our earlier paper if the incumbent knows how much a challenger would pay to enter and if the incumbent can preempt by outbidding its opponent. In the deterministic patent race, the incumbent can preempt by spending no more than a rival's value, and hence no more than the cost to the incumbent from entry.

In general, preemption need not occur when competition is limited. It can be more profitable for an incumbent to accommodate a (not too rivalrous) competitor rather than deter entry, *if* deterrence requires dissipating profits to make entry unattractive. This result emerges, for example, in Dixit's model of limit pricing, and conditions for which entry prevention is desirable are discussed in Gilbert (forthcoming). Another example where entry deterrence may not be profitable is a stochastic patent race with a single opponent (as in Reinganum). The incumbent may be forced to spend more than the opponent to deter entry. Suppose a challenger would spend X, but the total $R\&D$ expenditure required to make the challenger's profits

240   *THE AMERICAN ECONOMIC REVIEW*   *MARCH 1984*

negative would be NX. An incumbent has to spend at least $(N-1)X$ to deter the single opponent and this can cost more than the profit lost from the entry of a single competitor.

Finally, for free entry to make sense in these models, there has to be some mechanism limiting the number of firms which can coexist. In Reinganum's model, if entry is profitable for any one challenger at an $R\&D$ expenditure level x_C, it is profitable for any additional challenger who enters at the same $R\&D$ intensity. A challenger's instantaneous expected profit at date t, conditional on no discovery before t, is (using her notation)

$$(6) \qquad h(x_C)\pi_C - x_C,$$

and it is assumed that there exists an x_C such that this is positive. The present value of total expected profit for the challenger is

$$(7) \quad V^C(x_I, x_C) = \frac{h(x_C)\pi_C - x_C}{r + h(x_I) + h(x_C)}.$$

If expression (6) and hence the numerator in (7) are positive, there is no x_I that can make (7) negative. Additional expenditures on $R\&D$ by the incumbent decrease the probability that a challenger will successfully patent before any future date, but they do not lower the challenger's profit rate, conditional on no discovery. Since there are no fixed costs in the Reinganum model, a positive profit rate means that the challenger, and for that matter any other firm, can expect strictly positive profits from the patent race. With Reinganum's $R\&D$ technology, *entry deterrence is impossible*.

Given that an incumbent cannot keep out a potential competitor, it is not surprising that the incumbent acts in an accommodating way toward the challenger. Although it is useful to observe that an incumbent faced with unavoidable competition may invest less in $R\&D$, it does not imply that the firm would not prevent entry if it could. Also, it is not reasonable to cite uncertainty as the cause of the accommodative response to entry, when the assumed $R\&D$ technology does not allow for entry deterrence at all.

The absence of managerial diseconomies is central to the effectiveness of a preemption strategy. Without a clear argument why diseconomies arise in the management of productive resources, it seems reasonable in our view to assume that any firm can perform the activities of any other firm or collection of firms in the same industry at equal cost. Building in managerial diseconomies, as Reinganum does, guarantees that preemption is a decreasing returns activity.

We can extend Reinganum's model in various ways to examine the effect of allowing entry. If we retain her original model but allow firms to choose the number of parallel $R\&D$ activities which they operate, then it is necessary to impose a limit on the number of such activities any one firm can manage, as well as a limit on the number of potential entrants to avoid an infinite number of activities competing for the infinitesimal period before invention. If so, then with Reinganum's Nash equilibrium concept, the incumbent firm and all rivals will operate the maximum number of activities, and if the incumbent is allowed to operate more activities than all of his rivals put together, then he will probably win. If the incumbent can increase the number of activities he can operate without bound, while the rivals remain limited, then he will preempt with probability one.

However, these results only go to show that the original model is quite unsatisfactory for examining preemption. If, instead, we modify the model so that all of the expenditure X is incurred at time zero, which then generates a success probability of h per unit of time for no subsequent expenditure, then there is a maximum number of viable programs $\bar{m}$, which have nonnegative expected profits. Again following Reinganum's notation, if the incumbent runs m parallel programs, and the n entrants each operate one program, the incumbent's expected profits are

$$(8) \quad V^I(m, n) = \frac{mh\Pi + nh\pi_I + R}{r + (m+n)h} - mX,$$

while each challenger has expected profits

(per program)

(9) $\quad V^C(m,n) = h\pi_C/[r + (m+n)h] - X.$

If the incumbent moves first and incurs the sunk cost mX, then it can credibly preempt, for it can choose an $\bar{m}$ such that $V^C(\bar{m},1) < 0$, which first occurs at the integer value

(10) $\quad \bar{m} = \text{Int}\{\pi_C/X - r/h\}.$

If the incumbent chooses $m < \bar{m}$, then the number of rival programs will be $n = \bar{m} - m$, and the incumbent's profits will be given by (8). The incumbent's monopoly profits Π can be written

(11) $\quad\quad \Pi = \pi_I + \pi_C + L,$

where L is the loss from competition. If $\bar{m}$ is large, then there is little inaccuracy in ignoring the integer constraint of (10), in which case (10) and (11) can be substituted in (8) to give

(12) $\quad V^I(m, \bar{m} - m)$

$$= [mhL + \bar{m}h\pi_I + R]/[r + \bar{m}h].$$

This is increasing in m up to $\bar{m}$, and hence if the incumbent moves first he will choose $m = \bar{m}$ and deter entry, even though the innovation process is stochastic. Summarizing we have

PROPOSITION 1: *With free entry, no managerial diseconomies, and stochastic innovation, the incumbent's profits are maximized by committing to the entry-deterring R&D expenditure level whenever the loss from competition is positive.*

In this formulation the incumbent can commit by choosing to spend $\bar{m}X$ before the challenger can move, in which case no challenger would spend anything. Thus preemption is the Nash equilibrium of a game in which the incumbent firm can move first with a commitment.

If, on the other hand, the incumbent cannot move first, but must choose the number of programs m at the same time that the challengers choose their programs, then it is easy to see that preemptive R&D by the incumbent is not a Nash equilibrium. For at $m = \bar{m}$, $n = 0$.

$$\partial V^I(\bar{m},0)/\partial m$$

$$= rh[\Pi - R/r]/(r + \bar{m}h)^2 - X.$$

Substituting expression (10) gives

$$\partial V^I(\bar{m},0)/\partial m$$

$$= \{[r/(r + \bar{m}h)][(\Pi - R/r)/\pi_C] - 1\}X.$$

If the innovation is drastic, the incumbent's marginal profit is negative at $\bar{m}$, so that $m = \bar{m}$ cannot be a Nash equilibrium. Note that if the innovation is not drastic, preemption can be a Nash equilibrium in expenditure rates for the incumbent (without commitment) if the loss from competition is sufficiently large.

II

Preemption has to do with entry deterrence, and hence the conditions of entry and the timing of moves are of the essence. It makes little sense to consider preemption in a model in which assumptions are made that guarantee entry (i.e., by placing incumbent and challenger on equal footing and by specifying the number of firms and devising cost conditions to ensure interior equilibria as Reinganum does). If, on the other hand, the incumbent has the first move, and the number of entrants is endogenous to the model, then it becomes possible to deter potential competitors by reducing the benefits from entry to below the entry cost. If, in addition, there are no managerial diseconomies, then it is not only possible to deter entry, but desirable as well.

In any case, the assumption of a deterministic discovery function is neither necessary nor is it sufficient for the desirability of preemptive patenting. We have demonstrated that incentives for preemption persist when the discovery function is stochastic. We have also shown that with a deterministic discovery function and simultaneous Nash behavior, an incumbent cannot guarantee preemption. What Reinganum's model does illustrate is the importance of being able to move first and make credible commitments. Although preemptive patenting may be desirable, it need not be a *credible* response to potential competitors. The Nash formulation in the Reinganum model makes this clear. If preemption is successful, there will be no challengers. But if the challengers do no R&D, the incumbent is a monopolist in the R&D market and would not invest at the entry-deterring level.

Preemption is not a best response strategy in the Reinganum model, even though it might be desirable for the incumbent to preempt if it could. Whether preemption will occur ultimately rests on the extent to which firms can make prior entry-deterring commitments that are credible to potential competitors. We would argue that the incumbent has a natural temporal advantage since after all he is the incumbent, in which case the central issue is one of credibility. This in turn will depend on such questions as the extent to which R&D requires large irreversible investments (our paper, p. 517) and additional factors, not considered in this exchange, such as the scope of patent protection. We were careful in our original paper (Section IIIC) to point out that the incumbent might find it excessively costly to

preempt against multiple threats, and we only argued that in some cases monopoly may persist. We see nothing in Reinganum's 1983 article to cause us to change this conclusion, although we feel that her contrasting results have helped clarify our understanding of the circumstances required for persistence.

REFERENCES

Dixit, Avinash, "The Role of Investment in Entry-Deterrence," *Economic Journal*, March 1980, *90*, 95–106.

Fudenberg, Drew, Gilbert, Richard, Stiglitz, Joseph and Tirole, Jean, "Preemption, Leapfrogging and Competition in Patent Races," *European Economic Review*, June 1983, *22*, 3–32.

Gilbert, Richard J., "Preemptive Competition," in F. Mathewson and J. Stiglitz, eds., *New Directions in Industrial Organization*, International Economic Association, forthcoming.

_____ and Newbery, David M. G., "Preemptive Patenting and the Persistence of Monopoly," *American Economic Review*, June 1982, *72*, 514–26.

Reinganum, Jennifer F., "Uncertain Innovation and the Persistence of Monopoly," *American Economic Review*, September 1983, *73*, 741–47.

[4]

Uncertain Innovation and the Persistence
of Monopoly: Reply

By Jennifer F. Reinganum*

In my 1983 article in this *Review*, I reported results (based upon a stochastic model of invention) which were at variance with those (based upon a deterministic model of invention) reported previously in 1982 by Richard Gilbert and David Newbery (hereafter G-N).

In their comment, G-N claim that the differences in our respective results arise not due to the presence or absence of uncertainty, as I suggested, but due to (in my model) 1) a different assumption about the timing of moves in the $R\&D$ game, 2) the absence of free entry, and 3) assumed diseconomies in the management of the firm. The model in my paper was intentionally highly simplified, eschewing the issues of fixed costs and free entry, because the point was simple and intuitive. The point was *not* that preemption—or a weaker notion, stochastic preemption—would *never* occur. Nor did I claim that a deterministic invention process was either necessary or sufficient for preemption. My point was simply that when uncertainty is introduced into the G-N deterministic bidding model, the equilibrium outcome is quite different: in the deterministic model, the monopolist persists with probability one, while in the stochastic model, the monopolist will suffer entry—not just with positive probability—but with probability greater than one-half. Thus their conclusions regarding the likelihood of persistence are highly sensitive to the assumption of a deterministic invention process. Of course, this is not to say that their conclusions (or mine) are not equally sensitive to other modeling assumptions. In the sequel, I will examine the role of alternative assumptions regarding the order of play, free entry, and managerial diseconomies.

I. The Order of Play

There is no explicit discussion in G-N's 1982 article regarding the order of play in the game. However, indirect evidence tends to point toward simultaneous moves. For instance, "the strategy space for each firm is restricted to the research and development expenditure on product 2 and the price(s) the firm charges for the product(s) it sells" (p. 516). That is, monopolist and entrants alike each pick an investment level; in a sequential-move game, entrants would select a best-response function.[1]

Moreover, G-N assert that their model is formally equivalent to a particular type of auction model in which firms enter bids for the innovation; the winning bidder must then spend the amount of its bid on $R\&D$. This is essentially a first-price auction with complete and perfect information. It turns out that in this framework, there is no need to specify timing conventions at all. It is easy to show that the simultaneous-move equilibrium is identical to the equilibrium specified by G-N.[2] Thus, regardless of the sequential or simultaneous nature of the bidding, the equilibrium outcome is the same. The agent with the highest valuation (in this case the incumbent monopolist) wins; however, the winner needs to pay only (a tiny bit more than) the amount of the next-highest valuation.

---

[1] In a related model, Partha Dasgupta and Joseph Stiglitz explicitly assume a leader-follower structure; they state that "active firms work on the reaction function of potential entrants; i.e., entertain von Stackelberg conjectures regarding their behavior" (1980, p. 10).

[2] Technically, if we think of this as a first-price auction, then both the sequential-move and simultaneous-move equilibria are really "*epsilon*-equilibria," since there is no *minimum* winning bid.

---

*Division of Humanities and Social Sciences, California Institute of Technology, Pasadena, CA 91125. The financial support of the National Science Foundation is gratefully acknowledged.

244 *THE AMERICAN ECONOMIC REVIEW* *MARCH 1984*

Thus it is perfectly reasonable to compare G-N's bidding model with a stochastic invention model in which firms move simultaneously. However, in evaluating their conjectures about the effects of uncertainty on their model, it is important to keep in mind their (implicit) sequential-move assumption. I will postpone until Section IV my comments on the appropriateness of the sequential-move framework.

II. Unrestricted Entry

Gilbert and Newbery emphasize that their model includes free entry,[3] that mine doesn't, and that this is (at least in part) responsible for our differing results. The issue of free entry is a red herring. In their original paper they claim that free entry is *not* crucial to their result (and, indeed, it isn't). Immediately following their main argument, they state that "...the same argument holds if competition for the patent is less intense, so that the potential entrant anticipates positive profits instead of the zero profits implied by [free entry]" (pp. 516–17). Moreover, in their model it is only the most efficient challenger which provides any competition for the incumbent; theirs may as well be a two-firm model.

Nevertheless, consider what happens in my model if one adds fixed costs and allows unrestricted entry (obviously both must be added at once; due to the assumption of decreasing returns to investment, with no fixed costs the number of firms is infinite). The fixed cost, denoted F, does not affect equilibrium flow investment, only whether or not the challenger firm plays. Since $F = 0$ implies infinitely many firms, and since the equilibrium challenger payoff with n firms can be shown to be decreasing in n (see my forthcoming paper), for any n one can find an F_n such that only the incumbent and n challengers want to play. For one challenger, this fixed cost is $F_1 = V^C(x_I^*, x_C^*)$. When n challengers play, the results are even stronger; now the incumbent firm invests less than *each* challenger. Thus its probability of per-

sisting as a monopolist is less than $1/n$. Thus unrestricted entry can easily be accommodated without any weakening of my results.

III. Managerial Diseconomies

"Managerial diseconomies exist if the monopolist cannot conduct a research program or production plan as efficiently as any rival" (G-N, 1982, p. 518). This would not ordinarily seem to rule out decreasing returns to scale in the invention technology, as long as both incumbent and challengers alike are subject to the same decreasing returns. Actually, G-N want to say that if no managerial diseconomies exist, then the monopolist is as efficient as *all rivals put together*. Essentially, one needs to be able to run parallel *R&D* projects at no worse than constant returns to scale. Gilbert and Newbery "extend" my model to a number of parallel projects without including a fixed cost per project. Since this leads to an infinite number of parallel projects, they impose arbitrary upper bounds on the number of projects which may be undertaken by the incumbent and by challengers, and then discuss what happens when these bounds are differentially relaxed. In my earlier paper I reported results based on a model with parallel projects; the details of this model are available in an unpublished technical appendix. My own extension involved a fixed cost of K per project, and a flow cost, or research intensity, on each project. For simplicity, let the intensity be fixed at x, yielding hazard rate $h = h(x)$, and let n_I and n_C denote the number of parallel projects chosen by the incumbent and the challenger, respectively. The payoff functions now take the forms[4]

$$V^I(n_I, n_C)$$

$$= [n_I h \Pi(c) + n_C h \pi_I(c) + R - n_I x]$$

$$/ [r + n_I h + n_C h] - n_I K$$

---

[3] I interpret the term "free entry" as meaning *unrestricted*, but not necessarily *costless*, entry.

[4] The present value of profits to a monopolist using the new technology with unit cost c are $\Pi(c)$, capitalized profits to the incumbent and entrant if the entrant

and $V^C(n_I, n_C) = [n_C h \pi_C(c) - n_C x]$

$$/ [r + n_I h + n_C h] - n_C K,$$

where it is assumed that $h\Pi(c) - x > 0$, so that the challenger has at least a chance at positive profits if the innovation is drastic. Differentiating V^i with respect to n_i, $i = I, C$ and simplifying yields the following necessary conditions at an interior Nash equilibrium (n_I^*, n_C^*).

(1) $[r + n_C^* h][h\Pi(c) - x]$

$$- h[n_C^* h \pi_I(c) + R] - KB^2 = 0$$

(2) $[r + n_I^* h][h\pi_C(c) - x] - KB^2 = 0,$

where $B = r + n_I^* h + n_C^* h$.

PROPOSITION 1: *If the innovation is drastic and $R > 0$, then $n_I^* < n_C^*$; that is, the incumbent conducts fewer parallel projects than the challenger.*

PROOF:

If the innovation is drastic, then $\Pi(c) = \pi_C(c)$ and $\pi_I(c) = 0$. Combining equations (1) and (2) yields

(3) $(n_C^* - n_I^*)[h\Pi(c) - x] = R.$

Since $h\Pi(c) - x > 0$, equation (3) requires that $n_I^* < n_C^*$.

Again, a simple continuity argument establishes that there is an open set of technologies which are not drastic, but for which Proposition 1 remains valid.[5]

---

patents the new technology are $\pi_I(c)$ and $\pi_C(c)$, respectively. Current flow revenues to the incumbent are denoted R. An innovation is *drastic* if it would drive the incumbent from the market; i.e., if $c \leq c_0$ where c_0 is the maximum level of unit cost such that $\pi_I(c) = 0$. In the interest of brevity, the reader is referred to my 1983 article for more complete definitions and the derivation of payoff functions.

[5]Assuming that success in R&D is a function of *fixed* rather than flow costs, Richard Freeman (1982) finds that a single domestic entrant will conduct more parallel projects than an incumbent foreign monopolist. Thus this result does not depend upon the fixed vs. flow specification of costs.

IV. Conclusions

Gilbert and Newbery have argued that alternative assumptions regarding the conditions of entry, economies of scale and the order of play (and not uncertainty) are responsible for the differences in our respective results concerning the persistence of monopoly. It seems clear from the above discussion that at least the first two of these alternatives can be accommodated with no effect on the results. The models outlined in my original paper and in the preceding pages herein all describe circumstances in which, *were the invention process deterministic,* the incumbent would persist as the monopolist. But in the stochastic formulation, the incumbent enjoys a lower marginal benefit to invention than does the challenger when the innovation is drastic, or nearly so. Consequently, the incumbent invests less than the challenger and, *on average,* entry occurs.

All of my analysis is based upon interior Nash equilibria; that is, ones in which the challenger actually participates. Gilbert and Newbery object to assumptions which allow for the possibility of (or even guarantee) interior equilibria, saying that one cannot examine preemption and entry deterrence in such a framework. I think this takes an extremely narrow view of preemption and entry deterrence. When it is impossible to credibly preempt or deter entry with probability one, it still makes sense to ask whether stochastic preemption or stochastic entry deterrence are prevalent features of an industry. That is, are potential entrants discouraged *on average* from participating, or do they participate to a lesser extent than they would in the absence of the incumbent's strategic behavior?

I will concede that alternative assumptions regarding the order of play will typically yield different equilibrium results (G-N's deterministic bidding model is one example in which the order of play is of no consequence). But I do question the appropriateness of G-N's assumed order of play, and the attribution of the undesirable consequences to the patent system. In their comment, G-N extend their own model to the case of uncertainty, making explicit their sequential-move assumption. They show that in equilibrium the incumbent will choose an entry-deterring level of investment. However, this investment level will not be credible without some mechanism for commitment. They remark that

> Whether preemption will occur ultimately rests on the extent to which firms can make prior entry-deterring commitments that are credible to potential competitors. We would argue that the incumbent has a natural temporal advantage since after all he is the incumbent, in which case the central issue is one of credibility.   [p. 242]

That monopoly power per se should confer a first-mover advantage seems debatable at best. One could argue equally persuasively the obverse claim that the potential entrant should have the first move, since the incumbent may not be aware of its existence or intent to invest until it actually does so. The entrant's investment alerts the incumbent to its presence, and it is the incumbent who must respond.

Even if one concedes a first-mover advantage to the monopolist, there remains the issue of credibility. In their original paper, G-N state that their purpose is to determine "whether institutions such as the patent system create opportunities for firms with monopoly power to maintain their monopoly power" (p. 514). However, if the difference in our respective results is due to their assumption that the incumbent can credibly commit itself to a preemptive investment level, then the responsibility for persistent monopoly clearly does not reside with the patent system, but with the (implicit) institution which facilitates an otherwise noncredible threat.

REFERENCES

Dasgupta, Partha and Stiglitz, Joseph, "Uncertainty, Industrial Structure, and the Speed of R and D," *Bell Journal*, Spring 1980, *11*, 1–28.

Freeman, Richard, "A Model of International Competition in Research and Development," manuscript, Federal Reserve Board, December 1982.

Gilbert, Richard J. and Newbery, David M. G., "Preemptive Patenting and the Persistence of Monopoly," *American Economic Review*, June 1982, *72*, 514–26.

_____ and _____, "Uncertain Innovation and the Persistence of Monopoly: Comment," *American Economic Review*, March 1984, *74*, 238–42.

Lee, Tom K. and Wilde, Louis L., "Market Structure and Innovation: A Reformulation," *Quarterly Journal of Economics*, March 1980, *94*, 429–36.

Loury, Glenn C., "Market Structure and Innovation," *Quarterly Journal of Economics*, August 1979, *93*, 395–410.

Reinganum, Jennifer F., "Innovation and Industry Evolution," *Quarterly Journal of Economics*, forthcoming.

_____, "Uncertain Innovation and the Persistence of Monopoly," *American Economic Review*, September 1983, *73*, 741–48.

[5]

Preemptive Patenting and the Persistence of Monopoly: Reply

By Richard J. Gilbert and David M. G. Newbery*

Stephen Salant takes issue with a single paragraph of our 1982 paper (Section IIC, p. 518) and then claims that our conclusions result "either from faulty logic or from our implicit assumption that a market fails to operate." We respond by showing that our conclusions are logically consistent, and that Salant's argument is flawed by its incompleteness.

The preemptive patenting results hold whenever equally efficient firms compete with nonzero transaction costs (a point which is not contested by Salant), and whenever any cost disadvantage experienced by the incumbent is less than the transaction costs incurred in the process of bargaining for production rights. Furthermore, we will show that if the incumbent's cost disadvantage exceeds transaction costs, then the preemption result hinges on the *relative* transaction costs in the markets for $R\&D$ outputs and inputs. The conditions derived by Salant are erroneous, and indeed irrelevant to the incentives for preemption.

Salant mounts his main argument on the assumption that transaction costs are zero, but fails to realize the full implications of this counterfactual assumption. Ronald Coase told us many years ago that bargaining in the absence of transaction costs (broadly interpreted) will eliminate cost inefficiencies and yield a Pareto optimal allocation. By selecting excerpts from two different papers and then providing his own emphasis, Salant constructs the impression that our results contradict the Coase argument. We feel this creative journalism is an inaccurate representation of our conclusions.

The implications for preemptive patenting depend on transaction costs, as Salant shows.

*Department of Economics, University of California, Berkeley, CA 94720, and Churchill College, Cambridge, England CB3 ODS, respectively.

For any finite transaction cost, an equally efficient monopolist can preempt competitors (subject to the technological and strategic assumptions in our model). Salant argues that if a monopolist is less efficient than a rival, *and* if the cost penalty exceeds transaction costs, then the rival firm will preempt the monopolist. As it stands, this conclusion is false.

It is arbitrary to restrict bargaining, as Salant does, to a single market or group of markets. If firms can negotiate in the patent market, they can also negotiate in markets for inputs to the $R\&D$ process. Assuming (as we had explicitly done) no diseconomies that are solely due to management, technological inefficiency must be the result of inferior $R\&D$ inputs. These inputs can be bargained for as well.

I

Consider the case where a rival firm has, initially, a superior $R\&D$ technology. We shall examine the conditions that are necessary for the rival to succeed in obtaining from the incumbent an exclusive license on the existing product. Let X be the amount the rival would earn if it patents and bargains with the incumbent. Let Y be the amount the incumbent would receive by bargaining with the rival to transfer exclusive rights for the sale of the existing product. (We assume, as does Salant, that firms are equally efficient producers, so that only rights to sell, and not to manufacture, are important.)

The incumbent can remove the cost penalty by contracting with the suppliers of the superior technology. The incumbent can purchase the superior technology, either by contracting for the superior inputs or through purchase of the rival firm's assets. Let C be the cost for delivery of an innovation at date T. Since the cost net of transaction expenses

252   THE AMERICAN ECONOMIC REVIEW   MARCH 1984

should not exceed the innovation's value,

$$(1) \qquad C \leq X + \Gamma_1,$$

where Γ_1 is the transaction cost for this contract. (The cost could be less with competition for the supply of $R\&D$ inputs. The minimum, assuming free exit of suppliers, is the cost of producing the innovation at date T, plus transaction costs.)

Let Γ_2 be the transaction costs incurred in a contract for the rights to produce both the new and the established product. Monopoly profits from the sale of both products, less transaction costs for the bargain, must satisfy the inequality

$$(2) \qquad \Pi_m - \Gamma_2 \geq X + Y.$$

The incumbent should sell an exclusive license to the rival firm, and not preemptively patent, if the incumbent would thereby receive more when the rival firm patents. This condition is

$$(3) \qquad Y \geq \Pi_m - C,$$

or, in view of (1),

$$(4) \qquad Y \geq \Pi_m - (X + \Gamma_1).$$

Substitute for Y, the incumbent's receipts with entry, in equation (2) and rearrange terms to find that the incumbent would benefit from the sale of exclusive rights only if

$$(5) \qquad \Gamma_1 \geq \Gamma_2.$$

The incumbent would sell out to a rival only if transaction costs in the market for $R\&D$ inputs, Γ_1, exceed transaction costs in the output market, Γ_2. If transaction costs in the market for $R\&D$ inputs are less than transaction costs in the output market (and less than the loss due to competition), the incumbent should bargain for the most efficient $R\&D$ technology and preemptively patent. If transaction costs exceed the loss due to competition, bargaining is ineffective. The incumbent would preemptively patent if its cost disadvantage is less than the loss due to competition, and would allow entry otherwise.

Thus the results in our paper hold with bargaining whenever transaction costs are large, or whenever transaction costs in the output market exceed transaction costs in the market for $R\&D$ inputs.

Once we admit bargaining, then if it occurs we find that the incumbent's incentive to preempt is *independent* of the incumbent's (*ex ante*) cost disadvantage. What matters are the relative transaction costs: the transaction cost incurred by the incumbent in the market for $R\&D$ inputs compared to the transaction cost incurred by a rival in the incumbent's product market. This follows because bargaining gives the incumbent an opportunity to overcome its initial cost disadvantage. Provided transaction costs do not exceed the loss from competition, the incumbent should preempt whenever the rival can expect to incur greater costs bargaining for exclusive rights to the incumbent's product than the incumbent would incur by bargaining for the rival firm's assets (prior to patenting).

It is not obvious to us that transaction costs always favor the rival, since it is quite common for innovative entrepreneurs to sell out to established firms.

II

We have shown that, contrary to Salant's assertions, (initial) cost disadvantages are not a determinant of the gains to preemption. What matters are relative bargaining costs. Of course, this discussion ignores other important determinants of the bargaining process, including uncertainty, asymmetric information, and the inability to write, verify, and enforce complete contracts. Also, we continue to stress that successful preemption requires many restrictive assumptions with regard to technological opportunities and the ability to commit to preemptive $R\&D$ strategies (see our comment in this issue on the paper by Jennifer Reinganum).

Even if the rival buys out the incumbent and preemptively patents, there is no change in the market structure, nor in the persistence of (a) monopoly. Salant's only point is that there may be cases in which $R\&D$ is done by a more rather than less efficient firm, thus avoiding some social waste, though he failed to specify the correct conditions under which this would occur.

Salant's conclusions are faulty because he only looked at bargaining for the incumbent's assets. If we admit that transaction costs are low enough to permit bargaining, then the bargaining may lead the incumbent to acquire the necessary $R\&D$ resources, preserving our results. The gains from preemption in a bargaining situation then rest on relative transaction costs.

REFERENCES

Coase, Ronald H., "The Problem of Social Cost," *Journal of Law and Economics*, Oc-

tober 1960, *3*, 1–44.

Gilbert, Richard J., and Newbery, David M. G., "Preemptive Patenting and the Persistence of Monopoly," *American Economic Review*, June 1982, *72*, 514–26.

_____ and _____, "Uncertain Innovation and the Persistence of Monopoly: Comment," *American Economic Review*, March 1984, *74*, 238–42.

Reinganum, Jennifer F., "Uncertain Innovation and the Persistence of Monopoly," *American Economic Review*, September 1983, *73*, 741–48.

Salant, Stephen W., "Preemptive Patenting and the Persistence of Monopoly: Comment," *American Economic Review*, March 1984, *74*, 247–50.

[6]

The persistence of profits above the norm

A.   The hypothesis

As George Stigler (1963, p. 1) once observed, the issue of whether profit rates have a tendency to converge on a single, competitive level is fundamental to a normative evaluation of the competitiveness of a market economy. In an economy subject to uncertainty, profits and losses signal the existence of excess demand or excess supply at long-run competitive price. If resources are free to respond to market signals, they should move into areas where profits are being earned and out of areas suffering losses. This movement of resources continues until returns are equalized across all markets (with appropriate adjustment for risk). Of course, each new period brings new uncertainties and new positions of profits and loss, so that a point in time when all firm or industry profit levels are equal never obtains. But if the market is capable of responding to the signals of profits and losses, the long-run movement of individual firm and industry profit rates should be toward a common competitive level. All observed profits and losses should be short-run deviations around this trend.

Despite the central position that the persistence-of-profits issue must have in any normative evaluation of a market economy, it has received surprisingly little attention from economists. Yale Brozen has addressed the issue tangentially in his attack on the positive concentration—profit rate relationship found in much of the literature. Brozen (1970, 1971a, b) presents evidence that the correlation between concentration and profits is unstable over time. But he does not consider whether profits do converge completely to competitive levels (or move only part of the way), and, if convergence is complete, how quickly it occurs. Moreover, by focusing on the profits-concentration relationship, he leaves totally unanswered the question of whether profits due to factors unrelated to concentration disappear over time.[1]

In this chapter, we test the hypothesis that profits, whatever their cause, converge over time on a competitive level. We do not, at this

8

The persistence of profits above the norm   9

juncture, consider what factors prohibit or slow down the convergence process. Nor do we allow for risk differences across firms. These points will be taken up later. The results in this chapter simply test the hypothesis that all firm profit rates converge on a single competitive level, ignoring risk differences across firms.

The tests in this chapter are conducted using observations on individual firms. Although most studies of profit rate determinants have focused on industry profit levels, the competitive environment hypothesis of convergence on a single competitive level should be equally valid for firm-level profits and for industry profits. For a homogeneous product, all firms in an industry should charge the same price under competitive conditions. Free entry and exit should ensure that only the most efficient firms survive, that all firms have the same average costs as well as price. If all firms in the industry earn profits above the competitive level for long periods, then there must exist a barrier to entering the industry. If only some of the firms in a homogeneous product industry earn persistently supranormal profits, they must have access to a resource, technology, or special managerial talent that allows them to earn these higher profits. The competitive process would then appear to be thwarted in one or more of three possible ways: (1) other firms are banned from using the resource or technology that makes the more profitable firm have lower costs, (2) bidding for this special resource or talent is inhibited so that neither the assets of the firm nor the factor payments rise in value to bring the return on capital into line with competitive levels, (3) the more profitable firms do not exploit their competitive advantage by lowering price and expanding output at the expense of the other seemingly less efficient companies in the industry.

With differentiated products, both the definition of industries and the concept of entry barriers become more fuzzy, the use of firm-level profits more defensible. If a firm with a differentiated product can continually earn profits above the competitive level, other firms must be prevented from selling a sufficiently close substitute or adopting a sufficiently close technology to eliminate the price–cost margin advantage of the more successful firm. If other firms selling close substitutes in what is typically referred to as the same industry are not able to earn returns at competitive levels or suffer losses, this does not offset the fact that the persistently successful firm has some special advantage that others cannot duplicate. Our tests are designed to isolate firms with these special advantages, and to determine how significant they are.

10   **Profits in the long run**

B.   The models

We assume that a firm's returns on total assets at any point in time consist of three components: the competitive return on capital common to all firms; a long-run, permanent rent peculiar to the firm itself; and a short-run, quasi rent, which is also peculiar to the firm but varies over time and converges on zero in the long run. We wish to concentrate on those short- and long-run rents that are related to market structure and competitive forces. But profits can also vary over time because of business cycle factors. In a boom period, short-run rents are higher than average for any given market structure. We shall also assume that the competitive return on capital common to all firms and the permanent rent component of firm i's profits are also higher when business cycle conditions are favorable; that is, if an economy was always at full employment, all firms would earn higher returns on capital and enjoy higher short- and long-run rents, owing to market power advantages, than they would if the economy was continually characterized by excess supply in factor markets. We thus write firm i's return on capital at any point in time t as being proportional to the mean profit rate in the economy:

$$\Pi_{it} = (c + r_i + s_{it})\,\overline{\Pi}_t,\tag{2.1}$$

where c, r_i and s_{it} represent the fractions of average economy profits that correspond to the competitive return on capital, firm i's permanent rents, and its short-run rents, respectively. Subtracting $\overline{\Pi}_t$ from both sides of (2.1) and dividing by it, we obtain

$$\pi_{it} = \frac{\Pi_{it} - \overline{\Pi}_t}{\overline{\Pi}_t} = (c-1) + r_i + s_{it}.\tag{2.2}$$

The hypothesis that all firm and industry profit rates eventually converge on a single competitive level (risk questions aside), which we shall refer to as the competitive environment hypothesis, can now be stated as the twin predictions that

$$r_i = 0 \text{ and } \lim_{t \to \infty} E(s_{it}) = 0,$$

where E represents the expected value.

The deviation of a firm's profit rate from the sample mean at any point in time is composed of two components, the constant $(c + r_i - 1)$ and the time dependent, s_{it}. If s_{it} was assumed to be of sufficiently

The persistence of profits above the norm 11

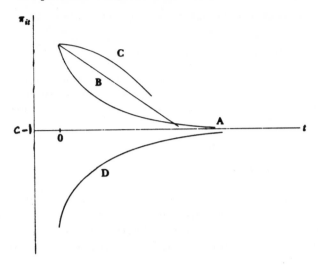

Figure 2.1 Possible profit paths.

short duration that its expected value in any year was zero, we could test the competitive environment hypothesis by simply comparing mean profit rates across firms on the basis of annual firm profits. But the disequilibria in markets that give rise to short-run rents cannot be reasonably assumed to vanish within a single year. A firm earning returns above the competitive level this year can be expected to earn above-normal returns next year without this implying that long-run permanent rents are being earned.

Now consider Figure 2.1. Suppose that i's profits at time $t = 0$ are above the competitive profit rate. If the competitive environment hypothesis is valid, π_{it} must fall to $(c-1)$ as the stochastic component of i's profits erodes. A return to $(c-1)$ along a path such as A is suggested. The two most obvious alternative routes, linear path B and *nonlinear* C, both must be rejected, since each implies a continual decline in profits, even after the competitive rate of return has been reattained. Similarly, less than competitive initial returns can be reasonably expected to return to $(c-1)$ along some path like D.

The curves in Figure 2.1 suggest a specification for the short-run rent component of a firm's profits of

$$s_{it} = \beta_i/t + \mu_{it}, \tag{2.3}$$

where μ_{it} is assumed to be a normally distributed error with the usual

12   Profits in the long run

error term properties (O, σ_μ). Substituting equation (2.3) into (2.2), we have

$$\pi_{it} = (c-1) + r_i + \beta_i/t + \mu_{it}. \tag{2.4}$$

Since c and r_i are constants, the competitive environment hypothesis can be tested – if we assume the short-run rents are specified as in (2.3) – by comparing the intercepts from the regressions of profits on the reciprocal of time

$$\pi_{it} = \alpha_i + \beta_i/t + \mu_{it}. \tag{2.5}$$

If the competitive environment hypothesis is valid, $r_i = 0$ for all firms, and the α_i $(= 1 - c + r_i)$ should be equal for all firms.

Specifying the short-run rents as in (2.3) presumes that the largest deviation of a firm's profits from their long-run level occurs in the first time period. This specification makes the estimates of α_i sensitive to the choice of time period. This deficiency can be removed by generalizing (2.3) to

$$s_{it} = \beta_i/t + \gamma_i/t^2 + \delta_i/t^3 + \mu_{it}. \tag{2.6}$$

Specifying the short-run rents as in (2.6) allows for the possibility that the peak or trough in the time series occurs at any point in time and allows for two changes in direction for the time path of profitability. Of course, more terms could be added to allow for more changes in direction, but these additional terms tend to introduce multicollinearity, while at the same time eating up degrees of freedom. We confine ourselves to estimating only up to third-order polynomials in time.

Equation (2.6) is only one of many that could be specified having the implication that as $t \to \infty$, the dependent variable is predicted to approach a constant. For example, one could replace t^2 and t^3 with t^4 and t^6 or with $t^{1/2}$ and $t^{1/3}$. These alternative formulations differ essentially in how rapid an adjustment process is presumed. I tried substituting $t^{1/2}$ and $t^{1/4}$ for t^2 and t^3 in (2.6). This more gradual convergence process gave quite implausible estimates of α. For example, (2.3) and (2.6) yield estimates for α with roughly the same range of values as the individual annual observations, but replacing the cubic and quadratic terms with $t^{1/4}$ and $t^{1/2}$ led to a range of α values far greater than the values actually observed. An examination of the plots of the data indicated that the equations using the simple powers of t fit the data much better than those assuming fractional powers.

This finding points to an important characteristic of equations (2.3) and (2.6). Each imposes on the data the property of convergence to some long-run, constant profit rate for each firm. It could be that the competitive environment hypothesis is valid not because the profit rates of all firms converge on some common return, $(c-1)$, but because they are so volatile that no central tendency can be discerned. By specifying the short-run rents as in (2.3) and (2.6), we presume a long-run central tendency for each firm's profit rate, where none may exist. We might, thereby, be biasing our results away from the competitive environment hypothesis.

An alternative formulation of s_{it} that avoids this characteristic is to assume that the rate of change in s_{it} over time is a function of the size of s_{it} rather than of time, as implied by (2.3) and (2.6). That is,

$$s_{it} = \lambda_i s_{it-1} + \mu_{it}, \tag{2.7}$$

where the competitive environment hypothesis implies $-1<\lambda_i<1$, if the process is to converge. The presence of μ_{it}, assumed to be a random error with the usual properties, in the adjustment equation allows for the possibility that profits move away from the long-run rate in any period while remaining on the convergence path. Substituting for s_{it} from (2.7) into (2.2) and writing $(1-c+r_i)$ as α_i once again, we have

$$\pi_{it} = \alpha_i + \lambda_i s_{it-1} + \mu_{it}. \tag{2.8}$$

Using (2.2) to eliminate s_{it-1},

$$\pi_{it} = \alpha_i(1-\lambda_i) + \lambda_i \pi_{it-1} + \mu_{it}. \tag{2.9}$$

The long-run profit rate for a firm can be estimated from the intercept term by estimating (2.9). If the competitive environment hypothesis is valid, the same α_i should be estimated for each company.

This completes our discussion of the models to be used to test the competitive environment hypothesis. Although other specifications for the erosion of short-run rents could be envisaged, the three proposed probably suffice to give a reasonable approximation to most other plausible convergence processes, two making the rate of change in the short-run rent a function of time, the other a function of the size of the rent itself.

Each model gives an estimate of the long-run projected profits of a firm, α_i, that is the sum of the competitive return on capital, and the firm's permanent rents r_i. In a fully competitive market environment, these latter rents should be zero. If we assume that the competitive return on capital is the same for all firms, all should have the same α_i. We test this hypothesis against the alternative hypothesis that there exist permanent rents, r_i, positive and negative, which result in

14   **Profits in the long run**

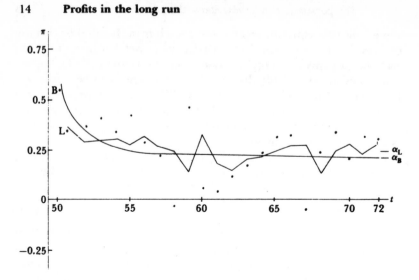

Figure 2.2 Observed and projected profits of Eaton Manufacturing.

systematic differences in the projected long-run profitability of companies.

C.   Some examples

Before we turn to the results for the entire sample, it may be helpful to illustrate the properties of the alternative models and the types of patterns they uncover.

Figures 2.2 through 2.9 present plots of the profit deviations used as dependent variables in each estimated profit projection for eight companies. In addition to the raw profit data (measured again as a relative deviation from the sample mean for each year), the predicted profit rates using the best fit of the three polynomials in $1/t$ (B), and the lagged dependent variable model (L) are presented. The dashes on the right labeled α_B and α_L are the projected long-run profit rates using each equation.

Figures 2.2 and 2.3 present companies that fit one's expectations of how the competitive process works. Both start with profit levels substantially above the norm and converge on profit levels considerably closer to the average, if not right on it. Figures 2.4 and 2.5 present data for companies that converged on the normal return from below. These four companies exhibit profit profiles that all companies

The persistence of profits above the norm 15

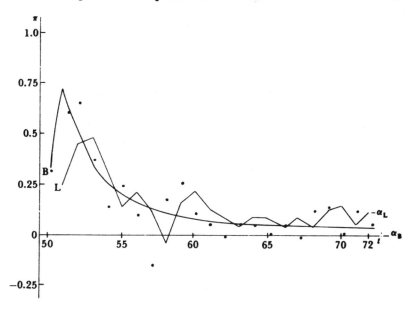

Figure 2.3 Observed and projected profits of Johns-Manville.

are expected to resemble if it is easy to enter into and exit from markets.

But all companies are not like these four. In Figures 2.6 and 2.7, data are presented for two firms that start with above-normal returns and move to levels of still higher returns. As the results in the following section will soon confirm, the profit profiles of Briggs and Stratton and Minnesota Mining and Manufacturing are not atypical. A substantial number of companies start the time period earning above-normal returns and persist in doing so throughout the period. More surprising, perhaps, is the reverse phenomenon – companies like Arden Farms (Arden-Mayfair) and Foster Wheeler persist in earning below-normal returns (see Figures 2.8 and 2.9). Firms like the four depicted in Figures 2.6–2.9 were sufficiently common in the United States between 1950 and 1972 to motivate this inquiry.

Whether the L and B lines fit the data well or not is perhaps a matter of taste. The profit rates they project lie fairly close to one another, and, at least to this observer, indicate more or less where each firm's profit series is going. As we shall soon see, the two projections are highly correlated.

16   **Profits in the long run**

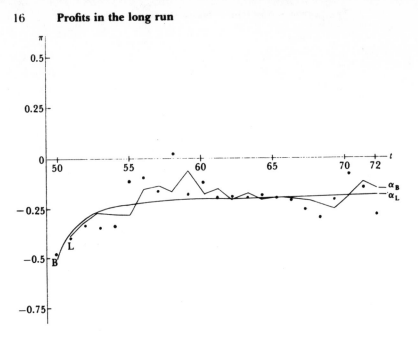

Figure 2.4 Observed and projected profits of Grolier.

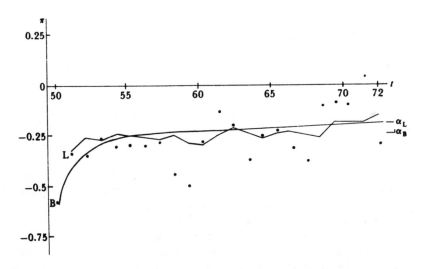

Figure 2.5 Observed and projected profits of Manhatten Shirt.

The persistence of profits above the norm   17

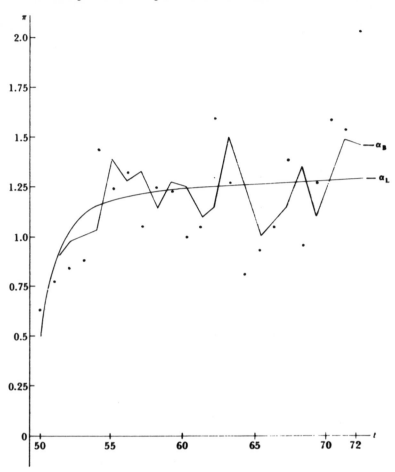

Figure 2.6 Observed and projected profits of Briggs and Stratton.

D.   The results

Long-run projected profit rates for each company were estimated in four ways consistent with the implications of the preceding section. The mean profit rate for each firm over the 23-year sample period, 1950–72, was also calculated (see Table 2.1). A firm's profit was defined as its net-of-tax profits plus interest divided by total assets. In a previous study, both net- and gross-of-tax measures were used, with similar results (Mueller 1977a). Net-of-tax profits have a conceptual

18   **Profits in the long run**

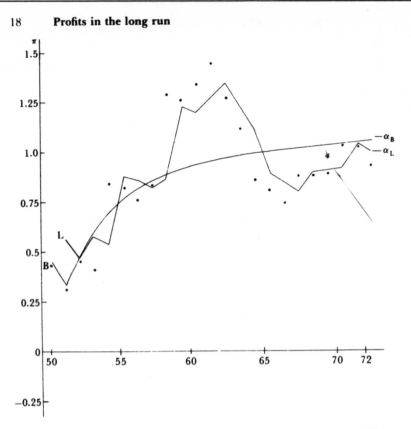

Figure 2.7 Observed and projected profits of Minnesota Mining and Manufacturing.

advantage in that net profits are presumably the appropriate signal for resource movement. Interest payments are added to profits to make the measure of profit independent of the source of funds used to create total assets.[2]

The sample used in this series of tests consists of 600 firms for which complete time-series data are available from 1950 through 1972. The starting point for constructing this sample was the surviving list of companies from the 1,000 largest manufacturing companies of 1950. To this list was added companies for which a full time series was readily available on the COMPUSTAT Tape. Most of these additional firms are in the 1972 sample of 1,000 largest companies. (The companies are listed in Appendix A-1.)

Equation (2.5) was estimated for each of the 600 firms. The full

The persistence of profits above the norm 19

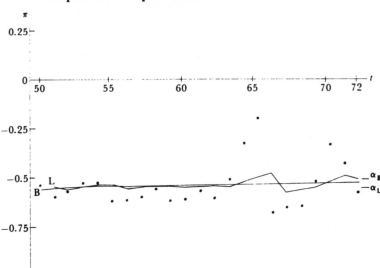

Figure 2.8 Observed and projected profits of Arden Farms.

sample was then divided into six subsamples on the basis of the average profit rates enjoyed during the first three years of the sample period: the 100 companies with the highest average profit rates of 1950–52 in sample 1, the 100 firms with the next highest profit rates in sample 2, and so on. Table 2.2 presents the mean αs and βs for each group. A distinct pattern is observed. On the average, both coefficients are positive and significantly greater than zero in the subsample with the highest initial profit rates and fall uniformly as one moves to subsamples with successively lower average profit rates in the initial three years. In the sixth (lowest initial profit rate) subsample, both coefficients are, on the average, significantly less than zero.

The mean values of $\bar{\beta}$ imply fairly rapid convergence to the long-run projected values for the profit rates. The mean β for the first subsample, for example, implies that although the profit rates for this group were, on the average, 45.5 percent greater than their long-run projected values in the first year of the sample period, they were only 4.55 percent higher after 10 years had elapsed (t being indexed at 1.23). All other mean βs in Table 2.2 imply an even smaller deviation from long-run projected values.

A similar picture emerges when the size of the adjustment in annual

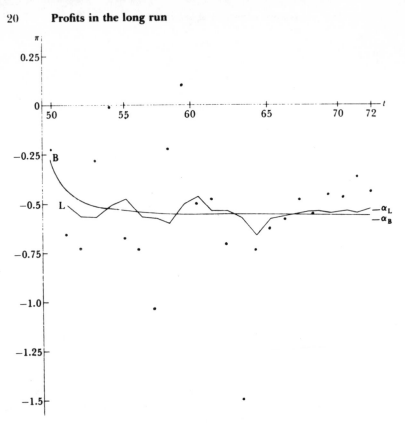

Figure 2.9 Observed and projected profits of Foster Wheeler.

profits is assumed to be proportional to the deviation of profits from their long-run value. Only 7 of the 600 $\hat{\lambda}$s estimated were greater than 1, and none was less than -1. The highest $\hat{\lambda}$ was 1.33. These numbers strongly suggest a process in which short-run rents disappear. Columns 3 and 4 of Table 2.2 present mean projected profit rates and $\hat{\lambda}$ parameters for each subsample. The mean $\hat{\lambda}$s are all around 0.5 and suggest no systematic pattern from subsample to subsample. This pattern is not what one expects to find if all deviations from the norm are short-run rents. If the latter were true, then the λs for companies earning normal returns would be relatively high, in that their normal returns should tend to persist. In contrast, companies with initially very high or low profits should have low λs, since their returns will be converging on the norm. The expected pattern of λs is weakly apparent in the bottom three subsamples, with the

Table 2.1. *Definitions of projected profitability variables*

Projected profitability symbol	Estimating equations	Notes
α	$\pi_t = \alpha + \beta/t + \mu_t$	
α_D	$\pi_t = \alpha + \beta/t + \mu_t$	If DW statistic indicates that the first-order zero autocorrelation hypothesis cannot be rejected (5 percent level, two tail test), $\alpha_D = \alpha$ as estimated from unadjusted data. Otherwise $\hat{\rho}$ was estimated from $\mu_t = \hat{\rho}\mu_{t-1} + \epsilon_t$, and α_D estimated from data transformed by subtracting $\hat{\rho}\pi_{t-1}$ from π_t.
α_B	$\pi_t = \alpha + \beta/t + \mu_t$ $\pi_t = \alpha + \beta/t + \gamma/t^2 + \mu_t$ $\pi_t = \alpha + \beta/t + \gamma/t^2 + \delta/t^3 + \mu_t$	All three equations estimated. Equation with highest $\overline{R}^2$ chosen as "best-fit" equation. (In about half a dozen cases, highest $\overline{R}^2$ suggested severe multicollinearity, i.e., large standard errors compared to lower-order equation. "Best-fit" equation then was lower-order equation with highest $\underline{R}^2$.) Same procedure vis-à-vis autocorrelation applied as well for α_D.
α_L	$\pi_t = \alpha(1 - \lambda) + \lambda\pi_{t-1} + \mu_t$	All $\lambda \geq 0.95$ set equal to 0.95. (This procedure resulted in slightly better fit to data.) Autocorrelation handled as for α_D and α_B.
$\bar{\pi}$	$\sum_{t=1}^{n} \pi_{t,n}$	

22   **Profits in the long run**

Table 2.2. *Mean αs and βs for two sets of projected profits estimates*
$[\pi_{it} = \alpha_i + \beta_i/t + \mu_{it}; \text{ and } \pi_{it} = \alpha_{Li}(1-\lambda) + \lambda_i\pi_{it-1} + \mu_{it}]$

1 Subsample (each of 100 OBS,)	2 $\bar{\alpha}$	3 $\bar{\beta}$	4 $\bar{\alpha}_L$	5 $\bar{\lambda}$	6 $\bar{\pi}$
1	.321 (.061)	.455 (.099)	.305 (.061)	.566 (.029)	.395 (.048)
2	.093 (.037)	.205 (.054)	.115 (.038)	.469 (.032)	.131 (.029)
3	−.018 (.033)	.085 (.052)	.005 (.036)	.514 (.027)	.001 (.026)
4	−.054 (.033)	−.094 (.050)	−.102 (.098)	.483 (.032)	−.067 (.025)
5	−.121 (.031)	−.201 (.042)	−.154 (.033)	.469 (.032)	−.155 (.026)
6	−.228 (.028)	−.448 (.051)	−.189 (.033)	.454 (.035)	−.302 (.022)

mean λ declining as one moves away from the mean, but the decline is very gradual and the differences between adjacent subsample mean λs are insignificant. More important, the highest mean λ in the table is for the highest initial profit group. Those firms that started with the greatest positive deviation from the mean exhibited the slowest average decline toward the mean.

Although both models present evidence of a general pattern of convergence to profit levels closer to the mean than initially observed rates, neither suggests that this process is complete. The mean long-run projected profit rates, $\bar{\alpha}$, for the 100 firms with the highest initial profit figures are more than 30 percent above the sample average under both models. The mean projected profit rates for the second subsample are around 10 percent above the mean, and the mean values of α and α_L both fall steadily as one moves to lower and lower initial profit groups. The lowest initial profit subsample is converging to profit rates that are, on the average, roughly 20 percent lower than the sample average.

Further evidence of both the existence of persistent differences in profitability and the tendency for above- and below-normal profits to converge toward the mean is obtained by comparing the mean values of the profit rates for each subsample over the period 1950–72 (column 6) with the mean projected values (columns 2 and 4). The mean

The persistence of profits above the norm   23

Table 2.3. *Correlation matrix, alternative projective profits measures*
$(n = 551)$

	α	α_D	α_B	α_L	$\bar{\pi}$
π_{50}	.42	.48	.20	.30	.61
α		.98	.80	.71	.97
α_D			.77	.66	.96
α_B				.55	.73
α_L					.69

profit rates exhibit the same pattern of relative magnitudes as do the mean *projected* rates, except in the highest and lowest initial profit groups, where the projected values are noticeably closer to zero than the simple mean values recorded in column 6. The two models imply convergence to lower (higher) profit levels for the companies with highest (lowest) initial profit ranks than are implied by simply examining the mean profit rates over the entire sample period, but further imply that the convergence process is incomplete.

Equation 5, in which profits are regressed on $1/t$, is the simplest of the time-dependent models by which to judge whether convergence toward the mean is taking place, since there is but one parameter whose sign must be examined. Positive βs are expected when initial πs are greater than their long-run values, negative $\bar{\beta}$s in the reverse case. As indicated in Table 2.2, on the average the $\bar{\beta}$s estimated corresponded to this expectation (column 3). But, as noted above, a second- or third-order polynomial in $1/t$ is more appropriate if the largest deviation in a firm's profits from normalcy occurs at a later point in time in the sample period. The α_B estimates are for the best-fitting polynomial in $1/t$ of the three estimates based on $\bar{R}^2$ (see Table 2.1).[3] Table 2.3 presents the correlation matrix for the various profit projections made, initial profits (π_{50}), and mean profits over the 23-year sample period. These correlations are for a subsample of 551 of the 600 companies on which Table 2.2 is based. The bulk of the empirical work throughout the remainder of this study is undertaken with this 551-firm subsample, and so we make the comparison of different profit projections over this group.

All profit projections correlate fairly well with one another and with mean profits for the sample time period. The profit projections based on the "best-fit" polynomial in $1/t$ have the poorest correlation with both initial profits and mean profits. Thus, the persistence of differences in profitability across firms is less pronounced when one projects

24   **Profits in the long run**

Table 2.4. *Regression of alternative projections of profitability on* π_{50}
(n = 551)

Dependent variables	Intercept	π_{50}	π^2_{50}	$\bar{R}^2$
α	.019	.461		
	1.18	10.91		.177
α	.725	.725	−.372	
	1.63	8.86	3.75	.196
α_D	.023	.485		
	1.59	12.83		.229
α_D	.030	.739	−.358	
	2.08	10.12	4.05	.336
α_B	.056	.302		
	2.34	4.87		.040
α_B	.053	.207	.134	
	2.22	1.70	.91	.039
α_L	.009	.455		
	.39	7.30		.087
α_L	.016	.704	−.351	
	.67	5.79	2.38	.095
π	.011	.588		
	.90	17.97		.369
$\bar{\pi}$	.018	.815	−.320	
	1.41	12.90	4.18	.387

Note: *t*-values under coefficients.

long-run profitability with the best fit of the three polynomials in
$1/t$. Nevertheless, a significant association between projected and initial
profits is evident even with the α_B projections. Table 2.4 presents the
results of regressing projected profits on initial values for both a linear
and quadratic specification. A significant relationship exists between
projected profitability and initial profits for all choices of projected
profits. For only the α_B projection is the linear formulation superior,
however. It indicates that for every 1 percent that a firm's profits were
above (below) the average profit rate of all firms in 1950–52, they are
projected to be 0.3 percent above (below) the average into the indefinite future.

The negative squared terms in all other equations in Table 2.4
indicate that after a point, the further a firm's profits are from the
mean, the greater the percentage movement toward the mean. All

The persistence of profits above the norm 25

Table 2.5. *Z-statistics for differences between mean firm profits across subsamples*

Subsample comparison	Z-value
1–2	3.84
2–3	4.28
3–4	3.14
4–5	3.18
5–6	2.74

Note: Each firm's mean profit rate, 1950–72, deflated by its standard deviation. For undeflated mean values see Table 2.2.

imply that a substantial fraction of a firm's profits at any point in time are rents, however. For example, the α_D equation implies that a firm earning double the average profit rate in 1950–52, will earn, on the average, 35 percent more into the indefinite future.

The results in Tables 2.2, 2.3, and 2.4 strongly suggest that a significant fraction of above- and below-average profits in 1950–52 represented permanent differences, that is, positive or negative long-run rents. Moreover, the fact that 593 of the 600 λ parameters estimated using the partial adjustment model fell in the range -1 to $+1$ indicates that profits do tend to converge on a single value for all but a handful of firms.[4] But to some extent the notion of a long-run projected profit rate has been imposed on the data by the choice of model for projecting profitability, at least for the α, α_D, and α_H specifications. How do we know that variations in profitability over time are not so great as to make the idea of a long-run projected profit rate illusory?

As one answer to this question, we divided each mean profit rate for the 23-sample period by its standard deviation and then compared the means as deflated between the six samples, as in Table 2.2. To the extent that profits move so erratically as to make projections of future profitability hopeless, standard deviations around the mean are large, and deflating the means by these standard deviations drives them toward zero. Significant differences between mean profitability figures thus deflated should disappear. Table 2.5 lists the Z-values from comparing the mean profit rates between subsamples after deflating each mean by its standard deviation. All subsample means are significantly different from the adjacent subsample mean(s) at the

26   **Profits in the long run**

Table 2.6. *Fractions of positive αs and βs by subsample*
$(\pi_{it} = \alpha_i + \beta_i/t + \mu_i)$

Subsample	Number of αs > 0	Number of αs significantly different from zero[a]	Number of βs > 0	Number of βs significantly different from zero[a]	n
1	70	71	67	53	100
2	53	64	67	32	100
3	44	60	55	30	100
4	33	71	49	24	100
5	28	67	31	29	100
6	17	69	17	45	100

[a] 5 percent level, two-tail test.

1 percent level. The test used allows for differences in subsample variances.

Further confidence in the meaningfulness of our profit projections can be obtained by examining Table 2.6. It lists the fractions of αs and βs significantly different from zero for each of the six subsamples for the full 600 firm sample. On the average, roughly two-thirds of the αs are significantly different from zero. Recalling that α = 0 implies a long-run projected return on assets equal to the sample mean, the finding that such large fractions of each subsample have αs significantly different from zero reinforces the conclusion that there are different profit rates to which companies converge over time.

The profit rate variables are deviations from sample means. If, on the average, observed profits contain elements of positive monopoly rents, convergence to the competitive rate of return should be to a return below the average profit rate. The results presented provide two possible ways to estimate long-run competitive rates. First, we might hypothesize that no company can survive indefinitely unless it earns the competitive return on capital. The lowest projected profit rate must then equal the competitive rate. Returning to Table 2.2, we see that both the π on 1/t and the partial adjustment model imply an average long-run projected return on total assets for the 100 companies with the lowest initial returns around 20 percent below the sample mean. Under this assumption, the competitive return on capital is some 20 percent below the average and the most profitable firms earn more than 50 percent above the competitive return on capital.

The logic of our second method of estimating the competitive return on capital is as follows: The competitive return on capital is earned by companies that receive zero rents. The profits of these companies differ from the competitive return by a random component assumed to be normally distributed around zero. Firms whose profits equal the normal return plus only a random component should be distributed normally about the competitive return and should exhibit an equal tendency to rise or fall over time. Thus, the competitive return is the long-run projected profits of that group of firms exhibiting equal tendencies for profits to rise and fall. The direction of movement of profits over time is easiest to discern from the simple π on $1/t$ model. Positive βs imply falling profit rates, negative βs rising profits. Table 2.6 reports the number of positive αs and βs for each group, as well as the number that were statistically significant. We are interested in the number of positive and negative βs. There are almost exactly the same number of positive (49) and negative (51) βs in the fourth profit group. This group also contains the fewest statistically significant βs, that is, the fewest equations in which there is a statistically significant tendency for profits to move up or down. Thus, by our second method of determining the competitive return, the average long-run projected profits of the fourth group equal the competitive return on capital. This average lies some 5 percent below the sample's mean profit rate, a figure quite close to the figure we obtained in the earlier study using the procedure, but dividing the sample into eight groups instead of six.

Note also that one-third of the βs of the top group are negative. Thus, in one-third of the 100 companies ranked highest on the basis of initial profits, profits tended to *rise* with the passing of time, a tendency starkly inconsistent with the hypothesis that all of the profits initially observed above the norm were transitory. Similarly, 17 of the lowest-ranked profitability firms witnessed a long-run tendency for their profits to *fall* still further. Although the general pattern of results in Tables 2.2, 2.4, and 2.6 is consistent with an overriding tendency for profits to regress back onto some normal, competitive level, the regression is not complete either in the sense that all firms exhibit such a regression, or that those that do experience a complete return to the competitive level.

E.   Predicting 1980 profitability

The projections of long-run profitability used in this study are based on time-series observations from 1950 through 1972. We stopped our time series in 1972 for several reasons:

28   **Profits in the long run**

1. The market share data are for 1950 and 1972 and we wished to have the profit projections based on data contiguous with the market share data.

2. Each year added to the data base reduces the number of observations in the sample owing to mergers, liquidations, and the other sources of disappearance discussed in Chapter 1. Since an important objective of the study is to try to explain differences in profit across firms with the market share and other data collected, extending the data base in time would hamper this goal.

3. The oil price shock of 1973 and the subsequent reverberations and economic malaise that befell the United States and other Western countries make the seventies a problematic period in which to test for the effects of competitive pressures on corporate profits. More than the normal market forces were at work in the seventies, driving some firms to near bankruptcy while showering huge windfalls on others. By stopping our time-series analysis of company profit performance in 1972, we avoid much of the randomness that seems likely to have been introduced into company profit trajectories following 1973.

4. We also avoid much of the inflation of the seventies that plays havoc with accounting profit rate measures (see Solomon 1970; Stauffer 1971).

Nevertheless, it is important to see what sort of predictors of future profitability the profit projectors are. Data for 456 of the 551 companies to be used throughout the study were available for 1980. Table 2.7 reports the results from regressing 1980 profitability on the various profit projectors. The 1980 profit figure is again the firm's deviation from the sample mean in 1980 divided by the sample mean. If short-run rents are normally distributed around the long-run profit rate, the coefficients on the projections of the long-run profit rate should, in the linear formulation, equal 1. They are significantly below 1. Indeed, there is generally a poorer association between 1980 profits and the projections of long-run profits than there is between the projections and the 1950–52 rates (see Table 2.4). Three factors seem likely to account for this difference. First, the independent variables are estimates of long-run profits and as such are subject to error. These errors in observing the true long-run projected profit rates bias the estimates of the coefficients in the equations in Table 2.7 toward

The persistence of profits above the norm 29

Table 2.7. *Regression of π_{80} on projected profits and π_{50}*
$(n = 456; \pi_{80} = a + bx + cx^2)$

Independent variables x	$\hat{a}$	$\hat{b}$	$\hat{c}$	$b\left(1 + \dfrac{\sigma_v^2}{\sigma_x^2}\right)$	$\bar{R}^2$
α	−.012	.256			
	.55	5.30		.267	.056
α	−.018	.111	.152		
	.86	1.14	1.72		.060
α_D	−.012	.256			
	.58	4.90		.309	.048
α_D	−.019	.082	.201		
	.91	.77	1.89		.054
α_B	−.016	.185			
	.76	5.14		.209	.053
α_B	−.022	.046	.111		
	1.04	.66	2.32		.062
α_L	−.005	.143			
	.24	4.23		.178	.036
α_L	−.011	.255	−.023		
	.53	4.83	2.75		.050
$\bar{\pi}$	−.009	.269			
	.41	4.91		.523	.048
$\bar{\pi}$	−.016	.105	.199		
	.75	.98	1.77		.053
π_{50}	−.0004	.129			
	.02	2.38			.010
π_{50}	.001	.183	−.07		
	.05	1.72	.59		.009

Note: t-values under coefficients.

zero. Some allowance for these errors in observation can be made using the standard errors of the estimates of each projected profit rate. If we treat these standard errors as rough estimates of the error in observing the true profit rate, σ_v, and compute the mean $\bar{\sigma}_v^2$ over the sample as a sort of average error of observation, then we can adjust the estimated coefficients in Table 2.7 by multiplying them by $(1 + \bar{\sigma}_v^2/\sigma_x^2)$, where σ_x^2 is the variance in the respective projector of profitability in each equation (Johnston 1972, pp. 281–91). The adjusted βs for the linear equations are presented to the right of the dotted line. They are somewhat closer to 1, of course, but still too far away to allow us to claim that any of the αs or $\bar{\pi}$ is a good predictor of 1980 profitability.

The projections of future profitability made in this chapter are based on the economic history of the fifties and sixties. They are legitimate projections of future profitability to the extent that the seventies resemble the two preceding decades in their economic evolution. As already noted, however, there is good reason to believe that significant structural changes in the seventies reduce the explanatory power of predictions based on the fifties and sixties. The macroevents of the seventies have undoubtedly added errors in our observations of true long-run rates of return of firms, which are several orders of magnitude above the standard errors of the estimates of projected profitability based on data from the 1950s and 1960s.

The third possible explanation for the low coefficients on the projected profit measures is that they may be biased in favor of finding significant differences in profitability across firms. The α estimates are based on the 23 observations from 1950–72 and thus include the years 1950–52. Some slight bias in favor of a positive correlation between αs and initial profits is certainly present. This property should not obscure our vision of the future, however. But, it may be that the αs, like mean profits over the 23-year period, are better statistics of past performance than predictors of the future. The coefficients on the α variables under this interpretation indicate that the process of convergence toward normal levels is continuing. The competitive environment hypothesis is sustained, provided one waits long enough.

Further support for this latter interpretation is provided by the last two equations reported in Table 2.7. The 1950 profitability can explain but 1 percent of the variation in 1980 profits. A company earning double the average profit rate in 1950–52 is predicted to earn about 12.9 percent more in 1980.

If one interprets the results in Table 2.7 as lending support for the competitive environment hypothesis, one is still left with the choice of a glass half empty and a glass half full in evaluating the findings. The earlier results suggested that as much as 70 percent of the differences in profit rates across firms in 1950–52 is transitory; that is, 30 percent or more of any profit differences observed are permanent. Table 2.7 implies that some 75 to 80 percent of these "permanent" differences also disappear over time and that the process of eroding profit differences continues until the job is done. But this process takes a long time. If one had no information upon which to predict 1980 profit differences across companies other than their 1950–52 profitability, one would be better off using this information than making a random guess.[5]

In addition to shedding additional light on the competitive environment hypothesis, the results in Table 2.7 allow us to evaluate the different profit projectors available. The best-fit α is slightly superior to the others because of its ability to predict 1980 profits. In view of this slight superiority in predictive performance, the fact that the equation estimates do provide the best fit to the 1950–72 data, and visual examination of the time-series plots of the data for each firm that suggested that α_B was, on the average, the closest estimate to what one would make oneself simply by looking at the data, we shall concentrate our subsequent empirical efforts on trying to explain differences in α_B across companies. The αs from the simple π on $1/t$ regressions run a close second to α_B. In the previous study, both α_D and α_B were employed as dependent variables, with rather similar results. In the present work, we confine our attention to the α_B variable since it best fits the data for 1950–72, and it best predicts 1980 profitability, even though ever so slightly.

F.   Summary and implications

In this chapter, we have defined and tested the hypothesis that the competitive process eliminates positive and negative rents over time; the hypothesis that the rate of return on total capital for all firms converges on some common competitive rate of return. Several alternative specifications of the possible adjustment paths profits might follow were proposed. All indicated that above- and below-average profits strongly tend to converge back toward the mean of the sample. But all specifications also projected persistent differences in corporate profitability into the indefinite future. A significant correlation existed between these projections and the initial profit rates earned by the companies in 1950–52. Since this starting point was more or less arbitrarily chosen, the present findings imply that an element of the profits of all firms at any point in time is a permanent rent, positive or negative, that the competitive process fails to erode.

These conclusions are based on a time-series analysis of 600 companies over the 23-year period 1950–72. The claim that the projected differences in rates of return across companies derived from this time-series investigation persist is called into question in the previous section in which we observed somewhat disappointing, albeit positive and significant, correlations between projections based on data through

32   **Profits in the long run**

1972 and actually observed profit rates in 1980. The results discussed in that section suggest that it may be necessary to redefine the projected differences in returns as quasi-permanent rents.

Whether the differences in projected returns are interpreted as permanent, quasi-permanent, or merely representative differences that existed for a generation, only to fade during the trying seventies, they are large enough and have lasted long enough to warrant further investigation into their causes. This task will preoccupy us for the remainder of the study.

Notes

1 For additional discussion and critique of Brozen's work, see Wenders (1971a, b:), MacAvoy, et al. (1971), Winn and Leabo (1974), Qualls (1974), and McEnally (1976).

2 Data were obtained from the Standard and Poor's COMPUSTAT Tape and conform to its definitions thus,

$$\Pi_i = (\text{INCOME (18)} + \text{INTEREST (15)/TOTAL ASSETS (6))}.$$

Where COMPUSTAT data were not available, but *Moody's* data were, the analogous definition based on *Moody's* data was used.

3 In about six cases, severe multicollinearity was observed in one of the higher-order polynomials in $1/t$ along with a higher R^2. The estimates from the lower-order regression were used in these few cases, both because they are less likely to be distorted by the multicollinearity, and because the standard errors that are particularly affected by this problem are used as weights in the subsequent work.

4 The estimate of λ exceeded 1 in seven cases. It was set equal to 0.95 for these firms.

5 Connolly and Schwartz (1984) test for the persistence of profit differences across firms by estimating probabilities that firms that start a 20-year time period a given distance from the mean converge to it. By and large, these results suggest that company returns do converge on the mean over time, but very slowly. Their conclusion is consistent with the interpretation offered here. It is also interesting that support for their regression-on-the-mean hypothesis is stronger for companies with initially below-average profits. Just as we found that, on the average, the coefficient on lagged profits is highest in the highest profit class, Connolly and Schwartz find some of the strongest evidence against the convergence-on-the-mean hypothesis in their top two profit groups. Firms in the highest group remain in the highest group with a significantly higher-than-expected probability. Firms in the second highest group enter the highest group with a significantly higher probability than predicted.

Profitability and market structure

In this chapter we begin to explore the determinants of persistent profitability. Over the last three decades, a large slice of the industrial organization literature has sought to explain industry or firm profitability on the basis of various industry or company characteristics (see Scherer 1980, Chapter 9; Weiss 1974). Virtually without exception, this literature has been cross-sectional in nature. The implicit assumptions underlying this research have been that the profit differences observed across industries and firms at any point in time are quasi-permanent differences, and that the cross-sectional estimation procedures capture *long-run* structural relationships. Although the interpretation of cross-sectional regression estimates as measures of long-run slopes and elasticities is rather standard in the literature (see Kuh 1963, pp. 182–6), the permanency of the profits observed in any cross section is open to question. Yale Brozen (1970, 1971a, b) launched his assault on the literature for that reason. The estimates of projected or long-run profitability derived in Chapter 2 should avoid much of the criticism Brozen has raised against previous studies. We use these estimates of projected profitability as the dependent variables in our subsequent work. Our independent variables are drawn from the same sets that other studies have employed, although we place a somewhat different interpretation on some of the variables. The estimating procedures are cross-sectional in nature and we also place a long-run interpretation on the estimated coefficients. Given the long-run nature of the profit measures used as dependent variables and the long-run interpretation of the structural relationships estimated, any support for the hypothesis we find should serve to confirm both the validity of the hypothesized underlying structure-performance relations and our interpretation of the profit projections as measures of long-run profitability of the firms.

As noted earlier, the basic conceptualization of how profits arise and why they might persist in the structure-performance literature focuses upon the industry. Boundaries are assumed to exist, separating one industry from another. Barriers may exist along these

Profitability and market structure   51

boundaries, which impede the entry, and maybe even the exit, of firms. Within an industry, all firms are treated essentially alike. A common technology is assumed for all firms that leads to a unique average cost function available to all firms in the industry. This average cost function is assumed to be U- or L-shaped with first a negatively sloped section up until some firm of minimum-efficient size, and then a horizontal section extending for a long, if not indefinite, range of firm sizes. All firms larger than the minimum-efficient size are assumed to have the same average costs; smaller firms have higher average costs.

The number of firms in an industry or level of concentration determines the degree of collusion in the industry and thereby the average height of prices. Although most studies do not confine themselves to homogeneous product industries, in their treatment of the concentration-collusion hypothesis and the role of product differentiation, they come close to imposing this assumption. Collusion is seen raising a common price umbrella over all firms in the industry. Product differentiation is seen not as a characteristic that differentiates one firm within an industry from another and thereby leads to different prices and profit levels across firms within an industry, but as a characteristic of the industry raising a barrier to the entry of other firms that benefits all companies in the industry alike (see, e.g., Comanor and Wilson 1974).

In contrast to this industry approach to market performance, one can envisage an alternative approach that makes the firm the centerpiece of analysis. Firms differ in the products they sell, their organizational form, and internal efficiency. It is the drive to be different that locomotes dynamic competition of a Schumpeterian sort. Those companies successfully differentiating their products or lowering their costs outpace their rivals and grow to be bigger and more profitable than those rivals. This firm approach to market performance reverses the causal link between size and efficiency. Under the industry approach, when an industry's technology dictates scale economies, the size of the firm determines its costs. Only if it is big enough does it have low average costs. Under the firm approach, efficiency determines size. The more efficient companies with superior products grow to be larger than other firms.

The firm approach to market performance is consistent with the criticisms of the traditional structure-performance literature by Harold Demsetz (1973, 1974) and Sam Peltzman (1977), which emphasize firm-specific efficiency advantages, and with the criticisms of W. Geof-

52   **Profits in the long run**

frey Shepherd (1972, 1975), which stress market-power advantages. Both lines of criticism concentrate on the individual firm as the basic unit of analysis.

It is difficult to test the validity of these criticisms of the traditional structure-performance models from the results these models themselves generate, since their very orientation toward the industry rather than the firm serves to obscure the measurement of differences across firms. To sort out the validity of the competing views, we thus develop two models: one that focuses on the industry and treats all firms within an industry alike, with respect to both their product and cost function characteristics, and another that focuses on the firm and allows each firm within an industry to produce a different product at different costs. We begin by developing the industry model.

A.   The industry approach to explaining firm profitability

Each firm in an industry is assumed to sell the identical product at the same price. Since each has access to the same production technology, the same cost function can be assumed for each firm. Since it is necessary to assume some linearity to obtain tractable results when product differentiation is introduced, we also assume linear demand and cost functions in the industry-approach case, although analogous results are obtainable here under rather general demand and cost function assumptions.

Thus, let industry demand be defined as

$$P = A - BX, \tag{4.1}$$

where P is price, X is industry output, and

$$X = \sum_{i=1}^{N} x_i. \tag{4.2}$$

We allow for oligopolistic interdependence by positing a "degree of cooperation" among sellers as the weight each firm places on the profits of other firms in its objective function. That is to say, we assume that each firm i maximizes an objective function, 0_i, that includes its profits, Π_i, and a weighted sum of the profits of the other $N-1$ companies in the industry:[1]

$$0_i = \Pi_i + \theta \sum_{j \neq i}^{N} \Pi_j. \tag{4.3}$$

Perfect collusion implies $\theta = 1$; each other firm j in the industry is given equal weight in i's objective function. Cournot independence

Profitability and market structure

occurs when the other firms are ignored, $\theta = 0$. Rivalry implies $\theta < 0$. This approach to modeling oligopolistic behavior differs somewhat from the more familiar conjectural variation approach. The two approaches are contrasted in Section C.

Each firm's total costs are $TC_i = Cx_i$. Substituting into (4.3), we obtain

$$
\begin{aligned}
0_i &= \Pi_i + \theta \sum_{j \neq i}^{N} \Pi_j \\
&= (P - C) x_i \\
&\quad + \theta \sum_{j \neq i} (P - C) x_j = (A - BX - C) x_i \\
&\quad + \theta \sum_{j \neq i} (A - BX - C) x_j.
\end{aligned}
\tag{4.4}
$$

Maximizing (4.4) with respect to x_i, and solving for x_i from the first order condition, one obtains

$$
x_i = \frac{A - C}{B(1 - \theta)} - \frac{1 + \theta}{1 - \theta} X.
\tag{4.5}
$$

Summing (4.5) over all i, we obtain industry output

$$
\begin{aligned}
X = \sum_{i}^{N} x_i &= N \left(\frac{A - C}{B(1 - \theta)} - \frac{1 + \theta}{1 - \theta} \right) X \\
&= \frac{N}{1 - \theta + N + \theta N} \frac{A - C}{B}.
\end{aligned}
\tag{4.6}
$$

From (4.6), we see immediately that $\theta = 1$ yields the perfect collusion industry output $(A - C)/2B$, and $\theta = 0$, the Cournot output $N(A - C)/(N + 1)B$.

The profits of any firm i are written as

$$
\Pi_i = (P - C) x_i = (A - BX - C) x_i.
\tag{4.7}
$$

Substituting for $A - C$ from (4.6), rearranging and defining the industry demand elasticity as

$$
\eta = \frac{P}{X} B,
$$

we obtain for the ith firm's profit-to-sales ratio

$$
\frac{\Pi_i}{S_i} = \frac{1}{\eta} \left(\frac{1 - \theta + N\theta}{N} \right).
\tag{4.8}
$$

54   **Profits in the long run**

Again, the perfect collusion ($\Pi_i/S_i = 1/\eta$) and Cournot ($\Pi_i/S_i = 1/\eta N$) outcomes emerge, when θ equals one, and zero, respectively.

Equations (4.5), (4.6), and (4.7) imply that the output of any firm and its profit-to-sales ratio are a function of only industry parameters A, B, C, θ, N, and η. The property that each company is of identical size holds for any choice of demand and cost-function structure as long as each firm has access to the same cost-function technology. Each firm, then, has the same objective function and solves a set of symmetric first-order-condition equations.

The implication that all firms in an industry are of the same size is sufficiently at odds with the facts of most manufacturing industries (see Hart and Prais 1956; and Simon and Bonini 1958) to call into question the basic assumptions upon which the industry approach rests, particularly if we assume nonlinear total costs. Although size differences within an industry might exist at any point in time because of historical factors, the freedom to vary plant and firm sizes in the long run should lead firms toward the lowest attainable point on the long-run average cost schedule, given the number of firms in the industry.

Different firm sizes can be reconciled with the assumption that all firms employ the same production technology when the total cost function is linear, as we have so far assumed. Given constant long-run average costs, different size distributions can be predicted to follow from different stochastic-growth assumptions, for example, the log normal from the Gibrat process (Ijiri and Simon 1977). Although postulating constant marginal costs and stochastic-growth processes can rationalize different size distributions of firms, this assumption does not alter the implication of equation (4.8) that all firms have identical profit-to-sales ratios. We thus conclude that the industry approach to explaining firm profitability leads, perhaps not surprisingly, to the implication that *firm* profit rates are a function of *industry* characteristics. All firms in a given industry have identical profit rates on industry sales.

B.   The firm approach to explaining firm profitability

We now wish to allow firms to be different with respect to both their product characteristics and their costs. We write the *i*th firm's demand schedule in a given industry as

$$p_i = a_i - bx_i - \sigma b \sum_{j \neq i} x_j \tag{4.9}$$

and its total cost function $TC_i = c_i x_i$. Thus we retain the linearity assumption with respect to both demand and cost functions. Each firm's demand schedule has the same slope, but the intercepts can differ. A larger a_i implies a greater willingness of buyers to pay for each unit of output. The a_i parameter is interpreted as an index of the perceived quality of the ith firm's product. The σ parameter is common to all firms in the industry and measures the degree of substitutability of one firm's product for another, $0 < \sigma < 1$. When $\sigma = 1$, an increase in the output of any firm in the industry has the same impact on the price the ith firm can charge as an increase in its own output; the products of all firms in the industry are perfect substitutes. If $\sigma = 0$, the ith firm is a monopolist. The objective function of the ith firm can now be written as

$$0_i = \Pi_i + \theta \sum_{j \neq i}^{N} \Pi_j = (a_i - bx_i - \sigma b \sum_{j \neq i} x_j - c_i) x_i$$
$$+ \theta \sum_{j \neq i} (a_j - bx_j - \sigma b \sum_{k \neq j} x_k - c_j) x_j. \quad (4.10)$$

Taking the first derivative of (4.10) with respect to x_i and solving for x_i, we obtain

$$x_i = \frac{a_i - c_i}{2b} - \frac{\sigma(1+\theta)}{2} \sum_{j \neq i} x_j. \quad (4.11)$$

The first term in (4.11) might be called the quality-efficiency index for firm i. Higher values of this term imply either higher levels of perceived quality for i's product (higher a_i), or lower per unit costs, c_i. Defining $r = \sigma(1+\theta)/2$, (4.11) can be rewritten as

$$x_i = \frac{a_i - c_i}{2b} - r \sum_{j \neq i} x_j = \frac{1}{1-r} \left(\frac{a_i - c_i}{2b} - rX \right). \quad (4.12)$$

The firm's sales are now a function of both industry- and firm-specific characteristics.[2] Firms with higher quality-efficiency indexes have greater outputs.

From (4.9) we can write the ith firm's profits as

$$\Pi_i = (a_i - (b - \sigma)x_i - b\sigma X - c_i)x_i. \quad (4.13)$$

Using (4.12) to remove $a_i - c_i$ and rearranging, we obtain

$$\Pi_i/x_i = bx_i - \sigma \theta bx_i + b\sigma \theta X. \quad (4.14)$$

56   **Profits in the long run**

If we sum p_i over all i, we have

$$\Sigma p_i = \Sigma a_i - (b-\theta)X - Nb\sigma X, \tag{4.15}$$

or

$$\overline{P}_i = \Sigma p_i/N = \Sigma a_i/N - (b-\sigma)\frac{X}{N} - b\sigma X, \tag{4.16}$$

with N large $(b-\sigma)X/N \simeq 0$, and

$$d\overline{P}/dX \simeq -b\sigma. \tag{4.17}$$

We can then define the industry demand elasticity for the case where we have differentiated products as the percentage change in quantity divided by the percentage in mean price and write

$$\eta = -\frac{dX}{d\overline{P}}\frac{\overline{P}}{X} = \frac{1}{b\sigma}. \tag{4.18}$$

If we now divide both sides of (4.14) by $\overline{P}$, and define $m_i = x_i/X$ as firm i's market share, we can use (4.18) to obtain

$$\frac{\Pi_i}{S_i} \simeq \frac{\Pi_i}{x_i\overline{P}} = \frac{1}{\eta}\left(\frac{m_i}{\sigma} - \theta m_i + \theta\right). \tag{4.19}$$

The ith firm's profit-to-sales ratio is approximately equal to three terms that include the three industry characteristics, demand elasticity, degree of cooperation, and degree of product substitution, and the one firm characteristic, market share. The firm approach to explaining profitability adds two variables not present in the profit-rate equation in the industry approach, the degree of product substitutability and the firm's market share.

C.   On modeling oligopolistic interdependence

Before examining the empirical estimates for the two models, we contrast the degree-of-cooperation approach to oligopolistic interdependence with the more familiar conjectural variation approach. In the latter, each firm i is assumed to make a conjecture, λ_i, of the aggregate response of all other firms in the industry to a change in its output

$$\lambda_i = \sum_{j \neq i} \frac{dx_j}{dx_i} \tag{4.20}$$

(see Cowling and Waterson 1976; Dansby and Willig 1979). If we assume a homogeneous product with demand schedule $P = A - BX$, and constant marginal costs C for all firms, as in the industry approach of Section A, then i's profit-maximizing output is

$$x_i = \frac{A - C - B\sum_{j \neq i} x_j}{B(2 + \lambda_i)} \tag{4.21}$$

and its price-cost margin is

$$\frac{P - C}{P} = -\frac{m_i(1 + \lambda_i)}{\eta}, \tag{4.22}$$

where m_i and η are i's market share and the industry demand elasticity, respectively. With homogeneous products and identical costs, it is reasonable to assume symmetric conjectures, so that $\lambda_i = \lambda$ for all $i = 1, N$. Then (4.21) and (4.22) imply that all firms are of the same size and have the same price–cost margin as in the results for the industry approach model. Indeed, the same range of price–cost margin predictions emerges with $\lambda = N - 1$ implying perfect collusion, $\lambda = 0$ Cournot independence, $\lambda = -1$ perfect competition (Bertrand independence).

Equation (4.21) implies that the profit-maximizing output of firm i is dependent upon the outputs of all other firms, the conjectured response of all other firms to a change in i's output, and the demand and cost parameters. Should all other firms change their output, i would change its output. Its optimal response would be

$$dx_i = -\frac{1}{2 + \lambda} d\sum_{j \neq i} x_j. \tag{4.23}$$

In particular, in Cournot's classic duopoly example, if $\lambda = 0$, firm i would respond to an increase in j's output by reducing its output by one-half of j's increase. At the Cournot equilibrium, each firm would hold expectations of what the other firm's output response would be ($\lambda = 0$) that were inconsistent with what their own response would be to a change in the other firm's output, as well as the other firm's response. A rational manager, recognizing the symmetric nature of the duopoly situation, would not choose outputs under the assumption that the other firm will not respond to a change in his or her company's output, while at the same time realizing that in precisely the same situation he or she would respond to a change in the other firm's output.

The seemingly irrational nature of holding inconsistent conjectures has led several writers to impose the requirement that the profit-maximizing response of each firm to a change in output be equivalent

58   **Profits in the long run**

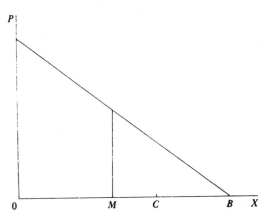

Figure 4.1 Outcomes in a Cournot duopoly game.

to the conjectured response of the other firm(s) (see, e.g., Laitner 1980; Bresnahan 1981b; Perry 1982; Kamien and Schwartz 1983; McMillan 1982; Ulph 1983). Thus, if $\bar{\lambda}$ is the profit-maximizing response of a firm to a change in the output of the other firm and λ remains the conjectured response, consistency requires that $\bar{\lambda} = \lambda$. In the symmetric, homogeneous product duopoly case, the only pair of outputs satisfying the consistent conjectures constraint is at the Bertrand equilibrium ($\lambda = -1$), that is, the competitive outcome where $P = C$.

Despite the obvious appeal of the assumption that rational managers hold consistent conjectures, I find the nature of the equilibria attained under this assumption implausible. Consider the classic Cournot duopoly example. Marginal costs are zero, AB is the demand schedule, M, C, and B are the joint profit-maximizing monopoly, Cournot, and Bertrand outputs, respectively (see Figure 4.1). Should the two firms be at some point to the right of M, say C, each would know that by jointly reducing their outputs they could increase their profits. Each faces a prisoner's dilemma situation, however, so that if one firm alone reduces its output, it is made worse off. Thus, we see the reasonableness of Cournot's assumption that each firm does not expect a cooperative response from the other, so that they remain locked into the noncooperative equilibrium at C.

Now, should the firms hold consistent conjectures, not only would they not try to move from C to M by reducing their outputs in the hopes that the other firms would also cooperate and would they not

Profitability and market structure 59

stay at C on the assumption that the other firm would not move, but *each* would *increase* its output on the expectation that the other firm would *reduce* its output. Thus, a movement from any point to the left of B to B must occur by each company behaving in a manner that is *inconsistent* with the conjectured behavior underlying the justification for claiming B as an equilibrium point, a property I find awkward, to say the least.

I think that the implausible nature of both the equilibria reached and the pseudodynamic movements toward these equilibria under the conjectural variation approach arises from the rather extreme context in which the oligopoly problem is posed. Each firm acts independently of the other, and each speculates on the other firm's output response without directly considering the effects on the other firm's profits. The setting is not unlike that posed by Sweezy (1939) in deriving the kinky oligopoly demand curve, and the results are equally implausible.

At first it might appear that the paucity of information each company is presumed to possess and the independence surrounding the output decision strengthen the analysis. The less one assumes and the more one proves, the stronger the theory is. But with respect to the oligopoly problem, imposing *weak* assumptions about the information available to each seller biases the results against reaching oligopolistic agreements. The more information the oligopolists have, the more likely they are to succeed in restricting industry output to some degree. Similarly, the independence built into the decision process is more compatible with Cournot–Nash–Bertrand outcomes than collusive ones. The emergence of equilibria falling in the Cournot–Bertrand outcome interval under a wide range of assumptions is less surprising than it first appears (see Bresnahan 1981b; Perry 1982; Kamien and Schwartz 1983; McMillan 1982; Ulph 1983).

With these criticisms in mind, modeling oligopoly by assuming a degree of cooperation among firms seems to have some conceptual advantages over assuming interdependence via conjectured output responses by rivals. In the degree-of-cooperation approach, each firm i is presumed to have sufficient information about the components of the demand and cost functions of other firms to allow it to choose its own output so as to maximize the weighted sum of company profits (4.3). The industry equilibrium arises at the set of individual firm outputs obtained from the simultaneous solution of the N first-order conditions. The strength of the assumptions embedded in this approach is now apparent. Each firm possesses enough information about the other $N-1$ companies' demand and cost functions to allow it to solve a set of N simultaneous equations for its own and every other firm's output. In the solution to this set of equations, all firms agree on the weight to be placed on all other firms' profits, θ. As just stated, the assumptions underlying the degree-of-cooperation approach may seem so strong that one is enticed back to positing conjectural variations by the seductive weakness of this approach's assumptions.

Indeed, one might object that the degree-of-cooperation approach presumes detailed information about one's competitors that no firm could possibly have, and if all firms within an industry did have this amount of information they would certainly be able to collude perfectly. This criticism resembles earlier critiques of profits maximization that argued managers do not know their marginal costs and revenues and thus cannot equate them (Lester 1946). The orthodox response has been that what is important in judging a model is whether the actors behave *as if* they had the required information, and the model's ability to describe and predict behavior vis-à-vis alternative models (Machlup 1946). This argument could be used to defend the present treatment of the oligopoly problem. Although no management has the information to maximize a weighted sum of the profits of all firms in an industry, a management that weighed the impact of its output choices on the profits of other firms might behave *as if* it were. Furthermore, in a world of imperfect information and imperfect coordination, the equilibria attained might resemble equilibria that would have occurred had all firms maximized objective functions with some common θ.

In the end, the choice of an oligopoly model from the existing set must be a matter of taste. Each has its faults and virtues. The conjectural variations approach with the added constraint that conjectures be consistent has the virtue of plausibly describing how an equilibrium once attained would be sustained. It has the fault of not describing how one would ever get there. Gone are the reaction curves from traditional duopoly theory since they presume inconsistent conjectured response. Gone, too, is the story about how equilibria are attained.

The degree-of-cooperation approach allows for any possible outcome in the range from perfect competition to full collusion. Any point between *B* and *M* in Figure 4.1 could be an equilibrium. Left unanswered is what it is that leads an industry to settle on a given degree of cooperation, θ, a given point between *B* and *M*.

Those who prefer the conjectural variation approach are reminded that analogous structural equations are derived under this model when the consistent conjectures constraint is not imposed (Long 1982). Initial efforts to estimate conjectural variations have ignored the consistency issue also (see Gollop and Roberts 1979; Bresnahan 1981a; Geroski 1982b; Roberts 1984).

D.   Empirical estimates: industry approach

The industry approach yielded an equation (4.8) to explain firm profits, as follows:

$$\frac{\Pi_i}{S_i} = \frac{1}{\eta}\left(\frac{1-\theta+N\theta}{N}\right). \tag{4.8}$$

If all firms were of the same size, $1/N$ would equal the Herfindahl index of concentration, and firm profitability would be a function of demand elasticity, the degree of cooperation, and the Herfindahl concentration measure. The usual assumption is that θ, the degree of cooperation, is also a function of the level of concentration. If we think of the problem of reaching collusive agreement in an industry as analogous to the problem of reaching a cooperative solution to a prisoners' dilemma game, then the most natural assumption to make about θ is that it increases with declining numbers of sellers, that is, that θ is positively related to concentration. This hypothesis underlies the traditional structure-performance literature. In Figure 4-2a, we depict θ as an S-shaped function of concentration, eventually approaching the perfect collusion value of one.

Howard Marvel (1980) has argued that collusion, like pregnancy, is an all-or-nothing affair. Firms either succeed in coordinating their outputs to achieve the pure monopoly industry output or do not, in which case pure rivalry reigns. This view of the collusion game is consistent with a critical concentration-ratio hypothesis (see White 1976; Sant 1978). Figure 4.2b depicts this hypothesis. Paul Geroski (1981) has argued in favor of a generalization of this assumption in which several concentration-ratio intervals are presumed to have different slope coefficients.

Finally, we allow for the possibility that rivalry may increase with increasing concentration, at least over some initial range of concentration levels. This hypothesis concerning concentration and rivalry is undoubtedly most compatible with rivalry in nonprice modes of competition (Cubbin 1983), where rivalrous expenditures on product differentiation can be expected to take the form of an inverted U (Cable 1972; Greer 1971). If nonprice competition is more difficult to coordinate than price competition, rivalry could increase with increasing concentration, at least to some point, and give rise to a U-

62   **Profits in the long run**

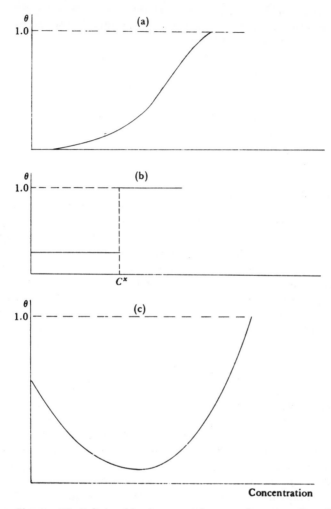

Figure 4.2 Relationship between degree of cooperation θ and concentration.

shaped relationship between concentration and rivalry (see Figure 4. 2c). Although we have not allowed for separate degrees of cooperation on price and nonprice competitive modes, as Cubbin does, it is obvious that the net effect of the two will be reflected in observed profit rates. Thus, if nonprice rivalry is sufficiently strong, we will capture the profit pattern that this mode of competition yields. Nonprice forms of competition lead to product differentiation and thus are incompatible with the industry approach set out here, but we allow for this possibility now for completeness.

A strong form of the structure-conduct hypothesis would assume that a single relationship between the degree of cooperation, θ, and concentration holds across all industries. One could then substitute for θ in (4.8), and using H as the measure of concentration, $H = 1/N$, one would have a relationship between firm profits and but two industry parameters, the price elasticity and concentration:

$$\frac{\Pi_i}{S_i} = \frac{f(H)}{\eta}. \tag{4.24}$$

If each firm sold in only one industry, both the industry demand elasticities and parameters of f could be estimated by regressing firm profit rates on industry concentration levels, assuming enough observations existed for each industry to give reasonable parameter estimates. Two difficulties exist with this approach. First, because almost all firms operate in more than one industry, firm profit rates are a weighted average of the profits earned in each industry. A weighted-average concentration index must be computed for each firm, therefore, but such an index slips in a linearity assumption concerning the concentration-profits relationship, where f might well be nonlinear. Second, f may not have the same functional form for all industries. In particular, the functional form that f takes may vary with the industry demand elasticity.

Equation (4.24) seems remarkably simple compared with the typical structure-performance equations estimated today. Particularly conspicuous is the absence of entry-barrier variables. One reason for their absence is that some variables usually considered as entry barriers (e.g., product differentiation proxies) are incompatible with the homogeneous product assumption underlying the industry approach. Similarly, an estimate of minimum-efficient size is not needed because of the long-run equilibrium assumption we impose, which in turn implies that either all firms are of equal size or marginal costs are constant. An additional problem with the most frequently used measures of minimum-efficient size, those based on the existing size distribution of firms, is that they are not independent of the concentration index (see Scherer et al. 1975, pp. 218–19).

The long-run equilibrium nature of the analysis suggests a more general interpretation of the demand elasticity parameter, η, that would allow for the inclusion of entry-barrier variables through η. The analysis of Section A assumes a fixed number of firms N choosing

64   **Profits in the long run**

quantities to maximize objective functions defined with respect to only these N companies; η measures the percentage change in price that follows from a change in quantity supplied by these N firms. If the number of firms in the industry does not change, η is the demand elasticity as usually defined. But we could think of firms outside of the N industry incumbents responding to changes in the incumbents' outputs in the long run, so that the price change that follows a given change in quantity by the incumbents is the result of the total change in quantity occurring, that is, the incumbents' change plus the outsiders' response. The ηs under these assumptions contain the anticipated reaction of outsiders to quantity changes by the incumbents. In this way, the ηs are themselves a reflection of the height of entry barriers. Lower barriers are indicated by larger values of η.

With these considerations as background, we are now prepared to proceed. We follow two paths:

1. We attempt to estimate the η from our data on firms' profits and industry concentration levels.
2. We employ external measures of η and use them to estimate the concentration–profit–relationship parameters.

Consider again (4.8), for example. Rewriting (4.8) with $H = 1/N$, we have

$$\frac{\Pi_i}{S_i} = \frac{1}{\eta}(H - \theta H + \theta). \tag{4.25}$$

If we assume that θ has the same functional form for all industries and attempt to approximate θ by the third-degree polynomial

$$\theta = a + bH + cH^2 + dH^3,$$

the term in parentheses in (4.25) becomes the fourth-degree polynomial

$$a + (1-a-b)H + (c-b)H^2 + (d-c)H^3 - dH^4. \tag{4.26}$$

A third-degree polynomial is a sufficiently general functional form to allow us to approximate almost any presumed relationship. Even the discontinuous relationship in Figure 4.1b is approximated fairly well by a third-degree polynomial, as in Figure 4.1a, with the parameters chosen to make the rising portion of the curve quite steep. There are several problems in trying to estimate (4.25) by replacing the term in parentheses with (4.26), however. First, we do not have measures of the Herfindahl index. We can use the market share data for the 1,000 largest companies to calculate a pseudo-Herfindahl index by summing the squared market shares for those companies that are in a given market and in the 1,000 largest companies. For big markets, the leading firms in the market must of necessity have sufficient sales in these markets alone to place them in the 1,000 largest companies. In these markets, our coverage of the leading firms is good and the H one can calculate using the 1,000 largest data is a close approximation of the true H. In small markets, we have but one or two firms and our pseudo-H is admittedly rough. Nevertheless, given that H appears in the equation independently of the θ term, we can simplify the analysis greatly by writing θ as a function of H.

We have individual company sales by five-digit industry for 1950 and 1972. We are thus able to calculate weighted-average Hs for each firm using their sales in each market in these two years. From these, two estimates of the long-run H in the industries for each firm were calculated: a simple average of the 1950 and 1972 Hs, and a projection of H assuming the same type of first-degree polynomial used to project profits in Chapter 2. That is to say, defining $HPRJ_i$ as the long-run projected H for firm i, we write

$$H'_i = HPRJ + \beta/t. \tag{4.27}$$

Since we observe H for only two points in time, we assume that (4.27) holds exactly for each firm in 1950 and 1972. From the two resulting equations, we can solve for the two unknowns $HPRJ$ and β. For $HPRJ$, we obtain

$$HPRJ_i = \frac{23}{22} H_i^{72} - \frac{1}{22} H_i^{50}. \tag{4.28}$$

Projections of a firm's market share and four-firm concentration ratio were made in a similar way. Since the projected values always performed somewhat better than the arithmetic mean of the 1950 and 1972 figures, we report here only the results for the projected indexes. Given the heavy weight placed on the 1972 H, we simply used this figure for those companies in the sample that were not in the 1,000 largest list for 1950.

1.   *Estimates using externally estimated demand elasticities*

The simplest method of estimating the parameters in (4.26) is to obtain independent estimates of the price elasticities and to multiply each term in (4.26) by $1/\eta$. This procedure allows us to estimate (4.26) using ordinary least squares and the elasticity-weighted concentration variables. Given that firms occupy more than one industry, the η variable

66   **Profits in the long run**

for each firm is a weighted average of the ηs in the industries in which it sells.

Very few studies have employed external estimates of demand elasticities in structure-performance tests and for good reason. Typically, one-third or more of any demand-elasticity estimates are of the wrong sign in any large-scale effort to estimate demand elasticities (see Comanor and Wilson 1974; Houthakker and Taylor 1970). Even when they are of the correct sign, individual estimates often seem rather implausible. For example, several of the estimates made by Pagoulatos and Sorensen (1981) for four-digit food and tobacco industries suggest implausibly inelastic demand schedules, and none of the industry elasticities they estimate exceeds one in absolute value. Given the very long-run orientation of this study, it seems extremely implausible that no food industry has an elastic demand schedule.

Michael Intriligator has kindly made available to me demand-elasticity estimates that he and H. DeAngelo calculated at the four-digit level. When these estimates were of the wrong sign, Intriligator and DeAngelo made new estimates at a higher level of aggregation. Their estimates thus have the twin advantages of spanning all industries in my sample and of being of the predicted sign at some level of aggregation. I have chosen to work with these estimates.[3]

As dependent variable, we wish to use the long-run profit projections from Chapter 2. These projections are rates of return on total assets, whereas (4.8), for example, predicts a relationship between concentration and the profit-to-sales ratio. If (4.8) is multiplied by sales over total assets, the left-hand side becomes profits over total assets, and the right-hand-side variables are all weighted by the ratio of sales to total assets. Our estimates of (4.8) are based on weighting all right-hand-side variables by sales over total assets.

Since the dependent variable is itself an estimated parameter, our confidence in its accuracy as a projection of long-run profitability varies across observations. This variability implies in turn that the variance in errors around an estimated regression line when $\hat{\alpha}$ is used as dependent variable cannot be expected to be constant, with the result that the estimates are inefficient. This problem is removed when each equation is estimated by a form of generalized least squares in which each observation is weighted by the reciprocal of the standard error of the estimate of $\hat{\alpha}_i$ for that observation (see Saxonhouse 1976). This procedure has the intuitively appealing feature of weighting each observation in proportion to our confidence in the accuracy of the estimate of the dependent variable.

Equation (1) in Table 4.1 presents the results from estimating a

Table 4.1. *Estimates of basic industry-approach model using external η estimates*

$$[\alpha_i = \frac{1}{\eta_i}(\beta_0 + \beta_1 H_i + \beta_2 H_i^2 + \beta_3 H_i^3 + \beta_4 H_i^4); \; n = 551]$$

Equation	$\frac{1}{\eta}$	$\hat{\alpha}_i$	β_0	β_1	β_2	β_3	β_4	$\bar{R}^2$
(1)		Best	.087	−.585	1.264	−1.513	1.028	.051
			.47	.35	.23	.21	.31	
(2)		Best	.102	−.571	.662			.053
			3.63	3.81	4.16			
(3)	1	Best	.445	−4.53	15.14	−21.37	11.31	.048
			1.26	1.32	1.29	1.30	1.40	
(4)	1	Best	.192	−.938	1.301			.047
			1.84	2.82	3.70			

68　　　**Profits in the long run**

fourth-degree polynomial in H using the projected profit rate from the best fit of the first-, second-, and third-degree polynomials using $1/t$ estimated in Chapter 2. All observations are weighted by the reciprocal of the standard error of the estimate of the dependent variable, σ_α. All right-hand-side variables are weighted by an estimate of the average elasticity of demand in the firm's markets and the ratio of its sales to total assets. We can calculate the parameters of (4.25) using the following formulas:

$$
\begin{aligned}
a &= \beta_0 \\
b &= \beta_1 + \beta_0 - 1 \\
c &= \beta_2 + \beta_1 + \beta_0 - 1 \\
d &= \beta_3 + \beta_2 + \beta_1 - 1 \\
d &= -\beta_4.
\end{aligned}
\tag{4.29}
$$

The estimates for equation (1) imply a positive intercept and negative coefficients on all other terms in the θ equation. The degree of cooperation appears to decline as concentration (as measured by the Herfindahl index) increases. The system of equations (4.29) is overdetermined, but both estimates of d are negative. Equation (1) is so obviously plagued by multicollinearity that I did not reestimate it constraining the coefficients as in (4.29).

Both the fourth- and third-degree terms must be dropped to break multicollinearity. The remaining coefficients again imply negative estimates for b and c. The degree of cooperation declines with increasing H at an increasing rate.

Equations (3) and (4) are the same as (1) and (2), except that all firms are given the same $\eta = 1$. The results indicate an only modest decline in $\bar{R}^2$. The same ordering of signs occurs, but multicollinearity appears to introduce more distortion in the estimates of the coefficients. The estimates in (4) again imply declining cooperation with increasing H.

These results are inconsistent with one's expectations concerning the relationship between concentration and cooperation, and one worries whether this may be due to the inadequacies in our measures of H. We therefore estimate polynomials between projected profits and concentration. For 1972, we were fortunate in having Leonard Weiss's (1981) recalculated concentration ratios adjusted for both imports and regional and local market differences. We again tried an arithmetic mean of 1950 and 1972 firm-level concentration ratios and a projected level using the same projection formula (4.27). We used the 1972 figure as the projected C_4 when no 1950 figure was available.

The estimates of the fourth-order polynomials again reveal multicollinearity (Table 4.2), and one observes a flip-flop in the signs of β_1 and β_2 as one drops the C_4^3 term (equations [2] and [3]). Thus, one is somewhat uncertain about the key parameters. The calculations in (4.29) cannot be used to solve for the parameters in the θ function because they are derived from (4.26), in which H plays two roles: as the reciprocal for the number of firms in the industry *and* as an argument in the θ function. It is only with respect to the latter that it is legitimate to substitute C_4 for H. If it were legitimate to use (4.29) to calculate the parameters of

$$\theta = a + bC_4 + cC_4^2 + dC_4^3,$$

then both equations (2) and (3) would imply declining cooperation with increasing concentration, even though profitability would increase over an initial range of concentration levels according to (2). This comes about because the first term in parentheses in (4.26), H, increases with increasing concentration, regardless of what happens to θ, and this can outweigh the impact of θ over some range of C_4 values.

The $\overline{R}^2$ of the equation in which $\eta = 1$ exceeds that for the analogous equation in which the right-hand-side variables have been weighted by $1/\eta_i$ and η_i is a weighted-average demand elasticity for each firm.

Whether this deterioration in performance is due to the quality of the demand-elasticity estimates, our use of a weighted average for each firm as opposed to figures for both profits and demand elasticity by industry, or the inadequacy of the theory itself cannot be ascertained. But both Tables 4.1 and 4.2 suggest that adding externally estimated demand elasticities does not improve the fit of the model.[4] We are thus driven to try to estimate the elasticities internally.

2.   Industry model with internally generated demand elasticities

Consider once again equation (4.25):

$$\frac{\Pi_i}{S_i} = \frac{1}{\eta_{ij}} (H_{ij} - \theta_j H_{ij} + \theta_j),$$

where the i stands for firm i and the j for industry j. Suppose that we were to approximate the term in parentheses by a polynomial in H as in the previous subsection. Suppose further that the same functional relationship between the degree of cooperation, θ, and concentration held across all industries, and that each firm operates in but one industry. We could then attempt to estimate both the parameters of

Table 4.2. *Estimates of basic industry-approach model using C_4 and external η estimates*

$$\hat{\alpha}_i = \frac{1}{\eta_i}(\beta_0 + \beta_1 C_{4i} + \beta_2 C_{4i}^2 + \beta_3 C_{4i}^3 + \beta_4 C_{4i}^4); \quad n = 551$$

Equation	$\frac{1}{\eta}$	$\hat{\alpha}_i$	β_0	β_1	β_2	β_3	β_4	$\bar{R}^2$
(1)		Best	-.264	2.471	-7.766	9.125	-3.159	.080
			1.55	1.59	1.54	1.32	.93	
(2)		Best	-.124	1.114	-3.159	2.686		.081
			1.54	2.07	2.83	3.62		
(3)		Best	.143	-.750	.843			.060
			4.41	4.59	4.92			
(4)	1	Best	-.446	3.791	-9.900	7.910		.082
			-2.69	3.13	3.70	4.37		

the θ function and the industry-demand elasticities by specifying separate dummy variable vectors for each firm (0 if the firm is not in
industry j, 1 if it is), and estimate (4.25) using a nonlinear estimation
technique.

There are several problems in proceeding this way. Perhaps the
easiest of these to get around is the one that arises because companies
operate in numerous industries. To deal with this difficulty, I generalized the dummy variable concept by constructing vectors for each
firm consisting of the percentage of sales in each industry.

More serious is the fact that the sample of 551 firms spans some
775 industries. It is impossible to estimate separate industry-demand
elasticities at this level. I thus aggregated each company's sales up to
the three-digit level, reducing the number of "industries" to 141.

Even so, one could not proceed directly. Estimating more than 140
parameters by a nonlinear regression technique would most likely
have exhausted the International Institute of Management's computer
budget for one year. Moreover, the SHAZAM package with which I
was working had a limit of 100 parameters that can be estimated with
any one regression. I thus had to follow another route.

Assume that the factor in parentheses in (4.25) could be approximated by a polynomial in concentration of, say, the second order.
Using C_4 instead of H because of its superior performance, as evidenced by comparing Tables 4.1 and 4.2, we have

$$\frac{\Pi_i}{S_i} = \frac{1}{\eta_j} (a + bC_{4j}^2 + cC_{4j}^2). \qquad (4.30)$$

Now, (4.30) can be estimated using ordinary least squares by estimating a separate intercept term and slopes on the concentration
terms for each industry and using the vector of percentages of sales
for each firm in each industry as a pseudo-industry dummy vector.
If the a, b, and c coefficients in (4.30) are the same for all industries,
then the ratio of the intercept to the slope on C_4 and C_4^2 should be
constants for all industries.

Given that we could not estimate more than 100 coefficients in a
single equation, we first broke the sample of industries into three
groups of roughly equal size: SIC industries 201–266, 271–339, and
341–399. Separate intercepts and slopes were estimated for all industries in the main subgroup, and the remaining two subgroups were
constrained to have the same intercepts and concentration slope. We
then combined all industries having neither an intercept nor a coefficient on the concentration term greater than their respective standard error, and reestimated separate intercepts and slopes across the

72   **Profits in the long run**

entire sample. Multicollinearity across industries did not appear to be very serious, but collinearity between an industry's intercept term and its concentration terms often was. When the concentration terms and intercept for an industry all had standard errors greater than their coefficients, the concentration terms were dropped to see whether the intercept by itself would have a coefficient larger than its standard error.

In all, some 65 of the 141 three-digit industries spanning the sample had at least one coefficient that exceeded its standard error in these first-pass regressions. About one-half of the intercepts were negative and less than $-.30$. Since it is unlikely that the competitive rate of return on capital is more than 30 percent below the sample mean, these negative intercepts can occur only if the η_j estimates for these industries are negative or if $\hat{a}$ in equation (4.30) is negative. But since $\hat{a}$ is presumed to be the same for all industries, if it is negative, then the η_j estimates for all those industries taking on positive intercepts must be negative. But we have defined η_j as the negative of the slope of the demand schedule. Thus, our first-pass estimates imply that roughly one-half of the estimated demand elasticities are of the wrong sign, or that the same $\hat{a}$ and, by implication, the same polynomial in C_4 do not represent the factor in parentheses in equation (4.30).

It is very difficult to accept the implication that roughly one-half of the industries have upward-sloping demand schedules. More plausible is the explanation that holding demand elasticity fixed, the same polynomial relationship between profitability and concentration does not hold across all industries. If this explanation is correct, then it will not be possible to isolate the separate influences of industry demand elasticity and concentration on a firm's profits. A firm having 10 percent of its sales in industry j has its profits shifted some h percent from the sample mean, where this h is determined by a combination of the industry j's long-run demand elasticity, concentration in j, and the degree of cooperation in j, but there is no way to sort out the given effects.

We can attempt to estimate the net effect of these factors, the h_j for each industry, by simply regressing firm profit rates on the vectors of percentages of firm sales in each industry. This technique is essentially an analysis-of-variance approach. We applied it to the 65 industries for which at least one coefficient in any one equation estimated exceeded its standard error. A common intercept was imposed on the remaining 76 industries, and a stepwise regression was employed to determine which of the 65 industries that appeared to be potentially important in explaining profitability would be so on a

Profitability and market structure 73

final pass. A 25 percent probability of significance criterion was used to enter and delete variables from the equation. The results are reported in Table 4.3. Column 1 of the results lists 32 industries that exhibited a 25 percent or better probability of having a coefficient significantly different from all other industries. The coefficient on all other industries is close to zero, so the coefficients as reported indicate roughly the deviation of a firm's projected profitability from the sample mean. The coefficient on the pharmaceuticals industry vector, for example, implies that a firm making 100 percent of its sales in the pharmaceutical industry is projected to earn a return on total capital 127 percent higher than the average profit rate earned in the 109 other industries not singled out in Table 4.3, and 134 percent (127 + 07) greater than the sample mean. All but 5 of the 32 coefficients in column 1 implied plausible projections of profitability differences as a result of participation in an industry; that is, the projections were plausible both with respect to sign (soaps and detergents, and photographic equipment earn above-normal returns, steel mills and railroad equipment below) and magnitude, in the sense that projected values for the industry fall within the range of observed projected values for all firms. But a couple of wild outliers exist. A firm lucky enough to have all of its sales in industry 235 (millinery and hats) is projected to earn more than 1,000 times the average company's return on capital.

Although the preliminary estimations of industry effects indicated that a common relationship between concentration and profitability did not hold across all industries, concentration is one of the industry characteristics that is likely to affect the level of profitability. It is of interest to see, therefore, what happens to the industry coefficients when concentration is introduced into the equation. Column 2 shows the result. Both C_4 and C_4^2 add significant explanatory power to the equation; the same U-shaped relationship between concentration and profitability is observed as was evident in equation (3) of Table 4.2. Two industries (212 and 281) on the borderline to entering the equation in Column 1 drop out, one industry (364) squeezes in. But basically very little change in either the identity of the industries included in the equation or the size of the coefficients follows from adding concentration. The most important exception to this generalization is industry 351 (generators, motors, and engines), whose coefficient and significance level drop sharply when C_4 and C_4^2 are included.

In columns 1 and 2 the right-hand-side variables were weighted by sales over total assets to adjust for the use of profits over assets as dependent variable, rather than profits to sales, as the theory requires.

Table 4.3. *Determinants of profitability, industries with significantly different projected profitability*

(n = 551)

Industry SIC codes	Industry names	Right-hand-side weighted by S/K		Right-hand-side unweighted	
		(1)	(2)	(3)	(4)
202	Dairy products		.168 (2.83)	-.179 (1.42)	-.152 (1.23)
203	Canned and frozen fruits, vegetables	.184 (3.06)	.181 (2.43)	.396 (3.33)	.347 (2.94)
204	Flour and cereals	.156 (2.04)	.138 (2.52)	.239 (1.81)	.263 (2.04)
206	Sugar and confectionery products	.184 (3.34)		.292 (3.78)	.150 (1.92)
208	Beer and distilled spirits			-.250 (1.81)	-.192 (1.43)
212	Cigars	-.267 (1.17)			
214	Tobacco	3.19 (2.65)	2.34 (2.00)	2.92 (2.79)	1.67 (1.62)
235	Millinery, hats	1098 (3.46)	1218 (3.93)	2518 (3.40)	2711 (3.76)
251	Furniture, wood and metal, mattresses	.208 (1.81)	.235 (2.09)	.363 (1.86)	.429 (2.24)
254	Wood and metal partitions	-2.28 (1.41)	-2.15 (1.36)	-2.43 (1.32)	-2.49 (1.39)
261	Wood pulp	1.59 (1.56)	1.76 (1.77)	1.76 (1.66)	2.00 (1.93)
262	Paper and newsprint	-.668 (2.77)	-.634 (2.69)	-.636 (2.43)	-.561 (2.17)
271	Newspapers	1.06 (1.28)	1.12 (1.38)	1.35 (1.29)	1.39 (1.36)
275	Commercial printing, magazines	.392 (2.61)	.398 (2.70)	.505 (2.88)	.546 (3.10)
278	Bookbinding				-2.03 (1.37)
279	Photoengraving, electrotyping, typesetting	-8.45 (1.69)	-7.66 (1.57)	-12.4 (1.75)	-12.7 (1.83)
281	Inorganic chemicals	-.314 (1.25)			

		(1)	(2)	(3)	(4)
283	Pharmaceuticals	1.27 (5.91)	1.32 (6.30)	1.40 (5.81)	1.48 (6.28)
284	Soaps, detergents, polishes, toilet preparations	.482 (4.81)	.471 (4.80)	.688 (4.27)	.668 (4.26)
307	Plastic products	.431 (2.40)	.420 (2.35)	.623 (2.52)	.691 (2.80)
313	Nonrubber shoes and boots	8.37 (4.68)	9.08 (5.16)	14.7 (4.37)	15.8 (4.75)
323	Mirrors and other products made from purchased glass	3.87 (2.14)	3.89 (2.21)	3.00 (1.23)	
324	Hydraulic cement	-.937 (2.69)	-1.02 (2.98)	-.722 (2.45)	-.871 (3.03)
331	Steel mill products	-.194 (2.46)	-.176 (2.18)	-.216 (2.33)	-.199 (2.17)
342	Cutlery, razors, hand tools	1.18 (3.70)	1.29 (4.13)	1.57 (3.76)	1.78 (4.38)
344	Fabricated structural metal products	-.218 (1.99)	-.245 (2.29)	-.411 (2.02)	-.460 (2.32)
349	Springs, valves, and pipe fittings	.375 (2.10)	.373 (2.13)	.522 (2.23)	.463 (2.02)
351	Turbine generators, gasoline and diesel engines	.546 (3.41)	.230 (1.37)	.759 (2.90)	
354	Machine tools	.656 (4.09)	.720 (4.59)	.788 (4.23)	.884 (4.86)
358	Laundry and refrigeration equipment	.359 (3.45)	.324 (3.16)	.572 (3.30)	.550 (3.28)
362	Motors and generators, electrical equipment	.569 (2.41)	.581 (2.49)	.804 (2.49)	.753 (2.37)
364	Electric lamps, light fixtures, and lighting equipment		.264 (1.34)	.348 (1.32)	.348 (1.32)
374	Locomotives and railroad equipment	-.451 (1.89)	-.387 (1.66)	-.527 (2.24)	-.414 (1.80)
381	Engineering and scientific instruments	-1.59 (1.62)	-1.53 (1.59)	-1.53 (1.45)	-1.41 (1.37)
384	Surgical and medical instruments	-.905 (1.35)	-.912 (1.40)	-1.04 (1.35)	-.983 (1.32)
386	Photographic and photocopying equipment	.825 (3.83)	.714 (3.37)	1.12 (4.75)	.865 (3.71)
Others		.071 (5.10)	.113 (1.74)	-.106 (4.89)	.097 (0.74)
C_4			-1.17 (3.97)		-1.45 (2.70)
C_4^2			1.52 (4.73)		2.07 (3.81)
R^2		.286	.322	.291	.330

76   **Profits in the long run**

Columns 3 and 4 report results following the same steps used to obtain columns 1 and 2, but without weighting the right-hand-side variables by S/K. The results are quite similar, with the second set exhibiting slightly higher $\bar{R}^2$s, as was true consistently for the earlier steps in obtaining the final list of industries. More or less the same industries appear with coefficients implying similar differences from other industries. The same industries appear as outliers. Introducing concentration results in an analogous overall U-shaped relationship between concentration and profitability. In addition to a sizable drop in the coefficient and significance of the intercept on industry 351 following the introduction of concentration, the tobacco industry 214 exhibits a decline in significance that is even more pronounced than when S/K is used to weight the variables on the right-hand side.

3.   Summary of industry model results

The attempt to estimate an industry model in which firm profits are a function solely of the two industry characteristics, demand elasticity and concentration, has been a mixed success. Imposing an externally estimated elasticity of demand provided generally somewhat weaker statistical fit than assuming all demand elasticities equal one. The multinomial used to approximate the concentration–profit relationship suffered from multicollinearity to the extent that the interpretation of this relationship was sensitive to the number of terms in the polynomial included in the equation. The most reliable estimates appeared to be for the quadratic and cubic specifications. Both indicated a declining portion of the profit–concentration curve over some range of concentration values. Both implied a positive relationship over the higher concentration values.

Trying to estimate the demand elasticities and the parameters in a collusion function from our data on firm sales by industry proved infeasible. But estimating separate intercepts for each industry participation vector did reveal significant differences in profitability across industries. Knowing the fraction of each firm's sales in all three-digit industries enabled us to explain 29 percent of the variation in profitability across firms. Unfortunately, it did not appear possible to determine whether it was demand elasticity, entry and exit conditions, concentration, or the degree of cooperation that accounted for these differences in projected profitability. Some light will be shed on this issue by the results on the firm-approach model.

E.   Empirical estimates: firm approach

Consider again equation (4.23), which we derived to explain a firm's profitability in the presence of product differentiation:

$$\frac{\Pi_i}{S_i} = \frac{1}{\eta}\left(\frac{m_i}{\sigma} - \theta m_i + \theta\right).$$

Let us approximate the degree of cooperation by the quadratic function

$$\theta = a + bC_4 + cC_4^2. \tag{4.31}$$

We now need an approximation for σ, the degree of substitutability among products. One variable frequently associated with product differentiation is advertising. Advertising is both cause and effect of product differentiation. Advertising is profitable only in industries in which some potentially perceivable differences in products exist, and advertising can enhance individual perceptions of the differences in products. We treat the level of advertising as a percentage of industry sales as one index of the extent of product differentiation across industries.

Although advertising is a reasonable index of differentiation for consumer products, it serves less well for producer's goods. Intuitively, one would like some measure of technical complexity or sophistication. There is more scope to differentiate computers than shovels. Although inventive activity is not a perfect index of this dimension of product differentiation, we employ it along with advertising.

The degree of substitutability among products ranges from 0 to 1 and is assumed to vary inversely with product differentiation. If we assume that the effects of advertising and inventive activity are additive, a particularly simple functional form that captures this dimensionality property of σ is

$$\sigma = \frac{d}{d + eA + fRD}. \tag{4.32}$$

When both advertising (A) and inventive activity (RD) are zero, $\sigma = 1$, and the sellers' products within the industry are presumed to be perfect substitutes. As advertising and inventive activity increase, σ falls toward 0.

Substituting from (4.31) and (4.32) into (4.23), one obtains

$$\frac{\Pi_i}{S_i} = \frac{1}{\eta}\left(a + (1-a)\, m_i + b\,(1-m_i)C_4\right. \\ \left. + c(1-m_i)C_4^2 + \frac{e}{d}Am_i + \frac{f}{d}RDm_i\right). \tag{4.33}$$

78   **Profits in the long run**

Equation (4.33) was estimated using projected market shares for each firm calculated in the same way that projected concentration ratios were calculated earlier in this chapter. A weighted-average ratio of industry advertising to sales was calculated for each company using its sales in each industry as weights and Internal Revenue Service three-digit industry advertising figures for 1963 (a point in time chosen because it lies roughly in the middle of the time period and in neither a boom nor a recession year). Two indexes of inventive activity were employed. National Science Foundation (NSF) figures for patents to sales by industry are available for as far back as 1967 and are at the three-digit level for technologically progressive industries. NSF research and development (R&D) expenditures are available for as far back as the mid-fifties (see NSF 1977), but are more aggregated.[5] We tried employing both the 1963 expenditure figures and 1967 patent numbers. Weighted averages for each firm were calculated as with advertising.

Table 4.4 presents results for which all η are assumed to equal one, and the dependent variable, $\hat{a}$, is measured as a return on assets. The model was also estimated weighting all right-hand-side variables by the reciprocal of the Intriligator-elasticities, and by the sales-assets ratio for each firm. Both sets of estimates provided a worse fit, which was quite pronounced when the $1/\eta$s were used, and neither set of results is reported here.

The first equation assumes a linear relationship between concentration and the collusion parameter, θ, and includes only advertising as an index of product differentiation. All coefficients are statistically significant except for the intercept, but the sign on the concentration variable implies that cooperation *declines* with increasing concentration. Both the market share variable and the market share–advertising interaction term have the predicted positive signs.

Equation (2) in Table 4.4 introduces the quadratic term in concentration. It takes on a negative sign and the linear term becomes positive but insignificant. Multicollinearity between the two concentration variables is apparent. The two coefficients on the concentration variable imply rising cooperation to a C_4 of .24 and then falling cooperation. Both market share and the market share–advertising term remain highly significant and of the predicted sign.

Equation (3) drops the linear concentration term, leaving in $(1 - m_i)C_4^2$. The explanatory power of equation (3) is identical to that of (2), and the implication is clearly that cooperation falls, and at an increasing rate, as concentration increases.

Table 4.4. *Firm-model results with* $\eta = 1$ *for all firms, right-hand-side variables not weighted by S/K,* α_i *as dependent variable*

$(n = 551)$

Equation	Int	m_i	$(1-m_i)C_4$	$(1-m_i)C_4^2$	m_iA	m_iPat	m_iRD	$\overline{R}^2$
(1)	.052	.568	-.491		.612			.249
	.95	2.52	3.66		8.11			
(2)	-.180	.859	.632	-1.291	.652			.252
	1.28	3.09	.99	1.79	8.30			
(3)	-.045	.707		-.596	.632			.252
	1.47	3.06		3.97	8.34			
(4)	.062	-.242	-.490		.719	1.48		.275
	1.15	.86	3.73		9.26	4.60		
(5)	-.081	-.032	.199	-.792	.739	1.43		.276
	.58	.09	.31	1.10	9.26	4.36		
(6)	-.039	-.088		-.573	.734	1.44		.277
	1.29	.31		3.88	9.42	4.67		
(7)	-.040			-.583	.718	1.38		.278
	1.38			4.04	12.20	5.44		
(8)	.048	.618	-.435		.624		-.051	.248
	.87	2.23	3.61		7.91		.54	

Equations (4)–(7) add the market share–patent intensity variable. It takes on the predicted positive coefficient and is significant.

The signs and significance of all other variables in the equation remain about as before, except for the market share variable, which now is insignificant. The m_iPat interaction is the fourth, in equation (5) the fifth, variable in the equation containing market share. Something had to give and it was the market share term by itself. The hypothesis that the intercept term and m_i coefficient sum to 1, in contrast to equations (1)–(3), is now rejected.[6] Whether this is because the model is wrong or because multicollinearity exists cannot be determined.[7] Equation (7), dropping market share, including m_iPat and including only the C_4^2 term, provides the best fit to the data of the eight equations in Table 4.4. Equation (8) adds the market share–industry R&D expenditure term in place of m_iPat. It does not have a statistically significant impact on projected profits. Since R&D expenditures and patent activity are highly correlated at the firm level (see Mueller 1966; Comanor and Scherer 1969) and both proxy the

80   **Profits in the long run**

same phenomenon, inventive activity, we attribute the weak performance of the R&D industry expenditure index to the more aggregated
nature of these data in contrast to the NSF patent intensity data.

Returning to equation (4.23) and ignoring demand elasticity, we
see that the determinants of profitability in the firm model consist of
two components: the one, m_i/σ, is related to the extent of product
differentiation, the other, $(1-m_i)\theta$, to the degree of cooperation.
Product differentiation leads to the introduction of market share and
market share–advertising and market share–inventive activity interaction terms. Collusion introduces the intercept and the concentration–$(1-m_i)$ interaction term. The collusion term implies that the
coefficient on market share equals one minus the intercept. Since the
intercepts in equations (1–3) are all insignificantly different from zero,
the large, positive, and significant coefficient on market share, entered
as a separate variable in these equations, must be attributed to the
product differentiation part of the story. When market share loses its
significance, it does so because another index of product differentiation is included, market share–patent intensity.

The collusion-related terms make a significant contribution to explaining profitability, but the impact of concentration on firm rivalry
is of the opposite sign from that assumed in most structure-performance discussions. That concentration might have a negative impact
on profitability was already suggested by the results for the industry
model discussed earlier in this chapter. The firm model suggests
strongly that, given a firm's market share, increasing industry concentration increases rivalry lowering profits.

Market share has a positive, marginal impact on profitability in every
term in Table 4.4 having a t-value greater than 1.0. Equation (7), the
equation providing the best fit to the data, implies that, when the
interaction variables are evaluated at their means, an increase in market share of 10 percentage points results in an increase in the long-
run projected return on capital of 20 percent of the sample mean.
(Recall that the dependent variable is the projected relative difference
between a company's returns on total assets and the sample mean.)

F.   Conclusions

The basic assumption of the industry approach model is that all firms
within an industry face identical demand and cost conditions. In the
long run, all firms should choose to be sufficiently large so that average
costs are minimized. If all firms are of the same size, $1/N = H$, the

Herfindahl index, and the basic industry approach equation (4.8) becomes

$$\frac{\Pi_i}{S_i} = \frac{1}{\eta}(H - \theta H + \theta). \tag{4.34}$$

This equation may be contrasted with its firm-approach analogue (4.19),

$$\frac{\Pi_i}{S_i} = \frac{1}{\eta}\left(\frac{m_i}{\sigma} - \theta m_i + \theta\right).$$

The firm approach replaces the industry characteristic H or $1/N$ with the firm's market share and adds industry product differentiation to the equation. If all firms are of the same size and the industry has a homogeneous product, $m_i = H$ and $\sigma = 1$. The firm approach then collapses into the industry approach. One way to judge the relative merits of the firm approach over the industry approach is to see whether firm market shares in conjunction with industry product differentiation add a significant amount of explanatory power to the basic industry-approach model. By this criterion, the firm-approach model wins hands down, as comparisons of Table 4.4 with Tables 4.1 and 4.2 quickly reveal. An F-test of whether relaxing the restriction that $\sigma = 1$ and $m_i = H$ results in a significant reduction in the sum of the unexplained residuals yields an F-statistic of 68.9, safely above the .05 level of critical value.

As an alternative way of allowing for industry-specific determinants of firm-level profits, we conducted an analysis of variance. Some 30 separate three-digit industry definitions proved to be important in explaining long-run differences in company profitability. Roughly 30 percent of the variance in long-run projected returns was explained by the industry participation vectors. Still on the basis of Occam's razor, the firm-approach model is probably to be preferred. The firm model explains some 28 percent of the profitability differences across firms with but four variables (three terms) in the equation.

Nevertheless, three of the four variables in the firm model are industry characteristics, and thus one might reasonably argue that the firm model, as estimated, is in large part an industry model. It must be stressed, however, that the advertising and patent intensity variables play a different role in the firm-approach model than is usually claimed for them in studies in which industry profits are the dependent variable. Typically, advertising in an industry profits equation is taken to be a barrier to entry (Comanor and Wilson 1967, 1974;

82   **Profits in the long run**

Porter 1974). By analogy, a similar role could be attributed to patent intensity (e.g., as in Grabowski and Mueller 1978). Something is inherently wrong with this interpretation, however. A variable's coefficient in a regression equation is usually taken to be an estimate of a partial derivative; that is, in the equation $Y = a + bX$, b is an estimate of the change in Y to be expected from a unit change in X. If X is industry advertising intensity, and Y industry profits, b measures the change in industry profits resulting from an increase in industry advertising. But since industry profits are defined net of advertising, a positive, linear relationship between advertising intensity and profitability under the barriers-to-entry hypothesis must imply that companies in all industries are underinvesting in advertising. Low advertising intensity industries would increase their profitability by advertising more and thereby raising the height of entry barriers. Presumably, even advertising-intensive industries might find it profitable to further heighten entry barriers by increasing advertising.

A more plausible assumption to make about the level of industry advertising is that it is at the optimal level for maximizing profits for each industry. Thus, *any* change in a given industry's advertising from the present level would *lower* its profits. Of course, oligopolistic coordination problems may prevent the firms in an industry from achieving the joint profit maximum advertising level, but if anything, these coordination problems probably lead firms to undertake too much advertising rather than too little, as implied by the entry-barriers interpretation. (For evidence with respect to advertising, see Grabowski and Mueller 1971; and Netter 1982. With respect to R&D, see Grabowski and Baxter 1973; Grabowski and Mueller 1978.) The easiest assumption to defend is, perhaps, that each industry's advertising or inventive activity level is at its optimum, plus or minus some random error with mean zero.

The latter interpretation is compatible with our use of industry advertising and patent intensity in the firm-approach model. Industry advertising and patent intensity capture the degree of product differentiation in the industry. That the cereals industry spends more on advertising than does the vegetable oils industry tells us something about the potential for product differentiation in cereals and vegetable oils. But vegetable oil manufacturers cannot simply advertise more and increase the degree of product differentiation to that of the cereal industry.

In this context, it is important to recall that industry advertising and patent intensity appear in the firm-approach model as interaction variables with firm-market share. It is the combination of the potential for product differentiation, as measured by industry advertising and patent intensity, along with high market share, which indicates success at differentiating one's product, that explains above-normal long-run profits. Thus, the strong performance of these two interaction terms (m_iPat and m_iA) reinforces the interpretation that the firm-specific product characteristics and cost advantages of the firm-approach model explain long-run profitability differences.

Both the firm-approach model and the industry models should include the industry demand elasticity as a multiplicative factor. But in the absence of good external estimates of industry price elasticities of demand, it is impossible to estimate the full firm model as specified in equation (4.23). Since industry demand elasticities appear in both the industry and the firm models, proxying these elasticities by industry intercept dummies does not help us sort out whether the assumptions underlying the firm or the industry model are more appropriate. Moreover, given the important role that product differentiation plays in the firm model, it is impossible to determine whether a separate industry slope or intercept is significant because it is capturing a significant difference in demand elasticities across industries, or a significant degree of product differentiation within the industry. We must base any claim we make that differences in product quality or efficiency across firms within an industry play an important role in explaining profitability differences across firms on the strong performance of market share–advertising and market share–patent intensity in Table 4.4, and on the rather perverse performance of concentration in all of the equations estimated throughout the chapter.

The present study adds to a short but rapidly growing set of studies that has found a negative relationship between profitability and concentration (e.g., Shepherd 1972, 1975; Gale and Branch 1982; Kwoka and Ravenscraft 1982; Ravenscraft 1983). They reinforce the importance of these findings in that they are not drawn from cross-sectional analysis of annual data, but are based on cross-sectional analysis using long-run projections of both profit rates and the key market structure variables. The profit data also do not include the post–oil crisis period, so that the results are not dependent on some unusual consequences of the seventies on accounting profit data or on the long-run structure-performance relationship across industries. Rather, the projections are based on a span of time, 1950–72, that, in retrospect, certainly appears to capture capitalism at its best. Finally, it should be noted that the negative relationship between profitability and concentration is not due to some collinearity between market share and concentration that forces the coefficient on the latter to be negative when market

84   **Profits in the long run**

share is included in the equation. The results for the industry-approach model also imply a largely negative impact of increasing concentration on projected profitability. Adding market share to the equation tends only to strengthen this interpretation.

Concentration appears in both the industry- and firm-approach models as a determinant of the degree of cooperation. Its negative impact on profitability in both models implies that cooperation declines as concentration increases. The greater the concentration in an industry, the greater the rivalry. Given the positive impact of the advertising– and patent intensity–market share interaction terms, it is natural to interpret the result that concentration leads to rivalry as implying that *nonprice* rivalry is encouraged by rising concentration. But a modeling of this conjecture would require industry data and an industry approach to nonprice competition and is beyond the scope of the present study.

Notes

1 The origins of this approach can be traced back to Fellner (1949) and Bain (1952). See also Bishop (1960), Cyert and De Groot (1973), Kuenne (1974), and Shubik (1980).

2 The number of firms drops out, since we have not explicitly constrained the sum of the demand schedules.

3 Richard Levin also kindly supplied me with demand elasticity estimates he made using an entirely different technique from that of Intriligator and DeAngelo. Levin's estimates do not cover all industries. The simple correlation between Levin's estimates and the Intriligator-DeAngelo estimates over those industries were both available as –.04, further increasing one's uneasiness of the gain to be made from including external estimates of demand elasticity in structure-performance studies.

It must be stressed that the reservations expressed are in no way meant as criticisms of the capabilities of the scholars making the estimates. Alas, obtaining demand elasticity estimates sufficiently comparable across industries to be of use in studies of the present kind seems beyond the limits of available data and estimating techniques. I have chosen not to make my own estimates because I do not feel I could do better.

4 We also substituted Pagoulatos and Sorensen estimates for the Intriligator-DeAngelo figures where the former were available. This measure performed even worse than the other.

5 No figures at all are given for unprogressive industries SIC 21, 23–27, 29, and 31. We assumed zero patent-to-sales ratios for these. (Other unprogressive industries had patent-to-sales ratios of 0.04–0.05 in comparison with some progressive industry ratios of around 1.0.)

6 The equations were estimated without restraining the intercept and the coefficient on market share to sum to one. Separate *t*-tests could not reject the

hypothesis as implied by equation (4.33) that these two parameters sum to one for equations (1)–(3) using a 5 percent level, two-tail test. Equation (1) failed the test at the 10 percent level. However, equations (4)–(7) all failed the test at the 5 percent level.

7 Ravenscraft (1983) found the coefficient on market share became insignificant when an interaction term between market share and advertising was included.

References

Bain, Joe S., *Price Theory*, New York: Henry Holt, 1952.

Bishop, Robert L., "Duopoly: Collusion or Warfare?" *American Economic Review*, December 1960, *50*, pp. 933–61.

Bresnahan, Timothy F., "Duopoly Models with Consistent Conjectures," *American Economic Review*, December 1981a, *71*, pp. 934–45.

———, "Departures from Marginal-Cost Pricing in the American Automobile Industry," *Journal of Econometrics*, 1981b, *17*, pp. 201–27.

Brozen, Yale, "The Antitrust Task Force Deconcentration Recommendation," *Journal of Law and Economics*, October 1970, *13*, pp. 279–92.

———, "Bain's Concentration and Rates of Return Revisited," *Journal of Law and Economics*, October 1971a, *14*, pp. 351–69.

———, "The Persistence of 'High Rates of Return' in High-Stable Concentration Industries," *Journal of Law and Economics*, October 1971b, *14*, pp. 501–12.

Cable, John, "Market Structure, Advertising Policy and Intermarket Differences in Advertising Intensity," in K. Cowling, ed., *Market Structure and Corporate Behavior*, London: Gray Mills, 1972, pp. 111–24.

Comanor, William S., and Scherer, F. M., "Patent Statistics as a Measure of Technical Change," *Journal of Political Economy*, May-June 1969, *77*, pp. 392–98.

Comanor, W. S., and Wilson, T. A., "Advertising, Market Structure and Performance," *Review of Economics and Statistics*, November 1967, *49*, pp. 423–40.

———, *Advertising and Market Power*, Cambridge: Harvard University Press, 1974.

Connolly, Robert A., and Schwartz, Steven, "The Intertemporal Behavior of Economic Profits," 1984, photocopy.

Cowling, K., and Waterson, M., "Price–Cost Margins and Market Structure," *Economica*, August 1976, *43*, pp. 267–74.

Cubbin, John, "Apparent Collusion and Conjectural Variations in Differentiated Oligopoly," *International Journal of Industrial Organization*, June 1983, *1*, pp. 155–63.

Cyert, Richard M., and DeGroot, Morris M., "An Analysis of Cooperation and Learning in a Duopoly Context," *American Economic Review*, March 1973, *63*, pp. 24–37.

Dansby, R. E., and Willig, R. D., "Industry Performance Gradient Indexes," *American Economic Review*, June 1979, *69*, pp. 249–60.

Demsetz, H., "Two Systems of Belief about Monopoly," in Harvey J. Goldschmid, H. M. Mann, and J. F. Weston, eds., *Industrial Concentration: The New Learning*, Boston: Little, Brown, 1974, pp. 164–84.

———, "Industry Structure, Market Rivalry, and Public Policy," *Journal of Law and Economics*, April 1973, *16*, pp. 1–9.

Fellner, William, *Competition Among the Few*, New York: Alfred A. Knopf, 1949.

Gale, Bradley J., and Branch, Ben S., "Concentration versus Market Share: Which Determines Performance and Why Does it Matter?" *Antitrust Bulletin*, Spring 1982, *27*, pp. 83–106.

Geroski, P. A., "Specification and Testing the Profits-Concentration Relationship: Some Experiments for the UK," *Economica*, August 1981, *48*, pp. 279–88.

———, "The Empirical Analysis of Conjectural Variations in Oligopoly," 1982b, photocopy.

Gollop, Frank M., and Roberts, Mark J., "Firm Interdependence in Oligopolistic Markets," *Journal of Econometrics*, August 1979, *10*, pp. 313–31.

Grabowski, Henry G., and Baxter, N. D., "Rivalry in Industrial Research and Development: An Empirical Study," *Journal of Industrial Economics*, July 1973, *21*, pp. 209–35.

Grabowski, Henry G., and Mueller, Dennis C., "Imitative Advertising in the Cigarette Industry," *Antitrust Bulletin*, Summer 1971, *16*, pp. 257–92.

———, "Industrial Research and Development, Intangible Capital Stock, and Firm Profit Rates," *Bell Journal of Economics*, Autumn 1978, *9*, pp. 328–43.

Greer, Douglas, "Advertising and Market Concentration," *Southern Economic Journal*, July 1971, *38*, pp. 19–32.

Hart, P. E., and Prais, S. J., "The Analysis of Business Concentration," *Journal of the Royal Statistical Society*, 1956, *119*, pp. 150–81.

Houthakker, H. S., and Taylor, L. D., *Consumer Demand in the United States*, 2d ed., Cambridge: Harvard University Press, 1970.

Iriji, Yuji, and Simon, Herbert A., *Skew Distributions and the Sizes of Business Firms*, Amsterdam: North-Holland, 1977.

Johnston, J., *Econometric Methods*, 2d ed., New York: McGraw-Hill, 1972.

Kamien, Morton I., "Conjectural Variations," *Canadian Journal of Economics*, May 1983, *16*, pp. 191–211.

Kuenne, Robert E., "Towards an Operational General Equilibrium Theory with Oligopoly: Some Experimental Results and Conjectures," *Kyklos*, 1974, *27*, pp. 792–820.

Kuh, Edwin, *Capital Stock Growth: A Micro-Economic Approach*, Amsterdam: North Holland, 1963.

Kwoka, John E., Jr., and Ravenscraft, David J., "Collusion, Rivalry, Scale Economics and Line of Business Profitability," Washington, D.C.: Federal Trade Commission, 1982, photocopy.

Laitner, J., "'Rational' Duopoly Equilibria," *Quarterly Journal of Economics*, December 1980, *95*, pp. 641–62.

Lester, Richard A., "Shortcomings of Marginal Analysis for Wage-Employment Problems," *American Economic Review*, March 1946, *36*, pp. 63–82.

Long, William F., "Market Share, Concentration, and Profits: Intra-Industry and Inter-Industry Evidence," Washington, D.C.: Federal Trade Commission, 1982, photocopy.

MacAvoy, Paul W., McKie, James W., and Preston, Lee E., "High and Stable Concentration Levels, Profitability and Public Policy: A Response," *Journal of Law and Economics*, October 1971, *14*, pp. 493–9.

Machlup, Fritz, "Marginal Analysis and Empirical Research," *American Economic Review*, September 1946, *36*, pp. 519–54.

Marvel, Howard P., "Collusion and the Pattern of Rates of Return," *Southern Economic Journal*, October 1980, *47*, pp. 375–87.

McEnally, Richard W., "Competition and Dispersion in Rates of Return: A Note," *Journal of Industrial Economics*, September 1976, *25*, pp. 69–75.

McMillan, John, "Collusion, Competition and Conjectures," June 1982, photocopy.

Mueller, Dennis C., "Patents, Research and Development, and the Measurement of Inventive Activity," *Journal of Industrial Economics*, November 1966, *15*, pp. 26–37.

———, "The Persistence of Profits above the Norm," *Economica*, November 1977a, *44*, pp. 369–80.

Netter, Jeffry, M., "Excessive Advertising: An Empirical Analysis," *Journal of Industrial Economics*, June 1982, *30*, pp. 361–73.

Pagoulatos, Emilio, and Sorenson, Robert, "A Simultaneous Equation Analysis of Advertising, Concentration, and Profitability," *Southern Economic Journal*, January 1981, *47*, pp. 728–41.

Peltzman, S., "The Gains and Losses from Industrial Concentration," *Journal of Law and Economics*, October 1977, *20*, pp. 229–63.

Perry, Martin K., "Oligopoly and Consistent Conjectural Variations," *Bell Journal of Economics*, Spring 1982, *13*, pp. 197–203.

Porter, Michael E., "Consumer Behavior, Retailer Power and Market Performance in Consumer Goods Industries," *Review of Economics and Statistics*, November 1974, *56*, pp. 419–36.

Qualls, P. David, "Stability and Persistence of Economic Profit Margins in Highly Concentrated Industries," *Southern Economic Journal*, April 1974, *40*, pp. 604–12.

Ravenscraft, David J., "Structure-Profit Relationships at the Line of Business and Industry Level," Review of Economics and Statistics, February 1983, *65*, pp. 22–31.

Roberts, Mark J., "Testing Oligopolistic Behavior," *International Journal of Industrial Organization*, December 1984, *2*, pp. 367–83.

Sant, Donald T., "A Polynomial Approximation for Switching Regressions with Applications to Market Structure-Performance Studies," Federal Trade Commission Staff Working Paper, Washington, D.C.: February 1978.

Saxonhouse, Gary R., "Estimated Parameters as Dependent Variables," *American Economic Review*, March 1976, *66*, pp. 178–83.

Scherer, F. M., *Industrial Market Structure and Economic Performance*, 2d ed., Chicago: Rand McNally, 1980.

Scherer, F. M., Beckenstein, A., Kaufer, E., and Murphy, R. D., *The Economics of Multiplant Operation*, Cambridge: Harvard University Press, 1975.

Shepherd, William G., "The Elements of Market Structure," *Review of Economics and Statistics*, February 1972, *54*, pp. 25–37.

————, *The Treatment of Market Power*, New York: Columbia University Press, 1975.

Shubik, Martin, *Market Structure and Behavior*, Cambridge, Mass.: Harvard University Press, 1980.

Simon, Herbert A., and Bonini, Charles P., "The Size Distribution of Business Firms," *American Economic Review*, September 1958, *48*, pp. 607–17.

Soloman, Ezra, "Alternative Rate of Return Concepts and Their Implications for Utility Regulation," *Bell Journal of Economics*, Spring 1970, *1*, pp. 65–81.

Stauffer, Thomas R., "The Measurement of Corporate Rates of Return: A Generalized Formulation," *Bell Journal of Economics*, Autumn 1971, *2*, pp. 434–69.

Stigler, George J., *Capital and Rates of Return in Manufacturing*, Princeton: Princeton University Press, 1963.

Sweezy, Paul M., "Demand under Conditions of Oligopoly," *Journal of Political Economy*, 1939, *47*, pp. 568–73.

Ulph, David, "Rational Conjectures in the Theory of Oligopoly," *International Journal of Industrial Organization*, 1983, *1*, pp. 131–54.

Weiss, Leonard W., "The Concentration-Profits Relationship and Antitrust," in H. J. Goldschmid, H. M. Mann, and J. F. Weston, eds., *Industrial Concentration: The New Learning*, Boston: Little, Brown, 1974.

————, "Corrected Concentration Ratios in Manufacturing–1972," Washington, D.C.: Federal Trade Commission, 1981, photocopy.

Wenders, John T., "Profits and Antitrust Policy: The Question of Disequilibrium," *Antitrust Bulletin*, Summer 1971a, *16*, pp. 249–56.

————, "Deconcentration Reconsidered," *Journal of Law and Economics*, October 1971b, *14*, pp. 485–8.

White, Laurence J., "Searching for the Critical Industrial Concentration Ratio," in Stephen Goldfield and Richard E. Quandt, eds., *Studies in Non-Linear Estimation*, Cambridge: Ballinger, 1976, pp. 61–75.

Winn, D. N., and Leabo, D. A., "Rates of Return, Concentration and Growth–Question of Disequilibrium," *Journal of Law and Economics*, April 1974, *17*, pp. 97–115.

Appendix 1   Companies studied

This appendix lists the companies that were part of our study. The first three subsections list the 1,000 largest sample for 1950, divided into three groups, the 200 largest, 201–500 largest, and 501–1,000 largest. Column 2 of these three subsections indicates each firm's status as of 1972, where SR ≡ survived, AQ ≡ acquired through merger, LQ ≡ liquidated, PI ≡ privately held (i.e., the firm survived, but because of private control of the firm not enough information was available to include it in the sample), ID ≡ insufficient data to include in sample, NI ≡ no information as to what happened to the firm. Column 3 reports the same information ·for firms that is available in the 1980 *Moody's Industrial Manual*. If the firm was in our sample of 600 companies used to obtain original profit estimates, its rank in 1950–52 is presented in column 4. Column 5 lists either the company's current name, if the company survived, or, in parentheses, the name of the firm that acquired it and the year of acquisition.

Subsection D lists the names and 1950–52 profit ranks of companies in the 1972 1,000 largest sample that were not in the 1950 1,000 largest included in the study. Subsection E lists firms and 1950–52 profit ranks that were included in our study and that were in neither the 1950 nor the 1972 1,000 largest groups.

234

Appendixes　　　　　　　　　　　　　　　　235

A. Largest 200 Companies	2	3	4	5
Admiral Corp.	SR	AQ	18	
Allegheny Ludlum Steel Corp.	SR	SR	418	ALLEGHENY LUDLUM IND.
Allied Chemical & Dye Corp.	SR	SR	225	ALLIED CHEMICAL
Allis-Chalmers Manufacturing Co.	SR	SR	395	
Aluminum Company of America	SR	SR	393	
American Can Co.	SR	SR	314	
American Cyanamid Co.	SR	SR	255	
American Home Products Corp.	SR	SR	138	
American Locomotive Co.	AQ			(RKO 1969)
American Radiator & Standard Sanitary Corp.	SR	SR	142	AMERICAN STANDARD
American Smelting & Refining Co.	SR	SR	159	
American Sugar Refining Co., The	SR	SR	496	AMSTAR
American Tobacco Co., The	SR	SR	468	AMERICAN BRANDS
American Viscose Corp.	AQ			(FMC 1963)
American Woolen Co.	AQ			(TEXTRON 1955)
Anaconda Copper Mining Co.	SR	AQ	471	
Anheuser Busch, Inc.	SR	SR	ID	
Archer-Daniels-Midland Co.	SR	SR	285	
Armco Steel Corp.	SR	SR	257	
Armour & Co.	SR	SR	572	
Armstrong Cork Co.	SR	SR	388	
Atlantic Refining Co., The (Pennsylvania)	SR	SR	292	
Avco Mfg. Corp.	SR	SR	427	
Babcock & Wilcox Co.	SR	AQ	348	
Baker & Co., Inc.	SR	SR	ID	
Baldwin Locomotive Works, The	AQ			
Beatrice Foods Co. (Delaware)	SR	SR	324	
Bemis Brothers Bag Co.	SR	SR	567	
Bendix Aviation Corp.	SR	SR	392	BENDIX CORP.
Bethlehem Steel Corp.	SR	SR	386	
Boeing Airplane Co.	SR	SR	424	
Borden Co., The	SR	SR	419	
Borg-Warner Corp.	SR	SR	169	
Briggs Manufacturing Co.	AQ			PANACON (CELOTEX 1972)
Budd Co., The	SR	SR	219	
Burlington Mills Corp.	SR	SR	441	BURLINGTON INDUSTRIES
California Packing Corp.	SR	AQ	467	DEL MONTE
Campbell Soup Co.	SR	SR	247	
Cannon Mills Co.	SR	SR	399	
Carnation Co.	SR	SR	277	
Case (J.I.) Co.	AQ			(TENNECO 1970)
Caterpillar Tractor Co.	SR	SR	246	
Celanese Corporation of America	SR	SR	366	
Champion Paper & Fibre Co.	AQ			(US PLYWOOD 1967)
Chrysler Corp.	SR	SR	198	
Cities Service Co.	SR	SR	442	

236 Profits in the long run

A. <u>Largest 200 Companies</u>	2	3	4	5
Coca-Cola Co., The	SR	SR	103	
Colgate-Palmolive-Peet Co.	SR	SR	359	
Colorado Fuel & Iron Corp.	SR	AQ	498	CF & I
Cone Mills Corp.	SR	SR	256	
Consolidated-Vultee Aircraft Corp.	SR	SR	598	GENERAL DYNAMICS
Container Corporation of America	SR	AQ	311	MARCOR
Continental Baking Co.	AQ			(ITT)
Continental Can Co., Inc.	SR	SR	489	
Continental Oil Co.	SR	SR	71	
Corn Products Refining Co.	SR	SR	183	
Corning Glass Works	SR	SR	136	
Crown Zellerbach Corp.	SR	SR	209	
Crucible Steel Company of America	AQ			(COLT INDUSTRIES)
Cudahy Packing Co., The	AQ			(GENERAL HOST 1971)
Curtis Publishing Co.	SR	SR	499	
Curtiss-Wright Corp.	SR	SR	524	
Dana Corp.	SR	SR	122	
Deere & Co.	SR	SR	173	
Douglas Aircraft Co., Inc.	SR	SR	155	
Dow Chemical Co.	SR	SR	412	
Dupont (E.I.) deNemours & Co.	SR	SR	69	DUPONT
Eastman Kodak Co.	SR	SR	197	
Eaton Manufacturing Co.	SR	SR	80	
Electric Auto-Lite Co.	AQ			(ELTRA CORP 1963)
Endicott Johnson Corp.	AQ			(McDONOUGH 1971)
Essex Wire Corp.	SR		ID	ESSEX INTERNATIONAL
Firestone Tire & Rubber Co.	SR	SR	274	
Ford Motor Co.	SR	SR	161	
General Electric Co.	SR	SR	152	
General Foods Corp.	SR	SR	337	
General Mills, Inc.	SR	SR	416	
General Motors Corp.	SR	SR	47	
General Tire & Rubber Co., The	SR	SR	270	
Glidden Co.	AQ			(SCM 1967)
Goodrich (B.F.) Co., The	SR	SR	188	
Goodyear Tire & Rubber Co.	SR	SR	443	
Gulf Oil Corp.	SR	SR	261	
Hearst Consolidated Publications, The	SR		ID	
Hercules Powder Company	SR	SR	151	
Hershey Chocolate Corp.	SR	SR	35	
Hormel (Geo. A.) & Co.	SR	SR	438	
Hudson Motor Car Co.	AQ			(AMERICAN MOTORS 1954)
Hygrade Food Products Corp.	SR	SR	469	
Inland Steel Co.	SR	SR	290	
International Business Machines Corp.	SR	SR	272	
International Harvester Co.	SR	SR	434	

Appendixes   237

A. Largest 200 Companies	2	3	4	5
International Paper Co.	SR	SR	109	
International Shoe Co.	SR	SR	371	INTERCO
Johns-Manville Corp.	SR	SR	48	
Johnson & Johnson	SR	SR	298	
Jones & Laughlin Steel Corp.	SR	SR	495	
Kaiser Aluminum & Chemical Corp.	SR	SR	378	
Kaiser-Frazer Corp.	SR	LQ	140	KAISER INDUSTRIES
Kaiser Steel Corp.	SR	SR	425	
Kellogg (Spencer) & Sons, Inc.	LQ			1961
Kennecott Copper Corp.	SR	SR	54	
Kimberly-Clark Corp.	SR	SR	396	
Kingan & Co., Inc.	AQ			(HYGRADE FOOD 1952)
Koppers Company, Inc.	SR	SR	413	
Lever Brothers Co.	SR	SR	534	UNILEVER
Libbey-Owens-Ford Glass Co.	SR	SR	37	
Liggett & Myers Tobacco Co.	SR	SR	481	LIGGETT GROUP
Lockheed Aircraft Corp.	SR	SR	518	LOCKHEED CORP.
Lorillard (P.) Co.	AQ			(LOEW'S)
Mayer (Oscar) & Co., Inc.	SR	SR	303	
Mead Corp., The	SR	SR	374	
Minnesota Mining & Mfg. Co.	SR	SR	84	
Monsanto Chemical Co.	SR	SR	304	
Morrell (John) & Co.	AQ			(AMK)
Morris (Philip) & Co. Ltd., Inc.	SR	SR	461	
Motorola, Inc.	SR	SR	38	
Murray Corporation of America, The	SR	SR	144	WALLACE-MURRAY
Nash-Kelvinator Corp.	SR	SR	268	AMERICAN MOTORS
National Biscuit Co.	SR	SR	220	NABISCO
National Dairy Products Corp.	SR	SR	382	KRAFT
National Distillers Products Corp.	SR	SR	458	
National Lead Co. (New Jersey)	SR	SR	157	NL INDUSTRIES
National Steel Corporation	SR	SR	244	
National Sugar Refining Co., The	SR	SR	522	
North American Aviation, Inc.	SR	SR	52	ROCKWELL INTERNATIONAL
Olin Industries, Inc.	SR	SR	592	OLIN CORP.
Owens-Illinois Glass Co.	SR	SR	271	
Paraffine Companies, Inc., (Pabco Products Inc.)	SR	AQ	242	FIBREBOARD
Pabst Brewing Co.	SR	SR	202	
Pacific Mills	AQ			(BURLINGTON IND. 1953)
Packard Motor Car Co.	AQ			(STUDEBAKER)
Pet Milk Co.	SR	AQ	494	
Phelps Dodge Corp.	SR	SR	92	
Philco Corp.	AQ			(FORD MOTOR 1961)
Phillips Petroleum Co.	SR	SR	264	
Pillsbury Mills, Inc.	SR	SR	529	

238   Profits in the long run

A. Largest 200 Companies	2	3	4	5
Pittsburgh Plate Glass Co.	SR	SR	177	PPG
Pittsburgh Steel Co.	AQ			(WHEELING 1968)
Procter & Gamble Co., The	SR	SR	94	
Pullman, Inc.	SR	SR	521	
Pure Oil Co., The (Ohio)	AQ			(UNION OIL 1965)
Quaker Oats Co., The	SR	SR	288	
Radio Corporation of America	SR	SR	226	RCA
Ralston Purina Co.	SR	SR	260	
Rath Packing Co., The	SR	SR	528	
Remington Rand, Inc.	AQ			(SPERRY 1955)
Republic Steel Corp.	SR	SR	343	
Revere Copper & Brass, Inc.	SR	SR	181	
Reynolds Metals Co.	SR	SR	449	
Reynolds (R.J.) Tobacco Co.	SR	SR	431	
Richfield Oil Corp.	AQ			(ATLANTIC 1966)
St. Regis Paper Co.	SR	SR	334	
Schenley Industries, Inc.	AQ			(RAPID AMERICAN 1972)
Schlitz (Jos.) Brewing Co.	SR	SR	ID	
Scott Paper Co.	SR	SR	120	
Scovill Manufacturing Co.	SR	SR	497	
Seagram (Joseph E.) & Sons, Inc.	SR	SR	179	DISTILLERS CORP.
Sharon Steel Corp.	SR	SR	222	
Shell Oil Corp.	SR	SR	67	
Sherwin-Williams Co.	SR	SR	344	
Simmons Co.	SR	AQ	326	
Sinclair Oil Corp.	AQ			(ATLANTIC-RICHFIELD 1969)
Smith (A.O.) Corp.	SR	SR	387	
Socony-Vaccum Oil Co., Inc.	SR	SR	273	MOBIL OIL
Spencer Kellug & Sons	AQ			(TEXTRON 1960)
Sperry Corp., The	SR	SR	10	SPERRY RAND
Staley (A.E.) Manufacturing Co.	SR	SR	515	
Standard Brands, Inc.	SR	SR	422	
Standard Oil Co. of California	SR	SR	70	
Standard Oil Co. of Indiana	SR	SR	381	
Standard Oil Company (N.J.)	SR	SR	145	EXXON
Standard Oil Co., The (Ohio)	SR	SR	376	
Stevens (J.P.) & Co., Inc.	SR	SR	389	
Studebaker Corp., The	SR		ID	STUDEBAKER-WORTHINGTON
Sun Oil Co. (New Jersey)	SR	SR	146	SUN CO.
Swift & Co. (Illinois)	SR	SR	573	ESMARK
Sylvania Electric Products, Inc.	AQ			(GTE 1959)
Texas Co., The	SR	SR	147	TEXACO
Tide Water Associated Oil Co.	SR	SR	546	GETTY OIL
Time, Inc.	SR	SR	316	
Timken-Detroit Axle Co., The	AQ			(NORTH AMER. ROCK.)

Appendixes   239

A. Largest 200 Companies   2   3   4   5

	2	3	4	5
Timken Roller Bearing Co.	SR	SR	129	TIMKIN
Union Bag & Paper Corp.	SR	SR	58	UNION CAMP CORP.
Union Carbide & Carbon Corp.	SR	SR	108	
Union Oil Co. of California	SR	SR	435	
United Aircraft Corp.	SR	SR	429	
United States Gypsum Co. (Illinois)	SR	SR	134	
United States Rubber Co.	SR	SR	426	UNIROYAL
United States Steel Corp.	SR	SR	486	
Wesson Oil & Snowdrift Co., Inc.	AQ			(HUNT FOOD 1959)
West Point Manufacturing Co.	SR	SR	63	WEST POINT PEPPERELL
West Virginia Pulp & Paper Co.	SR	SR	266	WESTVACO
Western Electric Co., Inc.	SR	SR	526	
Westinghouse Electric Corp.	SR	SR	391	
Weyerhaeuser Timber Co.	SR	SR	130	
Wheeling Steel Corp.	SR	SR	400	WHEELING-PITTSBURGH STEEL
Willys-Overland Motors, Inc.	AQ			(KAISER-FRASER 1952)
Wilson & Co., Inc.	AQ			(LTV)
Youngstown Sheet & Tube Co., The	SR	SR	394	
Zenith Radio Corp.	SR	SR	107	

B. Companies Ranked 201 to 500   2   3   4   5

	2	3	4	5
Abbott Laboratories	SR	SR	115	
Brandon Corp. (Abney Mills)	SR		PI	
Acme Steel Co.	AQ			(INTERLAKE 1964)
Air Reduction Co., Inc.	SR	AQ	437	AIRCO
Allied Mills, Inc.	SR	AQ	322	
American Agricultural Che. Co.,The (Del)	AQ			(CONTINENTAL OIL 1963)
American Brake Shoe Co.	AQ			(ILLINOIS CENTRAL)
American Car & Foundry Co.	SR	SR	531	ACF
American Chain & Cable Co. Inc.	SR	AQ	199	
American Enka Corp.	SR	SR	186	AKZONA
American Metal Co.,Ltd., The	SR	SR	398	AMAX
American Optical Co.	AQ			(WARNER LAMBERT 1967)
American Steel Foundries (New Jersey)	SR	SR	358	AMSTED
American Thread Co., Inc.	SR	SR	564	
American Zinc, Lead & Smelting Co.	SR	AQ	2	AZCON
Anchor Hocking Glass Corp.	SR	SR	217	
Arden Farms Co.	SR	SR	576	ARDEN-MAYFAIR
Armstrong Rubber Co., The	SR	SR	333	
Noblitt-Sparks Industries, Inc. (Arvin Ind.)	SR	SR	156	
Ashland Oil & Refining Co.	SR	SR	231	
Aurora Gasoline Co.	AQ			(ALLIED PRODUCTS)
Automatic Electric Co.	SR		PI	
Avondale Mills	SR	SR	476	
Bachmann Uxbridge Worsted Corp [3)]	AQ			(AMERACE, ESNA 1957)

240   **Profits in the long run**

B. Companies Ranked 201 to 500	2	3	4	5
Ballantine (P.) & Sons	AQ			(FALSTAFF 1972)
Barium Steel Corp	SR	SR	345	PHOENIX STEEL
Bates Manufacturing Co.	SR	LQ	491	
Beaunit Mills, Inc.	AQ			(EL PASO NATURAL GAS)
Beech-Nut Packing Co.	AQ			(SQUIBB 1968)
Bell Aircraft Corp.	AQ			(WHEELABRATOR-FRYE)
Berkshire Fine Spinning Associates,Inc.	SR	SR	535	BERKSHIRE-HATHAWAY
Best Foods, Inc. The	AQ			(CORN PRODUCTS 1958)
Bibb Manufacturing Co.	SR	SR	559	
Bigelow-Sanford Carpet Co.,Inc.	AQ			(SPERRY-HUTCHINSON)
Blaw-Knox Co.	AQ			(WHITE CONSOLIDATED,1968)
Blue Bell, Inc.	SR	SR	293	
Bohn Aluminum & Brass Corp.	AQ			(GULF & WESTERN)
Bridgeport Brass Co.	AQ			(NATIONAL DISTILLERS 1961)
Bristol-Myers Co.	SR	SR	307	
Brown Co.	SR	SR	240	
Brown Shoe Company, Inc.	SR	SR	306	BROWN GROUP
Brown & Williamson Tobacco Corp.	SR	SR	100	BRITISH AMER.TOBACCO
Bucyrus-Erie Co.	SR	SR	289	
Bulova Watch Co., Inc. (New York)	SR	SR	421	
Bunker Hill & Sullivan Mining & Concentrat.Co.	AQ			(GULF RESEARCH & CHEMICAL)
Burroughs Adding Machine Co.	SR	SR	547	BURROUGHS CORP.
Callaway Mills Co.	LQ			
Calumet & Hecla Consolidated Copper Co.	AQ			(UNIVERSAL OIL)
Carborundum Co. (Delaware)	SR	SR	174	
Carey (Philip) Manufacturing Co.	AQ			(GLEN ALDEN)
Carrier Corporation	SR	AQ	453	
Celotex Corp., The	AQ			(WALTER, JIM)
Central Soya Co.,Inc.	SR	SR	126	
Certain-teed Products Corp.	SR	SR	117	
Champion Spark Plug Co.	SR	SR	30	
Chase Bag Co.	SR		NI	
City Products Corp.	AQ			(HFC)
Clark Equipment Company	SR	SR	263	
Clinton Foods, Inc.	AQ			(STANDARD BRANDS 1956)
Cluett, Peabody & Co., Inc.	SR	SR	350	
Collins & Aikman Corp.	SR	SR	508	
Colorado Milling & Elevator Co.	AQ			(GREAT WESTERN UNITED 1962)
Combustion Engineering-Superheater,Inc.	SR	SR	383	
Commercial Solvents Corp.	SR	AQ	351	
Congoleum-Nairn, Inc.	AQ			(BATH INDUSTRIES 1968)
Consolidated Cigar Corp.	AQ			(GULF & WESTERN)
Consolidated Paper Co.	SR	SR	127	CONSOLIDATED PACKAGING
Consolidated Water Power & Paper Co.	SR	SR	249	CONSOLIDATED PAPERS
Crane Company	SR	SR	384	
Crowell-Collier Publishing Co.	AQ			

Appendixes

B. Companies Ranked 201 to 500	2	3	4	5
Crown Cork & Seal Co.,Inc.	SR	SR	582	
Cummins Engine Co., Inc.	SR	SR	245	
Cuneo Press, Inc.	SR	SR	581	
Curtiss Candy Co.	AQ			(STANDARD BRANDS 1964)
Cutler-Hammer,Inc.	SR	AQ	105	
Dan River Mills,Inc.	SR	SR	503	
Detroit Steel Corporation	AQ			(CYCLOPS 1971)
Devoe & Raynolds Co., Inc.	AQ			(CELANESE 1964)
Diamond Alkali Co.	SR	SR	411	DIAMOND SHAMROCK
Diamond Match Co., The	SR	SR	320	DIAMOND INTERNATIONAL
Doehler-Jarvis Corp.	AQ			(NATIONAL LEAD 1952)
Donnelley (R.R.) & Sons Co.	SR	SR	456	
Dresser Industries, Inc.	SR	SR	354	
Dubuque Packing Co.	SR		NI	
Du Mont (Allen B.) Laboratories,Inc.	AQ			(FAIRCHILD CAMERA)
Eagle-Picher & Co.	SR	SR	342	
Eastern States Petroleum Co. Inc.	NI			
Electric Storage Battery Co., The	SR	AQ	533	ESB INC.
Electrolux Corp.	AQ			(CONSOLIDATED FOODS)
Elgin National Watch Co.	SR	SR	575	
Emerson Radio & Phonograph Corp.	AQ			(NATIONAL UNION ELECTRIC)
Erwin Mills, Inc.	AQ			(BURLINGTON INDUSTRIES 1962)
Fairbanks, Morse & Co.	AQ			(COLT INDUSTRIES)
Fairchild Engine & Airplane Corp.	SR	SR	509	FAIRCHILD HILLER
Fairmont Foods Co.	SR	SR	594	
Field Enterprises, Inc.	SR		NI	
Flintkote Co., The	SR	SR	301	
Florsheim Shoe Co., The	AQ			(INTERNATIONAL SHOE 1953)
Food Machinery & Chemical Corp.	SR	SR	450	FMC
Forstmann Woolen Co.	AQ			(J.P. STEVENS 1957)
Fruehauf Trailer Co.	SR	SR	402	FRUEHAUF CORP.
Fulton Bag and Cotton Mills	AQ			(ALLIED PRODUCTS)
Gair (Robert) Co., Inc.	AQ			(CONTINENTAL CAN 1956)
Gardner Board & Carton Co.	AQ			(DIAMOND MATCH 1957)
Gates Rubber Co.	SR		NI	
Gaylord Container Corp.	AQ			(CROWN ZELLERBACH 1955)
General American Transportation Corp.	SR	SR	539	GATX
General Aniline & Film Corp.	SR	SR	553	GAF
General Baking Co.	SR	SR	406	GENERAL HOST
General Cable Corp.	SR	SR	361	
General Shoe Corp.	SR	SR	190	GENESCO
Gerber Products Co.	SR	SR	172	
Gibson Refrigerator Co.	AQ			(WHITE CONSOLIDATED 1955)
Gillette Safety Razor Co. (Delaware)	SR	SR	3	GILLETTE CO.
Globe Oil & Refining Co.	AQ			(MID-WEST REFINING)
Globe-Union, Inc.	SR	AQ	243	

242   **Profits in the long run**

B. Companies Ranked 201 to 500	2	3	4	5
Godchaux Sugars, Inc.	AQ			(NATIONAL SUGAR 1956)
Golden State Co., Ltd.	AQ			(FOREMOST-McKESSON 1953)
Goodall-Sanford, Inc.	AQ			(BURLINGTON INDUSTRIES 1953)
National Battery (Gould-National Batteries)	SR	SR	297	GOULD INC.
Granite City Steel Co.	AQ			(NATIONAL STEEL 1971)
Graniteville Co.	SR	SR	341	
Great Northern Paper Co.	SR	SR	368	
Great Western Sugar Co., The	SR		459	GREAT WESTERN UNITED
Greenwood Mills, Inc.	SR		NI	
Grumman Aircraft Engineering Corp.	SR	SR	385	GRUMMAN CORP.
Hall (W.F.) Printing Co.	SR	AQ	340	
Handy & Harmon	SR	SR	462	
Harbison-Walker Refractories Co.	AQ			(DRESSER INDUSTRIES 1967)
Harnischfeger Corp.	SR		ID	
Hazel-Atlas Glass Co.	AQ			(CONTINENTAL CAN 1956)
Heinz (H.J.) Co.	SR	SR	538	
Hills Bros. Coffee Co.	AQ			
Hinde & Dauch Paper Co., The	AQ			(WESTVACO 1953)
Houdaille-Hershey Corp.	SR		ID	HOUDAILLE
Hughes Tool Co.	SR		ID	
Hunt Foods, Inc.	SR	SR	452	NORTON SIMON
Industrial Rayon Corp.	AQ			(MIDLAND-ROSS 1960)
Ingersoll-Rand Co.	SR	SR	27	
Interchemical Corp.	SR	AQ	439	INMONT
Interlake Iron Corp.	SR	SR	403	INTERLAKE INC.
International Milling Co.	SR	SR	460	INTERNATIONAL MULTI-FOODS
International Silver Co.	SR	SR	250	INSILCO
Interstate Bakeries Corp.	SR	AQ	187	INTERSTATE BRANDS
Joanna Western Mills Co.	SR			
Joslyn Mfg. & Supply Co.	SR	SR	319	
Joy Manufacturing Co.	SR	SR	305	
Juilliard (A.D.) & Co., Inc.	AQ			(UNITED MERCH. & MFG. 1952)
Karagheusian (A.&M.), Inc.	AQ			(J.P. STEVENS 1963)
Kellogg Co.	SR	SR	16	
Kelsey-Hayes Wheel Co.	SR	AQ	204	KELSEY-HAYES
Kendall Co., The	SR	AQ	163	(COLGATE-PALMOLIVE 1972)
Keystone Steel & Wire Co.	SR	AQ	40	KEYSTONE CONSOLIDATED IND.
Kieckhefer Container Co.	AQ			(WEYERHAEUSER 1957)
Kohler Co.	SR		NI	
Kroehler Mfg. Co.	SR	SR	193	
Laclede Steel Co.	SR	SR	72	
Lees (James) & Sons Co.	AQ			(BURLINGTON INDUSTRIES 1960)
Lehigh Portland Cement Co.	SR	AQ	216	
Libby, McNeill & Libby	SR	AQ	552	
Liebmann Breweries, Inc.	SR		NI	
Lilly (Eli) & Co.	SR	SR	133	

Appendixes   243

B. Companies Ranked 201 to 500	2	3	4	5
Link-Belt Co.	AQ			(FMC 1967)
Lion Oil Co.	AQ			(MONSANTO 1954)
Lipton (Thomas J.), Inc.	SR		PI	
Lone Star Cement Corp.	SR	SR	148	LONE STAR INDUSTRIES
Long-Bell Lumber Co.	AQ			(INTERNATIONAL PAPER 1956)
Longview Fibre Co.	SR		ID	
Lowenstein (M.) & Sons, Inc.	SR	SR	258	
Luckens Steel Co.	SR	SR	401	
Mack Trucks, Inc.	AQ			(SIGNAL COMP.)
Magnavox Co., The	SR	AQ	86	
Mansfield Tire & Rubber Co., The	SR	SR	278	
Marathon Corp.	AQ			(AMERICAN CAN 1957)
Martin (Glenn L.) Co., The	SR	SR	601	MARTIN-MARIETTA
Masonite Corp.	SR	SR	192	
Massey-Harris Co.	SR	SR	139	MASSEY-FERGUSON
Mathieson Chemical Corp.	AQ			(OLIN)
Maytag Co., The	SR	SR	12	
McElwain (J.F.) Co. (major manufacturing subsidiary of Melville Shoe Corporation)	SR	SR	41	MELVILLE SHOE
McGraw Electric Co.	SR	SR	44	McGRAW-EDISON
McGraw-Hill Publishing Co., Inc.	SR	SR	282	
McLouth Steel Corp.	SR	SR	128	
Mengel Co., The	AQ			(MARCOR 1953)
Merck & Co., Inc.	SR	SR	215	
Mid-Continent Petroleum Corp.	AQ			(SUNRAY DX 1954)
Midland Steel Products Co., The	SR	SR	68	MIDLAND ROSS
Miller Brewing Co.	AQ			(PHILIP MORRIS 1969)
Minneapolis-Honeywell Regulator Co.	SR	SR	178	HONEYWELL INC.
Minneapolis-Moline Co.	SR		ID	DOLLY MADISON
Minnesota & Ontario Paper Co.	AQ			(BOISE-CASCADE)
Mohawk Carpet Mills, Inc.[1]	SR	SR	516	MOHASCO
Moore Business Forms, Inc.	SR		NI	MOORE CORP. LTD.
Motor Products Corp.	AQ			(WHITTAKER CORP.)
Motor Wheel Corp.	AQ			(GOODYEAR 1964)
Mount Vernon-Woodberry Mills, Inc.	AQ			(BOLLY)
Mrs. Tucker's Foods, Inc.	AQ			(ANDERSON-CLAYTON 1951)
Mullins Manufacturing Corp.	AQ			(AMERICAN STANDARD)
National Automotive Fibres, Inc.	SR	SR	218	CHRIS CRAFT
National Cash Register Co., The	SR	SR	318	NCR
National Container Corp.	AQ			(OWENS-ILLINOIS 1955)
National Cylinder Gas Co. (Delaware)	SR	AQ	207	CHEMETRON
National Gypsum Co.	SR	SR	279	
National Malleable & Steel Castings Co.	AQ			(MIDLAND ROSS 1964)
National Supply Company, The	AQ			(ARMCO STEEL 1958)
Nestle Co.	SR	SR	ID	
New Jersey Zinc Company	AQ			(GULF & WESTERN)
Newport News Shipbuilding & Dry Dock Co.	AQ			(TENNECO 1968)

244   Profits in the long run

B. Companies Ranked 201 to 500	2	3	4	5
Newport Steel Corp.	AQ			(ACME STEEL 1956)
Northern Paper Mills	AQ			(AMERICAN CAN 1952)
Norton Co.	SR		ID	
Ohio Oil Co., The	AQ			(MARATHON OIL)
Oliver Corp., The	AQ	SR	ID	(WHITE MOTOR 1960)
Oneida, Ltd.	SR	SR	227	
Owens-Corning Fiberglas Corp.	SR	SR	237	
Oxford Paper Co.	AQ			(ETHYL 1967)
Pacolet Manufacturing Co.	AQ			(DEERING MILLIKEN)
Parke, Davis & Co.	AQ			(WARNER-LAMBERT 1970)
Penick & Ford, Ltd., Inc.	AQ			(R.J. REYNOLDS 1965)
Pepperell Mfg. Co.	AQ			(WEST POINT MFG. 1965)
Pepsi-Cola Co.	SR	SR	353	PEPSICO
Pfizer (Chas.) & Co., Inc.	SR	SR	110	
Publicker Industries, Inc.	SR	SR	574	
Purity Bakeries Corp. 2)	AQ			(AMERICAN BAKERIES 1953)
Raybestos-Manhattan, Inc.	SR	SR	189	
Rayonier, Inc.	AQ			(ITT)
Raytheon Manufacturing Company	SR	SR	577	
Reeves Brothers, Inc.	SR	SR	433	
Reeves Steel & Mfg. Co.	AQ			(UNIVERSAL CYCLOPS 1958)
Reichhold Chemicals, Inc.	SR	SR	593	
Reliance Manufacturing Co. (Illinois)	LQ			
Reo Motors, Inc.	AQ			(WHITE MOTOR 1957)
Republic Aviation Corp.	LQ			
Rexall Drug, Inc.	SR	SR	587	DART IND.
Rheem Manufacturing Co.	AQ			(CITY INVESTING)
Riegel Textile Corp. (Delaware)	SR	SR	478	
Robertshaw-Fulton Controls Co.	SR	SR	112	ROBERTSHAW CONTROLS
Rockwell Mfg. Co.	SR	AQ	104	
Roebling's (John A.) Sons Co.	AQ			(CF & I 1951)
Rohm & Haas Co.	SR	SR	213	
Royal Typewriter Co., Inc.	AQ			(LITTON INDUSTRIES)
Ruberoid Company, The	AQ			(GAF 1967)
Russell-Miller Milling Co.	AQ			(PEAVEY)
St. Joseph Lead Co. (New York)	SR	SR	31	ST. JOSEPH MINERAL
Savannah Sugar Refining Corp.	SR	SR	339	SAVANNAH FOODS
Schaefer (F.M.) Brewing Co.	SR		ID	
Seeger Refrigerator Co.	AQ			(WHIRLPOOL 1955)
Servel, Inc.	AQ			(GOULD 1966)
Sheller Manufacturing Corp.	SR	SR	26	SHELLER-GLOBE
Singer Manufacturing Co., The	SR	SR	504	
Skelly Oil Co.	SR	AQ	75	
Smith (Alexander) & Sons Carpet Co. 1)	AQ			(MOHASCO 1955)
Spartan Mills	SR		NI	
Springs Cotton Mill	SR		ID	SPRINGS MILLS

Appendixes   245

B. Companies Ranked 201 to 500	2	3	4	5
Square D Co.	SR	SR	45	
Squibb (E.R.) & Sons	AQ			(MATHIESON 1952)
Standard Steel Spring Co.	AQ			(ROCKWELL SPRING & AXLE)
Stanley Works	SR	SR	251	
Stauffer Chemical Co.	SR	SR	548	
Sterling Drug, Inc.	SR	SR	176	
Stewart-Warner Corp.	SR	SR	405	
Stokely-Van Camp, Inc.	SR	SR	448	
Sunbeam Corp.	SR	SR	10	
Sunray Oil Corp.	AQ			(SUN OIL 1968)
Sunshine Biscuits, Inc.	AQ			(AMERICAN BRANDS 1966)
Sutherland Paper Co.	AQ			KALAMAZOO VEG.PARCH.(1959)
Swanson (C.A.) & Sons	AQ			(CAMPBELL SOUP 1954)
Tecumseh Products Co.	SR	SR	20	
Tennessee Corp.	AQ			(CITIES SERVICE 1963)
Textron, Inc.	SR	SR	591	
Thompson Products, Inc.	SR	SR	373	TRW
Times-Mirror Co.	SR	SR	556	
Tobin Packing Co., Inc.	SR	SR	451	
Todd Shipyards Corp.	SR	SR	537	
United Biscuit Co. of America	SR	SR	299	KEEBLER
United Engineering & Foundry Co.	AQ			(WEAN UNITED 1970)
United Merchants & Manufacturers, Inc.	SR	SR	300	
United Shoe Machinery Corp.	SR	AQ	472	USM
U.S. Industrial Chemicals, Inc.	AQ			(NATIONAL DISTILLERS 1962)
United States Pipe & Foundry Co.	AQ			(JIM WALTER 1969)
United States Plywood Corp.	SR	SR	182	CHAMPION INTERNATIONAL
Van Raalte Co., Inc.	AQ			(CLUETT PEABODY 1968)
Virginia-Carolina Chemical Corp.	AQ			(MOBIL OIL 1963)
Wagner Electric Corp.	SR	AQ	287	
Walker (Hiram) & Sons, Inc.	SR	SR	119	
Ward Baking Co.	SR	SR	295	WARD FOOD
Westinghouse Air Brake Co.	AQ			(AMERICAN STANDARD 1968)
Nineteen Hundred Corp. (Whirlpool Corp.)	SR	SR	85	
White Motor Co., The	SR	SR	502	
Wood (Alan) Steel Co.	SR		NI	
Worthington Pump & Machinery Corp.	SR		ID	STUDEBAKER-WORTHINGTON
Wrigley (Wm.), Jr. Co. (Delaware)	SR	SR	74	
Wyandotte Chemical Corp.	AQ			(BADISCHE-ANIL)
Wyman-Gordon Co.	SR		NI	
Yale & Towne Manufacturing Co., The	AQ			(EATON MFG. 1963)
Young (L.A.) Spring & Wire Corp.	SR		--	P. HARDEMAN INC.

C. Companies Ranked 501 to 1,000	2	3	4	5
Addressograph-Multigraph Corp.	SR	SR	82	
Affiliated Gas Equip., Inc.	AQ			(CARRIER 1955)

246   Profits in the long run

C. Companies Ranked 501 to 1,000	2	3	4	5
Alabama Mills, Inc.	AQ			(DAN RIVER 1955)
Allen-Bradley Co.	SR		NI	
Alpha Portland Cement Co.	SR	SR	208	ALPHA PORTLAND IND.
Alton Box Board Co.	SR		NI	
Aluminum Goods Mfg. Co.	SR	SR	160	MIRRO CORP.
Amalgamated Sugar Co.	SR	SR	369	
American Bakeries Company 2)	SR	SR	252	
American Bosch Corp.	SR	SR	541	AMBAC IND.
American Cast Iron Pipe Co.	SR		NI	
American Chicle Co.	AQ			(WARNER-LAMBERT 1962)
American Colortype Co. (New Jersey)	AQ			(RAPID AMERICAN)
American Crystal Sugar Co.	SR	AQ	532	
American Distilling Co., The	SR	SR	527	
American Hard Rubber Co. 3)	SR	SR	562	AMERACE ESNA
American Hardware Corp., The	SR	SR	570	EMHART
American Hide & Leather Co.	SR	SR	9	TANDY
American Laundry Machinery Co.	AQ			(McGRAW-EDISON 1960)
American Liberty Oil Co.	SR	SR	66	AMERICAN PETROFINA
American Machine & Foundry Co.	SR	SR	484	AMF
American Maize Products Co.	SR	SR	480	
American Manufacturing Co.	SR		NI	
American-Marietta Co.	AQ			(MARTIN GLENN)
American Meter Co., Inc.	AQ			(GENERAL PRECISION 1967)
American Potash & Chemical Corp.	AQ			(KERR-McGEE)
American Safety Razor Corp.	AQ			(PHILIP MORRIS 1960)
American Seating Company	SR	SR	281	
American Ship Building Co., The	SR	SR	551	
American Snuff Co.	SR	SR	447	CONWOOD
American Stove Co.	SR		ID	MAGIC CHEF
American Window Glass Co.	SR	SR	460	AMERICAN ST. GOBAIN
American Yarn & Processing Co.	AQ			(RUDDICK)
Ames Worsted Co.	SR		ID	AMES TEXTILE
Anderson-Prichard Oil Corp.	LQ			
Apex Electrical Mfg. Co., The	AQ			(WHITE CONSOLIDATED 1956)
Arrow-Hart & Hegeman Electric Co.	SR	AQ	60	ARROW-HART
Art Metal Construction Co.	AQ			(WALTER HELLER)
Artistic Foundations, Ind.	NI			
Arvey Corp.	SR		NI	
Aspinook Corp.	AQ			(BARKER BROS)
Associated Spring Corp.	SR		ID	
Associated Plywood Mills, Inc.	AQ			(US PLYWOOD 1954)
ATF, Inc.	AQ			(SCHULEMBERGER)
Atlas Plywood Corp.	AQ			(CONSOLIDATED ELECTRIC)
Atlas Powder Co.	AQ			(IMPERIAL CHEMICAL 1971)
Autocar Co.	AQ			(WHITE MOTOR)
Ball Brothers Co.	SR		ID	BALL CORP.

Appendixes 247

C. Companies Ranked 501 to 1,000	2	3	4	5
Bancroft (Joseph) & Sons Co.	AQ			(INDIAN HEAD 1961)
Barber-Colmon Co.	SR		NI	
Bassett Furniture Industries, Inc.	SR	SR	93	
Bath Iron Works Corp.	SR	AQ	488	BATH INDUSTRIES
Bausch & Lomb Optical Co.	SR	SR	563	
Bay Petroleum Corp.	AQ			(TEXAS GAS TRANS.)
Bayuk Cigars, Inc.	SR	SR	585	
Beacon Manufacturing Co.	AQ			(NATIONAL DIST. & CHEM. 1966)
Beech Aircraft Corp.	SR	AQ	542	
Bell Co., The	AQ			(PACIFIC COAST)
Bell & Howell Co.	SR	SR	365	
Beloit Iron Works	SR		NI	BELOIT CORP.
Berkshire Knitting Mills	AQ			(V.F. CORP.)
Bird & Son, Inc.	SR		NI	
Black & Decker Mfg. Co., The	SR	SR	178	
Black, Sivalls & Bryson, Inc.	AQ			(HUSTON OIL)
Blackstone Corp.	SR		NI	
Bliss, E.W., Co.	AQ			(GULF & WESTERN)
Blockson Chemical Co.	AQ			(OLIN 1955)
Blumenthal (Sidney) & Co., Inc.	AQ			(BURLINGTON INDUSTRIES)
Boston Woven Hose & Rubber Co.	AQ			(AMER. BILTRITE RUB.1957)
Botany Mills, Inc.	SR	NI	602	BOTANY INDUSTRIES
Cleveland Graphite Bronze Co., The	AQ			(GOULD 1969)
Cleveland Twist Drill Co.	AQ			(NATIONAL ACME 1967)
Cleveland Worsted Mills Co.	LQ			
Climax Molybdenum Co.	AQ			(AMERICAN METAL 1957)
Clow (James B.) & Sons	SR		ID	CLOW CORP.
Coleman Company, Inc. (Kansas)	SR	SR	123	
Columbia Broadcasting System, Inc.	SR	SR	485	
Columbia River Paper Co.	AQ			(BOISE CASCADE)
Columbian Carbon Co.	AQ			(CITY SERVICES 1962)
Conde Nast Publications, Inc.	AQ			(PATRIOT NAST)
Consolidated Chemical Industries, Inc.	AQ			(STAUFFER CHEMICAL 1951)
Continental-Diamond Fibre Co.	AQ			(BUDD 1955)
Continental Foundry & Machine Co.	LQ			
Continental Steel Corp.	SR	AQ	352	
Cook Paint & Varnish Co.	SR	PI	249	
Cooper-Bessemer Corp., The	SR	SR	235	
Coors (Adolph) Co.	SR	SR	NI	
Coos Bay Lumber Co.	AQ			(GEORGIA PACIFIC 1956)
Cornell Wood Products Co.	AQ			(ST. REGIS PAPER 1959)
Cosden Petroleum Corp.	AQ			(AMERICAN PETROFINA 1963)
Creameries of America, Inc.	AQ			(BEATRICE FOODS 1962)
Crocker Burbank & Co., Assn.	AQ			(WEYERHAEUSER 1962)
Crompton & Knowles Loom Works	SR	SR	180	
Crossett Lumber Co.	AQ			(GEORGIA PACIFIC 1962)

248   Profits in the long run

C. Companies Ranked 501 to 1,000	2	3	4	5
Crown Central Petroleum Corp.	SR	SR	469	
Cuban-American Sugar Co., The	LQ			
Darling & Co.	SR		NI	
Davison Chemical Corp.	AQ			(W.R. GRACE)
Dayton Malleable Iron Co.	SR	SR	430	
Dayton Rubber Co., The	SR	SR	347	DAYCO
De Laval Separator Co.	LQ			
Decca Records, Inc.	AQ			(M.C.A. 1966)
Deep Rock Oil Corp.	AQ			(NATIONAL INDUSTRIES)
Dennison Manufacturing Co.	SR	SR	114	
Detroit Harvester Co.	AQ			(WALTER KIDDE)
Detroit Steel Products Co.	AQ			(SPACE INDUSTRIES 1971)
Dewey & Almy Chemical Co.	AQ			(W.R. GRACE)
Diamond T Motor Car Co.	LQ			
Dierks Lumber & Coal Co.	AQ			(WEYERHAEUSER 1969)
Disston (Henry) & Sons	AQ			(H.K. PORTER 1962)
Dixie Cup Co.	AQ			(AMERICAN CAN 1957)
Dixie Mercerizing Co.	SR		NI	
Doniger (David D.) & Co. Inc.	NI			
Doubleday & Co., Inc.	SR		NI	
Doughnut Corp. of America	NI			
Draper Corp.	AQ			(NORTH AM. ROCKWELL)
Dunlop Tire & Rubber Corp.	SR		PI	
Duplan Corp.	SR	SR	555	
Duquesne Brewing Co. of Pittsburgh	AQ			(SCHMIDTS BREWING 1972)
Durez Plastics & Chemicals, Inc.	AQ			(OCCIDENTAL PETROL.)
Dwight Manufacturing Co.	AQ			(CONE MILLS 1951)
Eastern Corp.	AQ			(STANDARD PACKAGING)
Easy Washing Machine Corp.	AQ			(MURRAY 1955)
Eddy Paper Corp.	AQ			(WEYERHAEUSER 1957)
Edison (Thomas A.), Inc.	AQ			(McGRAW-EDISON 1957)
Ekco Products Co. (Illinois)	AQ			(AMER. HOME PRODUCTS 1965)
El Dorado Oil Works	AQ			(FOREMOST DAIRIES 1955)
Elliott Co.	AQ			(CARRIER 1957)
Emerson Electric Manufacturing Co.	SR	SR	321	
Emhart Manufacturing Co.	AQ			(AMER. HARD RUBBER 1964)
Emsco Derrick & Equipment Co.	AQ			(YOUNGSTOWN S & T 1955)
B.V.D. Corp., The (Erlanger Mills Corp.)	LQ			
Evans Products Company	SR	SR	505	
Eversharp, Inc.	AQ			(WARNER-LAMBERT 1970)
Ex-Cell-O Corp.	SR	SR	205	
Fafnir Bearing Co.	AQ			(TEXTRON 1968)
Falstaff Brewing Corp.	SR	SR	118	
Falk Corp.	AQ			(SUNSTRAND)
Farrel-Birmingham Co., Inc.	AQ			(USM 1968)
Federal-Mogul Corp.	SR	SR	61	

Appendixes   249

C. Companies Ranked 501 to 1,000	2	3	4	5
Federal Paper Board Co.	SR	SR	332	
Ferguson (Harry), Inc.	AQ			(MASSEY-HARRIS CO. 1953)
Ferro Corp.	SR	SR	356	
Firth Carpet Co.	AQ			(MOHASCO 1962)
Fisher Flouring Mills Co.	SR		NI	
Florence Stove Co.	SR	SR	440	ROPER GEO.
Flotill Products, Inc.	AQ			(OGDEN)
Flour Mills of America, Inc.	SR		NI	
Follansbee Steel Corp.	AQ			(UNION CHEM. & MAT.)
Foremost Dairies, Inc.	SR	SR	336	FOREMOST-McKESSON
Fort Wayne Corrugated Paper Co.	AQ			(CONTINENTAL CAN 1959)
Free Sewing Machine Co.	NI			
French Sardine Co. of Calif.	NI			
Froedtert Grain & Malting Co., Inc.	SR	AQ	230	SOLA BASIC
Fruit Growers Supply Co.	SR		NI	
Fry (Lloyd A.) Roofing Co.	SR		NI	
Fuller Brush Co.	AQ			(CONSOLIDATED FOODS)
Fuller (W.P.) & Co.	AQ			(NORTON SIMON)
Gardner-Denver Co.	SR	AQ	125	
Garlock Packing Co.	SR		ID	GARLOCK INC.
General Cigar Co.*	SR	SR	590	
General Fireproofing Co.	SR	SR	56	
General Portland Cement Co.	SR	SR	21	
General Precision Equipment Corp.	AQ			(SINGER 1968)
General Refractories Co.	SR	SR	196	
General Steel Castings Corp.	SR	SR	482	GENERAL STEEL INDUSTRIES
General Time Corp.	AQ			(TALLY INDUSTRIES)
Georgia-Pacific Plywood & Lumber Co.	SR	SR	194	
Gladding McBean & Co.	AQ			(INTERPACE 1962)
Glenmore Distilleries Co.	SR	SR	409	
Goebel Brewing Co.	AQ			(STROH's BREW.)
Gordon Baking Co.	AQ			(AMERICAN BRANDS 1956)
Gorham Mfg. Co.	AQ			(TEXTRON 1967)
Great Lakes Carbon Corp.	AQ			(KENNECOTT COPPER)
Greenbaum (J.) Tanning Co.	NI			
Green Giant Co.	SR	AQ	362	
Greif Brothers Cooperage Corp.	SR	AQ	408	
Griesedieck Western Brewery Co.#	AQ			(CARLING)
Grinnell Corp.	SR	AQ	210	
Gruen Watch Co.	SR	NI	317	GRUEN INDUSTRIES
Gulf States Paper Corp.	SR		ID	
Hall Brothers, Inc.	NI			
Hamilton Watch Co.	SR	SR	506	HMW
Hamm (Theo.) Brewing Co.	AQ			(HEUBLIN 1965)
Hammermill Paper Co.	SR	SR	455	
Hammond Lumber Co.	AQ			(GEORGIA PACIFIC 1956)

250   Profits in the long run

C. Companies Ranked 501 to 1,000

	2	3	4	5
Hanes (P.H.) Knitting Co.	SR		ID	
Harbor Plywood Corp.	AQ			(HUNT FOODS 1960)
Harley Davidson Motor Co.	AQ			(AMF 1969)
Harris-Seybold-Potter Co.	SR	SR	101	HARRIS INTERTYPE
Harshaw Chemical Co., The	AQ			(KEWANEE OIL 1966)
Hart, Schaffner & Marx	SR	SR	566	
Hathaway Manufacturing Co.	AQ			(BERKSHIRE-HATHAWAY 1955)
Heil Co.	SR		ID	
Heintz Mfg. Co.	AQ			(KELSEY-HAYES 1957)
Hercules Motors Corp.	AQ			(WHITE CONSOLIDATED 1960)
Hewitt-Robins, Inc.	AQ			(LITTON INDUSTRIES)
Heyden Chemical Corp.	AQ			(TENN. GAS TRANS.)
Heywood-Wakefield Co.	SR	NI	457	
Hines (Edward) Lumber Co.	SR	SR	51	
Hobart Manufacturing Co., The	SR	SR	214	
Hoe (R.) & Co., Inc.	SR	NI	150	
Hoffman-LaRoche, Inc.	SR	SR	PI	
Holeproof Hosiery Co.	AQ			(KAYSER-ROTH 1954)
Hollingsworth & Whitney Co.	AQ			(SCOTT PAPER 1953)
Holly Sugar Corp.	SR	SR	568	
Hooker Electrochemical Co.	AQ			(OCCIDENTAL PETROL.)
Hoover Co., The (Ohio)	SR	SR	291	
Howes Leather Co., Inc.	SR		ID	
Hubbard & Co.	AQ			(DYSON CORP.)
Huber (J.M.) Corp.	AQ			(A-T-O INC)
Hudson Pulp & Paper Corp.	SR	AQ	465	
Huron Portland Cement Co.	AQ			(NATIONAL GYPSUM 1959)
Ideal Cement Co.	SR		62	IDEAL BASIC INDUSTRIES
Imperial Paper & Color Corp.	AQ			(HERCULES 1960)
Imperial Sugar Co.	SR		NI	
Ingalls Iron Works Co., The	SR		NI	
Inland Container Corp.	SR		ID	
Inspiration Consolidated Copper Co.	SR	AQ	185	
International Latex Corp.	AQ			(GLEN ALDEN)
International Minerals & Chemical Corp.	SR	SR	284	
International Salt Co.	AQ			(AKZONA 1970)
I-T-E Circuit Breaker Co.	SR	AQ	377	I-T-E IMPERIAL
Jack & Heintz Precision Industries, Inc.	AQ			(LEAR-SIEGLER)
Jacobs (F.L.) Co.	SR	SR	600	
Jeffrey Mfg. Co.	SR		ID	
Jergens (Andrew) Co.	AQ			(AMERICAN BRANDS 1970)
Johnson (S.C.) & Son	AQ			
Kalamazoo Vegetable Parchment Co.	AQ			(GEORGIA PACIFIC 1967)
Kayser (Julius) & Co.	SR	AQ	540	KAYSER ROTH
Keasbey & Mattison Co.	AQ			(CERTAIN-TEED 1961)
Kendall Refining Company	AQ			(WITCO CHEMICAL 1966)

Appendixes   251

C. Companies Ranked 501 to 1,000   2   3   4   5

King-Seeley Corp.	AQ			(HFC)
Koehring Co.	SR	SR	302	
Ladish Co.	SR		NI	
Lambert Co., The	SR	SR	536	WARNER-LAMBERT
Lamson & Sessions Co.	SR	SR	200	
Landers, Frary and Clark	AQ			(J.B. WILLIAMS)
Lavino (E.J.) & Co.	AQ			(INT. MIN. & CHEM. 1965)
Le Tourneau (R.G.), Inc.	SR		NI	
Lee (H.D.) Co., Inc.	AQ			(V.F. CORP. 1969)
Lee Rubber & Tire Corp.	SR		ID	LEE NATIONAL
Lennox Furnace Co., The	SR		NI	
Leviton Manufacturing Co., Inc.	SR		NI	
Lewin-Mathes Co.	AQ			(CERRO-deFASCO 1956)
Life Savers Corp.	AQ			(SQUIBB 1955)
Lily-Tulip Cup Corp.	AQ			(OWENS-ILLINOIS 1968)
Linen Thread Co., Inc.	AQ			(INDIAN HEAD 1959)
Lincoln Electric Co.	SR		NI	
Liquid Carbonic Corp., The	AQ			(GENERAL DYNAMICS)
Lock Joint Pipe Co.	AQ			(INTERPACE)
Lone Star Steel Co.	AQ			(NORTHWEST INDUSTRIES)
Lorraine Mfg. Co.	AQ			(GREAT AM. INDUSTRIES)
Lowe (Joe) Corp.	AQ			(CONS. FOODS 1964)
Lucky Lager Brewing Co.	SR		ID	LUCKY BREWING
Ludlow Manufacturing & Sales Co.	SR	SR	578	LUDLOW CORP.
M & M Wood Working Co.	SR		PI	
Magee Carpet Co.	SR			
Mallinckrodt Chemical Works	SR		ID	
Mallory (P.R.) & Co., Inc.	SR	AQ	221	
Manhattan Shirt Co., The	SR	SR	525	
Manitowoc Shipbuilding Co.	SR		NI	
Manning, Maxwell & Moore, Inc.	LQ			
Marion Power Shovel Co.	LQ			UNIVERSAL MARION
Marlin-Rockwell Corp.	AQ			(TRW 1963)
Marquette Cement Mfg. Co.	SR	AQ	191	
Mars, Inc.	SR		ID	
Masland (C.H.) & Sons	SR		ID	
Matthiessen & Hegeler Zinc Co.	SR		ID	
McCall Corp.	AQ			(NORTON SIMON 1968)
McCord Corp.	SR	AQ	39	
McCormick & Co.	SR	SR	212	
Mead Johnson & Co.	AQ			(BRISTOL MYERS 1967)
Medusa Portland Cement Co.	SR	SR	310	MEDUSA CORP.
Meredith Publishing Co.	SR	SR	64	
Mergenthaler Linotype Co.	SR	AQ	510	ELTRA
Mesta Machine Co.	SR	SR	97	
Metal & Thermit Corp.	AQ			(AMERICAN CAN 1962)

252 Profits in the long run

C. Companies Ranked 501 to 1,000

	2	3	4	5
Miehle Printing Press & Mfg. Co.	AQ			(NORTH AM. ROCKWELL)
Milprint, Inc.	AQ			(PHILIP MORRIS 1956)
Mississippi Cottonseed Products Co.	SR	NI		
Moloney Electric Co.	AQ			(COLT INDUSTRIES)
Monarch Mills	AQ			(DEERING MILLIKAN)
Moore (Benjamin) & Co.	SR	NI		
Mooresville Mills	AQ			(BURLINGTON IND. 1954)
Morton Salt Co.	AQ			(NORWICH 1969)
Mueller Brass Co.	SR	AQ	171	UV INDUSTRIES
Munsingwear, Inc.	SR	SR	414	
Murray Company of Texas, Inc.	AQ			(NORTH AM. AVIATION)
National Acme Co., The	SR	SR	232	ACME CLEVELAND
National Can Corp.	SR	SR	557	
National Coop. Refinery Association	SR	ID		(ASHLAND OIL)
National Electric Products Corp.	AQ			(McGRAW-EDISON 1958)
National Pressure Cooker Co.	SR	SR	331	NATIONAL PRESTO
National Screw & Manufacturing Co.	AQ			(MONOGRAM INDUSTRIES)
National-Standard Company	SR	SR	143	
Naumkeag Steam Cotton Co.	SR	AQ	596	INDIAN HEAD
Nekoosa-Edwards Paper Company	AQ			(GREAT NORTHERN PAPER 1970)
Neptune Meter Company	SR	AQ	81	NEPTUNE INTERNATIONAL
Nesco, Inc.	AQ			(N.Y. SHIPBUILDING 1954)
New York Air Brake Company, The	AQ			(GENERAL SIGNAL)
New York Shipbuilding Corporation	AQ			(MERRITT, CHAPMAN 1970)
Newport Industries, Inc.	AQ			(TENN. GAS TRANS.)
Nicholson File Co.	AQ			(COOPER INDUSTRIES 1971)
Niles-Bement-Pond Co.	AQ			(COLT INDUSTRIES)
Noma Electric Corp.	AQ			(SIRNAL CORP.)
Nopco Chemical Company, Inc.	AQ			(DIAMOND-SHAMROCK 1967)
Nordberg Mfg. Co.	AQ			(REXNORD 1970)
Northwest Engineering Co.	SR	SR	223	
Northwest Paper Co., The	AQ			(POTLATCH FORESTS 1964)
Northwestern Steel & Wire Co.	SR	SR	106	
Ohio Boxboard Co.	AQ			(CENTRAL FIBRE PROD.)
Ohio Brass Co., The	SR	AQ	14	
Ohio Crankshaft Co.	SR	AQ	487	PARK-OHIO
Ohio Match Company	AQ			(NORTON SIMON)
Ohio Rubber Co., The	AQ			(EAGLE PITCHER 1952)
Okonite Co.	AQ			(KENNECOTT COPPER 1957)
Oswego Falls Corporation	AQ			(PHILLIPS PETROLEUM 1964)
Otis Elevator Co. (New Jersey)	SR	AQ	102	
Outboard, Marine & Manufacturing Co.	SR	SR	111	
Pacific American Fisheries, Inc.	AQ			(UNITED PACIFIC 1966)
Pacific Car & Foundry Co.	SR	SR	428	PACCAR
Pacific Lumber Co.	SR	SR	137	
Parker Pen Co., The	SR	SR	118	

Appendixes   253

C. Companies Ranked 501 to 1,000	2	3	4	5
Pasco Packing Co.	SR		ID	
Peerless Woolen Mills	AQ			(1952)
Pennsylvania-Dixie Cement Corp.	SR	SR	76	PENN-DIXIE INDUSTRIES
Pennsylvania Salt Manufacturing Co.	SR	SR	436	PENNWALT
Perfection Stove Co.	AQ			(WHITE CONSOLIDATED 1954)
Permanente Cement Co.	AQ			(KAISER CEMENT)
Peter Paul, Inc.	SR	AQ	239	
Petroleum Heat & Power Co.	LQ			
Pettibone Mulliken Corp.	SR	SR	454	PETTIBONE CORP.
Phillips-Jones Corp.	SR	SR	463	PHILLIPS-VanHEUSEN
Pittsburgh Coke & Chemical Co.	AQ			
Pittsburgh Forgings Co.	SR	AQ	149	
Pittsburgh Screw & Bolt Corp.	SR	SR	77	AMPCO-PITTSBURGH
Planters Nut & Chocolate Co.	AQ			(STANDARD BRANDS 1960)
Plymouth Cordage Co.	AQ			(EMHART 1960)
Pope & Talbot, Inc.	SR		ID	
Potlatch Forests, Inc.	SR	SR	275	POTLATCH CORP.
Powdrell & Alexander, Inc.	SR		PI	
Premier Petroleum Co.	NI			(SUN OIL)
Proctor & Schwartz, Inc.	AQ			(SCM 1966)
Publication Corp.	AQ			(CROWELL, COLLIER)
Puget Sound Pulp & Timber Co.	AQ			(GEORGIA PACIFIC 1963)
Quaker State Oil Refining Corp.	SR	SR	380	
Rahr Malting Co.	SR		NI	
Readers Digest Associates, Inc.	SR		NI	
Reed Roller Bit Co.	SR		238	REED TOOL
Reliance Electric & Engineering Co., The	SR	AQ	229	
Rhinelander Paper Co.	AQ			(ST. REGIS PAPER 1956)
Rice-Stix, Inc.	LQ			
Richardson Co.	SR	SR	364	
Richman Brothers Co.	AQ			(WOOLWORTH)
Riegel Paper Corp.	AQ			(FEDERAL PAPERBOARD 1972)
Robbins Mills, Inc.	AQ			(TEXTRON 1954)
Robertson (H.H.) Co.	SR	SR	83	
Rome Cable Corp.	AQ			(ALCOA 1959)
Ronson Art Metal Works, Inc.	SR	SR	253	RONSON CORP.
Royster (F.S.) Guano Co.	SR		ID	
Ruppert (Jacob)	AQ			(KRATTER CORP. 1962)
Russell, Burdsall & Ward Bolt & Nut Co.	SR		NI	
Saco-Lowell Shops (Maine)	AQ			(MAREMONT)
Sangamo Electric Co.	SR	AQ	262	
Savage Arms Corp.	AQ			(EMHART 1957)
Sayles Finishing Plants, Inc.	SR		NI	
Schweitzer (Peter J.), Inc.	AQ			(KIMBERLY-CLARK 1957)
Scullin Steel Company	LQ			
Seabrook Farms Co. (N.J.)	SR	AQ	554	

254   **Profits in the long run**

C. Companies Ranked 501 to 1,000

	2	3	4	5
Seiberling Rubber Co.	SR	SR	410	SEILON
Shamrock Oil & Gas Corp., The	AQ			(DIAMOND ALKALI 1967)
Sharp & Dohme, Inc. (Maryland)	AQ			(MERK 1953)
Sheaffer (W.A.) Pen Co.	AQ			(TEXTRON 1966)
Shellmar Products Corp.	AQ			(DIAMOND GARNER)
Shenango Furnace Co.	SR		NI	
Shuford Mills, Inc.	SR		NI	
Shwayder Bros., Inc.	NI			
Simonds Saw & Steel Co.	AQ			(WALLACE-MURRAY 1966)
Simpson Logging Co.	SR		NI	
S.K.F. Industries, Inc.	SR		PI	
Smith (L.C.) & Corona Typewriters, Inc.	SR	SR	390	SCM
Smith-Douglass Co., Inc.	AQ			(BORDEN 1964)
Smith, Kline & French Laboratories	SR	SR	15	SMITHKLINE
Sonoco Products Co.	SR	SR	158	
Sorg Paper Company	SR	SR	512	
Soundview Paper Company	AQ			(SCOTT PAPER 1950)
South Penn Oil Co.	SR	SR	78	PENNZOIL
Southern Advance Bag & Paper Co., Inc.	AQ			(CONTINENTAL CAN 1954)
Southland Paper Mills, Inc.	SR	AQ	50	
Southwestern Portland Cement Co.	AQ			(SOUTHDOWN)
Spalding (A.G.) & Brothers, Inc.	AQ			(QUESTOR 1969)
Standard-Coosa-Thatcher Co.	SR	SR	313	
Standard Lime & Stone Co.	NI			
Standard Railway Equipment Mfg. Co.	SR	AQ	33	STANRAY
Standard Screw Co.	SR	SR	269	STANADYNE
Stanley Home Products, Inc.	SR	SR	32	
St. Joe Paper Co.	SR		NI	
St. Paul & Tacoma Lumber Co.	AQ			(ST. REGIS PAPER '56)
Stetson (John B.) Co.	SR	AQ	500	
Stromberg-Carlson Co.	AQ			(GENERAL DYNAMICS)
Sun Chemical Corp.	SR	SR	372	
Superior Steel Corp.	AQ			(COPPERWELD STEEL 1956)
Surface Combustion Corp.	AQ			(MIDLAND-ROSS 1956)
Swisher (Jno. H.) & Son, Inc.	AQ			(AMERICAN MAIZE 1966)
Talon, Inc.	AQ			(TEXTRON 1968)
Taylor Forge & Pipe Works	AQ			(GULF & WESTERN)
Tennessee Products & Chemical Corp.	AQ			(MERRITT, CHAPMAN)
Textile Machine Works	NI			
Textiles-Incorporated	SR	SR	73	
Thatcher Glass Manufacturing Co.	AQ			(REXALL DRUG 1966)
Thermoid Co.	AQ			(H.K. PORTER)
Thew Shovel Co.	AQ			(KOEHRING 1964)
Thomaston Mills	SR	SR	19	
Thor Corp.	AQ			(SCM 1967)
Toledo Scale Co.	AQ			(RELIANCE ELECTRIC 1967)

Appendixes   255

C. Companies Ranked 501 to 1,000   2   3   4   5

Torrington Co., The	AQ			(Ingersoll-Rand 1969)
Trailmobile Co.	AQ			(PULLMAN 1951)
Trane Company	SR	SR	116	
Triangle Conduit & Cable Co.	SR		ID	TRIANGLE INDUSTRIES
Trico Products Corp.	SR	SR	164	
True Temper Corp.	AQ			(ALLEGHENY LUDLUM 1967)
Twin Coach Co.	AQ			(WHEELABATON)
Underwood Corp.	AQ			(OLIVETTI)
United Carbon Co.	AQ			(ASHLAND OIL 1963)
United Carr Fastener Corp.	AQ			(TRW 1968)
United Drill & Tool Corp.	AQ			(TRW 1968)
United Elastic Corp.	AQ			(J.P. STEVENS 1968)
United States Envelope Co.	AQ			(WESTVACO 1960)
United States Hoffman Machinery Corp.	NI			
United States Playing Card Co.	AQ			(DIAMOND INTERNATIONAL 1963)
U.S. Printing & Lithograph Co., The	AQ			(DIAMOND INTERNATIONAL 1959)
United States Radiator Corp.	AQ			(NATIONAL U.S. RADIATOR 1954)
United States Tobacco Co.	SR	SR	327	
Universal-Cyclops Steel Corp.	SR	SR	121	CYCLOPS CORP.
Upjohn Co., The	SR	SR	599	
Utah-Idaho Sugar Co.	SR	SR	580	U & I INC.
Utica & Mohawk Cotton Mills, Inc.	AQ			(J.P. STEVENS 1952)
Van Norman Co.	AQ			(GULF & WESTERN)
Vanadium Corp. of America	AQ			(FOOTE MINERAL)
Verney Corp.	AQ			(GLEN ALDEN)
Vick Chemical Co.	SR	SR	154	RICHARDSON-MERRILL
Victor Chemical Works	AQ			(STAUFFER-CHEMICAL 1959)
Visking Corp.	AQ			(UNION CARBIDE 1955)
Waldorf Paper Products Co.	AQ			(HOERNER-WALD 1966)
Walworth Co.	AQ			(INTERNATIONAL UTILITIES 1972)
Wanskuck Co.	SR		ID	
Warner & Swasey Co., The	SR	AQ	232	
Warren (S.D.) Co.	AQ			(SCOTT PAPER 1967)
Washburn Wire Co.	SR	NI	328	
Waukesha Motor Co.	AQ			(BANGOR PUNTA)
Weatherhead Co., The	SR	AQ	473	
Welch Grape Juice Co.	SR		ID	
Werthan Bag Corp.	SR		NI	
Western Printing & Lithographing Co.	SR	AQ	206	WESTERN PUBLISHING
White Sewing Machine Corp.	SR	SR	507	WHITE CONSOLIDATED
Whitin Machine Works	AQ			(WHITE CONSOL. 1965)
Whitman (William) Co., Inc.	LQ			(GULF OIL 1960)
Wilshire Oil Co.	AQ			
Wiscassett Mills Co.	SR	NI		
Wood (Gar) Industries, Inc.	AQ			(SARGENT IND. 1970)
Wood (John) Mfg. Co., Inc.	AQ			(MOLSON IND.)

256   **Profits in the long run**

C. Companies Ranked 501 to 1,000   2   3   4   5

Woodside Mills	AQ			(DAN RIVER 1956)
Woodward Iron Co.	AQ			(MEAD 1968)
Wurlitzer (Rudolph) Co.	SR	SR	558	
York Corp.	AQ			(BORG-WARNER 1956)

---

* Through an error in the company's report General Cigar Co. was considered to have manufacturing shipments too small to be included among the 1,000 largest manufacturing companies. Subsequently the tabulations on the cigar industry were amended to include it.

Through an error in the company's report Griesedieck Western Brewery Co. was considered to be among the companies ranked 201 to 500. The tabulations on the beer industry are based on the company's amended report.

1) Smith acquired Mohawk Carpet in 1955, but Mohawk is regarded as surviving to avoid dropping observation.

2) American Bakeries acquired by Purity in 1953, but American regarded as surviving to avoid losing observation.

3) Bachmann Uxbridge acquired American Hard Rubber in 1957. Name changed to Amerace, Amerace sold Bachman Uxbridge in 1960.

D. Companies in 1000 largest of 1972 but not in 1000 largest 1950, and in sample of 603.

Name	Profit Rank 1950-1952	Name	Profit Rank 1950-1952
Air Products & Chemicals	475	Faberge	211
Allied Products	203	Fairchild Camera & Instrument	561
Amcord	99	Fairchild Industries	509
American Biltrite	474	Fansteel	363
Ametek	233	Fedders	89
Anderson, Clayton	404	Foster Wheeler Corp.	565
Armada Corporation	8	Central Foundry	259
Atlantic Steel	571	Culbro	590
Avon Products	59	General Dynamics	597
Bangor Punta	423	General Instrument Corp.	544
Beckman Instruments	325	General Signal	375
Beech Aircraft	542	Grace, W.R. & Co.	549
Belden Corp.	170	Grolier, Inc.	514
Belding Hemingway	470	Grumman Corp.	385
Bliss & Laughlin Industries	501	Gulf & Western Industries	141

Appendixes

D. Companies in 1000 largest of 1972 but not in 1000 largest 1950, and in
sample of 603.

Name	Profit Rank 1950–1952	Name	Profit Rank 1950–1952
Boeing	424	National Union Electric Corp.	367
Boise Cascade	335	Northrop Corp.	323
Briggs & Stratton	22	Noxell Corp.	7
Carling Brewing Co.	309	Ogden Corp.	595
Cerro Corp.	338	Oxford Industries	479
Cessna Aircraft	519	Parker-Hannifin Corp.	513
Chesebrough-Pond's Inc.	90	Pitney-Bowes, Inc.	357
Collins Radio Co.	483	Polaroid	65
Colt Industries	598	Porter, H.K. Co.	355
CBS	485	Purex Corp.	308
Consolidated Foods	530	Purolator, Inc.	79
Cont. Copper & Steel Ind.	543	Ranco, Inc.	25
Copeland Corp.	91	Rapid-American Corp.	517
Copper Range	420	Rockwell International Corp.	52
Curtis-Wright Corp.	524	Rohr Industries	167
Diebold	445	Royal Crown Cola	36
Dr. Pepper	330	Rubbermaid, Inc.	5
Ethyl	407	Schering-Plough Corp.	296
Halliburton Co.	49	Searle, G.D. & Co.	4
Hammond Corp.	12	Signal Companies	589
Heileman, G. Brewing Co.	29	Signode Corp.	236
Helena Rubinstein	255	Skil Corp.	46
Helme Products	360	Sprague Electric Co.	23
Hercules Incorporated	151	Standard Pressed Steel	86
Heublein Corp.	520	Stone Container Corp.	43
Interpace	379	Sucrest Corporation	545
Kaiser Cement & Gypsum	24	Sundstrand Corp.	254
Kerr-McGee Corp.	417	Tenneco	224
Kidde, Walter & Co.	493	Thiokol Corp.	511
LTV	508	Thomas & Betts Corp.	53
Lehigh Valley Industries	584	Trans Union Corp.	477
Lockheed Aircraft Corp.	518	UMC Industries	397
Marathon Oil	28	United Technologies Corp.	429
Maremont Corp.	241	United Brands Co.	57
Martin Marietta	601	V.F. Corp.	312
Masco Corp.	34	Victor Comptometer Corp.	124
McDonnell Douglas Corp.	155	Walter, Jim Corp.	444
Miles Laboratories	96	Whittaker Corp.	1
Mohawk Rubber Co.	201	Wickes Corp.	166
Monroe Auto Equipment Co.	446	Witco Chemical Corp.	349
Norton-Norwich Products	132	Xerox Corp.	464
Nalco Chemical Co.	55		

258   **Profits in the long run**

E.   Companies in 603 firm sample but in neither the 1,000 largest sample of
     1950 nor the 1,000 largest sample for 1972.

Name	Profit Rank 1950–1952
Adams-Mills	415
Bond Clothing	523
British Petroleum	267
Baldwin	492
Freepont Minerals	42
Foote	195
Giant Portland Cement	95
Giddings Lewis	490
Hazeltine	294
Helene Curtis	466
Howmet	168
Leesona	579
Mississippi Portland Cement	280
Moly Corp.	315
Monarch Machine	286
Pittston	583
Tootsie Roll	98
Standard Kollsman	6
Starrett	432

[7]

ELSEVIER

Research Policy 24 (1995) 233–257

research
policy

(US/

Explaining the attacker's advantage: technological paradigms, organizational dynamics, and the value network [1]

Clayton M. Christensen *, Richard S. Rosenbloom

Harvard University Graduate School of Business Administration, Morgan Hall, Soldiers Field, Boston, MA 02163, USA

(Final version received November 1993)

Abstract

Understanding when entrants might have an advantage over an industry's incumbent firms in developing and adopting new technologies is a question which several scholars have explained in terms of technological capabilities or organizational dynamics. This paper proposes that the value network—the context within which a firm competes and solves customers' problems—is an important factor affecting whether incumbent or entrant firms will most successfully innovate. In a study of technology development in the disk drive industry, the authors found that incumbents led the industry in developing and adopting new technologies of every sort identified by earlier scholars —at component and architectural levels; competency-enhancing and competency-destroying; incremental and radical—as long as the technology addressed customers' needs within the value network in which the incumbents competed. Entrants led in developing and adopting technologies which addressed user needs in different, emerging value networks. It is in these innovations, which disrupted established trajectories of technological progress in established markets, that attackers proved to have an advantage. The rate of improvement in product performance which technologists provide may exceed the rate of improvement demanded in established markets. This mismatch between trajectories enables firms entering emerging value networks subsequently to attack the industry's established markets as well.

1. Introduction

From the earliest studies of innovation, scholars exploring factors influencing the rate and direction of technological change have sought to distinguish between innovations launching new directions in technology—'radical' change—and those making progress along established paths—

* Corresponding author. Tel. 617-495-6723.
[1] The authors gratefully acknowledge the financial suppport of the Harvard Business School Division of Research.

often called 'incremental' innovations. In an empirical study of a series of novel processes in petroleum refining, for example, John Enos [19, p. 299] found that half of the economic benefits of new technology came from process improvements introduced after a new technology was commercially established. Continuing this pattern, and borrowing Thomas Kuhn's [26] notion of scientific 'paradigms', Giovanni Dosi [17, p. 147] distinguished between 'normal' modes of technological progress—which propel a product's progress along a defined, established path—and the introduction of new 'technological paradigms'.

234   *C.M. Christensen, R.S. Rosenbloom / Research Policy 24 (1995) 233-257*

Dosi characterizes a technological paradigm as a 'pattern of solution of selected technological problems, based on selected principles derived from natural sciences and on selected material technologies' (p. 152). New paradigms represent discontinuities in trajectories of progress which were defined within earlier paradigms. They tend to redefine the very meaning of 'progress', and point technologists toward new classes of problems as the targets of ensuing 'normal' technology development.

The question examined by Dosi—how new technologies are selected and retained—is closely related to the question of why firms succeed or fail as beneficiaries of such changes. Chandler [7, p. 79] has shown that, in a variety of industries, leading firms have prospered for extended periods by exploiting a series of incremental technological innovations built upon their established organizational and technical capabilities. When challenged by radically different technologies, however, dominant incumbents frequently lag behind aggressive entrants, sometimes with fatal consequences to their established businesses. Students of innovation have long sought to understand the circumstances that will determine the outcomes under such conditions [13]. Richard Foster [20] argues that there is an 'attacker's advantage' in bringing new technologies to market, which incumbents must act to offset.

To explain that advantage, most studies have focused on two sets of factors: (1) the characteristics or magnitude of the technological change relative to the capabilities of incumbent and entrant firms, and (2) the managerial processes and organizational dynamics through which entrant and incumbent firms respond to such changes. We undertake to expand those explanations by arguing that the success and failure of entrants and incumbents with respect to strategic technological innovations is largely shaped by three interlocking sets of forces. To the two identified above we add a third, which we call the value network—the context within which the firm identifies and responds to customers' needs, procures inputs and reacts to competitors. Building on Christensen's [8] notion of a nested system of product architectures, we argue that the firm's

competitive strategy, and particularly its past choices of markets to serve, determines its perceptions of economic value in new technology that in turn shape the rewards it will expect to obtain through innovation.

The first two sections of this paper review the two perspectives on innovation mentioned above, and the third presents the concept of nested systems and the value network. In the fourth section, we develop these ideas further by analyzing the series of technological innovations that have underpinned frequent and substantial changes in the market position of leading firms throughout the history of the disk drive industry. The final section summarizes the paper and describes the sorts of innovations in which incumbents or attackers might be expected to enjoy an advantage.

2. Studies focused on the characteristics of a technology in relation to technological capabilities

Upon the emergence of some new technological paradigms, the inability of incumbent practitioners of the prior technology to acquire the capabilities required to compete within the new paradigm is a clear cause of some incumbents' decline. For example, cotton spinners simply lacked the financial, human and technical resources required to compete in synthetic fibers when that radically different technology was brought into the apparel industry by Dupont. Tushman and Anderson [40, p. 439] label such innovations 'competence-destroying', because they destroy the value of the competencies an organization has developed. The relationship between firms' capabilities and different types of technological change has been clarified by Henderson and Clark [24, p. 9]. They note that the core technologies upon which products are generally built are manifest in the components used in a product. Differences between analog and digital circuitry, optical and magnetic recording, and autos powered by electric motors instead of internal combustion engines are reflected in fundamentally different technological concepts embod-

C.M. Christensen, R.S. Rosenbloom / Research Policy 24 (1995) 233–257 235

ied in componentry. A product's design architecture defines the patterns through which components interact with each other. For example, both front-wheel-drive cars and rear-wheel-drive cars employ similar component technologies, but the components interact within the two automobile architectures in quite different ways.

Henderson and Clark propose a four-fold classification of innovations, shown in Fig. 1, according to the degree to which innovations reinforce or diminish the value of a firm's expertise in two respects—componentry and architecture. Incremental changes build upon and reinforce the producer's expertise in both product architecture and component technologies. Modular innovation denotes the introduction of new component technology inserted within an essentially unchanged product architecture, as when an antilock braking system is added to automobile design. Architectural innovation alters the ways that components work together. In the fourth category, radical innovation, a new core technology—for example, using optical fiber instead of metal for communications cables—leads to significant changes in both components and architecture.

The use of a given set of core technologies in a given architecture can be said to constitute the technological paradigm for the class of products. The cost and capabilities of products within a given technological paradigm evolve along a certain trajectory of improvement, generally building upon prior innovations. Within an established paradigm, innovation may either alter the partic-

ular materials and components employed, or the detailed design thereof. The higher in the design hierarchy these changes occur, the more trenchant the consequences [11, p. 235]. A shift to a new technological regime throughout the system (e.g. from electro-mechanical to electronic cash registers) is more profound than a similar shift in a single component (e.g. from LED to liquid crystal display) because new capabilities are required, and the value of established ones may be diminished or eliminated [40, p. 439]. These concepts suggest an ordering of difficulty of technological change to individual incumbent and entrant firms.

The early stages of the emergence of a new technological paradigm are characterized by diverse technical approaches and fluid designs, but once a dominant design has been established [1, p. 40] incumbent firms strengthen their positions by pursuing normal modes of innovation. Henderson and Clark [24, p. 9] predict that in this process, incumbent firms' abilities to develop and employ new component technologies and refine established product architectures will be strengthened and refined, but that their abilities to create novel product architectures will atrophy. Abernathy and Utterback [1] propose that the focus of incumbents' innovative efforts will shift from product to process innovations. Such evolution to normal modes of innovation ill equips successful incumbent firms to succeed when newer technological paradigms emerge—thus giving certain attackers an advantage.

Fig. 1. Types of technological innovation identified by Henderson and Clark [24].

236   *C.M. Christensen, R.S. Rosenbloom / Research Policy 24 (1995) 233–257*

Foster [20] characterized technological change in relation to the trajectory over time of salient attributes (performance, cost, etc.) rather than in terms of technological hierarchies and architectures. He argued that performance, mapped in relation to cumulative engineering effort, follows an S-shaped path as initial exponential improvement encounters diminishing returns. In the terms used above, this improvement path is driven by modular and incremental innovation—generally the result of learning by both producers [25] and users [34]. Foster notes that new paradigms, drawing on different core technologies or employing innovative architectures, may then emerge to challenge established techniques. When viewed in terms of the preferences of established markets, these challenging technologies often display inferior characteristics, and therefore find their earliest application in new or remote market segments where preferences are more closely aligned with the capabilities of the new technology. As normal advances are made in the new technology in its initial market, the new paradigm may return to overtake and surpass established paradigms in the original market as well [9].

The new competencies intrinsically required by new technological paradigms clearly provide part of the explanation for why once-successful firms may fail at such technological transitions. There are, however, innovative phenomena for which a technology-centered perspective cannot account —phenomena in which the experiences of leading incumbent firms facing the same technological transition have been shown to be very different. For example, the advent of radial tires brought opportunity to some tire-makers and disaster to others [15], and when electronics transformed office information equipment, Burroughs prospered, National Cash Register struggled and eventually triumphed, and Addressograph was destroyed [36]. In these and many other examples, some incumbent firms were able to muster the resources and skills to develop competitive capability in the new technology in question, while competing firms were unable to do so.

Attempts to explain these phenomena have elicited a second line of research, in which another set of scholars have used the dynamics and culture of the organization as their root cause explanatory variable. Rather than asking what types of technological changes are most difficult for incumbent firms to manage, these scholars take a given technology and examine the organizational dynamics which may explain why some incumbent firms successfully develop the capabilities required in the new technology, while other, similar organizations seem unable to do so.

3. Studies of the organizational dynamics of technological innovation

Clark [12] and Henderson and Clark [24, p. 9] have each postulated that once a new technological paradigm has become established, an organization's attention tends to shift to the sorts of incremental and modular innovations which drive performance and cost improvement within that paradigm. Groups within the engineering organization are chartered to focus on improvements to particular components, and the pattern of interactions amongst these groups tends to mirror the way the components themselves interact within the product's architecture. The organizational structure facilitates improvements at the component level and refinements in the interaction amongst components within the architectural paradigm. Conversely, such organizations can lose their capabilities to develop new architectural technologies because their positions in maturing markets do not require such capabilities to be exercised and honed. For example, RCA and Ampex had access to capabilities that would have made them contenders in VCR manufacture, but strongly held beliefs and inappropriate organizational structures frustrated their strategic commitments to do so [38,22]. Other detailed case studies of paradigmatic industry transitions in photolithographic equipment [23], video recording [37] and medical imaging [29] demonstrate that the structure, culture and dynamics of the incumbent's organization can modulate its engagement with a new technological paradigm.

Schein [39] argues that a work group's success in problem-solving contributes to the consensus about the best approach to problem-solving. Re-

C.M. Christensen, R.S. Rosenbloom / Research Policy 24 (1995) 233–257   237

peated success strengthens such beliefs until it is no longer necessary to explicitly decide on the approach; the decision is made by cultural fiat. The stronger and more sustained the firm's success, the stronger these culturally embedded, 'pre-determined' decisions will become. When key choices are made by culture rather than by explicit decision, an organization's ability to respond to new technologies becomes circumscribed: it becomes difficult for insiders to perceive that such decisions are even being made— and they therefore become very difficult to alter. For example, Henderson [23] found that engineers of photolithographic aligners steeped in one particular architectural technology perspective were not even able to see what was different about a superior competitive machine when they examined it. Also in a study of development projects in a single firm, Maidique and Zirger [27] found that technical teams tended to apply historically successful approaches to new problems until they failed badly. Failure forced reappraisal and development of new approaches which, when successful, became incorporated in the culture.

Another factor affecting an organization's perceptions of the returns obtainable through different sorts of innovations is its economic structure, which becomes shaped and hardened through its competitive experience. This is often reflected in its patterns of integration [21,33]. For example, for more than half a century, National Cash Register (NCR) produced a wide variety of electromechanical cash registers and accounting machines—some models containing as many as 10000 parts—at its huge Dayton, Ohio, headquarters complex. To assure adequate, cost-effective and timely supply of necessary components, NCR created an extensive vertically integrated manufacturing organization. It took these products to market through a direct sales force, and supported its vast customer base with a highly effective field service organization. When emerging microelectronics technologies rendered NCR's mechanical calculating technologies obsolete, acquiring the requisite electrical engineering expertise was the simplest of the barriers to innovation NCR faced: engineers could be hired. Much more difficult were the tasks of dismantling large and

powerful organizational units which had once been keys to NCR's competitive success, and of terminating old patterns of organizational interaction and communication which had once been effective and efficient, and forging new patterns in their stead [36].

These phenomena support the widespread observation that technical progress is largely path dependent—that established firms are more likely to "search in zones that are closely related to their existing skills and technologies" [30]. It is not just that a firm's technological expertise is shaped through its experience. The technological capabilities its engineers are able to perceive, pursue and develop can be limited by its culture and its organizational structure, even though the technological expertise per se may not be beyond the reach of the firm's human and financial resources.

So far, we have identified two broad classes of explanations for why attackers may hold the upper hand at points of paradigmatic technological change. Both relate to capabilities. At the first level, the nature or sheer magnitude of a new technology may make it impossible for incumbents to succeed. At a deeper level, we see that the structure and dynamics of an organization may facilitate or impede a firm's efforts to overcome the technological barriers which scholars using the first perspective cite as the driver of incumbents' fortunes.

Christensen's [8] research into the history of technological innovations in the rigid disk drive industry, however, indicates that just as organizational dynamics can affect an organization's ability to develop the requisite technological capabilities, its position in the marketplace may profoundly affect its organizational dynamics—which in turn drives the sorts of technologies a firm can and cannot develop successfully. This research suggests that successful incumbents' engagements in the marketplace and the influence of those engagements in creating informational asymmetries may determine their relative willingness to make strategic commitments to the development and commercialization of new technology. This mechanism is described conceptually in the following section. The history of the disk drive in-

238   *C.M. Christensen, R.S. Rosenbloom / Research Policy 24 (1995) 233-257*

dustry, in which the following framework is grounded, is then summarized.

4. Nested hierarchies and value networks

The viewpoint that differences in firms' market positions drive differences in how they assess the economics of alternative technological investments is rooted in the notion that products are systems comprised of components which relate to each other in a designed architecture. This is an established concept in studies of innovation [28,2]. It is important to note, however, that each component can also be viewed as a system, comprising sub-components whose relationships to each

other are also defined by a design architecture. Furthermore, the end-product may also be viewed as a component within a system-of-use, relating to other components within an architecture defined by the user. In other words, products which at one level can be viewed as complex architected systems act as components in systems at a higher level. Viewed in these terms, a given system-of-use comprised a hierarchically nested set of constituent systems and components.

This is illustrated in Fig. 2 by the example of a typical management information system (MIS) for a large organization. The architecture of the MIS ties together various 'components'—a mainframe computer; peripheral equipment such as line printers, tape and disk drives; software; a large,

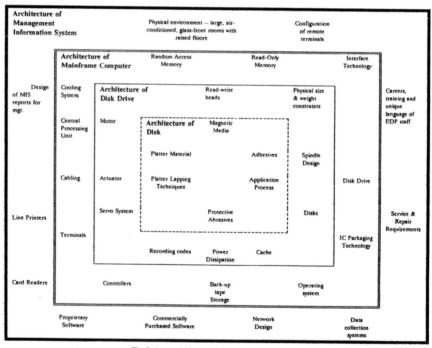

Fig. 2. A nested hierarchy of product architectures.

C.M. Christensen, R.S. Rosenbloom / Research Policy 24 (1995) 233–257   239

air-conditioned room with cables running under a raised floor; a staff of data processing professionals whose training and language are unique. At the next level, the mainframe computer is itself an architected system, comprising components such as a central processing unit, multi-chip pack-

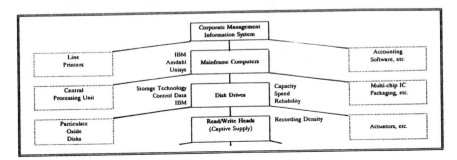

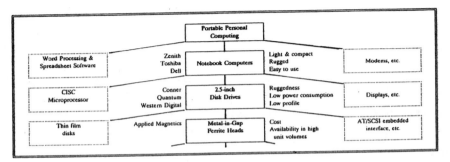

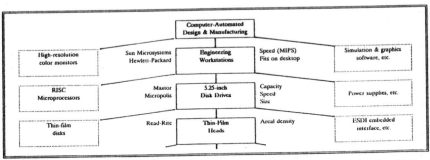

Fig. 3. Examples of three value networks: a corporate MIS system, portable personal computing, and CAD/CAM (dated approximately 1989).

ages and circuit boards, RAM circuits, terminals, controllers, disk drives and other peripherals, and telescoping down still further, the disk drive is a system whose components include a motor, actuator, spindle, disks, heads and controller. In turn, the disk itself can be analyzed as a system composed of an aluminum platter, magnetic material, adhesives, abrasives, lubricants and coatings.

Although the goods and services which constitute the system of use illustrated in Fig. 2 may all be made or provided within a single, extensively integrated corporation such as AT&T or IBM, most of these goods and services are tradeable—especially in more mature markets. This means that, while Fig. 2 is drawn to describe the nested physical architecture of a product system, it also implies the existence of a nested network of producers and markets through which the tradeable architected components at each level are made and sold to integrators at the next higher level in the system. For example, firms which are the architects and assemblers of disk drives—such as Quantum, Conner Peripherals and Maxtor—procure read–write heads from a group of firms which specialize in the manufacture of those heads, disks from a different set of disk manufacturing firms, and spin motors, actuator motors and cache circuitry from different, unique sets of firms. Firms which design and assemble computers at the next higher level may buy their integrated circuits, terminals, disk drives, IC packaging and power supplies from unique sets of firms focused upon manufacturing and supplying those particular products. We call this nested commercial system a value network. Three illustrative value networks for computing applications are shown in Fig. 3. The top network depicts the commercial infrastructure which creates the corporate MIS system-of-use depicted in Fig. 2. The middle network depicts a portable personal computing value network, while the bottom one represents a computer automated design/computer automated manufacturing (CAD/CAM) value network. These depictions are drawn only to convey the concept of how networks are bounded and may differ from each other, and are not meant to represent their complete structure.

The scope and boundaries of a value network

are defined by the dominant technological paradigm and the corresponding technological trajectory [17, p. 147] employed at the higher levels of the network. As Dosi suggests, the very definition of value is a function of the dominant technological paradigm in the ultimate system of use in the value network. The metrics by which value is assessed will therefore differ across networks. Specifically, associated with each network is a unique rank-ordering of the importance of various performance attributes, which rank-ordering differs from that employed in other value networks. As illustrated in Fig. 3, this means that parallel value networks, each built around a different technological paradigm and trajectory, may exist within the same broadly defined industry. Note how each value network exhibits a very different rank ordering of important product attributes, as shown at the right of the center column of component boxes. In the top-most value network, performance of disk drives is measured in terms of capacity, speed and reliability. In the portable computing value network depicted beneath it, important performance attributes are ruggedness, power consumption and physical size.

Although many of the constituent architected components in these different systems-of-use carry the same labels (each network involves read–write heads, disk drives, RAM circuits, printers, software, etc.), the nature of components used in the three networks is quite different. Generally, there is a set of competing firms, each of which has its own value chain [32], associated with each box in the network diagram. Often, the firms which supply the products and services used in each network are different, as illustrated by the listings of firms to the left of the center column of component boxes in Fig. 3.

Finally, we note that the juxtaposed depiction of value networks in Fig. 3 represents their structure at a given moment. As will be shown below, the value network is not a static structure—it can be highly dynamic. The rates of performance improvement which manufacturers of the constituent components are able to achieve may exceed the rate of improvement in performance demanded by downstream users within a value

C.M. Christensen, R.S. Rosenbloom / Research Policy 24 (1995) 233–257   241

network. This enables technologies which may initially have been confined to one value network to migrate into other networks as well. In addition, the rank orderings of performance attributes which define the boundaries of a network may change over time.

The position of a given established producer within a value network—the pathways it is supplying through downstream markets and producers to ultimate users, and its upstream supply network—therefore influences, and even defines to a considerable degree, the nature of the incentives associated with different opportunities for technological innovation which are perceived by the firm's managers. For example, the value placed on certain attributes of an automotive engine will differ depending upon whether the engine is destined for a delivery van, a family sedan, or an Indy 500 racing car. Since value and product performance are defined differently in these instances, we suggest that each of these vehicles is associated with a unique value network.

In another example, throughout the 1970s, Xerox Corporation's product and customer base was dominated by large, high-speed plain paper copiers used in large, central copying centers. It sold products direct to its customers, and supported them through an extensive, capable field service organization. Speed (pages per minute), resolution and cost per copy were among the most important of the performance attributes in that market. Technological improvements which enhanced these aspects of performance were of great value to Xerox, because they helped defend an established, profitable business. In general, few infrastructural investments were required to realize value from such innovations. Products embodying these innovations could be sold and serviced through established capabilities without having to build a different customer base. Often they could be produced in existing facilities.

On the other hand, simplicity, low machine cost, small size and relative ease of self-service are attributes which, though of great potential value in other value networks dominated by alternative technological paradigms, were accorded less worth within Xerox's value network. From an engineering standpoint, they could generally be obtained only by sacrificing along other, more important performance dimensions like speed and per-copy costs, and therefore were not viewed as improvements by Xerox's most important customers. Furthermore, they did not enhance the value of the company's downstream investments in direct sales, service and financing. Commercializing the sorts of component and architectural technologies associated with these attributes would have entailed for Xerox the expense in time and money of creating new market applications for photocopying, and new channels of distribution. In other works, Xerox's position in its value network, skewed its perceptions of return and risk associated with a marginal dollar of investment toward those technologies which addressed downstream needs in its own value network.

The position of a potential entrant to the photocopying value network could bias its perception of risks and rewards in just the opposite fashion. The costs and risks of replicating parallel and competitive capabilities throughout Xerox's large/fast copier value network made development of technologies for small copiers, and the creation of a new small business and office-based copying value network, a much more attractive option for entrants like Canon.

In this example of two photocopying value networks, note that the boundaries of such networks may not coincide with what marketers call 'market segments'. For example, one might well regard small businesses as a different market segment than large corporations, but some of the former will buy high-performance copiers for particular needs, while the latter may buy smaller copiers for distributed use in office areas throughout their facilities. The rank-ordering of preferred attributes (the definition of what constitutes improved product performance) will differ according to the application sought by each type of buyer, thus giving rise to two distinct systems of use, and hence two value networks.

We argue that both the perceived attractiveness of a technological opportunity and the degree of difficulty a producer will encounter in exploiting it are determined, among other factors,

242   *C.M. Christensen, R.S. Rosenbloom / Research Policy 24 (1995) 233–257*

by the firm's position in the relevant value network. As firms gain experience within a given network, they are likely to develop their capabilities, structures and cultures to 'fit' that position better by meeting that network's distinctive requirements. Manufacturing volumes, the slope of ramps to volume production, product development cycle times and organizational consensus about who the customer is, and what the customer needs, may differ substantially from one value network to the next. Competitors may therefore become progressively less well suited to compete in other networks. Their abilities and the incentives to create new market applications for their technology—giving rise to new value networks—may atrophy. While successful incumbents will become more cognizant of relevant information pertaining to the networks in which they compete, they will have greater difficulty acquiring and assessing information about others. The longer the firm has been in a given position, and the more successful it has been, the stronger these effects are likely to be. Hence it faces significant barriers to mobility [6]—barriers to those innovations whose intrinsic value is greatest within networks other than those with which it is already engaged.

These considerations provide a third dimension for analyzing technological innovation. In addition to required capabilities inherent in the technology and in the innovating organization, we argue that one should examine the innovation's implications for the relevant value network. The key consideration is whether the performance attributes implicit in the innovation will be valued within networks already served by the innovator, or whether other networks must be addressed or new ones created in order to realize value for the innovation.

In the case of the disk drive industry to date, one observes that most architectural innovations have imparted attributes to products which appealed to different intermediate buyers and end users from the ones which established firms were already serving. In other words, they constituted new technological paradigms, which were initially rejected within established value networks, but enabled the emergence of new ones. Component innovations, on the other hand, have generally addressed the needs of existing customers and downstream users. Established firms have historically excelled at component-level innovations, while new entrants generally succeeded at architectural innovations. We contend that the manifest strength of established firms in component innovation and their weakness in architectural innovation—and the opposite manifest strengths and weaknesses of entrant firms—are consequences not of differences in technological or organizational capabilities between incumbent and entrant firms, but of their positions in the industry's different value networks. Indeed, established disk drive manufacturers were the industry leaders in every sort of innovation—incremental, modular and architectural; competency-enhancing and competency-destroying—which addressed the needs of downstream actors in their value network, and they lagged behind the industry, in developing (or often failed to develop altogether) those technologies which addressed performance needs in other value networks. Details of this history of incumbent and entrant firms' successes and failures in the face of different types technological changes in the disk drive industry are recounted in the following section.

5. Technological history of the rigid disk drive industry [1]

Disk drives are magnetic information storage and retrieval devices used with most types of computers and a range of other products, such as high speed digital reprographic devices and medical imaging equipment. The principal components of most disk drives are: the disk, which is a substrate coated with magnetic material format-

---

[1] The following section draws upon a recent study of the industry by one of the authors (Christensen, 1992, [8]). The database rests on field-based studies of six leading disk drive manufacturers, which historically have accounted for over 70% of industry revenues, and detailed technical specifications of every disk drive model announced in the world between 1975 and 1990. Technical data come from *Disk / Trend Report, Electronic Business Magazine*, and manufacturers' product specification sheets.

ted to store information in concentric tracks; the read–write head, which is a tiny electromagnet positioned over the spinning disk which, when energized, orients the polarity of the magnetic material on the disk immediately beneath it; a motor which drives the rotation of the disk; an actuator mechanism which positions the head precisely over the track on which data is to be read or written; electronic circuitry and software, which control the drive's operation and enable it to communicate with the computer. These components work together within a particular product architecture. From the industry's inception there have been significant technological changes both within each component and in the architecture.

Magnetic recording and storage of digital information was pioneered with the earliest commercial computer systems, which used reels of coated mylar tape. IBM introduced the use of rigid rotating disks in 1956 and flexible ('floppy') disks in 1971. The dominant design for what are now called 'hard' drives was provided by the IBM 'Winchester' project, introduced as the Model 3340 in 1973.

While IBM pioneered in disk drive technology and produced drives to meet its own needs, an independent disc drive industry grew to serve two distinct markets. A few firms developed the plug-compatible market [PCM] in the 1960s, selling to IBM customers. Although most of IBM's initial rivals in the computer market were vertically integrated, the emergence in the 1970s of smaller, non-integrated computer makers spawned an OEM market for disk drives as well. By 1976 the output of rigid disk drives was valued at about $1 billion, in which captive production accounted for 50% of unit production, and PCM and OEM segments each accounted for about 25%.

The next dozen years tell a remarkable story of rapid growth, market turbulence, and technology-driven 'creative destruction'. The value of drives produced rose to more than $13 billion by 1989. By the mid-1980s the PCM market had become insignificant, while OEM output grew to represent two-thirds of world production. Of the 17 firms which populated the industry in 1976—all

of which were relatively large, diversified corporations—fourteen had failed and exited or had been acquired by 1989. During this period an additional 124 firms entered the industry, and exactly 100 of those also failed. Some 60% of the producers remaining by 1989 had entered the industry as de novo start-ups since 1976. All this took place within the context of the established core technology, i.e. magnetic digital recording. [2] However, components changed, and so did architectures, and therein lies the story.

Successive waves of technological change permitted dramatic improvements in performance at constantly decreasing cost. The impact on the industry of innovations in componentry and architecture was very different. In general, component innovations, such as thin-film heads, embedded servo systems and run length limited [RLL] recording codes, were developed and introduced by well-established incumbents. Component innovations sustained established trajectories of performance improvement within each architecture —an annual increase in capacity per drive which often approached 50%. Several waves of architectural innovation swept through the industry in this period, usually introduced by entrant firms. In contrast to the role played by component innovation, these new architectures often disrupted established trajectories of performance improvement, and redefined the parameters along which performance was assessed. For example, in the architecture used for portable computers, size, weight, ruggedness and power consumption, were all important attributes of performance. None of these attributes were critical in the architectures used in mainframe or minicomputers. These parallel streams of component and architectural innovation were symmetrical in one respect: new components were first introduced in the context of established architectures, while new architectures generally embodied proven componentry.

Both types of innovation were important to the growth and development of the industry in the

---

[2] An alternative core technology, digital optical recording, was widely perceived as a potential substitute through the 1980s, but by 1992 had made few substantial inroads.

244   *C.M. Christensen, R.S. Rosenbloom / Research Policy 24 (1995) 233–257*

1980s, but it is only in architectural innovation—and a particular class of architectural innovation at that—that attackers proved to have any advantage. Entrants rarely tried to pioneer innovative components, and most that did failed. In contrast, the predominant pattern for new architectures was for the innovation—and subsequent market leadership in the next generation—to belong to an entrant firm.

Until the late 1970s, 14-inch drives were the only rigid drive architectures available, and nearly all were sold to mainframe computer manufacturers. The hard disk capacity provided in the median priced, typically configured mainframe computer system in 1976 was about 170 megabytes (Mb) per computer. The hard disk capacity supplied with the typical mainframe increased at a 15% annual rate over the next 15 years. At the

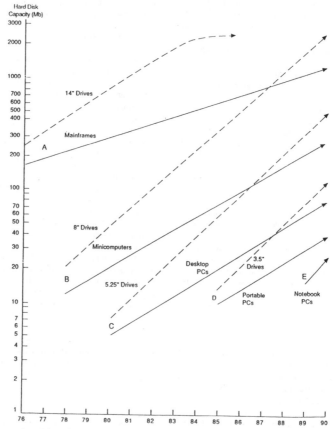

Fig. 4. A comparison of the trajectories of disk capacity demanded per computer, vs. capacity provided in each architecture.

C.M. Christensen, R.S. Rosenbloom / Research Policy 24 (1995) 233–257   245

Table 1
A comparison of the average attributes of 8-inch drives introduced in 1981 by established vs. entrant firms

Attributes	Level of performance		Annual rate of performance improvement (%)	
	Established firms	Entrant firms	Established firms	Entrant firms
Capacity (Mb)	19.2	19.1	61.2	57.4
Areal density (Mb sq in.)	3.213	3.104	35.5	36.7
Access time (milliseconds)	46.1	51.6	−8.1	−9.1
Price per megabyte	$143.03	$147.73	−58.8	−61.9

Source: Analysis of *Disk / Trend Report* data, from Christensen (1992, [8]).

same time, the capacity of the average 14-inch drives introduced for sale each year increased at a faster 22% rate, reaching beyond the main-frame market to the large scientific and super-computer markets. This is shown in Fig. 4 [3].

Between 1978 and 1980, several entrant firms —Shugart Associates, Micropolis, Priam and Quantum—developed new architectural families of 8-inch drives with 10, 20, 30 and 40 Mb capacity. These drives were of no interest to mainframe computer manufacturers, who at that time were demanding drives with 300–400 Mb capacity. These 8-inch entrants therefore sold their small, low-capacity drives into a new application—minicomputers. [4] The customers—Wang, DEC, Data General, Prime and Hewlett Packard—were not the firms which manufactured mainframes, and their customers often used software which was substantially different from programs used by mainframe computer users. In other words, 8-inch drives found their way into a different value network, leading to a different system-of-use. Al-though initially the cost per megabyte of capacity of 8-inch drives was higher than that of 14-inch products, these new customers were willing to pay a premium for other attributes of the 8-inch drive which were important to them—especially its smaller size. This attribute had little value to mainframe users.

Once the use of 8-inch drives became estab-lished in minicomputers, the hard disk capacity

shipped with the median-priced minicomputer grew about 25% per year—a trajectory driven by the ways in which minicomputers came to be used in their value networks. At the same time, how-ever, the 8-inch drivemakers found they could increase the capacity of their products at over 40% per year—nearly double the rate demanded by their original 'home' minicomputer market. In consequence, by the mid-1980s, 8-inch drive mak-ers were able to provide the capacities required for lower-end mainframe computers, and by that point, unit volumes had grown significantly so that the cost per megabyte of 8-inch drives had declined below that of 14-inch products. Other advantages of 8-inch drives also become appar-ent. For example, the same percentage mechani-cal vibration in an 8-inch drive caused the head to vary its absolute position over the disk much less than it would in a 14-inch product. Within a 3–4 year period, therefore, 8-inch drives began to invade an adjacent, established value network, substituting for 14-inch drives in the lower-end mainframe computer market.

When 8-inch products began to penetrate the mainframe computer market, most of the estab-lished manufacturers of 14-inch drives began to fail. Two thirds of these manufacturers never introduced an 8-inch model. The one-third of the 14-inch drive manufacturers which did introduce 8-inch drives did so with about a 2-year lag be-hind the 8-inch entrant manufacturers.

Interviews with industry participants and anal-ysis of product data suggest that destruction of engineering capabilities by the new architecture, as posited by Henderson and Clark [24, p. 9] and Tushman and Anderson [40, p. 439], does not explain the failure of the established producers.

---

[3] A summary of the data and procedures used to generate Fig. 4 is included in the Appendix.
[4] The minicomputer market was not new in 1978, but it was a new application for Winchester-technology disk drives.

246   *C.M. Christensen, R.S. Rosenbloom / Research Policy 24 (1995) 233–257*

Table 1, for example, shows that the population of 8-inch models introduced by the established firms in 1981 possessed performance attributes which, on average, were nearly identical to the average of those introduced that year by the entrant firms. In addition, the rates of improvement (measured between 1979 and 1983) in those attributes were stunningly similar between established and entrant firms. [5] This evidence supports the view that the 14-inch drive manufacturers were fully capable of producing the new architecture; their failure resulted from delay in making the necessary strategic commitments. By 1981 the entrants had already created barriers to entry around their new value network, and were surmounting the barriers which had protected the old one.

What explains the incumbents' strategic lag? Interviews with marketing and engineering executives close to these companies suggest that the established 14-inch drive manufacturers were held captive by customers within their value network. Mainframe computer manufacturers did not need an 8-inch drive. In fact, they explicitly did not want it—wanting instead drives with increased capacity at a lower cost per megabyte. The 14-inch drive manufacturers were listening and responding to their established customers, and their customers—in a way that was not apparent either to the disk drive manufacturers or their customers—were pulling them along a trajectory (22% capacity growth in a 14-inch platform) which would ultimately prove fatal.

This finding is similar to the phenomena observed by Bower (1970, [3], p. 254), who saw that

explicit customer demands have tremendous power as a source of impetus in the resource allocation process. 'When the discrepancy (the problem to be solved by a proposed investment) was defined in terms of cost and quality, the projects languished. In all four cases, the definition process moved toward completion when capacity to meet sales was perceived to be inadequate .... In short, pressure from the market reduces both the probability and the cost of being wrong'. Although Bower's specific reference is to manufacturing capacity, we believe that we observed the same fundamental phenomenon which he saw: the power of the known needs of known customers in marshalling and directing the investments of a firm.

Figure 4 also maps the disparate trajectories of performance improvement demanded in the subsequent, sequentially-emerging computer product categories which defined market segments for the disk drive suppliers, versus the performance made available within each successive architecture by changes in component technology and refinements in system design. Again, the solid lines emanating from points A, B, C, D and E measure the disk drive capacity provided with the median-priced computer in each category, while the dotted lines emanating from the same points measure the average capacity of all disk drives introduced for sale in each architecture for each year. Brief accounts of these transitions are presented below.

5.1. The advent of 5.25-inch drives

In 1980, Seagate Technology introduced the next architectural generation, 5.25-inch drives, as shown in Fig. 4. Their capacities of 5 and 10 Mb were of no interest to minicomputer manufacturers, who were demanding drives of 40 and 60 Mb from their suppliers. Seagate and other firms which entered with 5.25-inch drives in the 1980–1983 period (such as Miniscribe, Computer Memories and International Memories) had to pioneer new applications for their products—primarily desktop personal computers. Once the use of hard drives was established in the desktop PC application, the disk capacity shipped with the

---

[5] This result is very different from that observed by Henderson (1988, [23]), where the new-architecture aligners produced by the established manufacturers were inferior on a performance basis to those produced by the entrant firms. One possible reason for these different results is that the successful entrants in the photolithographic aligner industry which Henderson studied brought with them a well-developed body of technological knowledge and experience which had been developed and refined in other markets. In the case studied here, none of the entrants brought such well-developed knowledge with them. Most, in fact, were de novo start-ups comprised of managers and engineers who had defected from established drive manufacturing firms.

C.M. Christensen, R.S. Rosenbloom / Research Policy 24 (1995) 233–257   247

median-priced desktop PC increased about 25% per year. Again, the technology improved at nearly twice the rate demanded in the new market—the capacity of new 5.25-inch drives increased about 50% per year between 1980 and 1990. As in the 8- for 14-inch substitution, the first firms to produce 5.25-inch drives were entrants; on average, the established firms lagged the entrants by 2 years. By 1985, 50% of the firms which had produced 8-inch drives had introduced 5.25-inch models. The other 50% never made the transition. Growth in 5.25-inch drives occurred in two waves. The first was in the establishment of a new application for rigid disk drives—desktop computing, where product attributes which had been relatively unimportant in established applications were highly valued. The second wave was in substituting for the use of larger drives in established minicomputer and mainframe computer markets, as the rapidly increasing capacity of 5.25-inch drives intersected the more slowly-growing trajectories of capacity demanded in these markets. Of the four leading 8-inch drive-makers listed above, only Micropolis survived to become a significant manufacturer of 5.25-inch drives, and that was accomplished only with Herculean managerial effort.

5.2. The pattern is repeated: the emergence of the 3.5-inch drive

The 3.5-inch drive was first developed in 1984 by Rodime, a Scottish entrant. Sales of this architecture were not significant, however, until Conner Peripherals, a Seagate/Miniscribe spin-off, started shipping product in 1987. Conner had developed a small, lightweight drive architecture, which was much more rugged than its 5.25-inch ancestors, by handling functions electronically which had previously been managed with mechanical parts, and by using microcode to replace functions which had previously been addressed electronically. Nearly all of Conner's record first-year revenues of $113 million came from Compaq Computer, which had funded most of Conner's start-up with a $30 million investment. The Conner drives were used primarily in a new application—portable and laptop machines, in addition

to 'small footprint' desktop models—where customers were willing to accept lower capacities and higher costs per megabyte in order to get the lighter weight, greater ruggedness and lower power consumption which 3.5-inch drives offered.

Seagate engineers were not oblivious to the coming of the 3.5-inch architecture. [6] By early 1985, less than 1 year after the first 3.5-inch drive was introduced by Rodime and 2 years before Conner Peripherals started shipping its product, Seagate personnel had shown working 3.5-inch prototype drives to customers for evaluation. The initiative for the new drives came from Seagate's engineering organization. Opposition to the program came primarily from the marketing organization and Seagate's executive team, on the grounds that the market wanted higher capacity drives at a lower cost per megabyte and that 3.5-inch drives could never be built at a lower cost per megabyte than 5.25-inch drives.

The customers to whom the Seagate 3.5-inch drives were shown were firms within the value network already served by Seagate: they were manufacturers of full-sized desktop computer systems. Not surprisingly, they showed little interest in the smaller drive. They were looking for capacities of 40 and 60 megabytes for their next generation machines, while the 3.5-inch architecture could only provide 20 Mb—and at higher costs. [7]

In response to these lukewarm reviews from customers, Seagate's program manager lowered his 3.5-inch sales estimates, and the firm's executives canceled the 3.5-inch program. Their reasoning was that the markets for 5.25-inch products were larger, and that the sales generated by spending the engineering effort on new 5.25-inch

---

[6] This information was provided by former employees of Seagate Technology.

[7] This finding is consistent with what Robert Burgelman has observed. He noted that one of the greatest difficulties encountered by corporate entrepreneurs was finding the right 'beta test sites', where products could be interactively developed and refined with customers. Generally, the entrée to the customer was provided to the new venture by the salesman who sold the firm's established product lines. This helped the firm develop new products for established markets, but did not help it identify new applications for its new technology. [5, pp. 76–80].

248   *C.M. Christensen, R.S. Rosenbloom / Research Policy 24 (1995) 233–257*

products would generate greater revenues for the company than would efforts targeted at new 3.5-inch products.

In retrospect, it appears that Seagate executives read the market—at least their own market —very accurately. Their customers were manufacturers and value-added resellers of relatively large-footprint desktop personal computers such as the IBM XT and AT. With established applications and product architectures of their own, these customers saw no commercial value in the reduced size, weight and power consumption, and the improved ruggedness of 3.5-inch products.

Seagate finally began shipping 3.5-inch drives in early 1988—the same year in which the performance trajectory of 3.5-inch drives shown in Fig. 4 intersected the trajectory of capacity demanded in desktop computers. By that time nearly $750 million in 3.5-inch products had been shipped cumulatively in the industry. Interestingly, according to industry observers, as of 1991 almost none of Seagate's 3.5-inch products had been sold to manufacturers of portable/laptop/notebook computers. Seagate's primary customers still were desktop computer manufacturers, and many of its 3.5-inch drives were shipped with frames which permitted them to be mounted in computers which had been designed to accommodate 5.25-inch drives.

The fear of cannibalizing sales of existing products is often cited as a reason why established firms delay the introduction of new technologies. As the Seagate–Conner experience illustrates, however, if new technologies are initially deployed in new market applications, the introduction of new technology may not be an inherently cannibalistic process. When established firms wait until a new technology has become commercially mature in its new applications, however, and launch their own version of the technology only in response to an attack on their home markets, the fear of cannibalization can become a self-fulfilling prophecy.

Although the preceding discussion focused on Seagate's response to the development of the 3.5-inch drive architecture, its behavior was not atypical; by 1988, only 35% of the drive manufacturers which had established themselves making 5.25-inch products for the desktop PC market had introduced 3.5-inch drives. As in earlier product architecture transitions, the barrier to development of a competitive 3.5-inch product does not appear to have been engineering-based. As illustrated in table 1 above for the 14- to 8-inch transition, the new-architecture drives introduced by the incumbent, established firms in the 8- to 5.25 inch and 5.25- to 3.5-inch transitions were fully performance-competitive with the entrants' drives. Rather, it seems that the 5.25-inch drive manufacturers were misled by their customers, who themselves seemed as oblivious as Seagate to the potential benefits and possibilities of the new architecture. These only became apparent in the desktop market after the 3.5-inch products had been proven in a new application.

Table 2 shows that in the 1984–1989 period, when the 3.5-inch form factor was becoming firmly established in portable and laptop applications, Seagate had in no way lost its ability to innovate. It was highly responsive to its own customers. The capacity of its drives increased at about 30% per year—a perfect match with the pace of market demand and a testament to the firm's focus on the desktop computing market, rather than the markets above or below it. Seagate also introduced new models of 5.25-inch drives at an accel-

Table 2

Indicators of the pace of Seagate engineering activity within the 525-inch architecture, 1984–1987

	No. of new models announced	No. of new models as % of No. of models offered in prior year	% of new models equipped with thin-film disks	SCSI interface introduction	RLL codes introduction
1984	3	50	0		
1985	4	57	25	X	
1986	7	78	71		X
1987	15	115	100		

Source: Analysis of *Disk / Trend Report* data, from Christensen (1992, [8]).

C.M. Christensen, R.S. Rosenbloom / Research Policy 24 (1995) 233-257   249

erated rate during this period—models which employed many of the most advanced component technologies such as thin film disks, voice-coil actuators [8], RLL codes and embedded SCSI interfaces.

Seagate's experience was an archetype of the histories of many of the disk drive industry's leading firms. Its entry strategy employed an innovative architectural design with standard, commercially available components. Its appeal was in an emerging value network—desktop computing. Once it was established in that value network, Seagate's technological attention shifted toward innovations in component technology, as the work of Henderson and Clark [24, p. 9] suggests that it would. This is because improvements in component technology and refinements in system design —that is, modular and incremental innovations (see Fig. 1)—were the primary drivers of performance improvement within its value network. They were the drivers behind each of the dotted-line technological trajectories plotted in Fig. 4, and were the means by which firms attentive to customers' demands for improved performance addressed those needs. It is not surprising, therefore, that throughout the history of the industry, the leading innovators in the development and use of component technology were the industry's established firms, as we describe in the following section.

5.3. Leadership in component technology development by incumbent firms

As in other data processing sub-systems, disk drive technology advanced rapidly through the 1970s and 1980s, increasing drive capacity and performance, and reducing size and cost, at rates that would have been astonishing in almost any other industry. One of the primary technical trends behind increasing capacity was the relentless increase in the recording density achieved—a trend which was largely driven by improvements in component technology. The earliest drives could hold only a few kilobytes of data per square inch of drive surface; by 1967 this had risen to 50

kilobytes; within 6 years, the first Winchester design held 1.7 megabytes per square inch; by 1981 the IBM 3380 boasted a density greater than 12 Mb per square inch. In 1990, densities of 50 Mb per square inch were common, marking a 3000-fold increase in 35 years. As in other applications of magnetic technology (e.g., video recording) greater density led to smaller, less expensive devices. Costs were also driven down by a constellation of incremental improvements in components and materials, by manufacturing experience, and by huge scale increases in demand.

In the 1970s, some manufacturers sensed that they were approaching the limits of recording density obtainable from conventional particulate iron oxide disk coating technology, and began studying the use of thin film metal coatings to sustain improvements in recording density. While the use of thin-film coatings was then highly developed in the integrated circuit industry, its application to magnetic disks presented substantial challenges because of the disks' greater surface area and the need to make the relatively soft metal coatings as durable as the much harder iron oxide coatings. Industry participants interviewed by Christensen estimate that development of thin film disk technology required approximately 8 years, and that the pioneers of thin film disk technology—IBM, Control Data, Digital Equipment, Storage Technology and Ampex— each spent over $50 million in that effort. Between 1984 and 1986, a total of 34 firms—roughly two to three times the number of producers active in 1984—introduced drives with thin-film coatings. The overwhelming majority of these were established industry incumbents. Nearly all new entrants which used thin film disks in their initial products failed to establish themselves in the industry.

The standard recording head design employed small coils of wire wound around gapped ferrite (iron oxide) cores. A primary factor limiting recording density was the size and precision of the gaps forming electromagnets on the head. Ferrite heads had to be ground mechanically to achieve desired tolerances, and by 1981 many believed that the limits of precision would soon

----

[8] These were not new to the market, but were new to Seagate.

250 *C.M. Christensen, R.S. Rosenbloom / Research Policy 24 (1995) 233–257*

be reached. As early as 1965, researchers had posited that smaller and more precise electromagnets could be produced by sputtering thin films of metal on the recording head and then using photolithography to etch the electromagnets, thus enabling more precise orientation of smaller magnetic domains on the disk surface. Although thin film photolithography was well-established in the semiconductor industry, its application to recording heads proved extraordinarily difficult. Read–write heads required much thicker films than did integrated circuits, and the surfaces to be coated were often at different levels, and could be inclined.

Burroughs in 1976, IBM in 1979, and other large, integrated, established firms were the first to incorporate thin-film heads successfully in disk drives. In the 1982–1986 period, when over 60 firms entered the rigid disk drive industry, only four of them (all commercial failures) attempted to do so using thin-film heads as a source of performance advantage in their initial products. All other entrant firms—even aggressively performance-oriented firms such as Maxtor and Conner Peripherals—found it preferable to learn their way with ferrite heads before tackling thin-film technology. As was the case with thin-film disks, the introduction of thin-film heads was a resource-intensive challenge which only established firms could handle. IBM spent over $100 million developing its thin film heads, and competing pioneers Control Data and Digital Equip-

ment spent amounts of a similar order of magnitude. The rate of adoption was slow; a decade after Burroughs first established the technology's commercial feasibility, only 15 producers employed thin-film heads. Thin-film technology was costly and difficult to master.

The established firms were the leading innovators not just in undertakings to develop risky, complex and expensive component technologies such as thin film heads and disks, but in literally every component-level innovation. Even in relatively simple but important innovations—such as RLL recording codes (which took the industry from double- to triple-density disks), embedded servo systems, zone-specific recording densities and higher RPM motors—established firms were the successful pioneers, while entrant firms were the technology followers.

5.4. Leadership in architectural technology innovation

As noted above, Henderson and Clark found that in the photolithographic aligner industry attackers consistently had the advantage in architectural innovation. In contrast to their unambiguous findings, and to the clear pattern of component technology leadership by established firms described above, entrant firms led the disk drive industry in the introduction of three of the five new architectural technologies, while established firms led in the other two. The industry's first architectural technology transition was the

Table 3
Number of entrant vs. established firms offering new product architectures

		Number of firms offering one or more models of the new product architecture							
		First year		Second year		Third year		Fourth year	
		No. of firms	Percent	No. of firms	Percent	No. of firms	Percent	No. of firms	Percent
8-inch drives	Entrants	1	100	4	67	6	55	8	62
(1978)	Established	0		2	33	5	45	5	38
	Total	1	100	6	100	11	100	13	100
5.25-inch drives	Entrants	1	50	8	80	8	50	13	54
(1980)	Established	1	50	2	20	8	50	11	46
	Total	2	100	10	100	16	100	24	100
3.5-inch drives	Entrants	1	100	2	67	3	75	4	50
(1983)	Established	0		1	33	1	25	4	50
	Total	1	100	3	100	4	100	8	100

Source: Author's analysis of *Disk / Trend Report* data, reported in Christensen (1992, [8]).

switch from removable disk packs to the fixed-disk Winchester architecture between 1973 and 1980. The subsequent four architectural transitions involved the reduction in disk diameter from 14 to 8, 5.25, 3.5 and 2.5 inches between 1978 and 1990. These four new architectures reduced size by 'shrinking' individual components, by reducing part count, and by re-arranging the way the components interacted with each other in the system design. For example, in the 8-inch drive, a 110 volt AC motor was typically positioned in the corner of the system, and drove the disks by pulleys and a belt. In reducing the size to 5.25-inches, the motor was changed to a 12 volt DC 'pancake' design and positioned beneath the spindle.

Table 3 shows that the 8-, 5.25- and 3.5-inch generations embodied the architectural technolo-

gies which entrant firms pioneered. For example, in 1978 an entrant offered the industry's first 8-inch drive. Within 2 years, six firms were offering 8-inch drives; four of them were entrants. At the end of the second year of the 5.25-inch generation, eight of the ten producers were entrants. A similar pattern characterized the early population of firms offering 3.5-inch drives. Note that these transitions correspond to the movements from point A to points B, C and D in Fig. 4.

There were two significant architectural innovations in the industry's history in which the incumbent firms, and not entrants, were the leading innovators. The first was the substitution of sealed, fixed-disk Winchester-technology 14-inch drives for removable disk-pack drives, which was the first architectural transition after the emergence of a group of independent disk drive manu-

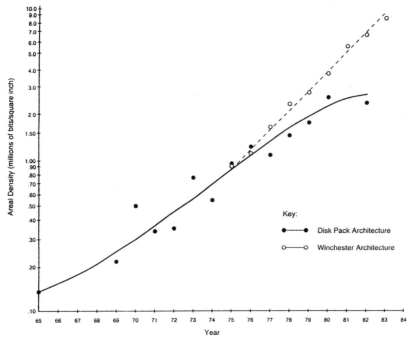

Fig. 5. Impact of Winchester architecture on the average areal density of 14-inch disk drives.

facturers in the 1960s. The first Winchester model was introduced by IBM, an established manufacturer of disk-pack drives, in 1973. The second and third firms to introduce a Winchester-architecture drive were Control Data and Microdata— also established firms—in 1975. Seven of the first eight firms to introduce 14-inch Winchester drives were established manufacturers of the prior architectural generation of disk-pack drives. Entrant firms were the followers in this transition. An indication of why the incumbent leaders successfully maneuvered across this architectural transition is found in Fig. 5, which plots the average recording density for all disk-pack models introduced in the industry each year (the solid black points), and the average density of Winchester-technology drives introduced in the same years (the open circles). Note the contrast between this architectural change and the transitions to 8-, 5.25- and 3.5-inch drives charted in Fig. 4. Whereas those architectural approaches disrupted established trajectories of performance improvement, the 14-inch Winchester architecture sustained the trajectory of improvement which had been established within the disk pack architecture. As a consequence, this new architecture was valued within the same value network as had used the prior-architecture products—in this case, mainframe computers. By listening to their customers, the leading incumbent manufacturers of disk pack drives seem to have been led, rather than misled, in the development of the 14-inch Winchester technology.

Sixteen years later, in 1989, Prairietek Corporation, a spin-off of Miniscribe, introduced a 2.5-inch drive as its first product. Its customers were almost exclusively manufacturers of notebook computers. Conner Peripherals, the leader of the 3.5-inch generation, introduced its own 2.5-inch product in 1990, however, and by 1991 it controlled over 85% of the worldwide 2.5-inch market. [9] Did Conner somehow manage its product development and deployment process differently from its predecessors to help it stay atop this industry?

---

[9] Miniscribe was in bankruptcy proceedings in 1989, and Prairietek declared bankruptcy and ceased operations in 1991.

Again, our interpretation is that it did not. In the three preceding architectural transitions, the new, smaller drives were sold to new customers in new applications—in new value networks. In the transition from 3.5-inch drives sold to laptop computer applications to 2.5-inch drives sold in notebook computers, however, the leading customers were largely the same firms. Toshiba, Zenith, Compaq and Sharp, which were the leading laptop computer manufacturers, became the leading notebook PC makers. Their customers, and the spreadsheet and word processing software they used, were the same. In other words, the system of use was the same; hence, and most importantly, the way disk drive performance was assessed—capacity per cubic inch and per ounce, ruggedness, power consumption, etc.—was unchanged. Whereas attentiveness to established customers led the leaders of earlier disk drive generations to attend belatedly to the deployment of new architectures, in this instance attentiveness to its established customers led Conner through a very smooth transition into 2.5-inch drives. Although the 2.5-inch drive represents a new engineering architecture, it was developed and deployed within the same value network as the 3.5-inch product, and Conner seems to have negotiated this development with competitive agility [10].

---

[10] Burgelman's account (1991, [4]) of Intel Corporation's development of Reduced Instruction Set Computing (RISC) microprocessors can be understood even more clearly in the context of the value network framework. According to those who Burgelman interviewed, chips made with the RISC architecture generally addressed the needs of "a customer base (which was) different than the companies who purchased (Intel's) 486 chips ... a lot of customers who before did not even talk to Intel." (p. 247). RISC's champion within the Intel organization, Les Kohn, had tried but failed to convince management to back the RISC technology. He had failed because "RISC was not an existing business and people were not convinced a market was there" (p. 246). Finally, Kohn decided to present the RISC chip as a coprocessor which enhanced the performance of Intel's 486 chip—as one which addressed the needs of the customers within Intel's primary value network, which was personal computing. Positioned as such, the RISC project got funding. Once it was funded, Kohn was able to begin selling the RISC chip to customers outside the 486 personal computing value network, to the customers who valued RISC's attributes most highly—engineering workstation manufacturers.

C.M. Christensen, R.S. Rosenbloom / Research Policy 24 (1995) 233–257   253

It does not seem from this evidence that the established disk drive manufacturers were constrained to prosper only within the value networks in which they were born. Firms such as Maxtor, Micropolis, Quantum and Conner proved themselves to have remarkable upward mobility, in terms of Fig. 4. Conner, for example, has moved from portable computing upwards to the desktop business computing market and the engineering workstation market. Micropolis and Maxtor are now the major suppliers of 5.25-inch drives to the mainframe market—even the large arrays employed by supercomputer manufacturers such as Thinking Machines. In other words, upward visibility and understanding towards other known, existing value networks seems not to have presented an insurmountable barrier to mobility. The differing slopes of the trajectories of technology supplied vs. performance demanded seem to be what facilitated the mobility of technologies and the firms practising them across the boundaries of value networks. Firms which led in the introduction of the 5.25-inch drive in desktop computing applications, for example, have been able to ride that technological paradigm across network boundaries into minicomputer, and now mainframe and supercomputer value networks.

In observing these firms' attacks across the boundaries of value networks, it is important to note that switching to new architectural paradigms per se was not the difficulty the incumbent firms faced which gave the attackers their advantage. When the new paradigms invaded the earlier established value networks, the leading incumbent firms at each transition quite rapidly introduced architecturally novel products which were fully performance competitive with those of the attackers. To repeat, as long as a technological innovation was valued within the incumbents' value network, they seemed perfectly competent and competitive in developing and introducing that technology—whether it was incremental, modular or architectural, competency enhancing or competency destroying, in character.

The problem established firms seem to have been unable to confront successfully is that of downward vision and mobility, in terms of Fig. 4. Finding new applications for new architectures,

and aggressively entering latent value networks, which necessarily are not well understood, seem to be capabilities which each of these firms exhibited once, upon entry, and then seems to have lost.

One final point about mobility within and across value networks merits mention. It appears, from the history of disk drive manufacturers and their suppliers, that the farther removed a firm is from the ultimate system-of-use which defines the dominant performance paradigm in a value network, the greater is its mobility across networks. For example, the firms which manufacture the aluminum platters on which magnetic material is deposited seem to have been able to sell platters to disk manufacturers regardless of the ultimate value network in which the disks were destined to be used. The firms which coated platters with magnetic material, and sold those completed disks to disk drive manufacturers, seemed more aligned than were their platter suppliers to specific value networks—but not nearly as captive within specific networks as the disk drive companies themselves seem to have been.

6. Conclusions and propositions

The history summarized in Fig. 4 seems to be a relatively clear empirical example of the emergence of a sequence of what Dosi [17, p. 147] calls 'technological paradigms' and their associated new trajectories. At points B, C and D, product performance came to be defined differently, new trajectories were established, and engineers began to focus, within each new paradigm, on new sets of problems. For example, power consumption, ruggedness and weight simply were not on the development agendas of any practitioners of the 14- and 8-inch generations, whereas they became the dominating issues on the technology agendas of every firm competing within the 3.5- and 2.5-inch generations. Interpreting Dosi further, in the light of Henderson and Clark's [24, p. 9] framework, it would appear that in the history of disk drive technology, innovations on the left-hand side of the Fig. 1 matrix—incremental and

254　　　　　　*C.M. Christensen, R.S. Rosenbloom / Research Policy 24 (1995) 233–257*

modular technological changes—would constitute normal technological progress. Note that we would include discontinuous, competency-destroying modular innovations in component technology as elements of this normal progress—because they sustained, rather than redefined, the established technological trajectory. Some innovations on the right-hand side of the Henderson–Clark matrix would also fall within the 'normal' rubric—such as the 14- and 2.5-inch Winchester architectures. Yet in the instances of 8-, 5.25- and 3.5-inch generations, it seems that new architectural technologies alone were sufficient to herald the emergence of a new paradigm.

Each of these new technological paradigms emerged within a new value network—mainframes, minicomputers, desktop PCs and portable computers. The forces which defined the trajectories of performance demanded in each value network tended to be at the broader, higher system-of-use levels in each network—the software used, the data processed, the training level of operators, the locations of use, etc.

Dosi theorized that within an established technological paradigm, the pattern of technological change would become endogenous to the 'normal' economic mechanism. He anticipated, in other words, that there would be a strong fit between customers' demands with respect to the rate and direction of improvement in cost and performance, and producers' abilities to meet those needs. That harmony, governed by market forces, is the fundamental driver of innovation within an established paradigm, according to Dosi's theory. Figure 4 suggests, however, that there seem to be two distinct, independent trajectories at work. The first is a trajectory of product performance improvement demanded in the ultimate system-of-use in each value network—the solid lines in Fig. 4. The second is a trajectory of performance improvement which the technology is able to supply—represented by the dotted lines in Fig. 4. There seems to be no reason why the slopes of these trajectories should be identical: the first is driven by factors at higher system-of-use levels in the value network, while the latter is driven by the inventiveness and ingenuity of scientists and engineers, and the willingness of mar-

keters and managers to make product commitments targeted at existing markets above them.

Likewise, Dosi theorized that the creation of new technological paradigms were events which occurred largely exogenously to the economic system—that institutional forces were largely responsible for their emergence. Our research suggests that although the factors governing selection of a new paradigm can be seen as 'outside' the 'normal' market mechanisms as perceived by established producers, they are nevertheless essentially economic in character.

Accordingly, in addition to classifying innovations according to their technological character and magnitude, and according to the requirements they place on an organization's culture and structure, as prior scholars have noted, we propose that innovations be categorized also by the degree of mobility they enable or require across value networks. If no mobility or change in strategic direction is required—if the innovation is valuable within a firm's established value network—the character of the innovation can be considered straightforward, regardless of its intrinsic technological difficulty or riskiness. If realization of inherent value requires the establishment of new systems of use—new value networks—the innovation is surely complex even if it is technologically simple. This is because such innovation requires far more than technological activity. It involves creating markets, and focusing on commercial opportunities which are small and poorly defined, rather than large and clear.

In summary, then, we argue that the context in which a firm competes has a profound influence on its ability to marshall and focus the resources and capabilities required to overcome the technological and organizational hurdles other scholars have identified as impediments to firms' ability to innovate. An important part of this context is the value network in which the firm competes. As we stated earlier, the boundaries of a value network are determined by a unique definition of product performance—by a rank-ordering of the importance of various performance attributes which differs from that employed in other systems-of-use in a broadly defined industry. In other words, the importance of such product attributes as size,

C.M. Christensen, R.S. Rosenbloom / Research Policy 24 (1995) 233–257   255

weight, power consumption, heat generation, speed, ruggedness and ease of repair will be ranked very differently by users, and hence in the markets comprised by different networks.

This implies that a key determinant of the probability of commercial success of an innovative effort is the degree to which it addresses the well-understood needs of known actors within the value network in which an organization is positioned. Incumbent firms are likely to lead their industries in innovations of all sorts—in architecture and components—which address needs within their value network, regardless of their intrinsic technological character or difficulty. These are straightforward innovations in that their value and application are clear. Conversely, incumbent firms are likely to lag in the development of technologies—even those where the technology involved is intrinsically simple—which address customers' needs as defined in emerging value networks. Such innovative processes are complex because their value and application are uncertain, according to the criteria used by incumbent firms.

Extending Dosi's [17, p. 147] notion of a 'technological trajectory' associated with each technological paradigm, we also suggest that two distinct trajectories can be identified—one which defines the performance demanded over time within a given value network, and one which traces the performance which technologists are able to provide within a given technological paradigm. In some cases, as in the disk drive industry, the trajectory of performance improvement which a technology is able to provide may have a distinctly different slope from the trajectory of performance improvement which is demanded in the system-of-use by downstream customers within any given value network. When the slopes of the two trajectories are similar, we expect the technology to remain relatively contained within the value network in which it is initially used, but when the slopes of these trajectories differ, new technologies, which initially are performance-competitive only within emerging or commercially remote value networks, may migrate into other networks, providing a vehicle for innovators in new networks to attack established ones.

When such an attack occurs, it is because technological progress has made differences in the rank-ordering of performance attributes across different value networks less relevant. For example, size and weight are attributes of disk drives which are far more important in the desktop computing value network than they are in the mainframe and minicomputer value networks. When technological progress in 5.25-inch drives enabled manufacturers of those products to satisfy the attribute prioritization in the mainframe and minicomputer networks (which prize total capacity and high speed) as well as the attribute prioritization in the desktop network, the boundaries between those value networks ceased to be barriers to entry by 5.25-inch drive makers.

A characteristic of almost all innovations in component technology is that they are an important engine of improvement within a given technological paradigm and its corresponding value network. Component innovation, although often 'competency-destroying', rarely changes the trajectory of performance improvement. As such, the risk of commercial error in component innovation is lower relative to architectural innovations. Thus, we expect incumbent firms to be the leaders in component innovations.

No such general statement can be made about innovations in architectural technologies. Some may reinforce or sustain the trajectory of performance improvement as it is defined within an established value network, while others may disrupt or redefine that trajectory. We expect incumbent firms to lead their industries in the sorts of architectural technology changes which sustain or reinforce the trajectory of performance within an established value network.

When architectural or radical innovations redefine the level, rate and direction of progress of an established technological trajectory, entrant firms have an advantage over incumbents. This is not because of any difficulty or unique skill requirements intrinsic to the new architectural technology. It is because the new paradigm addresses a differently ordered set of performance parameters valued in a new or different value network. It is difficult for established firms to marshall resources behind innovations that do not address the needs of known, present and powerful customers. In these instances, although this 'attacker's advantage' is associated with an architectural technology change, the essence of the attacker's advantage is in its differential ability to identify and make strategic commitments to attack and develop emerging market applications, or value networks. The issue, at its core, may be the relative abilities of successful incumbent firms vs. entrant firms to change strategies, not technologies.

7. References

[1] W.J. Abernathy and J.H. Utterback, Patterns of Innovation in Technology, *Technology Review* 80 (July, 1978) 40–47.

[2] C. Alexander, *Notes on the Synthesis of Form* (Harvard University Press, Cambridge, MA, 1964).

[3] J. Bower, *Managing the Resource Allocation Process* (Richard D. Irwin, Homewood, IL, 1970).

[4] R.A. Burgelman, Intraorganizational Ecology of Strategy Making and Organizational Adaptation: Theory and Field Research, *Organization Science* 2 (August, 1991) 239–262.

[5] R. Burgelman and L. Sayles, *Inside Corporate Innovation* (The Free Press, New York, 1986).

[6] R. Caves and M. Porter, From Entry Barriers to Mobility Barriers, Quarterly Journal of Economics 91 (May, 1977) 241–261.

[7] A.D. Chandler, Organizational Capabilities and the Economic History of the Industrial Enterprise, Journal of Economic Perspectives 6 (Summer, 1992) 79–100.

[8] C.M. Christensen, The Innovator's Challenge: Understanding the Influence of Market Environment on Processes of Technology Development in the Rigid Disk Drive Industry (Unpublished Doctoral Dissertation, Harvard University Graduate School of Business Administration, 1992).

[9] C.M. Christensen, Exploring the Limits of the Technology S-Curve, *Production and Operations Management* (Fall, 1993) 334–366.

[11] K.B. Clark, The Interaction of Design Hierarchies and Market Concepts in Technological Evolution, *Research Policy* 14 (1985) 235–251.

[12] K.B. Clark, *Knowledge, Problem-Solving and Innovation in the Evolutionary Firm: Implications for Managerial Capability and Competitive Interaction* (Working Paper, Harvard Business School Division of Research, Boston, MA, 1987).

[13] A.C. Cooper and D. Schendel, Strategic Response to Technological Threats, *Business Horizons* 19 (February, 1976) 61–69.

[15] D.L. Denouel, The Diffusion of Innovations: An Institu-

tion Approach. (Unpublished Doctoral Dissertation, Harvard University Graduate School of Business Administration, 1980).

[17] G. Dosi, Technological Paradigms and Technological Trajectories, *Research Policy* 11 (1982) 147–162.

[19] J.L. Enos, Invention and Innovation in the Petroleum Refining Industry, in: *The Rate and Direction of Inventive Activity: Economic and Social Factors* (National Bureau of Economic Research report, Princeton University Press, Princeton, NJ, 1962) 299–321.

[20] R. Foster, *Innovation: The Attacker's Advantage* (Summit Books, New York, 1986).

[21] P. Ghemawat, *Commitment: The Dynamic of Strategy* (The Free Press, New York, 1991).

[22] M.B.W. Graham, *RCA and the VideoDisc: the Business of Research* (Cambridge University Press, Cambridge, 1986).

[23] R.M. Henderson, The Failure of Established Firms in the Face of Technological Change: A Study of the Semiconductor Photolithographic Alignment Industry (Unpublished Doctoral Dissertation, Harvard University, 1988).

[24] R.M. Henderson and K.B. Clark, Architectural Innovation: The Reconfiguration of Existing Systems and the Failure of Established Firms, *Administrative Science Quarterly* 35 (1990) 9–30.

[25] S. Hollander, *The Sources of Increased Efficiency: A Study of DuPont Rayon Plants* (MIT Press, Cambridge, MA, 1965).

[26] T. Kuhn, *The Structure of Scientific Revolutions* (University of Chicago Press, Chicago, IL, 1962).

[27] M. Maidique and B.J. Zirger, The New Product Learning Cycle, *Research Policy* 14 (1985) 299–313.

[28] D.L. Marples, The Decisions of Engineering Design, *IEEE Transactions on Engineering Management* EM8 (1961) 55–71.

[29] J. Morone, *Winning in High-Tech Markets: The Role of General Management* (Harvard Business School Press, Boston, MA, 1993).

[30] K. Pavitt, Technology, Innovation and Strategic Management, in: J. McGee and H. Thomas, (Editors), *Strategic Management Research: A European Perspective*, (Wiley, Chichester, 1986).

[32] M. Porter, *Competitive Advantage* (The Free Press, New York, 1985).

[33] M. Porter, Towards a Dynamic Theory of Strategy, *Strategic Management Journal* 12 (1991) 95–117.

[34] N. Rosenberg, *Inside the Black Box: Technology and Economics* (Cambridge University Press, Cambridge, 1962).

[36] R.S. Rosenbloom, From Gears to Chips: The Transformation of NCR and Harris in the Digital Era (Working Paper, Harvard Business School Business History Seminar, 1988).

[37] R.S. Rosenbloom and M. Cusumano, Technological Pioneering and Competitive Advantage: The Birth of the VCR Industry, *California Management Review* 29 (Summer, 1987) 51–76.

[38] R.S. Rosenbloom and K. Freeze, Ampex Corporation and Video Innovation, *Research on Technological Innovation, Management and Policy* 2 (1985).

[39] E. Schein, *Organizational Culture and Leadership: A Dynamic View* (Jossey-Bass, San Francisco, CA, 1988).

[40] M.L. Tushman and P. Anderson, Technological Discontinuities and Organizational Environments, *Administrative Science Quarterly* 31 (1986) 439–465.

8. Appendix: A note on the data and methods used to generate Fig. 4

The trajectories mapped in Fig. 4 were calculated as follows. Data on the capacity provided with computers was obtained from *Data Sources*, an annual publication which lists the technical specifications of all computer models available from each computer manufacturer. Where particular models were available with different features and configurations, the manufacturer provided *Data Sources* with a 'typical' system configuration with defined RAM capacity, performance specifications of peripheral equipment (including disk drives), list price, and year of introduction. In instances where a given computer model was offered for sale over a sequence of years, the hard disk capacity provided in the typical configuration typically increased. *Data Sources* divides computers into mainframe, mini/midrange, desktop personal, portable and laptop, and notebook computers. For each class of computers, all models available for sale in each year were ranked by price, and the hard disk capacity provided with the median-priced model identified for each year. The best-fit line through the resultant time series

is plotted as the solid lines in Fig. 4. These single solid lines are drawn in Fig. 4 for expository simplification to indicate the trend in typical machines. In reality, of course, there is a wide band around these lines. The *frontier* of performance —the highest capacity offered with the most expensive computers—was substantially higher than the typical values shown.

The dotted lines in Fig. 4 represent the best-fit line through the unweighted average capacity of all disk drives introduced for sale in each given architecture for each year. This data was taken from *Disk / Trend Report*. Again, for expository simplification, only this average line is shown. There was a wide band of capacities introduced for sale in each year, so that the frontier or highest capacity drive introduced in each year was substantially above the average shown. Stated in another way, a distinction must be made between the full range of products available for purchase, and those in typical systems of use. The upper and lower bands around the median and average figures shown in Fig. 4 are generally parallel to the lines shown.

Because drives with higher capacities were available in the market than the capacities offered with the median-priced systems, we state in the text that the solid-line trajectories in Fig. 4 represent the capacities 'demanded' in each market. In other words, the capacity per machine was not constrained by technological availability. Rather, it represents a choice for hard disk capacity, made by computer users, given the prevailing cost.

Part II
Evolution and Horizontal Market Structure

[8]

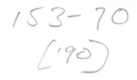

RAND Journal of Economics
Vol. 21, No. 1, Spring 1990

The evolution of new industries and the determinants of market structure

(US/

Steven Klepper*

and

Elizabeth Graddy**

LII

L25

L60

Several empirical regularities concerning firm growth rates and industry firm-size distributions have been developed by studying primarily mature industries. The primary purpose of this article is to bring together and extend empirical regularities on the evolution of new industries and to use these regularities to gain further insight into the forces governing industry evolution. To explain these regularities, a model is constructed which emphasizes how factors governing the early evolution of industries may shape their market structure at maturity. It stresses how chance events and exogenous factors that influence the number of potential entrants to the industry, the growth rate of incumbents, and the ease of imitation of industry leaders will influence the ultimate number and size distribution of firms in the industry.

1. Introduction

■ An impressive body of empirical regularities has emerged from the study of firm-size distributions and the relationship between firm growth rates and firm size (Scherer, 1980). A number of theories about how industries evolve over time have been developed to explain these regularities.[1] Nearly all the regularities that have been addressed by the theories, however, involve older, more mature industries, due, in large part, to the greater accessibility of data for such industries. The primary purpose of this article is to bring together and extend the empirical regularities concerning the evolution of new industries and to use these regularities to gain further insight into the forces governing industry evolution.

Building on the work of Gort and Klepper (1982), we establish that the number of

---

* Carnegie Mellon University.

** University of Southern California.

We thank Timothy Bresnahan, Mark Kamlet, Jonathan Leland, Leonard Lynn, David Mowery, Richard Nelson, and three anonymous referees for helpful comments. We especially thank Wesley Cohen for many valuable discussions and comments.

[1] Some of the early studies include Gibrat (1931), Champernowne (1953), Simon (1955), Hart and Prais (1956), Simon and Bonini (1958), Mansfield (1962), and Ijiri and Simon (1977). In recent years, Peltzman (1977), Loury (1979), Futia (1980), Flaherty (1980), Dasgupta and Stiglitz (1980, 1981), Jovanovic (1982), Telser (1982), Lippman and Rumelt (1982), Nelson and Winter (1978, 1982), and Winter (1984), among others, have developed similar theories to explain the various correlations between profitability, market structure, market share, and innovative input and output across industries and firms.

28 / THE RAND JOURNAL OF ECONOMICS

firms in new industries follows a distinctive path: first it grows, then declines sharply, and finally levels off. Trends in prices and output indicate that output rises and prices fall at decreasing percentage rates during both the growth phase and the decline phase for the number of firms; both trends then level off. We also synthesize from the literature a number of qualitative regularities concerning the evolution of new industries. These quantitative and qualitative regularities are used to reflect on the nature of industry evolution and to construct a simple model of industry evolution similar to those developed by Jovanovic (1982) and Winter (1984). We demonstrate that with suitable structuring, our model can explain all the regularities.

A distinctive feature of the model is that it predicts that the factors governing the early evolution of industries will shape their market structure at maturity. It stresses how chance events and exogenous factors that influence the number of potential entrants to the industry, the growth rate of incumbent firms, and the ease of imitation of the industry leaders will influence the ultimate number and size distribution of firms in the industry.

The article is organized as follows. In Section 2 we develop the quantitative and qualitative regularities characterizing the evolution of new industries. In Section 3 we use these regularities to reflect on the principal forces that shape new industries, and we construct a model to explain these regularities. In Section 4 we consider the forces that shape the evolutionary process and that determine the industry's concentration ratio at maturity.

2. Regularities in the development of new industries

■ **Quantitative regularities.** Scattered evidence has been presented suggesting that output in developing industries tends to rise over time at a decreasing percentage rate and price tends to fall over time at a decreasing percentage rate (Burns, 1934; Boston Consulting Group, 1972; Gort and Klepper, 1982). It has also been noted that a number of developing industries have experienced a shakeout in the number of producers at some point in their history (Porter, 1980; Gort and Klepper, 1982). In this section we reanalyze a data set assembled by Gort and Klepper (1982). We demonstrate that in fact, each of these patterns appears to characterize the evolution of a diverse set of new industries.

Gort and Klepper assembled data on the number of firms, output, and price for 46 new products. The data extend from the date of the initial commercial introduction of the product through 1972. Some were introduced in the nineteenth century, while others were introduced as late as the post-World War II period. They tend to be important products that eventually developed a sizable market. They include both consumer and producer goods as well as goods developed primarily for the military.

Annual data on the number of producers were secured from *Thomas' Register of American Manufacturers.*[2] Whenever possible, we extended these series through 1981. The data are based on the register's industry definitions, which in some instances are quite narrow (i.e., comparable to seven-digit S.I.C. industries) and in other instances are apparently broad enough to encompass certain types of component suppliers.[3] The initial commercial introduction of the product is generally dated according to its first listing in the register,[4] although in some instances an earlier date was chosen based on information supplied by

---

[2] *Thomas' Register* attempts to cover all manufacturers. It uses company contacts, information mailings, and field representatives who solicit advertising business to compile its firm listings. Approximately 85% of its listings are unpaid, while the other 15% are paid advertisements. Firms are checked to insure that they are manufacturers.

[3] Conversations with personnel at the publishing company indicate that the definitions are modified over time to reflect technological changes in the products. They assured us, however, that no systematic definitional changes were employed that might create artificial patterns in the data.

[4] Products are first listed based on sales representative and manufacturer contacts.

industry sources.[5] Output and sales data were derived for a subset of the industries from government and trade sources.[6] They are usually annual data, although for some products there are gaps in the series. They begin sometime after the product was commercially introduced and generally extend through 1971 or 1972. In general, the output data were not adjusted for quality changes nor for changes in the mix of variants of the product. Constant dollar implicit price indices were derived by dividing sales by output and then deflating by the Consumer Price Index.

Analyzing first the data on the number of firms, each product history was divided into a maximum of three stages. Stage 1 is composed of the years in which the number of firms grows. Stage 2 is characterized by a decline or shakeout in the number of firms. Stage 3 is composed of the period after the shakeout when the number of firms stabilizes. While the division of a continuous history into stages is inevitably arbitrary, we adopted the following rules based upon an inspection of the 46 product histories. Stage 1 ends when the number of firms reaches a peak.[7] Stage 2 ends in the year, denoted by t^*, after which the average annual change in the number of producers is greater than -1.0% of the peak number of producers in each of the following periods: t^* through $t^* + 5$, t^* through $t^* + 10$, t^* through $t^* + 15, \ldots, t^*$ through the last year of the product's history.[8] For example, suppose that the number of firms in an industry with a twenty-year life follows the following pattern: 1, 3, 8, 15, 28, 21, 29, 22, 18, 16, 17, 15, 14, 16, 17, 13, 15, 16, 15, 15. Then stage 1 would be composed of years 1–7, as year 7 is the year that the number of firms reaches a maximum. Stage 2 would be composed of years 8–10, as year 10 is the first year after which the average change in the number of firms in the next five years (i.e., years 10–15) and in the next ten years (i.e., years 10–20) is greater than -1.0% of the peak number of firms. Stage 3 would be composed of the remaining years, or years 11–20.

Table 1 lists the 46 products and the number of years in each stage for each product. The table indicates that by 1981, all but 8 of the products had attained stage 2, and 22 of the 46 products had attained stage 3. The 8 products that had not attained stage 2 by 1981 are relatively young, with a mean birth year of 1945 versus 1926 for the other 38 products. Thus, it might be expected that eventually these products will also pass through a shakeout period before reaching maturity.

While the 46 products appear to follow a similar pattern in terms of the three stages in the number of producers, Table 1 indicates that the length of each stage varies considerably across products. This is particularly true for stage 1, where some products have a much longer gestation period before developing a sizable market.[9] The average number of years in stages 1 and 2 across all products attaining the next stage is reported at the bottom of Table 1.

Table 2 lists the mean annual change in the number of producers in each stage for each product. Not surprisingly, in each stage there is considerable variation across products

---

[5] In these instances, there is a gap in the data from the date supplied by industry sources to the date the product was first listed in *Thomas' Register.*

[6] The sources for these data and the series themselves are available from Professor Klepper.

[7] A year is defined as a peak year for the number of producers when no higher number of firms is recorded in any earlier year or in the subsequent twenty-five years (or all subsequent years if there are less than twenty-five subsequent years). If the same maximum number of firms is attained in more than one year, the peak year is the one for which the average number of firms in the subsequent three years is greatest. The exception is when one of the years in which the number of firms reaches a maximum is the last year, in which case the last year is chosen as the peak year.

[8] In cases where there are fewer than five years in the product's history after the year in which the average annual decline in the number of firms is less than 1.0% of the peak number of firms, all the years following the peak are classified as part of stage 2.

[9] Gort and Klepper (1982) present evidence indicating that the length of this gestation period has been falling over time.

TABLE 1   Number of Years in Each Stage

		Stage		
Product Name	Period	1	2	3
Baseboard Radiant Heating	1946–1981	25	10	
Compressors, Freon	1935–1981	45	1	
Computers	1935–1981	46		
Crystals, Piezo	1936–1981	31	4	10
DDT	1943–1981	9	22	7
Electrocardiographs	1914–1981	50	17	
Electric Blankets	1911–1981	51	13	6
Electric Shavers	1930–1981	8	4	39
Engines, Jet-Propelled	1943–1981	21	8	9
Engines, Rocket	1944–1981	37		
Fluorescent Lamps	1938–1981	2	1	40
Freezers, Home and Farm	1929–1981	25	18	9
Gauges, Beta Ray	1955–1981	18	8	
Gyroscopes	1911–1981	55	15	
Lasers	1960–1981	21		
Machinery, Adding and Calculating	1889–1981	38	19	35
Missiles, Guided	1950–1981	12	19	
Motors, Outboard	1908–1981	9	6	58
Nylon	1939–1973	34		
Paints, Rubber and Rubber Base	1933–1981	33	15	
Penicillin	1943–1981	7	23	8
Pens, Ball Point	1945–1981	36		
Photocopy Machines	1940–1981	25	11	5
Polariscopes	1906–1981	50	11	14
Pumps, Heat	1953–1981	28		
Radar	1940–1981	22	19	
Radio Transmitters	1922–1981	40	13	6
Reactors, Nuclear	1942–1981	22	17	
Readers, Microfilm	1929–1981	49	3	
Records, Phonograph	1887–1981	36	9	45
Saccharin	1906–1972	12	9	45
Shampoo	1898–1981	51	1	31
Streptomycin	1945–1981	8	19	9
Styrene	1935–1981	45	1	
Tanks, Cryogenic	1959–1981	8	1	13
Tape, Recording	1947–1981	32	2	
Telemeters	1928–1979	34	17	
Television Receivers, Monochrome	1929–1973	26	18	
Tents, Oxygen	1926–1981	32	23	
Tires, Automobile	1896–1981	26	10	49
Transistors	1948–1981	33		
Trees, Artificial Christmas	1912–1981	52	17	
Tubes, Cathode Ray	1922–1981	37	7	15
Turbine, Gas	1936–1981	45		
Windshield Wipers	1914–1981	11	9	47
Zippers	1904–1981	55	13	9
Average (across products attaining the next stage)		29.3	10.5	

in the mean annual change in the number of producers, particularly in stages 1 and 2. What is more surprising is the severity of stage 2 (the shakeout) and the relative stability in the number of producers in stage 3. The severity of stage 2 is conveyed by Table 3, which reports the net decrease in the number of producers in stage 2 as a fraction of the peak number of producers for the 22 products attaining stage 3 by 1981. On average, Table 3 indicates there was a net decrease of 52% of the producers in stage 2, with some industries

TABLE 2   Mean Annual Change in the Number of Firms by Stage

Product Name	Stage 1	Stage 2	Stage 3
Baseboard Radiant Heating	1.0	−0.9	
Compressors, Freon	0.5	−2.0	
Computers	6.7		
Crystals, Piezo	1.4	−4.3	−0.4
DDT	4.1	−1.5	−0.1
Electrocardiographs	0.3	−0.5	
Electric Blankets	0.3	−0.9	0.2
Electric Shavers	3.9	−4.5	−0.2
Engines, Jet-Propelled	1.5	−1.1	−0.2
Engines, Rocket	0.4		
Fluorescent Lamps	16.0	−14.0	0.4
Freezers, Home and Farm	5.8	−2.1	0.3
Gauges, Beta Ray	0.5	−0.8	
Gyroscopes	0.8	−1.5	
Lasers	6.0		
Machinery, Adding and Calculating	2.3	−1.5	−0.5
Missiles, Guided	21.6	−11.5	
Motors, Outboard	2.2	−1.3	0.1
Nylon	0.8		
Paints, Rubber and Rubber Base	3.6	−4.6	
Penicillin	3.9	−1.0	−0.3
Pens, Ball Point	2.6		
Photocopy Machines	1.7	−2.1	0.0
Polariscopes	0.2	−0.5	0.1
Pumps, Heat	1.5		
Radar	8.1	−4.7	
Radio Transmitters	1.3	−4.2	5.0
Reactors, Nuclear	4.5	−1.7	
Readers, Microfilm	0.8	−2.3	
Records, Phonograph	1.3	−3.3	0.7
Saccharin	3.0	−3.1	−0.1
Shampoo	2.6	−5.0	0.0
Streptomycin	1.5	−0.6	0.0
Styrene	0.9	−3.0	
Tanks, Cryogenic	10.4	−29.0	0.2
Tape, Recording	1.8	−2.0	
Telemeters	0.7	−0.7	
Television Receivers, Monochrome	23.5	−10.2	
Tents, Oxygen	0.8	−0.9	
Tires, Automobile	12.3	−21.1	−1.0
Transistors	2.6		
Trees, Artificial Christmas	0.3	−0.5	
Tubes, Cathode Ray	1.5	−1.6	0.5
Turbine, Gas	0.9		
Windshield Wipers	4.6	−3.3	0.2
Zippers	0.9	−0.7	0.3
Average	3.8	−4.1	0.2

experiencing a shakeout of over 80% of their producers. In contrast, there is no clear trend in the number of producers in stage 3 for the same 22 products: 11 experience a net increase, 8 a net decrease, and 3 no change at all in the number of producers.[10]

---

[10] Two of the products that experienced an increase in the number of producers in stage 3—outboard motors and phonograph records—appear to have proceeded through a second cycle of growth and decline in the number of producers after initially attaining stage 3. No pronounced pattern in stage 3 is apparent for the other 20 products.

TABLE 3   Severity of Net Exit in Stage 2 for Those Industries Attaining Stage 3 by 1981

Product Name	Peak Number of Firms	Net Decrease in Number of Firms in Stage 2	Net Decrease/Peak
Crystals, Piezo	45	17	.38
DDT	38	33	.87
Electric Blankets	17	11	.65
Electric Shavers	32	18	.56
Engines, Jet-Propelled	29	9	.31
Fluorescent Lamps	34	14	.41
Freezers, Home and Farm	61	38	.62
Machinery, Adding and Calculating	55	28	.51
Motors, Outboard	21	8	.38
Penicillin	30	24	.80
Photocopy Machines	43	23	.53
Polariscopes	16	6	.38
Radio Transmitters	76	55	.72
Records, Phonograph	49	30	.61
Saccharin	39	28	.72
Shampoo	114	5	.04
Streptomycin	13	11	.85
Tanks, Cryogenic	84	29	.35
Tires, Automobile	275	211	.77
Tubes, Cathode Ray	39	11	.28
Windshield Wipers	51	30	.59
Zippers	49	9	.18
Average			.52

Although our classification procedure ensures that the average annual change in the number of producers is positive in stage 1, negative in stage 2, and close to zero in stage 3 for each product, it does not guarantee that all of the years classified in each stage conform to these patterns for each product. For instance, in the earlier example of the industry with a twenty-year life span, the number of firms fell during two of the years classified in stage 1. To convey the extent of such irregularities, we computed the ratio of the number of irregularities in the stage divided by the number of years classified in the stage for each product. We then averaged this across all products in each stage. The results indicate that for the average product, 11% of the years in stage 1 are characterized by a decline in the number of producers, 11% of the years in stage 2 are characterized by a rise in the number of producers, and 13% of the years in stage 3 are characterized by a monotonic fall or rise in the number of producers over the following three years, which is our definition of a stage 3 irregularity. Thus, a relatively small percentage of the years are subject to some kind of irregularity. Moreover, an unknown portion of these irregularities may be attributable to random errors in Thomas' listings rather than systematic departures from the general pattern.

While the number of these irregularities is small, they are not evenly distributed throughout stages 1 and 2. Approximately 70% of the stage 1 irregularities occur in the second half of the stage, while approximately 54% of the stage 2 irregularities occur in the first half of the stage. This suggests a possible hiatus between the growth stage and the shakeout stage during which the trend in the number of producers is not pronounced. Thus, a conservative assessment about the time path of the number of firms is that the typical new product does seem to experience pronounced periods of growth, shakeout, and stability in the number of firms, but there may be some time between the primary growth and shakeout stages during which the number of firms does not change sharply.

The trends in the output and price data are reported in Tables 4 and 5. The mean annual percentage change in output and price for successive five-year intervals is reported

TABLE 4   Annual Average Percentage Change* in Output by Five-year Intervals**

Product Name	Period	Order of Five-year Interval											
		1	2	3	4	5	6	7	8	9	10	11	12
Baseboard Radiant Heating	1954–1972	12.8	8.1	−6.8									
Computers	1955–1971	65.1	31.2	11.2									
Crystals, Piezo	1963–1971	9.9											
DDT	1944–1971	28.3	18.2	9.6	−2.9	−22.2							
Electrocardiographs	1961–1972	27.8	−0.9										
Electric Blankets	1946–1972	27.1	19.8	14.5	0.5	−0.8							
Electric Shavers	1931–1972	120.2	−2.1	13.1	0.8	22.0	−0.3	9.9	−0.7				
Engines, Jet-Propelled	1946–1972	47.7	−6.2	−4.5	9.9	−35.6							
Fluorescent Lamps	1938–1972	106.6	14.4	1.1	4.9	8.5	7.2	3.1					
Freezers, Home and Farm	1945–1972	75.9	4.2	−1.0	2.1	6.1							
Gyroscopes	1963–1972	4.8	−19.4										
Lasers	1962–1971	58.6	33.1										
Motors, Outboard	1925–1974	−2.6	25.3	27.2	−6.7	16.3	−12.5	5.0	2.7				
Nylon	1940–1972	44.8	21.1	22.8	10.5	15.8	7.8						
Penicillin	1945–1971	65.0	12.2	2.8	13.9	11.4							
Pens, Ball Point	1951–1972	32.3	21.4	9.0	3.4								
Records, Phonograph	1909–1972	18.8	29.6	−4.2	−19.5	14.9	−5.1	4.9	10.9				
Streptomycin	1946–1965	57.8	28.1	21.8	−3.0								
Styrene	1942–1971	68.5	3.1	11.1	9.8	8.4	7.2						
Tape, Recording	1961–1972	16.7	13.8										
Television Receivers, Monochrome	1939–1972	135.7	6.5	−3.6	3.1	−4.4							
Tires, Automobile	1910–1973	35.8	19.6	12.9	−3.6	−0.8	3.7	−5.4	14.5	3.7	1.4	6.7	3.5
Transistors	1954–1972	83.0	32.0	14.3									
Tubes, Cathode Ray	1934–1972	40.3	−3.5	1.6	−8.4	−13.0							
Zippers	1917–1972	64.4	62.0	20.0	34.4	14.2	7.5	3.3	14.7	−2.7			
Average		49.8	15.5	8.6	3.4	2.7	1.9	3.9	8.4	0.5	1.4	6.7	3.5

* Percentage changes are computed as the first differences in logarithms.

** In some instances the intervals exceed five years because of the unavailability of data or because there is less than a four-year interval at the end of a product's history (in which case the residual years are included with the previous five).

for each product for which data were available. Examining output first, Table 4 clearly indicates that for each product, output generally increases in each five-year interval. While the rate of growth in output differs considerably across products within each five-year interval, there appears to be a general tendency for output growth to be greatest in the first five-year interval and then to decline over successive five-year intervals. This can be seen from the average mean annual percentage change in output across products within each five-year interval, reported at the bottom of Table 4. The average annual mean percentage growth in output is greatest in the first five-year interval and then declines over the next five five-year intervals. Note, however, that in contrast to the patterns for the number of firms, there are a number of departures from the general pattern of decline in the percentage growth in output. In 29 of the 100 pairwise comparisons between consecutive five-year intervals for all the products, the percentage growth in output is higher in the later five-year interval.

A similar pattern for prices is recorded in Table 5. For each product, the mean annual

34 / THE RAND JOURNAL OF ECONOMICS

TABLE 5   Annual Average Percentage Change* in Price by Five-year Intervals**

Product Name	Period	Order of Five-year Interval							
		1	2	3	4	5	6	7	8
Computers	1955–1971	−16.5	−0.8	−0.6					
Crystals, Piezo	1963–1971	−9.0							
DDT	1944–1970	−26.3	−8.5	−5.1	−7.5	−3.8			
Electrocardiographs	1961–1972	9.6	−0.9						
Electric Blankets	1946–1972	−4.5	−9.2	−9.7	−3.8	−2.9			
Electric Shavers	1931–1972	−6.5	−1.9	−2.5	1.6	−4.0	−6.3	−4.2	−3.3
Fluorescent Lamps	1938–1972	−23.5	−5.2	3.2	0.8	−0.6	−4.7	−1.8	
Freezers, Home and Farm	1947–1972	1.6	−0.9	−8.4	−4.6	−5.9			
Gyroscopes	1963–1972	−15.6	−3.0						
Lasers	1963–1971	−1.9							
Motors, Outboard	1925–1974	4.0	−8.1	−0.3	5.9	11.2	0.2	1.7	
Nylon	1940–1971	−12.2	−6.2	−2.1	−4.7	−1.3	−4.2		
Penicillin	1945–1972	−55.7	−29.3	−1.0	−39.0	−6.8			
Pens, Ball Point	1951–1972	−2.2	−17.2	−3.0	−3.2				
Records, Phonograph	1914–1972	−11.6	−4.5	−1.7	−1.4	−2.7	2.7	−9.0	
Streptomycin	1946–1965	−63.4	−30.6	−17.0	−18.2				
Styrene	1943–1971	−17.9	7.8	−4.5	−7.3	−9.1			
Tape, Recording	1961–1972	2.9	−14.0						
Television Receivers, Monochrome	1939–1972	−10.6	−4.4	−7.6	−2.6	−5.8	−7.5		
Tires, Automobile	1915–1972	−3.0	−4.1	−6.8	6.9	0.7	0.2	−2.5	−1.0
Transistors	1954–1972	−11.4	−18.2	−19.8	−15.1				
Tubes, Cathode Ray	1948–1972	−3.5	−5.3	−2.3	−6.8	−2.6			
Zippers	1920–1972	−1.8	6.7	−20.7	−2.3	−5.9	−1.5	0.8	
Average		−12.6	−8.1	−6.6	−6.0	−3.2	−2.6	−2.9	−2.2

* Percentage changes are computed as the first differences in logarithms.

** In some instances the intervals exceed five years because of the unavailability of data or because there is less than a four-year interval at the end of a product's history (in which case the residual years are included with the previous five).

percentage change in price is generally negative, with considerable variation across products in the mean annual percentage change in price in each five-year interval. The average mean annual percentage change in price across products for each five-year interval, reported at the bottom of Table 5, indicates that the annual percentage change in price is most negative in the first five-year interval, after which it declines (in absolute value) over the next five five-year intervals. However, like the time path of output, there are a considerable number of departures from this general pattern. In 41 of the 86 pairwise comparisons between consecutive five-year intervals for all the products, the percentage fall in price is greater in the later interval.

Note that after the first five five-year intervals, both the mean percentage rise in output and mean percentage fall in price tend to level off and remain relatively constant over the subsequent five-year intervals. These means are based upon the 8 products with over twenty-five years of output and price data. Virtually all of these products had attained stage 3 after the twenty-fifth year of the output and price data. This suggests that the decline in the percentage fall in price and the percentage rise in output over time are confined to stages 1 and 2 and that once stage 3 is reached, the percentage fall in price and the percentage rise in output stabilize.

In summary, the new products in our sample appear to follow a common pattern in terms of changes over time in the number of firms, output, and price. Initially, the number of firms in the industry grows, then at a later point there is a shakeout in the number of firms, followed by a period in which the number of firms is stable. During both the growth and shakeout stages in the number of firms, output grows at a decreasing percentage rate and price falls at a decreasing percentage rate. Once the number of firms stabilizes, the percentage fall in price and the percentage rise in output level off and remain constant over time. While there is considerable variation in the pace and severity of this process, it appears that nearly all of the new products experience an initial rise followed by a shakeout in the number of producers. In contrast, it is not uncommon for a product to depart from the pattern of a fall in the percentage growth in its output and percentage decline in its price at some point in its history.

□ **Qualitative regularities.** The qualitative nature of the evolution of new products has been studied under the rubric of the product life cycle. An early article by Dean (1950) discussed the implications of the product life cycle for the pricing of new products. Subsequent articles explored the marketing implications of the product life cycle (Levitt, 1965; Cox, 1967) and its implications for international trade (Vernon, 1966; Wells, 1972). More recently, the nature of technological change over the product life cycle has been investigated (see especially Abernathy and Townsend (1975), Utterback and Abernathy (1975), Abernathy (1978), and Utterback (1979)), and its implications for firm strategies for evolving industries has been explored. (See, for example, Hayes and Wheelwright (1979a, 1979b) and Porter (1980, 1983).) In this section we review the general features of the product life cycle, particularly as summarized by Abernathy (1978) and Utterback (1979).

The prototypical new industry tends to develop as follows. Initially, little is known about the attributes of the new product desired by demanders. The early entrants into the industry are typically small and have experience in related technologies. Sometimes they are users of the new product, while in other instances they are spinoffs of incumbent firms. They often introduce major product innovations based on information about users' needs and/or the technological means available to satisfy them. Market shares often change rapidly as successful innovators displace less efficient rivals, as was the case in the early history of the auto, aircraft engine, and airframe industries (Klein, 1977).

The initial uncertainty that characterizes new industries appears to restrain the growth of incumbent firms.[11] Over time, the uncertainty abates as "dominant designs" emerge for various features of the product. Firms able to produce these designs prosper and grow, while firms that are unable to adapt exit the industry. Innovations in the industry become more incremental and tend to embody a smaller degree of inventiveness (Utterback and Abernathy, 1975). The slowdown in major innovations tends to cause market shares to stabilize, as Klein (1977) documents for the automobile and airframe industries and Mansfield (1962) demonstrates for the steel, petroleum, and tire industries.

While new industries tend to follow a prototypical pattern, not all firms in an industry follow the same strategy over time (Hayes and Wheelwright, 1979a, 1979b), and not all industries proceed at the same pace (Abernathy, 1978; Porter, 1983). Two factors appear to have an important effect on the pace of the prototypical evolutionary process: the characteristics of the product's technology and the nature of buyers' preferences. Products characterized by limited opportunities for technological change tend to be subject to less uncertainty and to reach maturity faster. Where products are characterized by considerable diversity in buyers' preferences, it is more difficult for dominant designs to emerge, which tends to lengthen the time it takes to reach maturity.

3. The determinants of the evolution of new industries

■ **General forces.** In this subsection we consider what the quantitative and qualitative regularities tell us about industry evolution. While it is not possible to reach definitive conclusions, the regularities are suggestive of a number of factors at work in new industries.

---

[11] See Porter and Spence (1982) for evidence concerning the effects of uncertainty on firm growth in the corn wet-milling industry.

Consider first the entry of firms. In the discussion of the qualitative regularities, it was noted that entrants into new industries typically have experience in related technologies. This suggests that firms require a certain expertise to enter an industry, which implies that the number of firms that could potentially enter a specific new industry is limited. The prototypical path of the number of producers suggests that at a given moment, only a fraction of these potential entrants actually enter. One explanation for this is that potential entrants differ in terms of their potential average costs of production and product qualities and that the potential entrants with the better product qualities and lower average costs are those who enter the industry at any given moment. Given the typical fall in price of new products over time, this explanation also requires that there be some possibility for potential entrants who do not enter the industry at a given moment to reduce their costs or improve their product quality subsequently. Otherwise, a potential entrant that did not enter the industry initially would never enter the industry later, in which case entry would not be dispersed over time.

The time path of the number of producers indicates that both exit and entry are dispersed over time. This suggests that not only do potential entrants differ in terms of their product qualities and average costs, but also that firms that enter the industry differ on these same dimensions. The incumbents with the highest costs and lowest product qualities presumably exit the industry first, followed by those firms with lower costs and higher product qualities that cannot compete as the price of the new product falls. Consistent with the qualitative regularities, this also suggests that on average, incumbents are limited in their ability to imitate more efficient rivals.

The fact that new industries ultimately reach a point where the number of firms stabilizes suggests that there is a narrowing over time in the range of costs and product qualities of incumbents, so only the firms that attain sufficiently low costs and/or high product qualities survive. But it is notable that in virtually all of our new industries, stability in the number of firms is not reached for many years. This implies that the rates of capacity growth for even the most efficient firms are quite limited during the evolution of the industry. One explanation for this is that firms are uncertain of their costs and product qualities relative to those of their competitors, so that no firm is able to predict with certainty that it will survive once the industry reaches maturity. Consistent with the findings of Porter and Spence (1982), this uncertainty might well inhibit the growth in capacity of all firms in the industry at any given moment.

The paths of prices and output also suggest important factors present in the evolution of new industries. If the demand curve for the new product does not systematically shift over time, then the price and output paths must be directly linked.[12] Indeed, if the price elasticity of demand does not change systematically over time, whatever forces account for the decline over time in the percentage growth in output must also account for the decline over time in the percentage fall in price. Focusing on the path in output, the rate of growth in output is attributable to two sources: the change in the number of producers and the expansion of capacity by incumbent producers. Both factors could contribute to a decline over time in the percentage growth in output. The growth in output attributable to the change in the number of producers will fall over time as exit eventually overtakes entry and the industry experiences a shakeout in the number of producers. The rate of capacity expansion of incumbents will be a function of the expected profit from expansion. If this expected profit is a function of the firm's current price-cost margin, and these margins decline over time as the industry price declines, then the rate of growth of incumbents will

---

[12] Shifts in the demand curve could result from potential adopters learning about the new product over time. However, the diffusion literature (see, for example, Mansfield (1968)), predicts that as the number of adopters of the new product increases initially, the rate of growth of new adopters, and hence output, should accelerate, which does not conform with the prototypical time path of output.

decline over time. This would reinforce the decline in the growth of industry output attributable to the change in the number of producers. If the price elasticity of demand does not change systematically over time, these same factors will also contribute to a decline over time in the percentage fall in price.

A last observation concerns the enormous variation across new industries in the pace and severity of the prototypical pattern of industry evolution. This suggests that there are important differences across industries in the factors that condition the evolutionary process. More fundamentally, it suggests that there are exogenous factors that differ across industries that affect the pace and severity of the evolutionary process.

□ **A model of industry evolution.** In the prior subsection we speculated on some of the principal forces driving the evolution of new industries. In this subsection we develop a general model that reflects these forces. We demonstrate that a number of the quantitative regularities can be explained by this general model but that the model needs to be structured further to explain the remaining regularities.

The following notation and conventions are used. The price at the beginning of period t is denoted by p_t, and industry output at the beginning of period t is denoted by Q_t. The number of firms at the beginning of period t is denoted by N_t. The number of entrants during period t that are still in the industry at the end of the period is denoted by E_t, and the number of incumbents at the beginning of period t that exit by the end of period t is denoted by X_t. Then N_t is defined as

$$N_t = N_{t-1} + E_{t-1} - X_{t-1}. \tag{1}$$

The product is introduced in period 0, so $N_0 \equiv 0$.

Consider first the specification of entry. It is assumed that in each period t, there are a finite number of potential entrants, denoted by K_t, that could conceivably enter the industry. For now, we impose no structure on how K_t is determined in each period; subsequently, we shall assume that entry of new firms causes the number of potential entrants to fall. It is assumed that there is a lump-sum cost associated with entry that can be interpreted as the cost of setting up a new organization. Once a firm has entered, however, it is assumed that production is subject to constant returns to scale. We abstract from scale economies because the available evidence suggests that in most industries, scale economies are exhausted at a low output relative to the size of the market.[13]

It is assumed that in each period, potential entrants differ in the average costs and product quality they would realize if they entered the industry. To accommodate both cost and product quality differences, average cost is calibrated per unit of quality of the good, so that differences across entrants can be expressed simply in terms of their average costs per unit of quality. (Hereafter, the qualification "per unit of quality" is omitted.) The cost differences between entrants are modelled by assuming that in each period, entrants that have not yet entered the industry receive a random draw from an "information urn." The information they draw may concern market opportunities, technology, or anything else that provides firms with a competitive advantage. The information qualifies each potential entrant to achieve some average cost of production, c.[14] The distribution function governing the cost draws is denoted by $G(c)$. It is assumed that the lowest possible cost of production is y, so $G(c) = 0$ for all $c < y$.

We assume that all firms maximize profits and that a potential entrant will enter the industry only if its cost draw is such that its expected discounted profits from entry are nonnegative; we also assume that all firms expect the industry price, p_t, to fall over time.

---

[13] See Scherer *et al.* (1975) and the evidence from the literature on plant and firm growth rates and survival probabilities (Stigler, 1958; Saving, 1961; Weiss, 1964; Simon and Bonini, 1958; Mansfield, 1962).

[14] Note that since potential entrants that have not yet entered receive a new cost of production each period, their costs can be lower in later periods, which, as we noted earlier, is necessary for entry to be dispersed over time.

38 / THE RAND JOURNAL OF ECONOMICS

Once a firm enters, it is assumed to be limited in its ability to reduce its cost after entry.[15] All postentry cost reductions are assumed to be realized through the imitation of more efficient rivals. For simplicity, all imitation is assumed to occur immediately after entry. Firms entering during period t with a cost $c > y(1 + \delta)$ are assumed to reduce their cost to $c/(1 + \delta)$ by the end of period t, where δ is a parameter representing the ease of imitation. Firms entering in period t with a cost $c \le y(1 + \delta)$ are assumed to reduce their cost to y, the lowest attainable cost, by the end of period t. After the period of entry, it is assumed that firms do not lower their costs any further.

Entrants to the industry are assumed to enter with a capacity to produce one unit of output. If they are still in the industry at the beginning of period t, they are assumed to change their capacity in period t at a rate that is determined by their cost, c, relative to the price at the beginning of period $t + 1$, p_{t+1}. If $c = p_{t+1}$, they are assumed to maintain their capacities. Alternatively, if $c < p_{t+1}$, they are assumed to grow at positive rates which are bounded in all periods from above and below. Later we also assume that in each period, the greater the industry price, the greater each firm's growth rate will be.

All firms are assumed to be price takers. The market demand curve, which is assumed to be fixed over time, is denoted by $Q_t(p_t) = f(p_t)$, where $df(p_t)/dp_t < 0$ for all p_t. It is assumed that the market clears in every period.

This model captures a number of the factors emphasized in the prior subsection. It assumes that the number of potential entrants is limited, that potential entrants differ in terms of their costs and product qualities, that potential entrants receive new information over time which alters their costs and product qualities, and that the rates of growth of incumbents are finite. As we show below, the model also predicts a number of aspects about the evolution of new industries that we highlighted, such as dispersed entry and exit, a narrowing over time in the range of costs and product qualities of incumbents, and an abatement in industry output growth due to a fall over time in entry and possibly declines in incumbent growth rates.

The model is similar to the evolutionary models of Jovanovic (1982) and Winter (1984), who also allow for random cost differences across firms, limited (or no) imitation, price taking, and the finite growth of incumbents. Because their objectives differ from ours, however, their models differ from ours in important respects. Jovanovic assumes an infinite number of atomistic potential entrants in all periods. This abstracts from the influence of randomness in the cost draws of potential entrants in each period. It also precludes analyzing the path of the number of firms and the associated paths of price and output. Winter, on the other hand, allows for randomness in the cost draws but uses simulation techniques to analyze his model rather than deriving general analytic results. In contrast, we analyze the extent to which general results can be derived by allowing both for randomness in the cost draws and a finite population of potential entrants.

The first result we derive concerns the direction of the change in price and output over time.

Proposition 1. There exists a period T such that for all periods $t < T$, $p_t > p_{t+1}$ and $Q_t < Q_{t+1}$, and for all periods $t \ge T$, $p_t = p_{t+1}$ and $Q_t = Q_{t+1}$.

Proof. We first establish that if $p_t \ne p_{t+1}$ for some t, then $p_t > p_{t+1}$ and $Q_t < Q_{t+1}$. To see this, suppose instead that $p_t < p_{t+1}$. Given that all firms are price takers, they will produce to capacity in period t as long as p_t exceeds their costs. Therefore, if $p_t < p_{t+1}$, then all of

---

[15] See Arrow (1974), Hannan and Freeman (1977), and Nelson and Winter (1982) for a discussion of the factors limiting the ability of firms to change over time. Among other things, there must be limits on the ability of firms to sell information (Arrow, 1962; Williamson, 1975). Otherwise, firms would be able to sell the information that qualifies them for a particular cost, in which case the opportunity cost of the information would equal its market value and all firms would effectively have the same cost.

the incumbents at time t will produce to capacity in period $t + 1$. Since the capacity of all incumbents that remain in the industry cannot decline, this implies that the output of the incumbents at time t must be less than or equal to the output of these same firms at time $t + 1$. But since entry can only add to the industry's output, this implies that $Q_t \leq Q_{t+1}$, which is inconsistent with $p_t < p_{t+1}$ and the fact that the industry demand curve is fixed over time. Therefore, if $p_t \neq p_{t+1}$, then p_t must be greater than p_{t+1}, which implies that $Q_t < Q_{t+1}$.

Eventually, p_t must equal y. To see this, suppose instead that $p_t > y$ for all t. Then all firms that attain cost y after imitation will remain in the industry and produce to capacity in every period. Furthermore, they will expand their capacity in every period by rates which are bounded from below. Consequently, these firms will eventually produce an output equal to $f(y)$, the total quantity demanded at price y. But this is not possible if the market clears in every period and $p_t > y$. Therefore, p_t must eventually equal y. Let T denote the period in which $p_t = y$.

Once p_t equals y, the only firms that will still be in the industry (i.e., that will still be producing nonzero output) are those that attained cost y after imitation. Since each of their costs equals the industry price, they will not grow. No new firms will enter the industry since the expected profits from entry will be negative no matter what cost a potential entrant draws. Therefore, after period T, total industry output will not change over time; hence, p_t will not change over time. This establishes the second part of the proposition.   *Q.E.D.*

Thus, we see that the model, without any further structuring, is capable of explaining the fall in price, the rise in output, and the eventual levelling off of both that characterizes the evolution of new industries.[16] The remaining aspect of the price and output regularities that needs to be explained is the decline over time in the percentage change in both price and output. We defer consideration of this and first demonstrate that the current form of the model can explain the regularities in the number of firms.

Proposition 2. There exists periods $t_1 \leq t_2 < T$ such that: (i) if $t < t_1$, then $N_{t+1} - N_t \geq 0$; (ii) if $t_2 \leq t < T$, then $N_{t+1} - N_t \leq 0$; and (iii) if $t \geq T$, then $N_{t+1} - N_t = 0$.

Proof. Consider first Part (i). Let e_t denote the highest cost in period t that a potential entrant could attain after imitation such that the expected discounted profit from entry is nonnegative. Given the lump-sum cost associated with entry, $e_t < p_t$ for all t. Moreover, if potential entrants (correctly) expect price to fall over time, then $e_t > e_{t+1}$ for all t. Now, let t_1 be the period in which $p_{t_1} = e_1$.[17] Then for all $t < t_1$, p_t must exceed the costs of all firms in the industry, in which case it will be profitable for all incumbents to remain in the industry prior to period t_1. Therefore, no firm will exit the industry prior to t_1, which implies that $N_{t+1} - N_t \geq 0$ for all $t \leq t_1$.

Next consider Part (ii). Since $e_t < p_t$ for all t, there must be some period $t_2 \geq t_1$ in which $p_{t_2} > y = e_{t_2}$. After this point, e_t will be less than y, and there will be no further entry. Since p_t is expected to fall over time and firm costs after imitation are fixed, firms will exit the industry once the industry price falls below their costs. Consequently, given that $p_t > y$ for all $t < T$ and $p_{t+1} < p_t$, all firms that entered prior to period t_2 that attained a cost after imitation between p_t and p_{t+1} will exit the industry during period t. Hence, for all t such that $t_2 \leq t < T$, $N_{t+1} - N_t \leq 0$.

---

[16] Note that the output and price patterns in Tables 4 and 5 suggest that, in contrast to the predictions of the model, it is the percentage change in output and price, and not price and output, that stabilize. However, the model can easily be modified to accommodate this by assuming that in every period the costs of all firms and potential entrants fall by a constant percentage rate (Klepper and Graddy, 1988). This could result from, among other things, technological change in the inputs to the industry which causes the price of the inputs to decline over time.

[17] The length of a period can always be defined so that for each i, there exists a period $j > i$ such that $e_i = p_j$.

Finally, consider Part (iii). For all $t \geq T$, $p_t = y$. Then there will be no entry, firm growth will be zero, and no firm will exit the industry. Consequently, for all $t \geq T$, $N_{t+1} - N_t = 0$. *Q.E.D.*

Proposition 2 indicates that in the initial years of the evolution of the industry, the number of firms will grow; at some later point in the industry's evolution, the number of firms will decline, and following this period, the number of firms will stabilize. This conforms precisely with our earlier empirical findings concerning the time path of the number of firms. Moreover, the model is compatible with the inferences we made in the prior subsection about the dispersion of entry and exit and the narrowing of the range of costs of incumbent firms over time. In each period, potential entrants differ in terms of their costs. Only those potential entrants with sufficiently low costs enter the industry. In the initial evolution of the industry, no prior entrants exit the industry, and the number of firms rises. Eventually, however, the price falls below e_1, and some firms—those with the highest costs—exit. As price falls, firms with successively lower costs exit the industry. Entry eventually ceases but exit continues, causing the number of firms to decline. Stability is reached only when there is no longer any disparity in costs between the firms in the industry, with those firms that attained the lowest possible cost of production after imitation surviving.

The only regularity left to explain is the decline over time of the percentage change in price and output up to time T. The model needs to be structured further to explain this regularity. We proceed by making the following four assumptions: (1) the distribution of the actual cost draws in each period is equal to the population distribution, $G(c)$, and $G(c)$ is uniform, so that $G(c) = k(c - y)$, where k is a factor of proportionality; (2) in each period t all incumbents with a cost less than p_{t+1} expand their capacity by $g\%$, where g is the same for all periods; (3) entry depletes the ranks of potential entrants, so that $K_{t+1} \leq K_t$ for all t; and (4) the price elasticity of the industry demand curve, $(df(p_t)/Q_t)/(dp_t/p_t)$, is the same for all Q_t. We also simplify the model by assuming that the cost associated with entry is zero.[18] Using these assumptions, we can now establish the last regularity.

Proposition 3. For all $t < T$, $(p_{t-1} - p_t)/p_{t-1} > (p_t - p_{t+1})/p_t$ and $(Q_t - Q_{t-1})/Q_{t-1} > (Q_{t+1} - Q_t)/Q_t$.

Proof. Consider the percentage change in industry output during period t. Given the assumptions, we can represent the output at time $t + 1$ of the firms in the industry at time t as $Q_t(1 + g)(p_{t+1}(1 + \delta) - y)/(p_t(1 + \delta) - y)$.[19] The output of the entrants to the industry during period t equals $K_t k(e_t - y)$, the number of entrants times their output at entry of one unit. Then the percentage change in industry output during period t can be expressed as

$$\frac{Q_{t+1} - Q_t}{Q_t} = \frac{(p_{t+1}(1 + \delta) - y)}{(p_t(1 + \delta) - y)}(1 + g) + \frac{K_t k(e_t - y)}{Q_t} - 1.$$

---

[18] If the cost of entry is positive, at time t some firms will have entered the industry during periods j for which $e_j < p_{t+1}$, whereas others will have entered in periods i for which $e_i \geq p_{t+1}$. As a result, the distribution of costs for firms within each of these two groups would differ, which would require dealing separately with these two different groups of firms. Assuming the cost of entry is zero obviates having to make this distinction, which greatly simplifies the subsequent discussion without compromising the generality of the analysis.

[19] In order for a firm to be in the industry at the beginning of period t, it must have drawn a cost prior to imitation that was less than or equal to $p_t(1 + \delta)$. Of these firms, only the ones that drew a cost prior to imitation that was less than $p_{t+1}(1 + \delta)$ will still be in the industry at the end of period t. Given our assumptions, this implies that the fraction of firms in the industry at the beginning of time t that are still in the industry at the end of time t equals $(p_{t+1}(1 + \delta) - y)/(p_t(1 + \delta) - y)$. Since all of the firms are assumed to grow by the same percentage rate, there will be no difference between the size of the firms from each cohort that do and do not exit the industry in any given period. Therefore, the total output at the beginning of period t of the firms that remain in the industry during period t must equal $Q_t(p_{t+1}(1 + \delta) - y)/(p_t(1 + \delta) - y)$. Increasing this by $g\%$ to reflect the growth of these firms during period t yields the expression in the text.

Now, suppose that the percentage fall in price actually increases over time. Then the first term above will decline over time. The second term will also decline over time since K_t is assumed to be nonincreasing over time and e_t falls and Q_t rises over time. Then the percentage growth of output will decline over time. But this cannot occur if the percentage fall in price increases over time and the price elasticity of the industry demand curve is constant. Therefore, the percentage fall in price must decline over time, and the percentage growth of output must also decline over time given the constant price elasticity of demand.   *Q.E.D.*

Intuitively, the uniform distribution of the cost draws in each period ensures that if the percentage fall in price rises over time, then the percentage of firms exiting the industry will also rise over time. As long as the growth rates of incumbent firms do not rise over time, this ensures that the percentage growth of output of incumbent firms will decline over time. If K_t is nonincreasing over time, the rise in industry output from new entrants must also decline over time. Consequently, if the percentage fall in price increases over time, then the percentage growth of industry output must fall over time. But this cannot occur if the price elasticity of the industry demand curve is constant. Therefore, both the percentage fall in price and growth of output must decline over time.

This explanation indicates that the assumptions we added to the model are sufficient but not necessary to explain the decline over time of the percentage fall in price and the percentage growth of output. For example, it is not necessary that $G(c)$ be uniform, just of a form that guarantees that the percentage of firms exiting the industry is a monotonic function of the percentage fall in price.[20] Similarly, it is not necessary that g be constant over time, just that the weighted average growth rate of incumbent firms does not increase over time. Indeed, it takes a systematic set of departures from the assumed conditions for the model *not* to explain the decline over time of the percentage fall in price and the percentage growth of output. But there is no way to rule out the possibility of such systematic departures. This may explain why on average the percentage fall in price and the percentage growth of output declined over time for the products in our sample, but many products departed from this pattern at some point in their evolution.[21]

4. Implications

■ The time path of the number of firms indicates that eventually the number of firms in new industries stabilizes. This is consistent with the qualitative regularities, which indicate that firm market shares in new industries tend to stabilize over time. This suggests that the market structures of industries are importantly shaped by their early experiences. Our model provides insights into how differences in the early experiences of industries might result in persistent differences in industry market structures.

One factor bearing on the evolutionary process is chance. In each period, potential entrants randomly receive information that qualifies them for a particular cost. The realization of this random process will have an important effect on an industry's ultimate market structure. To see this, note that the model predicts that the industry will eventually

---

[20] A sufficient condition for this is that $G(c)/(c - y)$ is a nondecreasing function of c, which is satisfied by a wide range of distributions.

[21] This explanation is consistent with the fact that there are few departures from the predictions of the model concerning the direction of the change in price and output over time and the time path of the number of firms, all of which hold under very general conditions. Alternatively, the greater number of departures from the predictions about the percentage change in price and output may be attributable to the fact that both the price and output series are measured with considerable error, introducing a lot of noise into both series, especially when expressed in percentage change form. Indeed, the price data are implicit price indices computed from indexes of sales and output, and thus errors can be introduced from either component. This may explain why there are more departures from the pattern of a decline over time in the percentage fall in price than the pattern of a decline over time in the percentage growth of output.

be composed of only those firms that attain the lowest possible cost after imitation, with the largest firms being those that were among the first to attain this cost. If, after the first N firms attain this cost, there is an unexpectedly long period before other firms receive the information required to attain this cost, then the N-firm concentration ratio of the industry will be high, *ceteris paribus*. Indeed, if there is an unexpectedly long delay after the first firm attains the lowest possible cost, then the industry could end up as a virtual monopoly.[22]

There are also nonrandom factors that can cause the evolutionary process to differ across industries. In the model, the key factors driving the evolutionary process are the number of potential entrants in each period, the rates at which firms grow in each period, and the ease of imitation of rivals. While the number of potential entrants and the growth rates of incumbents in each period will be endogenously determined, there are no doubt exogenous factors that cause them and the ease of imitation to differ across industries. For example, if potential entrants tend to be users of the new product and firms with experience in related technologies, as noted in the discussion of the qualitative regularities, then the number of potential entrants in any given period is likely to be greater the more diverse the users of the product and the greater the number of disciplines underlying the new industry's technology. Porter and Spence's (1982) results suggest that the growth rates of incumbents are tied to the degree of uncertainty (both technological and market related) characterizing the new product. Finally, the ease of imitation is likely to be related to the abilities of firms to appropriate the value of their innovations through devices like patents.

We can use the model to analyze how exogenous differences in the number of potential entrants, the growth rates of incumbent firms, and the ease of imitation affect the number of firms and the industry N-firm concentration ratio. In the Appendix, we show that exogenous forces in any period that lead to a greater number of potential entrants, greater ease of imitation, or lower rates of growth of incumbent firms will cause the number of firms to be greater and the industry N-firm concentration ratio to be lower in the next period. Analyzing the effect of these factors on the number of firms and the industry N-firm concentration ratio at maturity requires much more structuring of the model, which is beyond the scope of this article. But intuition suggests that the effect of these factors on the number of firms and the industry N-firm concentration ratio at maturity would be in the same direction as the effect of these factors on the number of firms and the industry N-firm concentration ratio in the next period. Indeed, Klepper and Graddy (1988) confirm this intuition using a simplified version of the model.

While it is possible to come up with examples of industries that conform with the predictions of the model concerning the determinants of the number of producers and the industry N-firm concentration ratio (Klepper and Graddy, 1988), this hardly constitutes a test of the predictions. But as we have demonstrated, the model is able to account for a wide range of regularities concerning the evolution of new industries. Moreover, similar models developed by Jovanovic (1982) and Winter (1984) are capable of explaining other important patterns. This suggests that the kind of evolutionary forces highlighted in our model play an important role in shaping industries. In its current form, however, the model provides a highly simplified account of industry evolution, ignoring such factors as innovation by incumbents, firm-specific learning, scale economies, and strategic behavior. An important question is whether these factors could be incorporated into the model without compromising the ability of the model to explain the regularities. A more fundamental question is whether the regularities could be explained by these factors alone and not by the evolutionary forces we emphasized. Hopefully, our efforts will galvanize others to develop and test alternative explanations of the regularities.

---

[22] These results are consistent with the simulation results of Nelson and Winter (1982) and Winter (1984).

[23] We assume that the growth rates of incumbent firms during period t are such that the greater p_{t+1}, the greater each firm's growth rate. An exogenous shift in the growth rates of incumbent firms during period t means that *for a given* p_{t+1}, the growth rates of incumbent firms will shift relative to what they otherwise would have been.

Appendix

■ In order to analyze the effects of an exogenous change in period t in the number of potential entrants, the growth rates of incumbent firms,[23] and the ease of imitation of rivals on the number of firms and the industry N-firm concentration ratio in period $t + 1$, we first consider the effects of these changes on the price in period $t + 1$. Consider first the effect of a rise in K_t on p_{t+1}. This must cause p_{t+1} to fall (relative to what it would have been). To see this, suppose instead that p_{t+1} were unaffected. Then the rate of exit and the growth rates of incumbent firms (i.e., firms in the industry at the beginning of period t) would be unaffected; hence, the output of incumbent firms in period $t + 1$ would be unaffected. If p_{t+1} were unaffected, then e_t would also be unaffected. But, given the rise in K_t, the number of entrants during period t would rise. Then Q_{t+1} would rise (relative to what it would have been), which cannot occur if p_{t+1} were unaffected. Therefore, p_{t+1} must be affected. Using the same argument, it is easy to show that p_{t+1} must fall. A similar argument can be used to show that an exogenous rise in δ or in the growth rates of incumbent firms in period t will also cause p_{t+1} to fall.

Now, consider the effect of the changes on N_{t+1}. If K_t rises, causing p_{t+1} to fall, then the exit rate of incumbents during period t will rise, causing the number of incumbent firms still in the industry during period t to fall (relative to what it would have been). Suppose this fall is balanced by an equal rise in the number of entrants during period t due to the rise in K_t. Then N_{t+1} would be unaffected (relative to what it would have been). Since incumbents are always at least as big as entrants, however, this implies that Q_{t+1} would fall (relative to what it would have been). But this cannot be if p_{t+1} is less than it would have been. Consequently, the number of entrants during period t must rise by an amount greater than the rise in the number of firms that exit the industry during t, implying that N_{t+1} must rise (relative to what it would have been). The same argument shows that a rise in δ in period t will lead to a rise in N_{t+1}. If the growth rates of all of the incumbent firms rise, causing p_{t+1} to fall, then the exit rate of incumbents during period t will rise, and the number of entrants during period t will fall. This implies that N_{t+1} will fall.

Finally, consider the effect of the changes on the industry N-firm concentration ratio in period $t + 1$. If K_t increases, the resulting fall in p_{t+1} will cause the growth rates during period t of all incumbents, including the N-largest firms, to fall. It will also cause Q_{t+1} to rise. Therefore, the industry N-firm concentration ratio in period t will fall (relative to what it would have been). The same argument establishes that a rise in δ during period t will cause the industry N-firm concentration ratio in period $t + 1$ to fall. Lastly, if the growth rates of all of the incumbent firms rise, causing p_{t+1} to fall, then the rate of exit among the incumbent firms during period t will rise and the number of entrants during period t will fall (relative to what it would have been). But since Q_{t+1} must rise if p_{t+1} falls, the only way this could occur is if the output of incumbent firms during period t rises (relative to what it would have been), both absolutely and as a percentage of Q_{t+1}. Assuming that all of the incumbent firms are affected similarly, this implies that the output of the N-largest firms in period $t + 1$ will rise as a percentage of Q_{t+1}, which means the industry N-firm concentration ratio will rise.

References

ABERNATHY, W.J. *The Productivity Dilemma*. Baltimore: The Johns Hopkins University Press, 1978.
———— AND TOWNSEND, P.L. "Technology, Productivity, and Process Change." *Technological Forecasting and Social Change*, Vol. 7 (1975), pp. 379–394.
ARROW, K.J. "Economic Welfare and the Allocation of Resources for Invention." in R.R. Nelson, ed., *The Rate and Direction of Inventive Activity: Economic and Social Factors*. Princeton: Princeton University Press, 1962.
————. *The Limits of Organization*. New York: W.W. Norton and Company, Inc., 1974.
BOSTON CONSULTING GROUP. *Perspectives on Experience*. Boston: Boston Consulting Group, 1972.
BURNS, A.F. *Production Trends in the United States Since 1870*. New York: National Bureau of Economic Research, 1934.
CHAMPERNOWNE, D.G. "A Model of Income Distribution." *Economic Journal*, Vol. 63 (1953), pp. 318–351.
COX, W.E., JR. "Product Life Cycles As Marketing Models." *Journal of Business*, Vol. 40 (1967), pp. 375–384.
DASGUPTA, P. AND STIGLITZ, J.E. "Entry, Innovation, Exit: Towards a Dynamic Theory of Oligopolistic Industrial Structure." *European Economic Review*, Vol. 15 (1981), pp. 137–158.
———— AND ————. "Industrial Structure and the Nature of Innovative Activity." *Economic Journal*, Vol. 90 (1980), pp. 266–293.
DEAN, J. "Pricing Policies for New Products." *Harvard Business Review*, Vol. 28 (1950), pp. 45–53.
FLAHERTY, M.T. "Industry Structure and Cost-Reducing Investment." *Econometrica*, Vol. 48 (1980), pp. 1187–1209.
FUTIA, C.A. "Schumpeterian Competition." *Quarterly Journal of Economics*, Vol. 94 (1980), pp. 675–695.
GIBRAT, R. *Les Inégalités Economiques*. Paris: Receuil Sirey, 1931.
GORT, M. AND KLEPPER, S. "Time Paths in the Diffusion of Product Innovations." *Economic Journal*, Vol. 92 (1982), pp. 630–653.
HANNAN, M.T. AND FREEMAN, J. "Population Ecology of Organizations." *American Journal of Sociology*, Vol. 82 (1977), pp. 929–964.
HART, P.E. AND PRAIS, S.J. "The Analysis of Business Concentration: A Statistical Approach." *Journal of the Royal Statistical Society*, Vol. 19 (Series A), (1956), pp. 150–181.

44 / THE RAND JOURNAL OF ECONOMICS

HAYES, R.H. AND WHEELWRIGHT, S.C. "Link Manufacturing Process and Product Life Cycles." *Harvard Business Review,* Vol. 57 (1979a), pp. 133–140.

—— AND ——. "The Dynamics of Process-Product Life Cycles." *Harvard Business Review,* Vol. 57 (1979b), pp. 127–136.

IJIRI, Y. AND SIMON H.A. *Skew Distributions and the Sizes of Business Firms.* New York: North Holland Publishing Co., 1977.

JOVANOVIC, B. "Selection and the Evolution of Industry." *Econometrica,* Vol. 50 (1982), pp. 649–670.

KLEIN, B.H. *Dynamic Economics.* Cambridge, Mass.: Harvard University Press, 1977.

KLEPPER, S. AND GRADDY, E. "Industry Evolution and the Determinants of Market Structure." Mimeo, Carnegie-Mellon University, 1988.

LEVITT, T. "Exploit the Product Life Cycle." *Harvard Business Review,* Vol. 18 (1965), pp. 81–94.

LIPPMAN, S.A. AND RUMELT, R.P. "Uncertain Imitability: An Analysis of Interfirm Differences in Efficiency Under Competition." *The Bell Journal of Economics,* Vol. 13 (1982), pp. 418–438.

LOURY, G.C. "Market Structure and Innovation." *Quarterly Journal of Economics,* Vol. 93 (1979), pp. 395–410.

MANSFIELD, E. "Entry, Gibrat's Law, Innovation, and the Growth of Firms." *American Economic Review,* Vol. 52 (1962), pp. 1023–1051.

——. *Industrial Research and Technological Innovation: An Econometric Analysis.* New York: W.W. Norton and Company, Inc., 1968.

NELSON, R.R. AND WINTER S.G. *An Evolutionary Theory of Economic Change.* Cambridge, Mass.: Harvard University Press, 1982.

—— AND ——. "Forces Generating and Limiting Concentration Under Schumpeterian Competition." *Bell Journal of Economics,* Vol. 9 (1978), pp. 524–546.

PELTZMAN, S. "The Gains and Losses From Industrial Concentration." *Journal of Law and Economics,* Vol. 20 (1977), pp. 229–263.

PORTER, M.E. *Competitive Strategy: Techniques for Analyzing Industries and Competitors.* New York: The Free Press, 1980.

——. "The Technological Dimension of Competitive Strategy." In R.S. Rosenbloom, ed., *Research On Technological Innovation, Management, and Policy.* Greenwich, Conn.: JAI Press, Inc., 1983.

—— AND SPENCE, A.M. "The Capacity Expansion Process in a Growing Oligopoly." In J.J. McCall, ed., *The Economics of Information and Uncertainty.* Chicago: University of Chicago Press, 1982.

SAVING, T.R. "Estimation of Optimum Size of Plant by the Survivor Technique." *Quarterly Journal of Economics,* Vol. 75 (1961), pp. 569–607.

SCHERER, F.M. *Industrial Market Structure and Economic Performance.* Chicago: Rand McNally, 1980.

——, BECKENSTEIN, A., KAUFER, E., AND MURPHY, R.D. *The Economics of Multiplant Operation: An International Comparisons Study.* Cambridge, Mass.: Harvard University Press, 1975.

SIMON, H.A. "On A Class of Skew Distribution Functions." *Biometrika,* Vol. 52 (1955), pp. 425–440.

—— AND BONINI, C.P. "The Size Distribution of Business Firms." *American Economic Review,* Vol. 48 (1958), pp. 607–617.

STIGLER, G.J. "The Economies of Scale." *Journal of Law and Economics,* Vol. 1 (1958), pp. 54–71.

TELSER, L.G. "A Theory of Innovation and Its Effects." *The Bell Journal of Economics,* Vol. 13 (1982), pp. 69–92.

THOMAS PUBLISHING COMPANY. *Thomas' Register of American Manufacturers.* New York: Thomas Publishing Co., various issues, 1906–1981.

UTTERBACK, J.M. "The Dynamics of Product and Process Innovation in Industry." In C.T. Hill and J.M. Utterback, eds., *Technological Innovation for a Dynamic Economy,* Elmsford, N.Y.: Pergamon Press, 1979.

—— AND ABERNATHY, W.J. "A Dynamic Model of Process and Product Innovation." *Omega,* Vol. 3 (1975), pp. 639–656.

VERNON, R. "International Investment and International Trade in the Product Life Cycle." *Quarterly Journal of Economics,* Vol. 80 (1966), pp. 190–207.

WEISS, L.W. "The Survival Technique and the Extent of Suboptimal Capacity." *Journal of Political Economy,* Vol. 72 (1964), pp. 246–261.

WELLS, L.T. "International Trade: The Product Life Cycle Approach." In L.T. Wells, ed., *The Product Life Cycle and International Trade.* Boston: Graduate School of Business Administration, Harvard University, 1972.

WILLIAMSON, O.E. *Markets and Hierarchies: Analysis and Antitrust Implications.* New York: The Free Press, 1975.

WINTER, S.G. "Schumpeterian Competition in Alternative Technological Regimes." *Journal of Economic Behavior and Organization,* Vol. 5 (1984), pp. 287–320.

[9]

Journal of Economic Literature
Vol. XXXVI (December 1998), pp. 1947–1982

Industrial Organization and New Findings on the Turnover and Mobility of Firms

RICHARD E. CAVES[1]

1. Introduction

ALTHOUGH RESEARCH on the turnover of business units has a long tradition, primary data on the full populations of business units (firms, establishments) present in nations' markets were inaccessible until recently. Only in the past decade have economists picked the locks on the doors of numerous national census bureaus and organized the primary records so that the births, deaths, and life trajectories of individual business units can be traced. Commercial data bases that claim similar coverage have also come into use for research on turnover and mobility.

This research has borne as its first fruit a great outpouring of stylized facts where no more than impressions had existed before. Although the importance of these facts for economic behavior and performance is manifest, their development has not been theory-driven. Indeed, identifying the theoretical models on which the stylized facts shed light is itself an exercise in hunting and gathering. The empirical evidence aligns with some obviously salient models of (e.g.) the effect of firms' random growth rates on their industry's concentration and the decisions of potential entrant firms uncertain about their prospective cost levels. But it also spotlights some nonobvious theoretical referents, such as the theory of real options (to explain the varying resource commitments made by entering firms) and the theory of job-matching (to explain the productivity of changes in control of business units).

The newly accessible data on turnover and mobility have attracted economists specializing in several fields. This survey's emphases are driven by the field of industrial organization, although with passing attention to work attuned to labor economics and macroeconomics.[2] Accordingly, the first section summarizes the recently accumulated stylized facts about entry, exit, and the mobility

[1] Harvard University. Thanks for helpful comments and suggestions to David Audretsch, John R. Baldwin, Tito Boeri, Steve Davies, Paul Geroski, Michael Gort, John Haltiwanger, John E. Jackson, Steve Klepper, Jose Mata, Anita McGahan, Robert McGuckin, Ariel Pakes, Mark J. Roberts, Frank Wolak, and anonymous referees.

[2] A sociology-based literature on organizational ecology (e.g. Michael T. Hannan and John Freeman 1989) will be neglected. To an economist's eyes, its treatment of turnover in business populations suffers from eschewing simple priors about business behavior: intended profit-maximization and the need to cover costs to keep a firm's coalition together. But there are compensating strengths, such as the analysis of reasons why a failing coalition frequently cannot imitate the *modus operandi* of a winner (Hannan and Freeman 1989, chap. 4).

1948   *Journal of Economic Literature, Vol. XXXVI (December 1998)*

of business units. Some of the findings are conditioned on the unit's specific market environment, but most of them deal in overall or average patterns. The second section brings this market context to the fore and seeks to integrate the new findings about turnover and mobility with industrial organization's traditional framework, based on static partial-equilibrium models of markets. The third section relates the new evidence to other lines of empirical research on productivity and productive efficiency, again in the context of firms competing in particular markets.

The data bases that researchers have employed are mostly longitudinal versions of national census data bases. A number of countries are represented, including developing nations. The bulk of the research, and hence this survey's attention, pertains to the United States and Canada; an effort will be made to expose international comparative conclusions, although the market mechanisms at work appear overwhelmingly similar from country to country. Some proprietary data bases have also been employed, and until recently most research on turnover unavoidably depended on data for large, publicly traded companies. Important differences exist among these data bases. Some of them are organized around firms, some around establishments or business units. Many pertain only to manufacturing industries, some to all nonfinancial sectors. They differ importantly in their coverage of small business units: some only sample small units or cut off at some threshold (such as 10 employees), while a few include single-person enterprises. Integrating this research requires many judgment calls on where data-base differences are and are not important. In the first section of this paper, the reader should assume that stated conclusions describe un-

weighted-average patterns drawn from censuses that include quite small firms; because of the sharply skewed distribution of firm sizes, smaller units therefore dominate the conclusions. That fact somewhat mitigates another difference among the data bases: some focus on firms, some on plants that might be either independent firms or dependent units of a multiplant firm. Most small establishments are independent firms, diluting any distortions due to units' heterogeneous independence.

Several forms of turnover are addressed in this research, and terminology for identifying them is not fully standardized. We use "turnover" as a general term to embrace three processes: the births and deaths of business units ("entry and exit"), variations in sizes and market shares of continuing units ("mobility"), and shifts between enterprises in the control of continuing business units ("changes in control"). An "establishment" is a plant (in some instances a line of business), and a firm is an independent legal entity (in some instances a set of plants under common control). A "business unit" might be either an establishment or a firm; research in this field commonly employs populations of establishments that include both free-standing single-plant firms and those plants controlled by multiplant firms. We shall not stress the firm/plant distinction except where appropriate to point out differences between the behavior of single-plant firms and of multi-plant firms' dependent plants.

2. Mobility, Entry, and Exit in Populations of Firms and Establishments

2.1 Background: The Law of Proportionate Effect

Although the research on turnover is not strongly theory-driven, many earlier empirical studies of the mobility of firms were shaped by a purely statistical model resting on the hypothesis known as the Law of Proportionate Effect (LPE) or Gibrat's Law: if growth rates of firms in a fixed population are independent of their initial sizes, the variance of growth rates shows no heteroskedasticity with size, and serial correlation of growth rates is absent, then the concentration of the population increases without limit. Many studies sought to test the independence and serial-correlation assumptions themselves, the implication of lognormally distributed firm sizes, or the implication of increasing concentration as the variance of the firm size increases. We can rely on John Sutton's (1997) survey of "Gibrat's legacy" for a review of recent econometric and theoretical advances from Gibrat's beachhead. The original formulation abstracted from the occurrence of entry and exit, which can be integrated into the random-process model in various ways. For organizing the recent profusion of stylized facts, what matters are the empirically established exceptions to and extensions of Gibrat's simple model (basic references include David S. Evans 1987a, 1987b; Bronwyn Hall 1987; Jonathan S. Leonard 1986; M. S. Kumar 1985; and surveys by Tito Boeri 1989 and Joachim Wagner 1992).

1. The variance of firms' proportional growth rates is not independent of their size but diminishes with it. This heteroskedasticity is not always evident among the largest firms but appears in samples that reach below Fortune 500 giants (see Peter E. Hart and Nicholas Oulton 1996; David B. Audretsch 1995a, chap. 4; and Jose Mata 1994). Evans (1987a) reported that the variability over time of a firm's growth rate decreases with size in

85 of 100 U.S. manufacturing industries.[3]

2. Mean growth rates of surviving firms are not independent of their sizes but tend to decline with size and also with the unit's age (given size). Evans (1987a) found the mean growth rate to decline significantly with size in 89 percent of the individual industries that he studied. The pattern is consistent with Galtonian regression and of course removes Gibrat's implication of increasing concentration (for example, Jozef Konings 1995b).

3. Entry and exit are intimately involved in growth–size relations. Entry is more likely to occur into smaller size classes, and the likelihood of a unit's exit declines with its size.

4. Units' growth rates may well be serially correlated, but earlier studies disagreed on the pattern. This is not surprising, as autocorrelation of changes in units' sizes may be regarded either as a statistical error-correction process (negative autocorrelation) or a cumulative economic response to the unit's perceived competitive advantage or disadvantage (positive). For large British firms, Kumar (1985) observed autocorrelation in growth rates measured over blocks of several (usually five) years that is positive but declining over time. Paul Dunne and Alan Hughes (1994), also working with a large sample of British companies and five-year periods,

[3] Sidney S. Alexander (1949) and subsequent researchers investigated whether the decline in the variance of firms' growth rates with size might have a statistical explanation. If a firm of size k is regarded as a portfolio of k independent unit-size businesses, we can predict the magnitude of the decline of growth's variance with size. Just as this assumption obviously marks an upper bound on the diversification of larger firms, so does the predicted rate of variance decline exceed those actually estimated (Boeri 1989). In this context S. W. Davies pointed out (personal communication) that it would be attractive to compare this variance-size relation in firms' overall sizes and in their sizes (shares) in individual markets.

detected weak positive autocorrelation for large firms and weak negative autocorrelation for small ones. Bruno Contini and Riccardo Revelli (1989) reported negative autocorrelation for small Italian firms, as did Boeri and Ulrich Cramer (1992) for all German non-agricultural establishments employing 20 or more. In a sample of the larger British firms, Geroski, Stephen Machin, and Chris Walters (1997) estimated significant positive regression coefficients of one year's growth on the growth rate in each of the three preceding years, but they observed that the partial correlation with growth in the preceding year was negative. Wagner's (1992) results for German firms appear consistent with Geroski, Machin, and Walters'. A possible resolution of these conflicting results is suggested in Section 2.2.

2.2 Mobility Patterns: Recent Evidence

Recent research has turned from a preoccupation with LPE to the direct measurement of turnover itself, recognizing that its significance extends beyond concentration to a broad range of behavioral and normative properties of product (also labor) markets. This new approach addresses both the mobility of continuing firms (this subsection) and turnover due to entry and exit (the next subsection).

Mobility in the shares of a set of continuing firms is usually measured by summing the absolute values of the differences between their activity (output, employment) levels at t and $t + 1$ and dividing by the sum of their activity levels at t. This mobility measure is equivalent to the sum of absolute values of their growth rates weighted by their initial shares, so mobility remains closely linked to the LPE literature (Boeri 1994). These changes are commonly large. Steven J. Davis, John C. Haltiwanger, and Scott Schuh (1996,

Fig. 2.3), working with absolute growth rates of employment, documented that about half of all job changes in U.S. manufacturing are accounted for by units making annual changes of 25 percent or more. John R. Baldwin (1995, Table 4.1) divided Canadian manufacturing firms that survived from 1970 to 1982 into those gaining and those losing employment. While the average continuing firm increased its employment by 1.5 percent annually, the average gainer grew by 7.8 percent while the average loser shrank by 6.3 percent. Findings for other countries are similar: for German nonagricultural sectors during 1977–90, expanding incumbents' employment on average grew 6.2 percent annually, while contracting ones shrank by 5.8 percent (Boeri and Cramer 1992). Although the changes tend to be cyclically sensitive, Baldwin noted that even in the decade's most expansionary year, 34 percent of the continuing firms reduced employment (though not necessarily output). Negative year-to-year autocorrelation appears in the typical firm's employment changes around any long-term trend, shown by comparing average rates of growth for firms that expanded employment in a given year to annualized growth rates for those that expanded cumulatively over longer periods. For example, continuing Canadian firms that expanded over 1970–81 grew by 27.2 percent, equivalent to 2.2 percent annualized, but firms growing in each year within 1970–81 had average annual growth of 8.2 percent. Continuing firms that contracted over 1970–81 (32 percent of all continuing firms) shrank by 11.0 percent, 1.05 percent annualized, but firms shrinking in each year contracted by 5.9 percent on average (Baldwin 1995, Table 4.3).

A second important feature of the mobility pattern is long-run regression to the mean. For example, the initial average size of Canadian firms that contracted over 1970–76 was 71 percent greater than the initial average size of those that expanded. The difference increases with the length of time over which the gainers and losers are identified. However, when continuing firms are divided into quintiles on the basis of their initial sizes, subsequent gainers predominate at the small end and subsequent losers in the top quintile, but both are well represented throughout; the ratio of the gainers' mean proportional gain to the losers' mean proportional loss rises rapidly and smoothly from the largest to the smallest quintile (Baldwin 1995, Table 4.6). Although many findings in this literature are consistent with pervasive mean regression, other countries' data have not been analyzed to check the short-run (error correction) and long-run (presumably behavior) mean regression found in Canada.

One might suppose that the mobility of firms results from their discrete and unequal adjustments to whatever aggregate expansion or contraction their market is experiencing. However, mobility seems largely independent of the direction and magnitude of the industry-wide change. Timothy Dunne, Mark J. Roberts, and Larry Samuelson (1989a) compared gross rates of increase in employment in expanding plants and of contraction in shrinking plants, after sorting industries into those that (in a five-year period) exhibit growing and shrinking employment overall. Within four-digit industries they found that for every job gained in a growing industry 0.604 are lost, and for every job lost in a contracting industry 0.644 are gained. Davis and Haltiwanger (1992) compared this intraindustry turnover to interindustry shifts. They broke down employment shifts (beyond those needed to accomplish a sector's net overall ex-

TABLE 1
AVERAGE ANNUAL RATES OF JOB TURNOVER
(GROSS GAINS PLUS GROSS LOSSES, PERCENTAGE OF
TOTAL EMPLOYMENT), SELECTED COUNTRIES AND
TIME PERIODS

Country	Time period	Turnover rate (%)
A. Selected industrial countries		
Canada	1984–90	22.6
Denmark	1984–89	29.8
Finland	1988–91	24.2
France	1985–87	26.3
Germany	1977–89	15.9
Italy	1985–91	23.4
Norway	1976–86	15.6
Sweden	1985–91	22.7
United Kingdom	1982–91	15.2
United States	1976–91	21.5
B. Manufacturing sector, selected countries		
Chile	1979–86	26.8
Colombia	1977–91	24.6
Morocco	1984–89	30.7
Canada	1973–86	20.5
United States	1973–86	19.6

Source: Panel A, Boeri (1994); panel B, Roberts and Tybout (1996, Table 2.1). Sectoral coverage for countries in panel A varies between manufacturing only (United States) and all employment (Germany).

pansion or contraction) into those occurring between and within four-digit U.S. manufacturing industries. Inter-industry shifts accounted for only 12 percent, and a more elaborate set of controls (region, plant size, plant age, ownership) still left 61 percent to be explained by random intraindustry mobility.[4]

To explain this high incidence of intraindustry mobility, one can look to

[4] Employment rather than output is widely used as a turnover measure, and it is important to keep in mind that a unit's falling employment might be associated either with falling output or with rising output and productivity. Martin Neil Baily, Eric J. Bartelsman, and Haltiwanger (1996) showed that the distribution of firms by rising and falling employment is largely independent of their distribution by rising and falling productivity.

differences among both countries and industries. The comparisons of countries' average turnover rates in Table 1 are based on employment turnover (jobs created in expanding units plus jobs lost in contracting units, as percentage of total employment). They vary in sectors covered and other details, and they include newly opened and closed business units as well as continuing ones. Variations among industrial countries do not submit to easy explanations, but developing countries seem to experience more turnover.[5] Among the industrial countries there is a weakly evident inverse relationship between average establishment sizes and mobility, consistent with the findings of the LPE literature already mentioned.[6] Table 1's information on selected developing countries supports this interpretation. The work of John E. Jackson et al. (1996) on Poland suggests that turnover in the transition economies is very high.[7]

Other evidence on the correlations of turnover comes from cross-section tests

within countries. Geroski, Machin, and Walters (1997) measured the dependence of British firms' sales growth on changes in their market values, the growth rates of their industries' outputs and of gross domestic product, and the occurrence of innovations within the firm and industry. Industry-level growth and innovations and aggregate growth exhibit some explanatory power, but instantaneous individual shocks account for most of the variance in growth rates of firms' sales. As they concluded, "corporate growth rates are not quite random." Working with data on plants in 23 four-digit U.S. manufacturing industries, Baily, Charles Hulten, and David Campbell (1992) sought to test competing models of the turnover process on patterns of change in plants' productivity rankings within their industries. They found some evidence of capital vintage effects (a plant's productivity declining with its age), as had T. Y. Shen (1968). These rankings show a lot of continuity, however, and the authors' preferred explanation is that each plant's productivity varies randomly around its own productivity intercept, with regression to the mean evident.

More could be done to pin down industry-specific determinants of mobility, and theoretical models offer help. In "active learning" models, such as Richard Ericson and Ariel Pakes (1995), firms invest in uncertain but expectedly profitable innovations or cost reductions. The firm grows if successful, shrinks or exits if unsuccessful. Capital vintage effects, already mentioned, can account for productivity dispersions that result from a plant's descent through the productivity rankings as it ages, eventually to be refurbished or retired and replaced by a new-vintage plant. Val Eugene Lambson (1991) demonstrated how, even without capital-embodied technical progress, vintage

---

[5] International comparisons will not be emphasized in this paper because of pervasive differences in national data sets. The most important is the varying truncation of small firms: some include even single-person businesses, while others omit firms smaller than ten employees.

[6] Baldwin and Garnett Picot (1995) compared labor mobility rates between Canada and the United States, broken down by changes in small and large units. The gross flows tend to be larger in Canadian than U.S. small units, and greater for U.S. than Canadian large ones. They conjectured that the Canadian plant-size distribution, more concentrated in small sizes than that of the United States, causes the burden of adjusting to disturbances to be pushed toward the smaller units.

[7] Other noteworthy findings are that privatized and reformed state enterprises have lost less than unreformed ones, and that the annual numbers and sizes of new enterprises have fallen as (perhaps) the richest and most obvious opportunities exposed in the transition were picked off first. The ending of a large disequilibrium has provoked temporary bursts of entry in other settings, such as the United States following World War II (Betty C. Churchill 1954a) and Chile after a massive liberalization of international trade (James R. Tybout 1996a).

effects could account for plants' dispersed productivity levels: firms choosing (sunk) technologies must guess about future prices of variable inputs, and the dispersion of firms' average variable costs at any point in time reflects the historic dispersion of those guesses. Interindustry associations between mobility and industry structure or technology are considered in Section 3.

The heteroskedasticity of firms' growth rates with size noted in the LPE literature suggests that the mobility of an industry's member firms decreases with their market shares. That heteroskedasticity might result from some form of entrenchment of leading firms (suspected although not well explained in the literature of industrial organization), from greater diversification of larger firms even within a well-defined product market, or simply from the way adjustment costs vary with firm size. Baldwin (1995, chap. 5) divided firms in each Canadian manufacturing industry into large and small (around the 50th percentile of output), confirming that the small firms show somewhat more variable shares. The largest four firms, however, do regress toward the mean: over 1970–79 on average they experienced declines in shares. The declines do not vary with rank within the top four, although the variance is somewhat greater for those ranked third and fourth. Nonetheless, thanks to the spread-out distribution of leaders' shares, the predicted duration of tenure in a top rank is quite long: 28, 17, 14, and 12 years for firms ranked 1, 2, 3, and 4 respectively. Geroski and Saadet Toker (1996) performed a similar calculation for 54 British industries, obtaining 17, 10, 11, and 9 years. Is the stickiness of leaders' positions just a reflection of the ubiquitous heteroskedastic variance of growth with size, or is there "something more"? As

Baldwin pointed out, the heteroskedasticity explanation appears sufficient, and an inquiry based on interindustry differences is needed to pin down any structural rigidities or first-mover advantages that might also weigh in. Earlier contributors to the LPE literature concluded that growth rates are almost independent of size among larger firms, but their failure to sort firms into industry groups deprives the result of clear implications.

An important dividend of the studies of mobility is indirect evidence of the character of costs of adjusting actual to desired levels of input or activity. The standard assumption of convex adjustment costs implies that the mass of the distribution of time rates of change will be concentrated around zero. The alternative of fixed costs of adjustment implies a dispersed distribution with modes away from zero. The evidence summarized in Haltiwanger's (forthcoming) survey clearly supports nonlinear adjustment. For example, one inference holds that about 70 percent of a 10 percent disequilibrium between a plant's actual and desired employment will remain three months later, while only 50 percent of a 60 percent disequilibrium will remain. This finding has important implications for macroeconomics as well as supplying a general explanation for high mobility rates. The same literature demonstrates the asymmetry in the adjustment upward and downward of plants' actual to desired capital stocks that is implied by the sunkenness of capital. We do not know whether this asymmetry imprints itself on market-share changes and (if so) over what range of industries.

To summarize this section, recent research documents wide variance of business units' rates of growth consistent with fixed costs of adjustment. Large minorities of units contract in

TABLE 2
AVERAGE RATES OF INDUSTRIES' GROSS ENTRY AND EXIT, EIGHT COUNTRIES (PERCENT)

Country	Time period	Entry rate		Exit rate	
		Number of firms	Market share	Number of firms	Market share
Belgium:	1980–84				
manufacturing		5.8	1.6	6.3	1.9
services		13.0	4.4	12.2	4.1
Canada	1971–79	4.0	3.0	4.8	3.4
Germany	1983–85	3.8	2.8	4.6	2.8
Korea	1976–81	3.3	2.2	5.7	n.a.
Norway	1980–85	8.2	1.1	8.7	1.0
Portugal	1983–86	12.3	5.8	9.5	5.5
UK	1974–79	6.5	2.9	5.1	3.3
US	1963–82	7.7	3.2	7.0	3.3

Source: Cable and Schwalbach (1991, Table 14.1).

an industry or economy that is expanding (and vice versa). The sustained trends in size (share) shown by many units coexist with long-run regression to the mean, although at a rate slow enough for firms to enjoy long tenure in leading positions. Much turbulence in the form of job changes occurs within rather than between industries. The variance of growth rates decreases strongly with the sizes of business units and apparently with the sunkenness of capacity.

2.3 Entry Rates and Entrants' Survival

An important line of research on turnover has tracked entrants to determine their subsequent growth and mortality rates. Studies have documented substantial rates of entry and exit in a number of countries. Data in Table 2 assembled by John Cable and Joachim Schwalbach show average annual entry rates (number of firms) of about 6.5 percent, claiming about 2.8 percent market shares in manufacturing industries; average exit rates are very similar to entry rates.

Entrants suffer from high rates of infant mortality. Churchill (1955) reported that half of all businesses established in the United States during 1946–54 were sold or discontinued within two years; hazard rates declined steadily after the first year. Baldwin's (1995, chap. 2) data show that entrants to Canadian manufacturing experience a first-year hazard rate of about 10 percent; it declines irregularly over a decade to the 5–7 percent range, which still exceeds the 3.5–5 percent range for firms more than one decade old. When the age structure of firms exiting in a given year is analyzed, again about 10 percent entered in the previous year, but about half were more than ten years old. Other studies that confirm the decline of hazard rates over time include Audretsch (1991), who worked with the U.S. Small Business Administration data based on establishment-level records of Dun & Bradstreet.[8]

---

[8] This data base has been controversial, because the Dun & Bradstreet records are biased toward covering only those establishments and single-plant firms that need to establish credit ratings, and they are updated infrequently. Audretsch and Zoltan J. Acs (1994) summarized the evidence on the quality of this data base, concluding that in practice the patterns that it yields agree with those based on data from official census records.

The hazard rates for entrants reported for various countries seem rather similar, except that Portugal's are distinctly higher: 25 percent in the first year, 16 percent in the second, 13 percent in the third (Mata, Pedro Portugal, and Paulo Guimarzes 1995). Portugal's development status and the coverage of very small firms are both sufficient explanatory factors. Although the pattern of declining hazard rates for an entering cohort is widely reported, Rajshree Agarwal and Michael Gort (1996) showed that it can be overridden by the industry's life cycle associated with the development, maturation, and ultimate displacement of its basic product. Hazard rates, they found, increase over time for early entrants as an industry-wide shakeout eventually sets in. Firms' hazard rates also increase at the end of the cycle. When hazard rates can be measured by month, they increase for the most of the first year; entrant firms likely start with enough resources to sustain themselves that long (Josef Brüderl, Peter Preisendörfer, and Rolf Ziegler 1992). There exists one unexplained exception: hazard rates increase persistently with the ages of small Belgian firms (Konings, F. Roodhooft, and L. Van der Gucht 1996).

Although entrants' rates of infant mortality are high, so are the growth rates of the survivors. Baldwin (1995, pp. 21–27) found that during the 1970s each entrant cohort's share of manufacturing value added increased over time (up to the ten years he could observe), so entry cumulatively contributes a lot to turnover in the enterprise population. Entrants surviving over the years 1970–81 made up 35.5 percent of manufacturing firms in 1981 and accounted for 10.9 percent of employment. If entry and exit are defined not for manufacturing as a whole but for individual (four-digit) industries, plants that are switched from one industry to another also become exits and entries (respectively). In the average industry, new firms' entries over a decade account for only about one-third as much of employment as existing firms that switched or built new plants.

Similar to Baldwin's findings are those of Timothy Dunne, Roberts, and Samuelson (1988; hereafter DRS) for the United States. They observed firms' entries into individual (four-digit) industries over five-year intervals only, but could extend coverage over a maximum of two decades (1963–82). Their quinquennial hazard rates cannot be compared to Baldwin's annual values, but they appear consistent. In the average industry and five-year period, DRS found that entrants (both new firms and "switchers") account for 39 percent of end-of-period firms (16 percent market share); at the start of a period those destined to exit similarly make up 35 percent of firms (also 16 percent market share). The combined employment share of a given cohort of entrants declines over time, and that decline occurs about equally in the new-firm entrants and the diversifying entrants that have either switched existing capacity or built new plants. In their intensive study of entry into the chemical processing industries, DRS (1989b) established the same conclusion by a different route, using a regression procedure to control for variation in industries' growth rates.

DRS (1989b) investigated the degree to which the enlarged sizes attained by surviving entrants are due to individual firms' fast growth rather than higher mortality rates of the initially smaller entrants. The initial-size factor is statistically significant for all entrants in their first five-year period and for multi-plant entrants through their observed lives, so survivors' growth and gains in

1956   *Journal of Economic Literature, Vol. XXXVI (December 1998)*

size relative to incumbent firms stem partly from a selection process.[9]

One is curious about the contrasting findings on whether an entrant cohort's combined output share rises or falls. This outcome is the net result of an initially high but declining hazard rate and high but declining average growth rates of survivors. For Canada, Baldwin (1995, chap. 2) found a net increase; for the United States, DRS (1988, 1989b) reported a net fall. Cohort shares in Portugal decline at rates similar to those in the United States (Mata, Portugal, and Guimarzes 1995). In both the U.S. and Canadian data a fringe of the smallest firms was excluded. Baldwin dealt with annual observations over a shorter period and with the whole manufacturing sector rather than individual industries. Quite possibly entrant cohorts in some settings enjoy short-run gains in aggregate share: for German nonagricultural firms, Boeri and Cramer (1992) found that the level (not share) of employment of an entrant cohort increases for a year or two but then drops below its initial value; for Michigan firms (all industries) Jackson (1996) reported cohort shares of employment to rise for eight years. Given that some early entrants to an industry typically grow large and live a long time, it is almost necessary that the typical entrant cohort's combined share ultimately declines. There is obviously room for further research on the short-run trajectories of entrant cohorts and their variation from industry to industry.

The evidence on entrants' growth and failure rates clearly suggests a stochas-tic process in which firms make their entry investments unsure of their success and do not initially position themselves at a unique optimal size. By general agreement, a fruitful explanation lies in Boyan Jovanovic's (1982) model of "passive learning" (also Hugo A. Hopenhayn 1992 and Luis M. B. Cabral 1993). The potential entrant is assumed to know the mean and standard deviation of all firms' costs but not its own mean expectation. Upon paying a (nonrecoverable) entry fee, it starts to receive noisy information on its true cost level, which in any one period might induce it to expand, contract, or even exit. The consistency of the preceding evidence with Jovanovic's model is clear.[10] Researchers have tested specific implications for the dependence of a firm's growth on its size and age. The link is the proposition that the younger the firm, the more does each observation contribute to its knowledge of its costs. Evans (1987b) analyzed the growth of young firms as a function of their age and initial size, finding that growth diminishes with size (at a decreasing rate) and decreases with age when firm size is held constant. The decrease with age holds both overall and within most individual industries (Evans 1987a), so the passive-learning model is well supported. DRS (1989c) obtained similar conclusions about U.S. manufacturing plants from the Census Bureau's longitudinal data base. As a firm ages and grows more confident about its costs, the mean and variance of its growth rate should decline. Indeed, DRS found that mean rates of (employment) growth decline with age for every

---

[9] The chemicals sector is not necessarily a representative one for analyzing the fate of entrants. DRS (1989b) showed that in the average manufacturing industry firms operating in 1963 retained in 1982 a 58 percent market share, while in the chemicals industries they retained 70 percent.

[10] Pakes and Ericson (forthcoming) pointed out that the passive-learning model does not necessarily predict hazard rates falling from the outset. They could rise at first, if ill-fated firms need some experience to be sure of their unfitness. This is confirmed in a few studies cited previously.

plant size group except the largest, and failure rates (indicating variance) also decline with age given size.[11] Growth rates and failure rates also decline with size given age. The patterns differ in small ways between single-plant firms and plants belonging to multiplant enterprises, but the basic conclusions seem insensitive to the plant/firm distinction. Intercountry differences are not evident: Roberts (1996a) reported for Colombia the same conclusions about survival's relation to age and size.

Pakes and Ericson (forthcoming) sought to test the passive-learning model in competition with their own active-learning model. The test (on Wisconsin state data) suggests that the passive-learning model fits the retailing sector well, while manufacturing shows patterns that suggest active learning. The test is adroit and suggestive, but suffers in that passive and active learning are not mutually exclusive: opportunities for both could be abundant in one industry, scarce in another.

A consequence of entrants' high rates of early mortality is that, as many cross-section studies have reported, industries with high entry rates will also show high exit rates. That is, the data reject the model that pervades our textbooks: optimal-size firms enter an industry when its equilibrium output expands, exit when it contracts, but never do both at the same time. Cable and Schwalbach (1991, Table 14.2) provided evidence for eight countries. Positive correlations between contemporaneous rates of entry and exit were also reported by Michael E. Beesley and R. T.

Hamilton (1984) for manufacturing industries in Scotland, Geroski (1991a, 1991b) for British industries, and Timothy Dunne and Roberts (1991) for the United States. David I. Rosenbaum and Fabian Lamort (1992) confirmed the positive relationship after controlling for other determinants of entry and exit; for U.S. manufacturing industries they found exits much more responsive to entries over a five-year period than are entries to exits. Agarwal and Gort (1996) observed that these positive entry/exit correlations make most sense for samples of industries in steady states of maturity but varying in structural entry barriers and the sunkenness of resource commitments. In early and late phases of a product's life cycle these correlations indeed reverse to negative.

Further evidence of entrants' uncertain fates lies in the association between rates of entry and rates of exit from a given industry over time. DRS (1988, Table 7) observed the usual positive correlations between rates of entry and exit among four-digit U.S. manufacturing industries over a common five-year period. The correlations turn negative when fixed effects confine the variation to temporal changes, but even then the entry rate in a given five-year period is positively correlated with the exit rate in the following five years. For Germany, Boeri and Lutz Bellmann (1995) found a positive entry shock to be followed by an increase in the next year's hazard rate (10 percent significance), although the hazard rate is unrelated to the current year's number of entrants. Leo Sleuwaegen and Wim Dehandschutter (1991) found the same lagged pattern in annual data on Belgian manufacturing industries. Baldwin and Joanne Johnson (1996) employed a hazard-rate analysis of individual entrants' fates to establish that

[11] Kenneth R. Troske (1996) confirmed from Wisconsin unemployment insurance data that the mean and variance of growth rates fall off as entrants age, with services firms reaching a steady state sooner than manufacturers. Contini and Revelli (1989) found growth to decline with age for Italian firms, with age variations beyond 6 or 7 years having no effect.

members of a larger entrant cohort are more likely to exit, and exit is also higher in an industry with a highly concentrated core and a numerous fringe. These studies of intertemporal entry-exit linkages control for macroeconomic conditions in various ways and degrees, but they leave the impression that recent entrants' hazard rates are rather insensitive to the observed variation in the macro environment.

Research on exit has mainly addressed infant mortality, and the prevalent decline of hazard rates with age suggests that geriatric problems are not serious for firms. Fröystein Wedervang (1965, pp. 168–75) early observed that age (i.e., youthfulness) is the more important factor explaining small firms' high exit rates, although size per se may be influential. Troske (1996) found that manufacturing firms five years before their exit are only half the sector's average size, while finance, insurance, and real estate firms destined to exit are then still at the average; both groups' mean growth rates go negative starting three years before exit, with manufacturers plunging more rapidly. Audretsch (1995a, chap. 7) observed that exits by older firms are less sensitive to industry growth disturbances than are exits by younger firms, and the elderly are preserved by the sunkenness of resources committed to industries with large minimum efficient scales (MES) of production (also Beesley and Hamilton 1984). Mark Doms, Timothy Dunne, and Roberts (1995) found that firms in machinery industries using various advanced technologies are less likely to exit; because these users do not grow significantly faster than their competitors, sunkenness is again suggested. For businesses small enough to be tied to their proprietors' life cycles, the manager's age positively predicts the business's survival in the prime working

years, but eventually age leads to discontinuance or sale of the business (Wedervang 1965, pp. 183–85; Timothy Bates 1990; Thomas J. Holmes and James A. Schmitz, Jr. 1996). Turnover in managers of small businesses tends to predict sales or closures shortly afterward, which suggests that job-matching for managers plays a role in the turnover of small businesses (Holmes and Schmitz 1995).[12]

Casual observation suggests that the oldest firms owe their longevity to trademarks (newspapers, simple consumer goods) that demand little organizational continuity. Organizational geriatrics has received little attention, although firms' exit rates have been studied in the context of industry or product life-cycles. Agarwal and Gort formulated the survival of mature firms as a trade-off between depreciation or obsolescence of their original endowments and the benefits of cumulative learning. Analyzing ten-year survival rates of firms entering during various (of the five) stages of their industry life-cycle, they found hazard rates increasing through the third stage, sufficiently explained by the fading growth opportunities offered by the product market. Hazard rates fall for late entrants, however, consistent with reduced rates of obsolescence of their initial endowments or increased efficacy of cumulative experience. Hazard rates for incumbents are lower than for entrants through all stages of the cycle in "nontechnical" products (where experience advantages might be great), higher for "technical" products, where entrants

[12] These patterns point to the ambiguities of defining exit and entry in small businesses that are often bought and sold, or their facilities transformed from one activity to another. Jack's Bar becomes Jill's Bar, a business exit and an entry have occurred, an establishment continues unchanged, and Jack's business did not necessarily fail. See Bruce A. Kirchhoff (1994, chaps. 6, 8).

bring the continuing flow of innovations (see also Audretsch 1991). Although their data base gives only limited leverage, Agarwal and Gort were able to calculate "senility points": ages at which hazard rates for incumbents entering in given stages of the life cycle stop falling and turn up again.

Steven Klepper and John H. Miller (1995) focused on the shake-out phase of the industry life cycle, in which the number of firms offering a product declines from its maximum to its long-run "mature" level. The data do not well support a simple model of overshot entry. The shake-out is prolonged and continues at a steady (rather than declining) pace, suggesting instead a process of continuing competition among incumbents to reduce costs, modeled by Klepper and Elizabeth Graddy (1990) and Klepper (1996). Industry life cycles are considered further in Section 3.

In summary, entrants experience high hazard rates (infant mortality) that decline over time. Successful entrants also achieve high average rates of growth (that also decline as they age). The combined market share of an entering cohort, the net effect of these forces, eventually declines, but may increase for a time after the cohort's entry. The pattern is highly consistent with theoretical models of both passive and active learning. Industries that experience high rates of gross entry also tend to show high rates of exit. Over time, variations of the exit rate lag behind those of the entry rate; there is no strong evidence that exogenous disturbances to the exit rate induce subsequent entry (perhaps indicating just the infrequency of exogenous exit-causing disturbances). Units that exit have experienced declining growth rates for several years but (whether young or old) are still of substantial size relative to their competitors.

2.4 *Interpreting Entry Patterns: Initial Commitments and Subsequent Options*

Firms enter an industry at different initial sizes, and the entrants' size distribution varies from industry to industry. That pattern invites interpretation in terms of entrants' diverse expectations and real options: entrants holding more positive expectations about their untested capabilities—their costs, or the qualities of their assets—make larger initial commitments. Even if the industry's technology supports a large optimal scale, the less confident entrant might rationally start out small, incurring a unit-cost penalty but limiting its sunk commitment while it gathers evidence on its unknown capability. Initially smaller entrants would then be expected to show higher exit rates.[13] Entrants' hazard rates should decline with the size of the minimum sunk resource commitment required to enter (roughly, the amount of costs that must be precommitted), but hazard rates could increase with the size of the irretrievable outlay needed to move from minimal or fringe entry to optimal-scale operation.

The empirical evidence neatly fits this framework of dispersed expectations and real options. First, Churchill (1954b) long ago showed that the size distribution of entrants to the typical industry is stable over time, suggesting some behavioral foundation. Furthermore, the distribution is aligned with the structure (entry barriers) of the entered industry (Mata 1991). Audretsch and Talat Mahmood (1995) as well as

---

[13] There is an evident problem of distinguishing between the entrant that limits its own initial commitment from self-knowledge of its long-shot status and the small entrant that fails because input-market imperfections denied it access to the optimal entry strategy. For a theoretical model of self-limiting entrants see Murray Z. Frank (1988).

1960   *Journal of Economic Literature, Vol. XXXVI (December 1998)*

Wagner (1994a) found that entrants' hazard rates decrease with their initial sizes, and Audretsch (1995b) established an inverse relation among industries between entrants' survival rates and the rates at which the lucky survivors grow. Mata (1996) found that better qualified Portuguese entrepreneurs (more schooling, older up to a point) start initially larger firms. Brüderl, Preisendörfer, and Ziegler (1992) found the hazard rates of German entrant firms to be lowered by the entrepreneur's general and industry-specific work experience, after controlling for the business's initial size and access to a broad (national) market; with these factors controlled, access to start-up capital was not a significant additional factor—lenders themselves apparently take these same success factors into account. Baldwin and Mohammed Rafiquzzaman (1995a) observed among Canadian industries a trade-off between the initial productivity levels of entrants who would subsequently survive (for at least ten years) and the rate at which their labor productivity subsequently grew. In each industry they compared the productivity in the first three years of survivors destined to last for a decade and ill-fated entrants who would not; the less the survivors' initial advantage over the quitters, the greater is the productivity growth subsequently achieved by the survivors. There is also an inverse relation between a survivor's initial labor productivity (relative to the productivity of incumbent firms) and the rate at which that productivity subsequently grows. The Baldwin-Rafiquzzaman findings invite the interpretation that successful entrants know or quickly learn their potential for rapid productivity growth. The invitation may be too seductive, because the Canadian data base lacks capital stocks, and Wedervang's (1965, pp. 194–96) study of Nor-

way showed that entrants have low labor productivity but high capital productivity. The winning entrants' labor-productivity gains might derive either from increasing their residual efficiency or exercising the option to make a major capital commitment.[14]

Further evidence of self-selected variation in initial commitments appears in the findings of DRS (1989b, 1989c) about differences between single-plant and multi-plant entrants, and between entries by new firms and firms established elsewhere. Single-plant entrants suffer much higher attrition than multi-plant entrants, consistent with the latter's much larger initial size commitments, reflecting greater confidence about prospects. Correspondingly, new-firm multi-plant entrants do much less well than diversifying multi-plant entrants, who likely have more accurate information on their ability to operate profitably in the entered industry. Capricious capital constraints or the hazards of undiversified life might explain this pattern, but differences in rational self-assessments are strongly suggested.

This real-option perspective is strengthened by evidence of industry-structure influences that both reduce survival and speed the survivors' growth. Audretsch (1995a, pp. 57–62; 1995b) confirmed several: the importance of MES in production[15] and the importance of innovation, both in the

---

[14] Laura Power (forthcoming) showed that post-entry investment bursts by successful entrants are far from the whole story. She concluded that in general plant-level labor productivity responds only weakly and slowly to "spikes" of machinery investments, even those undertaken after the plant's initial "birth" investment. Substantial and immediate effects turn up only in chemical-process industries. Elsewhere, investment may chiefly expand capacity rather than raise productivity.

[15] It also increases the mobility of small firms relative to large ones (Acs and Audretsch 1990, chap. 7).

industry as a whole and for its smaller firms. Audretsch (1995a, chap. 4) and Audretsch and Mahmood (1995) found that entrants' hazard rates increase with the industry's capital intensity (while older firms' rates decrease).[16] Two considerations let us make sense of this odd-sounding result. First, there is abundant evidence that manufacturing production functions are not homothetic, and capital intensity increases strongly with scale in the typical manufacturing industry (e.g., Caves and Thomas A. Pugel 1980), so small-scale entry need not entail a large sunk capital investment.[17] Second, if factors such as scale economies, capital intensity, and successful innovation can sustain rents to capable incumbents, they induce firms to enter for at least a "look" at their chances of ultimate success (see the model of S. A. Lippman and R. P. Rumelt, 1982).[18] Similar to Audretsch's finding on capital intensity is Marvin B. Lieberman's (1989) conclusion that the learning-curve advantages of leading incumbents of U.S. chemical processing industries do not deter the entry of new competitors but do lower their survival rates. A final evidence of entry as an options purchase lies in Audretsch and Mahmood's (1995) comparison of hazard-rate models fitted to entrant single-plant firms and to new establishments of established firms: the dependent establishment is more likely to exit (with all other factors controlled), consistent with lower sunk costs associated with the entrepreneurial unit; but its survival is not predictable by any of the factors that cogently determine the start-up firm's decision to stick or exit.[19]

With this evidence of entrants' options noted, it still holds (for Portuguese manufacturing, Mata and Jose A.F. Machado 1995) that the initial sizes chosen by entrants increase with the industry's MES, and that (among entrants) the sizes of the larger ones are more strongly influenced by MES in its relation to the market's size and growth.

In summary, the new evidence imputes more rationality to entrants' decisions than has generally been assigned to them. To put the point provocatively, we have thought many entrants fail because they start out small, whereas they may start with small commitments when they expect their chances of success to be small. At the same time, small-scale entry commonly provides a real option to invest heavily if early returns are promising. Consistent with this, structural factors long thought to limit entry to an industry now seem more to limit *successful* entry: if incumbents earn rents, it pays the potential entrant to invest for a "close look" at its chances.

---

[16] Wagner (1994a, 1994b), however, found for Germany the more conventional conclusion that capital-intensity of the industry raises entrants' survival rate while lowering the entry rate. Boeri and Bellmann (1995) also investigated the joint determinants of entrants' hazard rates and survivors' growth in German industry.

[17] Interestingly, Audretsch and Mahmood (1995) did find that entrants' hazard rates decrease with the industry's human capital intensity measured by its average wage rate. Either human capital is a component of the initially sunk costs, which seems unlikely, or it measures the entrant's opportunity to raise productivity through learning by doing. Nonhomotheticity was confirmed by Bartelsman and Phoebus J. Dhrymes (1992), who found that labor productivity residuals increase with plants' sizes but those from total factor productivity do not.

[18] It would be most desirable to know how much money unsuccessful entrants lose, but dead firms post no losses.

[19] The testing of this model of entrants' options is aided by what appear to be major differences between the typical manufacturing and the typical services industry in the abundance of post-entry growth options. Pakes and Ericson (forthcoming) and Troske (1996) suggested that services entrants quickly settle at their steady-state sizes, while manufacturers take time to grow into them.

2.5 *Entry and Exit through Control Changes*

Turnover also occurs in the control of business units through acquisitions, mergers, and sell-offs of plants. From the perspective of static equilibrium models, these changes are commonly regarded as without consequence for industries' behavior and performance. However, control changes can have substantial effects. Large U.S. firms' diversified acquisitions in the 1960s and 1970s drew a justifiably bad press for the subnormal subsequent performance of the acquired business units (e.g., David J. Ravenscraft and F.M. Scherer 1987). When comprehensive census records of control changes came available for analysis, however, a positive relation emerged between control changes and productivity changes. The productivity levels of plants fated for changes in control tend to fall before the change and to recover afterward (Frank R. Lichtenberg and Donald Siegel 1987; also Lichtenberg 1992). Baldwin (1995, chap. 3) analyzed the consequences of control changes for both the market shares and normalized productivity levels of transferred Canadian plants, distinguishing between mergers and spinoffs and between combinations with diversified activities unrelated and related to the unit's industry base. When a firm enters an industry by acquiring a plant, that plant's market share grows somewhat for six years but then drops sharply. The productivity of continuing plants that underwent control changes in the 1970s was typically above average in 1970 but nonetheless higher still at the decade's end. This improvement occurred for all types of control changes except unrelated mergers, and even these showed improvement when the aggregate effect was calculated using plant-size weights rather than unweighted.

Robert H. McGuckin and Sang V. Nguyen (1995) analyzed all plants in the U.S. food and beverage sector that experienced control changes during 1977–82, following them until 1987 and comparing their labor productivity to plants in the same four-digit industry not undergoing control changes. Their main finding resolves an apparent contradiction between Ravenscraft and Scherer (1987) and Lichtenberg and Siegel (1987) concerning the initial (1977) productivity of plants fated for changes in control. Lichtenberg and Siegel, whose data pertain largely to big plants employing more than 250, observed deterioration prior to the control change, while Ravenscraft and Scherer found that control changed for many highly productive small plants. McGuckin and Nguyen concluded that both were right. In their comprehensive data set, the unweighted average initial relative productivity of plants that would undergo control change exceeds unity, and the higher the relative productivity, the more likely the control change. When the average is weighted, however, the ratio lies below unity. And when analysis is confined to large plants, the relation reverses: the likelihood of control change decreases with initial relative productivity. It appears that control changes can either lift the performance of an unproductive large unit or supply resources needed to leverage the strengths of a highly productive small one.

To explain the productivity of control changes, Lichtenberg and Siegel (1987) invoked the theory of job-matching: a continuous stream of disturbances renders some of the ownership links between enterprises and plants (or other major fixed assets) nonoptimal and induces reshuffling through the market for corporate control. Such a model is not only consistent with their overall result, but also can be extended to predict differences among industries in the incidence of control changes. For the reshuffling of plants (or lines of business) among firms to be productive, there must be sources of heterogeneity that allow the mismatches to crop up. Assets tied to plants or business units must have these traits: (1) Their qualities or attributes differ from unit to unit, in the sense of either vertical or horizontal differentiation. (2) These heterogeneities cause assets' productivities to vary substantially depending on the other business assets with which they collaborate within the firm. (3) These business assets must be "important"—lumpy or discrete, so that variations in their productivity can warrant incurring the transaction cost of a control change. (4) Transactions in these assets must be subject to market failures that prevent them from being rented or sold directly rather than as components bundled with plants or lines of business. (5) Disturbances continually affect an asset's productivity, not just overall but conditional on the other assets with which it is combined. Job-matching models such as Dale T. Mortensen and Christopher A. Pissarides (1994) seem close in spirit to these conditions. The conditions can be plausibly linked to observable traits of industries (importance of product differentiation, selling costs, or advertising; importance of science base and innovation; importance of scale economies in production). For Canadian manufacturing industries, Baldwin (1995, chap. 11) showed that the volume and productivity of control changes are greater in industries where such inputs are more important.[20]

---

[20] This result agrees with many findings in the literature on corporate diversification, which attributes the linking within the firm of businesses that serve different markets to just such assets that have the additional property that they can be used productively in more than one market.

3. Turnover, Mobility, and Static Elements of Market Structure

These findings on turnover and mobility pose an important challenge for empirical industrial organization, for both the traditional taxonomic (structure-conduct-performance, or SCP) approach and modern market-econometrics approach rest on comparative statics applied to models of market equilibrium. The emphasis here falls on the SCP approach. Its strategy, to inventory regular empirical relationships among elements of market structure, patterns of behavior, and levels of performance, is close in spirit to the turnover literature's quest for empirical regularities (see Richard Schmalensee 1989).[21] Are the stylized facts of the old SCP and the new turnover regularities mutually consistent? Can they shed light on and explain one another? The core of the SCP taxonomy is the causal relationships starting from the number and size distribution (concentration) of participants in a market and the factors limiting their number or access (entry barriers). Concentration itself is regarded as a consequence of factors limiting the equilibrium number of incumbent firms and/or supplying incumbents with first-mover advantages over subsequent entrants. It proves convenient first to align concentration and turnover, including concentration's dependence on entry barriers, then to consider how the structural entry barriers themselves relate to turnover.

3.1 Concentration and Turnover: Contemporaneous Relationships

In the SCP paradigm, sellers' concentration is thought to affect their

---

[21] Turnover does have important implications for the "new IO" that are illustrated by G. Steven Olley and Pakes (1996).

1964   *Journal of Economic Literature, Vol. XXXVI (December 1998)*

behavior patterns but also to depend on their past conduct. Concentration is thus both a potential influence on mobility and turnover and (as the LPE shows) a potential consequence of mobility. And it depends on entry and exit in the near-definitional sense that the number of incumbent firms equals cumulative entries minus cumulative exits.

An inverse relation between an industry's concentration and its average rate of turnover due to entry and exit seems well established. Baldwin (1995, Table 8.5) related four-firm concentration ratios in Canadian manufacturing industries in 1979 to both turnover from entry and exit and turnover from incumbents' mobility, each measured over the preceding decade. His regression model also includes the standard measures of structural entry barriers long established as significant determinants of concentration. Turnover due to entry and exit exerts a powerful negative effect. Baldwin (1995, chap. 8) also used principal components summarizing various turbulence measures to supplement the standard cross-section model of concentration's determinants. Again, a principal component weighted positively on turnover due to entry and exit wields a great deal of incremental explanatory power.

Concentration is also commonly included as a regressor in cross-section models seeking to explain entry rates or turnover from entry and exit. Given that such models usually include the structural forces (entry barriers) that limit the equilibrium number of incumbents, it is not clear what behavioral mechanism is being tested. Because of causal links among the regressors (and resulting high multicollinearity), perverse signs commonly appear even when concentration itself takes a significant negative coefficient. The appropriate conclusion about concentration's influence is moot until we can replace it with measures of the mobility-deterring conditions or policies (such as vertical restraints on distributors?) employed by concentrated producers.

The relationship between incumbents' mobility and concentration is more elusive. Contrary to LPE, changes in concentration have no simple empirical relation to the mobility of an industry's firms. In Canadian manufacturing, while concentration showed no trend on average, Baldwin (1995, chap. 7) could regard only about 15 percent of the industries as low in turnover. Although some forms of turnover seem positively correlated with absolute changes in concentration (Baldwin 1995, Fig. 7.2), high mobility and stable concentration are evidently compatible in industries that range widely in concentration levels. In Baldwin's cross-section regression analysis, mobility among continuing firms has a negative but insignificant effect on 1979 concentration levels. When principal components are used, entry/exit turnover remains the dominant influence, and the only significant component strongly weighted on a mobility measure seems to imply that when entry/exit turnover is raised, concentration declines more where incumbents' share changes are similar.

Evidence of relations running from concentration to mobility is similarly thin. Baldwin (1995, chap. 5) did find a negative relation between concentration and mobility of the *leading* firms. However, it turns up as greater mobility for leaders only in the least concentrated quintile of industries, which hardly suggests that collaboration among oligopolists fostered by concentration is what deters mobility. Acs and Audretsch (1990, chap. 7) reported a significant positive influence of concentration on mobility in U.S.

manufacturing industries, but the presence of collinear regressors makes it difficult to interpret. Whatever structural elements determine the differences among industries in incumbents' mobility, concentration is not the dominant one. Mobility's determinants are easily found, however, in more basic elements of market structure. Baldwin and Rafiquzzaman (1995b) employed a classification (originated in the Organization for Economic Cooperation and Development) of manufacturing industries into five broad groups: natural resource-based, labor intensive, scale economies-based, product differentiated, and science-based; partitioning industries into these classes captures a surprisingly large amount of variance in the fundamental conditions of technology and demand among narrowly defined manufacturing industries.[22] The mobility of incumbents tends be high in labor intensive and product differentiated industries, low in scale-based ones. The pattern is what one would expect if mobility increases with competitors' scope for making uncertain investments that affect their market share, and decreases with the sunkenness of costs (which leads to narrowly confined short-run capacities). Baldwin (1995, pp. 344–58) related measures of long-run profitability of Canadian manufacturing industries to various measures of turn over and appropriate control variables. Mobility among incumbents has a marginally significant negative effect, and *net* entry as expected is a highly significant negative influence. Turn over due to entry and exit surprisingly exerts a significant positive influence, perhaps due to causation running from the rents of

successful incumbents to the number of entrants willing to test their luck.[23]

Researchers were led on their quest for a causal influence of concentration on mobility and turnover by the hunch that competition in some sense is a source of turbulence that may be dampened by oligopolistic cooperation. One specific form of competition was tested by Baldwin and Richard E. Caves (1998): international rivalry, measured by imports' penetration of the national market and/or the share of domestic output exported. As to the mechanisms at work, the variance of disturbances might be greater for transactions crossing national borders, or (more subtly) international competition might increase the closeness of substitutes for varieties of a differentiated product, so that any given exogenous disturbance generates larger quantity responses and hence more mobility. They found that international competition does indeed increase mobility and (entry-exit) turnover in Canadian manufacturing industries. The relation is not a particularly strong one, however. Baldwin (1995, pp. 139–47) noted a similar effect of import competition on mobility in both Canada and the United States, although Davis, Haltiwanger, and Schuh (1996, pp. 47–49) reported negative results from a less closely targeted test. Roberts and Tybout (1996, p. 7) also mentioned obtaining negative results for several developing countries. In studying the effects of a large-scale trade liberalization on New Zealand manufacturing, John K. Gibson and Richard I. D. Harris (1996) concluded that "the plants likely to survive trade liberalization were larger, lower cost, older, used specialized capital and were owned by specialized firms

[22] Further evidence appears in the positive rank correlations reported by Roberts (1996b, Table 2.6) between turnover rates in industries matched between countries.

[23] Baldwin suggested industry life cycles as an explanation: at early stages both entry/exit turnover and profitability are high; in maturity both decline.

with few plants." In short, import competition shook out the less efficient and the less "sunk" (also see Joseph E. Flynn 1991, on trade liberalization in the United States).

3.2 Concentration and Turnover: Cumulative Effects

This completes the descriptive relations found in cross-section between concentration and entry-exit turnover and incumbents' mobility. Much remains to be said, however, about concentration as a *cumulative* result of random processes operating through turnover and mobility, in the manner of Gibrat and the LPE. Two separate theoretical and empirical literatures have evolved, one updating Gibrat, the other resting on the concept of a product life cycle. They lead to broadly similar conclusions but benefit from separate treatment.

That concentration might reflect both structural forces (notably minimum efficient scale [MES] interacting with the size of the market) and random disturbances was recognized theoretically by Herbert A. Simon and Charles P. Bonini (1958) and empirically by Edwin F. Mansfield (1962). Davies and Bruce Lyons (1982) developed this insight into an empirical interindustry test in which the n-firm concentration ratio is allowed to depend on a lower bound set by MES and market size plus an additional component increasing with the variance of random disturbances that lift leading firms above the MES threshold. Sutton (1997, forthcoming) developed an important theoretical synthesis, building on the approach of Yuji Ijiri and Simon (1977), that rests on two assumptions: (1) New market opportunities arise continually, and the likelihood that the next one will be seized by any incumbent firm is a nondecreasing function of that firm's size (this relaxes

Gibrat's proportionality between size and growth). (2) New firms enter at a constant rate. These assumptions predict a lower bound for concentration as a function of the number of firms in the market that is independent of the rate of entry (proportion of opportunities captured by new firms) but does depend on the assumption that the market grows over time. Sutton (forthcoming, chaps. 10–13) showed that this lower bound to the level of concentration conditional on the number of firms seems highly consistent with data on manufacturing sectors in several countries. In a related contribution Davies and Geroski (1997) linked the random factors determining each leading firm's market share to the random processes influencing an industry's concentration level overall. They devised a way to integrate the determinants of mobility—changes in the market shares of individual leading firms—with the determinants of the change in industry concentration. Thus, the change in each leading firm's share (in U.K. manufacturing industries) is treated as a function of its initial market share and the firm's own rate of spending on advertising and R&D relative to its competitors, so that both discretionary sunk outlays and Galtonian regression can play their roles (also Geroski and Toker 1996).

Sutton's two massive investigations of market structure's determinants (1991, forthcoming) cannot receive just treatment here, but we at least note their links to the literature on turnover and concentration. His investigation of the food-processing industries in various nations focused on the role of "endogenous sunk costs"—outlays establishing trademark goodwill or buyers' perceptions of superior product quality. For reasons indicated by the theory of vertical differentiation, such successful outlays greatly enlarge the innovator's market share and put pressure on rivals either to imitate the strategy or to exit. Either way, concentration tends to increase, and its minimum bound stays strictly positive as the market's size increases without limit, because a larger market increases the firm's expected returns from these discretionary fixed (and sunk) outlays. The outlays themselves, however, can be regarded as randomly arriving opportunities, and in that sense the concentration arising from endogenous sunk costs depends on the variance of random opportunities and the persistence of their consequences.

In shifting his attention to research-intensive industries, Sutton (forthcoming) retained from his previous study the central role of endogenous fixed costs—now, to develop a vertically differentiated product. The new study deals explicitly with horizontal differentiation and the substitution between innovative and established products. Suppose that an innovative industry offers a line of horizontally differentiated products. The payout (profit, market-share gain) to an endogenous sunk outlay on improving one of these products can still be high if (1) the innovation productivity of R&D outlays is high, (2) this product is an important one for the industry, and/or (3) substitutability in demand between this product and others in the industry's line is high. Implications for concentration then follow as in Sutton (1991), except that the lower bound for concentration now decreases with the heterogeneity of the industry's product line. Once more, the randomness of innovation opportunities and successes links this mechanism to the random-process model. As in Sutton (1991), the theoretical model is supported by an impressive array of statistical tests and case studies.

Sutton's work clearly revitalizes the random-process approach and gives it potential applicability to a wide range of markets (see William T. Robinson 1993). In ways suggested by the "active learning" models of Richard R. Nelson and Sidney G. Winter (1978) and Ericson and Pakes (1995), parameters of the distribution of random outcomes can be related to observable data to test hypotheses about the richness and variance of opportunities, the persistence of disturbances' effects (mean reversion), and the appropriability of favorable opportunities (alternatively, the contagion of crippling afflictions).

The other empirical and theoretical way to link random processes to concentration lies in the research starting from Gort and Klepper (1982) on the life cycles of industries that arose from important product innovations. Although the theoretical components of this literature grew out of its empirical observations, it is convenient to begin with theory (Klepper and Graddy 1990; Klepper 1996) in order to facilitate comparison to Sutton's approach. A market begins with some major and profitable but not fully appropriable innovation that attracts a queue of potential entrants. Firms that have entered can carry out product and/or process R&D. Product R&D yields modifications that are soon imitated (no enduring vertical differentiation). Process R&D lowers cost toward an (exogenous) attainable minimum and is more profitable for an incumbent, the larger its size. The competitively determined price falls with incumbents' costs. Over time fewer and fewer potential entrants enjoy positive expected profits. Incumbents less successful in lowering costs drop out. The cycle relies on random processes to determine the capabilities of potential entrants in the queue and the successes of incumbents in product and (especially) process innovation.

1968   *Journal of Economic Literature, Vol. XXXVI (December 1998)*

This model was devised to explain facts emerging from studies of a number of innovative products (Gort and Klepper 1982; Klepper and Graddy 1990; Agarwal and Gort 1996) and more intensive studies of five industries (Klepper 1995; Klepper and Kenneth L. Simons forthcoming). The large-sample studies show an impressive regularity in the gross flows of entrants and quitters as the product passes from an innovation to a mature good. The number of incumbents rises to a peak reached at a time when industry output is still growing. The number then falls off to a plateau level likely to persist until industry output actually declines. The rate of product innovation peaks early in the cycle, the rate of process innovation later. Within a few years after the industry's origin, the survival rates of the earliest entrants come to exceed those of all subsequent entering cohorts. Correspondingly, the leading firms in the mature industry were usually among the early entrants; the basis for this first-mover advantage (skill and luck at process innovation, in the model) does not come particularly clear in the empirical studies (Klepper 1995). Contrary to other authors, Klepper (1997; Klepper and Simons forthcoming) argued that the shakeout of firms in the latter part of the cycle arises not from exogenous developments (major product innovations, emergence of a standard product configuration) but is implied by the basic conditions that drive the whole cycle.

To conclude, Sutton's and the life-cycle approaches to turnover and evolving concentration differ in many ways, but are clearly complementary in the opportunities that they open for empirical research. In general, incorporating turnover into traditional industrial organization clarifies how underlying structure shapes the environment in which market outcomes are determined. However, the evidence on turnover also deepens our anxiety as to what measurable features of markets are truly exogenous. While making the problem harder, the turnover literature does tell us where to look: the random drawings come from distributions that differ from market to market. They vary in where the disturbances strike, how large are their means and variances, and how durable are their consequences. The relevant parameters can be related coherently to "bedrock" characteristics of technology and tastes, although pinning down the connections will be a major challenge for empirical researchers. Turnover also hurls down a considerable challenge to those who seek their empirical research agendas from modern game theory. The outcomes that reflect adroit play of strategic advantages may be few relative to the outcomes in which the winner of a commitment game is the one who guessed most accurately the magnitude of Nature's next draw.

3.3 *Structural Entry Barriers and Turnover*

Standard structural barriers to entry first identified by Joe S. Bain (1956) have a well-established ability to predict industries' concentration levels (even if the normative interpretation of those barriers remains a festering issue). The theory of contestable markets flagged the need to establish the basis in sunk or committed costs for anything labeled a barrier to entry, and Ioannis N. Kessides (1990a, 1990b) found that both entry and concentration depend on the sunkenness of incumbents' commitments.[24] The coefficient of variation among industries of entrants' survival

---

[24] Mata (1995) found entry into Portuguese manufacturing to decline with the sunkenness of incumbents' capital, but sunkenness deters exit only through its effect on gross entry.

rates exceeds that of entry rates (Audretsch 1995b), and barriers must clearly be regarded as affecting survival as well as entry.

To ensure the coherence of their mechanisms, these entry barriers need to be related to the uncertainty of entrants' investments and its consequences for the numbers of entrants and commitments they choose. Entry barriers based on scale economies we usually suppose to have no randomness in their effects (but cf. David E. Mills and Lawrence Schumann 1985). Those based on proprietary intangible assets (advertising and buyer goodwill, proprietary innovations) and even learning by doing are another story, as we saw in Section 2.4. Entry-deterring assets based on intangibles are related to random processes and turnover in two ways. First, incumbents' advantages acquired through luck or skill are potentially wasting assets, at risk of losing their quasi-rents and deterrence potential due to taste shifts, other firms' innovations, and the like. Second, before entrants commit to a market, their qualifications will differ in unknown ways. Occasionally the random entrant will turn up with assets that excel those of some incumbents, supplying them with what George S. Yip (1982) called "gateways to entry." The larger the rents earned by successful incumbents and the smaller the entrant's sunk admission charge, the more entrants will make the attempt, and the higher will be their infant mortality rate (compare Lippman and Rumelt 1982). Thus, the entry barrier more essentially deters *successful* entry than it does *gross* entry.

A good deal of empirical evidence confirms this integration of structural entry barriers with random processes. Acs and Audretsch (1987, 1988) addressed the issue of innovation as a barrier or a gateway to entry using data on the number of innovations introduced in 1982 and classified by four-digit U.S. industry and size of the innovating firm. Small firms on average have higher rates of innovation (per employee) than large firms. Small firms' innovation rates are lower, relative to their large competitors' rates, in the less innovative industries and those with "heavy industry" characteristics (high concentration, capital intensity, unionization).[25] When the determinants of the innovation rates themselves are analyzed (Acs and Audretsch 1988), the small firms' rate surprisingly is not less sensitive to the industry's level of company-financed R&D spending. The small firms' rate is reduced by the industry's advertising outlays but increased by the human capital of its labor force, consistent with small firms' rate being high early in a basic innovation's life cycle and declining (absolutely and relative to large competitors) as the cycle proceeds. Correspondingly, the opportunity to make and appropriate innovations, a gateway to entry early in the process, becomes a barrier to entry in the mature stage (this model was sketched by Dennis C. Mueller and John E. Tilton 1969; William J. Abernathy and James M. Utterback 1978 discussed its implications for the sunkenness of incumbents' resource commitments). With other factors controlled, the small firms' innovation rate is a significant positive influence on the rate of entry into industries (Audretsch 1995a, chap. 3). Klepper and Simons (forthcoming), studying a group of industries that ultimately became highly concentrated, confirmed innovation's

[25] Gort and Akira Konakayama (1982), although working with net-entry data, modeled entry and exit as gross flows determined in the setting of innovative, growing markets. They inferred that both entry and exit increase with the industry's rate of patenting and the growth rate of output per firm, while entry (but not exit) also increases with the industry's incidence of major innovations.

decline over the life cycle and conversion to an entry barrier; in these industries, process and (largely) product innovations were dominated by larger incumbents throughout the cycle.

Kessides (1986) concluded that the sunk (capitalized) value of industry advertising outlays serves as a goodwill entry barrier, but the current flow (including entrants' outlays) operates as a gateway. We lack direct tests of the barrier-vs-gateway duality comparable to Acs–Audretsch in product-differentiation entry barriers, but the parallel seems clear. Robinson and Claes Fornell (1985) identified high barriers with pioneering trademarks immune to obsolescence (also Mata 1995). The increase in the productivity of large-scale advertising associated with the rise of television increased concentration (Willard F. Mueller and Richard T. Rogers 1980) but it also increased mobility (Mark Hirschey 1981). Robert J. Stonebraker (1976) in a neglected paper showed that the uncertainty of profits of small (fringe) firms in an industry increases with the product differentiation entry barriers protecting large incumbents.

To complete the analysis of turnover and entry barriers, we refer briefly to the large literature on the determinants of *net* entry (surveyed by Geroski 1991a, 1995). It concludes that net entry should be represented as an adjustment process that depresses industry profits to the "limit" level that renders further entry unprofitable, or that (in the "free entry" case) increases the number of incumbents to their zero-profit equilibrium number.[26] When the

dependent variable becomes the *gross* number of entrants, another block of determinants is needed to model the replacement of incumbents, including expected failures among the entrants (Baldwin 1995, chap. 14). Most studies have modeled this replacement component rather crudely by including the number of incumbent firms, when the gross number of entrants is the dependent variable. Enrico Santarelli and Alessandro Starlacchini (1994) employed the prevalence of small firms (whose mortality accounts disproportionately for turnover). Boeri and Bellmann (1995) added the lagged number of entrants as an explanatory variable, though with only modest statistical success, and Sleuwaegen and Dehandschutter (1991) found that entry increases with lagged exit. Baldwin (1995, chap. 14) observed a positive effect of the variability of industry sales on the number of entrants, suggesting that it reflects the decreased survival rate and increased entry needed to sustain expected zero profits in equilibrium.[27]

A result regularly reported in the entry-determinants literature is that, while structural barriers deter entry by newly created firms, they have little significant effect (sometimes even a positive effect) on entry by initially large newcomers, by firms established in other industries, or by multinational

---

[26] Another element recently added to this model is a supply-side component to depict the individual's trade-off between selling labor services and undertaking the entrepreneurial role. The implication that (cet. par.) an increase in the unemployment rate should raise the number of entering firms was confirmed by Evans and Linda S. Leighton (1990), among others.

[27] The positive effect of sales variability on gross entry is complemented by its negative effect on new-plant construction by incumbent firms (Baldwin 1995, Table 3.7); the incumbents are likely to build larger plants that are low-cost but better suited to stable environments (Mills and Schumann 1985). Regarding gross entry studies in general, the consideration of entrants' turnover calls into question researchers' practice of measuring entry by the market share achieved by entrants arriving over some time interval. That variable is the outcome of the gross number of entrants, their early hazard rates, and the growth rates achieved by the survivors. These three components do not have identical determinants, and it seems desirable to address them one by one.

firms. Baldwin and Paul K. Gorecki (1987; also Geroski 1991b and Mata 1993) explicitly treated the different types of entrants as responding to different replacement incentives (e.g. foreign-controlled entrants expect to replace foreign-controlled incumbents). Short-run entry inducements (profits, market growth) typically have little statistical effect on these well-endowed entrants. The pattern is consistent with their entries being driven largely by a replacement mechanism: apparently they expect to pass successfully through an entry "gateway" and compel incumbents to contract or exit.

3.4 Market Structure, Mergers, and New Entry

Actual entry and structural entry barriers must also, in light of the new evidence on turnover, be related to the incidence of changes in corporate control. Control changes (see Section 2.5) are not neutral with respect to the productivity and market shares of the acquired business units. They are "entry-like" in their potential competitive effect on other firms, which makes their relation to structural entry barriers important for an understanding of those barriers' overall effect. Baldwin (1995, p. 48) found that during 1970–79 rates of entry by acquisition and "green field" among Canadian manufacturing industries were *negatively* correlated, −0.18, statistically significant. Furthermore (Table 3.6), while the green-field entry rate decreases with four-firm concentration (regarded as a proxy for structural entry barriers), entry by acquisition significantly increases with it. See Nils-Henrik Mørch von der Fehr (1991) for related results.

Behind the inverse relation between green-field and acquisition entry rates lies the fact that acquisition rates are high in just those industries surrounded by structural barriers to entry. Baldwin (1995, chap. 11) found that both the incidence and the productivity of control changes are high in industries that are surrounded by structural entry barriers—production scale economies, product differentiation, control of proprietary technologies. Structural entry barriers thus exert their effect not simply by limiting an industry's equilibrium number of firms but also by altering the gross number and failure rates of entrants trying their luck, the mixture of types of entrant, and the relative occurrence of entry via new plants (or plants switched from other industries) and acquisition of incumbent capacity.

4. Turnover, Productivity, and Efficiency

4.1 Contribution of Turnover to Productivity Growth

The simple Darwinian interpretation that we reflexively assign to business units' turnover implies that the more efficient units displace the less efficient, so that average productivity rises. Researchers on turnover have seized the opportunity to measure this contribution and impute industry-level productivity gains to increases in the productivity of the average unit and the displacement of the less by the more efficient. Bartelsman and Dhrymes (1992) dramatized the role of turnover. In U.S. manufacturing, the unweighted mean total factor productivity (TFP) of large plants (over 250 employees) showed a sustained decline through 1972–84, though with a definite upturn in 1984–86. Over the same period, aggregate (i.e., weighted) TFP at the two-digit industry level dipped in the early 1970s but subsequently achieved a sustained increase. Individual plants' rankings in the productivity distribution they found to be quite stable, so much of the

1972   *Journal of Economic Literature, Vol. XXXVI (December 1998)*

discrepancy depends on the process of reallocating shares toward the more efficient.

Baldwin (1995, Table 9.1) considered the responsiveness of turnover to productivity differences among units. He divided all plants in each industry around median labor productivity and found that units exiting in 1970–79 were significantly concentrated below the 1970 median, while the previous decade's (surviving) entrants were more prevalent above the 1979 median. The pattern holds for other classes of entrants and exits but with exceptions: plants closed by continuing firms, and entrants who switch plants previously classified to other industries. With their sizes controlled, entrant plants of new firms became 16 percent more productive than continuing plants by 1979, and new plants of continuing firms 31 percent more productive. Continuing plants that were less productive in 1970 had a somewhat higher chance of gaining market share during the following decade (regression to the mean, once again), but in 1979 the percentage above the median that had gained share greatly exceeded the percentage below the median that had gained (Baldwin 1995, Table 9.2). Continuing plants that gained share were in 1970 insignificantly more productive than those destined to lose share, but they wound up 34 percent more productive in 1979.

Another contribution to the relation between turnover and productivity is Byong-Hyong Bahk and Gort (1993), who investigated related issues concerning the maturation of new plants in fifteen manufacturing industries. There is potential inconsistency between the recent findings on the growth and maturation of new business units and the traditional presumption that a plant or firm has a unique or at least a minimum optimal scale of operation. One way to reconcile the dynamic evidence with the static presumption is to establish what role vintage effects and learning-by-doing play in the plant's productivity level. Bahk and Gort followed to 1986 plants that had begun operation between 1973 and 1982, establishing that (overall, and within most industries) both average capital vintage and cumulative output have significant effects; the evidence does not distinguish clearly between cumulative plant output and the passage of time as factors governing the rate at which productivity improves.[28] They also found that the explanatory power of cross-section regressions of plants' input-output relations increases with plants' ages, consistent with Jovanovic's process of time-related learning.

Imputing industrywide productivity growth to components of unit-level productivity growth, turnover, and mobility presents a problem of statistical decomposition. It can be done in various ways resting on different economic assumptions. For example, do the shares gained by entrants come at the expense of exiting firms, and those of expanding incumbents from the shrinking incumbents? Or do all the expanders push indiscriminately against all the contractors? Baily, Hulten, and Campbell (1992) decomposed five-year productivity growth for 23 U.S. manufacturing industries in a way implying that the mobility of continuing plants adds roughly 50 percent (their Table 1) to those plants' own productivity growth. Low-productivity plants are more likely to exit (although initial productivity does not predict a plant's switch to

---

[28] Their findings on learning must be treated with caution. An entrant discovering immediately that it is blessed with low costs will elect to produce a large output. A young firm's cumulative large output might therefore reflect either learning-by-doing or early confirmation of its innate efficiency.

another industry), but net entry-exit is inferred to add little because of the entrants' low initial levels of productivity. Haltiwanger (forthcoming) reported a somewhat different decomposition applied to all U.S. manufacturing industries over 1977–87. It attributes 54 percent of industrywide productivity growth to within-plant increases but divides the share-change contribution into two components: share changes weighted by the difference between the unit's initial productivity and industry productivity; and the covariance between share changes and productivity changes. The latter term isolates the productivity winners' share gains and accounts for 38 percent of industrywide productivity growth. The former picks up mean regression and accounts for -10 percent. Net entry accounts for 18 percent.

Results for other countries suggest roughly the same relative importance for turnover in industrywide productivity growth. Baldwin (1995, chap. 9) used both statistical inference and a series of alternative assumptions to pin down these replacement patterns, concluding that on any reasonable procedure, 40 to 50 percent of Canadian industries' productivity growth in the 1970s could be laid to turnover. Baldwin (1996) also analyzed turnover and productivity growth in various subperiods of the years 1973–90, finding little or no evidence of interrelation in their movements. Analyzing all manufacturing and mining establishments in Israel, Zvi Griliches and Haim Regev (1992) imputed a larger proportion of productivity growth to within-plant improvements and less to mobility, possibly because of shorter (three-year) periods of observation. Tybout (1996b) reported complex patterns in several developing countries.

The observation period's duration

conspicuously affects the estimated contribution of entry and exit on industry productivity. All studies agree that in the short run, turnover from entry and exit appears to make a minimal contribution to an industry's productivity growth, because the quitters' productivity and the initial productivity levels of the entrants are similar and both below those of continuing firms, and because entrants account for a small share of activity. The productivity of surviving entrants grows rapidly, however, as they exploit their revealed competence (including the small-firm innovations stressed by Acs and Audretsch) and exercise of their investment options (see section 2.4). Exiting firms have experienced declining productivity and would presumably have deteriorated further if not pushed over the edge. In the long run, therefore, entry-exit turnover is important for industry-level productivity gains. Roberts and Tybout (1996, chap. 1) stressed this conclusion for the developing countries that they studied. Besides the evidence on developed countries reviewed in section 2, Geroski (1989) found that overall productivity growth in 79 British manufacturing industries (1976–79) increased significantly with the lagged rate of gross entry of new firms.

4.2 Turnover and Productive Efficiency

Although comparing productivity gains through turnover and through improved performance in the individual unit puts turnover's importance in useful perspective, the underlying mechanisms are not really commensurate. Given random shocks to firms' or plants' productivity levels, mobility and turnover should continuously enlarge the winners and shrink the losers whether the industry's overall rate of productivity growth is high or low. More fundamental is the relation between turnover and the dispersion at a point in time of the efficiency levels of competing business units, for that dispersion provides the opening for turnover to raise productivity. If we regard the production function as defining an industry's efficient frontier, then the reshuffling of the units' shares should directly register the penalties that the market imposes on units whose performance is slipping relative to the frontier and the rewards to those climbing toward it. Mobility should reduce the weighted average shortfall from the frontier, just as disturbances that widen the efficiency distribution should increase turnover.

Research on productive efficiency has recently drawn upon the same primary industrial census records as the research on turnover. Studies in a number of countries have used one or another technique to infer a frontier of technical efficiency for each manufacturing industry and test in cross-section hypotheses about factors that might cause or perpetuate inefficiency (Caves and David R. Barton 1990; Caves and Associates 1992; David G. Mayes 1996). These studies assume that the gap between average and best-practice productivity for an industry's representative business unit measures an equilibrium outcome with determinants that are stable over time. On that assumption they perform cross-section (inter-industry) tests of hypotheses about structural and behavioral forces that could create a dispersion of units' efficiency levels beneath the frontier and either speed or delay its shrinkage through the mobility process. The results support the general framework and confirm a number of specific hypotheses (Caves and Associates 1992, chap. 1; also Mayes, Christopher Harris, and Melanie Lansbury 1994, chap. 6). The confirmed determinants include such factors as industries' R&D intensi-

ties and rates of productivity growth—sources of turbulence and obsolescence that continually drag some units beneath the productivity frontier. They also include others (competitiveness, unionization of its workforce, exposure to international competition) that should either speed or delay mobility processes. Thus, the evidence on productive inefficiency reveals the sources of opportunities for productivity-raising turnover, just as the evidence on turnover shows the strength of the forces keeping productive inefficiency in check.[29]

Baldwin's (1995, Table 12.6) data dramatize the interplay of turnover and individual units' productivity changes for Canadian manufacturing in the 1970s: while each class of share gainers displaced a less productive set of losers, average productive efficiency fell 5 percent because continuing plants that lost market share experienced large declines in their relative productivity, while continuing plants that gained share raised theirs only a little. He found some evidence on what causes units to slip farther beneath the frontier. The increase in an industry's overall labor-productivity level is negatively correlated with the change in its productive efficiency (10 percent significance), which in turn is negatively correlated with its productivity gain through the turnover of

---

[29] Studies of industries' productive efficiency estimated in successive years further underline the importance of the relation between efficiency and turnover. For both Britain in the 1960s and 1970s (Sheryl Bailey 1992) and Korea during 1978–88 (Seong Min Yoo 1992) annual estimates of productive inefficiency seem to vibrate around stable means, although for Britain in the 1980s Lansbury and Mayes (1996) found upward trends prevailing. In Korea Yoo observed that the rank correlations of industries' efficiency levels are low even between adjacent years. Bailey analyzed what determines the amount of intertemporal variation in an industry's efficiency level, concluding that variability increases with the incidence of disturbances and decreases with the industry's speed of adjustment and flexibility of resource use.

market shares. That is, faster technical advance pushes the laggards and nonadopters farther back and prompts more turnover to displace them. The new research on turnover has an important potential for extending our knowledge of what determines productivity dispersions. Timothy Dunne (1994), for example, concluded that the adoption of advanced production technologies is not biased away from old plants in the way vintage models suggest.

In a regression analysis, Baldwin (1995, pp. 318–26) related market shares gained by an industry's entrants and expanding incumbents to the productivity differentials that propel this turnover and the various types of disturbances that disperse plants' productivity levels. The exogenous variables were filtered through principal components, which makes the influences of the underlying regressors difficult to summarize. Nonetheless, it is clear that forces in both groups exert significant influences. Investigating the determinants of productive efficiency in U.S. manufacturing industries, Caves and Barton (1990, chap. 6) concluded that it decreases with the importance of product innovations to the industry and also with process innovations underlying capital-vintage effects (also Shen 1968). Lansbury and Mayes (1996) observed a negative influence of productivity growth on productive efficiency in Britain, but Akio Torii (1992) found a positive effect in Japan.

Another apparently important influence on mobility and entry–exit turnover, and thereby productivity, is the stage of the business cycle. Davis and Haltiwanger (1990, 1992) observed that gross turnover moves contracyclically, with the effects most pronounced in larger and older plants and plants belonging to multiplant firms (also see Jeffrey R. Campbell 1997). Apparently "creative destruction" is involved when

adverse macroeconomic conditions force the process of adjustment (and the incurring of adjustment costs). The same result was found for Canada (Baldwin 1995, chap. 6) and the United Kingdom (Konings 1995a). In Britain, turnover tends to occur within industries during booms, between sectors during recessions. In Belgium no contracyclical job destruction was found, but the authors noted that their data covered a period lacking the major recessions that occurred in Britain and the United States (Konings, Roodhooft, and Van de Gucht 1996).[30] Roberts (1996b) also found no evidence of it in the developing countries that he studied, which might well lack a core of larger and older units vulnerable to being dislodged in a recession. Indeed, in developing countries entry–exit turnover is substantially more important relative to incumbents' mobility than in developed countries.[31] Christopher L. Foote (1997) showed that these disparate results on gross turnover components might be an artifact of countries' different net growth rates.

5. Conclusions

Plus ça change, plus c'est la même chose. Turnover processes are ubiquitous among plants and firms classified to an industry. They are also stable, explicable, and can be embraced within the traditional thinking based on market-equilibrium models that underlies the bulk of empirical research in industrial organization. The abundant new evidence on turnover processes reviewed in this paper provides a deeper

[30] Also, the Belgian study, unlike the others, covered very small firms, and contracyclicality would be expected more in the larger units.
[31] However, job turnover is concentrated within (rather than between) industries and regions no less in developing than in developed countries, contrary to what one might expect.

1976   *Journal of Economic Literature, Vol. XXXVI (December 1998)*

understanding of why concentration levels are what they are, why they change when they do, and how structural entry barriers affect the behavior of actual entrants. We know much more about why industries contain firms of diverse sizes and not alike-as-peas incumbents reflecting some iron law of optimal scale. We understand that the diverse fates and frequent failures of new firms reflect hidden information and option-value considerations, and need not be written off to "cannon fodder" and "animal spirits."

It is difficult to summarize a summary. However, if in a biblical mood one seeks ten substantive conclusions, they would be these:

1. In the typical industry and overall, mean growth rates of firms decrease with their initial sizes among small firms; for initially large firms growth rates and size are unrelated. The variance of growth rates decreases with firm size. Entry into and exit from the distribution occur mainly in the smaller size classes. These processes are typically consistent with the size distribution of firms (concentration) being stable over time.

2. The mobility of incumbent firms is substantial and consistent with the assumption that adjustment costs are not smoothly convex but have a fixed component. Long-run regression to the mean is clearly evident, although at a rate consistent with slow turnover in the ranks of the typical industry's largest firms.

3. Gross entry is substantial in most industries. It is much larger than net entry, due to high rates of infant mortality. Successful entrants grow rapidly, so that an entrant cohort's initial market share falls slowly. The pattern is consistent with Jovanovic's model of entrants learning their specific capabilities.

4. Entrants select different initial sizes reflecting both the structure of the entered market and their own perceived capabilities. The process works as if entrants obtain options to make larger further investments after learning or confirming their capabilities.

5. The turnover processes described so far show very little qualitative difference among countries. Less developed countries appear to exhibit more turnover associated with their concentration on activities with smaller sunk costs. Large macroeconomic disturbances (wars, major trade liberalizations, major privatizations) explicably affect the turnover process.

6. Turnover through changes in the control of business units operates in the manner of a job-matching process driven by continual disturbances to the optimal match.

7. Concentration in manufacturing industries is negatively related to turnover from entry and exit but largely independent of incumbents' current mobility, except that mobility is greater in the *least* concentrated industries. Changes in concentration depend on mobility-related factors. Mobility depends strongly on basic features of an industry's technology and demand conditions. Concentration strongly depends, however, on cumulative effects of past mobility rates, in ways shown by modern random-process models and analyses of industry life-cycles.

8. The traditional structural entry barriers affect both the number of entries and the entrants' survival rate; for some barriers the latter effect seems more important. Due to random qualities of new firms' endowments, entry barriers can become entry gateways for lucky entrants.

9. Productivity growth for an industry as a whole depends to an important degree on the redistribution of shares toward the more productive units and not

just on growth of the units' individual productivity.

10. Research on productive efficiency (gap between an industry's average and best-practice productivity) shows what factors determine the opportunities for productivity-raising turnover, thus complementing the evidence on turnover that shows the strength of the forces keeping productive inefficiency in check.

Much has been accomplished in a short time to set the stylized facts about turnover, but the research opportunities remain rich. Hazard-rate analyses are just coming into use to isolate the causes and correlates of individual units' fates. In particular, little is known about what factors systematically trigger the expansion or contraction of incumbent business units, and what temporal relations exist between changes in their unit profitability and scales of operation. Substantial work has been done on the factors associated with the persistence of successful business units' high profits (e.g., Geoffrey F. Waring 1996; Anita M. McGahan and Michael E. Porter 1996), but it needs to be extended and related to the general properties of turnover processes. We have far to go in relating mobility to its determinants in basic conditions of technology and demand. Because reallocations of activity from the less efficient to the more efficient are so important for the optimal use of resources, more evidence is needed on how competitive conditions within an industry affect the speed with which the more efficient displace the less efficient.

Exogenous shocks to an industry provoke diverse responses in individual units, and the relation between the overall disturbance and the pattern of responses should be pursued. This is especially important for the foundations of macroeconomics. There, analysis has

begun on the relation between changes in aggregate demand and plant-level investment responses (Ricardo J. Caballero, Eduardo M. R. A. Engel, and Haltiwanger 1995) and on the relative roles for determining fluctuations in U.S. aggregate manufacturing employment's growth of aggregate shocks and of changes in the distribution of idiosyncratic shocks (Caballero, Engel, and Haltiwanger 1997). The same questions arise for shocks originating in major innovations, international comparative advantage, trade policy (especially the formation of free-trade areas), and others.[32]

Turnover in the control of business units, noted only briefly in section 2.5 of this survey, deserves much more attention than it has received. This turnover has been regarded chiefly through the lens of corporate governance and contract theory, not as a type of job-matching problem triggered by changes in the optimal combination of heterogeneous business assets under particular managerial roofs.

National differences noted in this survey suggest further leads. Major reforms in national economic systems generate enormously heterogeneous disturbances to the nation's plants and firms, as in the transition economies and developing economies that have undertaken broad-based privatizations. Understanding their consequences requires following the turnover of individual units. Indeed, economic development seems to involve raising the capability to coordinate and manage larger business units with more complex teams of inputs, and that process itself

[32] An important limitation of this survey from the viewpoint of macroeconomics is its emphasis on unweighted-average behavior patterns. Size-weighted patterns matter for aggregate activity, an important point in the dispute over firm size and job creation (Davis, Haltiwanger, and Schuh 1996, chap. 4)

appears primarily in the differential fates of diverse business units.

REFERENCES

Abernathy, William J. and James M. Utterback, 1978. "Patterns of Industrial Innovation," *Tech. Rev.* 80:7, pp. 40–47.

Acs, Zoltan J. and David B. Audretsch. 1987. "Innovation, Market Structure, and Firm Size," *Rev. Econ. Statist.*, 69:4, pp. 567–74.

———. 1988. "Innovation in Large and Small Firms: An Empirical Analysis," *Amer. Econ. Rev,* 78:4, pp. 678–90.

———. 1990. *Innovation and Small Firms.* Cambridge, MA: MIT Press.

Agarwal, Rajshree and Michael Gort. 1996. "The Evolution of Markets and Entry, Exit and the Survival of Firms," *Rev. Econ. Statist.*, 78:3, pp. 489–98.

Alexander, Sidney S. 1949. "The Effect of Size of Manufacturing Corporation on the Distribution of the Rate of Return," *Rev. Econ. Statist.*, 31:3, pp. 229–35.

Audretsch, David B. 1991. "New-Firm Survival and the Technological Regime," *Rev. Econ. Statist.*, 73:3, pp. 441–50.

———. 1995a. *Innovation and Industry Evolution.* Cambridge, MA: M.I.T. Press.

———. 1995b. "Innovation, Growth, and Survival," *Int. J. Ind. Organ.*, 13:4, pp. 441–57.

——— and Zoltan J. Acs. 1994. "New-Firm Startups, Technology, and Macroeconomic Fluctuations," *Small Bus. Econ.*, 6:6, pp. 439–49.

Audretsch, David B. and Talat Mahmood. 1995. "New Firm Survival: New Results Using a Hazard Function," *Rev. Econ. Statist.*, 77:1, pp. 97–103.

Bahk, Byong-Hyong and Michael Gort. 1993. "Decomposing Learning by Doing in New Plants," *J. Polit. Econ.*, 101:4, pp. 561–83.

Bailey, Sheryl D. 1992. "The Intraindustry Dispersion of Plant Productivity in the British Manufacturing Sector, 1963–79," in Caves and Associates 1992, pp. 329–84.

Baily, Martin Neil; Eric J.Bartelsman and John Haltiwanger. 1996. "Downsizing and Productivity Growth: Myth or Reality?" *Small Bus. Econ.*, 8:4, pp. 259–78.

Baily, Martin Neil; Charles Hulten, and David Campbell. 1992. "Productivity Dynamics in Manufacturing Plants," *Brookings Pap. Econ. Activity: Microeconomics*, pp. 187–249.

Bain, Joe S. 1956. *Barriers to New Competition.* Cambridge, MA: Harvard U. Press.

Baldwin, John R. 1995. *The Dynamics of Industrial Competition.* Cambridge: Cambridge U. Press.

———. 1996. "Productivity Growth, Plant Turnover and Restructuring in the Canadian Manufacturing Sector," in Mayes 1996, pp. 245–62.

——— and Richard E. Caves. 1998. "International Competition and Industrial Performance: Allocative Efficiency, Productive Efficiency, and Turbulence," in *The Economics and Politics of International Trade.* Gary Cook, ed. London: Routledge, Volume II, pp. 57–84.

Baldwin, John; William Chandler, Can Le, and Tom Papailiadis. 1994. *Strategies for Success.* Catal. No. 61–523RE. Ottawa: Statistics Canada.

Baldwin, John and Paul K. Gorecki. 1987. "Plant Creation versus Plant Acquisition: The Entry Process in Canadian Manufacturing," *Int. J. Ind. Organ.*, 5:1, pp. 27–41.

Baldwin, John and Joanne Johnson. 1996. "Survival of New Canadian Manufacturing Firms: The Importance of Financial Structure," working paper, Micro-Economic Studies and Analysis Division, Statistics Canada.

Baldwin, John and Garnett Picot. 1995. "Employment Generation by Small Producers in the Canadian Manufacturing Sector," *Small Bus. Econ.*, 7:4, pp. 317–31.

Baldwin, John and Mohammed Rafiquzzaman. 1995a. "Selection versus Evolutionary Adaptation: Learning and Post-Entry Performance," *Int. J. Ind. Organ.*, 13:4, pp. 501–22.

———. 1995b. "Restructuring in the Canadian Manufacturing Sector from 1970 to 1990: Industry and Regional Dimensions of Job Turnover," Research Paper Series No. 78, Analytical Studies Branch, Statistics Canada.

Bartelsman, Eric J. and Phoebus J. Dhrymes. 1992. "Productivity Dynamics: U.S. Manufacturing Plants, 1972–1986," Discussion Paper No. 92–1, Center for Economic Studies, U.S. Bureau of the Census.

Bates, Timothy. 1990. "Entrepreneur Human Capital Inputs and Small Business Longevity," *Rev. Econ. Statist.*, 72:4, pp. 551–59.

Beesley, Michael E. and R. T. Hamilton. 1984. "Small Firms' Seedbed Role and the Concept of Turbulence," *J. Ind. Econ.*, 33:2, 217–31.

Boeri, Tito. 1989. "Does Firm Size Matter?" *Gior. degli Econ. e Annali di Econ.*, 48:9–10, pp. 477–95.

———. 1994. "Why Are Establishments So Heterogeneous?" *Small Bus. Econ.*, 6:6, pp. 409–20.

——— and Lutz Bellmann. 1995. "Post-Entry Behavior and the Cycle: Evidence from Germany," *Int. J. Ind. Organ.*, 13:4, pp. 483–500.

Boeri, Tito and Ulrich Cramer. 1992. "Employment Growth, Incumbents and Entrants: Evidence from Germany," *Int. J. Ind. Organ.*, 10:4, pp. 545–65.

Brüderl, Josef; Peter Preisendörfer, and Rolf Ziegler. 1992. "Survival Chances of Newly Founded Business Organizations," *Amer. Soc. Rev.*, 57:2, pp. 227–42.

Caballero, Ricardo J.; Eduardo M. R. A. Engel, and John C. Haltiwanger. 1995. "Plant-Level Adjustment and Aggregate Investment Dynamics," *Brookings Pap. Econ. Activity*, 2, pp. 1–54.

———. 1997. "Aggregate Employment Dynamics: Building from Microeconomic Evidence," *Amer. Econ. Rev.*, 87:1, pp. 115–37.

Cable, John and Joachim Schwalbach. 1991. "International Comparisons of Entry and Exit," in Geroski and Schwalbach 1991, pp. 257–81.

Cabral, Luis M. B. 1993. "Experience Advantages and Entry Dynamics," *J. Econ. Theory*, 59:2, pp. 403–16.

Campbell, Jeffrey R. 1997. "Entry, Exit, Embodied Technology, and Business Cycles," Working Paper No. 5955, National Bureau of Economic Research.

Caves, Richard E. and Associates. 1992. *Industrial Efficiency in Six Nations*. Cambridge, MA: M.I.T. Press.

Caves, Richard and David R. Barton. 1990. *Efficiency in U.S. Manufacturing Industries*. Cambridge, MA: M.I.T. Press.

Caves, Richard and Thomas A. Pugel. 1980. *Intraindustry Differences in Conduct and Performance*. Monograph Series 1980–2. NY: Graduate School Bus. Admin., NYU.

Churchill, Betty C. 1954a. "Recent Business Population Movements," *Surv. Curr. Bus.*, 34:1, pp. 11–16.

——. 1954b. "Size Characteristics of the Business Population," *Surv. Curr. Bus.*, 34:5, pp. 15–24.

——. 1955. "Age and Life Expectancy of Business Firms," *Surv. Curr. Bus.*, 35:12, pp. 15–19.

Contini, Bruno and Riccardo Revelli. 1989. "The Relationship between Firm Growth and Labor Demand," *Small Bus. Econ.*, 1:4, pp. 309–14.

Davies, Stephen and Paul Geroski. 1997. "Changes in Concentration, Turbulence, and the Dynamics of Market Shares," *Rev. Econ. Statist.*, 79:3, pp. 383–91.

Davies, Stephen and Bruce R. Lyons. 1982. "Seller Concentration: The Technological Explanations and Demand Uncertainty," *Econ. J.*, 92:4, pp. 903–14.

Davis, Steven J. and John C. Haltiwanger. 1990. "Gross Job Creation and Destruction: Microeconomic Evidence and Macroeconomic Implications." *NBER Macroeconomics Annual*, pp. 123–68.

——. 1992. "Gross Job Creation, Gross Job Destruction, and Employment Reallocation," *Quart. J. Econ.*, 107:3, 819–63.

Davis, Steven; John Haltiwanger, and Scott Schuh. 1996. *Job Creation and Destruction*. Cambridge, MA: M.I.T. Press.

Doms, Mark; Timothy Dunne, and Mark J. Roberts. 1995. "The Role of Technology Use in the Survival and Growth of Manufacturing Plants," *Int. J. Ind. Organ.*, 13:4, pp. 523–45.

Dunne, Paul and Alan Hughes. 1994. "Age, Size, Growth, and Survival: UK Companies in the 1980s," *J. Ind. Econ.*, 42:2, pp. 115–40.

Dunne, Timothy. 1994. "Plant Age and Technology Use in U.S. Manufacturing Industries." *RAND J. Econ.*, 25:3, pp. 488–99.

—— and Mark J. Roberts. 1991. "Variation in Producer Turnover across US Manufacturing Industries," in Geroski and Schwalbach 1991, pp. 187–203.

Dunne, Timothy; Mark Roberts, and Larry Samuelson. 1988. "Patterns of Firm Entry and Exit in U.S. Manufacturing Industries," *RAND J. Econ.*, 19:4, pp. 495–515.

——. 1989a. "Plant-Turnover and Gross Employment Flows in the U.S. Manufacturing Sector," *J. Labor Econ.*, 7:1, pp. 48–71.

——. 1989b. "Firm Entry and Post-entry Performance in the U.S. Chemical Industries," *J. Law Econ.*, 32:2, Part 2, pp. S233–71.

——. 1989c. "The Growth and Failure of U.S. Manufacturing Plants," *Quart. J. Econ.*, 104:4, pp. 671–98.

Ericson, Richard and Ariel Pakes. 1995. "Markov-Perfect Industry Dynamics: A Framework for Empirical Work." *Rev. Econ. Stud.*, 62:1, pp. 53–82.

Evans, David S. 1987a. "The Relationship between Firm Growth, Size, and Age: Estimates for 100 Manufacturing Industries," *J. Ind. Econ.*, 35:4, pp. 567–81.

——. 1987b. "Tests of Alternative Theories of Firm Growth," *J. Polit. Econ.*, 95:4, pp. 657–74.

—— and Linda S. Leighton. 1990. "Small Business Formation by Unemployed and Employed Workers," *Small Bus. Econ.*, No. 4, 2:4, pp. 319–30.

Flynn, Joseph E. 1991. "The Determinants of Exit in an Open Economy," *Small Bus. Econ.*, 3:3, pp. 225–32.

Foote, Christopher L. 1997. "The Surprising Symmetry of Gross Job Flows," working paper, Harvard U.

Frank, Murray Z. 1988. "An Intertemporal Model of Industrial Exit," *Quart. J. Econ.*, 103:2, pp. 333–44.

Geroski, Paul A. 1989. "Entry, Innovation, and Productivity Growth," *Rev. Econ. Statist.*, 71:4, pp. 572–8.

——. 1991a. *Market Dynamics and Entry*. Oxford: Basil Blackwell.

——. 1991b. "Domestic and Foreign Entry in the United Kingdom: 1983–1984" in Geroski and Schwalbach 1991, pp. 63–88.

——. 1995. "What Do We Know about Entry?" *Int. J. Ind. Organ.*, 13:4, pp. 421–40.

Geroski, Paul; Stephen Machin, and Chris Walters. 1997. "Corporate Growth and Profitability," *J. Ind. Econ.*, 45:2, pp. 171–89.

Geroski, Paul A. and Joachim Schwalbach, eds. 1991. *Entry and Market Contestability*. Oxford: Blackwell.

Geroski, Paul A. and Saadet Toker. 1996. "The Turnover of Market Leaders in UK Manufacturing Industry, 1979–86," *Int. J. Ind. Organ.*, 14:2, pp. 141–58.

Gibson, John K. and Richard I. D. Harris. 1996. "Trade Liberalisation and Plant Exit in New Zealand Manufacturing," *Rev. Econ. Statist.*, 78:3, pp. 521–29.

Gort, Michael and Steven Klepper. 1982. "Time Paths in the Diffusion of Product Innovations," *Econ. J.*, 92(3), pp. 630–53.

Gort, Michael and Akira Konakayama. 1982. "A

1980   *Journal of Economic Literature, Vol. XXXVI (December 1998)*

Model of Diffusion in the Production of an Innovation," *Amer. Econ. Rev.*, 72:5, pp. 1111–20.

Griliches, Zvi and Haim Regev. 1992. "Productivity and Firm Turnover in Israeli Industry: 1979–1988," Working Paper No. 4059, National Bureau of Economic Research.

Hall, Bronwyn H. 1987. "The Relationship between Firm Size and Firm Growth in the US Manufacturing Sector," *J. Ind. Econ.*, 35:4, pp. 583–600.

Haltiwanger, John. Forthcoming. "Measuring and Analyzing Aggregate Fluctuations: The Importance of Building from Microeconomic Evidence," *St. Louis Fed. Reserve Bank Econ. Rev.*

Hannan, Michael T. and John Freeman. 1989. *Organizational Ecology.* Cambridge, MA: Harvard U. Press.

Hart, Peter E. and Nicholas Oulton. 1996. "Growth and Size of Firms," *Econ. J.*, 106:3, pp. 1242–52.

Hirschey, Mark. 1981. "The Effect of Advertising on Industrial Mobility, 1947–72," *J. Bus.*, 54:2, pp. 329–39.

Holmes, Thomas J. and James A. Schmitz, Jr. 1995. "On the Turnover of Business Firms and Business Managers," *J. Polit. Econ.*, 103:5, pp. 1005–38.

———. 1996. "Managerial Tenure, Business Age, and Small Business Turnover," *J. Labor Econ.*, 14:1, pp. 79–99.

Hopenhayn, Hugo A. 1992. "Entry, Exit, and Firm Dynamics in Long Run Equilibrium," *Econometrica*, 60:3, pp. 1127–50.

Ijiri, Yuji and Herbert A. Simon. 1977. *Skew Distributions and the Sizes of Business Firms.* Amsterdam: North-Holland.

Jackson, John E. 1996. "Firm Size and the Dynamics of a Market Economy," Working paper, Dept. Polit. Sci., U. Michigan.

———; Jacek Klich, Krystyna Poznanska, Leszek Zienkowski, and Józef Chmiel. 1996. "Economic Change in Poland: 1990–1994," Working paper, Dept. Polit. Sci., U. Michigan.

Johnson, Joanne; John Baldwin, and Christine Hinchley. 1997. *Successful Entrants: Creating the Capacity for Survival and Growth.* Catalogue No. 61-524-XPE. Ottawa: Statistics Canada.

Jovanovic, Boyan. 1982. "Selection and the Evolution of Industry," *Econometrica*, 50:3, pp. 649–70.

Kessides, Ioannis N. 1986. "Advertising, Sunk Costs, and Barriers to Entry," *Rev. Econ. Statist.*, 68:3, pp. 84–95.

———. 1990a. "Toward a Testable Model of Entry: A Study of the US Manufacturing Industries," *Economica*, 57:2, pp. 219–38.

———. 1990b. "Market Concentration, Contestability, and Sunk Costs," *Rev. Econ. Statist.*, 72:4, pp. 614–22.

Kirchhoff, Bruce A. 1994. *Entrepreneurship and Dynamic Capitalism: the Economics of Business Firm Formation and Growth.* Westport, CT: Praeger.

Klepper, Steven. 1995. "Evolution, Market Concentration, and Firm Survival," working paper, Carnegie Mellon University.

———. 1996. "Entry, Exit, Growth, and Innovation over the Product Life Cycle," *Amer. Econ. Rev.*, 86:3, pp. 562–83.

———. 1997. "Industry Life Cycles," *Ind. and Corp. Change*, 6:1, pp. 1–37.

——— and Elizabeth Graddy. 1990. "The Evolution of New Industries and the Determinants of Market Structure," *RAND J. Econ.*, 21:1, pp. 27–44.

Klepper, Steven and John H. Miller. 1995. "Entry, Exit, and Shakeouts in the United States in New Manufactured Products," *Int. J. Ind. Organ.*, 13:4, pp. 567–91.

Klepper, Steven and Kenneth L. Simons. Forthcoming. "Technological Extinctions of Industrial Firms: An Inquiry into their Nature and Causes," *Ind. and Corp. Change.*

Konings, Jozef. 1995a. "Job Creation and Job Destruction in the UK Manufacturing Sector," *Oxford Bull. Econ. Statist.*, 57:1, pp. 5–24.

———. 1995b. "Gross Job Flows and the Evolution of Size in U.K. Establishments," *Small Bus. Econ.*, 7:3, pp. 213–20.

———; F. Roodhooft, and L. Van de Gucht. 1996. "The Life Cycle of New Firms and Its Impact on Job Creation and Job Destruction," Working Paper No. 9669, Faculty Econ. and Applied Econ., Katholieke Universiteit Leuven.

Kumar, M. S. 1985. "Growth, Acquisition Activity and Firm Size: Evidence from the United Kingdom," *J. Ind. Econ.*, 33:3, pp. 327–38.

Lambson, Val Eugene. 1991. "Industry Evolution with Sunk Costs and Uncertain Market Conditions," *Int. J. Ind. Organ.*, 9:2, pp. 171–96.

Lansbury, Melanie and David Mayes. 1996. "Shifts in the Production Frontier and the Distribution of Efficiency," in Mayes 1996, pp. 66–88.

Leonard, Jonathan S. 1986. "On the Size Distribution of Employment and Establishments," Working Paper No. 1951, National Bureau of Economic Research.

Lichtenberg, Frank R. 1992. *Corporate Takeovers and Productivity.* Cambridge, MA: M.I.T. Press.

——— and Donald Siegel. 1987. "Productivity and Changes in Ownership of Manufacturing Plants," *Brookings Pap. Econ. Activity*, 3, pp. 643–73.

Lieberman, Marvin B. 1989. "The Learning Curve, Technology Barriers to Entry, and Competitive Survival in the Chemical Processing Industries," *Strategic Manag. J.*, 10:5, pp. 431–47.

Lippman, S. A. and R. P. Rumelt. 1982. "Uncertain Imitability: An Analysis of Interfirm Differences in Efficiency under Competition," *Bell J. Econ.*, 13:2, pp. 418–38.

Mansfield, Edwin F. 1962. "Entry, Innovation, and the Growth of Firms," *Amer. Econ. Rev.*, 52:5, pp. 1023–51.

Mata, Jose. 1991. "Sunk Costs and Entry by Small and Large Plants," in Geroski and Schwalbach 1991, pp. 49–62.
———. 1993. "Entry and Type of Entrant: Evidence from Portugal," *Int. J. Ind. Organ.*, 11:1, pp. 101–22.
———. 1994. "Firm Growth during Infancy," *Small Bus. Econ.*, 6:1, pp. 27–39.
———. 1995. "Sunk Costs and the Dynamics of Entry in Portuguese Manufacturing," in *Market Evolution: Competition and Cooperation across Markets and Time.* A. van Witteloostuijn, ed. Dordrecht: Kluwer Academic, pp. 267–84.
———. 1996. "Markets, Entrepreneurs, and the Size of New Firms," *Econ. Letters*, 52:1, pp. 89–94.
——— and Jose A. F. Machado. 1996. "Firm Start-up Size: A Conditional Quantile Approach," *European Econ. Rev.*, 40:6, pp. 1305–23.
Mata, Jose and Pedro Portugal. 1994. "Life Duration of New Firms," *J. Ind. Econ.*, 42:3, pp. 227–45.
Mata, Jose; Pedro Portugal, and Paulo Guimarzes. 1995. "The Survival of New Plants: Start-up Conditions and Post-Entry Evolution," *Int. J. Ind. Organ.*, 13:4, pp. 459–81.
Mayes, David G. 1996. *Sources of Productivity Growth.* Cambridge: Cambridge U. Press.
———, Christopher Harris, and Melanie Lansbury. 1994. *Inefficiency in Industry.* Hemel Hempstead: Harvester Wheatsheaf.
McGahan, Anita M. and Michael E. Porter. 1996. "The Emergence and Sustainability of Abnormal Profits," working paper, Harvard Business School.
McGuckin, Robert H. and Sang V. Nguyen. 1995. "On Productivity and Plant Ownership Change: New Evidence from the Longitudinal Research Database," *RAND J. Econ.*, 26:2, pp. 257–76.
Mills, David E. and Lawrence Schumann. 1985. "Industry Structure with Fluctuating Demand," *Amer. Econ. Rev.*, 75:4, pp. 758–67.
Mortensen, Dale T. and Christopher A. Pissarides. 1994. "Job Creation and Job Destruction in the Theory of Unemployment," *Rev. Econ. Stud.*, 61:3, pp. 397–415.
Mueller, Dennis C. and John E. Tilton. 1969. "Research and Development Costs as a Barrier to Entry," *Canad. J. Econ.*, 2:4, pp. 570–79.
Mueller, Willard F. and Richard T. Rogers. 1980. "The Role of Advertising in Changing Concentration of Manufacturing Industries," *Rev. Econ. Statist.*, 62:1, pp. 89–96.
Nelson, Richard R. and Sidney G. Winter. 1978. "Forces Generating and Limiting Concentration under Schumpeterian Competition," *Bell J. Econ.*, 9:2, pp. 524–48.
Olley, G. Steven and Ariel Pakes. 1996. "The Dynamics of Productivity in the Telecommunications Equipment Industry," *Econometrica*, 64:6, pp. 1263–97.

Pakes, Ariel and Richard Ericson. Forthcoming. "Empirical Implications of Alternative Models of Firm Dynamics," *J. Econ. Theory.*
Power, Laura. Forthcoming. "The Missing Link: Technology, Investment, and Productivity," *Rev. Econ. Statist.*
Ravenscraft, David J. and F. M. Scherer. 1987. *Mergers, Sell-offs, and Economic Efficiency.* Washington, DC: Brookings Institution.
Roberts, Mark J. 1996a. "Colombia, 1977–85: Producer Turnover, Margins, and Trade Exposure," in Roberts and Tybout 1996, pp. 227–59.
———. 1996b. "Employment Flows and Producer Turnover," in Roberts and Tybout 1996, pp. 18–42.
——— and James R Tybout, eds. 1996. *Industrial Evolution in Developing Countries: Micro Patterns of Turnover, Productivity, and Market Structure.* New York: Oxford U. Press for World Bank.
Robinson, William T. 1993. "Are Sutton's Predictions Robust? Empirical Evidence on Price Competition, Advertising, and the Evolution of Concentration," working paper, School of Business Administration, U. Michigan.
——— and Claes Fornell. 1985. "Sources of Market Pioneer Advantages in Consumer Goods Industries," *J. Marketing Res.*, 22:3, pp. 305–17.
Rosenbaum, David I. and Fabian Lamort. 1992. "Entry Barriers, Exit, and Sunk Costs: An Analysis," *Appl. Econ.*, 24:3, pp. 297–304.
Santarelli, Enrico and Alessandro Starlacchini. 1994. "New Firm Formation in Italian Industry: 1985–89," *Small Bus. Econ.*, 6:2, pp. 95–106.
Schmalensee, Richard. 1989. "Inter-Industry Studies of Structure and Performance," in *Handbook of Industrial Organization.* Richard Schmalensee and Robert D. Willig, eds. Amsterdam: North-Holland Publishing Co., 1989. II, pp. 951–1009.
Schwalbach, Joachim. 1991. "Entry, Exit, Concentration, and Market Contestability," in Geroski and Schwalbach 1991, pp. 121–40.
Shen, T. Y. 1968. "Competition, Technology, and Market Shares," *Rev. Econ. Statist.*, 50:1, pp. 293–310.
Simon, Herbert A. and Charles P. Bonini. 1958. "The Size Distribution of Business Firms," *Amer. Econ. Rev.*, 48:4, pp. 607–17.
Sleuwaegen, Leo and Wim Dehandschutter. 1991. "Entry and Exit in Belgian Manufacturing," in Geroski and Schwalbach 1991, pp. 111–20.
Stonebraker, Robert J. 1976. "Corporate Profits and the Risk of Entry," *Rev. Econ. Statist.*, 58:1, pp. 33–39.
Sutton, John. 1991. *Sunk Costs and Market Structure: Price Competition, Advertising, and the Evolution of Concentration.* Cambridge, MA: M.I.T. Press.
———. 1997. "Gibrat's Legacy," *J. Econ. Lit.*, 35:1, pp. 40–59.

————. Forthcoming. *Technology and Market Structure: Theory and History.* Cambridge, MA: M.I.T. Press.

Torii, Akio. 1992. "Technical Efficiency in Japanese Industries," in Caves and Associates 1992, pp. 31–119.

Troske, Kenneth R. 1996. "The Dynamic Adjustment Process of Firm Entry and Exit in Manufacturing and Finance, Insurance, and Real Estate," *J. Law Econ.,* 39:2, pp. 705–35.

Tybout, James R. 1996a. "Chile, 1979–86: Trade Liberalization and Its Aftermath," in Roberts and Tybout 1996, pp. 200–26.

————. 1996b. "Heterogeneity and Productivity Growth: Assessing the Evidence," in Roberts and Tybout 1996, pp. 43–72.

von der Fehr, Nils-Henrik Mørch. 1991. "Domestic Entry in Norwegian Manufacturing Industries," in Geroski and Schwalbach 1991, pp. 89–110.

Wagner, Joachim. 1992. "Firm Size, Firm Growth, and Persistence of Chance: Testing Gibrat's Law with Establishment Data from Lower Saxony, 1978–1989," *Small Bus. Econ.,* 4:2, pp. 125–31.

————. 1994a. "The Post-Entry Performance of New Small Firms in German Manufacturing Industries," *J. Ind. Econ,* 42:2, pp. 141–54.

————. 1994b. "Small Firm Entry in Manufacturing Industries: Lower Saxony, 1979–1989," *Small Bus. Econ.,* 6:3, pp. 211–23.

Waring, Geoffrey F. 1996. "Industry Differences in the Persistence of Firm-specific Returns," *Amer. Econ. Rev.,* 86:5, pp. 1253–65.

Wedervang, Fröystein. 1965. *Development of a Population of Industrial Firms: The Structure of Manufacturing Industries in Norway, 1930–1948.* Oslo: Universitetsforlaget.

Yip, George S. 1982. *Barriers to Entry: A Corporate-strategy Perspective.* Lexington, MA: Lexington Books.

Yoo, Seong Min. 1992. "Technical Efficiency over Time in Korea, 1978–88: Exploratory Analysis," in Caves and Associates, pp. 313–27.

[10]

N A except

From Theory to Measurement

4.1 Introduction and Summary

This chapter is primarily concerned with developing some relations between the theoretical categories introduced in the preceding chapters and their empirical counterparts. The first part of the chapter deals with some preliminary issues regarding industry definitions. A number of criteria are introduced, and all industries within the food and drink sector that meet these criteria are included in the study. The primary criterion is simply that it should be possible to arrive at an industry definition that can be applied in a consistent way across each country, so that cross-country comparisons are likely to be both valid and informative. The criteria determining the set of countries to be studied here are also discussed briefly, and some mention is made of a number of country-specific factors whose influence is noted occasionally in later chapters.

The central part of the chapter is concerned with finding empirical counterparts to the concepts of setup cost, market size, and market structure, and with classifying industries into two groups: those in which advertising plays a negligible role, so that the exogenous sunk cost model of chapter 2 may reasonably be applied, and those in which advertising outlays appear to play a potentially important role.

Problems of measurement, then, take up much of the discussion, and a wide range of empirical problems arise in relation to the measurement of each of the variables. The econometric tests set out in the next chapter have been designed with these difficulties in mind; in particular, it is argued below that an important distinction arises between two sets of measurement issues.

• The key predictions of the model are about the relationship between market size and market structure (concentration), and the way in which this varies between two groups of industries. It is very important, therefore, to obtain reliable measures of market size and industry concentration, suitably defined, and to arrive at a classification scheme that is well motivated a priori.

• On the other hand, quite severe problems of measurement arise in estimating the levels of sunk costs incurred in any particular industry. These problems relate both to (exogenous) setup costs and to (endogenous) advertising outlays. Fortunately, the more important test of the model employed in the next chapter is *independent* of any measures of setup cost. Moreover, all procedures used in the next chapter rely on measures of advertising intensity only as a classificatory variable in dividing the industries into two groups. Because the divide between the two groups is rather sharp, this classification scheme would not be affected by moderate errors in measuring advertising outlays in particular industries.

The final section turns to problems of data collection and related issues. The raw data take the form of a matrix of industry profiles, which were built up using a combination of published market research reports and official industry studies. The information thus collected was augmented and cross-checked by over 100 interviews with senior marketing executives in various companies. Further checks were made possible by the generous assistance of leading market research companies in several countries.

4.2 The Industries

It was noted in chapter 1 that the set of industries studied here has been drawn from the food and drink sector. As explained earlier, the reason for choosing this sector is that among all broadly defined industry groups (two-digit SIC level), the food and drink group has one of the lowest levels of R & D intensity, together with the highest level of advertising intensity. For this reason, it offers an opportunity to study the effects of advertising in isolation from the similar (but more complex) mechanisms associated with the role of R & D outlays as an endogenous sunk cost. Moreover, the intensity of advertising in the food and drink sector is not only high on average but varies extremely widely from one product market to another, thus providing an unusually good context in which to examine its effects.

Before turning to the question of defining individual industries within this sector, it may be helpful to remark on two familiar issues that arise in respect of industry definitions. First, an industry may be defined either by reference to market criteria (i.e., in terms of substitutability of products in consumption) or by reference to similarities in production techniques. Typically, official statistics tend to be influenced by the latter criterion: for example, the U.S. four-digit SIC classification distinguishes the beet sugar industry from the cane sugar industry on this basis, though from a marketing point of view both products are perfect substitutes. Given the aims of this study, it is appropriate to work in terms of industry definitions that are chosen primarily by reference to market criteria; but it is useful, nonetheless, to maintain a rough concordance between the list of industries used and the four-digit SIC industries described in (U.S. and other) official statistics. The reason for maintaining this concordance is to facilitate the estimation of setup costs by industry.

In seeking a suitable market-based definition, a second difficulty arises: if we define an industry broadly enough to include all close substitutes for its core products, then it is likely that the industry thus defined will in fact be segmented into a number of product areas, in the sense that many, or most, firms will confine their activities to one or more market segments and will effectively compete only with the set of firms operating within that segment. (In Caves's terminology, these sets of firms are dubbed "strategic groups.")

If we try, on the other hand, to narrow our definition so as to confine our attention to one such specific market segment, we may miss the fact that many of the industry's major firms operate across many, or all, segments, and that a firm's activities in one segment may influence its success in another. This can happen not only because some firm may enjoy a cost advantage (economies of scope, in the sense of Panzar and Willig 1981), but—more pertinently to the present analysis—that its image advertising for one product line may enhance the demand for its entire product range (indeed, such a firm may devote a substantial fraction of its advertising budget to range advertising, that is, advertising its product line as a whole, across all market segments).

Under these circumstances, it seems appropriate to adopt a compromise solution: define markets fairly broadly to begin with, and then look at the pattern of segmentation within each market, on a case-by-case basis.

Bearing these observations in mind, the aim was to identify as large and comprehensive a set of markets as possible, subject to a number of criteria designed to ensure that like is being compared to like in carrying out cross-country comparisons. A preliminary examination of the market research literature on the food processing industries suggested a set of market definitions that recurs, with few exceptions or modifications, across all of the countries studied here. The level of aggregation involved in these studies is not dissimilar to that of the standard four-digit SIC industry, and a rough concordance between the definitions is possible (table 4.2).

One potential shortcoming of this approach, however, is that it runs the danger of undercoverage in respect of commodity-type industries, in which advertising expenditure is virtually nil—and in which there is relatively little interest by the market research community. For this reason, the set of products examined here has been broadened to include a number of commodity-type products—salt, sugar, flour, and bread—for which market research reports are rarely available and for which information must be sought through other channels (including, in particular, company interviews). In the case of salt, only a modest fraction of output enters the food industry; the bulk of output is used in other areas (de-icing roads, the chemical industry, etc.). Nonetheless, the industry provides a valuable point of comparison with other industries.

In this way, a preliminary list of industries was compiled and a rough concordance with four-digit SIC definitions established. Four criteria were employed in excluding certain industries from this preliminary list or in modifying industry definitions to avoid problems of comparability.

1. The product mix within the industry should not vary so widely across countries as to render comparisons overly problematic or meaningless.

On the basis of this criterion, wine, spirits, and pasta products were excluded entirely. In less extreme cases, the use of a narrower industry definition than that customarily used permitted a reasonable degree of comparability across countries. Thus, the meat processing industry is here defined narrowly to encompass processed pork products only. The canning industries are represented here by canned vegetables. The SIC category "canned specialties" includes part of the prepared soups industry, as well as the baby food industry, both of which are treated as separate industries here. The canned vegetables industry is defined to exclude canned tomatoes, which constitutes a very large category in Italy but is relatively unimportant elsewhere. In the oils and fats sector, it was decided to use the narrowly defined margarine market as a representative of the group.

Finally, in a few instances, the market in a single country was anomalous, and this market alone was excluded (canned vegetables in Japan (see chapter 7), prepared soups in Italy (see chapter 9), and mineral water in the United States (see chapter 11)).

2.   Some industries include one or more segments that differ widely in respect of the level of setup cost incurred by entrants. It is necessary to formulate industry definitions in a way that respects these differences.

Here, two approaches were used. In some cases, it was possible to split the industry into two broad subindustries and to consider each of them independently (sugar and chocolate confectionery, instant and roast and ground coffee). In other cases, a subindustry with setup costs widely different from the rest of the industry was simply excluded from the industry definition. The production of chewing gum involves extremely high setup costs, but this activity is normally classified as part of the sugar confectionery, where setup costs are generally extremely low. For this reason, in defining the sugar confectionery industry, the market for chewing gum was excluded.

3.   Some food and drink markets lie midway between the industrial and agricultural sectors, and the institutional arrangements in the latter sector may vary widely, and in a complex manner, across countries.

Because of the difficulty of making satisfactory comparisons in this context, the dairy products sector as a whole was excluded from the study.

4.   The markets should be independent.

This analysis assumes that each market is supplied by producers who each incur a minimal setup cost in entering the market. In a few of the industries considered here this condition is violated, either because the market is very small and is largely supplied by imports from abroad, or because a group of adjacent countries have a highly integrated market. For example, in the ready-to-eat (RTE) breakfast

Table 4.1
The twenty industries (the number in parentheses indicates the chapter in which the industry is discussed)

Salt	(6)	RTE cereals	(10)
Sugar	(6)	Mineral water	(11)
Flour	(7)	Sugar confectionery	(12)
Bread	(7)	Chocolate confectionery	(12)
Processed meat	(7)	Roast and ground coffee	(12)
Canned vegetables	(7)	Instant coffee	(12)
Frozen food	(8)	Biscuits	(12)
Soup	(9)	Pet foods	(12)
Margarine	(9)	Baby foods	(12)
Soft drinks	(9)	Beer	(13)

cereals industry, the leading seller (Kellogg) supplies all continental European markets from a single plant located in Germany, and it would be inappropriate to treat these three markets as independent; all three are omitted from the data set used in chapter 5. Furthermore, several markets in which the import penetration ratio exceeds 20% are excluded (see below).

These criteria led to the list of twenty industries shown in table 4.1. Readers who wish to see how the above exclusion criteria were applied, in terms of the standard list of four-digit SIC industries within the food and drink sector, may consult table 4.5. Finally, certain of these industries are omitted from the data set employed in the next chapter on the basis of criterion 4 (independence of supply). These are

France:	RTE cereals
Germany (F.R.):	RTE cereals, canned vegetables
Italy:	RTE cereals, pet foods
Japan:	salt, RTE cereals, baby foods
United Kingdom:	processed meat.

Some brief comment on each of these cases will be found in the relevant appendix.*

The Countries

This study is confined to the six largest Western economies: the United States, Japan, Germany (Federal Republic), France, the

*Appendices not reproduced in this volume.

United Kingdom, and Italy. The primary reason for not extending the sample further relates to the problems posed by the fact that import penetration ratios are much larger in the case of small economies, so that structure is heavily influenced by the role of imported (leading) brands. As has just been noted, this would violate the maintained assumption that each seller incurs the same setup cost in commencing production, in each market in which it operates. A secondary reason for not extending the study to more countries lies in the lack of adequate coverage of many of these industries in the market research literature.

In comparing industrial structure across these six countries, it is of interest to ask whether any country-specific factors exist that might operate across the general run of the industries studied. It has sometimes been observed in cross-country comparisons of structure that concentration levels tend to be higher in the United States and United Kingdom than in France, Germany, and Italy (see, for example, George and Ward 1975). The reasons for this are not generally agreed, and while the present data set supports the existence of such a difference, the theory set out here does not offer an explanation.

Within the present framework, systematic cross-country differences would arise if institutional factors specific to some country or countries affected either the toughness of price competition in the market or the degree of effectiveness of advertising outlays. Differences of this kind do indeed operate in specific industries, and their influence will be traced (see especially chapters 6 and 13). As to the existence of other cross-country differences that might impinge in a systematic way on structure, two are worth noting:

• The much greater geographical extent of the U.S. market might make it easier to achieve a relaxation in the toughness of price competition by means of geographical market segmentation. This is indeed evident in several of the industries (see, for example, chapter 6).

• Another respect in which the six countries differ relates to the degree of success achieved by retailers in developing their own brands ("private label" products) in competition with the manufacturers of leading branded products. This appears to vary in line with the degree of concentration in the retail sector. The retail sector is relatively concentrated in the United Kingdom, France, and Germany, but is relatively fragmented in the United States, Japan, and Italy.[1]

The degree of success of retailers' own brands has been greatest in the United Kingdom, where they accounted for 28% of total retail sales in 1985. The degree of penetration by category varies widely, being greatest when brands are least strong (canned vegetables and frozen food) and weakest where brands are strongest (pet foods and RTE cereals). Some leading retailers in the United Kingdom, notably Sainsbury's and Tesco, now advertise their own brands quite heavily. In the United States, on the other hand, the impact of retailers' own brands has been extremely weak. The relevance of this difference between countries will be seen in several of the industry studies. In the United Kingdom, for example, the strength of retailers' own brands appears to have grown to the point when it may be more costly for manufacturers to achieve a given market share by dint of advertising support for a new brand.

4.3   Measurement Issues I: Market Size and Concentration

This section deals with the measurement of the two key variables on which the central econometric tests of the present model will rest: market structure, or concentration, and market size.

The Reference Year

Basic research for study was carried out over the period 1987–88, and the figures for market size and market shares were established for the reference year 1986, or, if that figure was unavailable, for a date as close as possible to 1986. In the large majority of markets studied here, year-to-year fluctuations in sales and market shares are not very

---

1. In the United Kingdom, ten leading retailers were estimated to hold about 42% of retail sales of food in 1986. The four largest chains were Tesco, J. Sainsbury, Dee (inc. Fine Fare) and the Co-op. In France, the major supermarket chains cooperate as buying groups, thereby enjoying considerable bargaining power vis-à-vis food-processing firms. The three largest buying groups, A.R.C.I., Contact, and Di Fra, together accounted for 28% of retail sales of food in 1984. In Germany, thirteen leading retail groups accounted for 53.2% of retail sales of food in 1986, the largest being Aldi, RGG Leibbrand, Co-op AG Frankfurt, and Tengelman Gruppe. At the other extreme, the largest food retailer in the United States (Safeway) accounts for only 2% of total sales. In Italy, only 12% of total retail sales of food occurs through supermarkets (or hypermarkets). See the report *Own Brands*, published by Keynote (U.K.), 1986.

great, and figures reported for 1985 or 1987 differ little from those reported for 1986. Where occasional exceptions arise, due either to an unusually volatile share pattern or to the occurrence of mergers or acquisitions during the mid-1980s, attention is drawn to this in the relevant chapter.

Relative Market Size

The problem of measuring market size and its relation to setup cost can be divided into two steps. Assuming that the setup cost incurred in entering the market in any industry is the same across all countries, it suffices to estimate setup cost relative to market size for a single reference country (the United States) and to estimate as a separate exercise the relative size of each market relative to the U.S. market. The former step is quite problematic and is deferred to the next section. The latter step, of estimating relative size, is dealt with here.

The procedure applied is to estimate relative market size on the basis of total output volumes, wherever this is appropriate. In fact, this turns out to be feasible for ten of the twenty industries. In the remaining cases, relative market size is computed by reference to measures of the value of total sales (retail and nonretail) in the various markets, converted to U.S. dollars at the average rate of exchange prevailing over the reference year chosen.

Measuring Concentration

Two questions arise in regard to the appropriate measure of concentration. The first relates to the choice of index; some summary measure is needed which will distinguish concentrated from fragmented patterns of market share. An a priori defense of a particular measure may be developed if one is willing to presuppose some specific (oligopoly) model underlying the observed share pattern.[2] Since the aim here is to avoid imposing any precisely specified oligopoly model on the data, it would clearly be inappropriate to seek some "ideal" measure. The most important of the results presented in chapters 2 and 3 were framed in terms of the maximal market share, this is, the share enjoyed by the single largest firm. In most of

2. The standard example relates to the imposition of the standard Cournot model as a basis for employing the Herfindahl index. For a particularly helpful approach to the choice of index, based on certain intuitively appealing criteria, see Hannah and Kay 1977.

what follows, we adopt the conventional course of using a more or less arbitrary summary measure; specifically, we use the most popular measure, the four-firm concentration ratio (the sum of the shares of the top four firms). The results obtained, however, are checked against various alternative measures. To allow readers to examine their preferred choice of measure, the data presented in the industry appendices include individual market shares for the four largest firms. Furthermore, since we focus some attention on the "tail" of small firms active in the industry, an estimate of the total number of firms active in the industry is also provided, wherever a reliable estimate is available.

The second question that arises in regard to a measure of concentration relates to the choice between a sales concentration ratio as defined, for example, by the sum of the market shares of the four largest firms; or a production concentration ratio, defined as the sum of their shares of industry production. It has already been noted that the former measure is more appropriate in the present context, and this is adhered to in almost all industries. A few exceptions arise, in which it is not possible to ascertain firms' shares in total sales, and, in these cases, shares in total production, or in industry capacity, have been used an an approximation.

It may be worth noting the reasons for the often very large discrepancies between the sales concentration ratios reported here and the official estimates for the corresponding four-digit SIC industries in official statistics. A minor problem arises insofar as some domestically produced output is exported, while part of domestic sales consists of imports, thus leading to a difference between sales- and production-based measures. A much more important problem relates to the fact that the procedures used in official census estimates rely on the convention that each plant (establishment) is allocated to a particular industry, as defined by an SIC code. All sales revenue deriving from the plant is then attributed to this industry. The census must, of its nature, aim to be comprehensive; every plant must be allocated to some industry. This means, however, that the range of products falling within a particular SIC definition may encompass not only a central core of products that are more or less close substitutes in consumption, but may also include ancillary products that share a common production technology with the core products but that are not substitutes in consumption with these products.

A final problem that arises in using production-based concentration measures relates to products that can be produced using different technologies. For example, beet and cane sugar, as noted earlier, are classified in different four-digit SICs in the United States. Official estimates of concentration ratios relate, therefore, to two separate "industries." Some sugar producers operate only in one of these, while others operate in both. Unless the firms in question can be identified, the concentration ratios for these two industries do not suffice to determine the concentration ratio for the combined sugar market.

But while these considerations underline the value of working with sales concentration ratios computed directly from the market research literature and related sources, it should be emphasized that this approach has a number of shortcomings too. The most obvious of these relates to the accuracy of available market share statistics. In the food and drink industry, the fact that well-established procedures for monitoring retail sales have been developed over the past two decades by leading agencies means that quite accurate and reliable measures are often available. On the other hand, quite serious limitations arise whenever the nonretail market is relatively important—for even among the leading companies themselves, considerable uncertainty often surrounds the market share pattern in the nonretail segment.

In the market share tables shown in appendix 1 a range of values, rather than a single figure, is indicated in many instances. In a few cases, shares are reported for both the retail market and (with less accuracy) the total market. In all but two of the industries it has been possible to obtain reasonably satisfactory share estimates for the total market (i.e., retail and nonretail), or else the nonretail segment is so small that the sales concentration ratio for the retail sector provides a reasonable approximation to that of the market as a whole. There are, however, two industries in which neither of these circumstances holds (margarine and frozen food). The econometric estimates in chapter 5 are presented with these two industries excluded. Their inclusion (using the best measures available) does not materially affect the results.

4.4   Measurement Issues II: Setup Cost

The difficulties that arise in estimating the level of setup cost by industry are of a different order than those encountered in the preceding section. In what follows, a simple proxy measure of the *relative*

level of setup costs across different industries is proposed. A number
of criticisms of this measure are then listed. It is argued, in light of
these criticisms, that it is desirable to proceed as far as possible in the
subsequent analysis without employing these estimates of setup cost.

Defining a Proxy for Setup Cost

In chapters 2 and 3, the setup cost σ was defined as the minimal
level of sunk cost that must be incurred by each entrant to the
industry prior to commencing production. In the present section, it
is argued that these sunk costs might reasonably be assumed to vary
across industries in proportion to the cost of constructing a single
plant of minimum efficient scale (m.e.s.).

This assertion raises two kinds of difficulty:

(i) It assumes that the proportion of initial outlays that might be
recovered on exiting the industry is constant across industries. A
less strict requirement, which would suffice in the present context,
is that the proportion of such costs which are recoverable should
not vary in a systematic way with the size of the market or the
structure of the industry. Even this latter condition, however, might
be challenged. No systematic body of data is available that throws
light on the way in which such recovery rates vary across the present
set of industries.

(ii) If some minimum efficient scale of operation could be identified,
and if all new entrants necessarily operated at or above that level,
then the present procedure would be justified, subject only to (i).
A less strict requirement, which is still sufficient for our purposes,
is that the ratio between the minimal outlay that must be incurred by
a new entrant and the cost of establishing a single m.e.s. plant does
not vary in a systematic way with the size of the market or the
structure of the industry. No data on the outlays incurred by new
entrants exist that allow this assertion to be directly tested.[3]

The two preceding assumptions, though not directly testable, appear
at least to be plausible. A more serious difficulty arises when we turn

---

3. Moreover, even if such data were available, it will be clear that new entrants will often
confine themselves to some single segment (niche) of the market, and setup costs may
vary across different segments. As noted, the principles of industry definition used here
are aimed at avoiding the most serious instances of such heterogeneity—but, even using
the present set of definitions, this issue remains serious.

to the measurement of minimum efficient scale.[4] The most natural measure of m.e.s., in the present context, is that provided by engineering estimates based on studies that aim to identify the level of average cost achievable using alternative technologies and plant sizes. The m.e.s. level is defined as corresponding to the smallest level of output at which, using any available technology or plant size, a firm can attain a level of average cost within a given percentage (usually 10%) of the lowest achievable level (see section 1.6).

Such an estimate falls short of providing information on the *degree* to which firms operating below this level will be penalized. In some studies, supplementary estimates give the percentage increase in average cost suffered by a firm operating at some specified fraction of the m.e.s. level. Estimates of this kind would be extremely useful,

---

4. Within the theory, what meaning can be attached to the notion of minimum efficient scale? This concept is normally defined in the empirical literature as the scale of operation at which average cost can be brought to, or within some specified percentage distance of, the lowest level achievable. The interpretation of this idea varies according as different assumptions are made about the nature of the underlying technology. It has been assumed here that only one technology is available, and that this requires a sunk outlay of σ, whereupon output may then be produced at constant marginal cost c. More generally, it might be assumed that a range of possible technologies were available, and that increases in σ were associated with decreases in c. Two cases now arise. In the first case, the effectiveness of increasing σ eventually diminishes as c reaches some point beyond which further efficiency improvements become arbitrarily costly. In the second case, the elasticity of c with respect to σ is bounded above; a proportionate increase in σ always achieves a certain minimal proportionate reduction in c.

In other words, it is possible to embed the choice of technology (σ) within the richer framework of the endogenous sunk cost model. This means that the maintained assumption of the theory, that σ is exogenously fixed, is replaced by the weaker assumption, corresponding to the first case identified above, that is, that increases in σ eventually become ineffective in reducing c. This is precisely analogous to the discussion of advertising as an endogenous sunk cost in section 3.5. There, it was noted that if a ceiling to the effectiveness of advertising was reached at some point, increases in market size would eventually lead to a structure in which an arbitrarily large number of firms all operated arbitarily close to that ceiling—and the model collapsed in the limit to the exogenous sunk cost model. (The complementary case, in which increases in σ continue indefinitely to exert an effect on c, is of independent interest. It offers a model appropriate to industries characterized by constant process innovation. The properties of this case were developed by Dasgupta and Stiglitz 1980.)

This, then, is a route along which a concept analogous to the traditional m.e.s. notion may be incorporated into the present framework. On this reading, different firms may choose to incur different outlays at equilibrium in setting up plant, but there is a minimal outlay below which firms will suffer a serious cost disadvantage in stage two of the game—and, at equilibrium, all firms will incur at least some minimal outlay on plant and equipment.

because they might in principle help to identify more precisely the minimal outlay needed for viability. Unfortunately, estimates of this kind are available for relatively few industries, and it is customary in the industrial organization literature to represent m.e.s. instead by a more easily available measure: the size of the industry's median plant.

The rationale underlying this proxy is less than compelling, but it can be claimed that—at least within the food and drink sector— median plant size correlates quite well with engineering estimates of m.e.s. For a set of thirteen four-digit SIC industries in the U.S. food and drink sector, Connor et al. (1985), using the results reported by Culbertson and Morrison (1983), report a correlation coefficient of 0.83 between median plant estimates based on the 1972 census of manufactures and engineering estimates published over the period 1970–80. In Figure 4.1, scatter diagrams of these estimates are shown, both for the 1970–80 period and for the period 1950–63 (as compared with 1958 Census data). While the overall correlation is good, one clear outlier occurs. The engineering estimate for the canned vegetables industry lies far above m.e.s. estimates for the latter period, though not for the earlier period. This may reflect the fact that demand in the canned vegetables industry has been stagnant or declining since the 1950s, and new plant construction embodying best-practice technology may have been slowed as a consequence (see appendix 7.4).

This exception apart, the correlation is quite good for both periods and, on the basis of this observation, it may not seem unreasonable to employ m.e.s. estimates. Median plant size estimates, unlike engineering estimates, are available for all four-digit SIC industries in the case of the United States (but not in the case of the other countries studied here); and, as noted, a rough concordance can be established with the present set of industries. The measure of m.e.s. used here, then, is the ratio between the output level of the industry's median plant, relative to industry output. The estimates used are those of Culbertson and Morrison (1983) for 1972, as reported by Connor et al. (1985, pp. 154–156).

In two of the industries studied here, coffee and confectionery, the industry subdivides into two subindustries that differ greatly in respect of their setup costs. In the case of confectionery, the median plant estimate can be identified with the m.e.s. appropriate to sugar confectionery: for the large majority of firms in the industry specialize

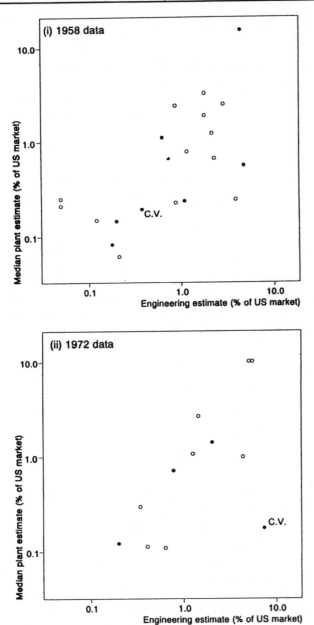

Key: Industries shown as • are among those included in the present study

C.V. denotes canned vegetables (see text)

Figure 4.1
Engineering estimates of m.e.s. versus median plant size estimates for a set of four-digit
SIC industries in the food and drink sector (double log scale). The estimates are those
reported by Connor et al. (1985), following Culbertson and Morrison (1983).

in only one segment, and the number of firms producing mainstream chocolate confectionery products, which involve relative high setup costs, is extremely small (<100) as compared with the number producing sugar confectionery (about 1,000). In the case of the coffee industry, however, the estimates for the combined U.S. industry are less easily identified with either subindustry (see chapter 12). In the table of estimated setup costs presented later in this chapter, the chocolate confectionery industry and both parts of the coffee industry have been omitted. A detailed discussion of these industries can be found in chapter 12.

Given some measure of m.e.s., we may proceed to estimate the level of setup cost relative to the size of the market as follows: Let μ denote the measure of m.e.s., that is, the output of the median plant relative to industry output. Assume (rather heroically) that the capital-output ratio of the median firm stands in the same proportion to the capital-output ratio of the industry as a whole, across all of the industries studied here. Let K/S denote the capital-output ratio of the industry as a whole, that is, the total value of plant and equipment[5] in the industry divided by the value of annual industry sales.

Under the above assumptions, the value of plant and equipment owned by the median firm is porportionate to μK, and an index of setup cost relative to market size is given by

$$\frac{\sigma}{S} = \frac{\mu K}{S}.$$

Estimates of this measure for the United States in 1976 are presented in table 4.2 for each of the relevant four-digit SIC industries. (This procedure is similar to that of Kessides 1988.)

The measure of capital stock used in deriving these estimates is the book value of plant and equipment, divided by annual industry sales. The book value of assets, valued at historic prices, seriously underestimates the current replacement cost of plant and equipment; this further reinforces the point that little weight should be attached to the absolute value of the index σ/S thus computed. Assuming that the age structure of plant and equipment does not vary greatly across the set of industries, however, this index still provides a (fairly crude) indicator of the *relative* level of σ/S across these industries.

---

5. The industries' capital stock will also include land; but this part of the firm's capital stock is likely to be more readily recoverable on exit and is here assumed not to constitute a sunk cost.

To compute the σ/S values for the remaining five countries, we estimate the ratio of the value of sales for the U.S. industry to the value of sales for the industry of the country in question. This ratio is labeled ρ_{ij} in what follows, where i is an industry index and j a country index. (In computing ρ_{ij}, the value of sales used for both countries is that of the industry as defined in the present study, and *not* that of the corresponding four-digit SIC industry.) Thus, if S_i/σ_i denotes the ratio of market size to setup cost for the U.S. industry, the corresponding ratio for country j is simply $\rho_{ij} \cdot (S_i/\sigma_i)$. The results of these computations are set out in table 4.3.

Criticisms

It will be clear at this point that the estimation of setup costs by industry poses serious difficulties. In addition to those problems raised above, a further objection may be added, which has some force: as Davies (1980) has noted, the use of median plant estimates in explaining differences in structure across industries may involve a potentially serious bias; put crudely, concentrated industries have large firms, and large firms tend to operate large plants. Thus even if the average cost schedule were flat above some minimal level of operation, median plant estimates would tend to be higher where concentration was higher.

This objection has considerable force where differences in m.e.s. are used to explain differences in structure *across industries* within a single country; and it is therefore worth emphasizing at this point that the primary focus of this study is to look at a *within-industry* relationship between market size and concentration by examining the same industry across several countries. In principle, the exercise could be carried out industry by industry, avoiding all interindustry comparisons, thus obviating the need for an estimate of σ. In practice, the paucity of data points means that some pooling of information from different industries is inevitable—but the key test in chapter 5 is independent of the σ_i/S_i measures and rests only on the relative market size estimates, ρ_{ij}.

4.5   Measurement Issues III: Advertising

The most serious measurement problems relate to advertising outlays; and, as with m.e.s. estimates, the design of the econometric

analysis is designed to rely as little as possible on problematic measures in this area. In this section, the difficulties involved are set out
at some length in order to motivate the route chosen in what follows.
This involves the use of measures of advertising intensity only as a
simple classificatory variable.

The Issues

The study aims to analyze the role played by advertising outlays in
influencing the development of structure; and this is carried out by
treating advertising as an endogenous sunk cost. It is doubtless true
that many other elements of sunk cost in these industries are also
endogenous; several elements of sunk cost may indeed be *complementary* to advertising outlays. Such elements include not only product development costs (which have been argued to be relatively
low in the food and drink sector) but also ancillary elements of sunk
cost incurred in such activities as building up a sales network. The
presence of such ancillary sunk costs will not vitiate the validity of
the model, but it would lead to a serious problem of measurement
if an attempt was made to estimate the total sunk costs incurred in
these industries.

   If attention is confined to the role of advertising alone, then matters
might appear more straightforward. In modeling advertising as an
endogenous sunk cost, what we would like to measure, ideally, is an
exogenous advertising response *function* analogous to the $F(u)$ of chapter 3. In practice, advertising response functions are extremely difficult to measure, both because (i) they will vary to a greater or lesser
degree over time and across product lines, within any industry, and
(ii) the response to any stream of advertising depends not only on the
level of outlay but on other factors (the quality or effectiveness of a
particular campaign), so that any function mapping outlays into
response for a particular industry, or group of firms, must be treated
as being stochastic in nature. (For a discussion of some aspects of this
problem from an economist's standpoint, see Lambin 1976; for some
attempts at estimation within particular advertising campaigns, see
Broadbent 1981.)

   In the present study, we eschew all attempts to estimate an equivalent of the function $F(u)$, and confine ourselves to looking at the
level of (endogenously determined) advertising outlays. This clearly
adds to the (already serious) limitations that arise in trying to formulate precise tests of the hypotheses. But even in estimating the level

of advertising outlays actually incurred by firms in a particular industry, some serious difficulties arise. The simple multistage structure of the games presented in chapter 3 embodies an analytically useful distinction between sunk costs incurred in product development over the long run and current costs incurred in the short run, over which it was assumed that the main focus of competition was on price. In practice, advertising outlays are incurred in a more or less continuous stream, both with a view to enhancing the product's image and in attempting to influence month-to-month fluctuations in share. In the latter context, price changes, promotional outlays (price support to retailers, etc.) involving variable costs, and advertising outlays that may properly be identified as a fixed cost are all involved.

In trying to suggest some suitable mapping from theoretical to empirical categories, it would in principle be appropriate to estimate the net present value of outlays incurred by firms over the history of the industry in supporting brands and products currently on offer. Even this modest task, however, lies outside the scope of the study. As was noted above, this book merely attempts a single broad-brush distinction between those industries that can be identified with the exogenous sunk cost model of chapter 2 and those in which endogenous advertising outlays play a substantial role. This is done by reference to a simple comparison of the range of current advertising-sales ratios observed for the industry across the six countries studied.

Even in regard to the relatively straightforward matter of estimating advertising-sales ratios, however, a number of routine difficulties arise that deserve mention. The advertising-sales ratio, which constitutes the most commonly used measure of advertising intensity, is defined as the ratio of total current advertising expenditure to industry sales. The level of advertising expenditure can be measured in two ways:

(i) by measuring the volume of advertising (seconds of TV time, numbers of magazine pages, and so on), and converting this to a value figure by using standard unit costs. This method tends to overstate total expenditure, insofar as (some) firms obtain rates more favorable than the list price of the advertising in question (the card rate). The values thus estimated may be compared either with total industry sales, or with the value of *retail sales* in the industry.

(ii) by computing the total expenditure on advertising reported by firms in their census returns. This figure, based on SIC definitions, can then be compared with the *value of production* in the industry in question.

We follow the first route. The values of A/S reported below are based on the ratio of measured advertising expenditure either to the total value of industry sales or to the value of retail sales. The reason for choosing a measured advertising value is that such advertising measures for most countries are based on market (industry) definitions close or identical to those employed here in computing the market share statistics. The reason for the use of a measure based on retail sales is that the impact of advertising falls primarily on the retail sector. As noted in chapter 3, it is widely argued that the industrial and catering buyers who constitute the nonretail sector tend to be less concerned about brand image, and their purchases appear to be more heavily influenced by reference to a comparison of price and intrinsic product characteristics.

The ratio of advertising outlays to retail sales for the six countries in 1986 are shown in table 4.4. The median reported values for six of the industries lies below 1%, and the remaining fourteen industries have values lying above this level. The six industries with levels below 1% are salt, sugar, bread, flour, canned vegetables, and processed meat. All of these are widely regarded as commodity products, and their identification as a low-advertising group appears reasonable a priori.

This split between the two groups is fairly sharp. Out of thirty values for the commodity group, only three lie above 1%. Of the seventy-one values for the advertising-intensive group, only two lie below 1%. A ranking of the twenty industries in terms of the advertising to *total* sales ratio for the United States, as shown in the first column of table 4.4, indicates that these six commodity products are again the six lowest ranked products. The split between the two groups of industries, then, appears to be a fairly sharp, and even fairly substantial measurement errors in advertising outlays would be unlikely to affect this classification. It seems reasonable, on the whole, to hypothesize that the structure of the first group of industries might be adequately described by the simple exogenous sunk cost model of chapter 2, whereas advertising outlays may play a potentially important role as an endogenous sunk cost in influencing the evolution of structure in the latter group.

A final remark is in order, regarding the fact that the A/S values shown in table 4.5 (whose magnitude corresponds to the values cited in the relevant market research literature), are substantially higher than certain values reported in the industrial economics literature (compare, for example, these values with those reported in Connor et al. 1985). There are three sources of discrepancy, which reflect the considerations noted above:

(i) The estimates usually cited in the industrial economics literature employ a sales value equal to the total sales revenue of the appropriate (four-digit) SIC industry.

This may lead to a *downward* bias in these figures, whenever (a) a nonretail segment is present, (b) the (four-digit) SIC industry encompasses activities peripheral to the narrower definition of the core market implicit in the definition used in the marketing literature.

(ii) Our values are biased *upward* by our failure to allow for the (often very substantial) discounts over card rates enjoyed by some firms.

(iii) Estimates based on official statistics will differ from those used here, due to the valuation of sales at producer rather than consumer prices.

One common reason for using SIC-based measures, in preference to the kind of estimates used here, is to take advantage of the large body of available data—notably in respect of concentration ratios. Once a decision is made to employ sales concentration ratios based on market research studies, rather than the official production-based figures, this consideration becomes less weighty.

In spite of these biases noted above, the *A/S* values reported here probably serve as a fairly reliable guide to the *relative* levels of advertising intensity across different industries. As to the absolute size of these values, it is worth noting that—qualifications regarding possible biases notwithstanding—the values reported in table 4.5 are very high in comparison with manufacturers' profit margins in the food and drink industries. The median value of the ratio of measured advertising outlays to total industry sales for the United States, over 11 advertising-intensive industries, is 3% (table 4.5). This figure can be compared with the ratio of net after-tax income to total industry sales, which stood at 4.2% in 1986.[6]

---

6. See the *Quarterly Financial Report for Manufacturing, Mining, and Trade Corporations*, First Quarter 1987, U.S. Dept. of Commerce, Bureau of the Census, p. 6. In comparing these figures, it should be borne in mind that these advertising-sales ratios may be biased upward (see section 4.5).

Table 4.2
Setup Costs for Equivalent Four-Digit SIC Industries (United States)

Industry	Nearest four-digit SIC (U.S.)	m.e.s.[a] (% of output)	Gross book value (plant and equipment) ($ millions, 1976)	Value of shipments ($ millions, 1976)	Estimated σ/S (%)[b] (based on m.e.s. of 0.8)
Salt	1476 Rock salt	0.8–3.52	103.2	159.8	0.52
	2899 Chemicals and chemical preps., n.e.c.	0.43			
Sugar[c]	2063 Beet sugar	1.87	622.1	1,483.2	0.78
	2062 Cane sugar refining	12.01	409.8	2,596.0	1.90
Flour	2041 Flour and other grain mill products	0.68	379.0	4,095.9	0.063
Bread	2051 Bread, cake, and related products	0.12	1,809.3	9,511.5	0.023
Processed meat	2013 Sausages and other prepared meats	0.26	533.8	7,098.7	0.020
Canned vegetables	2033 Canned fruit and vegetables	0.17	1,145.3	6,217.5	0.031
Frozen food[d]	2037/2038 Frozen fruit and vegetables, Frozen specialties	0.92	559.7	2,830.4	0.18
Soup[j]	2034 Dehydrated fruit and vegetables, soup	2.26	216.9	1,048.8	0.47
	2032 Canned specialties	2.59	439.7	2,863.5	0.40
Margarine	2079 Shortening and cooking oils	1.75	417.7	3,325.8	0.22
Soft drinks[h]	2086 Bottled and canned soft drinks	0.08	211.3	2,421.2	0.006
	2087 Flavoring extracts, syrups, etc.	1.23	211.3	2,421.2	0.11
RTE cereal	2043 Cereal breakfast foods	9.47	416.7	2,158.2	1.83
Mineral water	2086 Bottled and canned soft drinks[i]	0.08	1,810.7	8,780.1	0.016

Name	SIC	Description	m.e.s.			σ/S
Sugar confectionery / Chocolate confectionery }	2065	Confectionery products[e]	0.64	619.1	3,804.1	0.10
R & G coffee / Instant coffee }	2095	Roasted coffee[f]	5.82	442.7	4,623.6	0.56
Biscuits	2052	Cookies and crackers	2.04	459.8	2,718.2	0.35
Pet foods	2047	Dog, cat, and other pet food	3.02	475.9	2,675.6	0.54
Baby foods	2032	Canned specialties[g]	2.59	439.7	2,863.5	0.40
Beer	2082	Malt beverages	1.37	2,432.6	6024.5	0.55

a. The m.e.s. figure represents the ratio between the output of the median plant expressed as a percentage of industry shipments for the United States in 1977. All figures except that for salt are those estimated by Culbertson and Morrison (1983), as reported in Conner et al. 1985. The figures for salt are computed as described in appendix 5.1.

b. σ/S is estimated as m.e.s. × (gross book value of plant and equipment) ÷ (value of shipments). See text.

c. Sugar refining encompasses two four-digit SIC codes, 2062 (cane sugar refining) and 2063 (beet sugar refining). To estimate the *minimal* setup cost required to enter the industry, the value used is that for beet sugar refining, where scale economies and so estimated setup costs are both lower.

d. Frozen food encompasses two four-digit SIC industries, 2037 (frozen fruit and vegetables) and 2038 (frozen specialties). No m.e.s. estimates are available for the latter industry.

e. The number of sugar confectionery plants is very much greater than the number of chocolate confectionery plants in the United States, and the m.e.s. figure for SIC 2065 provides a good approximation to the value for sugar confectionery plants. This is used in what follows in estimating S/σ for sugar confectionery.

f. The estimate for SIC 2095 is *not* taken in the present study as providing a suitable measure for *either* R & G or instant coffee; see text, and chapter 12.

g. SIC 2032 (canned specialties) includes inter alia the five-digit industries 20321 (canned baby foods) and 20322 (canned soups).

h. The relationship between industries 2086 and 2087 is discussed in chapter 9. On the issue of combining the two industries, see Connor et al. 1985, p. 146. Here we take the higher setup cost associated with syrup manufacture as the appropriate figure; it can be argued that the lower value derived from 2086 is appropriate as a measure of the *minimal* outlay involved in entering the industry, as syrup is bought in by small drink firms. Under the latter interpretation, the arguments developed in this chapter and in chapter 9 are further strengthened.

i. The use of SIC 2086 as a point of reference in estimating setup costs in producing mineral water is somewhat arbitrary, but it appears to be the best available proxy.

j. Canned soup is included in SIC 2032 (see footnote g); dehydrated soup is SIC 2034. The associated values of σ are fairly close; the value 0.47 is used below.

Table 4.3
Market size to setup cost ratios, and four-firm sales concentration by country

Industry	France S/σ	France C₄(%)	Germany S/σ	Germany C₄(%)	Italy S/σ	Italy C₄(%)	Japan S/σ	Japan C₄(%)	United Kingdom S/σ	United Kingdom C₄(%)	United States S/σ	United States C₄(%)
Salt	39	~98	62	~93	24	~80	(*)	(*)	39	~99.5	194	82
Sugar	46	81	40	~60	31	72	49	41.5	41	94	128	46
Flour	392	29	580	38	652	6.7	392	67	346	78	1,590	55
Bread	2,845	4.5	3,824	7	3,015	~4	1,144	~48	2,114	~58	4,350	~25
Processed meat	745	~23	1,465	~22	1,245	~11	1,340	51	(*)	(*)	5,000	19
Canned vegetables	1,569	40	(*)	(*)	93	80	(*)	(*)	480	81	3,230	~50
Frozen food	(≠)	(≠)	(≠)	(≠)	(≠)	(≠)	(≠)	(≠)	(≠)	(≠)	556	(≠)
Soup	14	91	25	84	(*)	(*)	18	71	36	75	213	75
Margarine	79	(≠)	181	(≠)	34	(≠)	87	(≠)	154	(≠)	455	(≠)
Soft drinks	16	~70	89	57	20	84	53	88	47	~48	910	~89
RTE cereal	(*)	(*)	(*)	(*)	(*)	(*)	(*)	(*)	7.4	79	55	86
Mineral water	400	77	350	27	337	~55	9.8	62	9.4	73	(*)	(*)
Sugar confectionery	143	51	353	39	116	29	142	48	279	38	1,000	~27
Biscuits	88	62	43	49	69	46	57	49	130	62	286	68
Pet foods	30	86	16	93	(*)	(*)	9.3	39	33	83	185	64
Baby foods	50	88	40	83	41	88	(*)	(*)	27	80	250	90
Beer	18	82	68	~25	9.8	55	35	99.85	46	59	181	81

(*) Omitted from data set, see text. (≠) Figures relate to retail only, and the nonretail sector is large. See tables M7, M9 (appendix 1).

Table 4.4

Advertising to retail sales ratios for six countries, and advertising to total sales ratios for the United States. Figures are for 1986 except where indicated.

Product	Advertising/ total sales (%) United States	Advertising/retail sales (%)					
		France	Germany	Italy	Japan	United Kingdom	United States
Salt	0.26	—	—	—	(×)	0.45	1.3
Sugar	0.10	—	—	—	—	0.06	0.24
Flour	0.54	0.55	N.A.	N.A.	—	0.96	0.17
Bread	0.02*	0.12	0.40	0.04	1.14	0.29	0.42
Processed meat	0.32	0.70	0.30	0.40	3.2	(×)	0.54
Canned vegetables	0.71*	0.55	(×)	0.50	(×)	0.58	0.29
Frozen food	1.35	N.A.	1.2	7.1	2.5	2.6	2.0
Soup	N.A.	5.7	5.6	(×)	2.7	6.0	3.3
Margarine	3.04*	N.A.	2.6	N.A.	9.5	10.2	2.3
Soft drinks	2.80†*	2.2	3.8	5.4	4.4	1.2	3.2
RTE cereals	8.34	(×)	(×)	(×)	(×)	12.9	10.8
Mineral water	( )†	5.0	1.5	4.1	3.0	2.7	(×)
Sugar confectionery	2–3	~1.4	4.2	6.0	3.8	2.1	2–3
Chocolate confectionery	3–4	2.9	5.9	6.5	6.0	3.5	3–4
R&G coffee } Instant coffee }	2.19	14.0 11.1	2.9 3.5	~3 N.A.	16.7 9.6	1.9 6.4	~1 2.2
Biscuits	1.87	2.9	5.1	8.0	3.0	1.9	2.5
Pet foods	4.35	4.2	8.4	(×)	8.0	4.3	4.0
Baby foods	~0.9	1.3	1.2	4.2	(×)	2.2	0.9
Beer	5.43	~5	1.0	N.A.	2.7	1.0	3.6

Source: Author's estimates based on Leading National Advertisers (U.S.), MEAL (U.K.), Schmidt and Pohlman (Germany), Secodip (France), AGB Italia, and Fuji Keizai (Japan).
(−) Value very low and omitted from published statistics.
N.A. Not available.
(×) Market omitted from study.
† Soft drinks, including mineral water.
* 1985 figure.

Table 4.5
Relationship between four-digit SIC industries in the U.S. food and drink sector
and the present set of industries. The criteria referred to in the table are those set
out in section 4.2.

Four-digit SIC industries	Scope of industry group	Comment
2011–2017	Meat packing, processing	Represented by processed pork products
2021–2026	Dairy products	Excluded (criterion 3)
2032–3, 2091	Canning	Represented by canned vegetables, baby food, prepared soups
2034	Dehydrated fruits, vegetables, soups	Represented by prepared soups
2035	Pickles	Excluded (criterion 1)
2037–8	Frozen foods	Included
2941, 5	Flour	Included
2043	RTE cereals	Included
2044, 6	Rice milling, wet corn milling	Excluded (criterion 1)
2047	Pet foods	Included
2051	Bread, etc.	Included
2952	Cookies and crackers	Included
2061–3	Sugar	Included
2065–7	Confectionery	Represented as sugar confectionery and chocolate confectionery (criterion 2)
2074–9	Oils and fats	Represented by margarine
2082, 3	Malt, malt beverages	Represented by beer
2084, 5	Wines, spirits, liquors	Excluded (criterion 1)
2986	Soft drinks	Included
2092	Fish	Excluded (criterion 1)
2095	Coffee	Represented as R & G coffee and instant coffee (criterion 2)
2097	Manufactured ice	Excluded (criterion 1)
2098	Pasta products	Excluded (criterion 1)

The "miscellaneous" groups 2048, 2087, and 2099 were excluded under criterion 1.
In addition to the above, a number of specific industries were excluded, as follows:
Criterion 1: Canned vegetables in Japan; prepared soups in Italy; mineral water in
the United States.
Criterion 4: Salt in Japan; processed meat in the United Kingdom; canned vege-
tables in Germany; RTE cereals in France, Germany, Italy, Japan; baby foods in
Japan; pet foods in Italy.

4.6 Statistical Tables

Table 4.2 illustrates the concordance between the present set of industries and the equivalent four-digit SIC industries, together with the estimated σ/S values for the United States.

Table 4.3 shows the corresponding S/σ values for each country, the four-firm sales concentration ratio, as computed by multiplying the reciprocal of the σ/S value for the U.S. industry shown in table 4.2 by the ratio of industry sales in the country in question to the sales of the corresponding U.S. industry. Further statistical details on each industry are presented in the relevant industry studies presented in chapters 6–13.

Econometric Evidence

5.1 Introduction

This chapter presents some econometric evidence regarding the predictions of the theory, as summarized in the concluding sections of chapters 2 and 3.[1] Before turning to that evidence, it is of interest to first look at the way in which concentration ratios for each of the industries differ across the several countries. As noted in chapter 1, various earlier studies have found that the pattern of concentration levels across different industries is broadly similar from one country to another.

This relationship is illustrated in figure 5.1. The median value of the four-firm sales concentration ratio for each industry is plotted on the horizontal axis, and the actual values for each of the six countries on the vertical axis. Thus, each vertical bar in the figure indicates the range of concentration levels found for a particular industry.

It is clear that a substantial degree of correlation is present. This can be confirmed by regressing C_4 for the pooled sample on a set of industry and country dummies; the resulting R^2 equals 0.57 (a regression on industry dummies only yields an R^2 of 0.55). It is also clear from the figure that, in a small number of industries, the range of concentration levels is unusually high, and this in some instances reflects the presence of some obvious anomalies. Particularly noteworthy are the cases of beer (where Japan and Germany are outliers at the top and bottom of the range respectively) and flour (where

---

1. I would like to thank Richard Smith for his advice and help on the estimation of lower bounds, and Mark Schankerman and Hugh Wills, who suggested the proof set out in the annex.

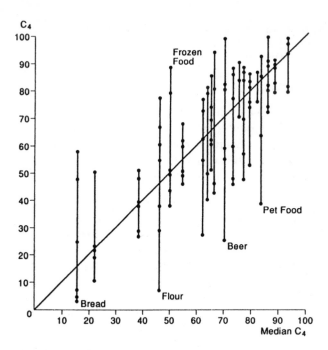

Figure 5.1
The range of four-firm sales concentration ratios across countries, for each product. For
each industry, the horizontal axis shows the median value, while individual values are
shown on the vertical axis. The height of the vertical bar indicates the range of values
for the industry.

the United Kingdom has the highest level of concentration). Other
outliers include the German and Italian frozen food industries, which
are both highly concentrated. These and other cases will be discussed
in later chapters. Some, but not all, of the variation observed in figure
5.1 can be attributed to differences in market size across different
countries; this issue forms the subject of the next section.

5.2 Testing the Theory

The central implication of the theory is that, where the level of
sunk costs is exogenously fixed, the minimal level of concentration
decreases to zero as market size increases; but within advertising-
intensive industries where sunk costs are endogenous this relationship
breaks down.

Specifically, there are two predictions that are of interest:

(a)   Within advertising-intensive industries, the minimal level of concentration is bounded away from zero independent of the size of the market.

(b)   The most distinctive proposition to emerge from the model is that, within advertising-intensive industries, the function describing the lower bound to concentration as a function of market size need not be monotonic. (See figure 3.4 and the accompanying discussion of the determinants of this function.)

The second prediction, despite its negative character, turns out to be very helpful in distinguishing this theory from the alternative view, that advertising may be treated as an exogenous barrier to entry. Under the latter view, the level of the barrier might of course vary from one industry to another, and it might also depend on certain country-specific factors. What is important is that its level is independent of the size of the market per se, as measured here by the value of total sales. Under this exogenous sunk cost view, the relationship between concentration and market size in advertising-intensive industries should be identical to that in homogeneous goods industries, except insofar as the setup cost σ is augmented by some unknown constant, representing the height of the advertising barrier. This prediction is tested in what follows.

5.3   The Evidence

The relationship between the four-firm concentration ratio, C_4, and the ratio of market size to setup cost, S/σ, is shown in figure 5.2. For the homogeneous goods group, shown in part (i) of the figure, a strong negative correlation is evident, and the minimal levels of concentration attained at large values of S/σ are quite small (less than 5%).

Among the advertising-intensive group, however, the lowest observed level of C_4 is 25%; several industries, all with relatively high values of S/σ, have values in the 25%–30% range.

The analysis that follows is developed in two steps. We take as our null hypothesis the traditional view under which advertising outlays constitute a barrier to entry whose size is exogenously fixed. Under

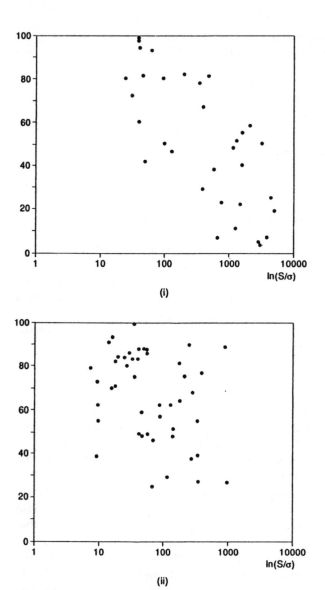

Figure 5.2
Scatter diagrams of the four-firm concentration ratio C_4 versus the market size to setup cost ratio S/σ (log scale) for (i) homogeneous goods industries and (ii) advertising-intensive industries.

the hypothesis, the presence of advertising outlays will shift the schedule that describes the lower bound to concentration as a function of market size, but this schedule will still approach zero as market size increases, just as it does in the homogeneous goods case.

The first part of this section is devoted to a preliminary exercise in which we estimate lower bounds to the scatters of points shown in figure 5.2, and we argue that the results do not support the null hypothesis; rather, the results are consistent with prediction (a). The schedule for the pooled sample of all advertising-intensive industries appears to tend to a different (higher) limiting value as market size increases.

Under our null hypothesis, the schedule describing the lower bound to concentration tends to the same limit (i.e., zero) for *all* industries as market size increases, and so estimating this schedule for the pooled sample of all advertising-intensive industries is reasonable. But under the present theory, this schedule will tend to a different limit in different industries. The paucity of observations in the sample makes it infeasible to estimate a separate schedule for each industry. We can, however, make further progress by turning to prediction (b), which forms the main topic of this section.

Estimating Lower Bounds

A lower bound to the scatters of observations shown in figure 5.2 can be estimated using standard techniques if we regard the chosen measure of concentration in each industry as generated by some underlying distribution function. A natural choice of distribution function is the Weibull distribution, for two separate reasons. First, the Weibull is a highly flexible functional form that has been widely and successfully used in fitting bounds to various empirical distributions. Second, some special features of the present data set make the Weibull form particularly attractive. This argument runs as follows: Suppose we regard a concentration ratio C_n as the sum of the n largest values in a sample (of firms' market shares) drawn from some distribution whose form is unspecified. Thus, C_1 can be treated as an extreme value of this unknown distribution. The limiting distributions of extreme values were first studied by Fisher and Tippett (1928). The classic reference to the use of such methods is Gumbel 1958. The central result is that the distribution of extreme values converges asymptotically to a distribution that takes one of three forms; only one of these three forms (the Weibull distribution) corresponds to the case in which the extreme values are bounded below. Thus, on this statistical model, a scatter of values of C_1 would be expected to converge asymptotically to a Weibull distribution. The case of C_n, $n > 1$, is more complicated, but the limiting form of distribution is closely similar to the Weibull distribution, and it would be difficult to distinguish the two in small samples.

Methods for estimating lower bounds using the Weibull distribution are well established. These methods can be extended to deal with the case where the lower bound b is a function of some independent variable z (see Smith 1989 for a recent review of the literature). These methods involve modeling the distribution of residuals between the observed values $y_i(z_i)$ and the bound $b(z_j)$, as a Weibull distribution, that is, $x_i = y_i - b$ should be distributed according to

$$F(x) = 1 - \exp\left[-\left(\frac{x - \mu}{s}\right)^\alpha\right] \qquad \alpha > 0, s > 0$$

on the domain $x \geq \mu$. The case $\mu = 0$ corresponds to the two parameter Weibull distribution. Nonzero values of μ correspond to a horizontal shift in the distribution illustrated in figure 5.3. The shape of the distribution varies with parameter α, a lower value of α corresponding to a heavier degree of clustering of observations at the lower

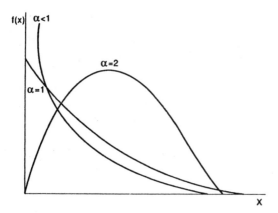

Figure 5.3
The form of the Weibull distribution.

bound, while the parameter s measures the dispersion (scale) of the distribution.

The obvious way to proceed here would be to fit a lower bound to the data using maximum likelihood methods. For $\alpha > 2$, the usual asymptotic results for maximum likelihood methods hold; they are consistent, asymptotically efficient, and asymptotically normally distributed. For $\alpha < 2$, however, these results break down, and an alternative approach is called for. For $1 < \alpha \leqslant 2$, a local maximum of the likelihood function exists, but it does not have the usual asymptotic properties; for $0 \leqslant \alpha \leqslant 1$, no local maximum of the likelihood function exists. (See Smith 1985, 1989 for details.) Low values of α correspond to the case in which observations are heavily clustered on the lower bound, and a visual examination of figure 5.2 suggests that it would be unwise to exclude this case a priori (an impression confirmed by the estimates presented below).

A method of fitting lower bounds that avoids these problems and is both computationally tractable and reasonably efficient[2] over the entire range of α has been suggested by Smith (1985, 1990).

It involves the use of a two-step procedure. As with any parametric method, some a priori decision must be made as to the form of the schedule $b(z)$ that describes the lower bound. Given some (one or many) parameter family of candidate schedules, a consistent estimator of the actual schedule may be obtained by choosing parameters to minimize the sum of the residuals $y_i - b(z_i)$ subject to the constraint that all residuals shall be non-negative. (Thus, a k-parameter bound will pass though k of the data points.) The second step in the procedure is to check that the pattern of residuals thus estimated (the k zero observations being deleted) fits the Weibull distribution and that the hypothesis $\mu = 0$ cannot be rejected.

The procedure rests on the assumption that the distribution of residuals is identical at all values of the independent variable (here S/σ). This would clearly be unreasonable if applied directly to the scatters shown in figure 5.2, given the presence of an upper limit of $C_4 = 1$; and so we first take a logit transformation of C_4, viz.,

$$\tilde{C}_4 = \ln \frac{C_4}{1 - C_4}.$$

---

2. Its rate of convergence is $n^{-1/\alpha}$, which is the optimal rate. More efficient (Pitman) estimators involve much more complex computations.

Chapter 5

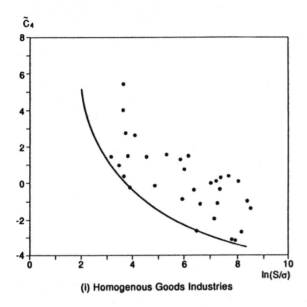

(i) Homogenous Goods Industries

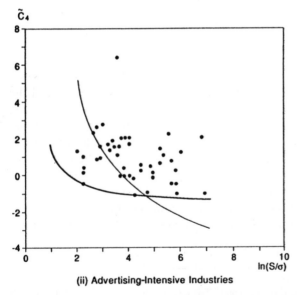

(ii) Advertising-Intensive Industries

Figure 5.4

Scatter diagrams of the logit transformation of C_4 against $\ln S/\sigma$ for (i) homogeneous goods industries and (ii) advertising-intensive industries. The fitted bounds are (i) $\tilde{C}_4 = -6.08 + 22.3/(\ln S/\sigma)$; (ii) $\tilde{C}_4 = -1.83 + 3.08/(\ln S/\sigma)$. The estimated bound (i) is shown also for comparison in panel (ii). The outlier in panel (ii) is the Japanese beer industry (see chapter 13).

Table 5.1
Estimation of lower bounds (standard errors in parentheses). The values of μ correspond to the three-parameter Weibull distribution, ΔNLLH indicates the difference in the negative log likelihood between the three-parameter Weibull and the two-parameter Weibull ($\mu = 0$). The two-parameter Weibull cannot be rejected (see text); the shape of parameter α reported in the table is that corresponding to the fitted two-parameter Weibull.

		$\tilde{C}_{\infty}$	μ	ΔNLLH	α
$\tilde{C}_4$	H	−6.08	−0.70 (1.51)	0.4	2.00
	A	−1.83	−0.03 (0.51)	0.0	2.90
$\tilde{C}_1$	H	−7.23	−0.54 (1.01)	0.5	1.66
	A	−3.71	−0.21 (0.10)	0.8	1.75

The scatters of $\tilde{C}_4$ are shown in figure 5.4. An examination of these scatters suggested that a reasonable family of candidate schedules would be

$$\tilde{C}_n = a + \frac{b}{ln(S/\sigma)}.$$

The fitted schedules are illustrated in figure 5.4. The associated set of residuals fits the Weibull distribution well in both cases, and the hypothesis $\mu = 0$ cannot be rejected.[3] Finally, the estimated values of α are below 2, in some cases, so that a maximum likelihood approach would not be appropriate (table 5.1). The lower panel of figure 5.4 shows the estimated schedule for the homogeneous goods group overlaid on that estimated for the advertising-intensive group. The relationship between the two schedules is *not* suggestive of a horizontal shift, as would be implied by the hypothesis that advertising was an exogenously determined element of sunk cost. On the

---

3. Checking that $\mu = 0$ amounts to testing the two-parameter Weibull against the three-parameter Weibull; this can be tested using a likelihood ratio test. Twice the difference of the fitted negative log likelihood (NLLH) has an approximate chi-square distribution with one degree of freedom. The 5% rejection point of this distribution is 3.84, corresponding to a difference of NLLH of 1.92. The NLLH values reported in table 5.1 are all far below this level; so that the two-parameter Weibull ($\mu = 0$) cannot be rejected. This conclusion is further supported by comparing the estimated values of μ in table 5.1 with their standard error.

other hand, the relationship between the two schedules does appear to conform nicely to that predicted on the basis of the present theory: this can be seen by comparing panel (ii) of figure 5.4 with figure 3.9. The limiting value of the estimated bound for the advertising group, as $S/\sigma \to \infty$, corresponds to a value of $C_4 = 19\%$. The corresponding limit of C_4 for the homogeneous goods group is 0.06%. These procedures were also applied to the scatter of maximal market shares, that is, to $\tilde{C}_1$, with closely similar results (table 5.1). To test the null hypothesis that the estimated schedules for both industry groups converge to the same value as $S \to \infty$, we can compare the difference in the estimated asymptotic values (shown as $\tilde{C}_\infty$ in table 5.1) with the standard errors on μ. It is clear that the difference in the means is very large compared to these standard errors in all cases, so that the hypothesis can be rejected.[4]

The procedure just described involves a pooling of observations for all advertising-intensive industries. As noted, this is satisfactory under the null hypothesis, but is not appropriate in the context of the present theory. To proceed further, we need to adopt a different approach.

The Second Prediction

A useful line of attack in discriminating between the present theory and the view of advertising as an exogenous barrier to entry lies in examining the second prediction set out above. Suppose that the level of sunk costs is exogenously fixed. Then, we predict that the expected level of concentration is negatively related to the ratio of market size to setup cost. An obvious specification for this relationship would be

$$C_{ij} = a_i + b_j + c\,ln\left(\frac{S}{\sigma}\right)_{ij}$$

$$= a_i + b_j + c\,ln\left[\left(\frac{S}{\sigma}\right)_i \rho_{ij}\right], \tag{1}$$

where C denotes the (n-firm) concentration ratio, and where industries are indexed by i and countries by j. As explained in chapter

---

4. In the case of the estimates for C_1, caution is needed in interpreting these standard errors, as the estimated α lies below 2, implying that the distribution of μ is not asymptotically normal.

4, the ratio of market size to setup cost for industry i in country j is computed by estimating S/σ for industry i in the U.S. market and multiplying by the ratio ρ_{ij} of the size of market i in country j to the size of the corresponding market in the United States. Hence it is the latter form of equation (1) that is estimated below.

One possible objection to specification (1) is that values of C_{ij} must lie between 0 and 1, so that this linear specification in inappropriate. This objection can be met by taking a logit transformation of C_{ij}, that is, by estimating

$$ ln \frac{C_{ij}}{1 - C_{ij}} = \tilde{C}_{ij} = a_i + b_j + c\, ln \left[\left(\frac{S}{\sigma} \right)_i \rho_{ij} \right]. \tag{2} $$

Now equation (2) can be written in the alternative form

$$ \tilde{C}_{ij} = a_i + b_j + c\, ln \left(\frac{S}{\sigma} \right)_i + c\, ln\, \rho_{ij} $$

$$ = a_i' + b_j + c\, ln\, \rho_{ij}. \tag{2'} $$

As equation (2′) indicates, errors in the estimated values of σ will affect equation (2) only via the industry dummy and will *not* affect the slope parameter c. In view of the difficulties surrounding the measurement of σ noted in chapter 4, this point deserves emphasis.

If advertising outlays can be treated as an (industry-specific) exogenous sunk cost, which merely augments the level of setup cost σ, then the coefficient c estimated in equation (2), (2′) should take the same negative value for both the homogeneous goods group and the advertising-intensive group. On the other hand, the theory predicts a negative relationship between ρ_{ij} and C_{ij} for the homogeneous goods group, but it implies that there is no reason to expect any systematic (negative or positive) relationship between ρ_{ij} and C_{ij} for the advertising-intensive group.

Estimates for specifications (1) and (2) for both groups of industries are shown in table 5.2. (A full set of industry and country dummies are included in all cases.) In the homogeneous goods group, the coefficient b is negative and statistically significant (at the 5% level) in both cases[5]; for the advertising-intensive group, the coefficient is

---

5. The estimates of the slope parameter for the first equation reported in table 5.2 imply that a doubling in S/σ implies a fall of 13 percentage points in C_4; the corresponding equation for the logit formulation indicates that a doubling of S/σ implies a fall of 19 percentage points in C_4.

Table 5.2
Regressions of concentration ratios on market size to setup cost ratios. A full set of industry and country dummies are included in all specifications; the table lists those that are significant at the 5% level. The estimated equations correspond to equations (1)–(2) in the text. $\tilde{C}_4$ denotes the logit transformation of C_4.

Dependent variable	Industry group	$\ln(S/\sigma)$	No. of obs.	R^2	Significant dummies*
C_4	H	−0.187	32	0.86	Sugar(−);
		(t = 3.2)			U.K.(+), U.S.(+)
	A	−0.02	58	0.49	Sugar con.(−)
		(t = 0.63)			
$\tilde{C}_4$	H	−1.12	32	0.89	Sugar(−);
		(t = 3.4)			Italy(−), U.K.(+), U.S.(+)
	A	+0.006	58	0.35	Sugar con.(−)
		(t = 0.02)			

small, its sign is unstable, and it is not statistically significant in any specification. These equations were reestimated using various alternative measures of concentration (C_3, C_2, etc.), and the same pattern of results was confirmed.

The equations shown for the advertising-intensive group in table 5.2 relate to the subsample of industries for which satisfactory measures of σ and C were available (table 4.3). Specification (2′) can also be estimated for various extended samples of industries. These results (not shown in the table) confirm the same lack of any relationship.[6] All in all, these results offer encouraging support for the predictions of the present theory, as against the view that advertising outlays constitute a barrier to entry whose size is exogenously fixed.

It would be attractive to try to probe the predictions of the theory further along these lines. What determines the slope of the lower bound to the size-structure relationship, for example? As shown in

---

6. Frozen food and margarine were omitted from the reported regressions, as nonretail market shares are difficult to estimate (see chapter 4). Their inclusion, using the C_4 for retail sales only, does not materially affect the results reported above. Chocolate confectionery, instant coffee and R&G coffee were also omitted from the reported regressions because of problems in measuring σ and/or ρ. The market size/market structure relationship for these industries is illustrated in chapter 12.

chapter 2, while this depends delicately on the details of the model, two influences are clear: the lower bound to the concentration-size relationship varies with the absolute size of setup cost and the responsiveness of demand to advertising outlays. While this might lead in principle to a more powerful test of the theory, the difficulties involved in obtaining satisfactory estimates of advertising response functions make this a rather problematic route.

References

Broadbent, Simon (ed.) (1981), *Advertising Works: Papers from the IPA Advertising Effectiveness Awards*, London: Holt, Rheinhart and Winston.

Connor, John M., Richard T. Rogers, Bruce W. Marion, and Willard F. Mueller (1985), *The Food Manufacturing Industries: Structure, Strategies, Performance and Policies*, Lexington, MA: Lexington Books.

Culbertson, John D., and Rosanna Mentzer Morrison (1983), "Economies of Scale Data for the Food Manufacturing Industries," Unpublished ms.

Dasgupta, P., and J. E. Stiglitz (1980), "Industrial Structure and the Nature of Innovative Activity," *Economic Journal*, vol. 90, pp. 266–293.

Davies, Stephen (1980), "Minimum Efficient Size and Seller Concentration: An Empirical Problem," *Journal of Industrial Economics*, vol. 28, pp. 287–302.

Fisher, R. A., and L. H. C. Tippett (1928), "Limiting forms of the frequency distributions of the largest or smallest member of the sample," *Proceedings of the Cambridge Philosophical Society*, vol. 24, pp. 180–190.

George, Kenneth, and T. S. Ward (1975), *The Structure of Industry in the EEC*, Cambridge: Cambridge University Press.

Gumbel, E. J. (1958), *Statistics of Extremes*, New York: Columbia University Press.

Hannah, Leslie, and John A. Kay (1977), *Concentration in Modern Industry: theory and measurement and the U.K. experience*, London: Macmillan.

Kessides, Ioannis N. (1988), "Toward a Testable Model of Entry: A Study of the U.S. Manufacturing Industries," unpublished (University of Maryland).

Lambin, Jean Jacques (1976), *Advertising, Competition and Market Conduct in Oligopoly over Time: An Econometric Investigation in Western European Countries*, Amsterdam: North Holland.

Panzar, John C., and Robert D. Willig (1981), "Economies of Scope," *American Economic Review*, vol. 71, pp. 262–272.

Smith, Richard L. (1985), "Maximum Likelihood estimation in a class of non-regular cases," *Biometrika*, vol. 72, pp. 67–92.

Smith, Richard L. (1989), "Extreme Value Analysis of Environmental Time Series: An Application to Trend Detection in Ground-Level Ozone," *Statistical Science*, vol. 4, pp. 367–393.

Smith, Richard L. (1990), "Nonregular Regression," *Biometrika* (forthcoming).

[11]

Scale, Scope, and Organizational Capabilities

The similarities in the beginnings and evolutionary paths of modern industrial enterprises in the United States, Great Britain, and Germany between the 1880s and the 1940s can be set out briefly by means of a dynamic framework. This analytical framework includes the definitions, concepts, and generalizations, that are needed to clarify a complex mass of historical detail, to make the comparisons between industries, countries, and time periods more precise, and to provide the ingredients for an explanatory theory concerning the creation and growth of the institution. The complexities, variations, and exceptions revealed by the detailed historical story will be described in later chapters.

The New Institution

In *The Visible Hand* I described the modern *business* enterprise (of which the modern industrial enterprise is a subspecies) as having two basic characteristics: it contains a number of distinct operating units, and it is managed by a hierarchy of full-time salaried executives. The modern *industrial* enterprise is the particular subspecies that carries out modern production processes. It has more than a production function, however. It is also a "governance structure," to use Oliver Williamson's term.[1] It governs units that carry out different production as well as commercial and research functions and so integrates these activities. In such an enterprise each unit—a factory, a sales or purchasing office, or a research laboratory—has its own administrative office, its own managers and staff, its own set of books, as well as its own resources (physical facilities and personnel) to carry out a specific *function* involved in the production or distribution of a specific *product* in a specific *geographical* area. Each unit—each factory, sales office, purchasing office, research laboratory—could theoretically act as an independent business enterprise. Indeed, many business

Scale, Scope, and Organizational Capabilities   15

enterprises still consist of just one such unit. In the modern multiunit enterprise the activities of the managers of these units (lower-level managers) are monitored and coordinated by middle-level managers. The latter, in turn, are monitored and coordinated by a full-time top-level executive, or a team of such executives, who plan and allocate resources for the operating units and the enterprise as a whole. The decisions of these top managers normally have to be ratified by a board of directors, legally defined as representatives of the owners (Figure 1).

Such boards of directors nearly always include both top managers (the inside directors) and part-time representatives of the owners (the outside directors). When the owners are an identifiable group of individuals or institutions, their representatives and the inside directors select the company's top management. When the owners are either widely scattered or have little interest in the details of the company's operations, the inside directors normally select the outside directors, and together they select the successors to top management.

Thus the institution under consideration, the modern industrial firm, can be defined as a collection of operating units, each with its own specific facilities and personnel, whose combined resources and activities are coordinated, monitored, and allocated by a hierarchy of middle and top managers. It is the existence of this hierarchy that makes the activities and operations of the whole enterprise more than the sum of its operating units.

As the definition of the institution suggests, its size, its managerial team or hierarchy, and the nature of the resources it controls are directly related to the number of its operating units; in fact, it is the number of these units, rather than total assets or the size of the work force, that determines the number of middle and top managers, the nature of their tasks, and the complexity of the institution they manage. Size in terms of assets, market value of shares, or labor force is the most readily available statistical proxy for such administrative complexity; but statistics cannot convey either the complexity or the nature and functions of the institution.

It then becomes critical to explain how and why the institution grew by adding new units—units that carried out different economic functions, operated in different geographical regions, and handled different lines of products. An initial explanation is that manufacturing enterprises became multifunctional, multiregional, and multiproduct because the addition of new units permitted them to maintain a long-term rate of return on investment by reducing overall costs of production and distribution, by providing products that satisfied existing demands, and by transferring facilities and skills to more profitable markets when returns were reduced by competition, changing technology, or altered market demand.

There were, of course, other reasons why the managers of an industrial enterprise invested in new units of production and distribution: to assure access

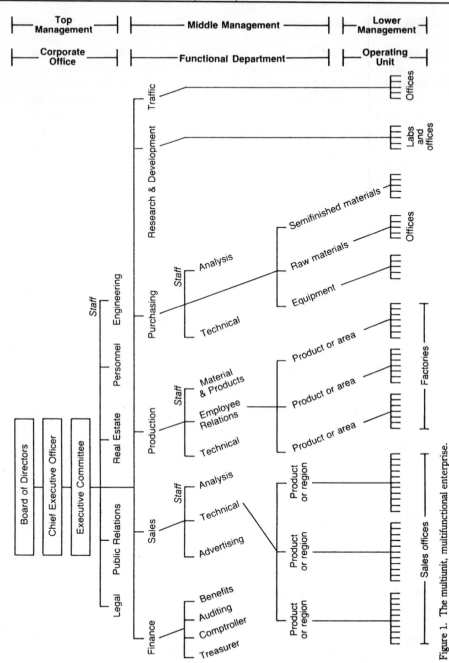

Figure 1. The multiunit, multifunctional enterprise.

to markets and supplies or to prevent competitors from obtaining such access, to obtain control over competitors, to eliminate competition in other ways, or merely to reinvest retained earnings. In more recent years financial reasons have played a role: to improve the firm's overall tax position, to alter the price of its securities, to carry out other financial manipulations, or merely to extend its portfolio of investments. Furthermore, managers have added units in order to acquire greater control over the work force, or simply to gain personal status and power.

Whatever the initial motivation for its investment in new operating units, the modern industrial enterprise has rarely continued to grow or maintain its competitive position *over an extended period of time* unless the addition of new units (and to a lesser extent the elimination of old ones) has actually permitted its managerial hierarchy to reduce costs, to improve functional efficiency in marketing and purchasing as well as production, to improve existing products and processes and to develop new ones, and to allocate resources to meet the challenges and opportunities of ever-changing technologies and markets. Such a process of growth has provided this bureaucratic institution with the internal dynamic that has made it powerful and enabled it to maintain its position of dominance as markets and technologies have changed and as world wars and depressions have come and gone.

Reductions in costs and efficient resource utilization have resulted, the explanation continues, from the exploitation of economies of scale in production and distribution, from exploiting economies of joint production or joint distribution, or from reduction in the costs of transactions involved.

Economies of scale may be defined initially as those that result when the increased size of a single operating unit producing or distributing a single product reduces the unit cost of production or distribution.

Economies of joint production or distribution are those resulting from the use of processes within a single operating unit to produce or distribute more than one product. (I use the increasingly popular term "economies of scope" to refer to these economies of joint production or distribution.)[2]

Transaction costs are those involved in the transfer of goods and services from one operating unit to another. When these transactions are carried out between firms or between individuals, they usually involve the transfer of property rights and are defined in contractual terms.[3] When they are carried out within the enterprise, they are defined by accounting procedures. The costs of such transactions are reduced by a more efficient exchange of goods and services *between* units, whereas the economies of scale and scope are closely tied to the more efficient use of facilities and skills *within* such units.

Transaction cost economies are, of course, closely related to those of scale and scope. The economies of scale and those of scope within a single unit of production or distribution permit that unit to expand the output of goods and services, which, in turn, increases proportionately the number of recurring commercial transactions and contractual relations the enterprise must carry on with other operating units. Just as changes in the processes of production and distribution within units have a powerful impact on the nature of transactions between units (as they are defined through contractual relations), so do changes in contractual relations affect the operations carried on within units.

Differences in economies of scale and scope in different industries, different countries, and different time periods result from differences in the technologies of production and distribution and differences in the sizes and locations of markets. Thus changes, particularly technological innovations in production and changes in market size, continually alter the economic environment (as differentiated from the political and social environment) in which the institution appears and grows. So do changes in per-capita income and demographic shifts, such as those from rural to urban areas and from city to suburb. External changes, by affecting the economies of scale and scope, alter contractual arrangements between units in production and those in distribution, finance, and other business activities.

It was the development of new technologies and the opening of new markets, which resulted in economies of scale and of scope and in reduced transaction costs, that made the large multiunit industrial enterprise come when it did, where it did, and in the way it did. These technological and market changes explain why the institution appeared and continued to cluster in certain industries and not in others, why it came into being by integrating units of volume production with those of volume distribution, and finally, why this multifunctional enterprise continued to grow (though not in all cases) by becoming multinational and multiproduct.

Historical Attributes

The ability of the modern industrial enterprise to exploit fully the economies of scale, scope, and transaction costs was the dynamic that produced its three most significant historical attributes. First, such enterprises clustered from the start in industries having similar characteristics. Second, they appeared quite suddenly in the last quarter of the nineteenth century. Finally, all were born and then continued to grow in much the same manner.

The industries in which the new institution first appeared, and in which it continued to cluster throughout the twentieth century, are indicated in Tables 5–8. The location, country by country and industry by industry, of all the industrial corporations in the world which in 1973 employed more than 20,000 workers is shown in Table 5. These industries are those defined by the U.S.

Table 5. Distribution of world's largest industrial enterprises with more than 20,000 employees, by industry and country, 1973.[a]

Group	Industry	United States	Outside United States	Great Britain	West Germany	Japan	France	Others	Total
20	Food	22	17	13	0	1	1	2	39
21	Tobacco	3	4	3	1	0	0	0	7
22	Textiles	7	6	3	0	2	1	0	13
23	Apparel	6	0	0	0	0	0	2	6
24	Lumber	4	2	0	0	0	0	2	6
25	Furniture	0	0	0	0	0	0	0	0
26	Paper	7	3	3	0	0	0	0	10
27	Printing and publishing	0	0	0	0	0	0	0	0
28	Chemicals	24	28	4	5	3	6	10	52
29	Petroleum	14	12	2	0	0	2	8	26
30	Rubber	5	5	1	1	1	1	1	10
31	Leather	2	0	0	0	0	0	0	2
32	Stone, clay, and glass	7	8	3	0	0	3	2	15
33	Primary metals	13	35	2	9	5	4	15	48
34	Fabricated metals	8	6	5	1	0	0	0	14
35	Machinery	22	12	2	3	2	0	5	34
36	Electrical machinery	20	25	4	5	7	2	7	45
37	Transportation equipment	22	23	3	3	7	4	6	45
38	Instruments[b]	4	1	0	0	0	0	0	5
39	Miscellaneous	2	0	0	0	0	0	0	2
—	Conglomerate	19	3	2	1	0	0	0	22
	Total	211	190	50	29	28	24	59	401

Sources: Compiled from "The Fortune Directory of the 500 Largest Industrial Corporations," *Fortune*, May 1974, pp. 230–257; "The Fortune Directory of the 300 Largest Industrial Corporations outside the U.S.," *Fortune*, August 1974, pp. 174–181.

a. The *Fortune* lists include enterprises of noncommunist countries only.

b. Medical equipment and supplies, photographic equipment and supplies, and watches and clocks.

Bureau of the Census as two-digit groups in its Standard Industrial Classification, or SIC. (The SIC divides its basic two-digit industry categories—those numbered from 20 to 39 for manufacturing—into three-digit categories. The appendixes show these three-digit classifications within the two-digit category.) In 1973, 289 (72.0%) of the 401 companies were clustered in food, chemicals, petroleum, primary metals, and the three machinery groups—nonelectrical and electrical machinery and transportation equipment.[4] Ninety-one, or just under 23%, were in three-digit subcategories of six other two-digit classifications— three-digit classifications which had the same industrial characteristics as those two-digit classifications in which the 72% clustered. These included cigarettes in tobacco; tires in rubber; newsprint in paper; plate and flat glass in stone, clay, and glass; cans and razor blades in fabricated metals; and mass-produced cameras in instruments. Only 21 companies (5.2%) were in the remaining two-digit categories—textiles, apparel, lumber, furniture, leather, printing and publishing, and miscellaneous.

A second fact illustrated by Table 5—one that is central to understanding the evolution of the modern industrial enterprise—is the predominance of American firms among the world's largest industrial corporations. Of the total of 401 companies employing more than 20,000 persons, over half (211, or 52.6%) were American. Great Britain followed with 50 (12.5%), Germany with 29 (7.2%), Japan with 28, and France with 24. Only in chemicals, primary metals, and electrical machinery did all the non-American firms outnumber the American firms by as many as four or five.

Earlier in the twentieth century the large industrial corporations in the United States had clustered in the same industrial groups as those in which they were concentrated in 1973 (Table 6). The pattern was much the same for Britain and Germany (Tables 7 and 8). The American firms, however, were bigger and more numerous than those in other countries (see appendixes). Well before World War II the United States had many more and many larger managerial hierarchies than did the other nations.

Basic differences within the broad pattern of evolution are also suggested by the tables. For example, in the United States throughout the twentieth century the great enterprises produced both consumer and industrial goods. Britain had proportionately more large firms in consumer goods than did the United States, while the biggest industrials in Germany concentrated much more on producer's goods. Even as late as 1973, close to one-third—sixteen of the fifty—firms in Great Britain employing more than 20,000 persons were engaged in the production and distribution of food and tobacco products, whereas Germany, and also France and Japan, each had only one firm in the same two categories (Table 5). On the other hand, before World War II Germany had had many more firms than Britain in chemicals and heavy machinery.

Scale, Scope, and Organizational Capabilities 21

Table 6. Distribution of the 200 largest industrial enterprises in the United States, by industry, 1917–1973.[a]

Group	Industry	1917	1930	1948	1973
20	Food	29	31	27	22
21	Tobacco	6	5	5	3
22	Textiles	6	4	8	3
23	Apparel	3	0	0	0
24	Lumber	3	4	2	4
25	Furniture	0	1	1	0
26	Paper	5	8	6	9
27	Printing and publishing	2	2	2	1
28	Chemicals	20	20	23	28
29	Petroleum	22	26	22	22
30	Rubber	5	5	5	5
31	Leather	4	2	2	0
32	Stone, clay, and glass	5	8	6	7
33	Primary metals	31	23	23	19
34	Fabricated metals	11	10	6	5
35	Machinery	17	19	23	16
36	Electrical machinery	5	5	7	13
37	Transportation equipment	24	23	29	19
38	Instruments	1	2	1	4
39	Miscellaneous	1	2	2	1
—	Conglomerate	0	0	0	19
	Total	200	200	200	200

Sources: Appendixes A.1–A.3 for 1917, 1930, and 1948; figures for 1973 compiled from *Fortune,* May 1974, pp. 230–257.

a. Ranked by assets.

Economies of Scale and Scope in Production

The major innovations made in the processes of production during the last quarter of the nineteenth century created many new industries and transformed many old industries. These processes differed from earlier ones in *their potential for exploiting the unprecedented cost advantages of the economies of scale and scope.*

In the older, labor-intensive industries, increases in the output of a manufacturing establishment came primarily by adding more machines and more workers to operate them. In newer industries, expanded output came by a drastic change in capital-labor ratios. It came by improving and rearranging inputs; by using new or greatly improved machinery, furnaces, stills, and other

Introduction: Scale and Scope   22

Table 7.   Distribution of the 200 largest industrial enterprises in Great Britain, by industry, 1919–1973.[a]

Group	Industry	1919	1930	1948	1973
20	Food	61	63	53	33
21	Tobacco	3	4	6	4
22	Textiles	26	21	17	10
23	Apparel	0	1	2	0
24	Lumber	0	0	0	2
25	Furniture	0	0	0	0
26	Paper	3	5	6	7
27	Printing and publishing	5	10	7	7
28	Chemicals	14	11	17	21
29	Petroleum	3	4	3	8
30	Rubber	3	3	2	6
31	Leather	1	1	1	3
32	Stone, clay, and glass	2	7	8	16
33	Primary metals	40	24	25	14
34	Fabricated metals	1	8	7	7
35	Machinery	7	6	10	26
36	Electrical machinery	6	10	11	14
37	Transportation equipment	23	17	21	16
38	Instruments	0	2	1	3
39	Miscellaneous	2	3	3	1
—	Conglomerate	0	0	0	2
	Total	200	200	200	200

Sources: Appendix B.1–B.3 for 1919, 1930, and 1948; figures for 1973 compiled from *The Times 1000, 1974/75* (London, 1974), table 15.

a. Ranked by market value of quoted capital.

equipment; by reorienting the processes of production within the plant; by placing the several intermediary processes employed in making a final product within a single works; and by increasing the application of energy (particularly that generated by fossil fuel).

The first set of industries remained labor-intensive. In industries such as apparel, textiles made from natural fibers, lumber, furniture, printing and publishing—in which the large modern firm remained relatively rare—improvements in equipment and plant design did bring economies of scale, but they were not extensive. A sharp reduction of unit costs did not accompany an increase in the volume of materials processed by the plant. In these industries the large mills, factories, or works often had observable, but not striking, cost advantages over the smaller ones.

In the second set, the more capital-intensive industries, new processes of

Scale, Scope, and Organizational Capabilities   23

Table 8. Distribution of the 200 largest industrial enterprises in Germany, by industry, 1913–1973.[a]

Group	Industry	1913	1929	1953	1973
20	Food	26	28	22	24
21	Tobacco	1	1	0	6
22	Textiles	15	24	26	4
23	Apparel	1	1	1	0
24	Lumber	1	0	0	0
25	Furniture	0	0	0	0
26	Paper	4	5	3	2
27	Printing and publishing	0	1	0	6
28	Chemicals	30	24	24	30
29	Petroleum	5	7	6	8
30	Rubber	4	2	5	3
31	Leather	2	5	2	1
32	Stone, clay, and glass	7	7	6	15
33	Primary metals	49	33	40	19
34	Fabricated metals	5	3	5	14
35	Machinery	25	19	28	29
36	Electrical machinery	7	11	8	21
37	Transportation equipment	16	24	18	14
38	Instruments	2	3	3	2
39	Miscellaneous	0	2	3	1
—	Conglomerate	0	0	0	1
	Total	200	200	200	200

Sources: Appendix C.1–C.3 for 1913, 1929, and 1953; figures for 1973 compiled from *Handbuch der deutschen Aktiengesellschaften, 1974–75.*

a. Ranked by sales for 1973 and by assets for the other three years.

production were invented or existing ones vastly improved in the late nineteenth century—processes for the refining and distilling of sugar, petroleum, animal and vegetable oil, whiskey and other liquids; for the refining and smelting of iron, steel, copper, and aluminum; for the mechanical processing and packaging of grain, tobacco, and other agricultural products; for the manufacturing of complex light, standardized machinery through the fabrication and assembly of interchangeable parts; and for the production of technologically advanced industrial machinery and chemicals by a series of interrelated mechanical and chemical processes. In these capital-intensive industries, investment in new facilities greatly increased the ratio of capital to labor involved in producing a unit of output. Production units achieved much greater economies of scale—that is, the cost per unit dropped more quickly as the volume of materials being processed increased. Therefore large plants operating at their "minimum efficient scale" (the scale of operation necessary to reach the lowest cost per unit) had an impressive cost advantage over smaller plants that did not reach that scale.[5]

The economies of joint production, or scope, also brought significant cost reduction. Here the cost advantage came from making a number of products in the same production unit from much the same raw and semifinished materials and by the same intermediate processes. The increase in the number of products made simultaneously in the same factory reduced the unit costs of each individual product.

These potential cost advantages, however, could not be fully realized unless a constant flow of materials through the plant or factory was maintained to assure effective capacity utilization. If the realized volume of flow fell below capacity, then actual costs per unit rose rapidly. They did so because fixed costs remained much higher and "sunk costs" (the original capital investment) were also much higher than in the more labor-intensive industries. Thus the two decisive figures in determining costs and profits were (and still are) rated capacity and throughput, or the amount actually processed within a specified time period. (The economies of scale theoretically incorporate the economies of speed, as I use that term in *The Visible Hand,* because the economies of scale depend on both size—rated capacity—and speed—the intensity at which the capacity is utilized.) In the capital-intensive industries the throughput needed to maintain minimum efficient scale requires careful coordination not only of the flow through the processes of production but also of the flow of inputs from suppliers and the flow of outputs to intermediaries and final users.

Such coordination did not, and indeed could not, happen automatically. It demanded the constant attention of a managerial team or hierarchy. The potential economies of scale and scope, as measured by rated capacity, are the physical characteristics of the production facilities. The actual economies of scale or of scope, as determined by throughput, are organizational. Such economies depend on knowledge, skill, experience, and teamwork—on the organized human capabilities essential to exploit the potential of technological processes.

The significance of economies of scale and those of scope in production, as measured by throughput, can be illustrated by two well-known examples: the Standard Oil Company, one of the very first modern industrial enterprises (as differentiated from transportation, communication, or distribution enterprises) in the United States; and the three oldest and largest German chemical companies.

In 1882 the Standard Oil alliance formed the Standard Oil Trust. (Its successor, Exxon, is still the world's largest oil company.) The purpose was not to obtain control over the industry's output: the alliance, a loose federation of forty companies, each with its own legal and administrative identity but tied to

Scale, Scope, and Organizational Capabilities   **25**

John D. Rockefeller's Standard Oil Company through interchange of stock and other financial devices, already had a monopoly. At that time, in fact, the members of the alliance produced 90% of America's output of kerosene.[6] Instead, the Standard Oil Trust was formed to provide a legal instrument to rationalize the industry and exploit economies of scale more fully. The trust provided the essential legal means to create a central or corporate office that could do two things. First, it could reorganize the processes of production by shutting down some refineries, reshaping others, and building new ones. Second, it could coordinate the flow of materials, not only through the several refineries, but from the oil fields to the refineries and from the refineries to the consumers.

The resulting rationalization made it possible to concentrate close to a quarter of the world's production of kerosene in three refineries, each with an average daily charging capacity of 6,500 barrels, with two-thirds of their product going to overseas markets. (At this time, refined petroleum products were by far the nation's largest nonagricultural export.) Imagine the *diseconomies* of scale (the increase in unit costs) that would result from placing close to one-fourth of the world's production of shoes, textiles, or lumber into three factories or mills! In those instances the administrative coordination of the operation of miles and miles of machines and the huge concentration of labor needed to operate those machines would make neither economic nor social sense.

The reorganization of the trust's refining facilities brought a sharp reduction in the average cost of producing a gallon of kerosene. In 1880 the average cost at plants with a daily capacity of 1,500 to 2,000 barrels was approximately 2.5¢ per gallon. By 1885, according to the industry's most authoritative history, the average cost for plants of that size had been reduced to 1.5¢.[7] Data compiled for the trust's Manufacturing Committee showed that the average cost of processing a gallon of crude for all its works had dropped from 0.534¢ in 1884 to 0.452¢ in 1885 with a resulting increase in the profit margin from 0.530¢ in 1884 to 1.003¢ in 1885. (That profit margin was the core of four of the world's largest industrial fortunes, those of the Rockefellers, Harknesses, Paynes, and Flaglers.) As these averages indicate, the unit costs of the giant refineries were far below those of any competitor. To maintain this cost advantage, however, these large refineries had to have a continuing daily throughput of 5,000 to 6,500 barrels, or a threefold to fourfold increase over the earlier daily flow of 1,500 to 2,000 barrels, with resulting increases in transactions handled and in the complexity of coordinating the flow of materials through the processes of production and distribution.

Even as Standard Oil was investing in its large refineries to exploit the economies of scale, the German dye makers were making still larger investments to permit them to exploit fully the economies of scope. The enlarged plants produced literally hundreds of dyes, as well as many pharmaceuticals, from the same raw materials and the same set of intermediate chemical compounds. The first three enterprises to make such investments to exploit the cost advantages of scale and then those of scope—Bayer, Hoechst, and BASF—were able to reduce the price of a new synthetic dye, red alizarin, from 270 marks per kilogram in 1869 to 9 marks in 1886, and to make comparable price reductions in their other dyes.[8] A new dye or pharmaceutical added little to the production cost of these items, and the additions permitted a reduction in the unit cost of the others. On the other hand, the development of new dyes and pharmaceuticals was not only costly, but each new product increased the tasks of quality control and coordination of product flow.

Standard Oil and the German chemical companies were by no means unique. In the 1880s and 1890s new mass-production technologies—those of the Second Industrial Revolution—brought a sharp reduction in costs as plants reached minimum efficient scale. In many industries the throughput of plants of that scale was so high that a small number of them could meet the existing national and even global demand. The structure of these industries quickly became oligopolistic, and the few large enterprises in each competed world-wide. In many instances the first company to build a plant of minimum efficient scale and to recruit the essential management team remained the leader in its industry for decades.

The differentials between the potential scale-and-scope economies of different production technologies indicate not only why the large hierarchical firms appeared in some industries and not in others, but also why they appeared suddenly in the last decades of the nineteenth century. It was not until the 1870s, with the completion of the modern transportation and communication networks—the railroad, telegraph, steamship, and cable—and of the organizational and technological innovations essential to operate them as integrated systems, that materials could flow into a factory or processing plant and finished goods move out at a rate of speed and volume and with the precise timing required to achieve substantial economies of throughput. Transportation that depended on the power of animals, wind, and current was too slow, too irregular, and too uncertain to maintain a level of throughput necessary to achieve the potential economies of the new technologies. Thus the revolution in transportation and communication created opportunities that led to a revolution in both production and distribution.

The essential first step in exploiting the new technologies of production—the step that led to the creation of the modern industrial enterprise—was, therefore, the investment in production facilities large enough to exploit the full potential of the economies of scale and scope inherent in the new or improved technologies. The critical entrepreneurial act was not the invention—or even the initial commercialization—of a new or greatly improved product or process. Instead it was the construction of a plant of the optimal size required to exploit fully the economies of scale or those of scope, or both.

Several points need to be made about such an investment. First, to repeat, different production technologies have different scale-or-scope economies. Costs decrease and increase more sharply in relation to volume in some production processes than in others. In some industries, such as oil, steel, and aluminum, the cost-curve gradient (to use an economist's term) was steep, and the penalties for producing below minimum efficient scale were severe. In others, such as soap, cereal, and similar branded packaged products, the cost gradient was less steep and the penalties for operating below minimum efficient scale were less severe. So too, the potential for exploiting the economies of scope varied widely from industry to industry.

Moreover, the optimal plant size for a specific product was related as much to existing demand as to the potential output of a technology. The number of plants in an industry that could operate at minimum efficient scale at a given point in time was limited by the size of the market for that industry's product. A plant, built at minimum efficient scale for an existing technology, that could produce more than the market could absorb had higher unit costs than a smaller plant whose output was more closely calibrated to market demand. In such a situation the optimal plant size would be smaller than the size of one built to the technology's minimum efficient scale. Therefore, I use the term "optimal plant size" to mean the most efficient size of a plant at a given time and place. The term reflects not only the state of the existing production technology but also the anticipated size of markets at the time the plant was built; furthermore, it reflects the elasticity of demand. Because the products of the new technologies were often new themselves (or much improved), the lower prices made possible by scale-or-scope economies greatly increased the demand, thus further increasing optimal plant size, at least until the technological limits were reached.

Both technologies and markets were dynamic. Changes in technology could increase or decrease minimum efficient scale. Changes in market size increased or decreased optimal plant size. In addition, the capital required to build a plant of optimal size varied from industry to industry. Steel mills needed much greater capital investments than did oil refineries, which in turn were more costly than factories producing cigarettes and other branded packaged products. For these reasons the sizes and costs of production plants differed widely from industry to industry.

Optimal size, as just defined, refers only to a production unit of the type described earlier, that is, a manufacturing establishment as defined in the U.S. Census, or its physically adjoining establishments, and not to the enterprise as a whole. Most enterprises became multiplant, for in few cases were single works of optimal size able to continue to meet the demand, particularly in growing markets. Decisions concerning where and when to build new plants involved a complex equation, one that changed as technology and markets changed. Key considerations included not only the cost advantages of operating at minimum efficient scale but also estimates of anticipated share of these markets, as well as size and location of markets plus transportation costs and other costs of distribution and supply. If the plant was to be in a foreign country, the costs resulting from tariff laws and other restrictive legislation needed to be computed. The relationship between the efficient size of plant and the efficient size of a multiplant enterprise is complex. But whatever the size of an investment in production, an enterprise could realize the cost advantages of that investment only if a management team effectively coordinated the fluctuating flow of a variety of materials into the several production facilities, through them, and then to the wholesalers, retailers, and final consumers.

Manufacturers quickly appreciated the importance of the relationship between cost and volume and the penalties of operating below minimum efficient scale. By the early twentieth century, managers, particularly in the United States, were using the concept of "over and under absorbed burden" as a way to place such variations in cost on their accounting sheets. If the plant operated at less than its standard volume (based on estimates of market size as well as anticipated throughput at rated capacity), the resulting loss was listed as "under absorbed burden"; if it operated at more than that volume the resulting gain was listed as "over absorbed burden."[9] Over and under absorbed burden became critical items on the cost sheets of individual plants and on the profit-and-loss accounts of the enterprise as a whole.

Economies of Scale and Scope in Distribution

The economies of scale and those of scope as measured by throughput in the production process help explain why large firms appeared in the industries where they did and when they did, but these economies do not explain why the firms initially grew in the way they did: that is, by integrating forward into distribution and backward into purchasing. The new mass producers might well have continued to buy from and sell to commercial intermediaries—particularly wholesalers and manufacturers' agents. By doing so they would have been spared the expense of investing in personnel and costly distribution and purchasing facilities. Explaining such vertical integration requires a more precise understanding of the processes of volume distribution—particularly why the wholesalers and other commercial intermediaries lost their cost advantage vis-à-vis the volume producer.

The intermediaries' cost advantage had resulted from exploiting the economies of both scale and scope. Because they handled the products of many manufacturers, they achieved a greater volume and lower costs per unit than did any one manufacturer in the marketing and distribution of a *single* line of products (scale). Moreover, they increased this advantage by the broader scope

Scale, Scope, and Organizational Capabilities 29

of their operation—that is, by handling a *number* of related product lines through a single set of facilities (scope). This was true of the new volume wholesalers and the new mass retailers—the department store, the mail-order house, and the chain store. These full-line wholesalers and mass retailers came into being only after the railroad, telegraph, steamship, and cable made possible new high-volume, high-speed, regularly scheduled transportation.

Both wholesalers and retailers were organized specifically to exploit the economies of scale and scope. The organizational core of a volume distributor was its buying departments, one for each major line handled. The buyers determined the price, the quantity, and the physical specifications (size, weight, and quality) of goods ordered. They were responsible for maintaining the high-volume flow of goods through the enterprise by working closely with its traffic department in arranging specific shipments and deliveries and with its selling force in arranging displays, catalogue copy, or advertising. The critical measure of performance in coordinating this flow through the enterprise was "stock-turn," that is, the volume of goods processed in relation to inventory by a single set of facilities and personnel within a specified period of time. Stock-turn was to mass distributors what throughput was to refiners and other mass producers. The greater the stock-turn, the more intensive the use of existing personnel, facilities, and capital invested in inventory; therefore, the lower the cost per unit. The buying departments, each coordinating the flow of a single line of products, were the units that permitted the new volume distributors to take advantage of economies of *scale*. The traffic departments, the selling facilities, and the geographically distant purchasing offices and facilities used by all the buying departments permitted the enterprise to achieve economies of *scope*—that is, to use the same facilities to market and distribute different products.

Yet the wholesalers' advantages of both scope and scale had their limits. When these limits were reached, it became more advantageous for the manufacturers themselves to make the investment in purchasing, marketing, and distribution facilities. When a manufacturer's volume attained a scale that would reduce the cost of transporting, storing, and distributing products to the level of that achieved by the wholesaler through his volume economies, the intermediary lost his cost advantage. As Scott Moss points out: "Provided that such a minimum efficient scale in transactions exists, the intermediary will have a cost advantage over its customers and suppliers only as long as the volume of transactions in which he engages comes closer to that scale than do the transactions volumes of his customers or suppliers."[10] A manufacturer of a single product rarely achieved such a volume in retailing, except in highly concentrated urban markets. On the other hand, he often did so in the wholesaling of both consumer and industrial goods.

Just as the volume distributor's cost advantages of scale were lost when the manufacturer increased his output to a volume that would bring comparable advantages, so the cost advantages of joint distribution or scope were reduced when products required specialized facilities and skills in their marketing and their distribution. (I use the term "marketing" to refer to promoting and selling goods and the term "distribution" to refer to the physical flow of goods from manufacturers to customers.) The more the products required such specialized skills and such specialized storage and transportation facilities, the less were the opportunities for the intermediary to achieve economies of scope resulting from the ability to handle a number of related products for a number of manufacturers. This was also true for transactions involved. If contractual arrangements for the sale and delivery of related products were relatively straightforward and standardized, then a single intermediary might easily handle all transactions involved in the distribution of a manufacturer's output. But if the transactions were complex, if specialized knowledge was required in order to sell, install, and maintain the products and to provide the necessary credit arrangements, and if costly specialized facilities were required to distribute the goods, then the intermediary had to hire personnel with these specialized skills and invest in these specialized facilities—skills and facilities that often were applicable to only one particular product line. Moreover, if the intermediary did make the investment in facilities and personnel, he became increasingly dependent on the few manufacturers of the product in question and on the cash flow needed to stay in business. The manufacturer, in addition, usually had a more accurate understanding of the specialized facilities, skills, and services required to distribute and market his specific products than did the wholesaler, who handled a variety of lines for a number of producers. Thus the increasing product-specificity of the investment required to market a product in volume reduced the intermediary's cost advantage and otherwise discouraged him from making the necessary investment. At the same time, of course, it increased the incentive of the manufacturer to make the expenditures.

Still another incentive for the manufacturer to invest in a sales force of his own was competition. The new production technologies with their historically unprecedented output created a new type of competition. In those industries where a few large plants could meet existing demand, these few quickly began to compete for a substantial share of national and often international markets. Cost advantages of scale reflected a manufacturer's market share. Normally, loss of share to a competitor not only increased his production costs but also decreased those of his competitor.

Thus in the new capital-intensive, oligopolistic industries the few large competitors could no longer afford to depend on commercial intermediaries who made their profits by handling products of more than one manufacturer. The manufacturers needed a sales force of their own to concentrate full-time on advertising, canvassing for customers, assuring delivery on schedule, and providing installation, service and repair, customer credit, and other services for their particular line of products. A sales force became the most dependable instrument for obtaining and holding a market share large enough to assure the cost advantages of scale. In addition, it provided a steady flow of information about markets and customer needs and tastes. In these ways the manufacturer's sales force reduced potentially high transaction costs.

For these reasons, as the scale of firms' output increased and as the specialized facilities and services required for volume distribution narrowed the intermediaries' potential to exploit the economies of scope, leading enterprises in the new capital-intensive industries invested in product-specific distribution facilities and recruited and trained personnel to provide specialized marketing services.

The motives for integrating backward by building a purchasing organization to take the place of commercial intermediaries were, of course, much the same as those for integrating forward into wholesaling. The establishment of a central purchasing office provided the enterprise with skilled, product-specialized buyers who searched out sources of supplies and contracted with suppliers on price, specification, and delivery date. They worked closely with their production departments to schedule flows and with the traffic departments which were responsible for the actual shipment of goods to the plants.

Although fewer product-specific services and facilities were needed in purchasing than in distribution, they were often quite essential in coordinating flows and reducing costs. The processors of branded packaged dairy and chocolate products and of canned milk, canned vegetables, and canned meat needed refrigerated storage facilities and careful scheduling to assure continuous year-in-and-year-out flows into the processing plants. Other processors, such as cigarette makers and distillers, whose raw materials required aging and curing, made comparable investments. Furthermore, the purchasing of manufactured supplies in volume directly from the manufacturers reduced costs just as it did for mass retailers. In these ways integrating backward into purchasing, like integrating forward into distribution, replaced the existing commercial intermediaries.

Building the Integrative Hierarchy

As I have emphasized, the initial step in the creation of the modern industrial enterprise was the investment in production facilities large enough to achieve the cost advantages of scale and scope. The second step, which often occurred almost simultaneously, was the investment in product-specific marketing, distributing, and purchasing networks. The third and final step was the recruiting and organizing of the managers needed to supervise functional activities pertaining to the production and distribution of a product, to coordinate and monitor the flow of goods through the processes, and to allocate resources for future production and distribution on the basis of current performance and anticipated demand.[11]

The resulting managerial hierarchies were established along functional lines. Each function was administered by a department (see Figure 1). The largest and first to be formed were those for production and sales, with a smaller one for purchasing. At the headquarters of these functional departments middle managers coordinated and monitored the activities of the lower-level managers who administered the enterprise's operating units—its several factories, its sales and purchasing offices, and its research laboratories. They also had to provide the incentive for plant and office managers to perform effectively, just as those lower-level executives had to motivate the operating personnel in their units. Normally, the functional departments were organized along the line-and-staff principle, with line officers having executive authority and staff officers having an advisory role. In production the line officers had charge of the specific processes used in the output of goods, and staff officers had charge of personnel records, labor relations, cost accounting, and quality and inventory control. In sales the line officers usually headed regions or managed specific products, while the staff officers were specialists in accounting, advertising, and market analysis. In addition, smaller departments were established to carry out other functional activities.

Of the smaller departments, research and development became one of the most significant in those enterprises operating in technologically advanced industries. The new enterprise's laboratories were created to assist in assuring proper control of production processes and in maintaining the quality of the product. The creation of a research organization geographically and administratively separate from production came only after the production and marketing organizations had been firmly established. In their early years such research departments concentrated on improving product and process; they also located new markets for existing products. Only in later years did they begin to develop new materials or finished goods for new markets.

The amount of investment in research reflected the technical complexities of the products and the production processes. Not surprisingly, industrial research in the United States and Europe remained concentrated in a small number of industries. In the United States in 1921 (the first year for which information is available), close to half the scientific personnel in industrial research were employed in two industries—chemicals and electrical equipment. Also not surprising was the close relation that developed between research managers and those in marketing and production.[12] The sales force maintained a careful watch on product performance and customer needs. Its managers worked closely with the product designers and plant managers, as well as laboratory chiefs, in improving both product and process. In the chemical and electrical machinery industries the resulting network of information flows became a major force in continuing technological innovation.

Scale, Scope, and Organizational Capabilities 33

Industrial firms invested in research and development for much the same reasons that they invested in marketing and distribution. Specialized firms existed in both areas, although there were far fewer specialized research firms than marketing firms. Like wholesalers and retailers, research and development firms made their profits by providing the same or related services to a number of manufacturers (scope). The manufacturer's primary interest, however, was in improving a specific product line. The improvement of products and processes required product-specific skills and facilities, as well as close coordination between marketing, plant, and laboratory personnel and the facilities handling that product. Moreover, in the technologically advanced industries, improved products and processes became major competitive weapons to maintain and enlarge market share. Whereas there was little incentive for a separate research firm to invest heavily in highly product-specific personnel and facilities, since its function was to serve many customers, the manufacturer with a strong proprietary interest in the development of his particular products had every incentive to do so. As a result, product-specific industrial research and development remained concentrated in the offices and laboratories of the integrated industrial enterprises. These firms, however, continued to use the specialized research companies, such as Arthur D. Little and Stone & Webster in the United States, for testing, setting standards, and other more routine, less proprietary activities. [13]

In addition to the departments for production and marketing and the smaller ones for purchasing and research and development, other smaller functional departments included traffic (to move goods over transportation networks), engineering (to construct plants and other facilities), legal, real estate, and, somewhat later, personnel and public relations. Again as in the case of research and development, the volume of activity and the product-specific nature of the tasks led to the creation of these smaller internal departments. The enterprise continued to rely on outside specialists for routine or part-time specialized assistance and advice.

The other large department was finance. Its functions were somewhat less product-specific. Its tasks were to coordinate the flow of funds through the enterprise's many units and to provide a steady flow of information to enable top management to monitor performance and allocate resources. The ability to plan and schedule cash flows was an important advantage gained from internalizing distribution units; for internalization eliminated the danger of delayed or intermittent payments from wholesalers—receipts whose steady flow was essential to pay suppliers and workers and to stabilize and reduce the costs of working capital. To provide information concerning performance and resource allocation, the financial department set up uniform accounting and auditing procedures. It also became responsible for external financial affairs, including the raising of new capital and the payment of dividends and interest on bonds.

The heads of the major functional departments, the president, and sometimes a full-time chairman of the board composed the senior decision-making unit of integrated industrial enterprises. In the United States these executives usually formed the Executive Committee of the Board; in Germany they made up the Vorstand. In Britain and Japan they became Managing or Executive Directors. Individually the full-time salaried top managers, the "inside directors" and their staffs, monitored the activities and performance of the middle managers who were responsible for the day-to-day operations of the functional departments. They supervised the flow of goods through the enterprise. Jointly they determined corporate policies, planned long-range strategy and allocated the resources—facilities and personnel—necessary to maintain the long-term health and growth of the enterprise. In making broad strategic decisions they worked closely with the "outside directors," the part-time representatives of families, banks, and other shareholders. The completed structures of these centralized, functionally departmentalized hierarchies were variations on the structure of the modern industrial enterprise (Figure 1), the central institution of managerial capitalism.

First-Mover Advantages and Oligopolistic Competition

The entrepreneurs who invested in plants big enough to exploit the economies of scale or scope in production, in product-specific facilities and skills in distribution (and also in research in technologically advanced industries), and in the managerial organization essential for coordination of those activities brought into being the modern industrial enterprise. The first to do so acquired powerful competitive advantages, or (to use the economists' term) "first-mover" advantages. This was particularly true in industries producing new or greatly improved products and using new and greatly improved processes. To compete with the first movers, rivals had to build plants of comparable size and make the necessary investment in distribution and, in some industries, in research. They also had to recruit and then train a managerial hierarchy. But to build a plant of the size needed to achieve comparable economies of scale or scope might mean that the total capacity of the industry would exceed the existing demand. Thus if latecomers were to maintain enough capacity utilization to assure competitive unit costs, they would have to take customers away from the first movers.

This was a challenging task. While the latecomer's production managers were learning the unique characteristics of what was usually a new or greatly improved technology and while its sales force was being recruited and trained, the first movers' managers had already worked out the bugs in the production processes. They had already become practiced in assuring prompt delivery. They knew how to meet customers' special needs and to provide demonstrations, consumer credit, installation, and after-sales repair and maintenance. In branded packaged products, where advertising was an important competitive weapon, the first movers were already investing some of the high profits resulting from low-cost operations in massive advertising campaigns.

The first movers had other advantages. In the more technologically complex industries the first to install research laboratories and to train technicians were the first to become fully aware of the attributes and intricacies of the new products and processes—an advantage that was often reinforced and expanded by patents. Moreover, in most of the new industries the latecomers had to make a much larger initial outlay of capital than their predecessors. They could rarely finance either the necessarily large investment in the scale of production or in the size of their marketing networks from retained earnings, as had the first movers, because to compete they had to build plants of comparable optimal size. The latecomers' investments not only had to be larger, they were also riskier, precisely because of the first movers' competitive strength.

Thus the first movers were not only the leaders in exploiting the cost advantages of scale and scope, but they had a head start in developing capabilities in all functional activities—production, distribution, purchasing, research, finance, and general management. Again to borrow a useful term from the economists, the first movers were apt to be well down the learning curve in each of the industry's functional activities before challengers went into full operation. Such advantages made it easy for first movers to nip challengers in the bud, to stop their growth before they acquired the facilities and developed the skills needed to become strong competitors. And such advantages could be and often were used ruthlessly.

This distinction between first movers and challengers is of major importance to this history. First in the development of a new set of improved products or processes came the inventors, usually the individuals who obtained the patent. Then came the pioneers, the entrepreneurs who made the investment in facilities needed to commercialize a product or process—to bring it into general use.[14] The first movers were pioneers or other entrepreneurs who made the three interrelated sets of investments in production, distribution, and management required to achieve the competitive advantages of scale, scope, or both, inherent in the new and improved products and processes. (I also use the term "first movers" for the enterprises thus created.) The challengers were the latecomers who took on the first movers by making a comparable set of investments and by developing comparable skills needed to obtain comparable competitive capabilities.

Although the barriers to entry into an industry that were raised by a first mover's investments were intimidating, challengers did appear. They came most often when rapid demographic changes had altered existing markets and when technological change had created new markets and diminished old ones. But in those industries where scale or scope provided cost advantages, the number of players remained small, and there was little turnover among the leaders. These industries quickly became and remained oligopolistic and occasionally monopolistic. A few large integrated firms competed for market share and profits in national and often world markets in what was a new, oligopolistic manner: they no longer competed primarily on price, as firms had done previously and as firms continued to do in the more fragmented labor-intensive industries. The largest firm (usually the first to make the three-pronged investment in production, distribution, and management) became the price leader, basing prices on estimates of demand in relation to its own plant capacities and those of its competitors.

Price remained a significant competitive weapon, but these firms competed more forcefully for market share and increased profits by means of functional and strategic efficiency, that is, by carrying out more capably the processes of production and distribution, by improving both product and process through systematic research and development, by locating more suitable sources of supply, by providing more effective marketing services, by product differentiation (in branded, packaged products, primarily through advertising), and finally by moving more quickly into expanding markets and out of declining ones.[15] The test of such competition was changing market share, and in most of the new oligopolistic industries market share and profits changed continually.

Competition for market share and profits tended to sharpen the skills of the middle managers responsible for the functional activities. It also tested and enlarged the skills of the top managers in their responsibilities for coordination, strategic planning, and resource allocation. The combined capabilities of top and middle management can be considered the skills of the organization itself. These skills were the most valuable of all those that made up the *organizational capabilities* of the new modern industrial enterprise.

These organizational capabilities included, in addition to the skills of middle and top management, those of lower management and the work force. They also included the facilities for production and distribution acquired to exploit fully the economies of scale and scope. Such capabilities provided the profits that in large part financed the continuing growth of the enterprise. Highly product-specific and process-specific, these organizational capabilities affected, indeed often determined, the direction and pace of the small number of first movers and challengers, and of the industries and even the national economies in which they operated.

Continuing Growth of the Modern Enterprise

Once the investment in production and distribution was large enough to exploit fully the economies of scale or scope, and once the necessary managerial hierarchy was in place, the industrial enterprise grew—it added new units—in four

Scale, Scope, and Organizational Capabilities   37

ways. One was by acquiring or merging with enterprises using much the same processes to make much the same product for much the same markets; that is, it grew by horizontal combination. Another was by taking on units involved in the earlier or later stages of making a product, from the mining or processing of raw materials to the final assembling or packaging; that is, it grew by vertical integration. The third way of growth was to expand geographically to distant areas. The fourth was to make new products that were related to the firm's existing technologies or markets. The initial motive for the first two strategies of growth was usually defensive, to protect the firm's existing investments. In the other two strategies, firms used their existing investments and above all their existing organizational capabilities—their facilities and skills—to move into new markets and into new businesses.

HORIZONTAL AND VERTICAL COMBINATION

In a large number of cases the incentive for acquisition or merger of enterprises producing competitive products was to gain more effective control of output, price, and markets. Such horizontal combination increased organizational capabilities and productivity *only* if a single, centralized administrative control was quickly established over the merged or acquired companies and then the facilities and personnel were rationalized to exploit more fully the economies of scale and scope. Such was the case, for example, when the Standard Oil associates legally consolidated to form the Standard Oil Trust. And such horizontal combination often permitted a number of pioneers to come together and then to make the investments in production and distribution and management necessary to achieve first-mover advantages. But if the companies acquired or those coming into the merger were not administratively centralized and rationalized but instead continued to operate autonomously much as they had before the change, the enlarged enterprise remained little more than a federation of firms. The resulting cost advantages were minimal.

The reasons for vertical integration—growth through obtaining facilities along the chain of production—were more complex. Faster throughput and with it significant cost reductions and increased productivity in terms of output per worker or unit of equipment rarely resulted from vertical integration unless the additional processes were directly connected to the firm's existing ones by its own rails, conveyors, or pipes. Such integration was particularly successful in the production of chemicals, metals, and machinery. Where the facilities to make related processes were located at a distance, increased throughput was less feasible.

The motive for such investments in growth by vertical integration was primarily defensive, but not in the same way as through horizontal combination. Sometimes the aim was to withhold supplies from competitors and so create barriers to entry in the industry. Far more often, however, the motive for such vertical integration was to assure a steady supply of materials into the enterprise's production processes, which was essential if the cost advantages of scale and scope were to be maintained. It provided insurance against great cost increases resulting from fluctuating production or even shutdown. It reduced the cost of high inventory storage and other carrying costs. It lowered the risk that suppliers would fail to carry out contractual agreements—risks from what economists and organizational theorists have termed "bounded rationality" (human fallibility) and "opportunism" (self-interest with guile). The greater the investment in capital-intensive facilities and the greater the optimal size of these facilities, the greater the incentive for insurance against such transaction costs. Thus the more concentrated the facilities of production and the more concentrated the sources of supply, the more likely was the integration of the two within a single enterprise.

Nevertheless, as long as such integration did not directly increase economies of scale or scope, as long as alternate sources of supply were available at a reasonable price, and as long as legal and personal ties and relationships helped to assure the fulfillment of contractual arrangements, manufacturers usually preferred to buy their supplies rather than invest in and manage the production of those supplies. If the investment was not made to reduce the cost of transaction risks, it might be made merely as a profitable portfolio investment. But most manufacturers preferred other routes to growth—those of adding units in areas and in products where their existing facilities and organizational capabilities gave them a distinct competitive advantage.

GEOGRAPHICAL EXPANSION AND PRODUCT DIVERSIFICATION

When managers of industrial enterprises combined horizontally or vertically for defensive or strategic reasons, they did so in response to specific historical situations that varied from time period to time period, from country to country, from industry to industry, even from firm to firm. For example, in the U.S. automobile industry during the interwar years, for specific historical reasons Ford remained fully vertically integrated, General Motors had a policy of controlling one-quarter of its suppliers, and Chrysler obtained nearly all of its supplies from independent producers (see Chapter 6).

Far more central to the continuing evolution of the modern industrial enterprise were the strategies that led to adding production units in distant places, usually abroad, and that led to manufacturing related products. Geographical expansion into distant markets provided a way for the enterprise to continue to exploit its competitive advantages, those based primarily on organizational capabilities that had been developed by exploiting economies of scale. Product diversification came from opportunities to use existing production, marketing, and research facilities and personnel by developing products for new and more profitable markets. Such expansion was based on organizational capabilities that

Scale, Scope, and Organizational Capabilities 39

had been developed by exploiting economies of scope. The efforts to utilize these organizationally based competitive advantages became the driving force—the underlying dynamic—in the growth of the modern industrial enterprise and industrial capitalism. The development and implementation of these two strategies of growth, carried out to employ more profitably the organizational capabilities that had been honed through functional competition, permitted the modern industrial enterprise to counter the bureaucratic inertia inherent in any hierarchical institution.

Obtaining distant production facilities obviously came after, not before, a first mover had made its initial investments in production, distribution, and management. The first expansion of production usually occurred at home with the enlargement of the original plant, particularly when such expansion brought greater economies of scale or scope. As the marketing organization was geographically extended and as the original plant reached minimum efficient scale, new plants were built to an optimal size based on the extent of the more distant domestic markets, on transportation costs, and on availability of materials and labor.

Much the same incentives led to direct investment abroad. In addition, tariff laws and other discriminatory legislation, by raising the cost of finished goods shipped across national borders, provided major reasons for constructing distant production facilities. At times factories were built to forestall competition in a new market, or to exploit potential market growth, or to produce a variation of the product line to meet local needs. In nearly every case, however, such investment was made on the assumption that the enterprise had a competitive advantage over local producers.[16]

The large integrated enterprise also expanded abroad, just as it did at home, for defensive reasons: to obtain assured sources of essential supplies, usually mineral or agricultural products, for its domestic and later its foreign processing plants. Again, it usually did so only when such supplies were not available at home and where local entrepreneurs had not developed the needed resource, as was often the case with direct investment in oil fields, mines, or rubber plantations.

The primary reason, however, for a firm's direct investment abroad was to expand its market share in distant countries and to lower the costs of making and selling its products in those markets. As I have already suggested, the decisions to establish plants abroad and to determine their size and location depended on a calculus that balanced, on the one hand, the costs of producing both primary and intermediate products in plants of optimal size with, on the other hand, the costs of transportation, distribution, tariffs, and other regulatory measures. For this reason most firms became multinational by building facilities to produce their basic lines in advanced rather than developing economies, for markets for new and improved industrial and consumer products were larger in those economies with high per-capita income. For this reason, too, such investment in distant production facilities followed, rather than preceded, that in marketing. [17]

Those first movers with the strongest competitive advantages went abroad most quickly. The first movers among American producers of mass-produced light machinery—sewing, office, and agricultural machines, automobiles (later), and a variety of comparable products, such as elevators and printing presses—were marketing and then producing abroad well before World War I. By that time the German producers of dyes and pharmaceuticals dominated world markets. By then, too, the first movers in Germany and the United States in the electrical equipment industry had taken over world markets. With the competitive advantages derived from economies of scale or scope these first movers long remained dominant firms in foreign countries, as well as in their own. By contrast, if an industry's technology of production provided little in the way of such competitive advantages, as was the case in the processing of natural fibers, the firms that went overseas rarely retained their initial market position.

Expansion by diversification into related industries—the other continuing strategy of growth—utilized the economies of scope at all three levels of the organization—the operating units, the functional departments, and the top or corporate office. And the stimuli for such diversification were both external and internal.

Changes in the environment often reduced demand for existing products and created markets for closely related ones. Basic technological innovations (electricity, electronics, and the internal combustion engine, for example), demographic shifts, and wars and depressions all affected product markets. In addition, as demand for existing products leveled off and as capacity became calibrated with or overreached existing demand, the search for new products intensified.

Internal stimulus came from the needs and opportunities to use existing facilities and capabilities more fully. [18] Indeed, the initial investment in facilities large enough to exploit the cost advantage of scale sometimes in itself encouraged new product development. Thus in the production of aluminum and synthetic ammonia the scale economies were so high that the aluminum and chemical companies had to search for new products that could take some of the output of the most efficient plants.

An impetus to diversification at the operating level was the emergence of by-products, such as fertilizer, soap, and glue in meatpacking and petrochemicals in oil refining. But unless the volume of output was high enough to warrant the creation of a new and separate marketing organization, these by-products remained by-products, and were marketed through wholesalers or other intermediaries who sold related products and so could continue to benefit from their economies of scope. Where the volume was large enough, as it was in the case

Scale, Scope, and Organizational Capabilities   **41**

of fertilizer and leather for the largest meatpackers, nationwide sales organizations were established, managers hired, and integrated subenterprises or divisions were thus formed to market such products and to coordinate the flow of goods through the enterprise.

The most common stimulus to diversification, however, was the potential for economies of scope existing in an enterprise's major functional units—production, distribution, and research. At most enterprises the first step toward such product diversification was the development of a full line that exploited the firm's facilities and capabilities in all three major activities. Thus a reaper company and a plow company began to compete directly as each moved into the other's markets by developing a full line of agricultural implements. So, too, automobile manufacturers embarked on producing and distributing a full line of cars, trucks, buses, and other commercial vehicles. Although the expansion of the line often required the building of new plants or even new sales departments, such growth relied primarily on expanding existing facilities or adding comparable ones using existing capabilities.

When diversification moved beyond producing a full line, the story was different. Where it came by exploiting the economies of scope in production to make goods sold in new and different markets, new marketing personnel and facilities had to be acquired. When American agricultural-equipment companies entered the construction-equipment business, when German dye makers moved into pharmaceuticals, or when Du Pont's rayon division developed cellophane, they all made more effective use of existing production facilities and personnel and of existing intermediate processes and materials. All also had to recruit and train new sales forces. Often, too, the resulting integration of production and distribution led to the formation of research and development units for each of the new product lines.

Where diversification resulted from the economies of scope in marketing and distribution, the establishment of new processing and purchasing units was often called for. Such economies existed because distribution and marketing networks, even though product-specific, could be used to handle more than a single product line. Thus the meatpackers began to send dairy products and fruit through their refrigerated networks. Distribution facilities created to assure daily delivery of fresh yeast to bakers and brewers were easily adapted to daily delivery of ground coffee to grocers. Nonrefrigerated facilities for moving one type of processed grain product could be used for others; and capabilities in marketing one set of branded packaged products were easily transferable to another.

In research and development, which was concentrated in the technologically advanced industries, facilities and organizational capabilities were even less product-specific and the opportunities to exploit economies of scope were even greater than in production and distribution. The knowledge required for research and development came from physics, chemistry, and other sciences, disciplines that far transcended the needs of one product line. The scientific disciplines acquired to improve processes and products in explosives were transferable to the development of new chemically produced fibers, fabrics, films, and plastics, as well as better paints, varnishes, and other finishes, since those products were all based on the same cellulose technology. The scientific training needed to improve machinery for the generation and transmission of electricity was applicable to developing electrical appliances, vacuum tubes, X-ray and electronic equipment, and other technologically complex devices.

Even more important, the chemical producers and electrical manufacturers had mastered the specialized technical and organizational skills needed to move a new or improved product into full commercial use: that is, they became even more skilled in development than in research. They understood the complexities that are inherent in market research, in building pilot plants and then in scaling up production facilities to minimum efficient size, and in recruiting and training a nationwide sales network—activities that absorb by far the greatest part of the cost of completing successfully the long haul from product innovation to volume production for world markets.

Finally, successful diversification required a team of experienced managers at corporate headquarters capable of monitoring and allocating resources for not one but several product lines. They not only had to evaluate current performance and functional competitive effectiveness in each of several product lines, but they also had to decide whether to expand or contract long-term investment in the lines. Of even more importance for the long-term performance of the enterprise, they had to determine whether or not to initiate research and development on a new product. Above all, they had to decide whether or not to make the extensive investment necessary to build production facilities of optimal size, and to recruit the management and the sales force needed to produce and sell a product that might not show a profit for many years after its development was authorized or even several years after the investment in production and other operating facilities had been made. Such evaluations and decisions called for managers experienced in the technological and marketing processes on which the competitive advantage of the new product rested. It was in carrying out a continuous strategy of growth through product diversification that the economies of scope at the enterprise level, as differentiated from the functional level, had their greatest significance.

Growth by adding units abroad or in related industries led to a modification of the enterprise's administrative structure.[19] Initially expansion abroad called for only a moderate adjustment—the formation of an international committee and then an international department to supervise distant marketing and distribution. In the few cases where overseas investment was primarily in basic materials, the supervisory body often became known as the raw materials

Scale, Scope, and Organizational Capabilities　　　　43

department. Only after extensive expansion overseas did an enterprise adopt a multidivisional structure by which major geographical regions were administered through integrated area divisions.

Diversification into related industries brought far more thoroughgoing administrative restructuring. Diversifying companies adopted, some more quickly than others, a multidivisional structure (see Figure 2). This structural change came when the senior managers realized that they had neither the time nor the necessary information to coordinate and monitor day-to-day operations and at the same time devise and implement long-term plans for the several product lines. The administrative overload had simply become too great. The solution was to establish a structure consisting of divisional offices to administer each of the major product lines and a general or corporate office to administer the enterprise as a whole.

Each divisional office included a general manager, his staff, and the heads of the functional activities involved. The general manager was fully responsible for his division's performance and profits. In other words, each division became a replica of the enterprise's original centralized, functionally departmentalized organization, except that the highest ranking officer in the division had become a middle manager reporting to the top executives in the corporate office. Each division competed functionally and strategically with other firms or with the divisions of other firms within the same industry.

At the corporate office the top managers became general executives without day-to-day operating responsibilities. They concentrated on continually evaluating performance of the operating divisions and on planning and implementing long-term corporate strategy through the allocation of funds, facilities, and personnel. They were assisted by a corporate staff who provided a constant flow of information and offered specialized skills, not only to the general executives at the corporate headquarters but also to the middle managers who headed the operating divisions. The corporate staff included the enterprise's enlarged financial department with its specialists in accounting, auditing, and other numbers-oriented activities. It also included a corporate personnel office that collected information on the training and experience of both employees and managers. Its central research laboratory helped to provide technological advice and develop new products and processes not clearly related to the work of the divisional laboratories. Its development department planned corporate strategy. Often there were corporate offices for marketing and production. These corporate staff departments remained only advisory, not decision-making offices, but they enhanced the capabilities of the organization as a whole by providing a systematic and continuous internal exchange of information on new developments in facilities, processes, and products.

The multidivisional structure was the administrative response to growth based on further utilization of firms' organizational capabilities. A division was

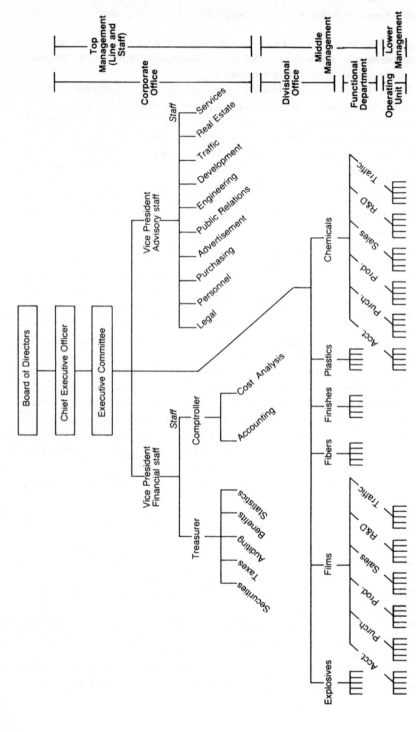

Figure 2. The multidivisional structure.

responsible for a single product line, or in some cases for a geographical area. In other words, the multidivisional structure provided the means to administer several different, though related, product lines; and it also provided the means to administer a single line which was sold worldwide by creating comparable integrated divisions for major geographical regions.[20] Thus the corporate office was able to monitor and advise and so to increase the competitive capabilities of the several divisions. In this manner diversified, multidivisional enterprises were able to intensify competition within the industry or region into which they moved and at the same time to transfer resources from older, more stable industries or markets to newer, more dynamic ones.[21]

The Modern Enterprise in Labor-Intensive Industries

It should be stressed that these broad descriptive patterns and the resulting explanations of the dynamics of the modern industrial enterprise relate to those industries where the technologies of production had the potential for extensive economies of scale and scope and where product-specific marketing organizations provided further competitive advantages. Where this was *not* the case— that is, in industries where, owing to their technology, the optimal size of plant was small, where mass distribution did not require specialized skills and facilities, and where coordination of flows was a relatively simple task—manufacturers had much less incentive to make the three-pronged investment in production, distribution, and management. In the more labor-intensive industries, such as publishing and printing, lumber, furniture, textiles, apparel, leather, seasonal and specialized food processing, and specialized instruments and machinery, the large integrated firm had few competitive advantages. In some, such as textiles and lumber, careful coordination of flows within manufacturing units did increase throughput and lower unit costs. Also costs were often lowered by producing a variety of differently designed items from the same machines and materials. But the resulting cost advantages were far fewer than those in the capital-intensive industries. They rarely created major barriers to entry. Indeed size, by making the large firm less flexible in meeting changes in demand and style, might be a competitive disadvantage. This was often the case in apparel (both cloth and leather) and in a number of industries processing food and drink. In the labor-intensive industries many small single-unit firms continued to prosper, and in them competition continued to be based on price and the ability to move quickly with changing demand.

Significantly, it was in several of these more fragmented industries—textiles, apparel, furniture, and some food processing—that the mass retailers (the department stores, mail-order houses, and chain stores) began to coordinate the flow of goods from manufacturer to consumer. In those industries where substantial economies of scale and scope did not exist in production, high-

Introduction: Scale and Scope   46

volume flows through the processes of production and distribution came to be guided—and the resulting cost reductions achieved—by the buying departments of mass retailers, retailers who handled a variety of related products through their facilities. Their efficiency, in turn, further reduced the economic need for the wholesaler as a middleman between the manufacturer and the retailer.

Where the economies of scale and scope and the creation of product-specific marketing organizations did bring competitive advantage, the history of the modern industrial enterprise followed in a general way the patterns outlined in this chapter. Here I have attempted to provide the framework—that is, the common terminology, the set of concepts, and the explanatory theory—that is needed to comprehend fully the complex, interrelated historical developments described in the following chapters.

Notes

1. Most succinctly defined by Oliver Williamson in his "Modern Corporation: Origins, Evolution, Attributes," *Journal of Economic Literature* 19:1539–44 (Dec. 1981); also in his "Organizational Innovation: The Transaction Cost Approach," in Joshua Ronen, ed., *Entrepreneurship* (Lexington, Mass., 1983), ch. 5.
2. David Teece, "Economies of Scope and the Scope of the Enterprise," *Journal of Economic Behavior and Organization* 1:223–247 (Sept. 1980); John C. Panzar and Robert D. Willig, "Economics of Scope," *American Economic Review* 71:268–272 (May 1981). See also Elizabeth E. Bailey and Ann F. Friedlaender, "Market Structure and Multiproduct Industries," *Journal of Economic Literature* 20:1084–1148 (Sept. 1982). The emphasis of this literature is on economies of scope in production, not in distribution.
3. Again the most succinct definition comes from Williamson, "The Modern Corporation," pp. 1547–49, which builds on Ronald Coase's classic article, "The Nature of the Firm," *Economica* 4:386–405 (Nov. 1937). In his piece Williamson states that "the criterion for organizing commercial transactions is assumed to be the strictly instrumental one of cost economizing. Essentially this takes two parts: economizing on production expenses and economizing on transaction costs. In fact, these are not independent and need to be addressed simultaneously." Williamson, however, does not differentiate between *distribution* expenses and transaction costs—costs that are largely defined in contractual terms. As Herman Daems has suggested, three types of transaction costs can be identified: contractual arrangements with customers, those with suppliers, and those with banks or other financial institutions or individuals.
4. A compilation by Herman Daems indicates that these firms generated an impressive share of the noncommunist world's employment in industry. Of the broad industrial categories in which the large firm clustered—food, chemicals, petroleum, metals, and the three machinery SIC groups—those firms employing more than 30,000 accounted in all the categories except food and nonelectrical machinery for from 39.5% to 72% of the total world's labor force in their industry. Herman Daems, "Power versus Efficiency: A Cross-Section Study of Chandler's *Visible Hand*," in François Caron, ed., *Entreprises et Entrepreneurs* (Paris, 1983).
5. I use the term "minimum efficient scale" as defined by such industrial organization economists as F. M. Scherer and William G. Shepherd, whose work, in turn, rests on that of George Stigler and Joe S. Bain, done in the 1950s and 1960s, on the relationship of "minimum optimal scale" to market share. This literature is effectively summarized by F. M. Scherer, "Economies of Scale and Industrial Concentration," in Harvey J. Goldschmid et al., eds., *Industrial Concentration: The New Learning* (Boston, 1974), esp. pp. 51–55; and by William G. Shepherd, *The Economics of Industrial Organization*, 2d ed. (Englewood Cliffs, N.J., 1985), chs. 9–10. My definition differs in emphasizing that minimum efficient scale depends on both capacity and throughput and thus can only be achieved by managerial coordination. An early and particularly useful application of these concepts to long-term development is Leonard W. Weiss, "The Survival Technique and the Extent of Suboptimal Capacity," *Journal of Political Economy* 72: 246–261 (June 1965). The

term "scale" as used in this chapter and the following ones refers primarily to continuous flow processes, but it can pertain to batch processes, as suggested in Armen Alchian, "Costs and Outputs," in Moses Abramovitz et al., *The Allocation of Economic Resources: Essays in Honor of Bernard Francis Haley* (Stanford, 1959), pp. 23–40.

6. Ralph W. Hidy and Muriel E. Hidy, in their *Pioneering in Big Business, 1882–1911* (New York, 1955), pp. 14–23, 44–46, describe the financial arrangements that unified the Standard Oil alliance.

7. Hidy and Hidy, *Pioneering in Big Business,* p. 107, gives costs and profits for 1884 and 1885; also Harold F. Williamson and Arnold R. Daum, *The American Petroleum Industry: The Age of Illumination, 1859–1899* (Evanston, Ill., 1959), pp. 482–484.

8. L. F. Haber, *The Chemical Industry during the Nineteenth Century: A Study of the Economic Aspect of Applied Chemistry in Europe and North America* (Oxford, 1958), pp. 128–136; and John J. Beer, *The Emergence of the German Dye Industry* (Urbana, 1959), p. 119; Sachio Kaku, "The Development and Structure of the German Coal-Tar Dyestuffs Firms," in Akio Okochi and Hoshimi Uchida, eds., *Development and Diffusion of Technology* (Tokyo, 1979), p. 78.

9. Alfred D. Chandler, Jr., *The Visible Hand: The Managerial Revolution in American Business* (Cambridge, Mass., 1977), p. 379.

10. Scott J. Moss, *An Economic Theory of Business Strategy: An Essay in Dynamics without Equilibrium* (Oxford, 1981), pp. 110–111. The application of the concept of minimum efficient scale to the understanding of the evolution of the enterprise is one of several major contributions of Moss's study. Particularly valuable are the concepts spelled out in his chapters 6 and 7 on vertical integration.

11. A detailed example of recruiting and organizing such a hierarchy is given in Alfred D. Chandler, Jr., and Stephen Salsbury, *Pierre S. du Pont and the Making of the Modern Corporation* (New York, 1971), pp. 132–148.

12. In the United States, General Electric, Westinghouse, Eastman Kodak, and Du Pont all provide good examples of this relationship during their pioneering years. See Harold C. Passer, *The Electrical Manufacturers, 1875–1900: A Study in Competition, Entrepreneurship, Technical Change, and Economic Growth* (Cambridge, Mass., 1960), pp. 263–264; Reese V. Jenkins, *Images and Enterprise: Technology and the American Photographic Industry, 1839–1925* (Baltimore, 1975), pp. 116, 120, 183–187 (esp. 184); Chandler and Salsbury, *Pierre S. du Pont,* pp. 140, 142–143; David A. Hounshell and John Kenly Smith, Jr., *Science and Corporate Strategy: Du Pont R&D, 1902–1980* (Cambridge, Eng., 1988), esp. chs. 1, 2, and 8. For German examples see Chapters 12 and 14 of this study.

13. David C. Mowery, "The Emergence and Growth of Industrial Research in American Manufacturing, 1899–1945" (Ph.D. diss., Stanford University, 1981), ch. 5, and Mowery, "The Relationship between Intrafirm and Contractual Forms of Industrial Research, 1900–1941" (Paper, Harvard Business School, July 1982).

14. The term "pioneers" as used here is close to "innovators" as used by Joseph Schumpeter, that is, entrepreneurs who put new processes of production and new products into use. Because the words "innovator" and "innovation" have been so widely used in so many contexts since Schumpeter's day, I prefer the more neutral descriptive term "pioneers."

15. The literature on functional and strategic competition is voluminous. Because such competition has been central in the administration of industrial companies, this literature has been used for decades in courses in production, marketing, purchasing, control, and policy taught in American business schools. Michael Porter,

Competitive Strategy: Techniques for Analyzing Industries and Competitors (New York, 1980), cogently describes the current thinking about such competition.

16. Stephen H. Hymer was the first to point out that the modern industrial enterprise moved abroad to exploit the competitive advantages based on the organizational capabilities of a managerial hierarchy. See particularly his "Multinational Corporation and the Law of Uneven Development," in J. W. Bhagwati, ed., *Economics and World Order* (New York, 1971), pp. 113–140, and his "Efficiency (Contradictions) of Multinational Corporations," *American Economic Review* 60:441–448 (May 1970). See also Charles P. Kindleberger, *American Business Abroad: Six Lectures on Direct Investment* (New Haven, 1969); and Richard E. Caves, "International Corporations: The Industrial Economics of Foreign Investment," *Economica* 38: 1–27 (Feb. 1971).

17. For example, S. J. Nicholas reports from a sample of 119 British firms: "In all cases for which information was available, 99% of all British multinationals had agency agreements and 70% had overseas travelers before the initial foreign investments." S. J. Nicholas, "British Multinational Investment before 1939," *Journal of Economic History* 11:620–621 (Winter 1982). This was true of both North American and German multinationals. Also, as John H. Dunning has noted concerning manufacturing subsidiaries established abroad by multinationals before 1914, 87.7% of those that were U.S.-based were in developed economies, as were 73.7% of those that were U.K.-based and 81.0% of those that were European-based. John H. Dunning, "Changes in Level and Structure of International Production: The Last One Hundred Years," in Mark Casson, ed., *The Growth of International Business* (London, 1983), p. 90.

18. Those stimuli to growth by diversification were first emphasized by Edith Penrose, *A Theory of the Growth of the Firm* (Oxford, 1959), esp. chs. 5 and 7; they were more fully developed by Scott J. Moss in his *Economic Theory of Business Strategy,* esp. pp. 51–64 (where he considers carefully the effect of the external environment). David Teece's excellent "Towards an Economic Theory of the Multiproduct Firm," *Journal of Economic Behavior and Organization,* 3:39–63 (March 1982), considers the economics of scope inherent in the modern industrial enterprise. Teece says (p. 47), "A specialized firm's generation of excess resources, both managerial and technical, and their fungible character is critical to the theory of diversification advanced here."

19. Alfred D. Chandler, Jr., *Strategy and Structure: Chapters in the History of the American Industrial Enterprise* (Cambridge, Mass., 1962), esp. chs. 2, 3, and 7.

20. Ibid., ch. 4.

21. This generalization refers, of course, to enterprises that moved into related products by direct investment and not, as did the conglomerates of the 1960s and 1970s, into unrelated products through acquisition. See the concluding chapter of this book.

[12]

ELSEVIER

European Economic Review 40 (1996) 511–530

EUROPEAN
ECONOMIC
REVIEW

Schumpeter lecture

Technology and market structure [1]

John Sutton [*]

The Toyota Centre, STICERD, London School of Economics, Houghton Street, London WC2A 2AE, UK

Abstract

This paper re-examines the relationship between the R&D intensity of an industry and its level of concentration, from the perspective of the Bounds approach to market structure. In so doing, it proposes an index which summarises those aspects of technology and tastes that are relevant to the determination of a lower bound to concentration.

JEL classification: L1; L11

Keywords: Technology; Market structure; Industrial structure

1. Background

This paper takes a new look at a widely-studied question: is there any systematic relationship between the nature of the technology in an industry, and its equilibrium market structure? It approaches this question from the point of view of the 'Bounds' approach to market structure, following Sutton (1991).

In order to provide a focus for what that follows, we begin by looking at a relationship that many authors have seen as providing an important clue in unravelling the relationship between technology and market structure: the alleged correlation across industries between R&D intensity (the ratio of R&D to Sales) and some measure of sales concentration. The search for a correlation between these variables has attracted ongoing attention in the literature over the past thirty years, but no clear consensus has emerged.

---

[*] Tel.: +44 171 955 7716; fax: +44 171 242 2357; e-mail: n.s.lippincott@lse.ac.uk
[1] This paper offers a brief sketch of an argument that will be developed at greater length in Sutton (1996); for fuller details, the reader is referred to that volume.

512   J. Sutton / European Economic Review 40 (1996) 511–530

One question raised in the early literature on this relationship was whether the 'direction of causation' ran from concentration to R & D intensity or vice versa. This dispute faded out in the late 1970s with the widespread acceptance of the view that these were both endogenous variables and they should be seen as being simultaneously determined within an equilibrium system (Phillips, 1971; Dasgupta and Stiglitz, 1980). This left open the question of what empirically identifiable characteristics of the technology might be used as exogenous 'explanatory variables'. Different industries clearly had quite different 'R & D technologies', but these technologies varied in so many different ways that it was not easy for researchers to agree on any description of the salient features of the different technologies that could command general acceptance [2].

Meanwhile, research continued on the empirical relation, which – these theoretical disputes notwithstanding – might be regarded as an empirically interesting 'reduced-form' relationship. The most authoritative review of the evidence is that of Cohen and Levin (1989) in the Handbook of Industrial Organisation. The authors note that most papers on the question report a positive relation, though some find a negative relation, while others argue for a non-monotonic relation. Results change substantially when industry-specific effects are controlled for, but there is no general agreement on what kind of control variables are appropriate, though many authors favour including some index of 'technological opportunity'. Most tellingly, once such control variables are included, the partial correlation between R & D intensity and concentration is very weak. The authors cite the example of the study by Scott (1984) which found that "line of business concentration and its square explained only 1.5 percent of the variance in R & D intensity across 3388 business units, whereas fixed two-digit industry effects explained 32 percent of this variance". Other studies, such as Levin et al. (1985), confirm the weakness of the observed effect. It is against this background that the conflicting claims as to the shape of the relationship should be judged.

Casual empiricism casts doubt on the existence of any simple relationship between concentration and R & D-intensity. Examples of industries that have low concentration but are highly R & D-intensive are familiar, especially in sectors such as Instrumentation. But examples of this kind are often dismissed on the grounds that they involve industries whose product lines are many and various, the implication being that if we only had data 'at the right level of aggregation', then they would be seen to consist of several sub-industries, each of which was highly concentrated. Whether this is so, is a question to which we turn in Section 4 below.

It will be suggested below that the mixed empirical results regarding the nature of the relationship between R & D-intensity and concentration are not surprising

---

[2] See, for example, Temin (1984). For attempts to control for industry differences by allowing for differences in 'technological opportunities', see Scherer (1980, pp. 434–436).

J. Sutton / European Economic Review 40 (1996) 511–530 513

for two reasons. First, it is claimed that measured R&D intensity does not serve as an adequate summary description of the relevant technological characteristic of an industry (and that the same is true of measures that combine R&D intensity with a measure of 'technological opportunity'). Second, it is claimed that the link between R&D intensity and concentration involves a 'Bounds' constraint, which is poorly captured by any regression specification.

In what follows, we propose a single index of industry characteristics that is sufficient for the purpose of determining a lower bound to concentration. This number, which is introduced in Section 3 and is referred to as 'alpha', can not be measured directly, but information about its value can be deduced from a pair of observable industry characteristics, one of which is the R&D/Sales ratio.

2. An example

We begin with an example that shows how an industry can have a high R&D/Sales ratio, together with an arbitrarily low level of concentration.

In the standard 'linear demand' model, a population of S identical consumers have a utility function defined over n substitute goods, as follows: [3]

$$U(x_1, x_2, \ldots x_n) = \sum_k (x_k - x_k^2) - 2\sigma \sum_k \sum_{\ell < k} x_k x_\ell + M \tag{1}$$

where M denotes money spent on outside goods, i.e.

$$M = M_0 - \sum_k p_k x_k .$$

The parameter σ, $0 \leq \sigma \leq 1$, is a measure of the degree of substitution between the goods. If $\sigma = 1$, the goods are perfect substitutes, and if $\sigma = 0$ the goods are independent in the sense that all cross-elasticities of demand are zero.

In what follows, we extend this standard example, following Sutton (1995), to the case in which goods differ in quality. The utility function becomes

$$U = \sum_k \left[x_k - \frac{x_k^2}{u_k^2} \right] - 2\sigma \sum_k \sum_{\ell < k} \frac{x_k}{u_k} \cdot \frac{x_\ell}{u_\ell} + M$$

---

[3] This expression defines utility over the domain of $\{x_k\}$ for which the marginal utilities u_k are non-negative. The consumer's optimal purchases will be inside this domain for all positive price vectors. It is assumed that the consumer's income M_0 is sufficiently large to ensure that the solution to the optimization problem is the interior solution defined by the set of first-order conditions, $u_k = p_k$, for all k. The demand schedule for each good k is linear, as follows by inspection of (1).

where $u_k \geq 1$ denotes the quality of good k. The individual consumer's inverse demand schedule now becomes

$$p_k = 1 - \frac{2 x_k}{u_k^2} - \frac{2\sigma}{u_k} \sum_{k \neq \ell} \frac{x_\ell}{u_\ell}$$

so that an increase in u_k shifts the (linear) demand schedule outwards.

Now suppose N firms each offer a single product to a population of S consumers, the quality of firm i's product being u_i. Let each good be produced at constant marginal cost c. Then at a Nash equilibrium in quantities (Cournot equilibrium), a routine calculation establishes that the profit of firm i is given by

$$\pi\left(u_i | N, \bar{u}\right) = \frac{1}{2} \left\{ \frac{u_i + \left[\sigma/(2-\sigma)\right] N(u_i - \bar{u})}{2 + (N-1)\sigma} \right\}^2 (1 - c)^2 S \qquad (2)$$

over the range of u_i such that good i, and at least one other good, have positive output at equilibrium, and where $\bar{u}$ denotes the average quality of all goods that have positive output at equilibrium. [4]

We now consider a 3-stage game as follows. At stage 1, firms decide whether or not to enter. At stage 2, each of the N firms that have entered offers a single product of some quality u_i, and incurs a fixed cost

$$F(u_i) = u_i^\beta, \qquad u_i \geq 1, \quad \beta > 2. \qquad (3)$$

In the final stage, firms compete à la Cournot and earn profits given by Eq. (2). A subgame perfect equilibrium is easily computed, following Sutton (1991, Ch. 3). The two necessary conditions for a symmetric equilibrium in which N firms offer quality $v > 1$ are as follows:

(Free entry)

$$\pi(v | N, v) = F(v), \qquad (4)$$

(Choice of quality)

$$\left. \frac{\partial \pi}{\partial u_i} \right|_{u_i = v} = \left. \frac{dF}{du_i} \right|_{u_i = v}. \qquad (5)$$

Now combining Eqs. (3), (4) and (5) we obtain

$$\left. \frac{u_i}{\pi} \frac{\partial \pi}{\partial u_i} \right|_{u_i = v} = \left. \frac{u_i}{F} \frac{dF}{du_i} \right|_{u_i = v} = \beta \qquad (6)$$

---

[4] Where $u_i \leq [N\sigma/(2 + (N-1)\sigma]\bar{u}$, good i has output zero at equilibrium, and $\pi(u_i | N, \bar{u}) = 0$. Where all of firm i's rivals offer qualities below $(\sigma/2)u_i$, good i is the only good with positive output at equilibrium, and $\pi(u_i | N, \bar{u}) = (S/8)u_i^2$.

J. Sutton / European Economic Review 40 (1996) 511–530   515

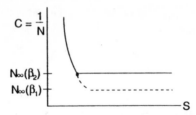

Fig. 1. Market size and concentration in the 'linear demand' example, for two values of β, where $\beta_2 < \beta_1$.

while from (2) we obtain, on writing $N\bar{u} = u_i + (N-1)v$, differentiating with respect to u_i, and simplifying, that

$$\frac{u_i}{\pi} \cdot \frac{\partial \pi}{\partial u_i}\bigg|_{u_i = v} = 2\left\{ 1 + \frac{\sigma}{2 - \sigma}(N - 1) \right\}. \tag{7}$$

We need to assume that β is 'sufficiently large' to ensure that these first-order conditions define a global maximum. Using Eq. (7) to express (6) in explicit form, we obtain an expression for the equilibrium number of firms, viz.

$$N = 1 + \left(\frac{2}{\sigma} - 1\right)\left(\frac{\beta}{2} - 1\right) \tag{8}$$

and so for the (one-firm) concentration ratio $C_1 = 1/N$.

The interesting feature of Eq. (8) is that N is independent of market size S. This is (a special case of) a well-known phenomenon: if market size is sufficiently small, firms find it optimal to enter with the lowest possible quality level $v = 1$, thereby incurring a fixed outlay of unity (Eq. (3)). [5] Once market size reaches a critical level, however, further increases in market size are associated, not with further entry, but with an escalation of fixed outlays. Given the functional form chosen for $F(u)$ here, we obtain a very simple outcome, under which N remains constant as S increases (Fig. 1). [6] We label this limiting value of N as N_∞, and the corresponding concentration level $1/N_\infty$ as $\underline{C}_1$.

What, then, determines the limiting level of concentration $\underline{C}_1$? From (8), we see that for a given value of β, $\underline{C}_1$ is lower according as σ is lower. A fall in the substitution parameter σ shifts the balance of incentives away from an escalation of spending aimed at raising u, and towards the introduction of new varieties. Conversely, for any fixed value of σ, a lower value of β implies a higher level of

[5] In this regime, $v = 1$ and (5) is replaced by an inequality constraint. Recall that the above characterisation applies to an equilibrium in which $v > 1$ (see Sutton, 1991, Ch. 3.)

[6] A slightly more general form for F allows the equilibrium value of N to rise or fall towards its asymptotic value as $S \to \infty$. What is general, in these models, is the idea that C_1 does not converge to zero as $S \to \infty$ (Sutton, 1991, Ch. 3).

516   J. Sutton / European Economic Review 40 (1996) 511–530

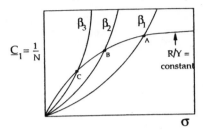

Fig. 2. Concentration and R&D intensity in the 'linear demand' example. The locus of constant R/Y is given by Eq. (9) of the text. The family of loci labelled by β correspond to Eq. (8) for different values of β, where $\beta_1 > \beta_2 > \beta_3$. The sequence of points labelled A, B, C correspond to different (β, σ) pairs for which R/Y is constant, while concentration declines.

concentration. The intuition here is that lowering β makes it cheaper to improve technical performance. Rather than attracting entry, this encourages escalation, leading to a rise in fixed outlays and a fall in the number of firms.

We now turn to the determination of R&D intensity in this example. Since the only fixed cost in this example is identified with R&D, it follows from the zero profit condition that total industry R&D must coincide at equilibrium with industry gross profit, whence the R&D/Sales ratio must equal the level of unit margins. In other words, if we denote equilibrium price by p, industry R&D spending by R, and industry sales by Y we have

$$\frac{R}{Y} \equiv \frac{NF}{Y} = \frac{N\pi}{Y} = \frac{N(p-c)x}{Npx} = \frac{p-c}{p}.$$

A routine computation of the level of unit margins at equilibrium yields

$$\frac{R}{Y} = \frac{p-c}{p} = \frac{1}{1 + [c/(1-c)] \cdot [2 + (N-1)\sigma]}. \tag{9}$$

The equilibrium level of unit margins depends on β only indirectly, through the effect of β on N, and so on $\underline{C}_1 = 1/N_\infty$. This follows from the fact that equilibrium margins are determined in the final stage subgame, in which N, but not β, enters as a parameter.

The point of this example is to show how high R&D intensity can coincide with low concentration. By combining a low value of β with a low value of σ, we can make $\underline{C}_1$ arbitrarily small, for a given level of R/Y (Fig. 2). [7]

---

[7] It is perhaps worth noting that these relationships take a particularly simple form in this example because of the link between R/Y and unit margins, the latter being linked to σ in an obvious way. This reflects two special features of this example: all fixed outlays are identified with R&D, and the equilibria are symmetric. In the general setting analysed in the next section, this identification of the R&D/Sales ratio with unit margins does not hold.

The intuition behind this result is as follows: R & D spending can be used either to enhance the quality of some existing variety, or to introduce a new variety. In this example, the substitution parameter σ and the parameter β serve to measure the relative profitability of raising the quality of some variety, versus introducing a new variety. When σ is small and/or β is high, 'proliferation' dominates 'escalation' and we get an outcome in which concentration is low. If we combine a reduction in σ with an offsetting reduction in β, we can keep concentration constant while raising the level of R & D intensity.

2.1. Towards a more general setting

This example, though useful in motivating ideas, is too restrictive to provide a basis for empirical analysis. In the next section, we turn to a more abstract setting. We look at some features of the above example that carry over to a general class of models which share some simple properties. One price we pay in moving to this more general setting is that we can not identify a unique 'equilibrium outcome'. We can only place some bounds on the set of outcomes that can be supported as equilibria.

3. A 'Bounds' approach

A central theorem within the Bounds approach to market structure (Sutton, 1991) specifies conditions under which concentration cannot converge to zero, no matter how large the market becomes. This theorem holds good over a wide range of models; it is couched in terms of a single abstract property which describes the returns earned by a firm that deviates by out-spending its rivals in its outlays of fixed costs (whether on R & D or advertising or otherwise). This basic non-convergence theorem (Shaked and Sutton, 1987) makes no reference to the behaviour of R & D-intensity. Here, we extend the theorem with a view to making statements about the joint behaviour of concentration and R & D-intensity.

The class of models that we consider share the following structure: [8] in a finite-horizon stage game, a number of firms introduce one or more products over

---

[8] This structure includes the familiar simultaneous entry case (where $T = 2$) It also includes many other specifications. It excludes the sequential entry structure, since in that setup each firm can enter products only at a specific, predetermined stage. This feature of the sequential entry setup leads to some properties that are considered 'unreasonable' (see Eaton and Ware, 1987). The present set of 'unrestricted' extensive forms avoids these objections (see Sutton, 1995). Nonetheless, these finite-horizon stage games have a rather special structure, and it is interesting to ask whether this structure can be relaxed. It is shown in Sutton (1996) that a similar nonconvergence theorem holds good for a broad class of dynamic games in which all firms present in the market are free to spend (additional) fixed outlays at any time.

stages 1 to $T - 1$. Each firm (potential entrant) is labelled with some date t, $1 \leq t \leq T$. The firm is free to enter any number of products of any specification at any date $t, t + 1, \ldots, T - 1$. At the end of the penultimate stage $T - 1$, the outcome of stages 1 to $T - 1$ can be summarised as a configuration of firms, each equipped with a set of products. At stage T, firms compete in price (à la Cournot, Bertrand, or otherwise). This configuration of products forms the argument of the final stage profit function $\pi(\cdot)$, and so determines the vectors of firms' sales revenues and firms' profits at equilibrium. We assume that the number of firms (potential entrants) is large relative to the size of the market, in the sense that if all firms enter, then at least one firm makes a loss. It follows that in any equilibrium, at least one firm does not enter.

We begin by introducing a condition on the final stage profit function of the model. Given any configuration of products, we denote by u_{M} the highest quality offered, and we denote by Y the total industry revenue in the corresponding equilibrium of the final stage subgame.

Condition. There exists some pair (a, k), with $a > 0$ and $k > 1$, such that given any configuration of firms and products, then in a modified configuration in which the quality of any one product is raised to ku_{M}, the firm offering this product achieves a final stage (gross) profit $\pi \geq aY$.

It is important to note that the number a defined in this condition holds for *any* product configuration in which qualities do not exceed u_{M}. In particular, it is independent of the *number* of firms, and of products offered.

We now introduce a cost function $F(u)$ that describes the fixed outlays incurred in introducing a product of quality u; and we assume that the elasticity of $F(u)$ is bounded above, i.e. there is some number β such that

$$\frac{u}{F}\frac{\mathrm{d}F}{\mathrm{d}u} \leq \beta \quad \text{for all } u.$$

Now consider some configuration in which the firm offering the highest quality product has a share of industry sales revenue of ε. We show that for ε sufficiently small, this configuration can not be supported as a (perfect) Nash equilibrium; for any firm that does not enter in the supposed equilibrium, will find it profitable to deviate by entering with a product of quality ku_{M}.

To see this, note that the entrant's profit is at least

$$aY - F(ku_{\mathrm{M}}) \geq aY - k^{\beta}F(u_{\mathrm{M}}) \quad (\text{since } uF'/F \leq \beta).$$

Denote the sales of the firm offering quality u_{M} in the initial equilibrium, the set of rivals' products being given, as y_{M}. Our definition of ε implies that $y_{\mathrm{M}} < \varepsilon Y$. It follows that

$$F(u_{\mathrm{M}}) = \frac{F(u_{\mathrm{M}})}{y_{\mathrm{M}}}y_{\mathrm{M}} \leq \frac{F(u_{\mathrm{M}})}{y_{\mathrm{M}}}\cdot \varepsilon Y$$

whence the deviant's profit is at least

$$aY - k^\beta F(u_M) \geq aY - k^\beta \frac{F(u_M)}{y_M} \varepsilon Y.$$

But the deviant's profit in the original equilibrium was zero, whence this deviation is profitable unless

$$aY - k^\beta \frac{F(u_M)}{y_M} \varepsilon Y \leq 0$$

or

$$\varepsilon \cdot \frac{F(u_M)}{y_M} > \frac{a}{k^\beta}. \tag{10}$$

The expression $F(u_M)/y_M$ represents the ratio of fixed outlays to sales incurred by the firm offering the top quality product. In what follows, we identify fixed outlays with R&D, and we write $F(u_M)/y_M$ as $(R/Y)_M$, to denote the R&D/Sales ratio of the firm offering the top quality product. [9] Since the (one-firm) sales concentration ratio C_1 cannot be less than ε, and since both C_1 and the equilibrium value of $(R/Y)_M$ cannot exceed unity, Eq. (10) implies that *neither C_1 nor $(R/Y)_M$ can be less than a/k^β.*

We can simplify matters further by looking at the role played by the constant k. Consider any model, as defined by a cost function $F(u)$ and a (final stage) profit function $\pi(\cdot)$. Associated with the model is a constant β, defined by reference to the cost function $F(u)$, and a set of pairs (a, k) that satisfy the preceding Condition. There will usually be many such pairs (a, k). A non-equilibrium configuration may in some cases be broken by a local deviation (so that k may be arbitrarily close to unity), but in other cases may be broken only by a global deviation [10] (so that k may have to be 'large'). We choose a pair (a, k) that maximises a/k^β; and we label this ratio as α. The result developed above can now be stated as

Theorem ('Nonconvergence'). The number α serves as a lower bound to C_1 and $(R/Y)_M$, i.e. in any (perfect Nash) equilibrium

$$C_1 \geq \underline{C}_1 = \alpha \quad and \quad \left(\frac{R}{Y}\right)_M \geq \alpha.$$

---

[9] The extension of the argument to allow for other forms of fixed outlay is straightforward.

[10] For an example, see Sutton (1991, p. 62).

520   *J. Sutton / European Economic Review 40 (1996) 511–530*

The nonconvergence theorem tells us that industries with a high value of alpha will have both high concentration and high R&D intensity. This statement is not very useful, however, unless we can relate the value of alpha to some observable industry characteristics.

3.1. Uncovering alpha

It is intuitively clear that alpha will be affected both by the pattern of technology and tastes in the industry, and by the nature of price competition. Any attempt at direct measurement of the determinants of alpha is likely to prove intractable. In what follows, we by-pass this issue by developing a relationship between alpha and a pair of observable industry characteristics. The first of these observables is the familiar R&D/Sales ratio. The industry-wide ratio, which we label R/Y, will serve as a proxy for $(R/Y)_M$ in what follows. The second observable that we introduce below is related to the degree of proliferation of different technologies and of different product groups in the industry.

In the example of Section 2, there were many different routes along which R&D could be pursued ('technologies'). Each route led to the production of one product. Each firm followed a different route, and produced a different product.

In this more general setting, it is appropriate to introduce a distinction between the set of technologies that can be used, and the set of products that can be produced. A simplified representation of this is shown in Fig. 3. A number of technologies are available, each of which leads to several products ('economies of scope in R&D'). A firm may focus all its spending on one technology, or it may spread its spending over many. (A specific example is described in Section 4 below.)

The non-convergence theorem can be applied straightforwardly in this setting.

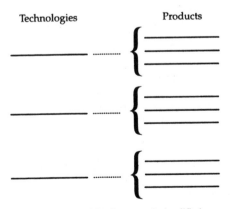

Fig. 3. R&D technologies and Product sets: A simplified representation.

J. Sutton / European Economic Review 40 (1996) 511–530   521

For each technology, we can define the set of pairs (a, k) satisfying the above Condition. The value of alpha for the industry is defined, as before, as the maximum of a/k^β, where this maximum is taken across all technologies.

The basic question is this: at equilibrium, will R & D spending be focussed on a small number of technologies, all with heavy spending, or will it be spread thinly across a large number of different technologies?

The non-convergence theorem shows how configurations where R & D is spread too thinly across many technologies cannot be stable, for it will be profitable for some firm to deviate by outspending rivals within one technology.

A 'dual' to this theorem is available, which shows how configurations where R & D is concentrated on too few technologies will be unstable, for it will be profitable for some firm to deviate by introducing a new technology.

The key point can best be seen by reference to the example of Section 2. If σ is very high, any firm can capture a large market share from its rivals by spending somewhat more than they do, however many rivals it has. But if a firm spends slightly less than its rivals, its market share falls sharply. On the other hand if σ is low, a firm cannot easily win market share from its rivals by raising its relative spending. But if the firm slightly underspends relative to its rivals, its profits will fall only slightly.

When we move to the more general setting, the parameter σ needs to be defined in a more abstract way. We omit the technical details here, beyond noting that σ is defined by direct reference to the ratio between the profit of an incumbent firm that offers a product of quality u, and the highest profit that an entrant can attain by offering a new but slightly inferior product (i.e. a product of some quality ku, where k is some constant that is strictly less than unity).

The formal analysis is based on a set of models, where a model is represented by a pair of functions $F(u|\beta), \pi(\cdot|\sigma)$. For each model, there is a value of α, which depends on β and σ. Decreases in β, or increases in σ, lead to an increase in α.

Within the theory, the notion of the 'number of technologies' and their associated 'sets of products' is straightforward, and we can treat the number of different technologies used, which we label n, as an equilibrium outcome. An index of 'proliferation' can be defined as $h = 1/n$, where $0 \le h \le 1$.

Two propositions characterise the link between α and the observables R/Y and h. The first is a corollary to the non-convergence theorem; this says that associated with any value of α is a maximum number of different technologies that will be in use, and so a minimum value of h. This, together with the result on (R/Y) in the nonconvergence theorem, ensures that a high value of α implies both a high value of R/Y and a high value of h.

The second proposition is the 'dual' to the nonconvergence theorem. This theorem places a lower bound on the number of different technologies in use, or the number of product categories offered. What it says is that, subject to weak regularity conditions on $\pi(\cdot)$, as $\alpha \to 0$, either $R/Y \to 0$ or $h \to 0$. It follows that

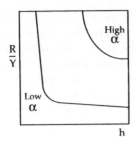

Fig. 4. The relation between alpha and the observables R / Y and h.

very low values of α will imply either very low values of R/Y or very low values of h.

These two results are illustrated in Fig. 4. They permit us to draw some conclusions as to the value of α by reference to the observables R/Y and h. This classification is only partial. There is no 1:1 mapping between α and this pair of observables. In practical terms, what is at issue is that any ordering of industries by $(h, R/Y)$ will not correspond to a well defined ordering in terms of α. All that can be done is to identify the two extremes.

The results shown in Fig. 4 suggest taking the following approach: suppose we examine the set of all industries for which R/Y exceeds some threshold value, and that we measure h for these industries. The results illustrated in Fig. 4 indicate that industries which have high values of R/Y and high values of h cannot be 'low alpha' industries; and so for these industries, concentration must be high. On the other hand, industries for which h is small may have low concentration, even though R/Y is high. This is the point that was illustrated in the example of Section 2. The properties are illustrated in Fig. 5.

In investigating this relationship empirically, a useful point of comparison is provided by those industries where R&D spending is zero, or very small. Here, the theory says that we should find industries with arbitrarily low levels of concentration *independently* of the value of h. This will be the case for those

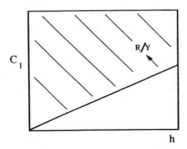

Fig. 5. The predicted relationship between concentration and the observables R / Y and h.

J. Sutton / European Economic Review 40 (1996) 511–530   523

industries where β is very high. Here alpha is close to zero (whatever the value of σ), and so also is $\underline{C}_1$. Such markets may use any number of technologies and produce any number of distinct product categories, so that h may take any value. But as market size increases, the lower bound to concentration converges to zero. The $(\underline{C}_1, h)$ locus illustrated in Fig. 5 collapses to coincide with the horizontal axis. (This case, where $\beta \to \infty$, is the special 'limiting' case of 'exogenous sunk costs'; see Shaked and Sutton (1987, p. 140)).

3.2. An empirical illustration

The results that follow are based on a sample defined by reference to the most comprehensive listing of R&D-intensities by business, the U.S. Federal Trade Commission Line of Business data set for U.S. manufacturing in 1977. This data-set is defined at a level of aggregation close to the 4-digit SIC level, and a concordance was established between all industries in this data-set that had an R&D/Sales ratio exceeding 4%, and the corresponding 4-digit SIC industries for 1977. The analysis was carried out by reference to the set of all 5-digit industries within this set of 4-digit industries.

In what follows, we use the industry R&D/Sales ratio as a proxy for the theoretical variable $(R/Y)_M$. Since this variable is used merely to classify industries as 'very high' or 'very low' spenders, this proxy is probably satisfactory.

We also need a proxy for h, and this is much more problematic. The approach taken here is crude. The proxy for h is calculated using data for sales by individual product lines reported in the Census (the 7-digit or 'product' listing). The number of product lines listed varies from a handful in some industries to ten or more in others. For each 5-digit industry, h is defined as the fraction of total shipments accounted for by the 7-digit product line with the highest value of shipments. In industries with only a few categories, this index will be close to unity; in industries containing a very large number of distinct product lines, all of them very small, h will be close to zero.

A caveat is needed, regarding the treatment of cases where the 5-digit industry includes only one recorded 7-digit product line. This happens under two different circumstances: where the industry produces a product that is homogenous, and where the products are so many and various as to preclude any sensible 7-digit breakdown. In the first of these cases the 'true value' of h is unity, but in the second case, its 'true value' is very small. To avoid arbitrariness, all 5-digit industries for which the shipments of only one 7-digit product line was recorded were omitted from the sample. [11]

---

[11] All 5-digit industries that refer to residual categories (labelled 'n.e.c.' or 'n.s.k.' in the Census classification) or which relate to 'repairs to...' or 'services to...' the products of the 4-digit industry, are also omitted.

The top panel of Fig. 6 shows a 'control group' consisting of all 5-digit industries within the fifty 4-digit industries that had the lowest ratios of R&D plus Advertising to Sales. Here, it seems that h has no effect on C_1. On the other hand, the theory predicts that for a sample of industries whose R&D intensity exceeds some threshold level, $\underline{C}_1(h)$ should increase from zero as h increases. The bottom panel of Fig. 6 shows those industries for which the 4-digit R&D/Sales ratio exceeds 4%. It appears that the lower bound to concentration increases with h for this group, as the theory suggests. [12]

4. A question of aggregation?

It is tempting to dismiss the proceeding analysis by saying that it is 'just a question of aggregation'. Suppose we split these industries into smaller sub-industries, each of which corresponds to a 'well defined' industry within which products are fairly good substitutes. Might we not then find that all the sub-industries with a high R&D/Sales ratio had high levels of concentration? This is a good idea, in principle. The first problem we meet, however, is that there is no 'right' level of aggregation. Even if we identify some set of distinct product categories, using a 7-digit classification or otherwise, we find that, for some groups of users, two categories may be good substitutes, while for another group of users, they may be poor substitutes. [13] No matter what classification we employ, there is no clean 'break in the chain of substitutes' that permits a 'good' definition of 'sub-industries'.

But this difficulty in finding a suitable level of aggregation might still be seen as a mere 'practical problem'. A close look at these industries suggests that this is not the case, but that the splintering of these markets into a multitude of ill-defined and overlapping submarkets is itself a reflection of the balance of incentives in R&D. The splintering of the market reflects the greater attraction of introducing new varieties, as opposed to pushing for higher performances on existing ones; this is the nature of what we characterised above as a 'low alpha' industry.

If we define the submarkets narrowly enough to ensure that all products within each submarket are substitutes, then we have defined them so narrowly as to preclude any allocation of R&D by submarkets: for in these industries, the larger part of R&D is often devoted to a search for new categories; these new types lie

---

[12] The relationship shown in Fig. 6 is just a first step in the statistical testing of the present theory. The main implications of the theory relate to the relationship between market size and concentration, and a test of these implications requires an extension of this discussion to a dynamic setting (see Sutton, 1996).

[13] This means that the response of relative sales of two rival products to marginal changes in their relative prices may differ widely at different levels of relative prices. As the technology evolves, relative unit cost and prices change. At some times, they 'look like good substitutes', at others not.

J. Sutton / European Economic Review 40 (1996) 511–530   525

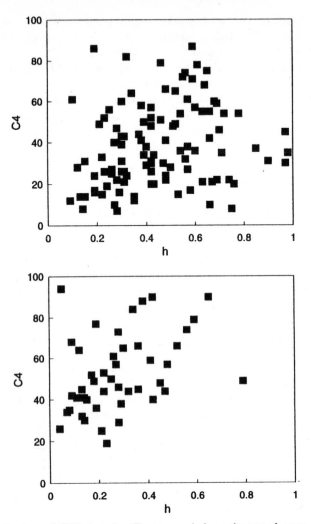

Fig. 6. Concentration and R&D intensity. The top panel shows the control group of low R&D industries. The bottom panel shows the industries for which the (4 digit) R&D/Sales ratio exceeds 4%. The outlier to the south-east in the lower panel is SIC 3573 (Electronic Computers). The recorded *h* index for this industry may be anomalous (Sutton, 1996).

outside any of the currently existing submarkets. They can often not be identified as a 'substitute' or 'next generation product' vis-à-vis any particular existing 'submarket', but may displace products for several of the existing submarkets in some, but not all, applications.

It is for this reason that attempts to tackle these problems by 'finding the right level of aggregation' are doomed to fail; the problem is one of principle, and is fundamental.

A good illustration of these issues is provided by the market for Flowmeters (SIC 38240). These devices are used to measure the flow of liquids and gases through pipelines, particularly in the chemicals industry, but also in many other areas. There are eight principle types of flowmeter, each based on a different physical principle. Every decade or so, a new type appears that carves out a position in some range of applications to which it is suited.

During the 1980s, developments in the design of electromagnetic flowmeters were leading to gains in market share at the expense of ultrasonic meters as design improvements in electromagnetic meters led to better performance, and to falling unit costs. The ultrasonic device is still preferred in many applications, however. An ultrasonic meter can be installed in a couple of hours by drilling into a pipeline without interrupting the flow, whereas the installation of an electromagnetic device requires cutting out a section of the pipe, into which the device will sit, and this may mean closing off the flow for a couple of days. This gives the ultrasonic device an important advantage in applications involving large pipes. Moreover, the electromagnetic meter is confined in its applications to conductive aqueous solutions, and this rules it out for use with hydrocarbons. Here, again, the ultrasonic device retains a strong advantage over alternatives.

Once a new type of flowmeter appears on the market, firms vie in solving design problems that limit the use of the original design in certain applications. Some innovations improve the performance in the eyes of all users; others are targeted at introducing the device into applications for which the original design was unsuited. As the design improves, and as unit costs fall, its total share of the market rises. But in due course a new type of device appears, eroding its share and carving out a position in some applications. In the 1980s, electromagnetic devices won market share from ultrasonics; now Coriolis meters are beginning to make headway against both these devices in certain applications.

The quintessential low-alpha industry, then, is one that combines two features:

1. buyers differ in the relative weight they place on different aspects of technical performance (product attributes);
2. many alternative technologies are available, which are based on different physical or chemical principles, and which therefore have different ultimate limitations in respect of each performance attribute.

Within this kind of setting, the focus of R&D efforts is directed away from the escalation mechanism, and towards a continuing proliferation of product varieties.

That said, it remains the case that there are some examples, within the low-alpha industries identified above, of well defined submarkets in which a group of businesses devote R&D to product improvement 'within the category'. Under the present theory, we would expect to find that in these cases, the sub-industry in question begins to resemble a high-alpha industry. Studies of such cases indicate that this is indeed so; and were such cases the norm rather than the exception among low-alpha industries, then the problems we have been addressing here could indeed be tackled by a simple dis-aggregation of the data.

5. Case studies

One of the main attractions of game-theoretic models lies in the absence of the fictional auctioneer of Walrasian theory. A Nash equilibrium is a configuration of strategies which admits of no profitable deviation; and so a game-theoretic model comes, of its nature, equipped with a prediction as to the qualitative form of deviation(s) that we should expect to see in an out-of-equilibrium situation.

In the present context, this leads to a search for 'natural experiments' within high alpha industries, i.e. situations in which certain shifts in the external environment lead to a rise in alpha, and so in the lower bound to concentration.

A 'natural experiment' of this kind arose, for example, in the photographic film industry during the shift from black-and-white to colour film in the 1960s. As firms vied for a position in the colour film market, a process of escalation of R & D spending led to a shakeout of firms, as rising R & D costs damaged profitability and induced a process of merger and exit – a basic 'fingerprint' of the escalation process (Sutton, 1991, Ch. 8). The end result was the dominance of the global market by just five firms: Kodak, Fuji, Konica, Agfa-Gevaert and 3M.

A useful function of case studies lies in pinning down the qualitative differences between the evolution of concentration in 'high alpha' and 'low alpha' industries. The issue here is whether these two types of market show a qualitatively distinct pattern of evolution, in accordance with the theory. A good illustration of the differences involved is provided by contrasting the shakeout of mid-size firms in the photographic film industry with the very different experience of firms producing flowmeters. The flowmeter industry supports a huge number of medium and small-sized firms, of widely varying size. The main difference between smaller and larger firms lies in the breadth of their product ranges. By confining its R & D efforts to a limited range, a mid-size flowmeter company can successfully compete on technical performance, even in new generation devices, with the industry's market leaders. For example, the KDG Mobrey company, whose U.K. R & D staff numbers 12–14 people, became one of the U.K. market leaders in the new ultrasonic ('time of flight') devices during the 1980s. Such examples recur throughout the low-alpha industries. The examples contrast sharply with the escalation environment that is characteristic of high-alpha industries. It is no accident that many studies of high technology small firms find them heavily clustered in sectors such as 'Instrumentation'; for these are typical 'low-alpha' industries. [14]

6. Implications

The present theory does *not* deny the possibility of linkages between concentration and R&D-intensity that go beyond those captured by the bound developed above. Nonetheless, the mere presence of this bound implies that a simple regression of R&D intensity versus concentration will detect a (very weak) positive correlation between these variables. Since most authors reporting results of this kind have claimed the existence of a weak positive correlation, it seems appropriate to ask whether a bound of the form shown in Fig. 6 might not be the only robust empirical relation linking these variables.

More broadly, the present analysis suggests that R&D-intensity does not constitute an adequate proxy for the technological factors relevant to the determinants of market structure; on the other hand, it suggests that the pair $(h, R/Y)$ does form an adequate if crude proxy. This provides a very simple classification procedure that avoids many potential problems that arise in 'classifying technologies'.

7. Concluding remarks: Theory and history

It is time to return to the central theme with which this paper has been concerned: the idea that cross-industry links between concentration and industry characteristics and between concentration and endogenous outcomes such as the degree of R&D intensity are best approached, not by way of the traditional regressions, which presuppose the existence of some identifiable 'true model', but rather by reference to the operation of a few strong mechanisms whose operation imposes certain bounds in the space of observed outcomes.

---

[14] The reader may wonder whether something more obvious is not at work in the Flowmeter industry, in that the unit development cost of a new device in this area falls far short of the unit development cost of a new colour film. Whether such differences provide an explanation for these outcomes requires a fuller exploration of cases. Here, we note that what matters analytically is the flow of R&D per unit time. Both unit development costs and the frequency with which one generation of products is replaced by the next, are endogenous. An examination of such industries as Pharmaceuticals, where unit development costs are high, but alpha is low, suggests that merely looking at unit development costs is not the right way forward. This observation does not, of course, imply that unit development costs are irrelevant, but merely that their role is secondary. For a full evaluation of their effects in the context of a 'natural experiment', see Sutton (1996).

This theme is closely related to an issue that greatly preoccupied Joseph Schumpeter and to which he returned again and again: the marriage of theory and history. Economics, he felt, lay midway between the domain in which formal modelling could prove valuable, and the domain of historical analysis, in which the influence of personalities and institutions loom large. His ideal involved a combination of historical, statistical and theoretical analysis, and their 'mutual peaceful penetration'. [15]

The pendulum has swung widely since Schumpeter's day. The dominant paradigm, over the past half-century, represents a triumph of 'equilibrium' over 'history'. This paradigm rests on the notion that observed outcomes should be modelled as the uniquely determined equilibrium outcomes of some 'true model', plus random noise. One (overly extreme) version of this paradigm claims that the constraints imposed on current outcomes by the working of the market mechanism are so tight that today's influences uniquely determine today's outcomes. But much less need be claimed: even if 'history matters', in the sense that past influences affect current outcomes, this paradigm may still be retained. What is needed is that all relevant factors, historical or otherwise, that impinge on outcomes are specified in the model.

But, in the area of 'Explaining Market Structure' at least, this will not do. For the key lesson we have learned from a decade of game-theoretic I.O. is that a wide range of subtle but crucial influences exert a systematic effect on outcomes. It is inappropriate to model these influences as random noise; where a lucky availability of documentation permits us to observe their role, their effects are both large and systematic. Yet faced with the task of explaining structure across a broad run of industries, we are reduced to treating these factors as 'unobservables'. If our theory is to be empirically useful, it must specify constraints on mappings of observables into observables. Constraints that are valid for any broad class of markets are likely to be relatively loose. By the same token, the notion that the structure of any interestingly broad class of markets can be represented by a single highly parameterised model with a unique equilibrium is probably a chimera. If this is so, then regression analyses of observed concentration levels on 'industry characteristics' would appear to be inappropriate.

Acknowledgements

The financial support of the Economic and Social Research council and the Leverhulme Trust is gratefully acknowledged. I would like to express my thanks

---

[15] This theme emerges repeatedly in his contemporaries' accounts of Schumpeter's views. See, for example, the contributions of Haberler, Machlup, Samuelson, Smithies and Usher to the volume of memorial essays edited by Harris (1951).

to Alison Hole, Michael Raith and George Symeonides for their thoughtful comments on an earlier draft. The shortcomings are mine alone.

References

Cohen, W.M. and R.C. Levin, 1989, Innovation and market structure, in R. Schmalensee and R.D. Willig, eds., Handbook of industrial organisation (North-Holland, Amsterdam).

Dasgupta, P. and J. Stiglitz, 1980, Industrial structure and the nature of innovative activity, Economic Journal 90, 266–293.

Eaton, B.C. and R. Ware, 1987, A theory of market structure with sequential entry, Rand Journal of Economics 18, 1–16.

Harris, S., 1951, Schumpeter, social scientist, (Harvard University Press, Cambridge, MA).

Levin, R.C., W.M. Cohen and D.C. Mowery, 1985, R&D appropriability, opportunity and market structure: New evidence on some Schumpeterian hypotheses, American Economic Review Proceedings 75, 20–24.

Phillips, A., 1971, Technology and market structure: A study of the aircraft industry (Heath Lexington Books, Reading, MA).

Scherer, F.M., 1980, Industrial market structure and economic performance, 2nd ed. (Rand McNally, Chicago, IL).

Scott, J.T., 1984, Firms versus industry variability in R&D intensity, in Z. Griliches, ed., R&D, patents and productivity (Chicago, IL, The University of Chicago Press for the National Bureau of Economic Research).

Shaked, A. and J. Sutton, 1987, Product differentiation and industrial structure, Journal of Industrial Economics 36, 131–146.

Sutton, J., 1991, Sunk costs and market structure (MIT Press, Cambridge, MA).

Sutton, J., 1995, One smart agent, STICERD discussion paper no. EI/8 (London School of Economics, London).

Sutton, J., 1996, Technology and market structure, in preparation.

Temin, Peter, 1984, Technology, regulation and market structure in the modern pharmaceutical industry, The Rand Journal of Economics 10, 429–446.

Part III
Regional Evolution

[13]

Growth in Cities

Edward L. Glaeser

Harvard University

Hedi D. Kallal

New York University

José A. Scheinkman

University of Chicago

Andrei Shleifer

Harvard University

Recent theories of economic growth, including those of Romer, Porter, and Jacobs, have stressed the role of technological spillovers in generating growth. Because such knowledge spillovers are particularly effective in cities, where communication between people is more extensive, data on the growth of industries in different cities allow us to test some of these theories. Using a new data set on the growth of large industries in 170 U.S. cities between 1956 and 1987, we find that local competition and urban variety, but not regional specialization, encourage employment growth in industries. The evidence suggests that important knowledge spillovers might occur between rather than within industries, consistent with the theories of Jacobs.

We are grateful to the National Science, Sloan, and Bradley foundations for financial support; to Robert Barro, Gary Becker, Carol Heim, Vernon Henderson, Lawrence Katz, Robert Lucas, Sherwin Rosen, Julio Rotemberg, T. W. Schultz, and George Tolley for helpful comments; and to Christopher Kim for research assistance.

[*Journal of Political Economy*, 1992, vol. 100, no. 6]

I. Introduction

Some historians have argued that most innovations are made in cities (Jacobs 1969; Bairoch 1988). The cramming of individuals, occupations, and industries into close quarters provides an environment in which ideas flow quickly from person to person. Jacobs (1969, 1984) argues that these interactions between people in cities help them get ideas and innovate. In fact, without an opportunity to learn from others and thus improve one's own productivity, there would be little reason for people to pay high rents just to work in a city. Easy flow of ideas might explain how cities survive despite the high rents.

Such a dynamic view of cities fits nicely with the recent work on economic growth, which views externalities (and particularly externalities associated with knowledge spillovers) as the "engine of growth" (Romer 1986; Lucas 1988). If geographical proximity facilitates transmission of ideas, then we should expect knowledge spillovers to be particularly important in cities. After all, intellectual breakthroughs must cross hallways and streets more easily than oceans and continents. This paper uses a new data set on American cities and industries to test the new growth theories. Because these theories are most compelling in the context of city growth, our focus on cities gives them the benefit of the doubt.

We focus on three theories. All these theories deal with technological externalities, whereby innovations and improvements occurring in one firm increase the productivity of the other firms without full compensation. The theoretical foundations of such knowledge spillovers have been modeled by many authors, starting with Loury (1979) and Dasgupta and Stiglitz (1980). Griliches (1979) surveys the empirical literature on the role of knowledge spillovers.

The Marshall-Arrow-Romer (MAR) externality concerns knowledge spillovers between firms in an industry. Arrow (1962) presents an early formalization; the paper by Romer (1986) is a recent and influential statement. Applied to cities by Marshall (1890), this view says that the concentration of an industry in a city helps knowledge spillovers between firms and, therefore, the growth of that industry and of that city. A good example would be computer chips in Silicon Valley (Arthur 1989). Through spying, imitation, and rapid interfirm movement of highly skilled labor, ideas are quickly disseminated among neighboring firms. The MAR theory also predicts, as Schumpeter (1942) does, that local monopoly is better for growth than local competition, because local monopoly restricts the flow of ideas to others and so allows externalities to be internalized by the innovator. When externalities are internalized, innovation and growth speed up.

Porter (1990), like MAR, argues that knowledge spillovers in specialized, geographically concentrated industries stimulate growth. He insists, however, that local competition, as opposed to local monopoly, fosters the pursuit and rapid adoption of innovation. He gives examples of Italian ceramics and gold jewelry industries, in which hundreds of firms are located together and fiercely compete to innovate since the alternative to innovation is demise. Porter's externalities are maximized in cities with geographically specialized, competitive industries.

Jacobs (1969), unlike MAR and Porter, believes that the most important knowledge transfers come from outside the core industry. As a result, variety and diversity of geographically proximate industries rather than geographical specialization promote innovation and growth. One example is the brassiere industry, which grew out of dressmakers' innovations rather than the lingerie industry. Jacobs also favors local competition because, like Porter, she believes that it speeds up the adoption of technology.

These theories of *dynamic externalities* are extremely appealing because they try to explain *simultaneously* how cities form and why they grow. MAR's and Porter's theories, in particular, predict that industries should specialize geographically to absorb the knowledge spilling over between firms. In addition, they predict that regionally specialized industries should grow faster because neighboring firms can learn from each other much better than geographically isolated firms. In contrast, Jacobs's theory predicts that industries located in areas that are highly industrially diversified should grow faster. Despite their differences, all these theories have implications for *growth rates* of industries in different cities. In this respect, they are different from the more standard location and urbanization externality theories that address the formation and specialization of cities (Henderson 1986) but not city *growth*.

We examine the predictions of the various theories of knowledge spillovers and growth using a new data set on geographic concentration and competition of industries in 170 of the largest U.S. cities. We focus on the largest industries because one of the strongest implications of growth models (such as MAR) is that externalities in these models are sources of permanent income growth. If such externalities are permanent and important, we should see them in the largest industries. If, alternatively, externalities are important only early in an industry's life cycle and disappear as an industry matures, our empirical work would not pick them up, but they are not sources of permanent growth either.

We ask which industries in which cities have grown fastest between 1956 and 1987 and why. All three theories of dynamic externalities focus on knowledge spillovers but differ in where they believe the source of externalities is and what makes the capture of these externalities most effective. The theories are not always mutually exclusive but rather offer different views of what is most important. By testing empirically in which cities industries grow faster, as a function of geographic specialization and competition, we can learn which, if any, externalities are important for growth.

Our results can be briefly summarized. Our findings are based on a cross section of city-industries (e.g., New York apparel and textiles, Philadelphia apparel and textiles, Philadelphia electrical equipment), where knowledge spillovers should be easier to find than by looking at whole cities. In a cross section of city-industries, we find that, as measured by employment, industries grow slower in cities in which they are more heavily overrepresented. For example, the primary-metals industry grew rapidly in Savannah, Georgia, where it was not heavily represented in 1956, and declined in Fresno, California, where it was heavily overrepresented. These results do not favor the local within-industry externality theory of MAR and Porter, according to which industries should grow faster precisely in places in which they are overrepresented.

We also find that industries grow faster in cities in which firms in those industries are smaller than the national average size of firms in that industry. If we take the view that spreading the same employment over more firms increases local competition between these firms and therefore the spread of knowledge, this result supports Porter's and Jacobs's view that local competition promotes growth. One could also take the view that smaller firms grow faster, which, however, is not strictly compatible with the MAR model or with other evidence. Finally, city-industries grow faster when the rest of the city is less specialized. This result supports Jacobs's view that city diversity promotes growth as knowledge spills over industries. The evidence is thus negative on MAR, mixed on Porter, and consistent with Jacobs.

If MAR externalities are not important, why are so many cities specialized in a few industries? There are many other externalities that explain regional specialization and city formation but that do not specifically focus on knowledge spillovers and growth. For example, Marshall (1890) has argued that firms in the same industry often locate next to each other to share various inputs, including specialized labor. Many other "localization" externalities are discussed by Lichtenberg (1960), Henderson (1986, 1988), Arthur (1989), and Rotemberg and Saloner (1990), among others. Henderson (1986) in particular presents empirical evidence indicating that output per labor-hour is higher in firms that have other firms from the same industry located nearby. Static localization externalities can thus easily account for city specialization, but not for growth.

Finally, some work also explains why firms might want to locate in places in which local demand is high, what Henderson (1986) calls "urbanization" externalities. These models tend to predict that firms in *different* industries should locate next to each other, which suggests that they cannot be the complete story of cities. Lichtenberg (1960), Murphy, Shleifer, and Vishny (1989), and Krugman (1991*a*, 1991*b*) all present models of such externalities. Like localization externalities, urbanization externalities explain patterns of industry location rather than of growth. Wheat (1986) finds strong evidence that manufacturing employment grows faster in regions with more rapid population growth. We present some less aggregate evidence also pointing to the importance of urbanization externalities.

Section II of the paper presents the predictions of different views of externalities and city growth. Section III describes the data. Section IV presents results for the growth of city-industries. Section V deals with localization and urbanization externalities. Section VI presents conclusions.

II. Theories of Dynamic Externalities

The models of city growth we consider stress the role of dynamic externalities, and more specifically knowledge spillovers, for city growth. According to these models, cities grow because people in cities interact with other people, either in their own or in other sectors, and learn from them. Because they pick up this knowledge without paying for it, these knowledge spillovers are externalities. The frequency of interaction with other people is ensured by their proximity in a city. Because this proximity makes externalities particularly large in a city, all the models predict that cities grow faster than rural areas in which externalities are less important because people interact less.

The theories of city growth that we present differ along two dimensions. First, they differ in whether knowledge spillovers come from within the industry or from other industries. Second, they differ in their predictions of how local competition affects the impact of these knowledge spillovers on growth.

The MAR theory of spillovers focuses on spillovers within industry. Knowledge accumulated by one firm tends to help other firms' technologies, without appropriate compensation. In Silicon Valley, microchip manufacturers learn from each other because people talk and gossip, products can be reverse engineered, and employees move between firms. In New York, fashion designers move between firms and take their knowledge with them. The same was true of the Bangladeshi shirt industry in the 1980s, where hundreds of firms were founded by people who were initially employed by *one* joint venture with a Korean firm. Physical proximity facilitates this free information transmission. In this case, industries that are regionally specialized and benefit most from the within-industry transmission of knowledge should grow faster. Cities that have such industries should grow faster as well.

In MAR models of externalities, innovators realize that some of their ideas will be imitated or improved on by their neighbors without compensation. This lack of property rights to ideas causes innovators to slow down their investment in externality-generating activities, such as research and development. If innovators had a monopoly on their ideas, or at least if they had fewer neighbors who imitated them immediately, the pace of innovation and growth would rise. The MAR models tend to imply that whereas local competition is bad for growth, local concentration is good for growth because innovators internalize the externalities (see Romer 1990).

The effect of local competition is the primary difference between MAR's and Porter's models. In Porter's model, local competition accelerates imitation and improvement of the innovator's ideas. Although such competition reduces the returns to the innovator, it also increases pressure to innovate: firms that do not advance technologically are bankrupted by their innovating competitors. Porter believes that the second effect is by far the more important. Ruthless competition between local competitors leads to rapid adoption of the innovations of others and to improvement on them, and so generates industry growth. In contrast, local monopolies lead a quieter life as their managers consume perquisites rather than risk innovation. Porter gives striking examples of Italian ceramics and gold jewelry industries, the German printmaking industry, and many others that grew through rampant imitation of new technologies and improvement on them. All these industries are highly geographically concentrated, presumably to facilitate the flow of ideas and imitation.

Because MAR and Porter agree that the most important technological externalities occur within industry, they also agree that regional specialization is good for growth both of the specialized industries and of the cities they are in. However, MAR would argue that local monopoly is good because it allows internalization of externalities. In contrast, Porter would argue that local competition is good because it fosters imitation and innovation. In our empirical work, we shall look at the effects of both specialization and local competition on the growth of industries in cities.

The third theory that stresses knowledge spillovers is that of Jacobs (1969). Jacobs's idea is that the crucial externality in cities is cross-fertilization of ideas across different lines of work. New York grain and cotton merchants saw the need for national and international financial transactions, and so the financial services industry was born. A San Francisco food processor invented equipment leasing when he had trouble finding financing for his own capital; the industry was not invented by the bankers. In a more systematic account, Rosenberg (1963) discusses the spread of machine tools across industries and describes how an idea is transmitted from one industry to another. Scherer (1982) presents systematic evidence indicating that around 70 percent of inventions in a given industry are used outside that industry. Much evidence thus suggests that knowledge spills over across industries. Because cities bring together people from different walks of life, they foster transmission of ideas.

In Jacobs's theory, industrial variety rather than specialization is conducive to growth, because in diversified cities there is more interchange of different ideas. She contrasts Manchester, a specialized textile city that eventually declined, with broadly diversified Birmingham, which eventually flourished. Bairoch (1988) supports Jacobs by arguing that "the diversity of urban activities quite naturally encourages attempts to apply or adopt in one sector (or in one specific problem area) technological solutions adopted in another sector" (p. 336).

In the debate between local monopoly and competition, Jacobs comes squarely on the side of competition. She writes that "monopolies gratuitously harm cities and suppress what their economies are capable of achieving . . . . Extortionate prices, harmful though they most certainly are, are the least of disadvantages of monopolies, for monopolies forestall alternate methods, products and services" (1984, p. 227). Like Porter, Jacobs favors local competition because it stimulates innovation.

The three theories can be summarized using a simple economic model that will guide the empirical work. Suppose that a firm in some industry in a given location has a production function of output given by $A_t f(l_t)$, where A_t represents the overall level of technology at time t measured nominally (so changes in A represent changes in technology and changes in price), and l_t is the labor input at time t. The basic production function $f(l_t)$ abstracts from capital inputs. Allowing for only one input means that we may not capture labor-saving technological innovations and that we shall not capture innovations that result only in further accumulation of physical capital. We unfortunately do not have a measure of total productivity that would allow us to measure different types of technological progress. Each firm in this industry takes technology, prices, and wages, w_t, as given and maximizes

$$A_t f(l_t) - w_t l_t, \tag{1}$$

and so it sets the labor input to equate the marginal product of labor to its wage:

$$A_t f'(l_t) = w_t. \tag{2}$$

We can rewrite (2) in terms of growth rates as

$$\log\left(\frac{A_{t+1}}{A_t}\right) = \log\left(\frac{w_{t+1}}{w_t}\right) - \log\left[\frac{f'(l_{t+1})}{f'(l_t)}\right]. \tag{3}$$

The level of technology A_t in a city-industry is assumed to have both national components and local components:

$$A = A_{local} A_{national}. \tag{4}$$

The growth rate will then be the sum of the growth of national technology in this industry and the growth of local technology:

$$\log\left(\frac{A_{t+1}}{A_t}\right) = \log\left(\frac{A_{local,t+1}}{A_{local,t}}\right) + \log\left(\frac{A_{national,t+1}}{A_{national,t}}\right). \tag{5}$$

The growth of the national technology is assumed to capture the changes in the price of the product as well as shifts in nationwide technology in the industry, and the local technology is assumed to grow at a rate exogenous to the firm but depending on the various technological externalities present in this industry in the city:

$$\log\left(\frac{A_{local,t+1}}{A_{local,t}}\right) = g(\text{specialization, local monopoly,}$$
$$\text{diversity, initial conditions}) + e_{t+1}. \tag{6}$$

In equation (6), *specialization* is a measure of concentration of that industry in that city, which MAR and Porter believe raises the rate of technological progress; *local monopoly* is a measure of appropriability of innovation, which raises technological progress according to MAR and reduces it according to Porter; and *diversity* measures the variety of activities that the city pursues, which according to Jacobs speeds up technological progress. In Section IV below, we discuss further the inclusion of certain initial conditions. In the analysis below, we try to measure specialization, local monopoly, and city diversity empirically.

If we set $f(l) = l^{1-\alpha}$, $0 < \alpha < 1$, we can combine (3), (5), and (6) to obtain

$$\alpha \log\left(\frac{l_{t+1}}{l_t}\right) = -\log\left(\frac{w_{t+1}}{w_t}\right) + \log\left(\frac{A_{national,t+1}}{A_{national,t}}\right)$$
$$+ g(\text{specialization, competition,} \tag{7}$$
$$\text{diversity, initial conditions}) + e_{t+1}.$$

Growth in nationwide industry employment is assumed to capture changes in nationwide technology and prices. Workers are assumed to participate in a nationwide labor market so that wage growth will just be a constant across city-industries. Equation (7) then allows us to associate the growth of employment in an industry in a city with measures of technological externalities given by the theories.[1]

We should note that this specification of the three models is restrictive in an important respect; namely, it assumes that knowledge spillovers are constant over time and therefore affect both mature and young industries. One could argue, alternatively, that industries have a life cycle, and externalities are important only at the beginning, when new products are introduced. In this case, the function g is different across industries and in particular depends on their point in the product cycle. This view of temporary externalities is broadly inconsistent with the theories like Romer's (1990), which use externalities to explain permanent growth. Since the main purpose of this paper is to shed light on these theories, we stick with the specification such as (7). Our empirical work includes many old as well as young industries, and hence our results can in no way reject any model of industry life cycle and temporary externalities.

III. The Data

Construction of the Data Set

Our data set was constructed from the 1956 and 1987 editions of *County Business Patterns* (CBP), produced by the Bureau of the Census. The year 1956 was chosen because it was the first year with comprehensive data; 1987 was the last year available. The 1956 data were assembled by hand from hard copy; 1987 data are available on computer tapes.

The data set contains the information on employment, payroll, and number of establishments[2] by two-digit industry for every county in the United States. We obtained wages by dividing payroll by employment. Since we focus on cities rather than counties, we aggregate data across counties into metropolitan area units as described below. When

[1] We are assuming a national labor market for simplicity. If workers participate in an industrywide labor market, then the growth in industrywide employment may pick up changes in these wages. If workers participate in local labor markets (which seems unrealistic given large amounts of migration and the long time periods involved in our data), then it would be wage changes, as much as employment changes, that reflect changes in local technologies. Our wage change regressions in table 4 below are based on this possibility.

[2] We use the 1956 census definition of an establishment, which is an actual firm rather than a plant. In later years, the census redefined the establishment to be a plant. For our purposes, a firm is what is appropriate, so the 1956 definition is good.

counties are aggregated, the wage number is total payroll in a city divided by total employment. Since we run cross-section regressions, we keep all variables nominal.

Cities were constructed from a list of the top 170 standard metropolitan areas (SMAs) in 1956 in the United States contained in CBP. In some cases, an SMA contains several counties; in others (only in New England), several SMAs split a single county. The problem is to decide which counties should be included in a given city since it would be impractical to include all counties in an SMA. We included in each city the largest counties that cover the SMA until their combined payroll added up to at least 80 percent of the total payroll of the SMA *in both 1956 and 1987*.[3] This procedure makes sure that if substantial growth of employment occurred in counties in an SMA that were small or nonexistent in 1956, these counties are included in the city. The multicounty unit arrived at using this procedure is the city we focus on.[4]

For each city constructed through aggregating counties, we use data on the six largest two-digit industries, where size is measured by 1956 payroll. We use only six industries because we are interested in regionally specialized industries; also, hand collection limits how many industries we can take. This choice of industries creates a bias against including small, young, and dynamic industries that have not yet made it into the top six. However, as we mentioned above, the theories we are testing do not just apply to industries in the early years of the product cycle.

In some cases in which an industry in a county has only a few establishments, for confidentiality reasons, CBP does not reveal exact information on employment in that county-industry. Instead, it typically presents the range in which the employment in a given industry in a given county lies, such as 0–20 or 5,000–10,000. In a few cases in which the employment in a given county-industry is below 50, CBP presents no employment number at all. To construct our sample, we had to address this problem of missing variables, which is particularly

---

[3] Including all the counties that are part of the SMA would be extremely time consuming because to find out which industries in an SMA are the largest—a procedure we use to construct the data—we would have to add up by hand employment in all the potentially largest industries over all the counties. Adding extra counties also significantly worsens missing data problems discussed below. To simplify the first problem and to avoid the second, we have restricted the subset of counties included in the city.

[4] This procedure for constructing a city might introduce errors for larger cities, which cover numerous counties. To test whether this problem is responsible for our results, we repeated the analysis for the smallest 75 percent of the cities in the sample. The results were very similar to the ones reported below. For this reason, we use the whole sample in the results reported in this paper.

severe when a city contains several counties only one of which has missing data.

We addressed this problem as follows. If exact data were missing for some county-industry in 1956, we simply omitted that industry from the sample and replaced it by the next largest industry in that city for which complete data were available for all counties. The missing data problem was not significant in 1956, however, since we are selecting the largest city-industries as of 1956.

If exact data were missing for some county-industry in 1987, we estimated the employment in that county-industry at the midpoint of the range provided by CBP. For example, if it reported the employment in a county-industry to be between zero and 20, we used 10; if the number was between 5,000 and 10,000, we used 7,500. In a multicounty city, we then added these estimates to precise employment numbers for the counties for which they were available. In the few county-industries with employment under 50 for which CBP did not even provide a range, we used 25 as the employment number. This procedure enabled us to compute employment for all but four of the $170 \times 6 = 1,020$ city-industries. The reason we had to drop four city-industries is that "ordnance and accessories," an industry that occurred four times in our sample in 1956, was discontinued as a qualified two-digit industry by 1987. Of the 1,016 city-industries in this sample, employment in 833 was provided exactly, and employment in the other 183 was estimated as described above.[5]

Although CBP presents ranges of employment by county-industry, it does not provide any information on payroll in the cases in which exact employment numbers are omitted. As a result, we cannot estimate wages for these observations. Consequently, the wage regressions we present below are estimated on 833 city-industries for which we have exact data on employment and payroll.

Description of the Data

Since we are using a new data set, it may be helpful to present a simple description of the data. This is done in table 1. Panel A of the table describes the five smallest and the five largest cities in our sample as of 1956, their employment in 1956 and 1987, and the six largest industries in each of them. Note first that the largest city— New York—has employment of over 4 million, and the smallest— Laredo, Texas—has under 7,500 employees. Clearly our procedure

---

[5] In addition, we adjusted for many three- and four-digit industries, which were reassigned among two-digit industries. The primary changes occurred with reassignments among industries 50 and 51.

TABLE 1

DESCRIPTION OF THE DATA

A. CITIES IN 1956

| CITY | EMPLOYMENT | | SIX LARGEST INDUSTRIES |
	1956	1987	
	Five Largest Cities in 1956		
New York	4,065,062	5,449,561	Apparel, business services, printing, special trade contractors, durable wholesale trade, nondurable wholesale trade
Chicago	1,919,757	2,778,180	Metal products, food and kindred products, electric equipment, nonelectric machinery, printing, durable wholesale trade
Los Angeles	1,710,325	3,546,393	Electric equipment, fabricated metal products, nonelectric machinery, special trade contractors, transportation equipment, durable wholesale trade
Philadelphia	1,085,524	1,287,820	Apparel, electric equipment, fabricated metal products, food and kindred products, nonelectric machinery, durable wholesale trade
Detroit	1,063,284	1,567,641	Fabricated metal products, nonelectric machinery, primary metal industries, special trade contractors, transportation equipment, durable wholesale trade
	Five Smallest Cities in 1956		
Laredo, Tex.	7,458	25,397	Apparel, apparel stores, auto dealers, general merchandise, transport services, durable wholesale trade
San Angelo, Calif.	12,188	29,720	Auto dealers, communications, general contractors, general merchandise, special trade contractors, nondurable wholesale trade
Ogden, Utah	13,958	40,715	Auto dealers, communications, general contractors, general merchandise, special trade contractors, durable wholesale trade
Fort Smith, Ark.	19,089	55,057	Auto dealers, food and kindred products, food stores, special trade contractors, durable wholesale trade, nondurable wholesale trade
Sioux Falls, S.D.	19,096	59,398	Auto dealers, food and kindred products, insurance, trucking, durable wholesale trade, nondurable wholesale trade

TABLE 1 (*Continued*)

B. 10 LARGEST CITY-INDUSTRIES

City	Industry	Employment
New York	Apparel	366,928
New York	Durable wholesale trade	241,754
Detroit	Transportation equipment	233,761
Los Angeles	Transportation equipment	228,619
New York	Nondurable wholesale trade	157,833
New York	Printing	151,905
New York	Business services	143,043
Chicago	Electric machinery	125,425
Chicago	Nonelectric machinery	121,847
New York	Special trade contractors	114,267

C. MOST COMMON CITY-INDUSTRIES

Industry	Number of Appearances in Sample
Durable wholesale trade	146
Food and kindred products	78
Nonelectric machinery	76
Special trade contractors	70
Transportation equipment	60
Nondurable wholesale trade	59
Automotive dealers and service stations	55
Fabricated metal products	48
Primary metal industries	46
Electric machinery	38

D. INDUSTRY GROWTH

City-Industry	Growth	Nondiversity	Competition	Concentration
	Five Fastest-Growing City-Industries*			
Albuquerque Business services	3.325	.217	1.500	1.090
San Jose, Calif. Electric machinery	2.765	.290	.835	2.582
San Jose, Calif. Durable wholesale trade	2.407	.310	1.008	.883
San Jose, Calif. Transportation equipment	2.403	.311	.930	.876
Atlantic City, N.J. Hotels	2.345	.373	.418	11.221
	Five Slowest-Growing City-Industries			
Scranton, Pa. Anthracite coal mining	−5.417	.387	.931	113.139
Manchester, N.H. Leather products	−5.161	.331	.272	19.559
Wilkes-Barre–Hazleton, Pa. Tobacco products	−5.078	.466	.279	21.193
Hamilton-Middletown, Ohio Primary metal industries	−4.813	.513	.326	4.271
Gadsden, Ala. Textile mills	−4.714	.406	.185	4.876

* Growth is log(employment in 1987/employment in 1956). Nondiversity is city's other top five industries' share of 1956 total city employment. Competition is establishments per employee relative to establishments per employee in the U.S. industry. Concentration is the city-industry's share of city employment relative to U.S. industry's share of U.S. employment in 1956.

of looking at SMAs gets us down to fairly small places. The panel
also shows a great variety of top industries across cities, although
wholesale durables and nondurables are big in many of them.

Panel B describes the 10 largest city-industries in our sample. New
York City apparel is the largest city-industry in the United States
in 1956 with over 350,000 employees. Transportation equipment in
Detroit, which is of course autos, is the third largest. New York City
appears six and Chicago two times on this list.

Panel C describes the most common city-industries in the sample.
Wholesale trade in durables is the most common: it appears in 146
cities. A few other service categories appear as well, but the predominant type of most common sector is manufacturing. In particular,
nonelectrical machinery, primary metals, fabricated metals, transportation equipment, and electric equipment all appear quite often. The
typical stories of externalities apply to many of these industries. In
most of our analysis, we have pooled manufacturing and services,
although we discuss below what happens when wholesale trade is
removed from the sample, as well as how services are different from
manufacturing.

Panel D lists the five fastest-growing and five fastest-declining city-
industries in terms of employment. The panel gives three impressions. First, rapidly declining city-industries were more regionally
concentrated than the rapidly growing ones. Second, industries grew
faster in diversified cities than in specialized ones. Third, fast-growing
city-industries were more competitive, as measured by establishments
per employee, than shrinking city-industries. All these three impressions turn out to be our general empirical findings.

The panel also shows that the fastest-growing city-industries tended
to be in the South, West, and Southwest, whereas the slowest-growing
city-industries were often in the East and the Midwest. This finding
points to some basic economic forces at work, such as capital moving
to low-wage areas. A cynic might say that temperature determined
city growth or only that we are observing the decline of U.S. manufacturing. These objections are not valid since we control for location in
the South and we compare how fast the same industry grows in different cities.

More important, the decline in certain industries (notably steel, but
possibly autos as well) may be related to the theories discussed in this
paper. Both steel and auto production were regionally concentrated
(autos in Michigan and steel in Pennsylvania). Both industries had
only moderate levels of competition. In both industries, innovation
was arguably lacking, particularly in areas in which these industries
were concentrated.

The steel industry, according to Reutter (1988), has missed opportunities that were exploited by their competitors in less sterile environments. Big steel lost market share not only to foreign competitors but to American minimills located in nontraditional areas such as Roanoke, Virginia, or Florida. Use of concrete in construction also hurt steel badly. The first major use of concrete took place in a Hempstead, Long Island, shopping complex, far away from the traditional steel mills. Both concrete and shopping malls were major postwar innovations coming not from the established building material centers (such as Pennsylvania) but from smaller, more diversified areas. The steel industry may have declined not just because of foreign competition or some exogenous decline in manufacturing but, in part, because of forces stressed by Porter and Jacobs. Our statistical work suggests that this story of steel is a rule rather than an exception.

IV. Results on the Growth of Industries across Cities

If externalities are important for growth, then the clearest way to find these effects is by looking at the growth of the same sectors in different cities and checking in which cities these sectors grow faster. The unit of observation is then an industry in a city, and we look at the growth rates of these industries as a function of our measures of knowledge spillovers. The sample includes 1,016 observations on the top six two-digit 1956 industries in 170 cities.[6] Table 2 describes the variables. The mean of employment growth is zero, indicating that in an average city-industry in our sample employment did not grow. The standard deviation of this number, one, indicates the enormous dispersion of growth records. This dispersion may reflect the decline of some mining and manufacturing industries and the growth of services.

Equation (7) suggests that employment growth in an industry in a city may depend on the specialization of that industry in that city, local competition in the city-industry, and city diversity. Our measure of specialization of an industry in a city is the fraction of the city's employment that this industry represents in that city, relative to the share of the whole industry in national employment:

$$\text{specialization} = \frac{\text{industry employment in city/total employment in city}}{\text{industry employment in U.S./total employment in U.S.}} \quad (8)$$

---

[6] We have also performed the analysis using cities as a unit of observation. These regressions have not produced any statistically significant coefficients on our measures of externalities, although these measures tend to be much cruder for cities than they are for city-industries.

TABLE 2

Variable Means and Standard Deviations

Variable	Mean	Standard Deviation	Number of Observations
Log(employment in 1987/employment in 1956) in the city-industry	.00236	1.004	1,016
Log(U.S. employment in 1987/U.S. employment in 1956) in the industry outside the city	.308	.459	1,016
Wage in the city-industry in 1956 in thousands of dollars per quarter	1.063	.244	1,016
Employment in the city-industry in 1956 (in millions)	.0097	.0228	1,016
City-industry's share of city employment relative to U.S. industry's share of U.S. employment in 1956	3.367	9.019	1,016
Establishments per employee in the city-industry relative to establishments per employee in the U.S. industry	.752	.416	1,016
City's other top five industries' share of 1956 total city employment	.351	.100	1,016
Log(wage in 1987/wage in 1956) in the city-industry	1.649	.208	833
Log(U.S. wage in 1987/U.S. wage in 1956) in the industry outside the city	1.645	.144	833
Wage in the city in 1987	4.600	.663	833
Log(employment in 1987/employment in 1956) in the city	.980	.424	170
Wage in the city in 1956	.864	.114	170
Employment in the city in 1956	.118	.298	170
Employment growth in the four biggest industries	−.0312	.648	170

This variable measures how specialized a city is in an industry relative to what one would expect if employment in that industry was scattered randomly across the United States. The variable corrects for situations in which a city-industry is large only because the city is large. Because we are looking at the largest industries and because of regional specialization, the mean of this variable is 3.37. In our cities, top industries are overrepresented relative to what one would expect if they were randomly scattered over the United States. It is interesting to note that the maximum of this variable is 182.35 for anthracite mining in the Wilkes-Barre and Hazleton (Pennsylvania) SMA. The prediction of both MAR and Porter is that high specialization of an industry in a city should speed up growth of that industry in that city.

Our measure of local competition of an industry in a city is the number of firms per worker in this industry in this city relative to the number of firms per worker in this industry in the United States:

$$\text{competition} = \frac{\text{firms in city-industry/workers in city-industry}}{\text{firms in U.S. industry/workers in U.S. industry}}. \quad (9)$$

A value greater than one means that this industry has more firms relative to its size in this city than it does in the United States. One interpretation of the value greater than one is that the industry in the city is locally more competitive than it is elsewhere in the United States. Alternatively, a value of the competition variable greater than one can mean that firms in that industry in that city are just smaller than they are on average in the United States. It is very hard to distinguish smaller firms from more competitive firms using our data. Unfortunately, we do not have data on the output of individual firms and so cannot construct concentration ratios. Since we are looking at industries with large employment in their respective cities, we expect the mean of this competition variable to be below one; in fact it is .75. In a liberal interpretation of Porter, a higher value of this measure of competition should be associated with faster growth.

Finally, to address Jacobs's theory, we need a measure of a variety of industries in the city outside the industry in question. The measure we use is the fraction of the city's employment the largest five industries other than the industry in question account for in 1956. The mean of this ratio is .35: cities are not well diversified. The lower this ratio, the more diverse the city is and the faster the industry in question should grow according to Jacobs.

Table 3 presents our results for employment growth across city-industries, with 1,016 observations. We include as controls in the regressions the 1956 log of wage and the log of employment in the city-industry, a dummy variable indicating a southern city, and the national employment growth in that industry. Some analysts have argued that firms move to low-wage areas (or workers move to high-wage areas). Including the 1956 wage controls for either of these effects, even though this control variable is not strictly consistent with the assumption of a national labor market. High observed initial employment reduces employment growth because of either measurement error or more serious economic factors. The MAR view is somewhat incompatible with the presence of real (as opposed to measurement-induced) mean reversion, but since we are not correcting for potential measurement problems, we do not use such mean reversion as evidence against the MAR externalities.

We also include national employment change in the industry to correct for demand shifts. Various studies, including Terkla and Doeringer (1991) and Blanchard and Katz (1992), show that changes

TABLE 3

CITY-INDUSTRY EMPLOYMENT GROWTH BETWEEN 1956 AND 1987

DEPENDENT VARIABLE	LOG(EMPLOYMENT IN 1987/EMPLOYMENT IN 1956) IN THE CITY-INDUSTRY			
	(1)	(2)	(3)	(4)
Constant	−.423	−.923	−.181	−.513
	(.129)	(.129)	(.159)	(.149)
Log(U.S. employment in 1987/	1.140	1.209	1.237	1.148
U.S. employment in 1956) in	(.059)	(.052)	(.055)	(.056)
the industry outside the city				
Wage in the city-industry in 1956	.0137	.0226	.0379	.027
	(.109)	(.104)	(.109)	(.104)
Employment in the city-industry	−2.898	−3.280	−3.91	−4.080
in 1956 (in millions)	(1.099)	(1.055)	(1.131)	(1.073)
Dummy variable indicating pres-	.426	.416	.370	.378
ence in the South	(.057)	(.054)	(.058)	(.055)
City-industry's share of city em-	−.0128	. . .	. . .	−.00799
ployment relative to industry's	(.003)			(.003)
share of U.S. employment in				
1956				
Establishments per employee in	. . .	.587	. . .	.561
the city-industry relative to es-		(.057)		(.057)
tablishments per employee in				
the U.S. industry in 1956				
City's other top five industries'	. . .	. . .	−.894	−.913
share of total city employment			(.259)	(.245)
in 1956				
Adjusted R^2	.392	.439	.387	.450
Number of observations	1,016	1,016	1,016	1,016

NOTE.—Standard errors of parameter estimates are in parentheses beneath these estimates.

in demand for a region's output are the principal determinant of employment growth in that region. Since we are looking at city-industries rather than whole regions, we must correct for changes in national industry demand, which we measure by national industry employment. We thus are looking at whether steel has grown faster or slower than average in particular cities, controlling for how steel employment changed in the nation as a whole. This correction is particularly important for traditional manufacturing industries, many of which have declined in the postwar United States.

The control variables tend to have the expected signs. High initial employment in an industry in a city leads to slower growth of that industry's employment. Employment in an industry in a city grows faster when employment in that industry in the whole country grows faster. It is interesting to note that the coefficient on national industry employment growth is above one. Factors shifting employment in national industries seem to be more influential in urban than in rural areas. Southern cities also grew significantly more than cities outside the South (see also Wheat 1986). Initial wages in a city-industry are uncorrelated with subsequent employment growth.

The results on externalities reveal several interesting findings. Equation 1 in table 3 shows that industries that are more heavily concentrated in the city than they are in the United States as a whole grow slower. The effect is statistically significant but qualitatively small. As we raise the measure of specialization by one standard deviation (9.02), cumulative growth of employment over 30 years slows by 12 percent total, which is about one-ninth of a standard deviation. This result is the opposite of the prediction of the MAR model. Not only do we fail to find positive evidence in favor of MAR, but the data point in the opposite direction: geographic specialization reduces growth.

In equation 2 in table 3, the coefficient on the competition variable is positive and very significant. More firms per worker in a city-industry relative to the national average leads to higher growth of that city-industry, consistent with Porter's and Jacobs's hypothesis. Going from as many to twice as many firms per worker as the national average (2.5 standard deviations) raises growth of employment in the city-industry by 59 percent over 30 years, which is almost two-thirds of a standard deviation. Of course, another interpretation of this finding is that smaller firms grow faster. However, recent evidence (Davis and Haltiwanger 1992) indicates that in fact smaller firms do not grow faster once one takes account of the fact that they have a higher probability of death than larger firms. We should also mention that the "small firms grow faster" model is inconsistent with the MAR view that monopolies that internalize externalities are good for growth. So even though the positive evidence in favor of competition is somewhat ambiguous, the negative evidence on MAR is more clear-cut.

Equation 3 in table 3 shows that industries in cities in which other large industries are relatively small grow faster. As we reduce the share of city employment taken up by the five largest industries other than the one in question by .1 (a standard deviation), cumulative employment growth in the city-industry over 30 years falls by 9 percent (one-tenth of a standard deviation). This result suggests that not having dominant industries as neighbors, or alternatively having a greater variety of neighbors, helps own growth. This finding is consistent with the importance of knowledge spillovers stressed by Jacobs from outside the industry.

Equation 4 in table 3 uses all measures of externalities simultaneously. The results remain statistically significant. They confirm our finding that industry overrepresentation hurts its growth. The fact that the coefficient has the wrong sign relative to what MAR predicts and is statistically significant is evidence against the importance of permanent within-industry knowledge spillovers for growth. Competition within the city-industry continues to exert a positive influence on growth of its employment, and the coefficient hardly changes from equation 2 in table 3. The result that concentration of other industries in the city hurts the growth of an industry's employment continues to be strong. The overall results are not favorable to MAR, mixed on Porter, and favorable to Jacobs.

It is also possible that our results support a neoclassical model rather than any kind of externality. Many of our findings are consistent with the observation that industries move to regions in which they are not present. Thus employment moves south, as Wheat (1986) has also found, and grows slower where it is high to begin with. The result that employment in an industry grows higher in a diversified city might reflect the fact that such cities are less crowded and hence cheaper to locate in. Competition for space and labor might thus explain many of our findings. At the same time, the very existence of cities despite the high rents is hard to explain without externalities. And if externalities do matter, our evidence points against intraindustry spillovers and in favor of knowledge spillovers across sectors à la Jacobs.

We have checked the robustness of these results in a number of ways. First, our results might be driven by the mining industries, which exhibit extraordinary regional specialization and have declined sharply in postwar years in part because prices fell and in part because mineral stocks were depleted. We have run the regressions in table 3 without the mining industries, and the results are similar in terms of sign patterns and statistical significance.

Second, one could argue that knowledge spillovers are more important in manufacturing than in services because technological progress is more rapid in manufacturing. Without subscribing to this objection, we tested it empirically by splitting the industries into manufacturing and nonmanufacturing. Our results hold qualitatively for both subsamples. All coefficients on the externality variables remain significant in the nonmanufacturing regression, and all but the coefficient on the urban variety variable are significant for manufacturing. If anything, the results appear to be stronger for nonmanufacturing.

Third, we divided manufacturing into ubiquitous industries (fabricated metals, nonferrous metals, nonelectrical machinery, etc.) and more specialized industries (electrical equipment, transport equipment, primary metals, pulp and paper, textiles and apparel, leather products, etc.). Specialized industries presumably produce primarily for export, so technological change can spur their growth, unfettered by the limits of local demand. Ubiquitous industries are presumably aimed toward local consumption, and their growth will be largely limited by local demand.[7] If this reasoning is correct, the effect of externalities should be more pronounced in more specialized manufacturing industries.

We have run our regressions using the two manufacturing subsamples separately. The negative effect of our specialization measure on industry growth is stronger and more statistically significant for ubiquitous manufacturing, but the effect remains negative, though insignificant, for more specialized manufacturing as well. There is certainly no evidence that the coefficient is positive, as MAR would suggest.

Although we have measured industry growth using employment growth, a better measure would be productivity growth. Since we do not observe output, it is hard for us to measure productivity. However, in the world in which some productivity gains accrue to labor, one rough measure of productivity growth might be city-industry wage growth. While this measure is not compatible with the model of national labor markets that we presented, it is compatible with models of locally more segmented markets. Even so, measuring productivity growth through wage growth is very imperfect. First, productivity increases might accrue only partly to labor, especially as migration occurs; in the long run, identical workers must be indifferent between cities. Second, declining industries might fire their less able and experienced workers first, creating an artificial rise in wages. Third, certain technological innovations (e.g., the assembly line) might make it easier to hire less expensive workers. Fourth, rent sharing might also be a factor, especially in those industries (steel, coal, or autos) with heavy union involvement. A further problem with the wage data is that we have no estimates of wages for counties without precisely reported employment numbers. The restriction of the sample to 833 observations could induce a sample selection bias. Given these objections, our results on wage growth should be interpreted as at best secondary to employment growth results.

Table 4 presents the findings in the same format as table 3. High initial wages in a city-industry reduce wage growth, but high initial employment in a city-industry helped wage growth, although as we saw before it hurt employment growth. This result might reflect a selection effect: high employment leads to employment cuts, which for reasons of seniority affect least well paid workers most, leading to an increase in the average wage of those who remain employed.

Equation 1 in table 4 shows that city-industry specialization has no

---

[7] This division was suggested by Vernon Henderson.

Innovation, Evolution of Industry and Economic Growth III

TABLE 4

CITY-INDUSTRY WAGE GROWTH BETWEEN 1956 AND 1987

VARIABLE	LOG(WAGE IN 1987/WAGE IN 1956) IN THE CITY-INDUSTRY			
	(1)	(2)	(3)	(4)
Constant	.332	.379	.398	.440
	(.065)	(.064)	(.069)	(.068)
Log(U.S. wage in 1987/U.S. wage in 1956) in the industry outside the city	.961	.975	.959	.973
	(.043)	(.042)	(.043)	(.042)
Wage in the city-industry in 1956	−.270	−.270	−.266	−.267
	(.027)	(.027)	(.027)	(.027)
Employment in the city-industry in 1956 (in millions)	1.025	1.111	.849	.938
	(.270)	(.266)	(.276)	(.271)
Dummy variable indicating presence in the South	.0175	.0161	.0094	.0085
	(.013)	(.013)	(.013)	(.013)
City-industry's share of city employment relative to industry's share of U.S. employment in 1956	.00053	...	...	−.00023
	(.0007)			(.0007)
Establishments per employee in the city-industry relative to establishments per employee in the U.S. industry in 1956	...	−.0850	...	−.0845
		(.014)		(.014)
City's other top five industries' share of 1956 city employment	...	...	−.172	−.161
			(.060)	(.059)
Adjusted R^2	.3832	.4099	.3889	.4139
Number of observations	833	833	833	833

NOTE.—Standard errors of parameter estimates are in parentheses beneath these estimates.

effect on wage growth, which does not support the MAR view, although the coefficient no longer has the wrong sign. When other measures of externalities are added in equation 4 in table 4, the coefficient is insignificant and has the wrong sign. City-industry competition reduces wage growth (the coefficient is significant), which is inconsistent with the view that competition contributes to productivity growth that accrues to the workers. We do not think that the latter position can be ascribed to Porter. Finally, diversity in a city helps wage growth of the industry, consistent with Jacobs's view that productivity growth is helped by diversity.

None of the evidence we have presented supports the importance of within-industry knowledge spillovers for growth. If such spillovers are particularly pronounced at geographical proximity, the evidence is detrimental to the theories of MAR and Porter that focus on these spillovers. We end this discussion with a word of caution, however. We are looking at large, mature cities that are not growing very fast and are in many cases declining, making ours a very special sample. Within-industry knowledge spillovers may not matter for such mature industries, though they may be much more important at the early stages of an industry. For example, these spillovers might be very important when a new industry is born and organizes itself in one location, but unimportant as this industry matures and geographical proximity becomes less important for the transmission of knowledge. Our data, unfortunately, cannot address this industry life cycle model. At the least, however, we are rejecting the strong version of the MAR theory, which predicts that within-industry knowledge spillovers lead to permanent self-sustaining growth in cities.

V. Static External Economies: Localization and Urbanization

Localization

The evidence we have presented suggests that diversity, and not specialization, contributes to growth. This result raises an important problem: If geographical specialization does not contribute to growth, why is it so prevalent? In this section, we address this problem. We also look for the evidence of urbanization externalities: those that make different industries locate next to each other to form a city.

There are several reasons for regional specialization that are not dynamic externalities that contribute to growth. Most obviously, natural resource or transport advantages often favor a particular location, and those apply equally to all firms in the industry. For example, the oil industry at the turn of the century was located in Ohio, near the discovered oil. Bairoch (1988) reports that during the Industrial Revolution many new cities located near the supplies of energy. One could also argue that the auto industry located in the Midwest in part to economize on transport costs of inputs.

But in addition to these natural reasons for specialization, there are several static externalities that contribute to specialization but not to growth. Perhaps most important is the idea of saving on moving inputs, suggested by Marshall (1890). A whole industry might locate near the place of common suppliers both to reduce the cost of getting supplies and to have a closer flow of information to suppliers. In addition, many firms producing specialized products that are subject to wildly fluctuating firm demand but more stable industry demand would locate together. By doing so, they enable specialized labor to move easily between firms without moving between cities, as in the previously mentioned case of the New York fashion industry. More generally, when firms share any input that is not costlessly mobile, it pays them to locate together near that input and so save on moving the input (see Lichtenberg 1960; Henderson 1986, 1988). More recently, Rotemberg and Saloner (1990) argued that firms locate together to commit to compete for labor and not pay monopsony wages. This effective commitment enables firms to attract labor in the first place. There are clearly many reasons for regional specialization other than knowledge spillovers.

Our findings are consistent with the importance of localization externalities as long as the location of firms next to each other to take advantage of these externalities is finished when our sample begins. In this case, there is no reason that regionally specialized industries should grow faster. If, in contrast, we observed young industries, in which entry of firms to take advantage of localization externalities was still taking place, we would still expect employment in regionally specialized industries to grow faster as entry takes place. Our results would then reject the importance of localization externalities, just as they reject the MAR-Porter models. Since we are focusing on the largest city-industries, however, the assumption that they are mature seems reasonable. Our findings do not reject the localization externalities playing a role in determining regional specialization.

Urbanization

Although cities are usually specialized in a few lines of work, they also typically pursue many other activities outside the main lines. Many of these activities are entirely unrelated to each other. This suggests another type of externality operating in a city. Firms locate in a city because local demand is high there, and so they can sell some of their output without incurring transport costs. This is obviously most important for high-fixed-cost industries. Lichtenberg (1960) argues that this externality explains why the insurance industry once located in New York City. Murphy et al. (1989) discuss such pecuniary externalities; Krugman (1991a, 1991b) models city formation based on local demand. Henderson (1986) refers to these effects as "urbanization" externalities and presents empirical evidence suggesting that they are not important for productivity.

These models imply that when an industry grows, it raises local payrolls and therefore local demand and so helps the growth of other possibly unrelated industries in that city, which adjust to higher demand. As a result, growth rates of different industries in a city are positively correlated. This argument is most compelling for local services, which probably grow when city exports grow.

The argument against urbanization externalities is crowding. When an industry in a city grows, it raises wages and rents and so makes it more expensive for other industries to expand in that city. Con-

TABLE 5

EMPLOYMENT GROWTH OF SMALLER INDUSTRIES BETWEEN 1956 AND 1987

Dependent Variable	Log(Employment in 1987/Employment in 1956) in the City Outside the Four Biggest Industries
Constant	1.410
	(.191)
1956 employment outside the four biggest industries (in millions)	−1.96
	(.083)
1956 wage outside the four biggest industries	−.455
	(.226)
Employment growth in the four biggest industries	.458
	(.033)
R^2	.5910
Number of observations	170

NOTE.—Standard errors of parameter estimates are in parentheses beneath these estimates.

versely, when an industry in a city shrinks, it frees up land and labor and so makes growth of other industries more attractive. Urbanization externalities and crowding have the opposite implications for the data.

Our data enable us to test these predictions, as shown in table 5. The dependent variable in the regression is employment growth in the city outside the four largest industries, and the key independent variable is employment growth in these four largest industries. The evidence indicates very strongly that small industries grow when large industries do. A 1 percent increase in the four-industry employment growth leads to a 0.5 percent increase in employment growth outside these industries. We replicated this result for several combinations of dependent and independent variables. The evidence consistently points in favor of aggregate demand spillovers and against crowding. Of course, another possible interpretation of this finding is that there are some city effects that attract all industries to some cities, but recall that we at least control for the 1956 wage level in our sample. Overall, the results support the role of urbanization externalities in city growth, consistent with the theoretical work of Murphy et al. (1989) and Krugman (1991a, 1991b) as well as with much of the empirical work in urban economics.

VI. Conclusion

The results presented in this paper allow some tentative conclusions. We have shown that at the city-industry level, specialization hurts, competition helps, and city diversity helps employment growth. Our best interpretation of this evidence is that interindustry knowledge spillovers are less important for growth than spillovers across industries, particularly in the case of fairly mature cities. The Jacobs-Rosenberg-Bairoch model, in which knowledge transmission takes the form of adoption of an innovation by additional sectors, seems to be the most consistent with the evidence.

An important objection to these results that we have mentioned already is that we are looking at a particular period in U.S. history in which traditional manufacturing industries have fared poorly because of import competition and at particular very mature cities. Our results may then not be applicable for more dynamic time periods or places. On this theory, MAR externalities matter the most when industries grow. We cannot address this objection with our data.

The evidence suggests that cross-fertilization of ideas across industries speeds up growth. The growth of cities is one manifestation of this phenomenon, but there may be others. The results would imply, for example, that open societies, with substantial labor mobility across industries, will exhibit a greater spread of ideas and growth. Similarly, the cross-fertilization perspective argues in favor of such labor flows as immigration and migration across areas. If Jane Jacobs is right, the research on growth should change its focus from looking inside industries to looking at the spread of ideas across sectors. As a final point, however, we recall that our evidence on externalities is indirect, and many of our findings can be explained by a neoclassical model in which industries grow where labor is cheap and demand is high.

References

Arrow, Kenneth J. "The Economic Implications of Learning by Doing." *Rev. Econ. Studies* 29 (June 1962): 155–73.

Arthur, W. Brian. "Silicon Valley Locational Clusters: When Do Increasing Returns Imply Monopoly?" Working paper. Sante Fe, N.M.: Santa Fe Inst., 1989.

Bairoch, Paul. *Cities and Economic Development: From the Dawn of History to the Present.* Chicago: Univ. Chicago Press, 1988.

Blanchard, Olivier J., and Katz, Lawrence F. "Regional Evolutions." *Brookings Papers Econ. Activity,* no. 1 (1992).

Dasgupta, Partha, and Stiglitz, Joseph E. "Uncertainty, Industrial Structure, and the Speed of R&D." *Bell J. Econ.* 11 (Spring 1980): 1–28.

Davis, Steve J., and Haltiwanger, John. "Gross Job Creation, Gross Job Destruction, and Employment Reallocation." *Q.J.E.* 107 (August 1992).

Griliches, Zvi. "Issues in Assessing the Contribution of Research and Development to Productivity Growth." *Bell J. Econ.* 10 (Spring 1979): 92–116.

Henderson, J. Vernon. "Efficiency of Resource Usage and City Size." *J. Urban Econ.* 19 (January 1986): 47–70.

———. *Urban Development: Theory, Fact, and Illusion.* New York: Oxford Univ. Press, 1988.

Jacobs, Jane. *The Economy of Cities.* New York: Vintage, 1969.
———. *Cities and the Wealth of Nations: Principles of Economic Life.* New York: Vintage, 1984.
Krugman, Paul. "Cities in Space: Three Simple Models." Manuscript. Cambridge: Massachusetts Inst. Tech., 1991. (*a*)
———. "Increasing Returns and Economic Geography." *J.P.E.* 99 (June 1991): 483–99. (*b*)
Lichtenberg, Robert M. *One-Tenth of a Nation: National Forces in the Economic Growth of the New York Region.* Cambridge, Mass.: Harvard Univ. Press, 1960.
Loury, Glenn C. "Market Structure and Innovation." *Q.J.E.* 93 (August 1979): 395–410.
Lucas, Robert E., Jr. "On the Mechanics of Economic Development." *J. Monetary Econ.* 22 (July 1988): 3–42.
Marshall, Alfred. *Principles of Economics.* London: Macmillan, 1890.
Murphy, Kevin M.; Shleifer, Andrei; and Vishny, Robert W. "Industrialization and the Big Push." *J.P.E.* 97 (October 1989): 1003–26.
Porter, Michael E. *The Competitive Advantage of Nations.* New York: Free Press, 1990.
Reutter, Mark. *Sparrows Point: Making Steel: The Rise and Ruin of American Industrial Might.* New York: Simon & Schuster, 1988.
Romer, Paul M. "Increasing Returns and Long-Run Growth." *J.P.E.* 94 (October 1986): 1002–37.
———. "Endogenous Technological Change." *J.P.E.* 98, no. 5, pt. 2 (October 1990): S71–S101.
Rosenberg, Nathan. "Technological Change in the Machine Tool Industry, 1840–1910." *J. Econ. Hist.* 23 (December 1963): 414–43.
Rotemberg, Julio, and Saloner, Garth. "Competition and Human Capital Accumulation: A Theory of Interregional Specialization and Trade." Manuscript. Cambridge: Massachusetts Inst. Tech., 1990.
Scherer, Frederic M. "Inter-Industry Technology Flows in the United States." *Res. Policy* 11 (August 1982): 227–45.
Schumpeter, Joseph A. *Capitalism, Socialism, and Democracy.* New York: Harper, 1942.
Terkla, D. G., and Doeringer, P. B. "Explaining Variations in Employment Growth: Structural and Cyclical Change among States and Local Areas." *J. Urban Econ.* 29 (May 1991): 329–48.
Wheat, Leonard F. "The Determinants of 1963–77 Regional Manufacturing Growth: Why the South and West Grow." *J. Regional Sci.* 26 (November 1986): 635–59.

[14]

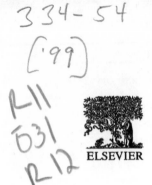

ELSEVIER

European Economic Review 43 (1999) 409–429

EUROPEAN ECONOMIC REVIEW

Innovation in cities:
Science-based diversity, specialization and localized competition

Maryann P. Feldman[a], David B. Audretsch[b,c,*]

[a] *Institute for Policy Studies, Johns Hopkins University, 3400 N. Charles St., Wyman Park 5th Floor, Baltimore, MD 21218-2696, USA*
[b] *Institute for Development Strategies, Indiana University, Bloomington, IN 47405-2100, USA*
[c] *Centre for Economic Policy Research, London, UK*

Received 1 September 1997; accepted 19 May 1998

Abstract

Whether diversity or specialization of economic activity better promotes technological change and subsequent economic growth has been the subject of a heated debate in the economics literature. The purpose of this paper is to consider the effect of the composition of economic activity on innovation. We test whether the specialization of economic activity within a narrow concentrated set of economic activities is more conducive to knowledge spillovers or if diversity, by bringing together complementary activities, better promotes innovation. The evidence provides considerable support for the diversity thesis but little support for the specialization thesis. © 1999 Elsevier Science B.V. All rights reserved.

JEL classification: O3, O1

Keywords: Innovation; Geography; Economic development; Agglomeration; Spillovers

* Correspondence address: School of Public and Environmental Affairs (SPEA), Institute for Developmental Strategies, Indiana University, Bloomington, IN 47405-2100, USA. Tel.: 1 812 855 6766; fax: 1 812 855 0184; e-mail: daudretsch@indiana ⁿᵈᵘ

1. Introduction

In proposing a new theory of economic geography, Paul Krugman (1991b, p. 5) asks, 'What is the most striking feature of the geography of economic activity? The short answer is surely concentration ... production is remarkably concentrated in space.' Perhaps in response to Krugman's concern, a literature has recently emerged which focuses on the implications of the concentration of economic activity for economic growth. Models posited by Romer (1986, 1990), Lucas (1993), and Krugman (1991a,b) link increasing returns to scale yielded by externalities within a geographically bounded region to higher rates of growth. The results of Jaffe (1989), Jaffe et al. (1993), Feldman (1994) and Audretsch and Feldman (1996) suggest that R&D and other knowledge spillovers not only generate externalities, but the evidence also suggests that such knowledge spillovers tend to be geographically bounded within the region where the new economic knowledge was created. New economic knowledge may spill over, but the geographic extent of such knowledge spillovers is bounded. Lucas (1993) emphasizes the most natural context in which to understand the mechanics of economic growth is in metropolitan areas where the compact nature of the geographic unit facilitates communication. Indeed, Lucas (1993) asserts that the only compelling reason for the existence of cities would be the presence of increasing returns to agglomerations of resources which make these locations more productive.

None of these studies, however, ask the question, 'Does the specific type of economic activity undertaken within any particular geographic region matter?' This question is important because a recent debate has arisen focusing precisely on the composition of economic activity within an agglomeration and how such externalities will be shaped by that composition of economic activity. One view, which Glaeser et al. (1992) attribute to the *Marshall–Arrow–Romer* externality, suggests that an increased concentration of a particular industry within a specific geographic region facilitates knowledge spillovers across firms.[1] By contrast, Jacobs (1969) argues that it is the exchange of complementary knowledge across diverse firms and economic agents which yields a greater return to new economic knowledge.

There are clear policy implications of this debate in terms of policies directed towards innovation and technological change. If the specialization thesis is correct, then policy should focus on developing a narrow set of economic activities within a geographic region in order to yield greater innovative output. On the other hand, if the diversity thesis is correct, then a geographic region comprised of a diverse set of economic activities will tend to yield greater output

---

[1] This mirrors an earlier debate summarized by Loesch (1954).

M.P. Feldman, D.B. Audretsch / European Economic Review 43 (1999) 409–429   411

in terms of innovative activity. The key policy concerns would then become how to identify the commonalties and how to foster such diversity.

The purpose of this paper is to penetrate the black box of geographic space by identifying the extent to which the organization of economic activity is either concentrated, or alternatively consists of diverse but complementary economic activities, and how this composition influences innovative output. To consider this question we link the innovative output of product categories within a specific city to the extent to which the economic activity of that city is concentrated ·in that industry, or conversely, diversified in terms of complementary industries sharing a common science base. We use results on the relevance of academic departments to R&D from Levin et al. (1987) to identify complementary industries across which knowledge spillovers may be realized. We find a tendency for innovative activity in complementary industries sharing a common science-base to cluster together in geographic space. Industries which use the same base of scientific knowledge exhibit a strong tendency to locate together for both the location of production and the location of innovation.

In Section 2, we introduce the main theories alternatively favoring diversity or specialization in generating innovative activity. Issues concerning the measurement of innovative activity, the geographic unit of observation and the concepts of science-based diversity and specialization are examined in Section 3. After the model is presented in the Section 4, the empirical results are provided in Section 5. To explore the validity of our results, we extend our analysis to consider the impact of specialization versus diversity of economic activity within the firm on innovative activity in Section 6. We find considerable evidence rejecting the specialization thesis and in support of the diversity thesis. Based on the findings for both industries within specific cities as well as for individual firms, an organizational structure of economic activities that are diverse, but still complementary, apparently yields a greater innovative output than a specialization of economic activity.

2. Diversity versus specialization

The importance of location to innovation in a world increasingly relying upon E-mail, fax machines, and electronic communications superhighways may seem surprising, and even paradoxical at first glance. The resolution of this paradox lies in the distinction between knowledge and information. While the costs of transmitting information may be invariant to distance, presumably the cost of transmitting knowledge, especially what Von Hipple (1994) refers to as *sticky knowledge*, rises with distance. Von Hipple persuasively demonstrates that highly contextual and uncertain knowledge is best transmitted via face-to-face interaction and through frequent contact. Proximity matters in transmitting

412   *M.P. Feldman, D.B. Audretsch / European Economic Review 43 (1999) 409–429*

knowledge because, as Arrow (1962) pointed out, such sticky knowledge is inherently non-rival in nature and knowledge developed for any particular application can easily spill over and be applied to different use and applications. Indeed, Griliches (1992) has defined knowledge spillovers as 'working on similar things and hence benefiting much from each other's research'.[2]

Despite the general consensus that knowledge spillovers within a given location stimulate technological advance, there is little consensus as to exactly how this occurs. Glaeser et al. (1992) characterize three different models from the literature that would influence the production of innovation in cities. The *Marshall–Arrow–Romer* model formalizes the insight that the concentration of an industry in a city promotes knowledge spillovers between firms and therefore would facilitate innovation in that city-industry observation. This type of concentration is also known as industry localization (Loesch, 1954). An important assumption is that knowledge externalities with respect to firms exist, *but only for firms within the same industry.* Thus, the relevant unit of observation is extended from the firm to the region in the theoretical tradition of the Marshall–Arrow–Romer model and in subsequent empirical studies, but spillovers are limited to occur within the relevant industry. The transmission of knowledge spillovers across industries is assumed to be non-existent or at least trivial.

Restricting knowledge externalities to occur only within the industry may ignore an important source of new economic knowledge–inter-industry spillovers. Jacobs (1969) argues that the most important source of knowledge spillovers are external to the industry in which the firm operates and that cities are the source of innovation because the diversity of these knowledge sources is greatest in cities. Thus, Jacobs develops a theory that emphasizes that the variety of industries within a geographic region promotes knowledge externalities and ultimately innovative activity and economic growth. Of course, there should be some basis for interaction between diverse activities. A common science base facilitates the exchange of existing ideas and generation of new ones across disparate but complementary industries. Thus, in Jacobs' view, diversity rather than specialization is the operative mechanism of economic growth.

A second controversy involves the degree of competition prevalent in the region, or the extent of local monopoly. The Marshall–Arrow–Romer model predicts that local monopoly is superior to local competition because it

---

[2] Considerable evidence suggests that location and proximity clearly matter in exploiting knowledge spillovers. Not only have Jaffe et al. (1993) found that patent citations tend to occur more frequently within the state in which they were patented but Audretsch and Stephan (1996) and Audretsch and Feldman (1996) found that the propensity for innovative activity to cluster geographically tends to be greater in industries where new economic knowledge plays a more important role.

M.P. Feldman, D.B. Audretsch / European Economic Review 43 (1999) 409–429   413

maximizes the ability of firms to appropriate the economic value accruing from their innovative activity. By contrast, Jacobs (1969) and Porter (1990) argue that competition is more conducive to knowledge externalities than is local monopoly.[3] It should be emphasized that by local competition, Jacobs (1969) does not mean competition within product markets as has traditionally en-visioned within the industrial organization literature. Rather, Jacobs is referring to the competition for the new ideas embodied in economic agents. Not only does an increased number of firms provide greater competition for new ideas, but in addition, greater competition across firms facilitates the entry of a new firm specializing in some particular, new, product niche. This is because the necessary complementary inputs and services are likely to be available from small specialist niche firms but not necessarily from large, vertically integrated producers.[4]

3. Measurement issues

Krugman (1991a, p. 53) has argued that economists should abandon any attempts at measuring knowledge spillovers because '...knowledge flows are invisible, they leave no paper trail by which they may be measured and tracked'. But as Jaffe et al. (1993, p. 578) point out, 'knowledge flows do sometimes leave a paper trail' – in particular in the form of patented inventions and new product introductions.

In this paper we rely upon a direct measure of innovative output, rather than on a measure of intermediate output, such as patented inventions.[5] This United States Small Business Administration's Innovation Data Base (SBIDB) is the primary source of data for this paper.[6] The database consists of new product

---

[3] Porter (1990) provides examples of Italian ceramics and gold jewelry industries in which numerous firms are located with a bounded geographic region and compete intensively in terms of product innovation rather than focusing on simple price competition.

[4] A recent series of country studies assembled by Reynolds et al. (1994) show that new-firm start-up rates tend to be greatest in those geographic regions where the average number of firms per employee is the greatest.

[5] Scherer (1983), Mansfield (1984) and Griliches (1990) have all warned that the number of patented inventions is not the equivalent of a direct measure of innovative output. For example, Pakes and Griliches (1984, p. 378) argue that 'patents are a flawed measure of innovative output; particularly since not all new innovations are patented and since patents differ greatly in their economic impact'. In addressing the question, 'Patents as indicators of what?' Griliches (1990, p. 1669) concludes that, 'Ideally, we might hope that patent statistics would provide a measure of the innovative output ... The reality, however, is very far from it. The dream of getting hold of an output measure of inventive activity is one of the strong motivating forces for economic research in this area'.

[6] A detailed description of the SBIDB is contained in Audretsch (1995).

introductions compiled form the new product announcement sections of over 100 technology, engineering and trade journals spanning every industry in manufacturing. From the sections in each trade journal listing new products, a database consisting of the innovations by four-digit standard industrial classification (SIC) industries was formed. These innovation data have been implemented by Audretsch (1995) to analyze the relationship between industry dynamics and technological change, and by Audretsch and Feldman (1996), Feldman (1994) and Feldman and Florida (1994) to examine the spatial distribution of innovation.

There are several important qualifications that should be made concerning the SBIDB. The trade journals report mainly product innovations. Thus, as is the case in the studies by Audretsch (1995) and Audretsch and Feldman (1996), the empirical analyses undertaken in this paper capture product innovation but not process innovation.

Another potential concern might be that the significance and 'quality' of the innovations vary considerably. In fact, each innovation was classified according to one of the following levels of significance: (1) the innovation established an entirely new category of product; (2) the innovation is the first of its type on the market in a product category already in existence; (3) the innovation represents a significant improvement in existing technology; and (4) the innovation is a modest improvement designed to update an existing product. About 87% of the innovations were in this fourth category and most of the remaining innovations were classified in the third category. However, the preliminary nature of such classifications leads us to treat the innovations as being homogeneous. While such an assumption will hopefully be improved upon in the future, it is consistent with the voluminous body of literature treating dollars of R&D, numbers of scientists and engineers, and numbers of patents as being homogeneous.[7]

An important strength of the database is that the innovating *establishment* is identified as well as the innovating *enterprise*. While this distinction is trivial for single-plant manufacturing firms, it becomes important in multi-plant firms. This is because some innovations are made by subsidiaries or divisions of companies with headquarters in other states. Even though the headquarters may announce new product innovations made by the company, the database still identifies the individual establishment responsible for the majority of the work leading to the innovation.

---

[7] An anonymous referee points out that the implicit assumption that innovations are homogeneous in their impact is found in most studies attempting to measure innovative activity. As Griliches (1990) emphasizes, this limitation has plagued studies using counts of patents, just as it has in those based on R&D expenditures or R&D scientists and engineers.

M.P. Feldman, D.B. Audretsch / European Economic Review 43 (1999) 409–429   415

The innovations from the SBIDB are then classified according to the four-digit SIC industry of the new product and the city where the innovating establishment was located. We adapt either the Consolidated Metropolitan Statistical Area (CMSA) or the Metropolitan Statistical Area (MSA) as the spatial unit of observation. The analysis here is based on 3969 new manufacturing product innovations for which the address of the innovating establishment could be identified.[8]

In 1982 the most innovative city in the United States was New York. Seven hundred and thirty-five, or 18.5%, of the total number of innovations in the country were attributed to firms in the greater New York City area. Four hundred and seventy-seven (12.0%) were attributed to San Francisco and 345 (8.7%) to the Boston area and 333 (8.4%) to the Los Angeles area. In total, 1890, or 45% of the innovations, took place in these four consolidated metropolitan areas. In fact, all but 150 of the innovations included in the database are attributed to metropolitan areas. That is, less than 4% of the innovations occurred outside of metropolitan areas. This contrasts with the 70% of the population which resided in these areas.

Of course, simply comparing the absolute amount of innovative activity across cities ignores the fact that some cities are simply larger than others. Cities vary considerably in terms of measures of city size, and we expect that city scale will have an impact on innovative output. Table 1 presents the number of innovations normalized by the size of the geographic unit. Population provides a crude but useful measure of the size of the geographic unit. Cities in Table 1 are ranked in descending order by innovation rate or the number of innovations per 100,000 population. While New York has the highest count of innovation, it has the third highest innovation rate. The most innovative city in the United States, on a per capita measure of city size, was San Francisco, with an innovation rate of 8.90, followed by Boston, with an innovation rate of 8.69. By contrast, the mean innovation rate for the entire country is 1.75 innovations per 100,000 population. The distribution of innovation rates is considerably skewed. Only 14 cities are more innovative than the national average. Clearly, innovation appears to be a large city phenomenon.

To systematically identify the degree to which specific industries have a common underlying science and technology base, we rely upon a deductive approach that links products on their closeness in technological space. We use the widely acknowledge and established *Yale Survey of R&D managers*. This survey is documented in great detail in Levin et al. (1987) and has been widely used in studies linking various mechanisms of appropriability to R&D activity (Cohen

---

[8] Feldman (1994) provides a description of the data collection procedure. The results are invariant to using PMSAs.

Table 1
Counts of innovation normalized by population

Consolidated metropolitan statistical area	Innovations (1982)	1980 population (thousands)	Innovations per 100,000 population
San Francisco – Oakland	477	5368	8.886
Boston – Lawrence	345	3972	8.686
New York – Northern New Jersey	735	17539	4.191
Philadelphia – Wilmington	205	5681	3.609
Dallas – Fort Worth	88	2931	3.002
Hartford	30	1014	2.959
Los Angeles – Anaheim	333	11498	2.896
Buffalo – Niagara	35	1243	2.816
Cleveland – Akron	77	2834	2.717
Chicago – Gary	203	7937	2.558
Providence – Pawtucket	25	1083	2.308
Portland – Vancouver	25	1298	1.926
Cincinnati - Hamilton	30	1660	1.807
Seattle – Tacoma	37	2093	1.768
Pittsburgh	42	2423	1.733
Denver – Boulder	28	1618	1.731
Detroit – Ann Arbor	68	4753	1.431
Houston – Galveston	39	3101	1.258
Miami – Fort Lauderdale	13	2644	0.492

Source: 1980 Population is from the Statistical Abstract.

and Levinthal, 1990; Levin et al., 1987). The survey uses a Likert scale of 1 to 7, from least important to most important, to assess the relevance of basic scientific research in biology, chemistry, computer science, physics, mathematics, medicine, geology, mechanical engineering and electrical engineering. We assume any academic discipline with a value greater than 5 to be relevant for a product category. For example, basic scientific research in medicine, chemistry and chemical engineering is found to be relevant for product innovation in drugs (SIC 2834).

We then identify six groups of industries which rely on similar rankings for the importance of the different academic disciplines. These six groups, shown in Table 2, reflect distinct underlying common scientific bases. To facilitate identification of the groupings we assigned a name to each group that reflects not only the underlying science base but also the application to which this knowledge is directed. Thus, what we term as the 'chemical engineering' and 'industrial machinery' groups actually include the same critical academic departments (ranked differently), but applied to different types of industries.

While each industry within the group shares a common scientific base, the geographic space and product space differ across industries. For example, there

M.P. Feldman, D.B. Audretsch / European Economic Review 43 (1999) 409–429   417

Table 2
The common science bases of industry clusters

Cluster	Critical academic departments	Most innovative industries
Agra-business	Chemistry (6.06); Agricultural Science (4.65); Computer Science (4.18); Biology (4.09).	SIC 2013: Sausages SIC 2038: Frozen Specialities SIC 2087: Flavoring Extracts SIC 2092: Packaged Foods
Chemical engineering	Materials Science (5.32); Chemistry (4.80); Computer Science (4.50); Physics (4.12).	SIC 3861: Photographic Equipment SIC 3443: Fabricated Plate Work SIC 2821: Plastic Materials SIC 3559: Special Ind. Machinery
Office machinery	Computer Science (6.75); Medical Science (5.75); Math (5.49); Applied Math (4.64).	SIC 3576: Scales and Balances SIC 3579: Office Machinery SIC 3535: Conveyors SIC 2751: Commerial Printing
Industrial machinery	Materials Science (5.03); Computer Science (4.76); Physics (3.94); Chemistry (3.88).	SIC 3551: Food Processing Equipment SIC 3523: Machinery SIC 3546: Hand Tools SIC 3629: Industrial Apparatus
High-tech computing	Materials Science (5.92); Computer Science (5.63); Physics (5.45); Math (4.76).	SIC 3573: Computing Machinery SIC 3662: Radio/TV Equipment SIC 3823: Process Control Instruments SIC 3674: Semiconductors
Biomedical	Chemistry (5.53); Medical Science (5.47); Computer Science (5.32); Materials Science (5.02).	SIC 3842: Surgical Appliances SIC 3841: Medical Instruments SIC 2834: Pharmaceuticals SIC 3811: Scientific Instruments

are 15 distinct industries included in the biomedical group. On average, each industry contributed 3.22 innovations. Their shared underlying knowledge base consists of chemistry, medical sciences, computer sciences and material sciences. Surgical Appliances (SIC 3842), Surgical and Medical Instruments (SIC 3841), and Pharmaceuticals (SIC 2834) are three of the 15 industries heavily dependent on this common underlying scientific knowledge base. There are 21 industries included in the Agra-Business group, 34 industries included in the Chemical Engineering group, 7 industries in the Office Machinery group and 11 industries included in the Industrial Machinery group. The largest science-based group is what we term High-tech Computing, which includes 80 industries.

The most innovative cities within each science-based industrial cluster are identified in Table 3. This recalls the well-known association between cities and

418 *M.P. Feldman, D.B. Audretsch / European Economic Review 43 (1999) 409–429*

Table 3
Innovation in science-based industry clusters

Cluster	Prominent cities	Mean industry innovations per 100,000 workers
Agra-business	Atlanta	92.40
	Dallas	41.15
	Chicago	33.03
	St. Louis	91.74
Chemical engineering	Dallas	38.09
	Minneapolis	66.67
	San Francisco	43.89
	Wilmington	85.47
Office machinery	Anaheim-Santa Ana	92.59
	Minneapolis	31.86
	Rochester	72.20
	Stanford	68.40
Industrial machinery	Anaheim-Santa Ana	54.95
	Cincinnati	66.01
	Cleveland	141.51
	Passaic, NJ	90.90
High-tech computing	Boston	73.89
	Houston	62.08
	San Jose	44.88
	Minneapolis	181.74
Biomedical	Boston	38.71
	Cleveland	68.76
	Dallas	35.22
	New York	188.07

industries. For example, Atlanta is a prominent center for innovative activity stemming from the common science base of agra-business. While the national innovation rate was 20.34 innovations per 100,000 manufacturing workers, agra-business in Atlanta was almost five times as innovative.

A Chi-Squared test on the independence of the location of city and science-based industrial activity reveals that neither the distribution of employment nor the distribution of innovative activity is random. Industries which rely on a common science base exhibit a tendency to cluster together geographically with regard to the location of employment and the location of innovation. We conclude that the distribution of innovation within science-based clusters and cities appears to reflect the existence of science-related expertise.

M.P. Feldman, D.B. Audretsch / European Economic Review 43 (1999) 409–429   419

4. Modeling framework

To test the hypothesis that the degree of specialization shapes the innovative output of an industry, we estimate a model where the dependent variable is the number of innovations attributed to a specific four-digit SIC industry in a particular city. To reflect the extent to which economic activity within a city is specialized, we include as an explanatory variable a measure of industry specialization which was used by Glaeser et al. (1992) and is defined as the 1982 share of total employment in the city accounted for by industry employment in the city, divided by the share of United States employment accounted by that particular industry. This variable reflects the degree to which a city is specialized in a particular industry relative to the degree of economic activity in that industry that would occur if employment in the industry were randomly distributed across the United States. A higher value of this measure indicates a greater degree of specialization of the industry in that particular city. Thus, a positive coefficient would indicate that increased specialization within a city is conducive to greater innovative output and would support the *Marshall–Arrow–Romer* thesis. A negative coefficient would indicate that greater specialization within a city impedes innovative output and would support Jacobs' theory that diversity of economic activity is more conducive to innovation than is specialization.

To identify the impact of an increased presence of economic activity in complementary industries, the presence of science-based related industries is included. This measure is constructed analogously to the index of industry specialization, and is defined as the share of total city employment accounted for by employment in the city in industries sharing the science base, divided by the share of total United States employment accounted for by employment in that same science base. This variable measures the presence of complementary industries relative to what the presence would be if those related industries were distributed across the United States. A positive coefficient of the presence of science-based related industries would indicate that a greater presence of complementary industries is conducive to greater innovative output and supports for the diversity thesis. By contrast, a negative coefficient suggests that a greater presence of related industries sharing the same science base impedes innovation and argues against Jacobs' diversity thesis.

The usual concept of product market competition in the industrial organization literature is typically measured in terms of the size-distribution of firms. By contrast, Jacobs' concept of *localized competition* emphasizes the extent of competition for the ideas embodied in individuals. The greater the degree of competition among firms, the greater the extent of specialization among those firms and the easier it will be for individuals to pursue and implement new ideas. Thus, the metric relevant to reflect the degree of localized competition is not the

420   *M.P. Feldman, D.B. Audretsch / European Economic Review 43 (1999) 409–429*

Table 4
Variable definitions and descriptive statistics

Variable name	Definition	Mean	Standard deviation
Specialization	$\dfrac{\text{Industry employment in city/total employment in city}}{\text{Industry employment in US/total employment in US}}$	0.96	1.47
Science base diversity	$\dfrac{\text{Employment in cluster in city/total employment in city}}{\text{Employment in cluster in US/total employment in US}}$	0.37	0.51
Competition	$\dfrac{\text{Firms in city} - \text{industry/workers in city} - \text{industry}}{\text{Firms in US industry/workers in US industry}}$	0.57	2.08

size of the firms in the region relative to their number (because, after all, many if not most manufacturing product markets are national or at least inter-regional in nature) but rather the number of firms relative to the number of workers. In measuring the extent of localized competition we again adopt a measure used by Glaeser et al. (1992), which is defined as the number of firms per worker in the industry in the city relative to the number of firms per worker in the same industry in the United States. A higher value of this index of localized competition suggests that the industry has a greater number of firms per worker relative to its size in the particular city than it does elsewhere in the United States. Thus, if the index of localized competition exceeds one then the city is locally less competitive than in other American cities.

The data for these measures are from County Business Patterns. Table 4 presents the variable definitions and descriptive statistics for the measures of science-based diversity, specialization and competition.

5. Results

Table 5 presents the regression results based on the 5946 city-industry observations for which data could be collected. The Poisson regression estimation method is used because the dependent variable is a limited dependent variable with a highly skewed distribution.[9]

---

[9] The number of innovations in a city and product category is either zero or some positive integer. The mean of the distribution is 0.26 and the standard deviation is 2.96.

M.P. Feldman, D.B. Audretsch / European Economic Review 43 (1999) 409–429   421

Table 5
Poisson regression estimation results

	Model 1	Model 2	Model 3	Model 4
Industry specialization	−0.209	−0.334	−0.527	−0.142
	(−8.360)	(−14.522)	(−17.684)	(−5.680)
Science-based related industries	0.168	0.104	0.089	0.069
	(3.812)	(2.122)	(2.405)	(2.091)
Localized competition	−0.175	0.576	0.221	0.168
	(−3.365)	(7.481)	(0.269)	(1.976)
City scale		1.044		1.004
		(28.216)		(20.917)
Technological opportunity			0.079	0.034
			(26.333)	(1.700)
n	5946	5946	5946	5946
Log-likelihood	−1296.793	−901.489	−693.046	−652.264

Note: The *t*-values of the coefficient is listed in parentheses.

Model 1 provides the results for the three measures which reflect the degree of specialization, diversity and localized competition. The negative and statistically significant coefficient of industry specialization suggests that innovative activity tends to be lower in industries located in cities specialized in economic activity in that industry. The positive and statistically significant coefficient for science-based related industries indicates that a strong presence of complementary industries sharing a common science base is particularly conducive to innovative activity. Taken together, these results provide support for the diversity thesis but not for the specialization thesis. The negative coefficient on the measure of localized competition suggests that less and not more localized competition promotes the innovative activity of an industry in a particular city.

One concern regarding the estimation of Model 1 is that larger cities might be expected to generate a greater amount of innovation in any particular industry, *ceteris paribus*, simply because of a greater degree of economic activity. In addition, the extent of localized competition might tend to be greater as the size of the city grows. Thus, when the total employment is included in the estimation of Model 2, the sign of the coefficient for localized competition switches from negative to positive, suggesting that a greater degree of localized competition is conducive to innovative activity. At the same time, the signs of the coefficients of the measures of industry specialization and science-based related industries remain unchanged.

Another concern regarding the estimation of Model 1 is that some industries are more innovative, or in a higher technological opportunity class than others. But even after controlling for the number of innovations recorded for the relevant industry in the estimation of Model 3 and Model 4, the basic results remain the same.[10]

The results in Table 5 generally provide support that it is diversity and not specialization that is more conducive to innovation. It should be emphasized here that even after we control for city scale and technological opportunity, specialization appears to have a negative effect on innovation, while science-based diversity has a positive impact on innovative output. In addition, the evidence suggests that a greater extent of localized competition and not monopoly tends to promote innovative output. Of course, the cross-sectional city level data do not provide any insight into whether these patterns are stable over time.

6. Diversity versus specialization at the firm level

The debate between specialization and diversity of economic activity and the impact on technological change is also relevant at the level of the firm and allows a further test of the effects of these influences on innovation. We expect a similar result in the organization of innovation within the firm – undertaking innovative activity across a range of science-based complementary activities will lead to greater innovative output than concentrating innovative activity within one industry. With this test we seek to ascertain if analogous processes operate at both the firm and the geographic level.

Jewkes et al. (1958) examined the histories of 61 innovations and found that a variety of different approaches within the firm are often pursued. It appears that diversity in terms of the number and the type of approaches used serves to reduce the uncertainty inherent in innovation by providing a greater number of unique ideas and outcomes. In an empirical examination of this question, Cohen and Malerba (1995) find a strong relationship between technological diversity and the rate of technical advance at the industry level. Our consideration of specialization examines the degree to which the firm focuses its innovative activity on one product category.

In order to model the effects of science-based diversity and specialization at the level, we follow the pioneering study of Scherer (1983) to estimate a

---

[10] The extent to which these relationships are non-linear was examined in the estimation with the inclusion of quadratic terms for industry specialization and localized competition. The results indicate that, in fact, cities which are highly specialized in economic activity may actually generate more innovative output in that industry. This result does not hold when city scale is included. It appears that scale is more important than the rate of change in the degree of specialization. The quadratic of localized competition suggests that there may be increasing returns to innovative output resulting for increased localized competition. Again, this result does not hold when urban scale is considered.

M.P. Feldman, D.B. Audretsch / European Economic Review 43 (1999) 409–429   423

non-linear model which links R&D[11] to innovative output:

$$I_i = \alpha + \beta_1 RD_i + \beta_2 RD_i^2 + \beta_3 Innovative\ Diversity_i$$

$$+ \beta_4 Innovative\ Specialization_i + \varepsilon,$$

where I represents the total number of innovations attributed to firm I in the 1982 SBIDB.[12] RD represents the R&D expenditures of firm I.[13] To measure the extent to which the innovative activity of firm I is diversified across related product categories we calculate the share of innovations in the same common science base product categories divided by the total number of innovations introduced by the firm. Similarly, specialization, or own industry share, is measured as the proportion's of the firm's innovative activity in the primary industry identified with the firm.

R&D expenditures are taken from the *Business Week* 1975 sample of over 700 corporations for which R&D expenditures play an important role. An important feature of this sample is that it included more than 95% of the total company R&D expenditures undertaken in the United States. There is a seven year lag between the 1982 innovations and the 1975 R&D expenditures. This lag may be somewhat long in view of a number of studies in the literature. However, as long as firm R&D expenditures are relatively stable over a short period of time, differences in the assumed lag structure should not greatly impact the results.[14]

Table 6 indicates the most innovative firms in the database along with the corresponding R&D expenditures, sales, R&D/sales ratio and the number of innovations per R&D dollar. As we might expect a positive relationship can be observed between the size of the R&D budget and innovative output, but there is also great variation in the productivity of R&D. Some firms such as Data General appear to obtain a relatively high degree of innovation per R&D dollar expended. Other firms such as General Electric and RCA exhibit a considerably lower R&D yield.

The regression results from estimating the model of firm innovative activity are shown in Table 7. The positive relationship between R&D inputs and

---

[11] R&D is generally observed to be the most decisive source of economic knowledge generating innovative activity.

[12] A log-log specification was estimated as well as the quadratic specification. The results for both specifications are consistent. We only report the results from the quadratic equations to facilitate comparisons with the earlier studies mentioned in the text.

[13] Note that the firm-level models are for the entire country and not for MSAs or states. It is not possible to identify firm-level R&D by location at this point.

[14] As an anonymous referee emphasizes, future research needs to explore distributed lags between R&D and innovative output.

Table 6
Firm innovation

	Number of innovations	R&D expenditure ($ million)	Sales ($ million)	R&D/ sales ratio	Innovation/ R&D[a]
Hewlett Packard Company	55	981.00	89.6	9.1	5.61
Minnesota Mining & Mfg.	40	3127.00	143.4	4.6	1.28
General Electric	36	13399.00	357.1	2.7	0.27
General Signal	29	548.00	21.2	3.9	5.29
National Semiconductor	27	235.00	20.7	8.8	11.49
Xerox	25	4054.00	198.6	4.9	0.62
Texas Instruments	24	1368.00	51.0	3.7	1.75
Pitney Bowes	22	461.00	10.5	2.3	4.77
RCA	21	4790.00	113.6	2.4	0.44
IBM	21	14437.00	946.0	6.6	0.15
Digital Equipment	21	534.00	48.5	9.1	3.93
Gould	20	773.00	23.1	3.0	2.59
Motorola	19	13112.00	98.5	7.5	1.45
Wheelabrator Frye	18	332.00	2.0	0.6	5.42
United Technologies	18	3878.00	323.7	8.3	0.46
Hoover	18	594.00	4.3	0.7	3.03
Honeywell	18	2760.00	164.2	5.9	0.65
Rockwell International	17	4943.00	31.0	0.6	0.34
Johnson & Johnson	17	2225.00	97.9	4.4	0.76
Eastman Kodak	17	4959.00	312.9	6.3	0.34
Data General	17	108.00	11.6	10.8	15.74
Exxon	16	4486.05	187.0	0.4	0.36
Du Pont	16	7222.00	335.7	4.6	0.22
Stanley Works	15	464.00	3.5	0.7	3.23
Sperry Rand	15	3041.00	163.5	5.4	0.49
Pennwalt	15	714.00	15.7	2.2	2.10
North American Philips	14	1410.00	22.5	1.6	0.99
Harris	14	479.00	21.1	4.4	2.92
General Motors	14	3572.05	1113.9	3.1	0.39

[a] Scaled by 100.

innovative output can be observed in Model 1. The negative coefficient of the quadratic term suggests that although innovative output tends to respond positively to increased investments in R&D inputs, the rate of increase in innovative output diminishes as R&D inputs increase.

· When the measure of innovation diversity within industries sharing a common science base is included in Model 2, the positive coefficient provides support for the hypothesis that diversification across complementary economic activities is conducive to greater innovative output. When the measure of innovation specialization is included in Model 3, the positive coefficient suggests

Table 7
Regression results estimating firm innovative activity

	1	2	3	4
R&D	0.02804	0.0119	0.0178	0.0081
	(6.051)	(3.320)	(1.624)	(2.481)
R&D^2	−1.6945	−0.4157	−0.8940	−0.0323
	(−2.603)	(−0.878)	(−1.732)	(−0.075)
Innovative diversity	–	3.3081	–	9.2466
		(9.510)		(9.988)
Innovative specialization	–	–	2.8116	−7.4357
			(6.218)	(−6.819)
Number of observations	209	203	203	203
R^2	0.189	0.466	0.350	0.568
F	23.980	57.905	35.677	64.980

Notes: The *t*-value of the coefficient is listed in parentheses. The coefficients of R&D^2 have been divided by 100,000 for presentation purposes.

that greater specialization in innovation yields greater innovative output. When both specialization and diversity are included together in Model 4, the coefficient of specialization exhibits a negative coefficient suggesting that greater innovation specialization is less conducive to greater innovative output. On the other hand, holding R&D expenditures constant, greater innovative diversity within the common science base results in more innovative output.

The firms can also be grouped according to major two-digit SIC sectors. Results for six specific industrial sectors are listed in Table 8. There is interesting variation in these results across manufacturing sectors. For example, in instruments and telecommunications diminishing returns to R&D inputs can be observed. By contrast, increasing returns to R&D can be observed in the group of firms classified as conglomerates, and in electrical equipment and transportation no significant relationship can be observed between R&D and innovative output.

While the links between R&D inputs and innovative output vary substantially across sectors in Table 8, the relationships between specialization, innovation diversity and innovation remain remarkably constant across sectors. For all six sectors the coefficient of the measure of science-based innovation diversity remains positive and statistically significant, and the coefficient of the measure of innovation specialization also remains negative and statistically significant in all six sectors. Thus, the main finding that diversity in innovation activities within a common science base tends to promote innovative output more than does the specialization of innovation within just one single industry holds across a broad range of industrial sectors.

Table 8
Regression estimating firm innovative activity for specific sectors

Sector	R&D	R&D^2	Innovative diversity	Innovative specialization	n	R^2	F
Instruments	0.1796	−46.7294	7.7780	−7.3747	23	0.756	13.918
	(2.863)	(−2.344)	(3.167)	(−2.311)			
Telecommunications	0.0426	−81.0826	12.1458	−10.5068	31	0.681	13.857
	(1.757)	(−1.955)	(3.995)	(−2.888)			
Pharmaceuticals	0.0579	−21.2919	5.0999	−4.1984	24	0.732	12.951
	(1.162)	(−0.496)	(1.840)	(−1.501)			
Electrical equipment	0.0328	−2.6788	11.8368	−9.5924	27	0.694	12.455
	(0.908)	(−0.249)	(3.471)	(−2.310)			
Transportation	0.0025	0.5888	10.1231	−8.7190	20	0.859	22.934
	(0.357)	(0.880)	(4.985)	(−3.960)			
Conglomerates	−0.1074	0.0019	7.5160	−5.5113	25	0.926	62.866
	(−2.671)	(6.970)	(3.941)	(−2.671)			

Notes: The t-value of each coefficient is listed in parentheses. The coefficients of R&D^2 are multiplied by 100,000 for presentation purposes.

Table 9
Regression results estimating firm innovative activity for specific science bases

	High-tech computing (1)	High-tech computing (2)	Biomedical (3)	Biomedical (4)
R&D	0.0100	0.0059	0.6000	0.0501
	(2.293)	(1.497)	(2.056)	(1.723)
R&D^2	−0.2928	−0.1683	−25.7484	−18.6446
	(−0.522)	(0.300)	(−1.222)	(−0.889)
Innovation share within science base	3.7691	9.8348	1.4761	5.2878
	(7.831)	(8.524)	(1.925)	(2.120)
Innovation share within industry	–	−8.2150	–	−4.0457
		(−5.670)		(−1.601)
Number of observations	134	134	32	32
R^2	0.454	0.563	0.680	0.708
F	35.983	41.493	35.677	64.980

Notes: The t-value of the coefficient is listed in parentheses. The coefficients of R&D^2 have been divided by 100,000 for presentation purposes.

The results are confirmed in Table 9, which groups the firms according to two of the largest science bases – high-tech computing and biomedical products. Not only is the knowledge production function found to hold for firms in each of these distinct science bases, but again, diversity in innovation across economic activities with a common science base is found to increase innovation.

7. Conclusions

The nature and utility of knowledge is at the heart of the economics of R&D, innovation and technological change. Whether diversity or specialization of economic activities better promotes technological change has been the subject of a heated debate in the economics literature. This paper has attempted to shed light on that debate by linking the extent of diversity versus specialization of economic activities to innovative output. By focusing on innovative activity for particular industries at specific locations, we find compelling evidence that specialization of economic activity does not promote innovative output. Rather, the results indicate that diversity across complementary economic activities sharing a common science base is more conducive to innovation than is specialization. In addition, the results indicate that the degree of local competition for new ideas within a city is more conducive to innovative activity than is local monopoly.

A second perspective explored in this paper is the effect of diversity and specialization at the firm level. The results indicate that innovative activity tends to be lower when that innovation is specialized within a narrow industry than when it is diversified across a complementary set of industries sharing a common science base. Thus, the results at both the level of the firm as well as for the industry across geographic space present a consistent view of the returns to specialization versus diversity of economic activity. Our results suggest that diversity across complementary industries sharing a common base – a crucial qualification – results in greater returns to R&D.[15]

Increasingly scholars of technological change realize that external sources of knowledge are critical to innovation. Our results suggest that the boundaries of the firm are but one means to organize and harness knowledge. An analogous means of organizing economic activity are spatially defined boundaries. Geographic location may provide another useful set of boundaries within which to organize innovation. Geography may provide a platform upon which knowledge may be effectively organized.

---

[15] We underscore the descriptive nature of these results since there may be alternative explanations. Specifically, the relationships may be endogenous in a way that we have not considered. Firms which are more innovative may be more profitable and therefore, more likely to be able to engage in diverse activities. Similarly, regions which are successful at innovation in one industry may attract other activities. The cross-sectional nature of the data we use here does not allow us to examine these issues.

Acknowledgements

We are grateful to the comments and suggestions of two anonymous referees and an editor of this journal, Elhanan Helpman. An earlier version of this paper was presented at the Center for Economic Policy Research (CEPR) conference on R&D Spillovers at Lausanne, Switzerland, 27–28 January 1995 and at the 1997 annual meetings of the American Economic Association at San Francisco. We would like to thank Zvi Griliches, Bronwyn Hall, Frank Lichtenberg and F.M. Scherer for their comments and suggestions.

References

Arrow, K.J., 1962. Economic welfare and the allocation of resources for innovation. In: Nelson, R.R. (Ed.), The Rate and Direction of Inventive Activity. Princeton University Press, Princeton, NJ, pp. 609–626.

Audretsch, D.B., 1995. Innovation and Industry Evolution. MIT Press, Cambridge.

Audretsch, D.B., Feldman, M.P., 1996. R&D spillovers and the geography of innovation and production. American Economic Review 86 (3), 630–640.

Audretsch, D.B., Stephan, P.E., 1996. Company-scientist locational links: The case of biotechnology. American Economic Review 86, 641–652.

Cohen, W., Levinthal, D., 1990. Absorptive capacity: A new perspective on learning and innovation. Administrative Science Quarterly 35, 1288–1352.

Cohen, W.M., Malerba, F., 1995. Is the tendency to variation a chief cause of progress? Unpublished manuscript, Carnegie-Mellon University.

Feldman, M.P., 1994. The Geography of Innovation. Kluwer Academic Publishers, Boston.

Feldman, M.P., Florida, R., 1994. The geographic sources of innovation: Technological infrastructure and product innovation in the United States. Annals of the Association of American Geographers 84, 210–229.

Glaeser, E.L., Kallal, H.D., Scheinkman, J.A., Shleifer, A., 1992. Growth of cities. Journal of Political Economy 100, 1126–1152.

Griliches, Z., 1990. Patent statistics as economic indicator: A survey. Journal of Economic Literature 28, 1661–1707.

Griliches, Z., 1992. The search for R&D spill-overs. Scandinavian Journal of Economics 94, 29–47.

Jacobs, J., 1969. The Economy of Cities. Random House, New York.

Jaffe, A.B., 1989. Real effects of academic research. American Economic Review 79, 957–970.

Jaffe, A.B., Trajtenberg, M., Henderson, R., 1993. Geographic localization of knowledge spillovers as evidenced by patent citations. Quarterly Journal of Economics 63, 577–598.

Jewkes, J., Sawers, D., Stillerman, M., 1958. The Sources of Innovation. MacMillan, London.

Krugman, P., 1991a. Increasing returns and economic geography. Journal of Political Economy 99, 483–499.

Krugman, P., 1991b. Geography and Trade. MIT Press, Cambridge.

Levin, R.C., Klevorick, A.K., Nelson R.R., Winter, S.G., 1987. Appropriating the returns from industrial research and development. Brooking Papers on Economic Activity, 783–820.

Loesch, A., 1954. The Economics of Location. Yale University Press, New Haven.

Lucas, R.E. Jr., 1993. Making a miracle. Econometrica 61, 251–272.

Mansfield, E.J., 1984. Comment on using linked patent and R&D data to measure interindustry technology flows. In: Griliches, Z. (Ed.), R&D, Patents and Productivity. University of Chicago Press, Chicago, pp. 415–418.

M.P. Feldman, D.B. Audretsch / European Economic Review 43 (1999) 409–429   429

Pakes, A., Griliches, Z., 1984. Patents and R&D at the firm level: A first look. In: Griliches, Z. (Ed.), R&D, Patents and Productivity. University of Chicago Press, Chicago, pp. 139–161.

Porter, M.P., 1990. The Comparative Advantage of Nations. The Free Press, New York.

Reynolds, P., Storey, D., Westhead, P., 1994. Cross-national comparisons of the variation in new firm formation rates. Regional Studies 28, 443–456.

Romer, P., 1990. Endogenous technological Change. Journal of Political Economy 94 (1), 71–102.

Romer, P., 1986. Increasing returns and long-run growth. Journal of Political Economy 94 (5), 1002–1037.

Scherer, F.M., 1983. The propensity to patent. International Journal of Industrial Organization 1 (1), 107–128.

Von Hipple, E., 1994. Sticky information and the locus of problem solving: Implications for innovation. Management Science 40, 429–439.

[15]

Geographic Concentration in U.S. Manufacturing Industries: A Dartboard Approach

Glenn Ellison

Massachusetts Institute of Technology and National Bureau of Economic Research

Edward L. Glaeser

Harvard University and National Bureau of Economic Research

This paper discusses the prevalence of Silicon Valley–style localizations of individual manufacturing industries in the United States. A model in which localized industry-specific spillovers, natural advantages, and pure random chance all contribute to geographic concentration is used to develop a test for whether observed levels of concentration are greater than would be expected to arise randomly and to motivate new indices of geographic concentration and of coagglomeration. The proposed indices control for differences in the size distribution of plants and for differences in the size of the geographic areas for which data are available. As a consequence, comparisons of the degree of geographic concentration across industries can be made with more confidence. Our empirical results provide a strong reaffirmation of the previous wisdom in that we find almost all industries to be somewhat localized. In many industries, however, the degree of localization is slight. We explore the nature of agglomerative forces in describing patterns of concentration, the geographic scope of localization, and the coagglomeration of related industries and of industries with strong upstream-downstream ties.

We would like to thank Richard Caves, Sara Fisher Ellison, Larry Katz, Bill Miracky, Wally Mullin, Peter Reiss, José Scheinkman, Sherwin Rosen, and two anonymous referees for helpful comments and Matt Botein, David Hwang, Rajesh James, Bruce Sacerdote, and Jacob Vigdor for research assistance. We both thank the National Science Foundation (SBR-9310009 and SBR-9515076, and SBR-9309808) and the Harvard Clark Fund for financial support.

[*Journal of Political Economy*, 1997, vol. 105, no. 5]

I. Introduction

The concentrations of high-tech industries in Silicon Valley and the auto industry in Detroit are two of the more famous examples of the geographic agglomeration of firms in a single industry. These examples for years have fascinated both practically minded urban planners and economic geographers who are interested in accounting for a striking feature of the economic landscape. More recently, it has been suggested by Krugman (1991a) and others that Silicon Valley–style agglomerations may be more the rule than the exception and that from them one may learn about the sources of increasing returns that have appeared in the literature following Marshall (1920). Given the central role increasing returns play in the new theories of growth and international trade, these suggestions have led to a surge of new work. Researchers who are primarily interested in international trade, growth, industrial organization, and business strategy have joined geographers and urban economists in investigating why agglomerations exist.[1] In this paper we step back a bit from this work and reexamine both how industry concentration over and above the general concentration of manufacturing (and industry group coagglomeration) can be measured and what the facts are to be explained.

We begin by proposing a "model-based" index of geographic concentration that has several useful properties. First, the index is scaled so that it takes on a value of zero not if employment is uniformly spread across space, but instead if employment is only as concentrated as it would be expected to be had the plants in the industry chosen locations by throwing darts at a map. Because production in many industries occurs mainly in a few large plants, accounting for lumpiness can be substantial. For example, in the U.S. vacuum cleaner industry (Standard Industrial Classification [SIC] 3635), about 75 percent of the employees work in one of the four largest plants. Thus we would not want to regard it as being concentrated simply because 75 percent of its employment is contained in only four states. Second, the index is designed to facilitate comparisons across industries, across countries, or over time. When plants' location decisions are made as in the model, differences in the size of the industry, the size distribution of plants, or the fineness of the geographic data that are available should not affect the index. Thus one may compare with more confidence, for example, the concentration of American and European industries, the concentration of

---

[1] For samples of work in these fields, see Creamer (1943), Florence (1948), Hoover (1948), Fuchs (1962), Carlton (1983), Henderson (1988), Enright (1990), Porter (1990), Krugman (1991a), and Jaffe, Trajtenberg, and Henderson (1993).

high- and low-tech industries, and the changes in levels of concentration over time.[2]

In our model of location choice, plants sequentially choose locations to maximize profits. We allow for two types of agglomerative forces, which we refer to as spillovers and natural advantage. By locational spillovers we mean both physical spillovers (as in Krugman [1991b], where the presence of one firm lowers transportation costs for a second) and intellectual spillovers (as in Glaeser et al. [1992]). Natural advantage includes the forces that lead the wine industry to concentrate in California and large shipyards to locate on bodies of water. When neither of these forces is present, the model reduces to one in which plants choose locations by throwing darts at an appropriately scaled map.

The first result of our theory section is an observational equivalence theorem that shows that the relationship between mean measured levels of concentration and industry characteristics is the same regardless of whether concentration is the result of spillovers, natural advantage, or a combination of the two. One may interpret this result as a warning that geographic concentration by itself does not imply the existence of spillovers; natural advantages have similar effects and may be important empirically. For our purposes, however, the result has a positive message: one can design an index that controls for differences in industry characteristics, regardless of the cause of concentration. The second part of the theory sections analyzes a similar multiple industry model to motivate an index of coagglomeration that may be useful in studies of cross-industry spillovers and shared natural advantages.

The largest portion of the paper uses our indices to describe concentration in U.S. manufacturing. Our first surprising result is that despite the fact that our index imposes more stringent standards for calling an industry concentrated, virtually every industry displays excess concentration (446 of 459 four-digit SIC industries). This does not mean, however, that we take our results as support for the view that Silicon Valleys are ubiquitous. While there are a number of industries that look like Silicon Valley or the auto industry, it is much more common for industries to be only very slightly concentrated. Our measurements suggest that explanations for concentration vary by industry and that natural advantage may often play a role. We also look at concentration at the county, state, and regional

---

[2] See Krugman (1991a) for a discussion of the first two questions and Fuchs (1962) for an analysis of the third. Florence's (1948) observation that industries with larger plants are more concentrated is a particularly clear example of the difficulties that can arise in interpreting results with other indices.

levels and at the coagglomeration of industries with related SIC codes. Here, we find evidence suggesting that spillover benefits are restricted neither to the county level nor to the most narrowly defined industries. Industries also appear to coagglomerate both with important upstream suppliers and with important downstream customers.

II. A Model of Location Choice

In this section, we develop a simple model in which the geographic concentration of an industry is one result of a sequence of profit-maximizing location decisions made by individual plants. Natural advantages of some locations and industry-specific spillovers lead plants to cluster together, and idiosyncratic plant-specific considerations provide the counterbalance that keeps the entire industry from concentrating at a single point.

A. *Natural Advantage, Spillovers, and Localization*

Suppose that an industry consists of N business units (best thought of as manufacturing plants) that choose sequentially to locate in one of the M geographic subunits of a larger entity (e.g., in one of the states of the United States). We assume that the kth business unit chooses its location v_k to maximize its profits given that it will receive profits π_{ki} from locating in area i. To make the model tractable, we assume that these profits are given by

$$\log \pi_{ki} = \log \bar{\pi}_i + g_i(v_1, \ldots, v_{k-1}) + \epsilon_{ki}, \tag{1}$$

where $\bar{\pi}_i$ is a random variable reflecting the profitability of locating in area i for a typical firm in the industry (as influenced by observed and unobserved area characteristics), g_i captures the effects of spillovers created by business units that have previously chosen locations, and ϵ_{ki} is an additional random component reflecting factors that are idiosyncratic to plant k.[3]

"Natural advantages" are included in our model to capture the fact that the plants in an industry will be geographically concentrated whenever their location choices have been influenced by common factors that make some locations more desirable than others. While natural advantage reasons for geographic concentration may

---

[3] Given the way in which we shall specify the model, one will also be able to regard location decisions as a rational expectations equilibrium of a process in which plants receive spillovers also from plants that choose locations later on.

not be exciting intellectually, they are clearly important when accounting for some of the agglomeration we observe. For example,
the localization of the wine industry in California is certainly attributable at least in part to California's favorable climate for growing
grapes, and some portion of the agglomeration of large shipyards
is due to their desire for locations on large bodies of water.

In our model, the effects of natural advantages on profits are captured by the random variables $\{\bar{\pi}_i\}$, which are chosen by nature at
the start of the process when it assigns resource endowments to each
area that fit well or poorly with the industry's needs. The expectation
$\bar{\pi}_i$ then reflects the average profitability of locating in area i, and the
variance of the $\{\bar{\pi}_i\}$ reflects how sensitive profits are to a good fit. For
example, these variances might be high in the shipbuilding industry
because the profitability of a state will depend greatly on whether
nature has put that state on the coast.

If we specify that the $\{\epsilon_{ki}\}$ are independent Weibull random variables independent of the $\{\bar{\pi}_i\}$ and there are no spillovers ($g_i \equiv 0$
for all i), then conditional on a realization of $\bar{\pi}_1, \ldots, \bar{\pi}_M$, our model
is a standard logit model and the firms' location choices are condi-
tionally independent random variables with

$$\text{prob}\{v_k = i | \bar{\pi}_1, \ldots, \bar{\pi}_M\} = \frac{\bar{\pi}_i}{\sum_j \bar{\pi}_j}.$$

We have therefore chosen to focus on models in which the distributions of the $\{\bar{\pi}_i\}$ satisfy two parametric restrictions.

First, so that on average across industries the model reproduces
the overall distribution of manufacturing activity (e.g., puts many
more plants in California and New York than in Wyoming), we assume that

$$E_{\bar{\pi}_1, \ldots, \bar{\pi}_M} \frac{\bar{\pi}_i}{\sum_j \bar{\pi}_j} = x_i, \tag{2}$$

where x_i is area i's share of overall manufacturing employment. In
practice, one can think of states with more manufacturing as having
higher average profit levels for any of several reasons: plants located
there may benefit from spillovers of aggregate activity that are not
industry-specific, they may have characteristics (such as nice weather
allowing lower equilibrium wages) desired by all industries, and they
may have more potential locations to choose from, increasing the
fit quality of the best location a plant is able to find.

894 JOURNAL OF POLITICAL ECONOMY

Second, we assume that the joint distribution of natural advantages is such that there is a single parameter $\gamma^{na} \in [0, 1]$ for which

$$\text{var}\left(\frac{\bar{\pi}_i}{\sum_j \bar{\pi}_j}\right) = \gamma^{na} x_i (1 - x_i). \tag{3}$$

We think of the parameter γ^{na} as capturing the importance of natural advantage to the industry. The $\gamma^{na} = 0$ extreme corresponds to a model in which unobserved state characteristics have no effect on profitability. In this case, the plant's location decisions are independent, with each choosing area i with probability x_i. At the other extreme, when $\gamma^{na} = 1$, state characteristics are so important that they completely overwhelm firm-specific idiosyncratic factors, and the one state that has the best set of endowments will attract all the firms. (The largest variance the random variable $\bar{\pi}_i / [\sum_j \bar{\pi}_j]$ can have consistent with its always being between zero and one and having mean x_i is $x_i[1 - x_i]$.)

One concrete specification of the distribution of the $\{\bar{\pi}_i\}$ consistent with these requirements is to assume that the $\{\bar{\pi}_i\}$ are independent random variables that are scaled so that $2[(1 - \gamma^{na})/\gamma^{na}]\bar{\pi}_i$ has a χ^2 distribution with $2[(1 - \gamma^{na})/\gamma^{na}] x_i$ degrees of freedom. In this case, we have $E(\bar{\pi}_i) = x_i$ and $\text{var}(\bar{\pi}_i) = [\gamma^{na}/(1 - \gamma^{na})] x_i$, so it is easy to see that unobserved state characteristics have a negligible effect on average profitability levels when γ^{na} is close to zero and that profits vary greatly with the realized suitability of state characteristics when γ^{na} is close to one.

The second class of explanations for agglomeration we examine are what we call "spillover" theories. We use the term broadly to refer to technological spillovers, gains from sharing labor markets, gains from interfirm trade, the effect of local knowledge on the location of spin-off firms, and any other forces that might provide increased profits to firms locating near other firms in the same industry. While it might be descriptively more accurate to suppose that a plant receives more benefits from locating near some plants than others and that the fraction of the potential benefits that are realized varies smoothly with proximity, we consider instead (to make the model tractable) spillovers of an "all or nothing" variety. For each pair of plants, either the plants receive no benefits from colocation or the spillovers between them have infinite magnitude and are extremely localized geographically, so the plants receive the full potential benefits if they choose identical locations and no benefits at all if they locate in separate areas (regardless of proximity).

Formally, we incorporate spillovers whose importance is indexed by a parameter $\gamma^s \in [0, 1]$ by assuming that

$$\log \pi_{ki} = \log(\overline{\pi}_i) + \sum_{l \neq k} e_{kl}(1 - u_{li})(-\infty) + \epsilon_{ki}, \tag{4}$$

where the $\{e_{kl}\}$ are Bernoulli random variables equal to one with probability γ^i that indicate whether a potentially valuable spillover exists between each pair of plants, and u_{li} is again an indicator for whether plant l is located in area i. We assume also that the existence of spillovers between plants is a symmetric, transitive relationship in the sense that $e_{kl} = 1 \Rightarrow e_{lk} = 1$ and $e_{kl} = 1$ and $e_{lm} = 1 \Rightarrow e_{km} = 1$.[4] This assumption is also motivated by the properties of the location decision process it induces: the process in which the kth plant chooses its location taking into account only the locations of the first $k - 1$ plants is also a rational expectations equilibrium of a model in which plants are forward looking, and the resulting distribution of locations is independent of the order in which the plants make their choices.

In describing this specification of spillovers, we sometimes extend the dartboard metaphor and imagine a two-stage process in which nature first randomly chooses to weld some of the darts into clusters (representing groups of plants that are sufficiently interdependent that they will always locate together) and then each cluster is thrown randomly at the dartboard to choose a location. The importance of spillovers is captured by the parameter γ^i, which indicates the fraction of pairs of firms between which a spillover exists.

Writing s_i for the share of the industry's employment in area i and x_i for the share of aggregate manufacturing employment in area i, one can construct a measure of an industry's geographic concentration by setting $G \equiv \sum_i (s_i - x_i)^2$. In the model we have described, the $\{x_i\}$ are taken as exogenous and the $\{s_i\}$ are determined endogenously by $s_i = \sum_k z_k u_{ki}$, where z_k is the kth plant's (exogenously fixed) share of the industry's employment and u_{ki} is an indicator variable equal to one if plant k chooses to locate in state i. The principal result of this section is a characterization of how the expected value of G is related to the parameters characterizing the strength of natural advantages and spillovers, the industry's plant size distribution, and the sizes of the areas for which employment breakdowns are available when location decisions are made in accordance with the model described above.

PROPOSITION 1. In any specification of the location choice model in which plants $1, 2, \ldots, N$ sequentially choose locations to maximize

---

[4] Note that we have *not* fully specified the joint distribution of the $\{e_{kl}\}$. The proposition below will apply to all distributions with these properties. To see that at least one such joint distribution exists, consider the case in which the $\{e_{kl}\}$ are perfectly correlated, so that with probability γ_0 all the firms are completely interdependent and with probability $1 - \gamma_0$ all their profits are independent.

profit functions that satisfy equations (2), (3), and (4),

$$E(G) = (1 - \Sigma x_i^2)[\gamma + (1 - \gamma)H],$$

where $H \equiv \Sigma_k z_k^2$ is the Herfindahl index of the industry's plant size distribution and $\gamma = \gamma^{na} + \gamma^s - \gamma^{na}\gamma^s$.

Proof. Writing p_i for $\bar{\pi}_i/(\Sigma_j \bar{\pi}_j)$ and p for $p_1, \ldots, p_M$, we can expand $E(G)$ using the law of iterated expectations as

$$E(G) = \sum_i E_p E[(s_i - x_i)^2 | p]$$

$$= \sum_i E_p \operatorname{var}(s_i | p) + E_p(s_i - x_i | p)^2.$$

Using the identity $s_i = \Sigma_j z_j u_{ji}$ and expanding the variance terms gives

$$E(G) = \sum_i E_p \left[\sum_j z_j^2 \operatorname{var}(u_{ji} | p) \right.$$

$$+ \sum_{j,k,j \neq k} z_j z_k \operatorname{cov}(u_{ji} u_{ki} | p) + E(s_i - x_i | p)^2 \Bigg]$$

$$= \sum_i E_p \left\{ \sum_j z_j^2 p_i(1 - p_i) \right.$$

$$+ \sum_{j,k,j \neq k} z_j z_k [\gamma^s p_i + (1 - \gamma^s) p_i^2 - p_i^2] + (p_i - x_i)^2 \Bigg\}.$$

Our specification of natural advantage ([2] and [3]) assumed $E(p_i) = x_i$ and $E[(p_i - x_i)^2] = \gamma^{na}(x_i - x_i^2)$, which together imply $E(p_i - p_i^2) = (1 - \gamma^{na})(x_i - x_i^2)$. Also, from our definition $H = \Sigma_j z_j^2$ we have $\Sigma_{j,k,j \neq k} z_j z_k = (\Sigma_j z_j)^2 - \Sigma z_j^2 = 1 - H$. Substituting each of these into the equation above gives

$$E(G) = \sum_i [H(1 - \gamma^{na})(x_i - x_i^2)$$

$$+ (1 - H)\gamma^s(1 - \gamma^{na})(x_i - x_i^2) + \gamma^{na}(x_i - x_i^2)]$$

$$= \left(1 - \sum_i x_i^2\right)[\gamma^{na} + \gamma^s - \gamma^{na}\gamma^s$$

$$+ (1 - \gamma^{na} - \gamma^s + \gamma^{na}\gamma^s)H].$$

Q.E.D.

The most interesting aspect of proposition 1 is that it establishes something of an observational equivalence result between the effects of natural advantages and spillovers on expected concentration levels. An analysis of the mean concentration of industries will allow one only to estimate $\gamma = \gamma^s + \gamma^{na} - \gamma^s\gamma^{na}$, and any estimated $\gamma \in [0, 1]$ is compatible with a pure natural advantage model, a pure spillover model, or models with various combinations of the two factors.[5]

The conclusion of proposition 1 is not a pessimistic statement. It is helpful in that it indicates that it will be possible to construct an index of concentration that "controls" for differences in industry and data characteristics without knowing what combination of natural advantages or spillovers is responsible for the agglomeration of each industry.

B. Coagglomeration

To discuss the degree to which pairs or groups of industries appear to be coagglomerated, we consider now a model in which N plants, each belonging to one of r industries in an industry group, choose locations. We use N_j, w_j, and H_j, respectively, for the number of plants in the jth industry, the jth industry's share of the total employment in those r industries, and the plant Herfindahl of the jth industry, and H for the plant Herfindahl of the group.

To produce a model in which these industries will exhibit some degree of coagglomeration, one could modify the discrete choice model above to allow for natural advantages that are correlated across industries or for spillovers that are not purely industry-specific. For example, plants in the cane sugar refining and shipbuilding industries might be coagglomerated because coastal locations provide higher profits both for shipyards and for importers of bulky commodities. On the other hand, the coagglomeration of various textile industries might be attributable to the presence of spillovers between plants in similar but not identical lines of business. Formally, this would involve making the average profits $\bar{\pi}_i^j$ and $\bar{\pi}_i^k$ that plants in the jth and kth industries receive when locating in area i correlated random variables and allowing the probability that a crucial spillover exists between two plants to depend on whether or not they belong to the same industry.

While such a model is not difficult to create, analyzing it is tedious and not particularly enlightening. Therefore, rather than character-

---

[5] While the result is limited in that only the effects on first moments of measured concentration are considered, we believe that attempts to distinguish natural advantage from spillover theories will not be fruitful because the higher moments of G will depend on a number of additional assumptions (e.g., on higher moments of the distribution of the area-specific average profit levels and on the full joint distribution of the indicator variables for whether spillovers exist between pairs of firms). Hence, pure natural advantage and pure spillover theories are each compatible with a range of findings for the higher moments.

ize expected concentration as a function of moments and so forth, we have chosen instead to give a more reduced-form theorem that relates the concentration of the group to the correlations in location choices induced by natural advantages and spillovers.

PROPOSITION 2. In an r industry location choice model, suppose that the distributions of average profit levels and spillovers are such that the indicator variables $\{u_{ki}\}$ for whether the kth plant locates in area i satisfy $E(u_{ki}) = x_i$ and

$$\text{corr}(u_{ki}, u_{li}) = \begin{cases} \gamma_j & \text{if plants } k \text{ and } l \text{ both belong to industry } j \\ \gamma_0 & \text{otherwise.} \end{cases}$$

Let $G = \sum_i (s_i - x_i)^2$, where s_i is area i's share of the aggregate employment in the r industries, and $H = \sum_j w_j^2 H_j$ be the plant Herfindahl of the aggregate of the r industries. Then

$$E(G) = \left(1 - \sum_i x_i^2\right)\left[H + \gamma_0\left(1 - \sum_{j=1}^r w_j^2\right) + \sum_{j=1}^r \gamma_j w_j^2 (1 - H_j)\right].$$

Proof. Write $z_{j1}, \ldots, z_{jn_j}$ for the sizes of plants in the jth industry. Our assumptions on correlations then give

$$E(G) = \sum_i \text{var}(s_i)$$

$$= \sum_i \left[\sum_{j,l} z_{jl}^2 \text{var}(u_{jli}) + \sum_{j,l,l',l \neq l'} z_{jl} z_{jl'} \text{cov}(u_{jli}, u_{jl'i})\right.$$

$$\left. + \sum_{j,j',l,l',j \neq j'} z_{jl} z_{j'l'} \text{cov}(u_{jli}, u_{j'l'i})\right]$$

$$= \left[\sum_i x_i(1 - x_i)\right]\left(\sum_{j,l} z_{jl}^2 + \sum_{j,l,l',l \neq l'} z_{jl} z_{jl'} \gamma_j + \sum_{j,j',l,l',j \neq j'} z_{jl} z_{j'l'} \gamma_0\right)$$

$$= \left(1 - \sum_i x_i^2\right)\left[H + \sum_j \gamma_j\left(w_j^2 - \sum_l z_{jl}^2\right) + \gamma_0\left(1 - \sum_j w_j^2\right)\right]$$

$$= \left(1 - \sum_i x_i^2\right)\left[H + \gamma_0\left(1 - \sum_j w_j^2\right) + \sum_j \gamma_j w_j^2 (1 - H^j)\right].$$

Q.E.D.

The proposition characterizes the expected concentration of the aggregate employment in an industry group in terms of two factors. The first is simply the tendency of plants in each individual industry to agglomerate as captured by the single parameter γ_j (for the jth industry), which reflects the influence of natural advantage and spill-overs as in proposition 1. The second, γ_0, captures the tendency for plants in one industry to locate near plants in the others. The $\gamma_0 = 0$ extreme corresponds with the case in which there are spillovers or shared natural advantages across industries within the group (beyond the spillovers from aggregate activity). At the other extreme, when $\gamma_0 = \gamma_1 = \cdots = \gamma_r$, average profit levels are perfectly correlated across industries and spillovers are group-specific rather than industry-specific. For example, a pure spillover model satisfying the conditions of the theorem would be one in which the probability that a pair of plants had a crucial spillover between them was γ_j if each belonged to industry j and γ_0 if they belonged to different industries.[6]

III. Indexes of Geographic Concentration

In this section, we propose indices that may be used to measure the geographic concentration of an industry and the coagglomeration of groups of industries, and we discuss the properties of these indices.

A. An Index of Industry Concentration

Beginning with the single-industry problem, suppose that we are given data containing the shares $s_1, s_2, \ldots, s_M$ of an industry's employment in each of M geographic areas, the shares $x_1, x_2, \ldots, x_M$ of total employment in each of those areas, and the Herfindahl index $H = \sum_{j=1}^{N} z_j^2$ of the industry plant size distribution. As an index of the degree to which an industry is geographically concentrated, we propose the use of a measure γ defined by

$$
\gamma \equiv \frac{G - \left(1 - \sum_i x_i^2\right) H}{\left(1 - \sum_i x_i^2\right)(1 - H)}
$$

$$
\equiv \frac{\sum_{i=1}^{M} (s_i - x_i)^2 - \left(1 - \sum_{i=1}^{M} x_i^2\right)^2 \sum_{j=1}^{N} z_j^2}{\left(1 - \sum_{i=1}^{M} x_i^2\right)\left(1 - \sum_{j=1}^{N} z_j^2\right)}. \tag{5}
$$

---

[6] Provided that $\gamma_0 \leq \min_j \gamma_j$, it is always possible to define such a joint distribution.

Note that if the plants' location decisions are made in accordance with the model of the previous section, then proposition 1 implies that the index γ is an unbiased estimate of the quantity $\gamma^{na} + \gamma^s - \gamma^{na}\gamma^s$ that captures the strength of the agglomerative forces in the model. For this reason the index has a number of desirable properties.

1. The index is easy to compute given the available data. In practice, the best available data on concentration are often a breakdown of total employment by some geographic subunits, for example, state-by-state employments for an industry in the United States or country-by-country employments for the European Community, and very little information is available on plant size distributions (on which our index requires only one moment).

2. The scale of the index allows one to make comparisons with a no-agglomeration benchmark in that $E(\gamma) = 0$ if the data are generated by the simple dartboard model of random location choices with no natural advantages or industry-specific spillovers.

3. The index is comparable across industries in which the size distribution of firms differs. Specifically, if each plant's location decision is made as in the model above, then the expected value of the concentration index is independent both of the number of plants and of their distribution.

4. The index is also comparable across industries regardless of differences in the level of geographic aggregation at which employment data are available in the different industries. While the geographic areas are built directly into the model specification, one can formalize this statement by supposing that the model describes how firms choose from a large set of M geographic areas (e.g., one for each square mile of the United States) and asking that the expected value of the index be unchanged no matter how the employment data are combined into M' larger aggregates before the index is computed.

To see that our index has this property given one specification of our location decision process, consider the example mentioned earlier in which $2[(1 - \gamma^{na})/\gamma^{na}]\bar{\pi}_i$ has a χ^2 distribution with $2[(1 - \gamma^{na})/\gamma^{na}]x_i$ degrees of freedom. The location process is then equivalent to drawing $(p_1, p_2, \ldots, p_M)$ from a Dirichlet distribution with parameters

$$\left(\frac{1 - \gamma^{na}}{\gamma^{na}} x_1, \frac{1 - \gamma^{na}}{\gamma^{na}} x_2, \ldots, \frac{1 - \gamma^{na}}{\gamma^{na}} x_M \right)$$

and then having each spillover-tied cluster of plants choose its location independently, with the probability of choosing area i being p_i.

When $(p_1, \ldots, p_M)$ has a Dirichlet distribution with parameters

$$\left(\frac{1 - \gamma^{na}}{\gamma^{na}} x_1, \ldots, \frac{1 - \gamma^{na}}{\gamma^{na}} x_M \right),$$

the distribution of $(p_1 + p_2, p_3, \ldots, p_M)$ is Dirichlet with parameters

$$\left(\frac{1 - \gamma^{na}}{\gamma^{na}} (x_1 + x_2), \frac{1 - \gamma^{na}}{\gamma^{na}} x_3, \ldots, \frac{1 - \gamma^{na}}{\gamma^{na}} x_M \right).$$

Hence, data generated by aggregating areas 1 and 2 in an M-location model with parameters $\gamma^{na}, \gamma^s, x_1, \ldots, x_M$ will have the same distribution as data generated from an $M - 1$ location model with parameters $\gamma^{na}, \gamma^s, x_1 + x_2, x_3, \ldots, x_M$. Repeating this argument as multiple areas are combined, we conclude that regardless of how areas are combined together, the expected value of an index computed from aggregated data remains $\gamma^{na} + \gamma^s - \gamma^{na}\gamma^s$.

When one makes the transition from the models to the real world, a caveat is necessary with regard to comparisons based on data at different levels of geographic aggregation. Our model imposes an extreme limitation on the geographic scope of forces that produce localization in two ways. First, when potential spillovers exist, they are realized only if firms choose to locate in the same geographic area. Second (at least in the χ^2 specification), natural advantages are drawn independently for each geographic area. In practice, we would expect that spillovers might provide some benefit also to plants locating in nearby areas. In this case, an estimate of γ that is computed from county-level data (and hence reflects only the added probability with which pairs of plants locate in the same county) would be expected to be smaller than an estimate that is computed from state-level data and reflects the additional colocations due to spillovers felt at some distance and to correlated natural advantages.

While the properties above can be taken as formalizing our motivation that an index should allow for meaningful comparisons across industries and with the null of no concentration, they are not axioms that determine our index uniquely. For example, any other unbiased estimator of $\gamma^{na} + \gamma^s - \gamma^{na}\gamma^s$ that could be computed from available data would also satisfy those properties. Our particular choice is to some degree arbitrary, although it does reflect a concern that the index reflects economically significant localizations. On these grounds, we would, for example, be uncomfortable with indexes based on plant count data (because such data tend to be dominated by very small plants that account for only a small portion of employment).

B.   Interpreting the Scale of the Index

While the scale of γ is such that one can interpret a value of zero as indicating a complete lack of agglomerative forces, we would also like to be able to talk about whether particular positive values of the index are "large" or "small." We discuss here several ways in which one might try to get a feel for the scale of γ.

First and most informally, we find it useful in trying to interpret values of γ to keep a mental list of the γ's of things with which we feel somewhat familiar so that they can be used for comparisons. Appendix C of the working paper version of this paper (Ellison and Glaeser 1994) contains a complete list of the γ's of each four-digit manufacturing industry. Looking at industries that have previously attracted attention for their concentration, one can find there, for example, that the measured γ's for the U.S. automobile and automobile parts industries (SICs 3711 and 3714) are 0.127 and 0.089. The photographic equipment industry (SIC 3861) has a γ of 0.174. The carpet industry's (SIC 2273) γ is 0.378. The computer industry is a bit harder to find in the SIC codes, but the γ's for SICs 3571 (electronic computers), 3572 (computer storage devices), and 3674 (semiconductors and related devices) are 0.059, 0.142, and 0.064, respectively. As a reference point at the other extreme, one can look up industries that one could not imagine to be concentrated and find that the γ's of the bottled and canned soft drink (SIC 2086), manufactured ice (SIC 2096), newspaper (SIC 2711), and miscellaneous concrete products (SIC 3272) industries are 0.005, 0.012, 0.002, and 0.012, respectively.

Another source of reference points is the agglomeration of aggregate manufacturing activity. The model and index of this paper can also be applied to measure the concentration of overall U.S. manufacturing activity relative to the land area of the states. We typically think of manufacturing concentration as substantial. Computing our index using state manufacturing employment for s_i and land area for x_i, we find a γ of 0.055. On the other hand, if we restrict our attention to the states east of the Mississippi, manufacturing employment is much closer to being proportional to land area: the largest states—Georgia, Michigan, and Illinois—have far more manufacturing than the smallest—the District of Columbia, Rhode Island, and Delaware—and the raw correlation between manufacturing employment and land area is .50. The measured γ of manufacturing employment shares relative to land area in this subset is 0.019.

While the comparisons above may help build intuition, they do not provide an estimated dollar magnitude for the impact of natural

GEOGRAPHIC CONCENTRATION 903

advantages/spillovers. One way to do this is to note that γ reflects the effect of natural advantages/spillovers on each state's share of manufacturing in an industry and that many previous studies have estimated the elasticity of plant locations with respect to cost differences. In the model (with a large number of plants), the effect of nature's allocation of natural advantage is to make the share p_i of plants that will locate in state i a random variable with mean x_i and variance $\gamma x_i(1 - x_i)$. For a state with $x_i = 0.02$ this means, for example, that when $\gamma = 0.01$, the standard deviation of p_i is $0.7E(p_i)$. A wide range of estimated new plant share–cost elasticities can be found in the literature.[7] If we assume the elasticity to be 25, the magnitude of the effects of natural advantages/spillovers on location decisions when $\gamma = 0.01$ is then similar to the effect of a cost shock whose standard deviation is 3 percent of total costs. The effect of natural advantages/spillovers with a γ magnitude of 0.10 would be similar to the effects of a cost shock with a standard deviation of 9 percent.[8] To put such differences in perspective, after one controls for education, tenure, and so forth in a log wage regression, the standard deviation of wage rates across states is about 8–10 percent of the level of wages. We would therefore regard a γ of 0.01 as indicating that cost differences are fairly small and a γ of 0.10 as indicating that cost differences are substantial.

Finally, we present a few magnitude calculations derived strictly from our model. In the model, the portion of γ due to spillovers is readily interpretable as an added colocation probability. For example, in an industry with 20 large plants, the expected number of large plants with which a given plant will colocate (on top of random colocations) is approximately 0.2 for $\gamma^s = 0.01$ and one for $\gamma^s = 0.05$. The magnitudes of natural advantages in the model are defined only in relation to the assumed magnitudes of the non-industry-specific advantages of the large states and the firm-specific idiosyncratic factors. To try to derive intuition from such a definition, table 1 records for several values of γ^{na} how likely it is that natural advantage will make Iowa a better location (for a firm with no idiosyncratic prefer-

[7] Given that energy costs are as small as 0.5 percent of total costs in some of the industries considered, the substantial energy price elasticities in Carlton's (1983) classic study imply elasticities of new plant shares to total costs in the 100–500 range. Carlton, however, finds much lower elasticities to wage differentials, and others (e.g., Bartik 1985) have failed to find significant responses to energy and other cost differences in other industries. In the literature on local tax rates and location decisions, Bartik's estimates imply elasticities with respect to total costs of around 50, whereas others (e.g., Schmenner, Huber, and Cook 1987) find very small elasticities. Crihfield (1990) finds the effects of taxes on growth rates to be small.

[8] These differences would be scaled up (down) linearly for smaller (larger) elasticities.

TABLE 1

EFFECT OF γ NATURAL ADVANTAGE RELATIVE TO STATE SIZE

γ^{na}	prob$\{\bar{\pi}_{IA} > \bar{\pi}_{GA}\}$	prob$\{\bar{\pi}_{IA} > \bar{\pi}_{MI}\}$	prob$\{\bar{\pi}_{IA} > \bar{\pi}_{CA}\}$
.005	.07	.006	.00
.01	.14	.03	.00
.02	.20	.08	.006
.05	.25	.14	.04
.10	.26	.15	.07
1.00	.27	.17	.09

ences) than Georgia, Michigan, and California.[9] For $\gamma^{na} = 0.01$, natural advantages are at times sufficiently powerful to make Iowa as attractive as Georgia, but they are rarely enough to overcome the non-industry-specific advantages of the larger states. Natural advantage becomes sufficiently important to make Iowa as good as Michigan with a reasonable probability when γ^{na} is between 0.02 and 0.05, and Iowa starts to be comparable to California at times when γ^{na} is between 0.05 and 0.10.

In describing our results, we shall generally adopt the convention of referring to those industries with γ's above 0.05 as being highly concentrated and to those with γ's below 0.02 as being not very concentrated.

C. Measurements of Coagglomeration

Suppose now that we are given area industry employment and plant size data for each of r industries belonging to some group. As in Section II*B*, use G^j, H_j, and w_j for the raw concentration, the plant Herfindahl index, and the employment share of the jth industry. Let $\hat{\gamma}_j$ be the value of our index of concentration as computed from the data on the jth industry. Write G for the raw concentration of employment in the group as a whole and $H = \sum_j w_j^2 H_j$ for the group's plant Herfindahl index. As an index of the degree to which the industries in the group are coagglomerated, we propose the use of a measure γ^c defined by

$$\gamma^c \equiv \frac{\left[G \Big/ \left(1 - \sum_i x_i^2\right)\right] - H - \sum_{j=1}^{r} \hat{\gamma}_j w_j^2 (1 - H_j)}{1 - \sum_{j=1}^{r} w_j^2}. \tag{6}$$

[9] The figures pertain to the χ^2 specification of average profits. Iowa has approximately 1 percent of manufacturing employment, Georgia 3 percent, Michigan 5 percent, and California 11 percent.

Note that proposition 2 implies that γ^c is an unbiased estimate of the parameter γ_0 in the model of Section II B, and as such, it has the same robustness properties as γ does with regard to changes in the firm size distribution and in the level of data aggregation. As a measure of the importance of group-specific natural advantages and spillovers, magnitudes have the same meaning as they do for γ. An estimate of $\gamma^c = 0$ may be interpreted as indicating that there is no more agglomeration of plants in the group than that attributable to the tendencies of plants to locate near other plants in the same industry and where aggregate manufacturing employment is high.

In discussing the scope of spillovers / natural advantages, we find it useful also to rescale this measure, defining an index, λ, of the degree to which spillovers are general by

$$\lambda \equiv \frac{\gamma^c}{\sum_j w_j \hat{\gamma}_j}. \tag{7}$$

We interpret a value of $\lambda = 0$ as indicating that any spillovers / natural advantages found within the industry group are completely industry-specific. We interpret a value of $\lambda = 1$ as indicating that they are perfectly general in the sense that any spillovers benefit firms in all industries equally and natural advantages are perfectly correlated.[10]

IV. Data

Our index requires the distribution of employment across a set of geographic areas for a set of industries and the Herfindahl index of plant employment shares for those industries. There is a trade-off between locational fineness and industrial fineness in the available data, and for this paper, we have chosen to focus on the most narrowly defined industries possible: the 459 manufacturing industries defined by the four-digit classifications of the Census Bureau's 1987 SIC system. Given this decision, we settled on the 50 states plus the District of Columbia as our geographic division, and even at this level of disaggregation, a complicated and somewhat speculative data construction process was necessary.

Our construction of state-industry employments relies on data from the *Census of Manufactures*. These data are incomplete in that some state-industry employments are categorized or top-coded to protect confidentiality. Moreover, employment data are not re-

---

[10] Note that because of the parameter estimates in the denominator, λ is not an unbiased estimator of $\gamma_0 / (\sum_j w_j \gamma_j)$ in our model.

ported for state-industries with fewer than 150 employees.[11] To complete our state-industry data set, we used a fairly elaborate computer program that tried to exploit the information contained in the across-state and across-industry adding-up constraints and in the state-industry plant count data when estimating employments in categorized and unreported state-industries. Some details on the process are provided in Appendix A.

Given our interpretation of the model as describing the location decision process of manufacturing plants, we must also construct an estimate of the Herfindahl index of plant employment shares in each four-digit industry. For this purpose, the relevant and available (subject to disclosure restrictions) census data consist of the number of plants and the total employment within plants in each of 10 employment size ranges.[12] We estimate Herfindahl indices from these data by a two-step procedure: employees were first allocated between the classes, and a Herfindahl index was then estimated by a procedure similar to that recommended by Schmalensee (1977), but taking into account the additional information available here in the form of the category divisions. The details of the data construction algorithm and a simulation analysis of the measurement errors it may create are discussed in Appendix B.

While we cannot be sure of the accuracy of our data-filling procedure, we do feel that it is an improvement over those that are typically used. The changes are likely to be particularly important in very small industries and highly geographically concentrated industries. The state employment data and the plant Herfindahl indices are available from the authors on request (the latter are listed also in app. C of Ellison and Glaeser [1994]).

Finally, to allow for a more thorough analysis of the geographic scope of concentration, we obtained a data set of 1987 county-level employments for three-digit industries. The data set had been constructed by filling in County Business Patterns data using an algorithm that consists largely of using mean plant sizes for nondisclosed employments (see Gardocki and Baj 1985). Some comparisons of these data with our main data set are also given in Appendix A.

V. Basic Results on Geographic Concentration

In this section we describe the patterns of geographic concentration in U.S. manufacturing industries. We begin at the broadest level with

---

[11] To give some idea of the magnitude of these restrictions, simply setting employment in each cell to its lower bound unequivocally identifies the location of 90 percent of employment in the median industry and 80 percent on average.

[12] The nondisclosures here are somewhat more problematic because they tend to obscure primarily the shares of the largest plants.

a discussion of whether any geographic concentration exists before moving on to discuss a few aspects in a little more detail.

A. Are Industries Geographically Concentrated?

The single most crucial question one must ask before further studying the geographic concentration of industries is whether geographic concentration really exists. While a number of previous writers have noted that localization appears to be widespread, we present here for the first time formal tests of the more stringent hypothesis that the extent of localization is greater than what would be expected to arise randomly.

In the simplest dartboard model in which the plants in an industry choose their locations in an independent random manner and there are no industry-specific spillovers or natural advantages, the result of proposition 1 is that $E(G) = (1 - \sum_i x_i^2) H$. The mean values of G and $(1 - \sum_i x_i^2) H$ across the 459 manufacturing industries in our data set are 0.74 and 0.27, respectively, and the difference between these two numbers is highly significant.[13]

When we look more closely at the industry-by-industry numbers, we find a prevalence of localization that we think is striking, even in light of the comments on the ubiquity of concentration found in Krugman (1991a) and so forth. The level of raw concentration G exceeds what would be expected to arise randomly in 446 of the 459 industries.[14] The flip side of this result—that in only 13 industries are plants more evenly distributed than would be expected at random—is interesting in that it indicates that the need to be near final consumers is rarely an overwhelming force in location decisions.

Because one might worry that manufacturing employment is not a good measure of the final demand in consumer goods industries, we performed this calculation also with population rather than manufacturing employment as the measure of state size. Such a calculation identifies 14 industries as being more evenly distributed than random (six of the 13 above and eight others), with the overall correlation between the two measures being .993.

---

[13] Under the null of $\gamma^i = \gamma^{na} = 0$, a lengthy calculation shows that

$$\text{var}(G) = 2\left\{ H^2[\sum x_i^2 - 2\sum x_i^3 + (\sum x_i^2)^2] - \sum_j z_j^4[\sum x_i^2 - 4\sum x_i^3 + 3(\sum x_i^2)^2] \right\}.$$

Using this formula, we estimate the standard deviation of the sample mean under the null to be 0.0005.

[14] The difference between G and $(1 - \sum_i x_i^2) H$ is larger than twice its standard deviation in 369 of the 446 industries in which the difference is positive and in none of the 13 industries in which the difference is negative.

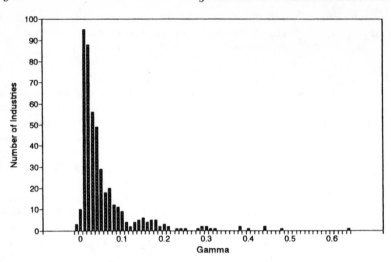

FIG. 1.—Histogram of γ (four-digit industries)

B.   How Concentrated Are They?

In this subsection, we try to use our models to get a feel for how much concentration there is. We begin by imposing no structure across industries and simply computing the index γ defined by (5) for each of the 459 four-digit industries in our sample. A complete list of the γ's we find can be found in appendix C of Ellison and Glaeser (1994) and is also available from the authors on request.[15]

A histogram illustrating the frequency distribution of these γ's is presented in figure 1. In the figure, each bar represents the number of industries for which γ lies in an interval of width 0.01. The distribution in the figure appears to be quite skewed, with the mean being 0.051 and the median being 0.026. The most striking feature of the figure is the large number of industries falling into the range we described as not very concentrated ($\gamma < 0.02$). The tallest bar is the one corresponding to values of γ between zero and 0.01, and 43 percent of the industries have $\gamma < 0.02$. On the other side, the figure displays a thick right tail, with slightly more than a quarter of the

[15] If one interprets γ's as estimates of $\gamma^{na} + \gamma^{s} - \gamma^{na}\gamma^{s}$ (as opposed to estimates of the realized sum of squared differences between the p's and the x's), these γ's are measured with substantial errors. To get a feel for the magnitudes, we computed standard errors by simulating a special case of our natural advantage model: that of Dirichlet-distributed state sizes. Among industries with $H < 0.02$, the mean of the estimated standard errors is 0.02. The means for industries with H in the ranges 0.02–0.05, 0.05–0.10, and 0.10–1.0 are 0.024, 0.041, and 0.072, respectively.

TABLE 2

Raw Concentration Attributable to
Spillovers / Comparative Advantage:
Fraction of Industries with
$(1 - \sum x_i^2)\gamma / G$ in Range

Range	All Industries	High-G Industries
<0	.03	.03
.00–.25	.09	.10
.25–.50	.22	.16
.50–.75	.32	.19
.75–1.00	.33	.53

industries having a γ of at least 0.05 and 59 having a γ of at least 0.10. While the automobile, computer, carpet, and other industries people have used as examples of concentration are far from typical, there are a substantial number of industries that have received less attention and are similarly concentrated. We would thus like to amend our earlier conclusion that concentration is remarkably wide-spread to read that slight concentration is remarkably widespread, with the more extreme concentration that has attracted attention existing in a smaller subset of industries.

To provide a rough idea of how important it is to account properly for random agglomeration when constructing an index of geographic concentration, table 2 lists the frequency with which the ratio $(1 - \sum_i x_i^2)\gamma / G$ falls into a number of intervals, both for all industries and for the subsample of those in the upper quartile of raw geographic concentration. We can think of the fraction as a rough measure of the portion of raw concentration that is legitimately attributable to some form of spillovers / natural advantage rather than to randomness. The table indicates that the two components are comparable in magnitude and that there is a great variation in the mix between them. In roughly one-third of the industries (both over-all and among the industries with high raw concentration), the fact that plants are discrete units and that some clusters appear at random accounts for at least as large a part of measured raw concentration as actual agglomerations of plants do. It is, therefore, not surprising that our index gives a somewhat different picture of geographic concentration than previous discussions of raw concentrations have.

C. Patterns of Concentration

While an attempt to explore formally the industry characteristics that tend to be associated with localization is well beyond the scope of this paper, we felt that a couple of simple tables would be of interest.[16]

Table 3 summarizes the levels of geographic concentration of the four-digit subindustries of each two-digit manufacturing industry. For each two-digit industry, the table lists the fraction of subindustries that fall in the not very localized ($\gamma < 0.02$), intermediate, and very localized ($\gamma > 0.05$) ranges. High levels of geographic concentration are most prevalent in the tobacco, textile, and leather industries and most rare in the paper, rubber and plastics, and fabricated metal products industries.

Table 4 lists the 15 most and the 15 least localized industries in terms of the index γ. As Krugman (1991*a*) has previously noted, there is no obvious single factor accounting for extreme concentration. The most concentrated industry, furs, is probably explained both by the local transfer of knowledge from one generation to the next and as a response to buyers' search costs. Furs also have an unusually high ratio of value to weight that may make physical transportation costs less important. The next most concentrated industry, wine, may be largely attributable to the natural advantage of California in growing grapes. Natural advantage may also be important in the carbon black, raw cane sugar, and phosphatic fertilizer industries (and perhaps very indirectly in the oil field machinery industry). While a single spillover-based explanation may account for the concentration of the various textile industries in the Southeast, the remaining industries seem quite disparate.

The list of the 15 least concentrated industries is also something of a mixed bag. The industries certainly do not stand out as being those in which spreading out to be close to final consumers is important, and the list contains several industries, for example, vacuum cleaners and small-arms ammunition, in which raw concentration is substantial, but employment turns out to be concentrated in a few very large (randomly scattered) plants.[17]

D. *The Geographic Scope of Concentration*

In Section III, we noted that the γ's estimated from county-, state-, or region-level data should be identical (in expectation) provided that the scope of spillovers is such that advantages are gained only

---

[16] For interesting work on this topic, see Henderson (1988) and Enright (1990).

[17] In interpreting these latter cases, the reader should keep in mind that the errors in measuring γ include both the inherent uncertainty of analyzing random dart throws and errors in filling in census nondisclosures. Each of these components is larger when H is larger, so the list may contain many industries with a large H simply because this is where we have made the largest errors in measurement.

TABLE 3

CONCENTRATION BY TWO-DIGIT CATEGORY

Two-Digit Industry	Number of Four-Digit Subindustries	Percentage of Four-Digit Industries with		
		$\gamma < .02$	$\gamma \in [.02, .05]$	$\gamma > .05$
20 Food and kindred products	49	47	18	35
21 Tobacco products	4	0	0	100
22 Textile mill products	23	9	13	78
23 Apparel and other textile products	31	13	42	45
24 Lumber and wood products	17	29	47	24
25 Furniture and fixtures	13	69	8	23
26 Paper and allied products	17	53	47	0
27 Printing and publishing	14	71	14	14
28 Chemicals and allied products	31	38	24	38
29 Petroleum and coal products	5	60	0	40
30 Rubber and miscellaneous plastics	15	73	27	0
31 Leather and leather products	11	0	36	64
32 Stone, clay, and glass products	26	58	27	15
33 Primary metal industries	26	39	35	27
34 Fabricated metal products	38	61	32	8
35 Industrial machinery and equipment	51	49	26	26
36 Electronic and other electric equipment	37	41	46	14
37 Transportation equipment	18	28	33	39
38 Instruments and related products	17	47	41	11
39 Miscellaneous manufacturing industries	18	44	22	33

TABLE 4

MOST AND LEAST LOCALIZED INDUSTRIES

Four-Digit Industry	H	G	γ
	15 Most Localized Industries		
2371 Fur goods	.007	.60	.63
2084 Wines, brandy, brandy spirits	.041	.48	.48
2252 Hosiery not elsewhere classified	.008	.42	.44
3533 Oil and gas field machinery	.015	.42	.43
2251 Women's hosiery	.028	.40	.40
2273 Carpets and rugs	.013	.37	.38
2429 Special product sawmills not elsewhere classified	.009	.36	.37
3961 Costume jewelry	.017	.32	.32
2895 Carbon black	.054	.32	.30
3915 Jewelers' materials, lapidary	.025	.30	.30
2874 Phosphatic fertilizers	.066	.32	.29
2061 Raw cane sugar	.038	.30	.29
2281 Yarn mills, except wool	.005	.27	.28
2034 Dehydrated fruits, vegetables, soups	.030	.29	.28
3761 Guided missiles, space vehicles	.046	.27	.25
	15 Least Localized Industries		
3021 Rubber and plastics footwear	.06	.05	−.013
2032 Canned specialties	.03	.02	−.012
2082 Malt beverages	.04	.03	−.010
3635 Household vacuum cleaners	.18	.17	−.009
3652 Prerecorded records and tapes	.04	.03	−.008
3482 Small-arms ammunition	.18	.17	−.004
3324 Steel investment foundries	.04	.04	−.003
3534 Elevators and moving stairways	.03	.03	−.001
2052 Cookies and crackers	.03	.03	−.0009
2098 Macaroni and spaghetti	.03	.03	−.0008
3262 Vitreous china table, kitchenware	.13	.12	−.0006
2035 Pickles, sauces, salad dressings	.01	.01	−.0003
3821 Laboratory apparatus and furniture	.02	.02	−.0002
2062 Cane sugar refining	.11	.10	.0002
3433 Heating equipment except electric	.01	.01	.0002

if firms choose identical locations, with natural advantages being independent across geographic areas. If, on the other hand, the effect of spillovers (or the spatial correlation of natural advantage) is smoothly declining with distance, then those γ's will reflect the excess probability with which pairs of firms tend to locate in the same county, state, and region, respectively. To investigate the geographic scope of spillovers, we estimated γ's from our county/three-digit data set using counties, states, and the nine census regions as the units of observation.

Figure 2 presents histograms of the γ's estimated from the three

County Level Gammas

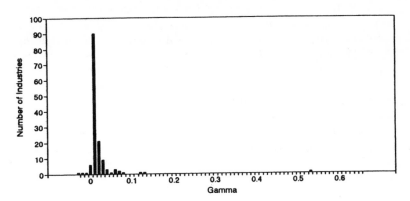

State Level Gammas

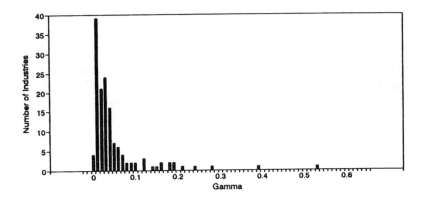

Region Level Gammas

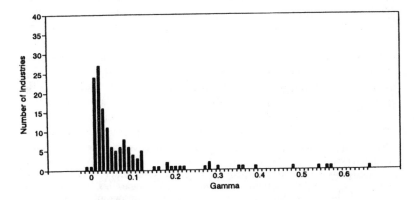

FIG. 2.—Concentration at the county, state, and regional levels

levels of data. Comparing the county- and state-level estimates, we find substantially more concentration at the state level. The median γ at the county level is 0.005, and the median γ at the state level is 0.023. The median of the ratio between them is 0.25, so typically the effect of spillovers is such that about one-fourth of the excess tendency of plants to locate in the same state involves plants' locating in the same county. We draw two conclusions. First, because one-fourth of all excess colocations do involve plants' locating in the same county (while states have many more than four counties), within-county spillovers are stronger than nearby-county spillovers. Second, "localized" spillovers are still quite substantial at a range beyond that of counties. In only a few cases do spillovers appear to be both substantial and limited in scope to the county level.[18] The rubber and plastics footwear industry seems to be the unique example in which concentration is substantially greater at the county level than at the state level, that is, where tightly grouped clusters of plants are spread (excessively) evenly across the states as though to minimize transportation costs.

Measured levels of state and regional concentration are more similar, although the regional data show a much thicker tail of very concentrated industries. (The mean γ's are 0.044 and 0.078.) The general pattern that slightly more than half of the tendency of firms to locate in the same region is accounted for by the tendency to locate in the same state appears to hold equally well for industries that are very unconcentrated and very concentrated at the state level, although there is considerable variation about this norm.[19]

VI. Evidence on Coagglomeration

In this section, we present some descriptive evidence on the coagglomeration of industries. First, we examine the extent to which geographic concentration tends to be a characteristic of broadly or narrowly defined industries by discussing the coagglomeration of SIC-similar industries. Next, to explore the importance of transportation costs or information flows between buyers and sellers, we look at the coagglomeration of pairs of industries with strong upstream-downstream relationships.

[18] The most notable cases are fur goods, building paper and board mills, and periodicals.
[19] Industries notable for unusually high (relative) regional concentration include ordnance and accessories, nonferrous foundries, and cigarettes. Industries in which state-level clusters are unusually dispersed include photographic equipment and supplies, radio and television receiving equipment, and periodicals.

TABLE 5

CONCENTRATION AND INDUSTRY DEFINITION

| | INDUSTRY MEANS | | |
INDUSTRY DEFINITION	H	G	γ
Two-digit	.007	.031	.026
Three-digit	.014	.056	.045
Four-digit	.028	.074	.051

A. *Industry Definition*

Table 5 provides a simple look at the concentration of two-, three-, and four-digit industries. While raw geographic concentration increases steadily as we move to finer industry definitions, the increase in γ appears to come more abruptly as we move from the two-digit to the three-digit level. This naturally raises two questions of scope. Is there any correlation in the location decisions of firms that share only a two-digit industry class, or is the concentration of two-digit industries entirely a consequence of the localization of their three-digit subindustries? Are location decisions influenced as strongly by the locations of plants belonging to different four-digit industries within the same three-digit class as they are by the locations of plants belonging to their own four-digit industry?

To address the latter question, we calculated for each of the 97 three-digit industries with more than one four-digit subindustry our measures γ^c and λ of the degree to which the four-digit subindustries are coagglomerated. Recall that the scale of γ^c is the same as that of γ, whereas λ measures the strength of coagglomerative forces relative to agglomerative forces. A value of $\lambda = 0$ would indicate that the subindustries exhibit no coagglomeration at all, and a value of $\lambda = 1$ would indicate that the natural advantages and spillovers that exist are (three-digit) group-specific rather than (four-digit) industry-specific. Figure 3 contains a histogram of the values of λ we estimate, which are fairly evenly spread between zero and 0.8. From this we conclude that there is some coagglomeration of four-digit industries, but it is rare for spillovers to be almost completely general to three-digit classes. Perhaps most interesting, the histogram suggests that there is considerable heterogeneity across industries in the specificity of spillovers.

Let us move on to yet broader industry classes. Table 6 reports the values of the γ^c and λ obtained from a similar calculation using the three-digit subindustries of each two-digit industry. The mean value of λ across two-digit industries is 0.29. There is again a great

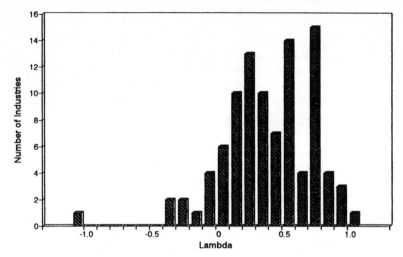

FIG. 3.—Histogram of λ: extent of spillovers between four-digit subindustries of three-digit industries.

TABLE 6

EXTENT OF SPILLOVERS BETWEEN THREE-DIGIT INDUSTRIES

Two-Digit Industry	γ^c	λ
Food and kindred products	.002	.14
Tobacco products	.151	.88
Textile mill products	.115	.61
Apparel and other textiles	.010	.29
Lumber and wood products	.016	.63
Furniture and fixtures	.001	.02
Paper and allied products	.005	.31
Printing and publishing	.005	.48
Chemicals and allied products	.007	.25
Petroleum and coal products	.007	.12
Rubber and miscellaneous plastics	.003	.38
Leather and leather products	.017	.31
Stone, clay, and glass products	.002	.20
Primary metal industries	.012	.41
Fabricated metal products	.003	.22
Industrial machinery and equipment	.000	.00
Electronic and other electric equipment	.000	.02
Transportation equipment	−.001	−.08
Instruments and related products	.013	.36
Miscellaneous manufacturing	.011	.34

variation across industries. In four cases (furniture, industrial machinery, electronic and electric equipment, and transportation
equipment), the data indicate that there is no coagglomeration at
all at the two-digit level. On the other hand, there is substantial coagglomeration of the three-digit subindustries within the two-digit tobacco, textile, and lumber industries.

B.   Coagglomeration and Upstream-Downstream Relationships

We examine here the coagglomeration of industries with strong
upstream-downstream ties in hopes that it may provide some suggestive evidence on economizing on transportation costs as a motivation
for agglomeration. Our analysis focuses on two lists of 100 industry
pairs that we constructed using data from the Census Bureau's six-
digit commodity-by-industry direct requirements table: one consisting of the 100 (downstream) industries that receive the largest
value of inputs per dollar value of output from a single upstream
industry (paired with that supplier) and the other consisting of the
100 (upstream) industries that sell the largest portion of their output
to one downstream industry. For example, the first list contains the
ice cream and frozen dessert industry paired with the milk industry
(from which it purchases a large amount of inputs per dollar of output), and the second contains the engine electrical equipment industry paired with the motor vehicle industry (to which it sells a large
portion of its output).

In the set of 100 industry pairs in which the downstream industry is
heavily dependent on an upstream input, we find clearly significant
evidence that there is a tendency to coagglomerate: for 77 of the
pairs, γ^c is positive. The mean level of γ^c for these pairs is 0.018, which
we would not regard as being particularly large, although nine of
the pairs have coagglomeration γ^c's in the range we would call very
concentrated (above 0.05). Of the 100 pairs in which the upstream
industry has an important customer, 68 exhibit some coagglomeration, with the mean of γ^c being 0.015 and 10 of the pairs having γ^c
above 0.05. Table 7 lists the top 15 pairs of each type (ranked on
input / output dependency) along with the γ^c and the λ of the pair.

VII.   Geographic Concentration within the Firm

In this section, we investigate the tendency of plants belonging to
the same firm to locate together. While our data set does not allow
us to provide detailed descriptive evidence on the topic, we felt that
some treatment of the issue was necessary to see whether such a

TABLE 7

COAGGLOMERATION OF UPSTREAM-DOWNSTREAM INDUSTRY PAIRS

Upstream Industry	Downstream Industry	γ^c	λ
	Pairs with Downstream Industry Relying on Upstream Input		
2026 Fluid milk	2021 Ice cream and frozen desserts	.005	1.05
2824 Organic fibers, noncellulosic	2296 Tire cord and fabrics	.078	.55
2011 Meat packing	2013 Sausages and prepared meats	.014	.50
3312 Blast furnaces and steel mills	3316 Cold finishing of steel shapes	.048	.74
3312 Blast furnaces and steel mills	3449 Miscellaneous metal work	.017	.28
2421 Sawmills and planing mills	2439 Structural wood members	.016	.44
3339 Primary nonferrous metals	3356 Nonferrous rolling and drawing	.014	1.20
3312 Blast furnaces and steel mills	3315 Steel wire and related	.019	.31
3312 Blast furnaces and steel mills	3412 Metal barrels, drums, pails	.015	.23
3312 Blast furnaces and steel mills	3465 Automotive stampings	.052	.48
3714 Motor vehicle parts, accessories	3711 Motor vehicles, car bodies	.107	1.02
3312 Blast furnaces and steel mills	3441 Fabricated structural metal	.004	.09
2075 Soybean oil mills	2079 Edible fats and oils not elsewhere classified	.033	.69
2421 Sawmills and planing mills	2941 Wood preserving	.027	.70
3312 Blast furnaces and steel mills	3448 Prefabricated metal buildings	-.006	-.11

Pairs with Upstream Industry Having Large Downstream Buyer

3313	Electrometallurgical products	3312 Blast furnaces and steel mills	.059	.85
2083	Malt	2082 Malt beverages	.032	87.19
3493	Steel springs except wire	3711 Motor vehicles, car bodies	.006	.05
3714	Motor vehicle parts, accessories	3711 Motor vehicles, car bodies	.107	1.02
2087	Flavoring extracts and syrups	2086 Bottled and canned soft drinks	.001	.19
3465	Automotive stampings	3711 Motor vehicles, car bodies	.149	1.05
2395	Pleating and stitching	3711 Motor vehicles, car bodies	-.028	-.23
3694	Engine electrical equipment	3711 Motor vehicles, car bodies	.011	.09
3292	Asbestos products	3714 Motor vehicle parts, accessories	-.019	-.22
3255	Clay refractories	3312 Blast furnaces and steel mills	.044	.64
2782	Book printing	2781 Book publishing	.000	.00
2076	Vegetable oil mills not elsewhere classified	2079 Edible fats and oils not elsewhere classified	.003	.10
2074	Cottonseed oil mills	2048 Prepared feeds not elsewhere classified	.020	.67
2399	Fabricated textile not elsewhere classified	3711 Motor vehicles, car bodies	-.017	-.15
3331	Primary copper	3351 Copper rolling and drawing	.000	-.01

920   JOURNAL OF POLITICAL ECONOMY

tendency could account for a significant portion of the localization
we have identified.

To analyze the potential for measuring agglomeration within the
firm, we consider an industry consisting of r firms with shares w_1, w_2,
..., w_r of the industry's employment. Let $H_f = \sum_j w_j^2$ be the Herfindahl index of the firms' employment shares. To avoid confusion, we
shall use H_p in this section for the Herfindahl index of the plants'
employment shares. Suppose that firm j consists of n_j plants having
shares z_{j1}, ..., z_{jn_j} of the industry's employment. Suppose that the
location choices of the plants are made analogously to those of our
multi-industry model (with the firms analogous to subindustries),
with the correlation of the location choice indicator variables u_{ki} and
u_{li} being γ_0 if plants k and l belong to different firms and $\gamma_1 > \gamma_0$ if
they belong to the same firm. A direct corollary of proposition 2 is
proposition 3.

PROPOSITION 3. In the model above,

$$E(G) = \left(1 - \sum_i x_i^2\right)[H_p + \gamma_0(1 - H_f) + \gamma_1(H_f - H_p)].$$

When one tries to apply the prediction of this model to recover
γ_1, a great obstacle arises: state-firm employments are much harder
to find than state-industry employments. As a result, we cannot separately estimate γ_0 and γ_1 for a single industry. What we try to do instead is to identify average values of γ_0 and γ_1 using cross-industry
variation. Specifically, we note that if one makes the heroic assump-
tion that the parameters γ_{0i} and γ_{1i} for industry i are random variables
whose conditional means are independent of H_{pi} and H_{fi}, then the
coefficients $\hat{\alpha}_0$ and $\hat{\alpha}_1$ from the ordinary least squares (OLS) regression

$$\frac{G_i}{1 - \sum_j x_j^2} - H_{pi} = \alpha_0(1 - H_{fi}) + \alpha_1(H_{fi} - H_{pi}) + \epsilon_i$$

are consistent for $E(\gamma_0)$ and $E(\gamma_1)$.

We estimated the regression above for our sample of 444 four-
digit industries. The parameter estimates for $\hat{\alpha}_0$ and $\hat{\alpha}_1$ are 0.046
(standard error 0.005) and 0.068 (standard error 0.067), respec-
tively. While the first coefficient estimate is highly significant, the
second is quite imprecise. Hence, while the point estimate is that
plants belonging to the same firm are slightly more agglomerated
than other plants in the same industry, we cannot rule out a substantially higher level of intrafirm agglomeration. Given that the mean

of $H_f - H_p$ is only 0.04, we can say fairly confidently that only a very small portion of total geographic concentration is attributable to intrafirm agglomerations.

VIII. Conclusion

In this paper, we have developed a model for the analysis of geographic concentration that captures both the "random" agglomeration a dart-throwing model would produce and additional agglomeration caused by localized industry-specific spillovers and natural advantages (which we feel have received less attention than they merit given their empirical importance). The model suggests that it is possible to control for industry characteristics in a fairly robust manner when measuring geographic concentration, and we have proposed new indices for the measurement of the localization of industries and the relative strength of cross-industry agglomerations.

While reaffirming that geographic concentration is ubiquitous and that there are many highly concentrated industries, the results are clearly not as proconcentration as some previous statements. Many industries are only slightly concentrated, and some of the most extreme cases of concentration are likely due to natural advantages. Clearly, though, there remains significant concentration to be explained. We have tried also to provide a quick summary of some of the patterns that exist in the coagglomeration of related industries, in the geographic scope of agglomeration, and so forth, and there remains in each case a great deal of heterogeneity to be explored.

Appendix A

This Appendix describes the process by which state-industry employment figures were constructed. For each state-industry with at least 150 employees, the 1987 *Census of Manufactures* reports employment rounded to the nearest multiple of 100 or categorizes employment as belonging to one of five ranges: 100–249, 250–499, 500–999, and 1,000–2,500. Table A1 indi-

TABLE A1

Extent of Withheld Data

	INDUSTRY DEFINITION		
	Two-Digit	Three-Digit	Four-Digit
Industries	21	141	460
Cells with ranges	153	1,776	5,700
Top codes	46	268	487
Average employment fraction	.02	.11	.20

cates the number of these state-industries for which data are categorized, the number of those that are top-coded at 2,500 or more employees, and the average across industries of the fraction of employees whose state cannot be determined simply by assigning each state its minimum possible employment.

Before beginning to fill in the data, we first adjust the upper or lower bounds on any two- or three-digit state-industry for which a sharper bound can be obtained by summing the upper or lower bounds of the subindustries that constitute it. This reduces the number of two- and three-digit state-industries without upper bounds to 13 and 157, respectively. In addition, a total of 82 and 680 bounds are tightened on cells in which a non-top-coded range had been given.

The filling process begins with the 21 × 51 matrix of two-digit data. First, a rough estimate of the total employment in cells that are reported as zero is made for each state and for each industry. The estimate is simply 35 times the number of missing firms with 20 or more employees plus 6 times the number of missing firms with fewer than 20 employees, provided that this total is less than 150 times the number of empty cells in the appropriate row or column. (Each of these estimates is fewer than 600 employees.)

The main part of the algorithm assigns values within the given range to each cell, trying to do so in a manner that makes the sums of the rows and columns as close as possible to those indicated by the reported totals for employment in each industry and manufacturing employment in each state. While this could be treated as a large optimization problem with a number of variables equal to the number of categorized state-industry employments, this approach was deemed intractable. Instead an admittedly ad hoc procedure was used to sequentially fill in cells. Essentially, the procedure repeatedly looks at the matrix of data, identifies the categorized cells for which there is the least uncertainty as to employment, fills in employment of those cells, and again looks at the matrix in which the filled-in numbers are accepted as fact.

The process of identifying which cells to fill in follows a set of priorities. First, if there are any rows or columns for which all categorized cells must be set to the minimum or maximum to satisfy adding-up constraints, those cells are chosen. Next, the algorithm looks for rows or columns in which only a single element is unknown. If all rows and columns have multiple unknown cells, the algorithm selects the row or column in which there is the least variance possible within the unknown ranges. As a result of the manner in which this is done, usually top codes are not filled in until virtually all active rows and columns contain a top code, and rows/columns with multiple top codes are not filled until there are no rows/columns with a single top code remaining. When filling cells in a row with multiple unknown elements, the algorithm looks at the departures from expected employment in the row and column of each unknown cell and adjusts the cells in a direction calculated loosely on the analogy of calculating conditional means of normal random variables. The amount by which a cell is adjusted is limited by the constraint that its row/column must be able to sum as well.

After the two-digit data are filled in, the process is repeated on the three- and four-digit data. The only difference is that instead of using the constraint that the state-industry employments should add up to the state total manufacturing employment, we use the set of constraints dictated, for example, by employment within each state in the three-digit subindustries of a two-digit industry adding up to the employment in that state in the two-digit industry.

In addition, the previously estimated state and industry total employments in states whose employments are reported as zero are allocated across state-industries by an algorithm identical to that described above. In the four-digit data, these rounded-to-zero employments are occasionally a nontrivial fraction of the total employment in an industry.

While there is no way to tell whether this algorithm is doing well, it is at least possible to tell whether it is doing badly to the extent that the algorithm is unable to make the state or industry totals add up (although because of rounding errors, totals are off by up to 400 employees in industries in which no data are withheld). Of the 21 two-digit industries, the maximum error in the adding-up constraints is 508 employees, with all other industries within 400. In the three-digit industries and four-digit industries, there are two and six industries in which the error is greater than 400; two four-digit industries have errors greater than 1,000 employees, the maximum being 2,010 (although these two are very big industries). The average errors in the state adding-up constraints are 31, 177, and 558 at the two-, three-, and four-digit levels. In all but one of the two-digit industries and in all but six of the three-digit industries, it was never necessary to fill in multiple top codes at the same time.

We would have liked to simulate a data-withholding process to provide rough estimates of the bias and variance of measurement error on the raw geographic concentration measure G induced by our data filling. However, the census's withholding process is not sufficiently transparent that we felt confident that we could reasonably simulate it. Without that, we present here a small test of the accuracy of our procedure based on data obtained separately from County Business Patterns (CBP) for the area in which our procedure is most suspect, filling in top codes in the four-digit data.[20]

Data were available from CBP on state-industry employment for 171 of the 487 four-digit state-industries in which employment was top-coded at 2,500 or more. The CBP's sample differs somewhat from the *Census of Manufactures*, and as a result the CBP reported that employment is below 2,500 in 30 of these state-industries. We dropped these state-industries from our test. (We chose not to use CBP data as an input to our algorithm precisely because they are often incompatible with range and adding-up constraints in the *Census of Manufactures* data.) Of the remaining 141 state-industries, four have very large employments; in each case our data fit extremely well, giving our estimates a misleadingly high .98 correlation with the CBP data. After we delete these four state-industries, the mean and standard deviation

[20] These data have previously been used by Enright (1990), among others, to fill in some of the top-coded *Census of Manufactures* data.

of employment in the remaining 137 state-industries are virtually identical in our data and in the CBP data; the correlation between the two is .74. (The means are 5,329 and 5,304; the standard deviations are 3,451 and 3,306.) For comparison, if the *Census of Manufactures* had reported ranges for these data using the CBP ranges (2,500–4,999, 5,000–10,000, and 10,000–20,000) and we had constructed estimates simply by filling in the mean of the appropriate range, the correlation coefficient would be higher (.93), but the sample means and variance would be much farther from those of the CBP data. (The mean would be 5,939 and the standard deviation 4,314.)

While the results above suggest that our procedure has some accuracy in filling in, the most important question is clearly what implications errors in assigning state employments have on the computation of G. Even a procedure that is quite inaccurate might yield reasonable estimates of G if it simply assigns clusters of employment to the wrong states. As a rough estimate of the effect that our filling in of top codes has on the computation of G, we constructed a measure of G_{CBP} by substituting the CBP employment totals for our filled-in employment totals for all top-coded cells in the 61 industries in which the CBP data allowed all top codes to be filled in (and where there was at least one top code). For this purpose we took the CBP data to report employment of 2,500 whenever it actually reported a smaller number. Comparing our previously estimated G with the value G_{CBP}, we find that the means are 0.052 and 0.048, with a correlation of .96. The absolute value of the difference between the two has a median of 0.0014, with the value being larger than 0.005 in 11 of the 61 industries. While this suggests that our filling in of top codes does not induce significant bias or large measurement errors, we should point out that the industries in which this test was performed may have been among the easier industries with top codes to fill in because they tended to have fewer top codes than the average industry with at least one top code (1.5 vs. 2.5). On the other hand, the majority of four-digit industries have no top-coded cells to begin with. Also, while the filled-in top codes would appear to be the greatest potential problem with our algorithm, this test says nothing about biases due to the filling in of non-top-coded ranges and of state-industry employments of fewer than 150.

For another look at the sensitivity of measured levels of concentration to the way in which we filled in the data, we compared the values of G obtained from state/three-digit industry calculations with our standard data set and with state totals from our county-level data set. (Recall that this latter data set had been constructed entirely from CPB data using mean establishment sizes to fill in missing values.) Because the latter data set is not based on the 1987 SIC revision, the comparisons below involve only the 96 SIC codes whose definitions were unchanged. The values of G from the two data sources differ (in absolute value) by less than 0.005 in 59 of the 96 industries. The difference is between 0.01 and 0.02 in 13 industries, and greater than 0.02 in eight. In several of these cases, however, the values of G are quite large, so that we may regard the two data sets as giving roughly similar measurements. The differences are both larger than 0.015 and larger than 20 percent of the larger G for only six SIC codes: 213, 315, 321,

375, 386, and 387. The data for these industries should perhaps be treated with some caution.

Appendix B

This Appendix discusses the manner in which an estimated plant Herfindahl index, H, was constructed from the census data and the potential implications for our measurements of geographic concentration. Given that a significant amount of information about the distribution of plant shares within each industry is available, we have chosen to construct H by a procedure that is much more akin to filling in data than to imposing any distributional assumptions and estimating parameters, and therefore will admittedly be ad hoc. The algorithm has two main steps: the first consists of allocating employees across size classes to obtain a regular data structure, and the second consists of computing an expected sum of squares for the plants within each class using a rule of thumb recommended by Schmalensee (1977).

When nondisclosure constraints do not bind, the *Census of Manufactures* reports for each industry the number of plants and the total employment in plants belonging to each of 10 employment size categories: 1–4, 5–9, 10–19, 20–49, 50–99, 100–249, 250–499, 500–999, 1,000–2,499, and 2,500 or more. In 316 of the 459 industries, however, the Census Bureau has withheld data on the total employment within a size class (typically one with three or fewer plants). In this case, the census data instead contain the combined employment in this class and another indicated class. To perform a rough separation of the employment in combined classes, for each size class we first used the sample of industries for which the total employment is reported to estimate the mean and variance of employment/plant as a function of the number of plants in the class. (The mean was assumed to have the form $a_0 + a_1 \log[1 + n]$ and the variance the form $b_0 + b_1[1/n]$, with the parameters estimated by OLS regressions.) Employment in each of the combined classes was then set so that departures from the predicted means were inversely proportional to the predicted variances, provided that this did not violate the upper and lower bounds on plant size.

The second step procedure essentially consists of assuming that the sizes of the plants within each class are discretely uniformly spread on a range centered on the mean, with its boundary at the closer of the two end points of the size range. The index H is estimated simply by taking the sum of the squares of the plant shares for this particular allocation of employees across plants. Schmalensee reports that this assumption of linear shares within a class seems to give the best estimates of the Herfindahl index in a similar problem.

We do not regard this procedure as an attempt to assign employments to plants, but just as a complicated function that approximates the Herfindahl index given the available data. To assess the accuracy of this procedure, we constructed a simulated data set of 5,000 industries. The simulated industries were created by assuming that the plant sizes in industry i consist of n_i draws from a lognormal distribution with mean μ_i and standard deviation σ_i. The parameters n_i, μ_i, and σ_i were themselves realizations of independent lognormal random variables with means (standard deviations) 527 (1,106), 143 (286), and 287 (2,101), respectively. These parameters were obtained from sample statistics (and the estimated H) of our 459-industry sample. The data produced by the simulations bear a superficial resemblance to the actual data, although they tend to contain far more extreme outliers (e.g., industries with over 95 percent of employment in a single plant). We created a simulated data set modified to preserve confidentiality by combining employment in any size class with two or fewer plants with the employment in the next lower nonempty size class. This modification involved withholding data in 3,200 of the 5,000 simulated industries.

We applied our algorithm to this data set to produce estimated plant Herfindahls, $\hat{H}$, and compared them to the true H. On average, the estimated Herfindahls were slightly smaller than the true values, the ratio of the means being 1.05. We principally use estimates of H in the paper as a part of the computation of γ for each industry. Note that if we set $\gamma = [G/(1 - \sum_i x_i^2) - \hat{H}]/(1 - \hat{H})$, where $G = (1 - \sum_i x_i^2)[\gamma_0 + (1 - \gamma_0)H + \epsilon]$ with $E(\epsilon|H, \hat{H}) = 0$, then

$$E(\gamma - \gamma_0|\hat{H}) = (1 - \gamma_0)E\left(\frac{H - \hat{H}}{1 - \hat{H}}\bigg|\hat{H}\right).$$

Hence, if $E(H|\hat{H}) = \hat{H}$, then our estimates of γ_0 will be unbiased.

One cannot estimate $E(H|\hat{H})$ without making assumptions about the distribution of H. While our simulated H's do not match the observed distribution of plant Herfindahls, we hope that they will at least provide results that are indicative of the magnitude of the bias our procedure produces. Over our 5,000-industry sample, an OLS regression of H on $\hat{H}$ yields an estimated constant of 0.0003 (t-statistic 1.3), with the estimated coefficient on $\hat{H}$ being 1.04 (t-statistic 228.9). Restricting the regression to the observations with $\hat{H} < 0.3$ to eliminate the effect of unreasonable industries gives estimates of 0.0001 (t-statistic 0.5) and 1.05 (t-statistic 173.8). Adding a quadratic term to this regression, we find the coefficient to be insignificant, suggesting that nonlinearity is not a problem. Regressing the squared error from the linear regression on a constant, $\hat{H}$, and $\hat{H}^2$ to get an idea of the magnitude of the measurement error in a typical industry gives the estimate $\hat{\sigma}^2 = 0.00003 + 0.003\hat{H} + 0.007\hat{H}^2$.

If we believe these results, then for a typical industry in which the true value of γ is small, we shall underestimate γ by about $0.05H$. Given that the mean of H is less than 0.03, this bias is fairly small. To correct this bias, one could simply multiply all our previous estimates of H by 1.05. The correction is not large, however, and given that we have limited confidence in the simulations, we decided not to impose it.

References

Bartik, Timothy J. "Business Location Decisions in the United States: Estimates of the Effects of Unionization, Taxes, and Other Characteristics of States." *J. Bus. and Econ. Statis.* 1 (January 1985): 14–22.

Carlton, Dennis W. "The Location and Employment Choices of New Firms: An Econometric Model with Discrete and Continuous Endogenous Variables." *Rev. Econ. and Statis.* 65 (August 1983): 440–49.

Creamer, Daniel. "Shifts of Manufacturing Industries." In *Industrial Location and National Resources.* Washington: Government Printing Office (for Nat. Resources Planning Board), 1943.

Crihfield, John B. "Manufacturing Supply: A Long-Run, Metropolitan View." *Regional Sci. and Urban Econ.* 20 (November 1990): 327–49.

Ellison, Glenn, and Glaeser, Edward L. "Geographic Concentration in U.S. Manufacturing Industries: A Dartboard Approach." Working Paper no. 4840. Cambridge, Mass.: NBER, August 1994.

Enright, Michael. "Geographic Concentration and Industrial Organization." Ph.D. dissertation, Harvard Univ., 1990.

Florence, P. Sargant. *Investment, Location and Size of Plant: A Realistic Inquiry into the Structure of British and American Industries.* Cambridge: Cambridge Univ. Press, 1948.

Fuchs, Victor. *Changes in the Location of Manufacturing in the United States since 1929.* New Haven, Conn.: Yale Univ. Press, 1962.

Gardocki, Bernard C., Jr., and Baj, John. "Methodology for Estimating Nondisclosure in County Business Patterns Data." Manuscript. De Kalb: Northern Illinois Univ., Center Governmental Studies, 1985.

Glaeser, Edward L.; Kallal, Hedi D.; Scheinkman, José A.; and Shleifer, Andrei. "Growth in Cities." *J.P.E.* 100 (December 1992): 1126–52.

Henderson, J. Vernon. *Urban Development: Theory, Fact, and Illusion.* New York: Oxford Univ. Press, 1988.

Hoover, Edgar M. *The Location of Economic Activity.* New York: McGraw-Hill, 1948.

Jaffe, Adam B.; Trajtenberg, Manuel; and Henderson, Rebecca. "Geographic Localization of Knowledge Spillovers as Evidenced by Patent Citations." *Q.J.E.* 108 (August 1993): 577–98.

Krugman, Paul. *Geography and Trade.* Cambridge, Mass.: MIT Press, 1991. (*a*)

———. "Increasing Returns and Economic Geography." *J.P.E.* 99 (June 1991): 483–99. (*b*)

McFadden, Daniel L. "Conditional Logit Analysis of Qualitative Choice Behavior." In *Frontiers in Econometrics,* edited by Paul Zarembka. New York: Academic Press, 1974.

Marshall, Alfred. *Principles of Economics: An Introductory Volume.* 8th ed. London: Macmillan, 1920.

Porter, Michael E. *The Competitive Advantage of Nations.* New York: Free Press, 1990.

Schmalensee, Richard. "Using the *H*-Index of Concentration with Published Data." *Rev. Econ. and Statis.* 59 (May 1977): 186–93.

Schmenner, Roger W.; Huber, Joel C.; and Cook, Randall L. "Geographic Differences and the Location of New Manufacturing Facilities." *J. Urban Econ.* 21 (January 1987): 83–104.

Part IV
International Competitiveness
of Industries

[16]

Econometrica, Vol. 61, No. 2 (March, 1993), 251–272

MAKING A MIRACLE[1]

By Robert E. Lucas, Jr.

This lecture surveys recent models of growth and trade in search of descriptions of technologies that are consistent with episodes of very rapid income growth. Emphasis is placed on the on-the-job accumulation of human capital: learning by doing. Possible connections between learning rates and international trade are discussed.

KEYWORDS: Growth, productivity, on-the-job training, learning.

1. INTRODUCTION

IN 1960, THE PHILIPPINES AND SOUTH KOREA had about the same standard of living, as measured by their per capita GDPs of about $640 U.S. 1975. The two countries were similar in many other respects. There were 28 million people in the Philippines and 25 million in Korea, with slightly over half of both populations of working age. Twenty seven percent of Filippino's lived in Manila, 28 percent of South Koreans in Seoul. In both countries, all boys of primary school age were in school, and almost all girls, but only about a quarter of secondary school age children were in school. Only 5 percent of Koreans in their early twenties were in college, as compared to 13 percent in the Philippines. Twenty six percent of Philippine GDP was generated in agriculture, and 28 percent in industry. In Korea, the comparable numbers were 37 and 20 percent. Ninety six percent of Philippine merchandise exports consisted of primary commodities and 4 percent of manufactured goods. In Korea, primary commodities made up 86 percent of exports, and manufactured goods 14 (of which 8 were textiles).

From 1960 to 1988, GDP per capita in the Philippines grew at about 1.8 percent per year, about the average for per capita incomes in the world as a whole. In Korea, over the same period, per capita income grew at 6.2 percent per year, a rate consistent with the doubling of living standards every 11 years. Korean incomes are now similar to Mexican, Portuguese, or Yugoslavian, about three times incomes in the Philippines, and about one third of incomes in the United States.[2]

I do not think it is in any way an exaggeration to refer to this continuing transformation of Korean society as a miracle, or to apply this term to the very similar transformations that are occurring in Taiwan, Hong Kong, and Singapore. Never before have the lives of so many people (63 million in these four areas in 1980) undergone so rapid an improvement over so long a period, nor (with the tragic exception of Hong Kong) is there any sign that this progress is

---

[1] Prepared for the 1991 Fisher-Schultz Lecture, given in September at the European meetings of the Econometric Society. I am grateful to Jose Scheinkman, T. W. Schultz, Nancy Stokey, Alwyn Young, and the referees for discussion and criticism.
[2] The figures in the first paragraph are taken from the 1984 *World Development Report*. The income and population figures in this paragraph and the next are from Summers and Heston (1991).

near its end. How did it happen? Why did it happen in Korea and Taiwan, and not in the Philippines?

Questions like these can be addressed at many levels. It is useful to begin simply by listing some of the features of these transformations in addition to their income growth rates. All of the East Asian miracle economies have become large scale exporters of manufactured goods of increasing sophistication. They have become highly urbanized (no problem for Singapore and Hong Kong!) and increasingly well-educated. They have high savings rates. They have pro-business governments, following differing mixes of laissez faire and mercantilist commercial policies. These facts—or at least some of them—must figure in any explanation of the growth miracles, but they are additions to the list of events we want to explain, not themselves explanations.

We want to be able to use these events to help in assessing economic policies that may affect growth rates in other countries. But simply advising a society to "follow the Korean model" is a little like advising an aspiring basketball player to "follow the Michael Jordan model." To make use of someone else's successful performance at any task, one needs to be able to break this performance down into its component parts so that one can see what each part contributes to the whole, which aspects of this performance are imitable and, of these, which are worth imitating. One needs, in short, a theory.

There has been a great deal of interesting new theoretical research on growth and development generally in the last few years, some of it explicitly directed at the Asian miracles and much more that seems to me clearly relevant. I will use this lecture to try and see what recent research offers toward an explanation for these events. My review will be sharply focused on neoclassical theories that view the growth miracles as *productivity* miracles. What happened over the last 30 years that enabled the typical Korean or overseas Chinese worker to produce 6 times the goods and services he could produce in 1960? Indeed, my viewpoint will be even narrower than the neoclassical theories on which I draw, since I intend to focus on issues of *technology*, with only cursory treatment of consumer preferences and the nature of product market competition. There is no doubt that the issue of who gets the rewards from innovation is a central one, and it is not one that can be resolved on the basis of technological considerations alone, so this narrow focus will necessarily restrict the conclusions I will be able to draw. But there is no point in trying to think through hard questions of industrial organization and general equilibrium without an adequate description of the relevant technology, so this seems to me the right place to start.

I will begin in Section 2, with a brief sketch of some recent theoretical developments and of the image of the world economy these developments offer. This image does not, as I see it, admit of anything one could call a miracle, but it will be useful in motivating my subsequent emphasis on the accumulation of human capital, and in particular on human capital accumulation on the job: learning by doing. In Section 3, I will review a piece of microeconomic evidence on learning and productivity, just to remind you how solid the evidence is and how promising, quantitatively, for the theory of growth. Yet establishing the importance of learning by doing for productivity growth on a specific production process is very different from establishing its importance for an entire economy as a whole, or even for an entire sector. This connection is much more problematic than I once believed. But it has been made, in research by Nancy Stokey and Alwyn Young, and I will sketch the main technological implications of their work in Section 4. There is good reason to believe, I will argue, that something like this technology provided the means for the productivity miracles to occur. Section 5 discusses some of the issues involved in developing market equilibrium theories in which differential learning rates account for observed growth rate differences, and offers some speculations about the implications of such a theory for the development prospects of poor countries. Conclusions are in Section 6.

2. THEORETICAL BACKGROUND

There has been a rebirth of confidence—stimulated in large part by Romer's (1986) contribution—that explicit neoclassical growth models in the style of Solow (1956) can be adapted to fit the observed behavior of rich and poor economies alike, interacting in a world of international trade. I do not believe we can obtain a theory of economic miracles in a purely aggregative set-up in which every country produces the same, single good (and a rich country is just one that produces more of it) but such a framework will be useful in stating the problem and in narrowing the theoretical possibilities.

Consider, to begin with, a single economy that uses physical capital, $k(t)$, and human capital, $h(t)$, to produce a single good, $y(t)$:

$$(2.1) \qquad y(t) = Ak(t)^{\alpha}[uh(t)]^{1-\alpha}.$$

Here I multiply the human capital input by u, the fraction of time people spend producing goods.[3] The growth of physical capital depends on the savings rate s:

$$(2.2) \qquad \frac{dk(t)}{dt} = sy(t),$$

while the growth of human capital depends on the amount of quality-adjusted

---

[3] One of the referees for this paper found my use of the term "human capital" in this aggregate context idiosyncratic, and I agree that aggregate theorists tend to use terms like "technology" or "knowledge capital" for what I am here calling "human capital." But the cost of having two terminologies for discussing the same thing, one used by microeconomists and another by macroeconomists, is that it makes it too easy for one group to forget that the other can be a source of relevant ideas and evidence.

It was the explicit theme of Schultz (1962) that the theory of human capital, then in its infancy, would prove central to the theory of economic growth, and Schultz included the stock of human capital accumulated on the job in his Table 1 (p. S6). His figures were based on estimates provided in Mincer (1962), whose estimation method "treats 'learning from experience' as an investment in the same sense as are the more obvious forms of on-the-job training, such as, say, apprenticeship programs" (p. S51). My usage in this paper is, I think, consistent with 30 years of practice in labor economics.

time devoted to its production:

$$(2.3) \quad \frac{dh(t)}{dt} = \delta(1-u)h(t).$$

Taking the decision variables s and u as given, which I will do for this exposition, the model (2.1)–(2.3) is just a reinterpretation of Solow's original model of a single, closed economy, with the rate of technological change (the average Solow residual) equal to $\mu = \delta(1-\alpha)(1-u)$ and the initial technology level equal to $Ah(0)^{1-\alpha}$. In this system, the long run growth rate of both capital and production per worker is $\delta(1-u)$, the rate of human capital growth, and the *ratio* of physical to human capital converges to a constant. In the long run, the level of income is proportional to the economy's initial stock of human capital.[4]

To analyze a world economy made up of countries like this one, one needs to be specific about the mobility of factors of production. A benchmark case that has the virtues of simplicity and, I think, a decent degree of realism is obtained by assuming that labor is completely immobile, while physical capital is perfectly mobile. That is, if there are n countries indexed by i, assume that the world stock of physical capital, $K = \sum_{i=1}^{n} k_i$, is allocated across countries so as to equate the marginal product in each country to a common world return, r. Then if each country has the technology (2.1) with a common intercept A, this world return is $r = \alpha A(K/H)^{\alpha-1}$, where $H = \sum_i u_i h_i$ is the world supply of effective labor devoted to goods production. Net domestic product in each country is proportional to its effective workforce:

$$(2.4) \quad y_i = A\left(\frac{K}{H}\right)^{\alpha} u_i h_i.$$

If everyone has the same constant savings rate s, the dynamics of this world economy are essentially the same as those of Solow's model. The world capital stock follows $(dK/dt) = sAK^{\alpha}H^{1-\alpha}$, and the time path of H is obtained by summing (2.2) over countries, each multiplied by its own time allocation variable u_i. The long run growth rate of physical capital and of every country's output is equal to the growth rate of human capital. Each country's income level will be proportional to its initial human capital, not only in the long run but all along the equilibrium path. The theory is thus consistent with the permanent maintenance of any degree of income inequality.

It would be hard to think of another theory as simple as this one that does a better job of fitting the postwar statistics in the back of the *World Development Report*. By reinterpreting Solow's technology variable as a country-specific stock

---

[4] Of course, essentially the same economics can be obtained from a model in which consumer preferences are taken as given and savings and time allocation behavior are derived rather than assumed. See Uzawa (1965), Lucas (1988), and Caballe and Santos (1991). The particular model sketched in the text is simply one rather arbitrarily selected example from the large number of similarly motivated models that have recently been proposed. See, for example, Jones and Manuelli (1990), King and Rebelo (1990), and Becker, Murphy, and Tamura (1990).

of human capital, a model that predicts rapid convergence to common income levels is converted into one that is consistent with permanent income inequality. But the key assumption on which this prediction is based—that human capital accumulation in any one economy is independent of the level of human capital in other economies—conflicts with the evident fact that ideas developed in one place spread elsewhere, that there is one frontier of human knowledge, not one for each separate economy. Moreover, as Parente and Prescott (1991) observe, if the model above is realistically modified to permit each economy to be subject to shocks that have some independence across countries, the assumption that each economy undergoes sustained growth due to its own human capital growth *only* would imply ever-growing inequality within any subset of countries. Relative income levels would follow random-walk-like behavior. I do not see how this prediction can be reconciled with the postwar experience of, say, the OECD countries or the EEC. The countries of the world are tied together, economically and technologically, in a way that the model (2.1)–(2.3) does not capture.[5]

One way to introduce some convergence into the model I have sketched, proposed and studied by Parente and Prescott (1991), is to modify the human capital accumulation technology (2.2) so as to permit any one country's rate of human capital growth to be influenced by the level of human capital elsewhere in the world. For example, let $H(t)$ be the world effective labor variable defined above, and let $Z(t) = H(t)/\Sigma_i u_i$ be the world average human capital level. Replace the human capital accumulation equation (2.2) with:[6]

$$(2.5) \qquad \frac{dh(t)}{dt} = \delta(1-u)h(t)^{1-\theta}Z(t)^{\theta}.$$

With this modification, the dynamics of the world stocks of physical and human capital are essentially unchanged, but now an economy with a human capital stock lower than the world average will grow faster than an above average economy. For example, if the time allocation is equal across countries, so that $H(t)$ and $Z(t)$ grow at the rate $\delta(1-u)$, a country's *relative* human capital, $z_i = h_i/Z$, follows

$$(2.6) \qquad \frac{d}{dt}z_i(t) = \delta(1-u)z(t)\left[z(t)^{-\theta} - 1\right].$$

Evidently, $z_i(t)$ converges to one, and from (2.4), this means that relative incomes converge to one at the same rate.

In the world as a whole in the postwar period, income dispersion across all countries appears to be increasing. But, of course, there are many reasons to believe that the assumption of free world trade that leads to (2.6) is a very bad

[5] An informative recent debate on income convergence has been stimulated by the exchange between Baumol (1986), De Long (1988), and Baumol and Wolff (1988). My statement in the text simply echos the shared conclusion of these authors.

[6] This external effect might better be captured through the human capital level of the most advanced countries, rather than the world average $Z(t)$. But the use of the latter variable keeps the algebra simple, and I don't think the distinction is critical for any conclusions I wish to draw here.

approximation for much of the world, and there are certainly differences across countries in the incentives people have to accumulate both kinds of capital, implying differences in savings rates and the allocation of time. Yet over subsets of countries, or regions of countries, where factor and final goods mobility is high (like the EEC or the 50 U.S. states) convergence can be observed.[7]

Barro and Sala-i-Martin (1992) obtain a regression estimate of an average convergence rate of relative incomes, conditioned on variables that may be interpreted as controlling for a country's adherence to the above assumptions, of slightly less than .02 (Table 3, p. 242). As they observe, if one interprets this coefficient as reflecting differential rates of physical capital accumulation in a world in which income differences reflect mainly differences in capital per worker, this rate of convergence is much too low to be consistent with observed capital shares. Alternatively, interpreting this figure as an estimate of $(1/z)(dz/dt)$ in (2.6), their estimate implies $\theta\delta(1 - u) = .02$. Since $\delta(1 - u)$ is the average rate of human capital growth, also about .02 in reality, this interpretation yields an estimated θ of unity, which from (2.5) would mean that human capital accumulation in any country depends on local effort together with worldwide knowledge, independent of the local human capital level. From this viewpoint, the Barro-Sala-i-Martin estimate seems high.

All of this is by way of a prelude to thinking about growth miracles—about deviations from average behavior. I have described a model of a world economy —reasonably realistic in its description of average behavior of countries at different income levels—in which everyone has the same savings rate and allocates time in the same way. What are the prospects for using the same theory to see how variations across economies in the parameters s and u can induce variation in behavior of the magnitude we seek to explain? Here the exercise begins to get hard.

The East Asian economies do indeed have high investment rates. The current ratio of gross domestic investment to GDP in Korea is about .29, as compared to average behavior of around .22. In Taiwan and Hong Kong, the investment ratios are .21 and .24 respectively. In Singapore, it is a remarkable .47. In the Philippines, for comparison it is .18.[8] In a world with the perfect capital mobility used in my illustration above, these differences in investment rates would have *no* connection with savings rates: any country's higher than average savings would simply be invested abroad. Even with no international capital mobility, to translate a given difference in savings rates into a differences in output growth rates one must multiply by the return on capital (since

$$\frac{\partial}{\partial s}\left(\frac{1}{y}\frac{dy}{dt}\right) = \frac{\partial}{\partial s}\left(\frac{1}{y}\frac{\partial y}{\partial k}\frac{dk}{dt}\right) = \frac{\partial y}{\partial k},$$

---

[7] See, for example, Ben-David (1991).
[8] All the figures cited are for 1984. The ratio for Taiwan is from the 1987 Taiwan *National Income*. The others are from the 1986 *World Development Report*.

from (2.2)). If the return on capital were ten percent, then, the Korea-Philippines investment rate difference of .11 can account for a difference of .011 in output growth rates, or about one percentage point. Even this effect is only transient, since in the long run differences in savings rates are level effects only.

Now applying the same rough calculation to the Singapore-Philippines investment rate difference of .29, one can account for a difference in output growth rates of nearly three percentage points (and more, if a higher and still defensible return on capital is used) which is close to the differentials I am calling "miraculous." Indeed, Young (1992) demonstrates that output growth in Singapore since the 1960's can be accounted for *entirely* by growth in conventionally measured capital and labor inputs, with nothing left over to be attributed to technological change. But Young's point, underscored by his parallel treatment of Singapore and Hong Kong, is the exceptional character of growth in Singapore, and not that the Asian miracles in general can be attributed to capital accumulation.

Growth accounting methods, applied country-by-country as in Young's study, can quantify the role of investment differentials in accounting for growth rate differences. In general, these differentials leave most measured output growth to be explained by other forces. This conclusion, which seems to me so clear, remains controversial. Correlations between investment ratios and growth rates, which tend to be positive, are frequently cited but do not settle anything. If growth is driven by rapid accumulation of human capital, one needs rapid growth in physical capital just to keep up: look at equation (2.4)! It may be that by excluding physical capital from the human capital accumulation equation (2.3) or (2.5) I have ruled out some interesting possibilities: One cannot accumulate skill as a computer programmer without a computer. Perhaps physical capital will assume a more important role when the technology for accumulating human capital is better understood, but if so, it will be at best a supporting part. Let us look elsewhere.

In the framework I am using, the other possible source of growth rate differentials is differential rates of human capital accumulation, stemming from differences in societies' time-allocation decisions. But human capital takes many forms and its accumulation occurs in many ways, so there are decisions in emphasis to be made here as well. The key choice, I think, is whether to stress human capital accumulation at school, or on the job.

If one interprets (2.3) or (2.5) as describing knowledge accumulation through schooling, these equations imply that doubling the fraction in school would double the human capital growth rate, adding only another .02 to the average rate of .02. And, of course, the linearity of (2.3) probably leads to an *overstatement* of the effect of so large a change. As I remarked in my introduction, the fast growing Asian economies are not, in general, better schooled than some of their slow growing neighbors. Emphasis on formal schooling, then, seems to involve the application of a modest multiplier to very slight differences in behavior, leading to the same discouraging conclusion for human capital that I arrived at in the case of physical capital.

This conclusion may seem an inappropriate inference from an oversimplified model, but I think it is in fact reinforced by thinking more seriously about the effects of schooling. Actual schooling decisions take place in a life-cycle context, with school preceding work and each individual deciding on the length of these two career phases. (This is a simplification, too, but a better one than thinking of a representative agent dividing his time in perpetuity.) Now in a steady state or balanced path of an economy in which everyone spends a fraction $1 - u$ of his working life in school, workers with schooling level $1 - u$ are retiring from the labor force at exactly the same rate as new workers with the same education level are entering. No matter what the value of u is in such a steady state, *all* of this investment is replacement investment and there is *no* increase in the average skill level of the workforce. Since (2.3) is an hypothesis about *net* investment, one cannot then identify the variable $1 - u$ with time spent in school. One is left with two choices. We can identify *increases* in average schooling levels with net human capital investment. Since schooling levels are increasing in virtually all societies today, this is a possibility worth developing, but it cannot be pursued within a steady state framework. This is an important and neglected respect in which neither advanced nor most backward economies can be viewed as moving along balanced growth paths.

Alternatively, we can think of a balanced path on which time spent in school is constant but the *quality* of schooling is improving due to increases in general knowledge. This possibility is analyzed in Stokey (1991a), from which the argument of the last paragraph is taken. In this paper, the rate of expansion of knowledge is taken to be an external effect of the time spent in school, the hypothesis that transforms a level effect into the needed growth effect. But this hypothesis does not salvage the multiplier arguments I applied above, unless one is willing to assume that increases in general knowledge accrue equally from time spent in primary schools and universities. To quantify a model like Stokey's, one would need a much sharper empirical identification of the set of activities that lead to new knowledge—to net investment in a society's human capital—than is provided by any aggregate index of total schooling time. This would be a most interesting avenue to explore but I am not prepared to do so here, so I will end this digression and move on.

Human capital accumulation also occurs at work, as we know from the fact the experienced workers and managers earn more than inexperienced ones. This aspect of human capital accumulation—on the job training—could also be (and has been) modeled as a time-allocation decision. Alternatively, in a multiple good world, one could think of on the job accumulation—learning by doing—as associated with the type of process one is engaged in. That is, one might think of some activities as carrying with them a high rate of skill acquisition and others, routine or traditional ones, as associated with a low rate. If so, the mix of goods a society produces will affect its overall rate of human capital accumulation and growth. For understanding diversity, I think this route has promise: The variation across societies, or at least those engaged in international trade, in the mix of goods produced is enormous. In this section, I have tried to motivate a focus on this source of diversity by a process of elimination: Neither physical capital accumulation nor human capital accumulation through schooling seems to have much potential, at least within the framework I have adopted. In this next section, I turn to much more direct, microeconomic evidence on the same point.

3. THE LIBERTY SHIP MIRACLE

In Lucas (1988) I used a multi-good model, adapted from Krugman (1987), in which different goods were associated with different learning rates to capture the idea that the choice of which goods to produce can be viewed as an implicit choice of a human capital accumulation rate. In a world of open economies, comparative advantage—previously accumulated, good-specific human capital holdings—will determine who produces what, and the mix of goods that this process assigns to a particular economy will determine its rates of human capital growth. This kind of formulation has been taken in interesting directions by Boldrin and Scheinkman (1988) and Matsuyama (1992). It is attractive, for present purposes, because there are such wide differences in product mix across countries and because the fast growing Asian economies have undergone such dramatic changes in the goods they produce.

But the hypothesis that different goods are associated with *permanently* different learning potentials conflicts sharply with available evidence in two respects. First, examination of growth in total factor productivity (Solow residuals) across both industries and time (as conducted, for example, by Harberger (1990), shows no decade-to-decade stability in the high productivity growth industries. Lumber and wood products can rank 14th in the 1950's, first in the 1960's, and disappear from the list of leaders altogether in the 1970's.[9] Second, evidence we have on learning on narrowly defined product lines invariably shows high initial learning rates, declining over time as production cumulates. These two kinds of evidence reinforce each other, and seem decisive against the formulation Krugman proposed. These observations have led Stokey (1988) and Young (1991a) to a very different formulation, one that is much more tightly grounded in microeconomic evidence. I will review this formulation in Section 4, but before doing so I want to reinforce the motivation with a reminder of just how impressive the evidence on the productivity effects of learning by doing can be.

The best evidence I know of that bears on on-the-job productivity change in a single, large scale production process, was utilized in studies by Allan D. Searle (1945) and Leonard A. Rapping (1965). Both studies used data on the production of a single type of cargo vessel—the Liberty Ship—in 14 U.S. shipyards during World War II. From December, 1941, through December, 1944, these yards produced a total of 2458 Liberty Ships, all to the same standardized design. For several individual yards, Searle plotted man-hours per vessel against

[9] Harberger (1990), Table 3.

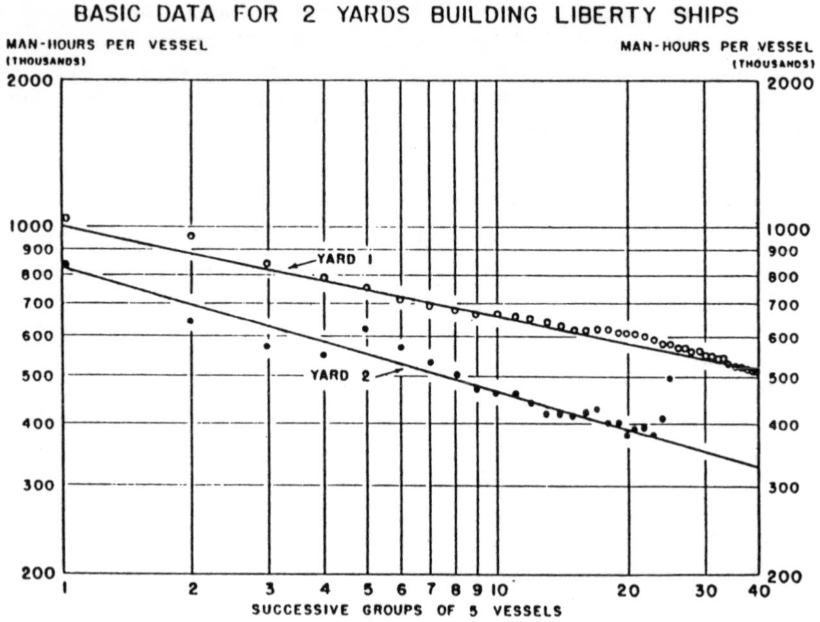

BASIC DATA FOR 2 YARDS BUILDING LIBERTY SHIPS

FIGURE 1.—Reductions in man-hours per vessel with increasing production.
Merchant shipyards.

number of vessels completed to date in that yard on log-log paper. His results
for two yards are reproduced here as Figure 1. Average results over ten yards
are given in Figure 2, along with results for three other vessel types. For Liberty
Ships, "the reductions in manhours per ship with each doubling of cumulative
output ranged from 12 to 24 percent."[10]

Stimulated in part by Kenneth Arrow's (1961) theoretical suggestion that
learning-by-doing might serve as the key factor in growth for an economy as a
whole, Rapping incorporated Searle's and other evidence within a neoclassical
production framework. He pooled the data for all yards and estimated a
Cobb-Douglas production function, controlling for changes in capital per yard,
with cumulated yard (not industry) production as an added regressor. He
obtained estimates of the learning effect, comparable to Searle's, ranging from
11 to 29 percent. He also showed that the inclusion of calendar time added
nothing (the trend came out slightly negative!) to these results.

I do not think there is anything unique to shipbuilding in the findings that
Searle and Rapping obtained. The Boston Consulting Group (1972) has ob-
tained fairly clean learning curves, with slopes similar to those estimated by
Searle and Rapping, for a variety of industries, and other researchers have done

[10]Searle (1945), p. 1144.

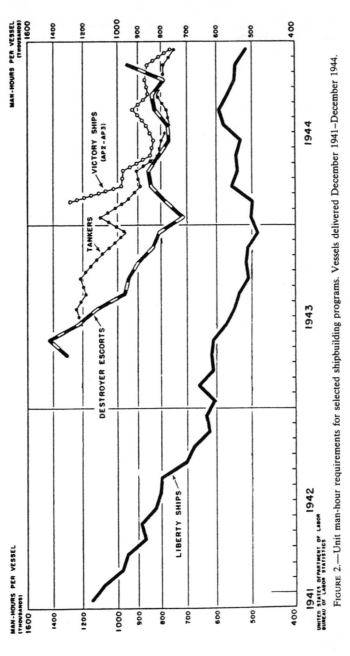

FIGURE 2.—Unit man-hour requirements for selected shipbuilding programs. Vessels delivered December 1941–December 1944.

so as well. What is unique about the Liberty ship data is that the ships were built according to exactly the same blueprints over a period of several years and that data were available yard by yard. Figure 2, which gives Searle's learning curve for the industry as a whole, is not nearly as sharp as the curves in Figure 1 for individual yards, presumably because industry expansion is a mix of increased production by existing yards and the entry of new, inexperienced yards. Production data even from narrowly defined industries mask continual model and other product mix changes over time, which makes it difficult to use them to identify even strong learning effects. What is exceptional about the Liberty ship evidence, I think, is the cleanness of the experiment, not the behavior it documents so beautifully.

Quantitatively, these results are interesting to an economist looking for possible sources of miracles. For the three year period covered by Rapping's study, industry output per manhour increased at a 40 percent annual rate! There is also considerable ambiguity about what this evidence means. Is it the individual worker who is doing the learning? The managers? The organization as a whole? Are the skills being learned specific to the production process on which the learning takes place, or more general? Does learning accrue solely to the individual worker, manager, or organization that does the producing, or is some of it readily appropriable by outside observers? These are questions that the theory of growth needs to address, but I will pass over them here.

A more urgent question, I think, is whether the kind of behavior Rapping and Searle documented, for one product line for one brief period, can be linked to productivity growth for an entire economy over periods of thirty or forty years. This is the topic of the next section.

4. LEARNING MODELS: TECHNOLOGY

In order to examine the possible connection between evidence of learning on individual product lines and productivity growth in an economy as a whole, consider the labor-only technology:

$$(4.1) \quad x(t) = kn(t)z(t)^{\alpha},$$

where $x(t)$ is the rate of production of a good, k is a productivity parameter that depends on the units in which labor input and output are measured, $n(t)$ is employment, and $z(t)$ represents cumulative experience in the production of this good. Cumulative experience is in turn defined by the differential equation:

$$(4.2) \quad \frac{dz(t)}{dt} = n(t)z(t)^{\alpha},$$

and the initial value $z(t_0)$, assumed to be greater than or equal to one, of the experience variable on the date t_0 when production was begun. The general solution to (4.2) is

$$(4.3) \qquad z(t) = \left[\left(z(t_0) \right)^{1-\alpha} + (1-\alpha) \int_{t_0}^{t} n(u) \, du \right]^{1/1-\alpha}.$$

The implications of this model for the dynamics of production of a single good are familiar enough. Suppose, to take the simplest case, that employment is constant at $\bar{n}$ over time. Then (4.1) and (4.3) imply that production follows

$$x(t) = k\bar{n} \left[z(t_0)^{1-\alpha} + (1-\alpha)\bar{n}(t - t_0) \right]^{\alpha/1-\alpha}.$$

Production grows without bound, and the rate of productivity growth declines monotonically from $\alpha\bar{n}(z(t_0))^{\alpha-1}$ to zero. For any initial productivity level $z(t_0) \geqslant 1$ and any employment level (or path) productivity at date t is an increasing function of the learning rate α.

Notice that the technology (4.2) implies a scale effect: a link between the level of employment and the rate of growth of productivity. This carries the unwelcome implication that a country like India should have an enormous growth advantage over a small country like Singapore. This is a feature of any learning by doing theory, but I agree with Matsuyama (1992) that if one is thinking about an entire economy or sizeable sector of an economy, it is a nuisance implication that we want to dispose of.[11] Matsuyama proposes thinking of a population as containing a fixed fraction of entrepeneurs, and of a technology that requires that each enterprise be headed by one of them. Then doubling the population means doubling the number of enterprises that are subject to the learning technology, keeping the size of each fixed, and has no growth effects. Insofar as learning effects are partly external to the firm, as I think they are, this device doesn't quite work, and one needs to think of some other limitation on scale—city size, say. I will simply ignore these scale economies in what follows, assuming that some explanation along the lines of Matsuyama's will be discovered to rationalize this neglect.

With the technology (4.1)–(4.3), one can obviously obtain miraculous rates of productivity growth by shifting a large amount of labor onto a single, new product line. Provided that $\bar{n}(t - t_0)$ is large relative to initial experience (which is the way most people interpret statistical learning curves), the rate of productivity growth t years after production is initiated is approximately $\alpha/((1-\alpha)t)$. Using the value $\alpha = 0.2$ estimated by Rapping and Searle, productivity growth one year after a product is introduced is $\alpha/(1-\alpha) = 0.25$. After two years, the growth rate is reduced by half to 0.125, and so on. A growth miracle sustained for a period of decades clearly must thus involve the continual introduction of new goods, not merely continued learning on a fixed set of goods. Even if new goods are introduced, a shift of workers from old goods with low learning rates to new goods with high rates involves an initial drop in productivity: people are

---

[11] Backus, Kehoe, and Kehoe (1991) is an empirical examination of scale effects on growth rates, formulated in a variety of ways. They find some evidence of such effects in manufacturing, and none for economies as a whole.

better at familiar activities than they are at novel ones. It is not even clear how these factors balance out.

To pursue this question, I follow Stokey (1988) and consider an economy in which a variety of goods, indexed by s, is produced, where a higher index s means a better good. In Stokey (1988) and, in different ways in Young (1991a) and Grossman and Helpman (1991b), specific assumptions on consumer prefer-ences or the technology give a precise meaning to the sense in which one good is better than another. For my immediate objectives, it will be adequate to consider a small, open economy and to use an assumed schedule $p(s, t) = e^{\mu s}$ of world prices to summarize the quality of goods: a better good means a good with a higher price on world markets. Assume that the economy progresses by introducing better quality (higher s) goods into production over time, and let $S(t)$ be the index of the good that is first produced at date t. (I will also use $\tau(s)$, where τ is the inverse function of the increasing function S, to denote the date on which good s is first produced.) Then if $x(s, t)$ is production of good s at date t, the value of the economy's total production is

$$(4.4) \qquad y(t) = \int_0^{S(t)} e^{\mu s} x(s, t) \, ds.$$

Let $n(s, t)$ be employment on good s at t, and $z(s, t)$ be cumulated experience. Then if learning proceeds independently, good by good, (4.1) and (4.3) imply

$$(4.5) \qquad x(s, t) = kn(s, t) \left[(z(s, \tau(s)))^{1-\alpha} + (1-\alpha) \int_{\tau(s)}^t n(s, u) \, du \right]^{\alpha/1-\alpha}.$$

Equations (4.4) and (4.5) together describe the implications for total production of a given way of allocating labor across product lines through time.

Consider the following specific labor allocation. Let the rate of new product introduction be a constant λ, so that $S(t) = \lambda t$ and $\tau(s) = s/\lambda$. Let φ be a density function with cdf Φ, and suppose that for all $s \in (0, \lambda t]$, $n(s, t) = \varphi(t - s/\lambda)$ (that $\varphi(t - s/\lambda)$ workers are assigned to produce the goods of age $t - s/\lambda$) and that the remaining $1 - \Phi(t)$ workers produce a good 0 on which no learning occurs. Assume that initial productivity is the same for all goods, at the level $z(s/\lambda, s) = \xi \geq 1$. Under these assumptions, (4.4) and (4.5) imply that the value of total production is

$$(4.6) \qquad y(t) = 1 - \Phi(t) + k\lambda e^{\mu\lambda t} \int_0^t e^{-\mu\lambda u} \varphi(u) \left[\xi^{1-\alpha} + (1-\alpha)\Phi(u) \right]^{\alpha/1-\alpha} du.$$

The asymptotic growth rate for this economy is evidently $\mu\lambda$. This rate does not depend either on the learning parameter α or on the distribution φ of the workforce over goods of different vintages. Changes in either of these factors are simply level effects. To obtain sustained growth at all in this framework, it is necessary to assume that better goods become producible at some exogenously given rate λ, which then along with the quality gradient μ dictates the long run growth rate of the system, independent of learning behavior.

Though the production of new goods is continuously initiated in this example, the rate at which this occurs through time is fixed. In Stokey (1988) this rate is made endogenous through the assumption that the experience accumulated in producing good s reduces the cost of producing good $s' > s$. (It may reduce the cost of producing $s' < s$, too, but the spillover effect is assumed to be loaded in the direction of improving productivity on the more advanced good.) As a specific instance of Stokey's hypothesis, very close to that proposed by Young (1991a), let us modify the last example by postulating that the initial value $z(s, \tau(s))$ in the learning curve (4.3) depends on the experience that has been accumulated on less advanced goods. Suppose that an economy at some fixed date t has experience summarized by $z(s, t)$ for $s < S(t)$, but has yet to produce any good with index above $S(t)$. Assume that if production of a good $s \geqslant S(t)$ is initiated at t (if $\tau(s) = t$) then its initial z-value is proportional to an average of the economy's experience on previously produced goods:

$$(4.7) \quad z(s, \tau(s)) = \theta\delta\int_0^s e^{-\delta(s-u)}z(u, \tau(s))\, du.$$

Equation (4.7) expresses the initial productivity on good s as an average of experience on lower quality goods. Equivalently, we can express the initial productivity on the good introduced at t, good $S(t)$, as an average of experience on goods introduced earlier:

$$(4.8) \quad z(S(t), t) = \theta\delta\int_0^t e^{-\delta[S(t)-S(t-v)]}z(S(t-v), t)S'(t-v)\, dv,$$

integrating over ages v instead of goods s.

Assume, next, that production on a new good is initiated whenever the expressions (4.7) and (4.8) reach a trigger value $\xi \geqslant 1$, taken as a given constant. Under this assumption, the left side of (4.8) is replaced with this constant ξ, implying that the function $S(t)$ whose derivative is the rate at which new goods are introduced must satisfy

$$(4.9) \quad \xi = \theta\delta\int_0^t e^{-\delta[S(t)-S(t-v)]}z(S(t-v), t)S'(t-v)\, dv.$$

As in the previous example, we continue to assume that the allocation of employment at any date is described by a density φ and cdf Φ, where $\Phi(u)$ is the fraction of people employed producing goods that were introduced less than u years earlier. In the present case, each good has the initial productivity level ξ, so inserting the solution (4.3) for $z(S(t-v), t)$ with this initial value into (4.9) yields a single equation in the function $S(t)$. For large values of t, the solution $S(t)$ to this equation will behave like $S(t) = \lambda t$, where the constant λ satisfies

$$(4.10) \quad \xi = \theta\delta\lambda\int_0^\infty e^{-\delta\lambda v}\left[\xi^{1-\alpha} + (1-\alpha)\Phi(v)\right]^{1/1-\alpha}\, dv.$$

The right side of (4.10) is just an average of the positive, increasing function $\theta[\xi^{1-\alpha} + (1-\alpha)\Phi(v)]^{1/(1-\alpha)}$, taken with respect to an exponential distribution with parameter $\delta\lambda$. Hence it is a positive, decreasing function of $\delta\lambda$, tending toward the value $\theta \xi$ as $\delta \lambda \to \infty$ and toward the value $\theta[\xi^{1-\alpha} + 1 - \alpha]^{1/(1-\alpha)}$ as $\delta \lambda \to 0$. (If the latter expression is less than ξ at $\lambda = 0$, then the economy does not accumulate relevant experience fast enough to introduce new goods in the steady state.) For fixed $\delta \lambda$, the right side of (4.10) is an increasing function of θ, α, and k, and it also increases as the distribution of labor $\varphi(v)$ becomes more concentrated on lower values of v (on newer goods). Hence if a positive solution λ exists, it is inversely proportional to the decay rate of spillover experience, an increasing function of the spillover parameter θ and the learning rate α, and increases as employment is more heavily concentrated on goods that are closer to the economy's production frontier.

The formula (4.6) for the value of total production continues to hold in this second example, and the economy's long run growth rate is $\lambda \mu$, as before. But under this second, spillover, technology, economies that distribute workers across goods of different ages in different ways will grow at different rates. Of course, this conclusion is not based purely on technological considerations: The value ξ of initial productivity that is assumed to trigger the initiation of production of a new good is of central importance, and needs an economic rationale.

One might view the spillover technologies of Stokey and Young as reconciling the Krugman hypothesis of a manufacturing sector with a constant rate of productivity growth, based on learning, with the fact that learning rates on individual production processes decline over time to zero. For example, one could interpret either of the examples in this section as describing a sector of an economy with a positive asymptotic rate of productivity growth. On this view, the contribution of Stokey and Young is to break down an assumed sectoral learning rate into its components, α, θ, and δ (in my notation), and to relate this rate to the way workers are distributed over goods of different vintages.

This interpretation seems fine to me as long as one is discussing the consequences of a *given* workforce distribution, but if one has in mind applying the theory of comparative advantage to *determining* the way workers in each country are allocated to the production of different goods it ceases to make sense. In Krugman's theory (as in Lucas (1988)) it is a sector *as a whole* that either has or does not have a comparative advantage. In a sectoral interpretation of Stokey and Young's theories, each sector consists of many goods and comparative advantage must be determined good by good. No country can be expected to have a comparative advantage in manufacturing in general, or even in crude aggregates like Chemicals and Allied Products or Printing and Publishing. Comparative advantage will be associated with categories, like acetylene or paperback editions of English poetry, that are invisible even in the finest industrial statistics. As we shall see in the next section, this feature—besides being a step towards greater realism—leads to an entirely different view of trade and growth than is implied by the Krugman technology, the superficial similarity of the two notwithstanding.

The main attraction of a learning spillover technology such as that described in the second example of this section is that it offers the potential of accounting for the great difference in productivity growth rates that are observed among low and middle income economies. Of course, little is known about the crucial spillover parameters δ and θ—on which the learning curve evidence described in Section 3 provides no information—but surely an essential first step is to find a formulation that is capable, under *some* parameter values, of generating the behavior we are trying to explain.

5. LEARNING AND MARKET EQUILIBRIUM

The objective of the last section was to set down on paper a *technology* that is consistent with a growth miracle, which is to say, consistent with wide differences in productivity growth among similarly endowed economies. This has been done, following Stokey and Young, in a way that I think is consistent with the main features of the East Asian miracles, all of which have involved sustained movement of the workforce from less to more sophisticated products. A fast growing economy or sector under this technology is one that succeeds in concentrating its workforce on goods that are near its own quality frontier, and thus in accumulating human capital rapidly through the high learning rates associated with new activities and through the spillover of this experience to the production of still newer goods. These hypotheses are consistent with commonly known facts, and have testable implications for many more. As yet, however, I have said nothing about the *economics* that determine the mix of production activities in which an economy or sector of an economy in fact engages.

The papers of Stokey (1988), (1991b) and Young (1991a) develop models of market equilibrium with learning technologies under the assumption the effects of learning are external—that all human capital is a public good. In this case, labor is simply allocated to the use with the highest current return, independent of learning rates. With the constant returns technology these authors assume, the competitive equilibrium is Ricardian and straightforward to calculate. This is the simplest case, so I will begin with it too.

In such a setting, Stokey (1991b), studies north-south trade, where "north" means relatively well-endowed with human capital. Under specific assumptions about consumer preferences for goods of different qualities, she obtains a unique world equilibrium in which the south produces an interval of low quality goods, the north produces an interval of high quality goods, and there is an intermediate range of goods that are produced in neither place. With free trade (as opposed to autarky) learning-by-doing is depressed in the poor country, which now imports high-quality goods from the rich country rather than attempting to produce them at home. One can see that with dynamics as assumed in Stokey (1988), both countries will enjoy growth but the poor country will remain forever poorer.

A similar equilibrium is characterized in Young (1991a), using a parameterization of preferences and the learning technology that permits the explicit calculation of the north-south equilibrium, including a full description of the equilibrium dynamics. There are many possible equilibrium evolutions of his north-south system, depending on the populations of the two regions and on their relative human capital holdings at the time trade is initiated. As in Stokey's (1991b) analysis, the advanced country produces high quality goods and the poor country produces low quality goods. Free trade slows learning and growth in the poor country and speeds it in the rich one. In Young's framework, there are equilibria in which the poor catch up to the rich, but only when their larger population lets them enjoy greater scale economies. Young does not emphasize this possibility and, as I have said earlier, I do not wish to either.

The equilibria of Stokey and Young, then, involve sustained growth of both rich and poor, at possibly different rates, and the continuous shifting of production of goods introduced in the north to the lower wage south. Initial comparative advantage is not permanent, as in Krugman's formulation, since a rich country's experience in producing any given good will eventually be offset by the fact that the good can be produced more cheaply in a less experienced but lower wage environment. Yet there are no growth miracles in these theories. Though these equilibria could readily be modified to include cross-country external effects, and hence catching up (for reasons unrelated to economies of scale), as I have done with the Solow model, there would be nothing one would wish to call miraculous about this process.

In the models of Stokey and Young, all human capital benefits are assumed to be external. The learning and growth that occurs is always, in a sense, accidental. Other models contain aspects of privately held knowledge, so that individual agents face the capital-theoretic problem of balancing current returns against the future benefits of learning of some kind. Matsuyama (1991) studies a two-sector system in which workers compare the present value of earnings in a traditional sector to the value of earnings in a manufacturing sector in which production is subject to external increasing returns. Young (1991b) augments learning with a research activity that yields patentable new products. Grossman and Helpman (1991a) postulate two R and D activities—innovation, done only in advanced economies, and imitation, done by poor economies too—with lags that let the discoverer or successful low-cost imitator enjoy a period of super-normal profits in a Bertrand-type equilibrium. Whether one calls the decision problems that arise in these analyses occupational choice, or research and development, or learning, all involve a decision on the allocation of time-at-work that involves balancing current returns against the benefits of increased future earnings, and all have a similar capital-theoretic structure.

Dropping the assumption that learning has external effects only is certainly a step toward realism, one that raises many interesting theoretical possibilities yet to be explored. It is thus only conjecture, but I would guess that the main features of the equilibria that have been worked out by Stokey and Young will turn out to stand up very well under different assumptions about the ownership, if I can use that term, of human capital. A learning spillover technology gives those who operate near the current goods frontier a definite advantage in moving beyond it. This advantage is decisive when decisions are taken myopically; I do not see why it should disappear when some of the returns from doing so are internalized and workers and firms look to the future in their individual decision problems.

In short, available general equilibrium models of north-south trade do not predict miraculous economic growth for the poor countries taken as a group, nor do I see any reason to expect that the equilibria of more elaborate theories will have this feature. This is a disappointment, perhaps, but it does not seem to me to be a deficiency of these models. These are theories designed to capture the main interactions between the advanced economies taken as a group and the backward economies as a whole, within a two-country world equilibrium framework. Since it is a fact that the poor are either not gaining on the rich or are gaining only very slowly, one wants a theory that does not predict otherwise.

A successful theory of economic miracles should, I think, offer the *possibility* of rapid growth episodes, but should not imply their occurrence as a simple consequence of relative backwardness. It should be as consistent with the Philippine experience as with the Korean. For the purpose of exploring these possibilities, the conventions of small, open economy trade theory are more suitable (as well as simpler to apply) than those of the theory of a closed, two-country system. If the technology available to individual agents facing world prices has constant returns, then anything is possible. Some allocations will yield high external benefits and growth in production and wages; others will not. There will be a large number of possibilities, with individual agents in equilibrium indifferent between courses of action that have very different aggregative consequences. Theoretically, one can shut off some of these possibilities by introducing diminishing returns in the right places, but I am not sure that these multiplicities should be viewed as theoretical defects, to be patched up. If our objective is to understand a world in which similarly situated economies follow very different paths, these theoretical features are advantageous. A constant returns (at the level of individual producing units) learning spillover technology is equally consistent with fast and slow growth. If our task is to understand diversity, this is an essential feature, not a deficiency.

A second attraction of the learning spillover technology is that it is consistent with the strong connection we observe between rapid productivity growth and trade or openness. Consider two small economies facing the same world prices and similarly endowed, like Korea and the Philippines in 1960. Suppose that Korea somehow shifts its workforce onto the production of goods not formerly produced there, and continues to do so, while the Philippines continues to produce its traditional goods. Then according to the learning spillover theory, Korean production will grow more rapidly. But in 1960, Korean and Philippine incomes were about the same, so the mix of goods their consumers demanded was about the same. For this scenario to be possible, Korea needed to open up a large difference between the mix of goods produced and the mix consumed, a difference that could widen over time. Thus a large volume of trade is essential to a learning-based growth episode.

One can use the same reasoning to see why import-substitution policies fail, despite what can initially appear to be success in stimulating growth. Consider an economy that exports, say, agricultural products and imports most manufactured goods. If this economy shifts toward autarky through tariff and other barriers, its workforce will shift to formerly imported goods and rapid learning will occur. But this is a one-time stimulus to productivity, and thereafter the mix of goods produced in this closed system can change only slowly, as the consumption mix changes. Note that this argument has to do only with the pace of *change* in an economy's production mix and does not involve scale, though it can obviously be reinforced by scale economies.

I do not intend these conjectures about the implications of a learning spillover technology for small countries facing given world prices to be a substitute for the actual construction of such a theory. To do this, one would need to take a realistic position on these issues touched on in my discussion of Rapping's and Searle's evidence. What is the nature of the human capital accumulation decision problems faced by workers, capitalists, and managers? What are the external consequences of the decisions they take? The papers cited here consider a variety of possible assumptions on these economic issues, but it must be said that little is known, and without such knowledge there is little we can say about the way policies that affect incentives can be expected to influence economic growth.

6. CONCLUSIONS

I began by asking what current economic theory has to say about the growth miracles of East Asia. The recent literature on which I have drawn to answer this question is fragmentary, and my survey of it more fragmentary still. Even so, the image of the growth process and the role of these remarkable economies within this process that emerges is, I think, surprisingly sharp, certainly compared to what could have been said on this subject ten years ago. I will conclude by summarizing it.

The main engine of growth is the accumulation of human capital—of knowledge—and the main source of differences in living standards among nations is differences in human capital. Physical capital accumulation plays an essential but decidedly subsidiary role. Human capital accumulation takes place in schools, in research organizations, and in the course of producing goods and engaging in trade. Little is known about the relative importance of these different modes of accumulation, but for understanding periods of very rapid growth in a single economy, learning on the job seems to be by far the most central. For such learning to occur on a sustained basis, it is necessary that workers and managers continue to take on tasks that are new to them, to continue to move up what Grossman and Helpman call the "quality ladder." For this to be done on a large scale, the economy must be a large scale exporter.

This picture has the virtue of being consistent with the recent experience of both the Philippines and Korea. It would be equally consistent with post-1960 history with the roles of these two economies switched. It is a picture that is consistent with any individual small economy following the East Asian example, producing a very different mix of goods from the mix it consumes. It does not appear to be consistent with the third world as a whole beginning to grow at East Asian rates: There is a zero-sum aspect, with inevitable mercantilist overtones, to productivity growth fueled by learning by doing.

Can these two paragraphs be viewed as a summary of things that are *known* about economic growth? After all, they are simply a sketch of some of the properties of mathematical models, purely fictional worlds, that certain economists have invented. How does one acquire knowledge about reality by working in one's office with pen and paper? There is more to it, of course: Some of the numbers I have cited are products of decades-long research projects, and all of the models I have reviewed have sharp implications that could be, and have not been, compared to observation. Even so, I think this inventive, model-building process we are engaged in is an essential one, and I cannot imagine how we could possibly organize and make use of the mass of data available to us without it. If we understand the process of economic growth—or of anything else—we ought to be capable of demonstrating this knowledge by *creating* it in these pen and paper (and computer-equipped) laboratories of ours. If we know what an economic miracle is, we ought to be able to *make* one.

Dept. of Economics, The University of Chicago, 1126 E. 59th St., Chicago, IL 60637, U.S.A.

Manuscript received April, 1992; final revision received August, 1992.

REFERENCES

ARROW, KENNETH J. (1961): "The Economic Implications of Learning by Doing," *Review of Economic Studies*, 29, 155–173.

BACKUS, DAVID K., PATRICK J. KEHOE, AND TIMOTHY J. KEHOE (1991): "In Search of Scale Effects in Trade and Growth," Federal Reserve Bank of Minneapolis Working Paper.

BARRO, ROBERT J., AND XAVIER SALA-I-MARTIN (1992): "Convergence," *Journal of Political Economy*, 100, 223–251.

BAUMOL, WILLIAM J. (1986): "Productivity Growth, Convergence, and Welfare," *American Economic Review*, 76, 1072–1085.

BAUMOL, WILLIAM J., AND EDWARD N. WOLFF (1988): "Productivity Growth, Convergence, and Welfare: Reply," *American Economic Review*, 78, 1155–1159.

BECKER, GARY S., KEVIN M. MURPHY, AND ROBERT TAMURA (1990): "Capital, Fertility, and Economic Growth," *Journal of Political Economy*, 98, S12–S37.

BEN-DAVID, DAN (1991): "Equalizing Exchange: A Study of the Effects of Trade Liberalization," National Bureau of Economic Research Working Paper No. 3706.

BOLDRIN, MICHELE, AND JOSE A. SCHEINKMAN (1988): "Learning-by-Doing, International Trade and Growth: A Note," in Santa Fe Institute Studies in the Sciences of Complexity, *The Economy as an Evolving Complex System*, 285–300.

BOSTON CONSULTING GROUP (1968): *Perspectives on Experience*. Boston: Boston Consulting Group.

CABALLE, JORDI, AND MANUEL S. SANTOS (1991): "On Endogenous Growth with Physical and Human Capital," Working Paper.

DE LONG, J. BRADFORD (1988): "Productivity Growth, Convergence, and Welfare: Comment," *American Economic Review*, 78, 1138–1154.

DIRECTORATE-GENERAL OF BUDGET, ACCOUNTING AND STATISTICS, EXECUTIVE YUAN (1987): *National Income in Taiwan Area. The Republic of China*. Taipei: Veterans Printing Works.

GROSSMAN, GENE M., AND ELHANAN HELPMAN (1991a): "Quality Ladders and Product Cycles," *Quarterly Journal of Economics*, 106, 557–586.

——— (1991b): *Innovation and Growth in the Global Economy*. Cambridge: MIT Press.

HARBERGER, ARNOLD C. (1990): "Reflections on the Growth Process," Working Paper, U.C.L.A.

JONES, LARRY E., AND RODOLFO E. MANUELLI (1990): "A Convex Model of Equilibrium Growth: Theory and Policy Implications," *Journal of Political Economy*, 98, 1008–1038.

KING, ROBERT G., AND SERGIO REBELO (1990): "Public Policy and Economic Growth: Developing Neoclassical Implications," *Journal of Political Economy*, 98, S126–S150.

KRUGMAN, PAUL R. (1987): "The Narrow Moving Band, the Dutch Disease, and the Consequences of Mrs. Thatcher: Notes on Trade in the Presence of Scale Economies," *Journal of Development Economics*, 27, 41–55.

LUCAS, ROBERT E., JR. (1988): "On the Mechanics of Economic Development," *Journal of Monetary Economics*, 22, 3–42.

MATSUYAMA, KIMINORI (1991): "Increasing Returns, Industrialization, and Indeterminacy of Equilibrium," *Quarterly Journal of Economics*, 106, 617–650.

——— (1992): "Agricultural Productivity, Comparative Advantage and Economic Growth," *Journal of Economic Theory*, 58, 317–334.

MINCER, JACOB (1962): "On-the-Job Training: Costs, Returns, and Some Implications," *Journal of Political Economy*, 70, S50–S79.

PARENTE, STEPHEN L., AND EDWARD C. PRESCOTT (1991): "Technology Adoption and Growth," NBER Working Paper.

RAPPING, LEONARD A. (1965): "Learning and World War II Production Functions," *Review of Economics and Statistics*, 47, 81–86.

ROMER, PAUL (1986): "Increasing Returns and Long-Run Growth," *Journal of Political Economy*, 94, 1002–1037.

SCHULTZ, THEODORE W. (1962): "Reflections on Investment in Man," *Journal of Political Economy*, 70, S1–S8.

SEARLE, ALLAN D. (1945): "Productivity Changes in Selected Wartime Shipbuilding Programs," *Monthly Labor Review*, 61, 1132–1147.

SOLOW, ROBERT M. (1956): "A Contribution to the Theory of Economic Growth," *Quarterly Journal of Economics*, 70, 65–94.

STOKEY, NANCY L. (1988): "Learning by Doing and the Introduction of New Goods," *Journal of Political Economy*, 96, 701–717.

——— (1991a): "Human Capital, Product Quality, and Growth," *Quarterly Journal of Economics*, 106, 587–616.

——— (1991b): "The Volume and Composition of Trade Between Rich and Poor Countries," *Review of Economic Studies*, 58, 63–80.

SUMMERS, ROBERT, AND ALAN HESTON (1991): "The Penn World Table (Mark 5): An Expanded Set of International Comparisons, 1950–1988," *Quarterly Journal of Economics*, 106, 327–368.

THE WORLD BANK (1984, 1986): *World Development Report*. Oxford: Oxford University Press.

UZAWA, HIROFUMI (1965): "Optimum Technical Change in an Aggregative Model of Economic Growth," *International Economic Review*, 6, 18–31.

YOUNG, ALWYN, (1991a): "Learning by Doing and the Dynamic Effects of International Trade," *Quarterly Journal of Economics*, 106, 369–406.

——— (1991b): "Invention and Bounded Learning by Doing," MIT Working Paper.

——— (1992): "A Tale of Two Cities: Factor Accumulation and Technical Change in Hong Kong and Singapore," NBER *Macroeconomics Annual 1992*, forthcoming.

[17]

ELSEVIER

Journal of Development Economics
Vol. 47 (1995) 313–332

JOURNAL OF
Development
ECONOMICS

Productivity and the export market:
A firm-level analysis

B.-Y. Aw [a,b,*], A.R. Hwang [c]

[a] *Department of Economics, Pennsylvania State University, 608 Kern Graduate Building,
University Park, PA 16802-3306, USA*
[b] *The World Bank, Washington, DC, USA*
[c] *The Institute of Economics, Academia Sinica, Taipei, Taiwan*

Received May 1993; final version received May 1994

Abstract

An empirical model is developed to distinguish the roles of resource-level differences from productivity differences in explaining output differences between exporters and non-exporters of Taiwanese electronic products. Our results indicate that the larger size of exporters relative to non-exporters explains the bulk of the difference in output between the two groups of producers. Nevertheless, there are significant differences in productivity levels between exporters and non-exporters in three out of the four products examined. The contribution of these differences to output differences between the two groups of producers vary from 3 to 20%, depending on the electronic product and model specification.

Keywords: Productivity; Export market; Firm-level analysis

JEL classification: F10; O12

---

* Corresponding author. We thank Judith Dean, Ann Harrison, Kala Krishna, J.T. Liu, Mark Roberts, and two anonymous referees for very helpful comments. We are extremely grateful to the Accounting and Statistics Section, Bureau of Census, Taiwan for making the microdata available to us. Partial funding from the World Bank and the National Science Council (NSC) for this project are gratefully acknowledged. The views expressed are those of the authors and should not be attributed to the World Bank or the NSC.

314   *B.-Y. Aw, A.R. Hwang / Journal of Development Economics 47 (1995) 313–332*

1. Introduction

It is often argued that developing countries that pursue export-oriented trade policies generally outperform those embracing import-substitution policies. That export-orientation is associated with higher output growth is relatively well-established in the empirical literature. [1] It is further argued that increases in productive inputs and/or greater average utilization of capacity play major roles in this higher output growth in many export-oriented developing countries. [2] More recently, researchers have focussed on the link between export-orientation and productivity. In the development literature, the arguments linking export-orientation positively with productivity are related to increasing returns to scale, or increasing returns to entrepreneurial effort with exposure to foreign competition. [3] However, more formal analysis of these arguments has shown that this positive relationship between export-orientation and productivity is far from an obvious one. [4]

In view of the diverse theoretical literature on the link between export-orientation and productivity, it is not surprising that the empirical evidence of this link in the existing literature is rather mixed. Some of these studies conclude that export growth is positively associated with productivity growth. [5] However, others have concluded that there is no strong evidence favoring such a linkage. [6] Pack (1988), in particular, conjectures that the primary difference between export-oriented and import-substituting countries is not so much in productivity growth rates as in the levels of productivity.

The mechanism that underlies the hypothesized link between export-orientation and productivity is that export markets are more competitive and therefore afford firms less opportunity for inefficient operation. While this explanation emphasizes firm differences, the bulk of the empirical verification has been conducted at the industry or country level, primarily by comparing output or factor productivity

---

[1] Among many of the papers on this subject are Balassa (1978, 1981) and Krueger (1978) and Syrquin and Chenery (1989).

[2] Chenery (1983) explores the relative significance of factor growth and productivity growth in explaining economy-wide growth, noting that factor growth plays a major role in the 'Gang of Four' (Hong Kong, South Korea, Singapore, and Taiwan). Kim and Kwon (1977) and Pack (1988) stress the importance of increases in capacity utilization in explaining rapid growth.

[3] These arguments are summarized in Tybout (1992).

[4] For a critical analysis of some of the arguments commonly made regarding the trade-productivity nexus, see Rodrik (1992).

[5] Krueger and Tuncer (1982) and Nishimizu and Robinson (1984).

[6] See Pack (1988) and Harvylyshyn (1990). Tybout (1992) and Rodrik (forthcoming) provide comprehensive and critical surveys of the recent theoretical and empirical literature linking trade-orientation and productivity.

B.-Y. Aw, A.R. Hwang / Journal of Development Economics 47 (1995) 313–332   315

growth with export growth or an index of openness. [7] Our study is based on a unique Census-based firm-level microdata set for the electronics industry in Taiwan which includes firm-level export participation. By focussing on the cross-sectional comparisons of exporting and non-exporting firms in a specific industry in a given country, we avoid differences or changes in macroeconomic factors that often complicate cross-country and time series analysis of the role of export-orientation. We estimate separate production functions for two groups of firms: those that sell primarily in the domestic market and those that sell their output primarily in the export market. We examine whether the observed differences in output between these two groups of firms can be attributed simply to level differences in the usage of inputs. More importantly, we distinguish the input-level effect on output from that due to productivity differences in the use of those inputs in the two groups of firms. [8]

Berry (1992) surveys the literature linking firm performance and trade policies and points to the great degree of intra-industry firm heterogeneity, particularly in developing countries. Berry shows that exports of manufactured goods come from relatively large firms. In this paper, we examine the issue of whether exporting firms are more productive. A related issue is with regard to the popular conjecture in the development and trade literature that increased exposure to international markets results in greater productivity given the potential benefits of exploiting plant-level scale economies. This paper examines the empirical evidence underlying this particular link between trade exposure and returns to scale.

Our results indicate that input differences of exporters relative to non-exporters explains the bulk of the difference in their mean value-added. Nevertheless, the contribution of productivity differences between exporters and non-exporters in three out of the four electronic products examined is quite significant. The contribution of these differences to value-added differences between the two groups of producers vary from 3 to 20%, depending on the electronic product

---

[7] There are a handful of papers using firm-level data, that examine the effects of trade liberalization on productivity, scale, and technical efficiency. Tybout et al. (1991) use Chilean plant-level panel data to examine the link between changes in trade regime and technical efficiency. He finds that, although no more than half of the three-digit industries registered overall productivity gains, the ones that are most exposed to foreign competition underwent the highest improvements in productivity. Similarly, Haddad (1993) demonstrates the link between trade liberalization in Morocco with higher firm-level total factor productivity.

[8] Chen and Tang (1987) compare the level of technical efficiency between foreign firms in Taiwan's electronics industry that are oriented to the domestic market and those constrained to export all of their output. They find that the export-oriented group exhibits a higher level of technical efficiency than those oriented to the domestic market. Two issues remain largely unresolved in their paper: the applicability of the results to domestic firms and the sensitivity of the results to differences in the product composition of exporters and non-exporters. In this paper, among other things, we address both issues by focussing on productivity differences between all firms operating in the export market and domestic market using data on four-digit product categories.

316   *B.-Y. Aw, A.R. Hwang / Journal of Development Economics 47 (1995) 313–332*

under consideration and model specification. It is important to note that our results do not allow us to infer the direction of causality at work. That more productive firms did more exporting is just as likely as the reverse, that higher exports led to higher productivity.

In Section 2 we provide some background information on the electronics industry in Taiwan and summary statistics on the distribution of production characteristics among plants oriented toward the domestic market compared to those oriented toward the export market. The empirical models used to estimate the production functions and distinguish the sources of performance differences in the two groups of plants are discussed in Section 3. Section 4 reviews the data and the empirical results are discussed in Section 5. The final section contains a summary of the major results and concluding remarks.

2. The electronics industry

Taiwan's electronics industry began in the 1960s when concerted efforts were made by the government to turn Taiwan into an 'electronics industry center' based initially, in the 1960s through the 1970s, on exports of labor-intensive consumer electronics. The industry was granted priority status as a strategic industry and as such became the beneficiary of low-interest finance, assistance in technical and operational management, exemption or reduction of tariffs on machinery imports, and income tax reductions. [9]

From the 1980s onwards, due to the increasing importance of the industry in the domestic and export markets, the government sought to move the industry from its concentration on consumer electronics like radios and TVs, toward more advanced electronics goods like monitors, computers, electronic software, semi-conductors, and telecommunications. Given their small size and limited capital, exporting firms in Taiwan have generally relied on public R&D organizations or foreign firms through subcontracting for advanced technologies. Joint ventures between local and foreign firms with state-of-the-art technology were actively sought after and encouraged by the government. Beginning in the early 1970s exporting firms benefitted from various government fiscal incentives and conces-sional credit. Considerable transfers of technology from foreign partners and public research organizations, including advice on production engineering, product design, and marketing, also occurred during the early 1980s. [10]

It is, therefore, quite clear that exporting firms have more inputs, or have greater access to more inputs, than their counterparts in the domestic market. This

---

[9] Of the 199 strategic products identified in 1987, 91 were electronics-related.

[10] See Wade (1992) for more details of the various stages of development and government incentives involving the electronics industry.

B.-Y. Aw, A.R. Hwang / Journal of Development Economics 47 (1995) 313–332   317

larger quantity of inputs makes possible opportunities for the exporting firms that are not open to firms producing for the domestic market.

In his analysis of the role of the government in the electronics industry in eleven countries, Dahlman (1990) rates the use of trade protection and public R&D by Taiwan as high relative to other countries with different strategies affecting different parts of the industry. Imports of Consumer Electronics were highly restricted in the early to mid-1980s. For instance, by 1986 import duties on VCRs were reduced to 35%, while those on Parts and Components remained at 50%. In contrast, the Data Storage and Processing subsector has been promoted primarily by developing a strong technological base while keeping an open import policy and encouraging the integration of local firms with the technology available in the international market.

In 1986, the Taiwanese electronics industry comprise of about 2832 firms that sell in the domestic and export markets. The electronics and electric industries led the manufacturing sector in terms of their contribution to total output (15%), total employment (19%), total exports (27%), and total R&D expenditure (32%). Over one-half of the electronic firms sell purely in the domestic market (54%) and 32% of these firms sell part of their output in the export market. The remaining 14% of the firms operate solely in the export market.

The electronics industry comprises four four-digit SIC products; Data Storage and Processing Units (3621), Consumer Electronics (3622), Parts and Components (3623), and Communication Equipment (3624). Table 1 shows the number of firms in each four-digit product and the proportions that sell in both the domestic and export markets, as well as the proportions that sell purely in either market. More than 85% of all electronic firms are engaged in the production of Electronic Parts and Components and Consumer Electronics. The rest of the firms in each group are approximately evenly distributed between the Data Storage and Processing Units, and the Communication Equipment groups. Over 60% of the firms in the largest product category (in terms of the number of firms), Parts and Components, sell solely in the domestic market while 70% of the firms in the smallest product category, Data Storage and Processing Units, sell part or all of their output in the export market.

Table 1
Firms in the electronics industry by market-orientation

Four-digit product	Number of firms	Proportion in export market only	Proportion in export and domestic markets	Proportion in domestic market only
Data Storage/ Processing Units	201	0.16	0.54	0.30
Consumer Electronics	765	0.16	0.35	0.49
Parts and Components	1661	0.08	0.31	0.61
Communication Equipment	205	0.16	0.44	0.40

Table 2
Product mix of domestic and export firms in the electronics industry

Four-digit product	Share of total firms	
	Domestic	Export
Data Storage and Processing Units	0.05	0.11
Consumer Electronics	0.23	0.31
Parts and Components	0.66	0.49
Communication Equipment	0.06	0.09

Tables 2 and 3 contain information on the product composition at the four- and seven-digit classifications, respectively. At the four-digit industry classification, the mix of products produced by firms that sell their output primarily in the domestic market does not differ significantly from those who operate primarily in the export market. The bulk of firms in either group are in the Parts/Components and Consumer Electronics categories – 89% of the domestic-market-oriented firms and 80% of the export-oriented firms.

Table 3 presents a more detailed look at the product composition of the firms with varying market-orientation. The seven-digit items listed within each four-digit product classification are the major contributors to the output in their respective product category as indicated by the figures in parentheses. For instance, although there are a total of 64 seven-digit product items under Data Storage and Processing, the five items listed, together contribute 50% to the share of the value of output in that product category. Similarly, between five to seven seven-digit products contribute between half to three-quarter of total output in each of the other three product categories. Given these representative samples of firms, the columns in Table 3 examine the mix of these seven-digit items in firms classified into three producer groups: those that only sell in the domestic or export market and those that sell in both markets. As in the more aggregate case in Table 2, there does not appear to be significant compositional differences in the three producer groups. Generally, more than half of the firms in each producer group is concentrated in one or two of the seven-digit items. For instance, in Communication Equipment, the share of firms in each group that is involved in the production of telephone sets ranges from 62 to 75%. The evidence from the data therefore tends to indicate a fairly similar composition of products among firms that are involved primarily in exports and those that are primarily in the domestic market.

Table 4 provides a summary of the average characteristics of the electronic firms in the domestic and export markets. By all measures of size (value of sales, employment, and value-added), the firms producing for the export market are several times larger than those producing for the domestic market. Exporting firms are also more capital-intensive and older than those in the domestic market. Average capital–labor ratio (measured as value of net assets per worker) among

B.-Y. Aw, A.R. Hwang / Journal of Development Economics 47 (1995) 313–332   319

Table 3
Product composition of firms in each product category by market-orientation

Four- and seven-digit products [a]	Percentage of firms [b]		
	Domestic only	Export only	Both export and domestic
Data storage processing units	(18 firms)	(27 firms)	(47 firms)
Microcomputers (11.4)	0.28	0.30	0.28
Terminals (16.1)	0.17	0.22	0.11
Calculators (10.7)	0.22	0.26	0.26
Small computers (9.3)	0.16	0.07	0.19
Keyboards (2.5)	0.17	0.15	0.17
	1.00	1.00	1.00
Consumer electronics	(90 firms)	(62 firms)	(91 firms)
Color TV sets (20.3)	0.10	0.07	0.09
Radio w/recorders (15.2)	0.30	0.32	0.23
Speakers (5.1)	0.32	0.36	0.52
Tuners (4.5)	0.04	0.10	0.03
Recorders (3.5)	0.19	0.05	0.09
B&W TV sets (2.3)	0.04	0.11	0.04
	1.00	1.00	1.00
Parts and components [c]	(252 firms)	(54 firms)	(207 firms)
Cathode ray tubes (11.7)	0.01	0.00	0.04
Micro motors (6.6)	0.08	0.09	0.05
Integrated circuits (11.2)	0.04	0.13	0.10
Capacitators (5.6)	0.28	0.30	0.35
Printed circuit boards (5.1)	0.35	0.19	0.16
Transformers (5.0)	0.14	0.17	0.15
Rheostat (4.3)	0.11	0.13	0.15
	1.00	1.00	1.00
Communication equipment	(50 firms)	(28 firms)	(60 firms)
Telephone sets (47.5)	0.62	0.67	0.75
Electronic exchanges (10.9)	0.08	0.00	0.08
Citizen band transceivers (7.6)	0.02	0.14	0.02
Radio transmitters (7.1)	0.06	0.00	0.02
TV antennas (5.0)	0.22	0.10	0.13
	1.00	1.00	1.00

[a] Figures in parenthesis represent the share of each seven-digit product in output of each four-digit product category.
[b] Figures in parenthesis represent the total number of firms sampled in each four-digit product category by market-orientation.
[c] Some of these items are aggregated to the six-digit in order to get a representative sample of the firms in this broad product category.

exporters is approximately 1.5 times larger than that of domestic-market producers. Given the relatively more capital-intensive nature of the export-oriented firms, it is not surprising that their output per worker is significantly higher on average.

320   *B.-Y. Aw, A.R. Hwang / Journal of Development Economics 47 (1995) 313–332*

Table 4
Mean characteristics of firms in the electronics industry by market-orientation

	Domestic	Export
Sales ('000 NT$)	17610	271440
Value added ('000 NT$)	7551	100825
Employment (number)	26.1	213.2
Capital–labor ratio ('000 NT$ per worker)	519.3	680.4
Output–labor ratio ('000 NT$ per worker)	697.7	1090.0
Age (years)	4.7	7.5
Utilization rate of capacity (%)	73.5	75.9

Our findings that exporters are larger and have higher capital-intensity relative to non-exporters in the Taiwanese electronics industry in 1986 are consistent with the findings of Berry (1992). He finds that, in the typical developing country, there is evidence that manufactured exports come mainly from firms that are both large and capital-intensive by the standards of the country. [11]

The above characteristics hold, in general, for all the four-digit products that comprise the electronics industry. There is more variability in the age and capacity utilization rate variables between exporters and non-exporters at the product level. At the aggregate level, exporting firms average at 7.5 years of age and operate at 75.9% of capacity. The corresponding figures for the non-exporting firms are 4.7 years and 73.5%. These figures hide important differences in both age and capacity utilization rates at the more disaggregated product level. In particular, firms in the Data Storage / Processing Units, irrespective of market-orientation, are significantly younger than those in the other three products. Moreover, the average difference in age between exporters and non-exporters in the former product is

---

[11] An exception is Chen and Tang (1986). They found that in 1980, export-oriented multinational firms were smaller and less capital-intensive than their counterparts that sold in the local market. According to the authors, these firms tended to specialize in off-shore assembly of imported components for re-exportation, using inexpensive labor. However, since 1980, wages in Taiwan has risen dramatically, reducing the incentive of labor-intensive foreign investment activities. Secondly, since our observations comprise of all electronic firms in Taiwan, it is very likely that our export-oriented firms are involved in a wider range of activities that include higher value-added activities. In short, the Chen and Tang characterization of the size and capital-intensity of export versus domestic market-oriented firms may be specific to multinational firms in Taiwan at that time rather than reflecting characteristics of export-oriented firms in general.

B.-Y. Aw, A.R. Hwang / Journal of Development Economics 47 (1995) 313–332   321

also significantly smaller than the corresponding figures for the latter products. Finally, unlike the other products in the electronics industry, non-exporting firms in the Data Storage/Processing Units operate at slightly higher rates of capacity utilization averaging at 71.4% relative to their counterparts in the export market at 67.6%. These differences may be important in reflecting the role of new technology for firms producing the different products that comprise the electronics industry.

In summary, firms that export electronics products from Taiwan are similar to those selling in the domestic market in terms of their product mix and utilization rate of capacity. Exporters are, on average, larger, more capital-intensive, older, and have higher levels of labor productivity than their counterparts that produce for the domestic market.

We are interested in the issue of how one might decompose variations in output among firms into various sources. There are three main possible sources of differences in output or value-added between exporting and non-exporting firms. First, exporters might have greater access than others to inputs like subsidized capital or imported machinery and equipment. Second, given equal inputs, exporters may be more productive due perhaps to better access to new and improved foreign technology or greater competitive pressure in the international market. [12] Finally, holding inputs and productivity constant, differences in output could arise from exporters being in particular industries or products. By focussing on a single industry we reduce the influence of industry-effects. Our examination of the product composition of firms of different market-orientations indicates that differences in product mix, at the most disaggregated product level for which data is available, is an unlikely source of differences in output among the firms that export the bulk of their output and those that sell primarily in the domestic market. Thus, we concentrate on the first two sources of output differences between exporters and non-exporters: input level differences and productivity differences. To do this, we estimate separate production functions for exporters and non-exporters in each four-digit product within the electronics industry. In our empirical model, productivity differences between the domestic-market-oriented firms and the export-oriented firms are measured as differences in the parameters of the production functions for these two groups of firms. Since these parameters are the elasticities of output with respect to the inputs, firm productivity is defined as the weighted average of the firm's output elasticities. The parameter estimates of these production functions are then used to quantify the roles of productivity and size differences in explaining output differences between exporters and non-exporters.

---

[12] It is also possible that the most productive firms choose to enter the export market because they are the only ones that can operate profitably in that market.

322   *B.-Y. Aw, A.R. Hwang / Journal of Development Economics 47 (1995) 313–332*

3. The empirical model

In this section, we discuss the framework used to estimate production functions for firms operating in the separate markets, the econometric issues involved, and describe the empirical model used to distinguish between the various factors affecting firm-level value-added.

The functional form chosen for our production function is the Translog production function developed by Christensen et al. (1971, 1973). This functional form is more general than the Cobb–Douglas production function in that there are no a priori constraints regarding homotheticity, homogeneity or the elasticities of substitution between factors.

The translog production function for firm i in the electronics industry is

$$\ln \, q_i = \beta_0 + \sum_j \beta_j \, \ln \, X_{ji} + \tfrac{1}{2} \sum_j \sum_k \beta_{jk} \, \ln \, X_{ji} \, \ln \, X_{ki} + \eta_i, \qquad (1)$$

where q_i represents real value-added and X_{ji} and X_{ki} are the inputs in production for firm i, η_i is a random error term. The inputs included in the production function are labor and capital service. From the production function in Eq. (1), we can derive the profit-maximizing input demand equations. Assuming that firms are price-takers in both the input and output markets, the output elasticities with respect to each input equal the revenue share of that input. That is,

$$\partial \ln \, q_i / \partial \ln \, X_{ji} = P_j X_{ji} / P q_i = \beta_j + \sum_k \beta_{jk} \, \ln \, X_{ki} + \epsilon_j, \qquad (2)$$

where P_j is the price of input j and P is the price of output and ϵ_j is a random error term.

Eqs. (1) and (2) form the estimating system and are estimated separately for the two groups of firms, domestic-market and exporting firms. [13] By so doing, we allow the coefficient estimates of the production parameters to differ for each group of producers. We assume that these disturbance terms capture any deviations of the actual production and share equations from the ideal ones. We jointly estimate the translog production function and the labor demand equation as a multivariate regression system using Zellner's seemingly unrelated regression estimator.

In the rest of this section, we show how production function estimates for the two groups of firms can be used to decompose differences in value-added that arise from differences in productive endowments and those that come from

---

[13] Due to the problem of multicollinearity it is often difficult to estimate parameters of the translog production function (1) with precision. Therefore, rather than estimating the production function as a single equation, we estimate it jointly with the factor demand equation (2), and exploit the cross-equation parameter restrictions to increase the precision of the estimates. Without this second equation, standard errors of the production parameters are significantly higher.

B.-Y. Aw, A.R. Hwang / Journal of Development Economics 47 (1995) 313–332   323

productivity differences. The econometric framework used here follows from models developed to study labor market discrimination by Blinder (1973) and Oaxaca (1973). In that literature, the authors decompose observed wage differences between white and black workers into differences due to workers' endowments and differences due to discrimination. The construction and interpretation of their model is summarized in Berndt (1990) and applied here in our examination of the observed differences in the value-added between exporting and non-exporting firms.

Productivity differences are revealed by differences in the estimated coefficients. These parameter estimates come from estimating the production functions separately for each group of firms. Denote the exporting firms by the superscript E, and the firms selling in the domestic market by superscript D, then their production functions, using the same notations as in Eq. (2) can be represented by

$$\ln q^E = X^E \beta^E + \mu^E, \tag{3}$$

$$\ln q^D = X^D \beta^D + \mu^D, \tag{4}$$

where q and μ are vectors of value-added and random disturbances, respectively, and X is a matrix of observations on inputs in production.

Let b^E and b^D be the estimates of β^E and β^D. The mean difference in the log value-added between the two groups can therefore be represented by

$$\overline{\ln q^E} - \overline{\ln q^D} = b^E(\overline{X}^E - \overline{X}^D) + \overline{X}^D(\Delta b), \tag{5}$$

where $\Delta b = b^E - b^D$. Eq. (5) states that the mean difference in log value-added between export and domestic market firms can be separated into the effects of differences in their average endowments (the first expression on the right-hand side) and the effect of productivity differences as revealed by differences in the estimated coefficients (the second expression). [14]

The main goal of this paper is to quantify the role of input level differences as distinguished from the differences in the productivity of the inputs in determining

---

[14] In this specification, average inputs are weighted by exporters' coefficient estimates and differences in estimated coefficients are weighted by average input levels of the domestic market-oriented firms. Alternatively, we can reverse the weights and use the domestic market oriented firms estimated coefficients as weights for the difference in average input levels and the average input level of exporters as weights for the difference in the estimated coefficients. The choice between the use of different weights is essentially a classic index number problem involving a decision on which weights to employ. See Cotton (1988) for a critique and reformulation of the original Oaxaca decomposition in the labor literature. He finds that his results are very sensitive to which weights are used to compute the decomposition. Following the practice of previous researchers, both sets of weights are employed here to yield an estimated range of the value-added effects of productivity differences between the two groups of firms. In our paper, we obtain a very small range (0–9%) using the different weights.

324   *B.-Y. Aw, A.R. Hwang / Journal of Development Economics 47 (1995) 313–332*

value-added differences between producers that sell primarily in the export market and those that concentrate their sales in the domestic market. It is important to note that the above methodology allows the data to indicate the relative importance of differences in input levels versus productivity of those inputs in explaining differences in value-added between exporters and non-exporters. However, it does not tell us how these differences in inputs and productivity arise in the first place. Moreover, in order to attribute any causality to the results, it is necessary to ascertain whether the extent of trade orientation of firms is exogenous or endogenous. If trade orientation and productivity are both endogenous variables that respond to unmodelled forces, then it is not possible with our data to determine the direction of the causality at work. Panel data would be required to do this.

4. Data

The basic data set to be analyzed is the cross section of plants in the electronics industry drawn from the 1986 Census collected by the Taiwanese Bureau of Statistics. In this industry, there are 2832 firms that sell in the domestic and export markets. Of this total, approximately 54% sell solely in the domestic Taiwanese market and 46% sell part or all of their output in the export market. [15]

In the estimation of the translog production function, value-added is measured as the difference between the value of output and the total expenditure on intermediate inputs, which includes raw materials, electricity, and energy. The inputs in the production function are labor, measured as total number of workers, and capital services. The usual practice is to use the value of net assets as a proxy for capital services. This ignores interfirm variation in the utilization of capital and can lead to the mismeasurement of capital services. [16] Our database contains information on the utilization rate of machines by firm. Thus, we are able to get a more accurate estimate of firm-level capital services by taking the product of machine value and the rate of capacity utilization rate. Since some firms did not report the rate of utilization, the number of observations used to estimate the production model is 2384 firms.

---

[15] Exporters are those whose export share in total firm sales exceeds 25%. This definition excludes about 17% of the total number of firms that export. Aw and Batra (1993) find strong evidence that the very activity (independent of levels) of exporting has significant positive productivity impacts.

[16] Recent literature on production function estimation has pointed to the importance of including capacity utilization in production function estimates given that output levels reflect both input levels as well as the utilization of capacity (Abbott et al., 1988). If the latter variable is omitted from the estimation, parameter estimates of the included variables are likely to be upward-biased.

B.-Y. Aw, A.R. Hwang / Journal of Development Economics 47 (1995) 313–332   325

Table 5
Parameter estimates of the translog production function of the electronics industry by products and markets

Independent variables	Data storage processing units		Consumer products		Parts and components		Communication equipment	
	Domestic-market firms	Export firms	Domestic-market firms	Export firms	Domestic-market firms	Export firms	Domestic-market firms	Export firms
Intercept	6.168 **	4.553 **	5.594 **	5.600 **	4.939 **	5.683 **	5.114 **	5.967 **
	(1.054)	(0.652)	(0.215)	(0.328)	(0.170)	(0.306)	(0.364)	(0.529)
Log labor	0.981 **	0.879 **	0.608 **	0.948 **	0.723 **	0.825 **	0.779 **	0.623 **
	(0.141)	(0.166)	(0.039)	(0.099)	(0.033)	(0.089)	(0.077)	(0.093)
Log capital service	-0.443	0.228	-0.038	-0.136	0.095	-0.085	-0.029	-0.022
	(0.317)	(0.177)	(0.062)	(0.093)	(0.050)	(0.085)	(0.100)	(0.123)
$(\text{Log labor})^2$	0.088 *	-0.111	0.082 **	0.050	0.066 **	-0.011	0.108 **	0.066 **
	(0.036)	(0.062)	(0.010)	(0.034)	(0.009)	(0.032)	(0.020)	(0.026)
$(\text{Log capital service})^2$	0.160 **	-0.002	0.061 **	0.083 **	0.046 **	0.046 **	0.081 **	0.062 **
	(0.050)	(0.031)	(0.011)	(0.019)	(0.008)	(0.016)	(0.018)	(0.018)
(Log labor)	-0.091 **	0.026	-0.035 **	-0.061 *	-0.044 **	-0.010	-0.069 **	-0.041 *
(Log capital service)	(0.028)	(0.037)	(0.008)	(0.022)	(0.006)	(0.020)	(0.015)	(0.017)
Standard error	31.39	51.11	134.54	96.67	331.12	134.75	36.17	32.94
R^2	0.95	0.94	0.97	0.97	0.96	0.97	0.98	0.98
Number of observations	65	95	366	268	1003	425	94	78

Standard errors of the parameter estimates are in parenthesis.
* Reject the hypothesis that the parameter equals zero at the 0.05 significance level using the two-tail test.
** Reject the hypothesis that the parameter equals zero at the 0.01 significance level using the two-tail test.

5. The empirical results

In order to control for differences in product mix between export and domestic-market firms, Table 5 reports separate production function estimates for each of the four product categories in the electronics industry. The coefficient estimates are generally reasonable and significantly different from zero. Capital service and value-added appear to have a non-linear relationship given that the capital-squared coefficients are generally significantly different from zero and the capital coefficients are not.

Productivity differences between the two groups of producers are reflected in both the intercept and slope coefficients of the production functions. The former is conventionally referred to in the literature as difference in total factor productivity (TFP). If exporters are more productive than non-exporters, then their estimated production technology should show a higher intercept term, or higher average slope coefficients, or both.

We perform the Chow test in each product market to test for the equality of regression coefficients between exporting and domestic-market firms. We reject the null hypothesis that the intercept and slope coefficients of the two groups of producers are identical for three (Consumer Electronics, Parts and Components and Communication Equipment) of the four electronic products. [17]

In the case of Data Storage and Processing Units, we do not reject the null hypothesis that the coefficient estimates are equal in the exporter and domestic-market equations. As noted earlier, this is also the product category that was comprised of relatively young firms, irrespective of market-orientation, producing personal computers, micro-computers, monitors, terminals, peripherals, and add-ons. These firms operate in a rapidly changing and highly competitive market, without any protection from imports or domestic content requirements. The higher intercept coefficients for the domestic-market firms suggest that these firms have higher levels of exogenous productivity that act to offset any productivity differences arising from more efficient input use among exporters in this product category. This result is consistent with the results of Dahlman (1990) and Mody (1990). In their analysis of the electronics industry, both point to the overall success of Taiwan in the Data Storage and Processing subsector relative to the other subsectors. At the very minimum, it is likely that productivity differences between exporters and domestic-market firms in this product category have been significantly reduced by deliberate government policy that sought to build technological competence in advanced electronics. This was achieved in two ways since the early 1980s; by promoting a greater integration between private firms and

---

[17] The critical F statistic at the 5% level is approximately 2.1. The computed F statistics are 1.21 for Data Storage and Processing Units, 2.8 for Consumer Products, 2.25 for Parts and Components and 2.2 for Communication Equipment.

public research labs and encouraging joint ventures with foreign multinationals to facilitate the transfer and assimilation of advanced technology. [18]

The parameter estimates of the production functions of domestic-market firms and exporters reported in Table 5 are used to measure the extent to which the difference in value-added between the two groups of firms can be attributed to differences in their productivity. Productivity differences between the two groups of producers are significantly different from zero and on average contribute 19.5% in Communication Equipment, 9.8% in Consumer Electronics, and 7.3% in Electronic Parts and Components to differences in their value-added. [19,20] Changing the definition of exporters does not alter the qualitative nature of the results in a significant way. [21]

Our results indicate that the activity of exporting is generally correlated with higher firm-level productivity but the pattern is product specific. This relationship is evident in three out of four products under study. In Parts and Components and Communication Equipment most of the observed higher productivity among exporters relative to domestic-market firms is captured in the higher intercept coefficients. This result suggests the important role played by exogenous productivity-enhancing factors favoring exporters, rather than greater efficiency in the use of inputs among exporters. The larger intercept coefficients for exporters may

---

[18] Dahlman (1990) and Wade (1992) discuss the central role of the state in growth of the computer industry in Taiwan. One of the main instruments is the Electronics Support Service Organization (ERSO), Taiwan's premier public research institution for industry. In addition to attracting foreign investments in technology-intensive products in the industry in general, the public R&D body often licenses foreign technologies itself and sublicenses to firms, therefore eliminating price-raising competition among firms for identical technologies.

[19] We repeated the analysis using a gross output production function instead of the value-added production function. The results did not change significantly. Productivity differences between exporters and domestic-market firms are not significantly different from zero in Data Storage/Processing, while contributing 17.7% in Communication Equipment and 6.6% in both Consumer Electronics and Parts and Components to differences in their gross output.

[20] The standard errors of the estimates are 0.039, 0.031, and 0.040, respectively. The figures are calculated only for three out of the four products in the electronics industry since we could not reject the equality of the coefficient estimates between exporters and domestic-market firms for the Data Storage/Processing Units category. Both sets of weights, discussed in footnote 14, are used yielding an estimated range of 15–24% and 9.5–10% for Communication Equipment and Consumer Electronics, respectively. The estimate for the Parts and Components is independent of the weights used. The figures in the text represent average estimates of the value-added effects of productivity differences between exporters and non-exporters.

[21] As the cutoff for our definition of exporters rises, from export shares in sales of 25% to 50% to 100%, the productivity differences between exporting and domestic-market-oriented firms rise from 19.5% to 23% to 28%, respectively, in Communication Equipment and 9.8% to 10% to 15%, respectively, in Consumer Electronics. In the case of Parts and Components, the corresponding figures are 7.3% and 5.1%, as exporters are defined as those with export shares equal to or greater than 25% and 50%, respectively. The number of pure exporters in this category was very small, leading to large standard errors and estimated coefficients that are generally insignificant.

328   *B.-Y. Aw, A.R. Hwang / Journal of Development Economics 47 (1995) 313–332*

capture, among other things, the transmission or diffusion of new or improved technology to exporters from foreign buyers of these products. [22] The large productivity difference between exporters and non-exporters in Communication Equipment is consistent with the observation in Dahlman (1990) that aside from telephones, production in this subsector is oriented to the domestic market and not particularly competitive. The domestic market in this subsector is highly regulated by the government and has the ''largest technological gap among the electronics industries with respect to the international frontier'' (San and Chen, 1989). In Consumer Electronics, there is no significant difference in the intercept coefficients between exporters and non-exporters, and the higher productivity among exporters appears to be related to more efficient use of inputs. The higher productivity for exporters relative to non-exporters in both the Consumer Electronics and Parts/Components is consistent with the liberal use of trade restrictions in these product categories (Dahlman, 1990).

In order to examine the role of returns to scale in accounting for the observed differences in productivity levels between exporters and domestic-market firms, we use the coefficient estimates of the production functions in Table 5 to obtain estimates of the output elasticities of labor and capital service in the respective markets. The sums of these output elasticities yield the estimates of returns to scale by market-orientation and product type. The last column in Table 6 reports the returns to scale estimates of each of the two groups of producers in each product category. [23] The estimates range from 0.87 to 0.99 among non-exporters and 0.88 to 0.96 among exporters. These estimates are reported for the average firm in each subgroup. [24] The decreasing returns to scale estimates are more likely

---

[22] The source of this so-called 'spillover' or 'externality' effect of exporting on the level of productivity of exporting firms is attributed to the inflow of foreign technology through contacts with foreign buyers in Dahlman and Sananikone (1990) and Westphal et al. (1979), or the presence of foreign investment in Blomstrom and Wolff (1989) and Haddad and Harrison (1993). Pack (1992) points to the critical role played by returning Taiwanese nationals in transmitting new knowledge in exporting firms rather than purely domestic-market firms. The latter, due to their smaller sales base are unable to offer sufficiently high wages to attract these returning nationals.

[23] Westbrook and Tybout (1993) show that estimates based on cross-sectional data tend to be upward biased due to unobservable plant-specific effects and downward biased due to measurement errors. Panel data is necessary to correct for these effects in the data. In the absence of panel data, and under the assumption that the extent of bias is the same for exporters and non-exporters alike, we focus on the relative magnitudes of returns to scale estimates rather than their absolute magnitudes.

[24] Using the cross-sectional data, we also estimated returns to scale by firm size. In Data Storage/ Processing Units, for both exporters and domestic-market firms, returns to scale begin at 1.04 and fall to about 0.94 as size categories grow. However, in the other two products, returns to scale rise from around 0.89 to 1.02 as size categories get larger but none is more than two standard deviations from constant returns to scale. More importantly for the purposes of this paper, the difference in the returns to scale estimates for exporters relative to domestic-market firms for any given size category is not significantly different from zero. A possible reason for the curious positive relationship between returns to scale and firm-size categories could be bias arising from unobservable heterogeneity among firms.

B.-Y. Aw, A.R. Hwang / Journal of Development Economics 47 (1995) 313–332   329

Table 6
Output elasticities of inputs [a] and returns to scale by product and market-orientation

Product and market-orientation	Output elasticity of labor	Output elasticity of capital	Returns to scale
Data Storage and Processing Units			
Domestic	0.634	0.353	0.988
Export	0.625	0.322	0.947
Consumer Electronics			
Domestic	0.616	0.258	0.874
Export	0.657	0.281	0.938
Parts and Components			
Domestic	0.611	0.279	0.900
Export	0.691	0.270	0.961
Communication Equipment			
Domestic	0.606	0.335	0.942
Export	0.575	0.309	0.884

[a] These elasticities are calculated by multiplying the relevant input coefficient estimates of the production functions in Table 5 with the ratio of mean input to mean output of each product category.

to reflect an estimation problem than technology given the cross-sectional nature of our data. In order to isolate the role of decreasing returns in our findings, we repeated the above analysis with constant returns to scale imposed on the production functions estimated. The contribution of productivity differential to value-added differences between exporters and domestic-market firms are significantly lower at 9.7%, 4.2%, and 3.3% in Communication Equipment, Consumer Electronics, and Parts and Components, respectively.

We also estimated the production functions without taking into account the rate of capacity utilization of capital. As predicted and shown by Abbott et al. (1988), the effect of its omission is to raise the output elasticities with respect to capital. However, in our case, this effect is fairly small, ranging from 0.01 to 0.04 across the different product categories. This is not surprising given the already high average rate of capacity utilization among the electronic firms in Taiwan (over 75%). The effect of capacity utilization could potentially be much greater in the other industries or the same industry in other countries. Within each product category, the effect of omitting the rate of capital utilization between exporters and non-exporters is even smaller. Again, this is not surprising since the capacity utilization rates between these two groups of producers are rather similar.

6. Summary and conclusions

In this paper, we examine the microfoundations of the performance of export-oriented relative to domestic-market-oriented firms. One possible explanation for the superior performance under the former strategy is that firms that are more subject to foreign competition are likely to be more efficient in their use of inputs than those oriented to a protected domestic market. Another rationale may be that exporting firms are bigger due, perhaps, to their better access to new, improved technology. In addition, bigger firms that are not already exporting are more likely to do so if they face downward-sloping domestic demand schedules, since they have the necessary resources to incur the extra costs of diversifying into foreign markets.

Our results shed light on the differential roles of resource-level differences and productivity differences in explaining value-added differences between export-oriented and domestic-market-oriented firms in the Taiwanese electronics industry. We note that our results cannot distinguish between the alternative hypotheses: whether the productivity difference between export-oriented and domestic-market-oriented firms are the result of or the cause of the export activity.

Our results indicate that the magnitude of the contribution of productivity differences to value-added differences between exporters and domestic-market firms are product specific. With the exception of Data Storage and Processing Units, productivity differences between exporters and domestic-market-oriented firms explain between 7 and 20% of the observed higher value-added among exporters. If we impose constant returns to scale in production, the corresponding range is 3 to 10%. [25] These results are consistent with the observations documented by previous researchers that, except for Data Storage and Processing Units, the local electronics market is more restricted by trade or entry barriers. [26]

Overall, our results indicate that input differences between exporters and non-exporters explain the bulk of the difference in their mean value-added. Nevertheless, the contribution of productivity differences between the two groups of firms to their differences in value-added in three of the four electronic products is significant. More importantly, our findings suggest that for 59% of all the firms that engage in the export market (those in Parts and Components and Communication Equipment) exogenous technological factors appear to play a critical role in their higher productivity. In the case of the electronics industry in Taiwan, Aw and Batra (1993) find some evidence that the greater exposure to the international market, particularly among exporting firms that do not undertake any formal investments in new technology, act as an important conduit for informal inflow of foreign technology and thus generating higher productivity levels.

---

[25] Chen and Tang (1987) find that export-oriented foreign firms are 6 to 11% closer to the production frontier than the import-substitution-oriented firm.

[26] See Dahlman (1990), San and Chen (1989), and Chen and Tang (1987). The latter authors observe that "local markets are more permissive not only because tariff protection is afforded (as Consumer Electronics and Parts/Components) but also because further entry to the markets may be blocked by the government (as in Communication Equipment) which tends to subject new firms to the full exportation constraint when markets are deemed 'crowded'."

Thus, we conclude that, relative to those who sell similar products primarily in the domestic market, exporters have higher levels of productivity, as conjectured by Pack (1988). It is likely that the higher productivity of exporters will shrink as input measures are redefined to account for say, labor skill differences. A panel data in the future will permit the examination of the link between export and productivity growth as well as how the contribution of the level differences in productivity between exporters and non-exporters change over time. A government policy that pumps more and more resources (or one that provides preferential access to these resources) into export-oriented firms at the expense of domestic-market-oriented firms may be more justified if the performance difference between the two groups of firms are increasingly explained by their productivity differences (rather than resource difference).

References

Abbott, T.A., III, Z. Griliches and J.A. Hauseman, 1988, Short run movements in productivity: Market power versus capacity utilization, Working Paper (National Bureau of Economic Research, Cambridge, MA).

Ahluwalia, I.J., 1985, Industrial Growth in India (Oxford Press, Delhi).

Aw, B.Y. and G. Batra, 1993, Linking export, technology and productivity: A new approach, Working Paper (The Pennsylvania State University).

Balassa, B., 1978, Exports and economic growth: Further evidence, Journal of Development Economics 5, 181–190.

Balassa, B., 1981, The newly industrializing countries in the world economy (Pergamon Press, New York).

Berndt, E., 1990, The practice of econometrics: Classic and contemporary (Addison-Wesley, Reading, MA).

Berry, R.A., 1992, Firm (or plant) size in the analysis of trade and development, in: G.K. Helleiner, ed., Trade policy, industrialization, and development: New perspectives (Clarendon Press, Oxford).

Blinder, A.S., 1973, Wage discrimination: Reduced form and structural estimates, Journal of Human Resources 18, 436–455.

Blomstrom, M. and E.W. Wolff, 1989, Multinational corporations and productivity convergence in Mexico, Working Paper (New York University, New York).

Chen, T.-J. and D.-P. Tang, 1986, The production characteristics of multinational firms and the effects of tax incentives, Journal of Development Economics 24, 119–129.

Chen, T.-J. and D.-P. Tang, 1987, Comparing technical efficiency between import-substituting and export-oriented firms in a developing country, Journal of Development Economics 26, 277–289.

Chenery, H., 1983, Interactions between theory and observation in development, World Development 11, 853–861.

Christensen, L.R., D.W. Jorgenson and L.J. Lau, 1971, Conjugate duality and the transcendental logarithmic production function, Econometrica 39, 255–256.

Christensen, L.R., D.W. Jorgenson and L.J. Lau, 1973, Transcendental production frontiers, Review of Economics and Statistics 55, 28–45.

Cotton, J., 1988, On the decomposition of wage differentials, Review of Economics and Statistics 70, 236–243.

Dahlman, C.J., 1990, Electronics development strategy: The role of government, Industries Series Paper no. 37 (The World Bank, Washington, DC).

Dahlman, C. and O. Sananikone, 1990, Technology strategy in the economy of Taiwan: Exploiting foreign linkages and investing in local capability, PSD Working Paper (The World Bank, Washington, DC).

Haddad, M., 1993, How trade liberalization affected productivity in Morocco, PRE Working Paper no. 1096 (The World Bank, Washington, DC).

Haddad, M. and A. Harrison, 1993, Are there positive spillovers from direct investment? Evidence from panel data for Morocco, Journal of Development Economics, forthcoming.

Harvylyshyn, O., 1990, Trade policy and productivity gains in developing countries: A survey of the literature, The World Bank Research Observer 5, 1–24.

Kim, Y.C. and J.K. Kwon, 1977, The utilization of capital and the growth of output in a developing country: The case of South Korean manufacturing, Journal of Development Economics 9, 265–278.

Krueger, A.O., 1978, Foreign trade regimes and economic development: Liberalization attempts and consequences (Ballinger, Lexington, MA).

Krueger, A.O. and B. Tuncer, 1982, Growth of factor productivity in Turkish manufacturing, Journal of Development Economics 11, 307–326.

Mody, A., 1990, Institutions and dynamic comparative advantage: The electronics industry in South Korea and Taiwan, Cambridge Journal of Economics 14, 291–314.

Nishimizu, M. and S. Robinson, 1984, Trade policy and productivity change in a semi-industrialized country, Journal of Development Economics 16, 177–206.

Oaxaca, R., 1973, Male female wage differentials in urban labor markets, International Economic Review 14, 693–709.

Pack, H., 1988, Industrialization and trade, in: H. Chenery and T.N. Srinivasan, eds., Handbook of development economics, Vol. 1 (Elsevier Science Publishers, Amsterdam).

Pack, H., 1992, Technology gaps between industrial and developing countries: Are there dividends for latecomers? Supplement to the World Bank Economic Review and World Bank Research Observer, Proceedings of the World Bank Annual Conference on Development Economics.

Olley, G.S. and A. Pakes, 1992, The dynamics of productivity in the telecommunications equipment industry, Working Paper no. 3977 (National Bureau of Economic Research, Cambridge, MA).

Rodrik, D., 1992, Closing the productivity gap: Does trade liberalization really help?, in: G. Helleiner, ed., Trade policy, industrialization and development: New perspectives (Clarendon, Oxford).

Rodrik, D., forthcoming, Trade and industrial policy reform in developing countries: A review of recent theory and evidence, in: J. Behrman and T.N. Srinivasan, eds., Handbook of development economics, Vol. 3 (North-Holland, Amsterdam).

San, G. and C.N. Chen, 1989, In service training in Taiwan, ROC, Economic Monograph Series no. 20 (Chung-hua Institute for Economic Research, Chung-hua).

Syrquin, M. and H. Chenery, 1989, Three decades of industrialization, The World Bank Economic Review 3, 145–181.

Tybout, J.R., 1992, Linking trade and productivity: New research directions, The World Bank Economic Review 6, 189–211.

Tybout, J.R., J. de Melo and V. Corbo, 1991, The effects of trade reforms on scale and technical efficiency: New evidence from Chile, Journal of International Economics 31, 231–250.

Tybout, J.R. and M.D. Westbrook, 1991, Trade liberalization and the structure of production in Mexican manufacturing, PRE Working Paper no. WPS 754 (The World Bank, Washington, DC).

Wade, R., 1992, Governing the market: Economic theory and the role of government in East Asian industrialization (Princeton University Press, Princeton, NJ).

Westbrook, M.D. and J.R. Tybout, 1993, Estimating returns to scale with large, imperfect panels: An application to Chilean manufacturing industries, World Bank Economic Review 7, 85–112.

Westphal, L., Y.-W. Rhee and G. Purcell, 1979, Foreign influences on Korean industrial development, Oxford Bulletin of Economics and Statistics, 41.

Part V
Public Policy

[18]

The Tradeoff Between Firm Size and
Diversity in the Pursuit of
Technological Progress

Wesley M. Cohen
Steven Klepper

1. Introduction

Since the writings of Schumpeter, the role of firm size in promoting technical advance has preoccupied scholars of technological change. As international competitive pressures have intensified in recent years, the role of firm size has emerged as a central concern of policymakers and industrialists as well. In the United States, some argue that the small entrepreneurial firm is the primary vehicle through which new ideas are introduced into the marketplace and that the diversity of ideas and approaches flowing from small firms represents American manufacturing's key competitive advantage (e.g., Gilder, 1988; Rodgers, 1990; Shaffer, 1990). On the other side, it is argued that only large firms or consortia can command the resources necessary to field the large research efforts required to keep up with the large, often cooperatively organized research operations of Japan, and, more recently, Europe (e.g., Ferguson, 1988; Norris, 1983; Noyce, 1990). Over the course of his career, Schumpeter himself spanned the poles of this debate. In his earlier work, Schumpeter (1934) saw the small-scale entrepreneur as the key to capitalism's vitality. Later Schumpeter (1942) argued that the large scale enterprise was the principal engine of technological progress, although he feared that the bureaucratic character of the large modern corporation would undermine entrepreneurial initiative and eventually sap capitalism of its technological vitality.

Final version accepted on June 13, 1991

Carnegie-Mellon University
Department of Social & Decision Sciences
Pittsburgh, PA 15213-3890, U.S.A.

In recent years, this controversy has been dominated, with some exceptions (e.g., Jorde and Teece, 1990), by industrialists and policy analysts. Most of the arguments advanced by both sides are based upon specific industries, most notably the semiconductor and computer industries. These arguments have largely failed to galvanize economists. Not only have the arguments been casually developed, but there are strong counterarguments to each, leaving us with little a priori basis for favoring either position. For example, proponents of large scale enterprise often allude to scale economies and capital market imperfections to rationalize the need for large firms and consortia. Scale economies, however, bear only on the optimal size of the R&D effort and relate only indirectly to the optimal size of the firm. With regard to capital market imperfections, there is no consensus among economists as to the import of such imperfections for investment in general, much less R&D in particular. Those arguing in behalf of small size have claimed that small firms, unencumbered by bureaucracy, provide both the freedom and economic incentives that stimulate creativity and agility in response to economic opportunity. On the other hand, while large firms may be more bureaucratic, they provide a superior human and capital infrastructure to support innovative activity.

To the extent that economists have probed the relationship between firm size and innovative activity, the evidence for either side of the debate has also not been compelling. Indeed, the predominant finding from a voluminous literature on the subject is that in most industries, above a modest threshold firm size large firms are no more research intensive than smaller firms. This implies that consolidation of firms above the threshold would have no effect on total industry R&D

Small Business Economics 4: 1—14, 1992.
© 1992 *Kluwer Academic Publishers. Printed in the Netherlands.*

expenditures, which has been widely interpreted to indicate that above a modest firm size neither small nor large firm size confers any advantage in R&D (e.g., Kamien and Schwartz, 1982; Scherer, 1980; Baldwin and Scott, 1987).

We propose that even if small and large firms are equally capable at R&D, there may nonetheless be important social advantages associated with *both* large and small firm size. We suggest that there is merit to both sides of the debate about the optimal firm size for R&D, but not for the reasons typically advanced. Our demonstration of the social advantages of small and large firm size proceeds in two stages. First, drawing heavily on prior work (Cohen and Klepper, 1990, 1991), we suggest that both firm size and technological diversity influence firm R&D expenditures within industries and we highlight evidence that supports this claim. In the second stage, we go beyond our earlier analysis, and, in a more speculative spirit, consider not only how firm size and diversity influence firm R&D expenditures, but also how they affect the technical advance generated by the expenditures. We argue there are virtues both to having a large number of small firms in an industry and to consolidating output in a few large firms.

The social advantages in our framework of an industry composed of numerous small firms rests on two notions suggested by Nelson's (1981) argument about the importance of competition and diversity for technological change. The first notion is that in the typical industry undergoing technological change, there are many productive ways of innovating. The other notion is that firms have different capabilities and perceptions which lead them to pursue different sets of approaches to innovation. In such a world, dividing up industry output over a greater number of small firms increases the chances that any given approach to innovation will be pursued, thereby increasing the diversity of technological efforts in the industry. While increasing the number of firms does not necessarily benefit individual firms in the industry, it promotes technical advance and, hence, benefits society by increasing the number of productive approaches to innovation that are collectively pursued in the industry. From this perspective, the source of the social advantage associated with small firm size is not smallness per se but the greater number of firms that small size implies given some industry demand.

Our argument about the social advantages of large firm size stems from the idea that large firms possess an advantage in appropriating the returns from innovation due, in part, to imperfections in the market for information (Arrow, 1962). This causes the returns to large firms from any given R&D effort to be greater than the returns to small firms, leading large firms to conduct more socially desirable R&D than smaller firms. Consequently, consolidating output over a smaller number of firms will result in the performance of more socially desirable R&D for each approach to innovation that is pursued. This benefit is realized independent of whether there are any economies of scale in the conduct of R&D or whether large firms have superior ability to finance R&D.

Given the social advantages associated with both large firm size and more numerous small firms, there will always be a tradeoff associated with changing the number of firms within an industry. Reducing the number of firms will increase the average firm size, which will increase the level of innovative effort applied to each approach to innovation that is pursued. This comes, however, at the cost of reducing the number of productive approaches to innovation that are collectively pursued in the industry. On the other hand, increasing the number of firms will increase the diversity of approaches that are pursued in the industry but reduce the level of effort for each approach. The optimal number of firms in each industry will depend on the relative importance of these two effects, which we argue will vary across industries.

We speculate that market forces alone are not likely to lead to the socially optimal average firm size and number of firms in each industry. For example, the eventual displacement of larger incumbent firms by smaller new firms will compromise the appropriability advantages of size. Alternatively, even when entry of new firms can enhance social welfare by increasing the diversity of approaches to innovation pursued within an industry, we argue that such entry will not necessarily be forthcoming. Although these opposing forces could conceivably balance out to yield some optimal number of firms, we have no reason to expect this to occur in the typical industry.

We discuss how the failure of private initiatives to lead to a socially optimal state will create a tension from a policy standpoint. Following recent trends, obstacles to cooperative R&D efforts within industries could be removed, which would encourage the development of larger scale innovating units. This will, however, reduce the diversity of technological approaches pursued. Alternatively, diversity could be stimulated by government subsidies to entrants. However, more entry will reduce average firm size, thereby compromising the advantages of size. We suggest that it may well be just this tension that, in part, has given rise to the recent policy debates. We argue that there are policies, however, that can to some degree preserve the benefits of size while at the same time maintain technological diversity.

The paper is organized as follows. In Section 2, we present our framework and briefly review the evidence that supports it. In Section 3, we suggest how larger firm size is tied to technical advance. In Section 4, we suggest how a larger number of firms may yield greater technological diversity and how that diversity, in turn, contributes to technical advance. In Section 5, we discuss the tradeoff implied by the existence of both an appropriability advantage of large firm size and a diversity-inducing advantage of having numerous small firms within an industry. In Section 6, we conclude by highlighting the limitations of our analysis and by suggesting issues for further research.

2. A model of R&D investment

In this section we consider how firms decide how much to spend on R&D. Our conception follows the model of R&D investment developed in Cohen and Klepper (1990, 1991). We discuss the basis for the model and provide a brief description of its implications. We refer the reader to Cohen and Klepper (1990, 1991) for the formal and more extensive development of the model.

The model is based on a distinctive conception of an industry. The industry is assumed to be subject to ongoing technological change. Following Nelson (1990) and others, it is assumed that technological advance can be achieved in many different ways. A distinction is commonly drawn, for example, between process and product innovations. Moreover, there are typically many different ways of improving technology within each of these categories. For example, a production process may be improved through automation and by increasing the scale of production. Similarly, a

product may be improved along a range of dimensions. For example, personal computers can be made more user-friendly and they can be made to work faster. These different approaches to enhancing product and process performance are often additive in their effect on technical advance; they do not represent competing or mutually exclusive approaches to satisfying the same performance objective. A firm in principle could pursue all of the approaches or any subset of them.

Firms are assumed to be uncertain about the profitability of pursuing any given approach to innovation, both in terms of the cost of the innovation and its gross returns. For simplicity, we assume that all approaches are profitable to pursue, although the firms do not know that in advance. The uncertainty concerning the profitability of the various approaches to innovation generates differences in firms' expectations about which approaches are worth pursuing. These differences are assumed to reflect the differences in the sorts of expertise possessed by each firm. The differing expectations cause the firms to make different bets on which approaches to pursue.

The firms that make the best bets will experience the greatest rate of innovation and technical advance. It is assumed that eventually all innovations (but not the approaches themselves) will be copied, so that ultimately all benefits from innovation will be passed on to buyers in the form of lower prices. In the interim, however, firms that innovate most will reap economic profits. They will grow at the fastest rates over time, although growth will tend to be incremental, reflecting, among other things, the impact of uncertainty on investment and convex adjustment costs. Those firms that innovate the least will find the price of their product falling below their costs and will eventually exit. Over time the expertise required to evaluate and exploit approaches to innovation will change as the industry's technology evolves. Firms will be limited in their ability to change their expertise,[1] and in the long run new firms with more suitable expertise will replace the industry leaders.

The consequence of this process is that at a given moment in each industry there will be an array of firms of different sizes and capabilities with different views about which approaches to innovation are worth pursuing. The model focuses on how these differences condition firm decisions about which approaches to pursue and about how much to spend on R&D for each approach pursued. The number of firms and the output of each firm are taken as given, having been determined by the evolutionary process leading up to that moment in the industry's history. For simplicity, firms are also assumed to be price takers and to choose their R&D expenditures independent of the R&D expenditures of their rivals.

With regard to the approaches a firm decides to pursue, we assume this choice is determined exclusively by the expertise of the firm. A firm is assumed to pursue a particular approach if it possesses the expertise that would enable it to exploit and recognize the value of the approach. Consequently, in each industry the environment governing the endowment of firms with expertise will ultimately determine the approaches to innovation that are pursued by firms in the industry. We use a very simple model to represent this environment. First, we assume that in each industry the likelihood of a firm possessing the expertise that would lead it to pursue any given approach is independent of the likelihood of the firm possessing the expertise that would lead it to pursue any other approach. This implies that the probability of a firm pursuing any given approach is independent of the probability of it pursuing any other.[2] Second, we assume that in each industry the likelihood of a firm being endowed with the expertise that would lead it to pursue any given approach is independent of the size of the firm. This implies that the probability of a firm pursuing any given approach is independent of its size.

The choice about how much the firm should spend on each approach to innovation it pursues is conceived as follows. Each approach to innovation is assumed to be characterized by a range of projects with different marginal products, where the marginal product of a project is defined in terms of the technical advance (measured in standard units) generated from the project. Ordering the projects by their marginal products defines a diminishing marginal product schedule that relates the marginal product of R&D expenditures on an approach to the level of R&D expenditures on the approach, where it is assumed that the level of R&D expenditures is proportional to the number of projects pursued. All firms that pursue an approach are assumed to face the same marginal product of R&D schedule for the approach.

Although the marginal productivity schedules for all approaches are assumed identical across firms, the marginal revenue schedules associated with the approaches will differ across firms. The marginal revenue a firm earns from a project depends on the marginal product of the project and the level of output over which the innovations from the project are applied. It is assumed that firms will typically not sell their innovations in disembodied form either due to imperfections in the market for information (Arrow, 1962) or because the innovations are more valuable to the innovator than to other firms (Cohen and Klepper, 1990).[3] This implies that firms will appropriate the returns to their innovations primarily through their own output.[4] We also assume that the firm expects its growth due to innovation to be incremental and conditioned by its pre-innovation output level. This implies that the returns a firm earns from any given R&D project will be proportional to its sales prior to the R&D project, which we refer to as the firm's *ex ante* sales.

The assumptions governing the choice of approaches to innovation and the amount spent per approach form the basis for predictions about firm R&D expenditures in an industry. First, assuming no economies of scale in R&D, Cohen and Klepper (1991) demonstrate that the assumption that the firm's expected returns to innovation are scaled by its *ex ante* output implies that in each industry all firms pursuing a particular approach will spend an amount on R&D on the approach that is proportional to their *ex ante* sales. The simple intuition behind this result is that the greater the firm's sales then the larger the returns from any given R&D effort and thus the larger the optimal R&D expenditures of the firm. Furthermore, if the number of approaches to innovation pursued by the firm is uncorrelated with its sales, Cohen and Klepper (1990) show that the overall R&D intensity of the firm (i.e., the ratio of the firm's R&D expenditures on all approaches to its sales) will be independent of its *ex ante* sales. Alternatively expressed, in each industry total firm R&D expenditures will vary across firms proportionally with the *ex ante* sales of the firms.

Second, Cohen and Klepper (1991) demonstrate that if it is assumed that in each industry the marginal product schedule of each approach to innovation is the same and firms are equally likely to adopt each approach to innovation, then the number of approaches to innovation pursued by firms and their overall R&D intensity will be binomially distributed. Intuitively, given that firms will pursue different numbers of approaches, the adoption of each approach by a firm can be thought of as an independent Bernoulli trial. As a consequence, in each industry the number of approaches pursued by firms will be binomially distributed. It was noted above that firms' R&D expenditures on any given approach will be proportional to their sales. Coupled with the assumption that the marginal product schedules of the approaches do not differ, Cohen and Klepper (1991) show that this implies that in each industry firm R&D intensities will also be binomially distributed, with the firms that pursue the greatest number of approaches having the largest R&D intensities and the firms that pursue the smallest number of approaches having the smallest number of approaches having the smallest R&D intensities.

Both sets of predictions of the model are supported by evidence on how firm R&D expenditures vary within industries. Cohen and Klepper (1990) note how the predictions of the model concerning the independence of firm R&D intensities and firm sales accords with the large body of evidence about the proportional relationship within industries between R&D expenditures and firm sales noted in the introduction. The predictions of the model concerning the nature of the distribution within industries of firm R&D intensities are supported by the empirical regularities in industry R&D intensity distributions documented by Cohen and Klepper (1991) for a sample of business units[5] belonging largely to the 1,000 leading American manufacturing firms as of 1974—1977. These distributions tend to be unimodal, positively skewed, and to contain a substantial number of nonperformers of R&D, which is consistent with firm R&D intensity being binomially distributed. Moreover, across industries the moments of the distributions are correlated, which is also compatible with the binomial. Indeed, as Cohen and Klepper (1991) show, the model is capable of explaining not only the fact that the moments are correlated but also the signs of the correlations.

Thus, the model can explain a fairly exacting set of regularities that characterize the distribution of R&D intensities within industries. This provides indirect support for the two central tenets of the model: (1) returns to R&D are scaled by the size of the firm; and (2) differences in firm R&D intensities are attributable to differences across firms in the number of approaches to innovation pursued.

3. The advantages of large size

In this section we consider the implications of our framework for the advantages of large firm size, where size refers specifically to the level of output of a particular product. Our discussion is largely based on Cohen and Klepper (1990). Following our earlier work, we assume that the mechanisms within an industry for appropriating rents due to innovation, such as patents, are given. We focus on the welfare implications of the link in our framework between firm size and the appropriability of the returns to innovation.

Since, in our framework, the firm earns returns on its innovations through its own output and growth tends to be incremental, the returns to R&D are scaled by the firm's *ex ante* sales. As we noted, this is the key in our framework to explaining the proportional relationship between R&D effort and firm size. This argument also implies that large firms will have an advantage over smaller firms in R&D competition. To see this, consider two firms that produce the same product and pursue the same number of approaches to innovation. Suppose, for simplicity, that all R&D expenditures result in innovations which lower the average cost of production.[6] If the two firms spend the same amount on R&D then our framework implies that they would achieve the same unit cost reduction. The larger firm, however, would apply the unit cost reduction over a larger level of output, enabling it to earn greater profits from its R&D.[7] Moreover, our framework implies that if two firms pursue the same number of approaches, they will have the same R&D intensity, which implies that the bigger firm will actually perform more R&D than the smaller firm. This reflects the greater return it earns from any given level of R&D due to its greater size, which provides it with an incentive to perform a greater level of R&D than its smaller rival. Since it will earn positive profits from this additional R&D, this reinforces its advantage over its smaller rival.

Our interpretation of the relationship within industries between R&D effort and firm size is quite unconventional. The standard interpretation is that the proportional relationship between R&D effort and firm size suggests no advantage or disadvantage of large firms in R&D, although Fisher and Temin (1973) caution against making inferences about the advantages of firm size in R&D from the relationship between R&D effort and firm size. Of course, all we have shown is that the evidence is compatible with a theory in which there is an appropriability advantage to large firm size in R&D. There is, however, no competing explanation for why R&D effort should be proportional to firm sales.

Our framework implies that the private advantage accruing to large firm size also represents a social advantage. Perhaps the easiest way to see this is to consider the merger of two firms that produce the same product, are the same size, pursue the same approaches to innovation, and spend the same amount on R&D on the same projects within each approach to innovation. The merger would result in two social dividends. First, duplicative R&D would be eliminated, a point suggested by other researchers (e.g., Spence, 1984). Second, and more novel, for each approach to innovation pursued by the two firms, the merger will increase the profitability of R&D *at the margin*, thereby leading the merged firm to undertake socially efficient R&D projects that were not undertaken by either firm before the merger. In effect, the merged firm will be better able to appropriate the returns from its innovations than either firm alone was able to do, causing it to undertake a greater number of socially efficient R&D projects than were collectively undertaken by the two firms before the merger.

Much of the empirical literature in the Schumpeterian tradition assumes that if R&D effort rises proportionally with firm size, then the size distribution of firms would have no effect on the amount of technological change achieved in the industry. In this view, technical advance is solely a function of the total amount of R&D performed in the industry, notwithstanding who performs it. In contrast, Cohen and Klepper (1990) argue that if innovations cannot be sold and lead to incremental growth, then the total amount of technological change generated in an industry will be a function of not only the total amount of R&D performed by all firms but also

the distribution of R&D effort across firms. By redistributing sales and R&D expenditures from smaller to larger firms, total R&D expenditures would not change but a greater number of socially efficient R&D projects would be collectively undertaken, thereby increasing the amount of technological change generated per unit of industry R&D expenditure.

If large firms have an advantage in conducting R&D, as our framework implies, then the appropriability advantage of size would be fully realized under monopoly. We do not, however, commonly observe the emergence of monopoly in R&D intensive industries despite the appropriability advantage of size. An explanation for this is that even successful firms grow only slowly, and that over time technology typically evolves in ways that favor either new firms or firms that were formerly less successful. Indeed, in his development of the notion of creative destruction, Schumpeter (1942) suggested that even monopolists will be displaced in the long run for such reasons.

In the absence of monopoly, firms will have an incentive to cooperate in R&D if they can appropriate the returns to their innovations only through their own output. For any given approach to innovation, all firms pursuing the approach could benefit by pooling their efforts. They would avoid the costly duplication of effort that would otherwise occur. Moreover, because they could apply innovations to their joint output, the firms would collectively profit from R&D expenditures that none of the firms could profit from individually. This suggests that it may be efficient for government to allow cooperative R&D ventures among competing firms pursuing the same approaches to innovation. Indeed, since the 1984 passage of the National Cooperative Research Act, prohibitions against cooperative R&D ventures have been relaxed. A large fraction of the cooperative ventures formed since that time, however, have brought together firms with complementary capabilities rather than firms pursuing the same approaches to innovation (Scott, 1988). This suggests that firms have a range of incentives to cooperate in their R&D efforts, and the one we have identified may not, in practice, be paramount.[8] Moreover, cooperation among firms pursuing the same approaches to innovation may be impeded by difficulties in communication and concerns about competitive advantage. If so, then a more active role for government may be indicated.

It is important to stress that the advantage of size in our framework is based solely on the assumption that firms' returns to innovation are scaled by their *ex ante* output. To the extent that innovations can be sold in disembodied form and/or that firms can reap the returns to their innovations through rapid growth, the advantage of *ex ante* large firm size will be less significant. It is likely that both of these factors will vary across industries and perhaps types of innovations (e.g., product versus process innovations).[9] The greater the extent to which the returns to innovation do not depend on *ex ante* output, then the lower will be the social benefits from cooperation.

4. The advantages of diversity

In this section we consider the role of technological diversity in technical advance and the link between diversity and the number of competitors.

Diversity across firms is incorporated in our framework through the assumption that firms pursue different sets of approaches to innovation. This in turn gives rise to differences in firm R&D intensities that reflect differences in the total number of approaches to innovation pursued by each firm. As we discussed, this form of technological diversity allows us to explain regularities characterizing the nature of the distribution within industries of firm R&D intensities. Of course, this does not mean that diversity is actually an important determinant of R&D intensities within industries, but it does provide indirect support for this view.

In our framework, diversity across firms' innovative activities stems from the existence of different noncompeting approaches to innovation within an industry. We conceive of these different approaches not as substitute or parallel ways of achieving the same technological objective but as independent ways of achieving technological change.[10] The total number of approaches to innovation in an industry can be thought of as being determined by the science and technology underlying R&D in the industry. Which of these approaches are actually pursued by firms in the industry at any given moment will depend upon

the expectations and capabilities of firms in the industry. It is certainly possible that some subset of the approaches will not be pursued by any firm in the industry. Indeed, if there are X firms in the industry and the probability of any approach being pursued by any given firm is p, then the likelihood of any approach not being pursued by any firm in the industry is $(1 - p)^X$.

A simple measure of technological diversity in our framework is the number of distinct approaches to innovation that are actually pursued by the firms in the industry. This measure corresponds well to the notion of diversity implicit in the arguments of proponents of small scale enterprise who stress the greater breadth of ideas and types of innovations pursued in industries composed of numerous small firms (e.g., Rodgers, 1990). It follows directly from this measure of technological diversity that the extent of diversity will be directly related to the number of firms in the industry. Since the likelihood of a potential approach to innovation in an industry not being pursued by any firm is $(1 - p)^X$, the expected number of different approaches to innovation pursued in an industry will be an increasing function of the number of firms, X. This implies that on average industries composed of a greater number of firms will be characterized by a greater amount of technological diversity. Note that this greater diversity does not emerge from any superior creativity on the part of smaller firms. It is simply the result of having a greater number of firms in the industry choosing which approaches to innovation to pursue.

The predicted relationship between the number of firms and technological diversity depends upon a key assumption of our framework, namely that the likelihood of a firm pursuing any given approach is independent of the size of the firm. If, alternatively, the probability of a firm pursuing any given approach increased with the size of the firm, it would no longer follow that increasing the number of firms would necessarily increase the expected degree of diversity.[11] While there are undoubtedly industries where the probability of pursuing an approach is correlated with firm size, the evidence concerning the regularities in the industry R&D intensity distributions suggests that the number of such industries is limited. Otherwise, our framework implies that there would be a large number of industries for which the largest firms are characterized by above average R&D intensities,[12] which does not conform with the evidence. Moreover, if the probability of pursuing an approach were an increasing function of the size of the firm, then based on our framework the distribution of firm R&D intensities within an industry would depend on the size distribution of firms and would, in all likelihood, not conform to the regularities in the industry R&D intensity distributions documented by Cohen and Klepper (1991).

If the likelihood of pursuing an approach to innovation is independent of the size of the firm then two firms of equal size would together be expected to pursue a greater number of distinct approaches to innovation than one firm twice their size. Having more firms provides more "independent minds" to consider the alternatives, which results in greater technological diversity. There are a number of organizational factors that might explain why the likelihood of pursuing any approach is independent of firm size and, hence, why diversity is promoted by a greater number of firms. We suspect it has something to do with the way R&D proposals are processed within firms. Following the argument suggested by Sah and Stiglitz (1986, 1988), suppose that proposals are initiated by technical staff and then subsequently considered by higher level decision makers. If large firms have more hierarchical levels than small firms and a proposed approach can be rejected at any level, an approach will have a greater chance of being approved by a smaller firm. As long as the number of proposed approaches in the two firms combined and the one large firm are equal, the two smaller firms would then be expected to pursue a greater number of distinct approaches than the large firm. Alternatively, suppose the probability of an approach being rejected is independent of the size of the firm. Even in this case, if all approaches proposed in the large firm are proposed in at least one of the two smaller firms and some are proposed in both of the smaller firms,[13] then the two smaller firms combined will approve a greater number of distinct approaches than the larger firm.[14]

Suppose we are correct and the number of firms is an important determinant of the diversity of approaches to innovation pursued in an industry. In order for there to be an advantage associated with small firm size, there must be some benefit associated with the greater diversity brought about by a greater number of firms. Our framework highlights an obvious benefit from the greater diversity — the exploitation of beneficial approaches to innovation that otherwise would not have been pursued. Indeed, this advantage of diversity was suggested long ago by Alfred Marshall when he stated that, "The tendency to variation is a chief source of progress" (Marshall, 1920, p. 355). Even if diversity does promote progress, as Marshall suggests, this does not mean that social welfare is necessarily promoted by the greater diversity associated specifically with an increase in the number of firms. Holding the output of the industry constant, if the number of firms is increased then the average size of each firm will decline. In the prior section, we showed how in our framework the consolidation of firms would yield social benefits. It follows that reducing the average firm size would impose a social cost. Assuming that the returns to innovation are scaled by *ex ante* output, each firm will spend less on R&D on the approaches it pursues, and for some amount of time, the innovations developed by each firm will be applied over a smaller level of output. The net effect on social welfare of increasing the number of firms depends on the magnitude of these costs relative to the benefits of having additional approaches to innovation pursued. We consider this tradeoff further in the next section.

While it is not straightforward to establish the social advantage of diversity in our framework, it is possible to imagine circumstances in which the increase in diversity brought about by a greater number of firms unequivocally promotes social welfare. For instance, suppose that firms are fully able to sell their innovations and there is no duplication among firms in their R&D efforts. In such a world, all innovations will be applied immediately to the entire output of the industry, and a reduction in the size of each firm will not diminish its incentives to conduct R&D. Then the decrease in firm size associated with the increase in the number of firms will have no effect on the R&D expenditures of the incumbent firms nor on the output over which any innovations resulting from these expenditures are applied. Consequently, any increase in the number of approaches pursued resulting from an increase in the number of firms will provide a net benefit to society. Intuitively, having a greater number of different minds (i.e., firms) evaluate the possible approaches to innovation will diminish the chance that a beneficial approach to innovation will be overlooked.

Our claim that diversity within an industry will increase with the number of firms implicitly assumes that at any given moment there may be firms outside of an industry that would pursue an otherwise unpursued approach if they entered the industry. Stated more baldly, it assumes that there may be potential entrants who recognize an opportunity but who do not enter the industry to exploit it. One reason this could occur is if there is some cost to entering the industry that exceeds the gross profit the entrant could make from pursuing the unexploited opportunity. From a social welfare perspective, however, this cost should be counted against the technical advance generated by the increase in the number of firms. If the social benefit of this technical advance was solely limited to the producer surplus resulting from the entrant's pursuit of a new approach, the net change in social welfare from the increase in the number of firms would be negative since the cost of entry would exceed the gross profits the producer could make from entering. Thus, for the increase in diversity to bring about an increase in social welfare, there must be some kind of wedge between the private and social returns from the pursuit of a new approach.

Our analysis of innovative activity, like many others (e.g., Arrow, 1962; Scherer, 1979; Spence, 1984), provides the basis for such a wedge. In laying out the framework, we noted that eventually all innovations are imitated. To the extent that the costs of imitation are less than the benefits, the social returns to innovation will exceed the private returns.[15] Consequently, it is possible that the pursuit of new approaches to innovation by entrants could be socially beneficial but not profitable to the entrant. In that case, the social benefits from greater diversity would not be realized through private initiative.

Our arguments suggest that if policies to increase the number of firms in an industry were undertaken, diversity would be expected to increase, which, in turn, could increase social welfare. Such policies could include prohibitions on horizontal mergers, subsidies of failing firms, and/or subsidies of entrants. Note that none of these policies requires the government to have any special insights about the sort of innovations an industry should pursue. Indeed, there is no reason to expect the government to be any more enlightened than firms about the best innovations to pursue. The rationale for these policies is simply that by getting more firms in the industry, there will be less chance that beneficial opportunities for technical advance will be unexploited.

It is important to note that the diversity-inducing effect of the presence of many small firms clearly depends upon the vitality of the science and technology underlying technical advance in any given industry, which we take as given. If this science and technology base is moribund, then the number of approaches to innovation that could be pursued will be few. In this case, the relationship between the number of firms and technological diversity, and, in turn, technical advance, will be weaker.

5. The tradeoff

In the last section we argued that it is not possible to bring about an increase in diversity through an increase in the number of firms without compromising some of the benefits associated with large firm size. Not surprisingly, it is also not possible to reap the benefits of large firm size without compromising the advantages associated with greater diversity. In this section we consider further the nature of this tradeoff.

When diversity is promoted through a greater number of firms, average firm size is reduced, which compromises the advantages associated with large size firms. Consider, alternatively, the costs associated with promoting the advantages of large firm size through the consolidation of firms. By reducing the number of firms in the industry, the expected number of approaches to innovation collectively pursued in the industry will decline. Then, on average, a smaller fraction of the beneficial opportunities for innovation will be pursued, which will reduce social welfare. Thus, just as increasing diversity through an increase in the number of firms has offsetting costs, so does increasing firm size through the consolidation of firms.[16]

Thus, in our framework, there is a tradeoff between the advantages associated with small firms and those associated with large firms. In order to have more approaches to innovation pursued, it is necessary to sacrifice some intensity of effort for each approach, and *vice versa*. The nature of this tradeoff is complicated and will depend on a number of factors. Analyzing the optimal average firm size for any industry in our framework requires a formal model of this tradeoff, which is beyond the scope of the paper. We can, however, use our framework to speculate about the role of factors that would be expected to shape the nature of the tradeoff: the extent to which firms can either sell their innovations or grow rapidly due to innovation, and the vitality of an industry's technology, as represented by the number of different approaches to innovation potentially available in the industry. To the extent that firms can realize rents due to innovation via rapid growth, licensing, and other mechanisms that do not exploit the firm's *ex ante* output, the appropriability advantage of size will be limited. In that case, an industry composed of a greater number of firms will be desirable. To the extent that the science and technology base of an industry is such that the potential number of approaches to innovation available to the industry is small, the diversity advantage associated with numerous small firms will be limited. In that case, an industry composed of a smaller number of firms will be desirable.

Consider the case of an industry in which there are a large number of approaches to innovation and firms can appropriate the returns to innovation only through their own *ex ante* output, which is the case where the tradeoff between the advantages associated with large and small firm size is the most acute. We suspect a substantial number of technologically progressive industries will be characterized by just such an acute tradeoff. There is no reason to believe that in these types of industries market forces alone will result in an optimal number of firms. In any given industry, there likely will be either too little entry to promote sufficient diversity or entry may be so unencumbered that the appropriability advantage of larger firm size is excessively compromised.

If market forces cannot be expected to lead to the optimal number of firms, policy makers will be faced with the challenge of deciding whether the number of firms in each industry is too large or too small. This will require making extremely difficult judgments. It is possible, however, that we have overblown the challenge posed by the tradeoff and policies can be designed to achieve the benefits of both diversity and large size. Consider, for example, current proposals that government condone firm cooperation on "generic" research (e.g., Nelson, 1990). Such proposals can be interpreted as suggesting that firms pursue separately R&D on approaches which they do not pursue in common and pursue together R&D on approaches which they do pursue in common. In this fashion, cooperative agreements could be crafted that would permit the industry and society to benefit from the appropriability advantage of large firm size without compromising the benefits of diversity. Indeed, cooperation on something resembling what we call generic research is apparently one of the models for cooperative research employed in the Japanese manufacturing sector.

6. Conclusion

Our analysis lends support to both sides of the debate concerning the optimal firm size for achieving technical advance. It provides a basis for why industries composed of many small firms will tend to exhibit greater diversity in the approaches to innovation pursued, and why greater diversity will contribute to more rapid technological change. It also provides a basis for why industries populated by larger firms will achieve a more rapid rate of technical advance on the approaches to innovation that are pursued. These arguments together suggest that a tradeoff exists between the appropriability advantage of large size and the advantages of diversity that accrue from numerous small firms.[17]

Our analysis has been more appreciative than rigorous and, indeed, often explicitly speculative. While we attempted to raise important questions, our framework requires more structuring before we can be confident about any of our conclusions. Even in its inchoate form, however, our analysis demonstrates that much needs to be done before the current debate about firm size can seriously inform policy. If we accept the plausibility of our basic framework, it focuses attention on a range of issues and questions. The fundamental premise of our analysis is that firm capabilities and perceptions differ within industries. This premise is not, however, widely reflected in analyses of industry behavior and performance, which typically take some representative firm as their starting point. Indeed, the analytic utility of our particular premise deserves scrutiny. Are differences in firm capabilities and perceptions as critical to explaining the industry patterns in innovative activity and performance as we suggest? Do these differences persist? Is our abstract characterization of these differences and their effects on innovative activity up to the task of providing a basis for policy?

These intraindustry differences in capabilities and perceptions underpin the hypothesized relationship in our framework between the number of firms within an industry and the number of distinct technological activities pursued by the industry as a whole. Surely this hypothesis should be tested. To establish the relationship between numbers of firms and technological diversity, we also made two important assumptions, which themselves should be examined. First, we assumed that firms independently decide upon which approaches to innovation to pursue. This assumption precludes the clustering of firms around innovative activities due to imitation, a phenomenon highlighted by Nelson (1981) and Scott (1991). To the degree that innovative activities yield relatively fast, public results, the assumption may be suspect. While our evidence indirectly suggests that such clustering may not be critical for explaining innovative activity in a wide range of industries, more research would be helpful. Second, we assumed that the number of approaches to innovation pursued by firms is independent of their size, implying large and small firms will tend to pursue the same number of approaches. This assumption probably does not apply to the smallest firms within an industry, particularly to the extent that such firms are often not full line manufacturing firms. Does it apply, however, to the medium to large firms that account for the preponderance of R&D and economic activity in the manufacturing sector? While our evidence again provides indirect support for this claim, more empirical and theoretical research is indicated.

We also made other claims and assumptions that deserve further attention. For example, we

argued that greater technological diversity stimulates technical advance and provides gross increments to social welfare. Assuming it exists, the mechanism linking diversity and technical advance has never been examined empirically and is not obvious. Our assumption that expected firm growth due to innovation is incremental played an important role in permitting us to hypothesize an appropriability advantage of large size. Again, both the assumption and its alleged effect on innovative activity are worth examining. Finally, we also need to test whether the relationship between R&D and firm size within industries depends upon appropriability conditions, particularly upon the extent to which firms can sell their innovations or grow rapidly due to innovation.[18] In conclusion, this litany of reasonable but unsubstantiated assumptions and arguments should make clear that this paper is only a modest beginning of a daunting research agenda.

Acknowledgements

We are indebted to Mark Kamlet, Jonathan Leland and F. M. Scherer for their suggestions.

Notes

[1] An important theme of the work on industry evolution is that it is difficult for a firm to change deliberately its core expertise (e.g., Nelson and Winter, 1982; Klepper and Graddy, 1990). The corporate strategy literature also implicitly makes this point when arguing that firms should exploit their "core competences" (e.g., Andrews, 1971; Porter, 1980), suggesting that it is difficult for firms to transform their capabilities.

[2] This is a strong assumption which we plan to relax in subsequent development of our model. It can be rationalized, however, by simply defining two approaches as distinct if the likelihood of the approaches being pursued by any given firm are independent.

[3] In recent years, it has been recognized that many innovations are most valued by the innovators themselves because they are either idiosyncratic to the innovator (Nelson, 1989) or require idiosyncratic expertise for their exploitation that is only generated in the course of the innovation process itself (Cohen and Levinthal, 1989, 1990).

[4] The survey results of Levin *et al.* (1987) provide a strong empirical basis for the claim. They find that the most effective mechanism for appropriating rents due to innovation are first-mover advantages, secrecy, and complementary sales and service, all of which are implemented via the firm's own sales.

[5] A business unit represents a firm's activity in a given industry.

[6] The following argument applies equally to product innovations (Cohen and Klepper, 1990).

[7] Cf. Nelson, Peck and Kalachek (1967) and Scherer (1970), who also note this potential advantage of size.

[8] See Scott (1988), Link and Bauer (1989), and Katz and Ordover (1990) for a discussion of the range of factors that may affect the benefits and costs of R&D cooperation.

[9] For example, the ability of firms to sell their innovations in disembodied form will vary across industries according to the ease of defining and enforcing property rights over innovations.

[10] To make the idea of different, noncompeting approaches to technological change within an industry more concrete, consider the semiconductor industry. Historically, research in semiconductors has been conducted in many areas, including silicon manufacture, low-cost methods for semiconductor manufacture, and the design of various devices such as MOS, bipolar, integrated circuit, and memory devices. Each of these can be thought of as different but complementary approaches to innovation in semiconductors. Also, consistent with our general framework, semiconductor firms have differed considerably in the sets of these approaches that they pursued. Texas Instruments, for example, possessed a broad range of expertise in solid state physics, materials properties and preparation, production process chemistry, advanced photolithographic processes, semiconductor device and design technologies, and pursued a broad range of approaches to innovation. In contrast, companies such as Mostek, American Micro-Systems and SEMI possessed more circumscribed expertise in device design technologies, and pursued a narrower range of approaches to innovation that focused on the design of MOS, bipolar, or memory devices.

Our characterization of approaches as noncompeting contrasts with others' conceptualization of different approaches to innovation. For example, in the analyses of Evenson and Kislev (1976) and Nelson (1982), different approaches represent distinct, competing ways of achieving the same technological end. Differentiating approaches in this way is relevant when there is uncertainty about how best to achieve a particular technological objective. In our framework, however, we abstracted from this kind of uncertainty. Our firms differ, in contrast, in the objectives (i.e., approaches) they pursue, reflecting differences in their expertise. While there is often uncertainty about how best to achieve a particular technological objective, we have abstracted from this kind of uncertainty because it would not readily explain the regularities in industry R&D intensity distributions. Indeed, it does not readily explain why R&D intensities of firms in an industry should differ at all in any systematic way (Cohen and Klepper, 1991).

[11] Holding industry output constant, an increase in the number of firms will reduce the average firm size. If the probability of a firm pursuing an approach were positively related to its size, then the increase in the number of firms would decrease the probability of any firm pursuing any given approach. Then the probability of any given approach not being pursued by any firm in the industry could fall with an increase in the number of firms, which would cause the expected amount of diversity to fall.

[12] In our framework, if the probability of pursuing an approach were positively related to the size of the firm, then larger firms would be expected to pursue a greater number of approaches to innovation, causing them to have above average R&D intensities.

[13] This is plausible if some of the approaches proposed in the large firm are proposed by multiple individuals. In that case, if the larger firm were broken into two firms, there would be some probability that the technical personnel in each of the smaller firms would propose the same approach.

[14] Another reason firms of equal size might pursue a greater number of distinct approaches than one firm twice their size is that most firms tend to funnel control over their R&D operations for a given industry through one individual, and that individual will naturally reflect his/her own expertise and perceptions in the decisions that are made. Thus, regardless of the firm's size, the approaches that are pursued will tend to reflect one individual's judgment. Indeed, a recent article in the *The Wall Street Journal* (Rigdon, 1991) about Kodak's research on filmless cameras highlighted the importance — and difficulty — of decentralizing high-level R&D decision-making authority when a firm becomes aware of a distinct and viable new approach to innovation within an industry. It noted that while the research team working on new filmless camera technology has been given its own budget and autonomy over hiring decisions, the same individual who oversees research on more conventional film technologies also oversees this research, which may ultimately inhibit Kodak's willingness or ability to pursue the new technology.

[15] In a static setting, imitation reinforces the gross social benefits accruing from greater diversity because the benefits from the pursuit of new approaches will be reaped by more than just the firms pursuing the new approaches. Imitation may also yield dynamic dividends. As noted by Marshall (1920, p. 271), ". . . if one man starts a new idea, it is taken up by others and combined with suggestions of their own; and thus it becomes the source of further new ideas . . ." Thus, pursuing a given approach may stimulate other firms "to improve it, variegate it, more generally contribute to its further advance," (Nelson, 1989, p. 6) even in ways that cannot be anticipated when the approach is first pursued. Von Weizsacker (1980) also recognized this point when he explored the implications of "sequential innovations" for the welfare effects of entry barriers.

[16] We managed to sidestep this cost in the example we used earlier to illustrate the benefits of large firm size by focusing on the merger of two firms that pursued the same approaches to innovation. This insured that the merger of the firms did not reduce the diversity of approaches pursued in the industry. However, firms generally will not pursue the identical set of approaches to innovation, so that consolidations will be expected to compromise the collective number of approaches to innovation pursued in the industry.

[17] Others, such as Nelson (1981), have also recognized a tradeoff between the diversity-inducing advantage of more competitive industry structures and advantages of large firm size, but not the particular tradeoff we have identified.

[18] Cohen and Klepper (1990) demonstrate that if firms can sell some fraction of their innovations in disembodied form or

if growth due to innovation is unconditioned by existing output levels, then large firm size will confer less of an advantage and R&D effort should rise less than proportionally with firm size.

References

Andrews, K. R., 1971, *The Concept of Corporate Strategy*, Homewood, Illinois: Dow Jones-Irwin.

Arrow, K., 1962, 'Economic Welfare and the Allocation of Resources for Inventions', in R. R. Nelson (ed.), *The Rate and Direction of Inventive Activity*, Princeton, NJ: Princeton University Press for the National Bureau of Economic Research.

Baldwin, W. L. and J. T. Scott, 1987, *Market Structure and Technological Change*, Chur: Harwood Academic Publishers.

Cohen, W. M. and S. Klepper, 1990, 'A Reprise of Size and R&D', mimeo, Carnegie Mellon University.

Cohen, W. M. and S. Klepper, 1991, 'The Anatomy of Industry R&D Intensity Distributions', *American Economic Review*, forthcoming.

Cohen, W. M. and D. Levinthal, 1989, 'Innovation and Learning: The Two Faces of R&D', *Economic Journal* 99, 569—596.

Cohen, W. M. and D. Levinthal, 1990, 'Absorptive Capacity: A New Perspective on Innovation and Learning', *Administrative Science Quarterly* 35, 128—152.

Evenson, R. E. and Y. Kislev, 1976, 'A Stochastic Model of Applied Research', *Journal of Political Economy* 84, 265—281.

Ferguson, C. H., 1988, 'From the People Who Brought You Voodoo Economics', *Harvard Business Review* (May—June), 55—62.

Fisher, F. M. and P. Temin, 1973, 'Returns to Scale in Research and Development: What Does the Schumpeterian Hypothesis Imply?', *Journal of Political Economy* 81, 56—70.

Gilder, G., 1988, 'The Revitalization of Everything: The Law of the Microcosm', *Harvard Business Review* (March—April), 49—61.

Jorde, T. M. and D. J. Teece, 1990, 'Innovation and Cooperation: Implications for Competition and Antitrust', *The Journal of Economic Perspectives* 4, 75—96.

Kamien, M. I. and N. L. Schwartz, 1982, *Market Structure and Innovation*, Cambridge: Cambridge University Press.

Katz, M. L. and J. A. Ordover, 1990, 'R&D Cooperation and Competition', *Brookings Papers on Economic Activity, Microeconomics*, 137—203.

Klepper, S. and E. Graddy, 1990, 'The Evolution of New Industries and the Determinants of Market Structure', *The Rand Journal of Economics* 21, 27—44.

Levin, R. C., A. Klevorick, R. Nelson and S. Winter, 1987, 'Appropriating the Returns from Industrial Research and Development', *Brookings Papers on Economic Activity* 3, 783—820.

Link, A. N. and L. L. Bauer, 1989, *Cooperative Research in U.S. Manufacturing — Assessing Policy Initiatives and Corporate Strategies*, Lexington, Mass.: Lexington Books.

Marshall, A., 1961, *Principles of Economics*, New York: The Macmillan Company, 9th (variorum) edition, Vol. 1, with annotations by C. W. Guillebaud (based on New York: The Macmillan Company, 8th edition, 1920).

Nelson, R. R., 1981, 'Assessing Private Enterprise: An Exegesis of Tangled Doctrine', *The Bell Journal of Economics* 12, 93—111.

Nelson, R. R., 1982, 'The Role of Knowledge in R&D Efficiency', *Quarterly Journal of Economics* 97, 453—470.

Nelson, R. R., 1989, 'What Is 'Commercial' and What Is 'Public' About Technology, and What Should Be?', mimeo, presented at the Conference on Economic Growth and the Commercialization of New Technologies, Stanford University, September 11—12, 1989.

Nelson, R. R., 1990, 'Capitalism as an Engine of Progress', *Research Policy* 19, 193—214.

Nelson, R. R. and S. G. Winter, 1982, *An Evolutionary Theory of Economic Change*, Cambridge: Harvard University Press.

Nelson, R. R., M. J. Peck and E. D. Kalachek, 1967, *Technology, Economic Growth, and Public Policy*, Washington: Brookings Institution.

Norris, W. C., 1983, 'How to Expand R&D Cooperation', *Business Week*, April 11, p. 21.

Noyce, R. N., 1990, 'Cooperation Is the Best Way to Beat Japan', *New York Times*, July 9, Section 3, p. 2.

Porter, M. E., 1980, *Competitive Strategy: Techniques for Analyzing a Business, Industry and Competitors*, New York: Free Press.

Rigdon, J. E., 1991, 'Kodak Tries to Prepare for Filmless Era Without Inviting Demise of Core Business', *The Wall Street Journal*, April 18, 1991, B1, B5.

Rogers, T. J., 1990, 'Landmark Messages from the Microcosm', *Harvard Business Review* (January—February), 24—30.

Sah, R. J. and J. E. Stiglitz, 1986, 'The Architecture of Economic Systems: Hierarchies and Polyarchies', *American Economic Review* 76, 716—727.

Sah, R. J. and J. E. Stiglitz, 1988, 'Committees, Hierarchies and Polyarchies', *Economic Journal* 98, 451—470.

Scherer, F. M., 1970, *Industrial Market Structure and Economic Performance*, 1st edition, Chicago: Rand McNally College Publishing Company.

Scherer, F. M., 1979, 'The Welfare Economics of Product Variety: An Application to the Ready-to-Eat Cereals Industry', *Journal of Industrial Economics* 28, 113—134.

Scherer, F. M., 1980, *Industrial Market Structure and Economic Performance*, 2nd edition, Chicago: Rand McNally College Publishing Company.

Scherer, F. M. and D. Ross, 1990, *Industrial Market Structure and Economic Performance*, 3rd edition, Boston: Houghton Mifflin.

Schumpeter, J. A., 1934, *The Theory of Economic Development*, Cambridge: Harvard University Press.

Schumpeter, J. A., 1942, *Capitalism, Socialism, and Democracy*, New York: Harper.

Scott, J. T., 1988, 'Diversification Versus Cooperation in

R&D Investment', *Managerial and Decision Economics* **9**, 173—186.

Scott, J., 1991, 'Research Diversity and Technical Change', in Z. Acs and D. Audretsch (eds.), *Innovation and Technical Change*, Ann Arbor: University of Michigan Press, pp. 132—151.

Shaffer, R. A., 1990, 'Let a Thousand Companies Fight', *New York Times*, July 9, Section 3, p. 2.

Spence, A. M., 1984, 'Cost Reduction, Competition, and Industry Performance', *Econometrica* **52**, 101—121.

Von Weizsacker, C. C., 1980, *Barriers to Entry*, New York: Springer-Verlag.

[19]

SOME LESSONS FROM THE EAST ASIAN MIRACLE

Joseph E. Stiglitz

The rapid economic growth of eight East Asian economies, often called the "East Asian miracle," raises two questions: What policies and other factors contributed to that growth? And can other developing countries replicate those policies to stimulate equally rapid growth?

This article, based on case studies, econometric data, and economic theory, offers a list of the ingredients that contributed to that success. But it is the combination of these ingredients, many of which involve government interventions acting together, that accounts for East Asia's success.

The remarkable success of the economies of East Asia raises the question: to what can that success be attributed? In most of the eight economies that are part of the "East Asian miracle"—Hong Kong, Indonesia, Japan, the Republic of Korea, Malaysia, Singapore, Taiwan (China), and Thailand—government undertook major responsibility for the promotion of economic growth. Which policies contributed to the success of these economies, and why? Ascertaining what would have happened in the absence of the specified policy is often difficult. That the government subsidized a sector that grew rapidly does not imply that the growth should be attributed to the government's action. The sector might have grown without government intervention.

This article is an interpretive essay based on case studies, econometric data, and economic theory. In formulating a coherent explanation of East Asia's experience, I do not present a formula or a simple recipe, but rather a list of ingredients. Because these ingredients are interactive, and because they were introduced in conjunction with other policies, the government's approach has to be evaluated as a package. Indeed, East Asia's success was based on a combination of factors, particularly the high savings rate interacting with high levels of human capital accumulation, in a stable, market-oriented environment—but one with active government intervention—that was conducive to the transfer of technology.[1]

Each of the economies is unique; each differs in its history and culture. Some, such as Singapore and Hong Kong, are small city-states. Others are large. Many

The World Bank Research Observer, vol. 11, no. 2 (August 1996), pp. 151–77

151

are racially and culturally homogeneous; some, such as Malaysia, are culturally diverse. But it seems implausible to attribute the success of each of these countries to special factors; the task instead is to discover the common threads.

Moreover, the unique factors typically refer to certain cultural aspects, such as a Confucian heritage, that are suspect: not that long ago, the Confucian heritage, with its emphasis on traditional values, was cited as an explanation for why these countries had not grown. To be sure, cultural factors may play an important role: the stress on education has contributed much to the success of these countries.

Statistical Explanations

Having expressed reservations about the usefulness of cultural explanations, it is important to note as well the limitations to the standard statistical techniques. For almost four decades (Solow 1957), the standard approach has been to ask to what extent this growth can be explained by increases in inputs, that is, human and physical capital, and expenditures for the acquisition of technology. In this approach, the "miracle" is the amount of this growth that cannot be so explained (the residual). Several such studies have argued that the East Asian experience can largely be explained by rapid increases in inputs—high levels of investment and heavy expenditures for education. Krugman (1994) and Young (1993, 1995) argue that essentially all of the growth in Singapore can be so explained. Others, such as Kim and Lau (1993) and World Bank (1993), find more evidence of a positive residual, but even then it is not unusually high. There are a variety of technical reasons why the applicability of this methodology to at least several of the East Asian countries should be suspect. Whatever their flaws, however, these studies still offer an important lesson: policies that increase the accumulation of physical and human capital are likely to lead to more rapid growth. The real problem is what these studies leave unanswered. The unique and changing circumstances of each country and the multitude of programs involved, each with a number of potentially important features, imply that a statistical study would be relevant only for addressing the broadest questions: were savings rates unusually high, or were financial restraints associated with faster rates of economic growth? Such studies do not identify those features that facilitated what in retrospect was a remarkable transformation of the economy. To understand this transformation, answers must be found to the following:

First, why were saving rates so high? Elsewhere, such saving rates had only been attained under the compulsion of strong government force, as in the Communist countries. Although studies suggest that these saving rates may be explained in part by economic factors—such as high growth rates that spurred high saving rates, as consumption lagged increases in incomes (Carroll, Weil, and Summers 1993; Stiglitz and Uy 1996)—government actions also played an important role in mobilizing savings (although this "virtuous cycle" between growth and savings was important as well).

Second, how was it possible to invest efficiently at such a rapid pace? To be sure, if life consisted of nothing more than adding homogeneous capital to a homogeneous production process, East Asia's success would hardly be remarkable. But in that case other countries that attempted to invest rapidly would have had far more success than they have had.

Third, how was it possible to reduce the technology gap so quickly? Clearly, more was entailed than just buying technology. To encourage the transfer of technology from foreign investors, the East Asian economies made enormous investments in human capital, educating large numbers of skilled engineers able to absorb and adapt the most advanced technology. And the East Asian economies were willing to accept foreign investment and create an economic atmosphere conducive to its entry.[2] Moreover, they combined these efforts with an emphasis on the most technologically advanced investment.

And finally how did East Asia ensure that the benefits of rapid growth were spread widely among the population? Previous theories suggested that rapid growth was associated with rapid capital accumulation, which in turn was associated with high degrees of inequality; and that growth would in fact be accompanied by an increase in the degree of inequality (Kuznets 1955). Not only did this assumption prove to be false, but there are reasons to believe that government policies that promoted greater equality contributed in no small measure to the remarkable growth of these countries.

Metaphors of Economic Growth

Several metaphors are used to describe the process of economic growth. These metaphors undoubtedly influence how we think about the subject.

An Engine Metaphor

Perhaps the most popular metaphor is that which refers to the engine of growth—as if there were a motor driving the performance of the economy. Capital accumulation is often given credit for being the engine of growth. And the countries of East Asia certainly have accumulated capital at an impressive rate. Sometimes the concept of capital accumulation is broadened to include human capital—the improvement in the skills of the labor force. And sometimes these two are given credit not only for their direct contribution, but also for the technical progress that might not have occurred in their absence.

Once one identifies the engine of growth, one tries to make the engine stronger. Thus, if capital accumulation is the engine, the task is to increase capital accumulation. The role of government is to rev up the engine to encourage a higher rate of capital accumulation. The engine metaphor has some important limitations: it encourages a search for particular factors that account for growth, although it may in fact be the system as a whole, including the interactions among the parts, that accounts for growth. If human capital accumulation is inadequate, even rapid physical capital accumulation may be ineffective. But if both are required, which one is *the* engine?

A Chemical Metaphor

I prefer two other metaphors for thinking about the growth process. One is borrowed from chemistry: the government as catalyst. The government can be a catalyst for growth without necessarily providing a great deal of resources. Indeed, that is the remarkable property of catalysts—having set off a chemical reaction, they are themselves not used up in the process. At the very least this metaphor warns that the effect of some government policy should not be measured simply by asking about the magnitude of the subsidy or what fraction of the funds was provided by the government. More concretely, investments in human capital and infrastructure, both physical and institutional, can increase the private return to investment and thereby promote growth.

A Biological Metaphor

The second metaphor, "adaptive systems," is borrowed from biological terminology. Species that survive adapt to changes in their surroundings. More advanced species survive in part because of their ability to learn. Thus the most important characteristic for survival is not a particular policy, but the ability to respond to changes in the environment and to learn from past mistakes. Adaptability is often said to distinguish private sector enterprises from government bureaucracy. But government, because of its monopoly powers, can survive even if it does not adapt well or quickly. The East Asian economies demonstrated that government too can be highly adaptive. When changes in the environment made previously adopted policies inappropriate, these governments changed course, and they learned quickly from their mistakes. As their economies grew and became more complex, the state's role clearly had to change: there was neither the need nor the capacity for active intervention on the scale previously assumed. And officials recognized the importance of adopting policies to promote higher levels of technology and higher value-added industries.

A Metaphor from Physics

One metaphor has been omitted from this list—the one that has in fact dominated the economics profession for almost a century—the economy as an equilibrium system. The omission is deliberate: it is a metaphor that provides little insight into the dramatic changes that occurred in these societies. The equilibrium metaphor suggests that individuals had (perhaps rational) expectations concerning future rates of return; given those expectations, they determined their saving rate; meanwhile, profit-maximizing firms scoured the world looking for the best products and technologies to employ, given the costs of adjustment. In this metaphor, too, government played at most an ancillary role. This metaphor leaves unasked—and unanswered—such fundamental questions as, What set the East Asian countries apart from other countries? Why is their experience so different?

Complementing Markets Rather Than Replacing Them

Before the East Asia miracle there were two dominant paradigms for development, one focused on markets, the other on government and planning. The first had its intellectual roots in Adam Smith's "invisible hand": markets lead to efficient outcomes. All that government needs to do to promote growth is get out of the way. The basic slogan is "get the prices right." With the right prices, everyone will have an incentive to make the right resource allocations. Undermining this particular religion was the disturbing observation that countries that seemed to get the prices right—to follow all the advice of the visiting preachers of the free market—too often failed to grow. To be sure, like medieval medicine, there was always the allegation that the patient had not followed the doctor's orders precisely, and it was this that accounted for the failure of the remedy.

At the opposite side were those who had little faith in the market and who looked to government to ensure through the planning process that resources were deployed in a way that promoted economic growth. The lack of success of those countries that followed this paradigm has led to the virtual extinction of this school of thought.

Ironically, almost none of the successful industrial countries followed either of these extreme strategies. They are mixed economies in which government plays an important role. The appropriate question to be asked is not whether government should play a role, but what role and how can it be performed most effectively.

At the same time that the success of the East Asian economies and the collapse of the socialist economies called into question the standard paradigm, advances in economic theory called into question the intellectual foundations of these two approaches. In the mid-1950s Arrow and Debreu (1954) identified several conditions that must be satisfied if markets are to yield efficient outcomes. These include, first, the absence of externalities (external economies or diseconomies that affect the activity in question) and of public goods (commodities or services that, once provided, can be obtained without payment by others); second, the presence of perfect competition; and, third, a complete set of markets, including markets extending infinitely far into the future and covering all risks. A market failure is said to occur where these conditions are not satisfied. This approach identified specific interventions by the government to correct each market failure, for instance, pollution taxes to correct for environmental damage. Government had a well-defined, highly circumscribed role.

It was not until thirty years later, however, that the full limits of the market mechanism became well understood. Hidden in Arrow and Debreu's framework were strong assumptions about information and technology. In their model information need not be perfect, but it could not change as a result of actions taken within the economy. Greenwald and Stiglitz (1986) showed that whenever information was imperfect or markets were incomplete, government could devise interventions that filled in for these imperfections and that could make everyone better off. Because information was never perfect and markets never complete, these results completely undermined the standard theoretical basis for relying on the market mechanism. Similarly the standard models ignored changes in technology; for a variety of reasons markets may underinvest in research and development (see, for example, Stiglitz 1987, 1988, and Arrow 1962). Because developing economies have underdeveloped (missing) markets and imperfect information and because the development process is associated with acquiring new technology (new information), these reservations about the adequacy of market mechanisms may be particularly relevant to developing countries (Stiglitz 1989).

The modern theory of market failures recognizes, however, that government interventions may not actually improve matters. Theories of regulatory capture and rent-seeking imply that government interventions may contribute to inefficient resource allocation, and whatever their weaknesses, these theories have sufficient plausibility to suggest that governments need to exercise caution. How the government intervenes may matter a great deal.

The fundamental mistake of the countries of the former Soviet Union and those developing countries that tried to rely on planning was that they sought to correct market failures by replacing the market. The governments of East Asia, by contrast, recognized the limitations of markets but confined the government's role to

- Policies that actively sought to ensure macroeconomic stability.
- Making markets work more effectively by, for instance, regulating financial markets.
- Creating markets where they did not exist.
- Helping to direct investment to ensure that resources were deployed in ways that would enhance economic growth and stability.
- Creating an atmosphere conducive to private investment and ensured political stability.

In short, rather than replacing markets, these governments promoted and used them. Such interventions had to be carefully balanced; if they were too heavy-handed, they might have squelched the market. This agenda required government to design interventions in a way that reduced the likelihood of rent-seeking behavior and that increased its ability to adapt to changing circumstances. One such mechanism was a performance-based reward structure that provided strong growth-oriented incentives and served as a basis for awarding government subsidies. This structure was relatively free from corruption and helped to direct resources to areas that produced high economic returns. Another essential step was to design a civil service system based on merit, which compensated employees well and built in provisions that reduced the dangers of corruption.

In this discussion, the interventions are organized around four major themes: industrial policies, cooperation and competition, equality, and export-led growth. Some of the most important actions to promote economic growth were directed to the financial market, and these interventions are the subject of the accompanying article in this journal by Stiglitz and Uy.

Industrial Policies

Industrial policies are directed at developing and encouraging certain sectors. What were these industrial policies? Why were they adopted? And did they work, either by directing resources to desired areas or, more broadly, in promoting economic growth?

What Policies Were Pursued?

Most countries shared three objectives: developing technological capabilities; promoting exports; and building the domestic capacity to manufacture a range of intermediate goods (such as plastics and steel). Support for particular industries and imports of the necessary foreign technology took several forms. First, the support for education—particularly engineering and science education—provided an intellectual infrastructure that facilitated technological transfer. Second, the decision to discourage (through financial market regulations) the allocation of capital to areas such as real estate meant that more capital was available for areas with higher technological benefits, such as plants and equipment. Third, as discussed later, the government encouraged exports. Fourth, in some industries, particularly those with many firms, government promoted technology programs, including science centers that offered services ranging from identifying new products to providing research and development for firms that had no facilities of their own. Taiwan (China) and Malaysia developed industrial parks for high-technology industries, both to allow firms to capture some of the diffuse externalities associated with these industries as well as to lower the barriers to entry. (Diffuse externalities arise when the actions of one firm benefit—or confer costs upon—many firms, rather than, say, just one upstream firm or one downstream firm.) And finally, the government provided explicit and implicit subsidies (through cheap credit) to industries it wished to support.

An important element in the expansion of certain industries was a receptivity to direct foreign investment. The East Asian economies not only resisted xenophobic aversions to foreign investments, but they also induced capital inflows by providing sound macroeconomic management, a stable political environment, and well-managed labor markets with educated workers. In many cases governments took explicit steps to ensure that a transfer of technological and human capital would accompany these inflows. Foreign investment increased the pace of expansion, reducing the constraints imposed by limitations on the availability of capital, domestic entrepreneurship, and technological know-how.

Why Were Industrial Policies Adopted?

Market failures are likely to be particularly significant in developing countries for several reasons.[3] Understanding these market failures helps explain the policies that were adopted and the reasons they were so effective.

WEAK AND NONEXISTENT MARKETS. In the early stages of development, markets often do not exist or work well, so prices may not provide good signals for resource allocation. In East Asia capital markets were particularly weak, leading government to create institutions to promote savings (the postal savings banks) and to extend long-term credit (the development banks). Governments also tried to develop the financial infrastructure by helping to establish bond and equity markets (Stiglitz and Uy 1996).

Having promoted savings, governments had to decide how to allocate these funds. If there had been well-established market institutions for allocating long-term capital, governments could have made use of those institutions. But because the governments had to decide how to allocate resources, it was natural to direct the funds to projects that would yield the highest level of social welfare.

TECHNOLOGICAL SPILLOVERS. Private markets have inadequate incentives for investing in the production and acquisition of technology, largely because it is difficult to appropriate the returns to knowledge. Developing countries typically operate at a level of technology far below that of industrial countries; development is, to a large extent, the process of acquiring and adapting existing technologies. Patent protection ensures that the seller can command some payment for new technology, but it does not provide much protection for a firm that transfers and adapts an existing technology. Adopting and adapting new technologies involves a risk. If successes are quickly imitated, then firms face a "heads I lose, tails you win" situation: when they succeed, there is little profit because of the force of competition; when they fail, they lose money.

MARKETING SPILLOVERS. Still another kind of valuable information concerns marketing. Knowing where there is a market for a product is not information that can be kept secret. If a firm spends money to discover that Americans like madras shirts, then any manufacturer of madras shirts can take advantage of that information. The converse is that the products of a country establish a reputation. Thus, Japan's reputation for high quality benefits all Japanese producers.

Such marketing spillovers have led governments to adopt programs aimed at promoting the country's products. (In Hong Kong these programs are financed by a special tax. In Singapore they are directed by the powerful Economic Development Board.) Spillovers have also resulted in an array of programs to improve the countries' reputation. Most notable in this respect is the recent effort by Taiwan (China) to encourage its domestic firms to obtain brand recognition.

RETURNS TO SCALE: a problematic explanation. Not all of the arguments advanced as rationales for industrial policies are persuasive, however. One that seemed particularly influential in Japan held that government intervention was required to rationalize industry. It was argued that without government support, firms would be too small, and the large number of such firms would reduce the profitability of all firms in a sector. (Thus, the Japanese government not only condoned the increased concentration in the steel industry in the late 1960s but, in one of its most famous mistakes, tried to discourage Honda—at the time a successful manufacturer of motorcycles—from entering the automobile market.) This argument is unpersuasive because if there truly were increasing returns to scale, then a single firm would benefit by increasing its production; in time its costs would be lowered, and it would then be able to undercut its rivals. Natural economic forces lead to the rationalization of industries without government intervention.

A slight variant of the argument about returns to scale does have some validity. Increasing returns combined with a shortage of capital may stunt small firms. They cannot expand to take advantage of increasing returns either because they cannot get access to capital or because the only form of capital to which they have access is credit, which imposes too high a risk. In this case, government intervention can lower the costs of capital and increase economic efficiency.

Increasing returns, especially when combined with capital market imperfections, provide the foundation for strategic trade policy. Historically, arguments for government trade interventions focused on industries with learning by doing. If today's production lowers future marginal costs, that creates a form of increasing returns akin to the more familiar static increasing returns. A firm that expands production lowers its future production costs and undercuts its rivals. The infant industry argument holds that protection is important so that the young firm can gain the experience required to lower its production costs and allow it to become viable. Critics of this argument claim that if the firm is to be profitable in the long run, it should incur any necessary losses today. But this assumption is based on the premise that capital markets are perfect. With imperfect capital markets, a firm may not be able to sustain the losses that would enable it to produce at a level at which it would eventually become profitable.

Moreover, if the firm is unable to appropriate all the returns to its learning, then social returns to production will exceed private returns (Dasgupta and Stiglitz 1988). In addition, dominant firms in industrial countries are likely to take advantage of the lack of competition that prevails when learning is important by raising prices and increasing their profits. Government policies may be directed at trying to appropriate some of these rents (the excess profits that result from a dominant competitive position).

COORDINATION FAILURES. The widespread absence of markets in developing countries means that prices cannot perform their coordination role. Government may thus have to assume a more active role in performing this function. The traditional examples relate to the development of downstream and upstream industries: developing a steel-manufacturing industry does not pay unless there is a steel-using industry; and developing a steel-using industry does not pay if there is no steel-manufacturing industry. If both wait, nothing happens. According to this view, the government has an important function in coordinating the two activities. Such coordination failures, it is argued, are likely to be most important when the returns to scale are large. For instance, if manufacturing steel is deemed to be desirable, it is necessary to build a large steel plant and a large steel-using industry. Other market failures, such as the absence of risk markets, interact with this failure: large risks are likely to accompany such large-scale investments, and the market provides no mechanism by which these risks can be divested. Moreover, no single entrepreneur could amass the capital required, and the imperfections of the capital market mean that it cannot supply the funds required. Developing countries are less likely than industrial countries to have the organizations capable of undertaking these large investments in a single sector, let alone the capacity to undertake the investments in both the upstream and downstream firms. Thus coordination problems may be larger in developing countries, and the capacity to deal with them may be smaller.

The earlier arguments for coordination failures (Rosenstein-Rodan 1943 and Murphy, Shleifer, and Vishny 1989) were rightly criticized as unpersuasive (Stiglitz 1994a). Such a problem could easily be addressed through trade—one of the solutions devised by the East Asian countries (without benefit of the theoretical literature). It is possible to develop a steel-using industry simply by importing steel and to develop steel producers without steel users simply by exporting steel.

In the early stages of rapid growth, the subsectors responsible for the takeoff in many, if not most, of the East Asian countries—textiles, footwear, sporting goods, toys—were not those in which economies of scale or coordination problems seemed important. But there was a more subtle form of returns to scale in which government intervention did matter and which affected growth even in these areas: the availability of a wide range of intermediate—often fairly complex—goods, tailored for the producers of final goods. The sellers of these intermediate goods do not capture all of the benefits that their greater availability provides. The improved two-way flow of information between the producer and the user, which permits better coordination in the development of the intermediate and final goods, is a benefit of proximity. That explains why importing the intermediate good does not serve as a perfect substitute for domestic production and also provides a rationale for government intervention. In Malaysia it is claimed that the local auto manufacturer has provided important spillovers to the intermediate goods firms that produce parts and that these firms, in turn, have benefited producers of other final goods.

STRATEGIC NEGOTIATIONS. In negotiations with other countries or companies, the governments of East Asia have often recognized—and taken advantage of— the nature of the market environment. The outcome of any bargaining depends on the strength of competition on both sides. By reducing competition among buyers of technology and trying to increase competition among sellers, the governments succeeded in appropriating more of the surplus associated with the transfer of technology than otherwise could have been captured. In Japan, for instance, a single firm was sometimes given the right to negotiate a licensing agreement; it might then be compelled to share the technology with other firms in the industry.

Did These Policies Work?

Industrial policies have been widely criticized, on the (somewhat contradictory) grounds that they were ineffective or distortionary. The first criticism suggests that industrial policies are more form than substance. Critics cite statistics such as the small percentage of loans made by the development banks. These statistics are unconvincing, however: the consequences of, say, a loan by the Industrial Bank of Japan may be far greater than the actual dollars lent, because of either its signaling or risk-sharing effect (Stiglitz and Uy 1996). Government policies that increase the equity of a firm can have immense effects through the power of leveraging. Beyond that, there was a wide range of instruments for effecting industrial policies; it is the cumulative effect of all of these that matters. The criticism is more properly directed at those who have suggested that Japan's Ministry of International Trade and Industry totally controlled the allocation of resources. This assumption is wrong on two counts. First, firms made most of the decisions about resource allocation—influenced, to be sure, by government policies, but not directly controlled by them. None of the East Asian countries is a command-and-control economy. Second, the view that government makes decisions on its own seems misguided. Consultation between business and government was extensive (and many of the top leaders of business were former government employees).

The charge that industrial policy was distortionary, however, is of more concern. Even if there is a rationale for government intervention, this view alleges that government does not do a good job at picking winners. Instances of mistakes by the government are typically cited. In some cases the government discouraged a firm (Honda, for example), when in retrospect it clearly should not have; and in others the government encouraged some industry (such as petrochemicals), when in retrospect it probably should not have.

There are four responses to this criticism. First, good decisionmaking by the government necessarily involves making mistakes: a policy that supported only sure winners would have taken no risks. The relatively few mistakes speak well for the government's ability to pick winners. Second, the government was not heavy-handed. Although it made mistakes of judgment, it did not force its opinions on others when they were willing to risk their own capital. This is one of the strengths of decentralized decisionmaking: it ensures that mistaken views will not dominate.

Third, to a large extent, government policies were not directed at picking winners in the narrow sense of the term. Several governments decided to support export-oriented industries. In a sense, that was choosing a winning development strategy; it did not necessarily entail micromanaging. Even when the government identified an industry for support, the banks seem to have had discretion to select which firms or projects within that industry to support.

Fourth, industrial policies were focused not so much on picking winners as on identifying market failures—instances where investors could not capture large potential spillovers. Concern about such spillovers helps explain the government's encouragement of high technology industries. Training provides another example. Firms would benefit from a trained labor force, but, because workers can leave for a better job once they are trained, firms have inadequate incentives to proceed with training. Yet a skilled work force is essential for economic growth, so government undertook to improve the quality of the labor force by emphasizing education.

Moreover, the criticism of industrial policies as misguided attempts to pick winners ignores the broader range of government actions, such as its role in spearheading the expansion of certain manufacturing sectors. "Picking winners" seems to imply culling from a fixed pool of applicants to find those with the highest long-run social returns. East Asian governments have instead performed an entrepreneurial role. Entrepreneurship requires combining technological and marketing knowledge, a vision of the future, a willingness to take risks, and an ability to raise capital. In early stages of development, these ingredients are typically in short supply. The governments in East Asia stepped in to fill the gap—but in a way that promoted rather than thwarted the development of private entrepreneurship.

Government was also effective in monitoring the recipients of its support and ensuring that they did not siphon off funds for private use. Other government policies, such as those that led to more equity financing, reduced the magnitude of the monitoring problem; that is, they resulted in firms having more appropriate incentives. Still other policies, such as those that enhanced the stability of the banking system, led to more effective monitoring by financial institutions.

Cooperation and Competition

Popular discussions of the success of Japan and several other East Asian countries have stressed the cooperative relations between government and business, between workers and employers, and between small and large businesses. Clearly, the extent of this cooperation (sometimes referred to as "Japan Inc."), has been exaggerated. Yet a variety of institutions and practices facilitate cooperation, and this kind of cooperation appears to have had beneficial effects. Adam Smith's "invisible hand" of perfect competition argues that because each individual, in pursuing his self-interest, is also maximizing the common welfare, cooperation is not necessary. But when market failures occur, it is not necessarily the case that the selfish pursuit of self-interest leads to efficient outcomes.

The governments of East Asia recognized that the business community had superior information about investment decisions, but they also recognized that the overall information base could be improved. The establishment of formal and informal councils gave rival firms and industries a way to exchange information with each other and with the government. (This information exchange process is sometimes described as akin to indicative planning, but the analogy is, at best, an imperfect one.) These exchanges conveyed far more information than the traditional format used to display planned sectoral inputs and outputs. What made them more meaningful than such exchanges in other countries? Why would businesses, or government for that matter, tell the truth?

To a large extent, good behavior is induced through long-term relationships and reputations. In the process of development, social sanctions become less effective in enforcing cooperative behavior, but establishing and maintaining alternative bases for cooperative relations may be difficult. The gains from cooperation are based on the perception that the future returns to cooperation exceed the short-run gains that might accrue from the pursuit of self-interest. But an environment of rapid change may heighten uncertainty about the value of the future relationship and the magnitude of the long-term gains from cooperation. Moreover, future cooperative gains have to be discounted (meaning that, because they may not materialize in the future, they are worth less in today's terms). Typically uncertainty is greater and discount rates higher in developing countries. Further, concerns about the potential bankruptcy of one or the other firm, which could terminate the relationship, heighten the likelihood that cooperative relationships will not materialize. Under these circumstances, future gains from cooperation must be greater to compensate firms for sacrificing the short-run gains from self-interested behavior.

Encouraging Cooperation

The Japanese government used both carrots and sticks to encourage cooperation and the exchange of truthful information. Although cultural characteristics are often credited with facilitating this harmonious result, other countries with similar cultural backgrounds have not displayed the same sort of cooperative behavior seen in Japan. It seems far more likely that government actions were more important than culture in shaping these behavioral patterns.

Of the institutions and mechanisms that facilitated cooperation, an important role was played by business councils set up to share reliable and timely information. Why did not some businesses try to "free ride," to obtain the information provided by others while providing no real information themselves? The answer is, in part, that they were in a longer-term relationship; a firm that "cheated" would be ostracized from the circle. The fact that the government was included in these circles was important: firms wanted to know what the government was thinking about specific projects or what policy changes were planned. Even if a firm's cooperative instincts went astray, self-interest was a strong incentive. Moreover, by paying attention to these councils, the government ensured that the gains from cooperation were even greater.

The government's discretionary powers enabled it to reward cooperation and honesty, and there was at least a fear that the lack of cooperation and the appearance of dishonesty would be punished. Government intervention in markets created rents that the government could then allocate to participants who behaved cooperatively. For example, by restricting the formation of branch banks, a large franchise value was associated with the right to have a branch. Similarly, restricting credit meant that access to credit had value. And the Bank of Japan (the central bank) could, on a discretionary basis, provide banks with additional funds when needed.

The relative stability of the East Asian governments increased the incentives for establishing long-term cooperative relations. At the same time, long-term relations enhanced the effectiveness of incentives (Stiglitz and Weiss 1983). Firms that performed well on one project could expect to be rewarded with another project.

The East Asian governments also tried to create an environment conducive to close cooperation among businesses. In Japan, for instance, the government tried to encourage mergers. To the extent that these programs were successful (and there is considerable controversy about that), they reduced the difficulties of cooperation. The smaller the group, the easier cooperation is to attain. Here the government was walking a fine line; a small group could—and may—have led to collusion by restricting competition. In some circumstances, the government approved the formation of so-called recession cartels. These cartels were an explicit attempt to deal cooperatively (and collusively) with the problems that arise in a recession when there is excess capacity in a capital-intensive industry. Under certain conditions, as demand shifts down, prices drop and firms are unable to recover their capital costs. Recession cartels were a way to restrict competition to enable the industry in question to avoid the low prices that would damage all the firms. Whether the gains were worth the costs of reduced competition, higher prices, and underutilized resources is not clear, however. Because of the strong incentives to cheat on such arrangements, cartels are seldom successful without legal sanctions from the government. In some cases the Japanese government paid firms to destroy equipment, and in others, to seal equipment shut. Even these tactics were not always successful; some firms did not completely dismantle their equipment.

Labor markets were similarly designed to encourage cooperative behavior. The Japanese pattern of lifetime employment was important because it meant that employees had long-term relationships with employers, which facilitated cooperative behavior. The rapid increase in wages that came with age and experience provided a strong incentive for workers to stay with their organizations. The average pay of each age cohort increased sharply, but differentiation within the age cohort remained smaller than in, say, the United States. Japan's prevalent compensation scheme, in which a large part of the salary was paid as an annual bonus (based largely on profits of the previous year), also encouraged cooperation because workers had, in effect, an equity stake in the firm. This form of risk-sharing may be particularly important in early stages of development when capital markets are underdeveloped. Because wages are based on the group's performance, the individual has an incentive to monitor his peers to make sure that his co-workers are working hard (Arnott and Stiglitz 1991; Stiglitz 1990b). One might even go further. Basing salary on individual performance encourages self-interested, noncooperative behavior. Conversely, paying wages based on group performance signals the importance of cooperative behavior.

Also important in Japan's labor market was the government-established Productivity Council, which dealt with the degree of inequality that could exist within a firm and limited salaries of top managers to no more than ten times the wages of the lowest-paid workers.[4] This compressed wage structure enhanced the sense that top management was not taking advantage of workers and led to greater effort and lower labor turnover.

Cooperative behavior between firms and their employees is particularly important in facilitating technological change. Workers are often in the best position to identify improvements in efficiency, although such improvements do not always redound to the benefit of the workers. Because labor-saving innovations may result in less demand for labor and higher unemployment, employees are often reluctant to disclose such ideas. If, however, the firm provides a guarantee of lifetime employment, existing employees will see no conflict between their interests and those of the firm. Moreover, when wages are based partially on firm profitability, interests coincide: if the productivity-enhancing innovation enhances profits in the long run, employees will share in the gain. Of course, when growth is rapid firms can more easily promise that labor-saving innovations will not result in reduced employment, which makes it more credible that all (existing) employees will benefit from such innovations.

Cooperative behavior between firms and their banks was also evident in the operations of capital markets. In Japan each firm had a long-standing relationship with a single bank, and that bank played a large role in the affairs of the firm. Japanese banks, unlike American banks, are allowed to own shares in the firms to which they lend, and when their client firms are in trouble, they step in. (The fact that the bank owns shares in the firm means that there is a greater coincidence of interest than there would be if the bank were simply a creditor; see Stiglitz 1985.) This pattern of active involvement between lenders and borrowers is seen in other countries of East Asia and was actively encouraged by governments.

Another important aspect of business-government cooperation in Japan has been the attempt to reduce bankruptcies, which have been markedly less cyclical than those in the United States and other countries. This pattern reflects not only the country's better macroeconomic performance and a legal structure that encourages actions short of bankruptcy but also an active government policy directed at avoiding the economic disruption caused by bankruptcy.

Combining Competition and Cooperation

The East Asian countries succeeded (not always, but with a remarkable frequency) in harnessing the advantages of cooperation while retaining the advantages of competition. Cooperation to increase efficiency can easily be turned into collusion to raise prices and restrict output and entry. Worse still, discretionary powers needed for cooperation can give rise to rent-seeking and corruption. Competition both enhanced efficiency and reduced the scope for abuses of discretionary powers. In fostering a competitive industrial structure, governments looked not so much at the number of firms in an industry, but at the effectiveness of the competition; competition may be more effective with two evenly matched firms than with one firm competing with many small rivals (Nalebuff and Stiglitz 1983).

By the same token, the process of identifying which workers to promote in Japanese firms may be more effective in encouraging competition than is the process in the United States. In Japan, where workers are less mobile, a cohort of workers hired together advances together. They all work hard; they all have to signal that they are committed to the firm; they all remain in the contest. In the United States decisions concerning who is on an upward career ladder often take place earlier. Under that system, incentives may be strong in the early stages of individual careers, but they may be greatly attenuated once these decisions are made. Those who know that they are not going to be "winners" have little reason to work hard.

One method introduced to stimulate competition was the use of contests. Governments rewarded firms that performed well relative to others (such as in exports) by, for example, providing them with access to capital and foreign exchange. In many instances, the value of the prize arose from the government intervention: if the government had not created artificial scarcity of capital or foreign exchange, an increase in availability would have had no incentive effect.

Well-functioning contests are characterized by rules that establish a clear criterion for rewards, such as export performance; specify the nature of the reward (the allocation of credit or foreign exchange); and indicate who will evaluate performance. This system reduced the scope for abuse of bureaucratic discretion at the same time that it provided strong incentives.

Ironically, licensing requirements put in place to restrict competition may give rise to more competitive behavior. At various times, the Japanese government imposed restrictions on the expansion of capacity in certain industries. It awarded licenses to expand capacity on the basis of firms' previous market shares. Thus performance—particularly growth—in one year may increase profits not only in that year, but also in subsequent years.

Growth with Equality

Although industrial policies attempt to direct resource allocations in ways that maximize growth, income distribution policies seek to promote greater equality. Historically, the development process has been characterized by marked increases in inequality (the Kuznets curve). It was alleged that the massive amounts of capital accumulation required could only be attained through significant inequality; the poor simply could not save enough. Moreover, growth creates winners (the owners of those firms that do well), and losers (workers displaced from lagging industries, in particular agriculture). The economies of East Asia were able to achieve rapid growth without an increase in inequality. Indeed, active policies promoting equality probably enhanced growth (figure 1).

In Korea, Japan, and Taiwan (China), land reforms—at least partially imposed from the outside—were important in the initial stages of development. These had three effects: they increased rural productivity and income and resulted in increased savings; higher incomes provided the domestic demand that was important in these economies before export markets expanded; and the redistribution of income contributed to political stability, an important factor in creating a good environment for domestic and foreign investment.

In later years policies to ensure more equitable distribution of income continued to contribute to economic growth, with positive effects that more than offset the possible negative effects of reduced capital accumulation upon which earlier discussions had focused. These policies continued to contribute to political stability. High and increasing wages reduced inequality, made workers not only more satisfied but also (by standard efficiency wage arguments) more productive, and promoted cooperative relations between workers and firms. Policies that attempted to restrict real estate speculation (by limiting lending for that purpose) can be viewed both as part of industrial policy and as part of income distribution policy. While they directed funds into industry, they limited the increases in the prices of housing relative to what would otherwise have occurred. Such price increases would have led to demands for further wage in-

Figure 1. *Income Inequality and Growth of Gross Domestic Product, 1970–93*

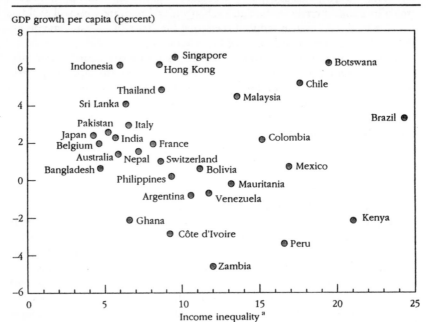

GDP growth per capita (percent)

a. Income inequality is measured by the ratio of the income shares of the richest 20 percent
and the poorest 20 percent of the population.
Source: World Bank data.

creases and would have had particularly adverse effects on the very poor, who
often seem unable to obtain adequate housing under such conditions.

Additionally, policies ensuring universal literacy both increased productivity
and promoted greater equality. The emphasis on female education led to reduced fertility, thus mitigating the adverse effects of population pressure felt in
so many developing countries, and it directly increased the supply of educated
labor. Most studies suggest that a worker's wage performance is more directly
related to nonschool factors, such as home background, than to education in
school. Education of women can be thought of as a roundabout but high-return
way of enhancing labor force productivity.

In Thailand a program to provide credit to the rural sector, although largely
motivated by concerns about communist insurgency, seemed not only to have
promoted equality but also to have yielded reasonably high economic returns.
And in Malaysia, policies that would be regarded as affirmative action elsewhere were able not only to draw upon a reservoir of human talent that had not

been well used before, but to weld together a nation that had already demonstrated a potential for ethnic strife.

There are positive relations between growth and equality. High rates of growth provided resources that could be used to promote equality, just as the high degree of equality helped sustain the high rates of growth. Although this may seem to be little more than common sense, until the experience of East Asia, "common sense" suggested quite the contrary: growth produced inequality, and inequality was necessary for growth.

Export-Oriented Growth

Why focus on exports? Should not countries simply produce the goods in which they have a comparative advantage, whether that happens to be products that are exported or substitutes for goods that are currently imported?[5] Success in exporting provided policymakers with an objective way to award credit and foreign exchange.[6] Two questions arise: why are exports a better measure of performance than profits? And second, do markets reward success in an appropriate way without government intervention?

In measuring performance to determine which firms to favor with credit and other scarce resources, governments faced an information problem. All governments face a similar problem, but in the context of development, the information problem is particularly severe for two reasons. First, relatively few firms may be engaged in similar activities, so bases of comparison are limited. Second, a host of problems must be overcome—new supplier relationships, new markets, and so on. In such circumstances, short-run profits may be imperfect indicators of long-term performance. Consider, for instance, the two sources of profits: those derived from exports, and those derived from domestic sales. The latter may reflect either the firm's efficiency or its monopoly position in the economy. The profits that result from imperfect competition in the domestic market accrue at least partially at the expense of consumers and should not be thought of as a social gain. By contrast, a firm that succeeds in the export market is more likely to be economically efficient. It can market a product at a lower price than can foreign rivals, or one better tailored for the world market. Export markets are more likely to be competitive. And even if they are not, it is of no concern: the profits of the firm are then at the expense of foreign consumers. Indeed, from the exporting country's perspective, finding a niche within which some market power can be exercised is to be rewarded, not condemned.

Other advantages are also associated with exports. Firms learn a great deal in international markets, benefiting from spillovers related to both marketing and production know-how. For instance, success in producing intermediate goods requires producing to standards that are typically higher than those that prevail within developing countries. This generates a demand for testing laboratories.

The recognition that standards are important and the knowledge about producing goods of higher quality has implications across a broad range of products. Moreover, the contacts established through exporting may be of value when the firm decides to enter related markets. It will, for instance, know where to turn to acquire advanced technology.

From a social perspective, success in exporting may be a better indicator of whether a firm merits additional funds than success in selling domestically, but banks have typically preferred lending to firms engaged in the domestic market, and for a simple reason. Banks do not care whether a firm makes social returns or private returns, as long as it can repay the loan. Banks are less informed about foreign markets and thus consider it riskier to lend for export projects than for the domestic market.

It has been argued that the preferences East Asian governments gave to exports were intended simply to offset the disadvantages of tariffs and other restrictions on imports. From this perspective, government was not promoting exports but simply "getting the prices right." Upon closer examination (even without a detailed scrutiny of the statistics), this argument appears faulty on two grounds. First, it refers to averages of exports; but what is relevant is the effective subsidy on particular exports. If some exports are encouraged and others (perhaps unintentionally) discouraged, it is apparent that government has intervened in the allocation of resources. Second, the government actually engaged in a wide range of activities beyond direct subsidies to promote exports.

Export Promotion Activities

Four activities were very important in promoting export growth: the provision of infrastructure; preferential access to capital and foreign exchange; the development of export markets; and licensing and other regulations designed to enhance the reputation of the country's exports. As noted previously, the close, long-term relationships between exporters and governments can be credited with making these mechanisms work.

THE PROVISION OF INFRASTRUCTURE. Because poor infrastructure is an important barrier to trade, East Asian governments have invested in infrastructure, including good port facilities and improved transportation systems to reduce the costs of shipping goods abroad. Transportation is not the only aspect of infrastructure that has received government attention. Singapore has been involved in efforts to provide an adequate supply of electricity and an effective telecommunications system, both vital to the country's development as a financial center.

PREFERENTIAL ACCESS TO CAPITAL AND FOREIGN EXCHANGE. Most of the countries of East Asia engaged in some degree of financial restraint, that is, capital markets were controlled to give priority industries preferential access to capital and foreign exchange (Stiglitz and Uy 1996). Although in some cases governments provided subsidies (including lower interest rates) to encourage the expansion of favored industries, most observers believe that the access to credit was far more important.

Critics of this access raise the issue of fungibility: what if the government did provide credit and funds for investment in export-oriented industries? So long as money is fungible, large conglomerates could simply divert to other uses those funds that would have been allocated to exports. Consequently, financing exports may have little incremental effect on exports. From this perspective, the allocation of capital to the export sector has no marginal effect. It has only an inframarginal effect on firms that are successful in exporting. This view, however, does not take account of the process by which funds are allocated. If past export performance is used as one of the criteria for judging the creditworthiness of the borrower, firms have an incentive to increase exports. And firms that were successful exporters had demonstrated some set of abilities. If those abilities were correlated with other abilities that enhanced the likelihood of high marginal returns to investment, then the use of export performance may have been an efficient selection mechanism.

DEVELOPING NEW EXPORT MARKETS. Information problems associated with the development of new export markets go beyond the problems of reputation. One noted earlier was the "public good" nature of information. As in the case of other public goods, a strong case can be made for public provision. And many of the East Asian economies have done just that. For instance, Singapore's Economic Development Board has actively worked on developing foreign markets and takes an active interest in what goods might be produced for export. Business executives are invited to join official trips abroad to persuade them that it is in their interests to enter into meaningful business relationships overseas.

ENHANCING THE REPUTATION OF THE COUNTRY'S EXPORTS. In the 1950s and early 1960s, Japanese products had a reputation for being shoddy. American and European buyers had little information about individual Japanese producers and were likely to make unfavorable inferences concerning any particular product. Because establishing a reputation is expensive for any firm seeking to export (particularly when consumers have strong negative prior beliefs), individual firms had little incentive to improve the quality of their products. The government conducted a concerted effort both to improve the quality of the products and to establish brand reputations for Japanese firms, so that they would have private incentives to maintain their reputation. Here is an example of an interaction between cooperative behavior and individual incentives. A similar process is occurring in Taiwan (China), where the government is effectively providing subsidies for firms to establish brand recognition. In doing so, firms will have a private incentive to maintain high quality, with positive effects on the reputation of Taiwanese products in general.

Conclusion

One of the reasons for attempting to delineate what East Asian governments did that resulted in such high growth rates is that other countries would like to replicate their success. If they did the same thing as the governments of East Asia, would they too grow at such rapid rates? To be sure, many countries did similar things, but often with adverse rather than positive effects. They created development banks, only to find that the development banks diverted scarce savings into projects with low returns and made investments that did more to line the pockets of politicians than to raise the welfare of the country. The East Asian miracle had many dimensions: rents were created, but they were used to encourage growth, not dissipated in rent-seeking. Government and businesses cooperated closely, but they collaborated without collusion. Many aspects of this transformation can be explained, and to the extent that they can be explained, it is possible that what they did can be replicated. A high rate of saving leads to high growth; allocating resources on the basis of contests and other performance-based measures can both provide high-powered incentives and reduce the scope for corruption; egalitarian policies, including active education policies, can contribute to a more stable political and economic environment and lead to faster growth through a more productive labor force. Governments that use markets and help create markets are likely to be more successful in promoting growth than governments that try to replace markets.

What generalizations can be drawn from the findings of this article? To be sure, not all of these generalizations are held with the same degree of confidence. In some cases, there are alternative interpretations of the events and evidence. But a combination of theory and evidence supports these conclusions. Included in the discussion below are several interventions in the financial market, which, although mentioned only briefly, are amplified in the accompanying article by Stiglitz and Uy in this issue. Because governments in different countries pursued somewhat different policies, not all the statements hold with equal validity in all countries; some may not even hold within all sectors of a given country. These conclusions are organized around six themes.

- *Making society function better.* Economic growth required the maintenance of macroeconomic and political stability. Policies that sustained a more equitable distribution of income—and that supported basic education for women as well as men—contributed to economic progress by encouraging political stability and cooperative behavior within the private sector. The result was a better business climate for investment and more effective use of human resources.
- *Adaptability of government policies.* Government policies adapted to changing economic circumstances, rather than remaining fixed. As the East Asian economies grew more complex, government had less need to assume an active role and found it more difficult to act effectively on a broad scale.

- *Government and markets.* Governments played an active role in creating market institutions, such as long-term development banks and capital markets to trade bonds and equities, and in establishing an institutional infrastructure that enabled markets to work more effectively. These institutions and markets helped ensure that the high volume of savings was invested efficiently. Governments also used their control of financial markets to help direct resources in ways that stimulated economic growth. This control was probably more important than direct subsidies or low interest rates. Credit was directed not only toward priority areas, but away from speculative real estate and consumer durables.

  Policies to improve government-business cooperation enabled governments to design programs that served the needs of the business community, created a favorable business climate, and encouraged business to direct its energies in ways that contributed to high social returns. Sharing information enhanced the quality of decisionmaking.

  By using, directing, and supplementing markets rather than replacing them, the private sector remained the center of economic activity in most of the East Asian countries; when the private sector disagreed with the government, it was permitted to go ahead and risk its own capital.

- *Promoting accumulation of physical and human capital.* The introduction of postal savings institutions and provident funds resulted in higher domestic savings. At the same time, measures that established prudential regulations (and in some cases, entry restrictions) enhanced the safety and soundness of financial institutions and promoted financial deepening. A variety of programs increased the returns to private investment and facilitated the development and transfer of technology; these included policies that promoted education and training, provided infrastructure, and, in most countries, established a receptivity to foreign investment.

- *Altering the allocation of resources.* Governments in East Asia used industrial policies to affect the allocation of resources in ways that would stimulate economic growth. They took an entrepreneurial role in identifying industries in which research and development would have high payoffs. Support for industry, such as the establishment of research and science centers and quality control standards, was important both in attracting foreign investment and in encouraging domestic investors. Emphasizing industries with strong backward and forward links and large externalities may have helped long-term growth. In the short term, the lack of profitability does not provide a good measure of the potential long-run contribution to growth, precisely because it is the discrepancy between private and social returns that motivates government intervention.

  Governments actively encouraged firms to export. Exports provided a performance-based criterion for allocating credit, encouraged the adoption of international standards, and accelerated the diffusion of technology. Contests among exporters were used widely as incentive devices. The essential ingredients of contests are rewards (here the allocation of credit), rules (measures of performance), and referees (who evaluate performance). In a world short of perfect competition, contests can provide strong incentives with limited risks, and, if the rules are well specified, reduce bureaucratic abuses.

- *Government policies supporting investment.* Mild financial repression had a positive effect on economic growth. The effects on national savings and on the efficiency with which scarce capital was allocated were likely positive; positive incentive effects may have been associated with the contest for scarce credit, and the increased equity of firms and banks (because of lower interest rates) enhanced their ability to bear risks. Equally important were other government programs that led to more effective risk-sharing within the economy. Risk-sharing reduced the effective cost of capital, thus stimulating investment. Government intervention in international economic relations (for instance, in bargaining for foreign technology, in impeding certain capital movements, and in insisting on certain transfers of technology as part of foreign investment) may have enhanced the national interest, promoted economic stability, and enhanced savings.

No single policy ensured success, nor did the absence of any single ingredient ensure failure. There was a nexus of policies, varying from country to country, sharing the common themes that we have emphasized: governments intervened actively in the market, but used, complemented, regulated, and indeed created markets, rather than supplanted them. Governments created an environment in which markets could thrive. Governments promoted exports, education, and technology; encouraged cooperation between government and industry and between firms and their workers; and at the same time encouraged competition.

The real miracle of East Asia may be political more than economic: why did governments undertake these policies? Why did politicians or bureaucrats not subvert them for their own self-interest? Even here, the East Asian experience has many lessons, particularly the use of incentives and organizational design within the public sector to enhance efficiency and to reduce the likelihood of corruption. The recognition of institutional and individual fallibility gave rise to a flexibility and responsiveness that, in the end, must lie at the root of sustained success.

Notes

Joseph E. Stiglitz is chairman of President Clinton's Council of Economic Advisers, on leave from Stanford University, where he is professor of economics. This is a shortened version of a paper written as part of the World Bank project on The East Asian Miracle and Public Policy. Financial and technical support of the World Bank is gratefully acknowledged. The author is particularly indebted to Marilou Uy. He has also benefited from discussions with Nancy Birdsall, John Page, Richard Sabot, Howard Pack, Edward Campos, Masahiro Okuno, Masahiko Aoki, Daniel Okimoto, Lawrence Lau, Professor Gato, Professor Baba, and dozens of other government officials, academics, bankers, and industrialists who gave generously of their time during this research project. Research assistance from Thomas Hellman is also gratefully acknowledged.

1. In the literature on this subject, particular reference should be made to the work of Alam (1989), Aoki (1988), Wade (1990), Amsden (1989), Okimoto (1989), Lau (1990), Agrawal and others (1992), Johnson (1982), Pack and Westphal (1986), Itoh and others (1984), Komiya, Okuna, and Suzumura (1988), and Vogel (1991), as well as to the country studies of the World Bank. The information theoretic foundation of the analyses presented here is set forth in greater detail in Greenwald and Stiglitz (1986, 1988, 1992), Arnott, Greenwald, and Stiglitz (1993), and Stiglitz (1994b). The implications for government policy are discussed in greater length in Stiglitz (1990a, 1991a, 1991b).

2. The contrast between India and Singapore could not bring this point home more clearly: India, with a population 300 times that of Singapore and a gross domestic product ten times as large, has a cumulative foreign investment one-fifteenth that of Singapore's.

3. The discussion of this section focuses on standard market failures associated with externalities, missing markets, and competition. The Greenwald-Stiglitz theorems, which go beyond these standard market failures, establish that whenever information is incomplete, a discrepancy may exist between social and private returns. An important application of this principle arises in the context of capital markets: the ratio of the private return to the supplier of capital to the social return may differ markedly (even in the absence of the traditional market failures). For instance, private lenders may be able to appropriate a larger fraction of the total returns to real estate lending than to other lending. For a fuller discussion of the implications, see Stiglitz and Uy (1996).

4. This should be contrasted with the United States, where, for instance, in recent years top executives often received 100 times the pay of recent hires. Within rapidly growing areas of China, the degree of inequality is even lower, with managers getting paid approximately three times the amount received by workers.

5. Note that several of the countries went through an import substitution phase, during which they were very successful. It is questioned whether this phase was necessary, whether it helped (or hindered) the growth process, or whether it was primarily a consequence of the particular economic doctrines that were fashionable at the time.

6. The arguments here are not those provided by government officials at the time (or even subsequently). These focused on more immediate concerns: for instance, in the postwar era, with an overvalued foreign exchange rate, Japan was short of foreign exchange. To some extent, it saw export activities as offsetting the disadvantages exporters faced as a result of the overvalued exchange rate.

References

The word "processed" describes informally reproduced works that may not be commonly available through library systems.

Agrawal, P., S. Gokarn, V. Mishra, K. Parikh, and K. Sen. 1992. "Learning from Tigers and Cubs." Discussion paper. Indira Gandhi Institute of Development Research. Bombay. Processed.

Alam, M. S. 1989. *Governments and Markets in Economic Development Strategies.* New York: Praeger Publishing.

Amsden, Alice H. 1989. *Asia's Next Giant.* New York: Oxford University Press.

Aoki, Masahiko. 1988. *Information, Incentives, and Bargaining in the Japanese Economy.* Cambridge, U.K.: Cambridge University Press.

Arnott, Richard, Bruce Greenwald, and Joseph E. Stiglitz. 1993. "Information and Economic Efficiency." NBER Working Paper 4533. National Bureau of Economic Research, Cambridge, Mass. Processed.

Arnott, Richard, and Joseph E. Stiglitz. 1991. "Moral Hazard and Non-Market Institutions: Dysfunctional Crowding Out or Peer Monitoring." *American Economic Review* 81(March):179–90.

Arrow, Kenneth. 1962. "Economic Welfare and the Allocation of Resources for Invention." In National Bureau of Economic Research, *The Rate and Direction of Inventive Activity: Economic and Social Factors*. Princeton, N.J.: Princeton University Press.

Arrow, Kenneth, and Gerard Debreu. 1954. "Existence of Equilibrium for a Competitive Economy." *Econometrica* 22:265–90.

Carroll, Chris, David N. Weil, and Lawrence H. Summers. 1993. "Savings and Growth: A Reinterpretation." Paper presented at the Carnegie-Rochester Public Policy Conference, Bradley Policy Research Center, Rochester, N.Y. April 23–24. Processed.

Dasgupta, Partha, and Joseph E. Stiglitz. 1988. "Learning by Doing, Market Structure and Industrial and Trade Policies." *Oxford Economic Papers* 40:246–68.

Greenwald, Bruce, and Joseph E. Stiglitz. 1986. "Externalities in Economies with Imperfect Information and Incomplete Markets." *Quarterly Journal of Economics* 101(May):229–64.

———. 1988. "Pareto Inefficiency of Market Economies: Search and Efficiency Wage Models." *American Economic Review* 78(2):351–55.

———. 1992. "Information, Finance, and Markets: The Architecture of Allocative Mechanisms." *Journal of Industrial and Corporate Change* 1(1):37–63.

Itoh, Motoshige, Kazuharo Kiyono, Masahiro Okuno-Fujiwara, and Kotaro Suzumura. 1984. "Economic Analysis of Industrial Policy." *Kikan Gendai Keizai (Contemporary Economy)*. Tokyo.

Johnson, Chalmers H. 1982. *MITI and the Japanese Miracle*. Palo Alto, Calif.: Stanford University Press.

Kim, Jung, and Lawrence J. Lau. 1993. "The Sources of Economic Growth of the East Asian Industrialized Countries." Paper presented at a Conference on the Economic Development of Republic of China and the Pacific Rim in 1990 and Beyond, Stanford University, Calif. Processed.

Komiya, Ryutaro, Masahiro Okuno, and Kotaro Suzumura, eds. 1988. *Industrial Policy of Japan*. San Diego: Academic Press.

Krugman, Paul. 1994. "The Myth of Asia's Miracle." *Foreign Affairs* 73(November/December):62–78.

Kuznets, Simon. 1955. "Economic Growth and Income Inequality." *American Economic Review* 45(1):1–28.

Lau, Lawrence J. 1990. *Models of Development: A Comparative Study of Economic Growth in South Korea and Taiwan*. San Francisco: Institute for Contemporary Studies Press.

Murphy, K. M., A. Shleifer, and R. W. Vishny. 1989. "Industrialization and the Big Push." *Journal of Political Economy* 97(5):1003–26.

Nalebuff, Barry, and Joseph E. Stiglitz. 1983. "Prizes and Incentives: Towards a General Theory of Compensation and Competition." *Bell Journal* 14(1):21–43.

Okimoto, Daniel. 1989. *Between MITI and the Market*. Palo Alto, Calif.: Stanford University Press.

Pack, Howard, and L. E. Westphal. 1986. "Industrial Strategy and Technological Change." *Journal of Development Economics* 22:87–128.

Rosenstein-Rodan, P. N. 1943. "Problems of Industrialization in Eastern and South Eastern Europe." *Economic Journal* 53(June-September):202–11.

Solow, Robert M. 1957. "Technical Change and the Aggregate Production Function." *Review of Economics and Statistics* 39 (August):312–20.

Stiglitz, Joseph E. 1974. "Theories of Discrimination and Economic Policy." In George M. von Furstenberg and others, eds., *Patterns of Racial Discrimination*. Lexington, Mass.: D.C. Heath.

———. 1985. "Credit Markets and Control of Capital." *Journal of Money, Banking and Credit* 17(1):133–52.

————. 1987. "On the Microeconomics of Technical Progress." In Jorge M. Katz, ed., *Technology Generation in Latin American Manufacturing Industries*. New York: Macmillan Press.

————. 1988. "Technological Change, Sunk Costs, and Competition." In Martin Neil Baily and Clifford Winston, eds., *Brookings Papers on Economic Activity*, 3 (special issue on Microeconomics):883–947. Washington, D.C.: Brookings Institution.

————. 1989. "Markets, Market Failures, and Development." *American Economic Review* 79(2):197–203.

————. 1990a. "On the Economic Role of the State." In A. Heertje, ed., *The Economic Role of the State*. Oxford, U.K.: Basil Blackwell and Bank Insinger de Beaufort NV.

————. 1990b. "Peer Monitoring and Credit Markets." *World Bank Economic Review* 4(3):351–66.

————. 1991a. "The Invisible Hand and Modern Welfare Economics." In D. Vines and A. Stevenson, eds., *Information, Strategy and Public Policy*. Oxford, U.K.: Basil Blackwell.

————. 1991b. "Social Absorption Capability and Innovation." Paper prepared for Korean Development Institute 20th Anniversary Symposium, Seoul. June. Processed.

————. 1994a. "The Role of the State in Financial Markets." In Michael Bruno and Boris Pleskovic, eds., *Proceedings of the World Bank Annual Conference on Development Economics 1993*. Washington, D.C.: World Bank.

————. 1994b. *Whither Socialism?* Cambridge, Mass: MIT Press.

Stiglitz, Joseph E., and Marilou Uy. 1996. "Financial Markets, Public Policy, and the East Asian Miracle." *World Bank Research Observer* 11(2):249–76.

Stiglitz, Joseph E., and Andrew Weiss. 1983. "Incentive Effects of Termination: Applications to the Credit and Labor Markets." *American Economic Review* 73(December):912–27.

Vogel, Ezra F. 1991. *The Four Little Dragons: The Spread of Industrialization in East Asia*. Cambridge, Mass.: Harvard University Press.

Wade, Robert. 1990. *Governing the Market: Economic Theory and the Role of the Government in East Asian Industrialization*. Princeton, N.J.: Princeton University Press.

World Bank. 1993. *The East Asian Miracle: Economic Growth and Public Policy*. New York: Oxford University Press.

Young, Alwyn. 1993. "Lessons from the East Asian NICs: A Contrarian View." NBER Working Paper 4482. National Bureau of Economic Research, Cambridge, Mass. Processed.

————. 1995. "Growth without Scale Effects." NBER Research Working Paper 4211. National Bureau of Economic Research, Cambridge, Mass. Processed.

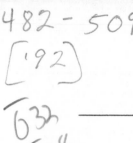

[20]

National Innovation Systems:
*A Retrospective on a Study**

RICHARD R. NELSON

(School of International and Public Affairs, Columbia University, 420 West 118th
Street, New York, NY 10027, USA)

1. *What is the Study About?*

In this essay I will describe a large comparative study of national innovation systems that has just been completed, tell something of what motivated the study and how it was organized and undertaken, and highlight some of the more interesting findings. This is a difficult task, for the project was not only large but also complex.

The heart of the project consisted of studies of 15 countries, including all of the prominent large market oriented industrialized ones, several smaller high income countries, and a number of newly industrializing states. The studies were carefully designed, developed, and written to illuminate the institutions and mechanisms supporting technical innovation in the various countries, the similarities and differences across countries and how these came to be, and to permit at least preliminary discussion of how the differences seemed to matter. No other project has come remotely close to treating the range of countries considered here. Moreover, many of the individual studies stand as major contributions in their own right to the

*A volume, containing the full study, will be published in the fall of 1992, under the title of *National Innovation Systems: A Comparative Study*, by the Oxford University Press. Funding for the project was provided by the American Enterprise Institute, Columbia University's Center for Japanese Economy and Business, the German Marshall Fund of the United States, and the Sloan Foundation through its support of the Consortium on Competition and Cooperation. Conferences which played an essential role in the progress of the project were hosted by the School of International and Public Affairs of Columbia University, MERIT, SPRU, and CEPR of Stanford University.

The authors of the country studies were: US—David Mowery and Nathan Rosenberg; Japan—Akira Goto and Hiroyuki Odagiri; Germany—Otto Keck; UK—William Walker; France—Francois Chesnais; Italy—Franco Melerba; Denmark and Sweden—Charles Edquist and Bengt Åke Lundvall; Canada—Donald McFetridge; Australia—Robert Gregory; Korea—Linsu Kim; Taiwan—Chi-ming Hou and San Gee; Brazil—Carl Dahlman and Claudio Frischtak; Argentina—Jorge Katz; Israel—Morris Teubal.

I was joined on the steering committee that guided the project by Claude Barfield, Carl Dahlman, Giovanni Dosi, Christopher Freeman, Luc Soete, Hugh Patrick, Keith Pavitt, and Nathan Rosenberg.

Industrial and Corporate Change   Volume 1   Number 2   1992

——————— *National Innovation Systems: A Retrospective on a Study* ———————

understanding of the innovation systems of particular countries, going far behind anything written on those countries before. To describe and summarize in compact form what came out of the project simply is impossible. I must pick and choose and hint.

The project was undertaken to try to throw some light on a very complicated and important set of issues. The slowdown of growth since the early 1970s in all of the advanced industrial nations, the rise of Japan as a major economic and technological power, the relative decline of the United States, and widespread concerns in Europe about being behind both, has led to a rash of writing and new policy departures concerned with supporting the technical innovative powers of national firms. At the same time the enhanced technical sophistication of Korea, Taiwan, and other newly industrializing countries (nics) has broadened the range of nations whose firms are competitive players in fields which used to be the preserve of only a few, and led other nations who today have a weak manufacturing sector to wonder how they might emulate the performance of the successful nics. There clearly is a new spirit of what might be called 'techno-nationalism' in the air, combining a strong belief that the technological capabilities of a nation's firms are a key source of their competitive performance, with the belief that these capabilities are in a sense national, and can be built by national action.

It is this climate that has given rise to the current strong interest in national innovation systems, their similarities and differences, and in the extent and manner that these differences explain variation in national economic performance. There now may be more awareness and research about such national differences than on any other area where comparative institutional analysis would seem interesting and illuminating.

The project on which I report here was born of this intellectual climate, and came out of belief on the part of the participants that much of the writing and argument were somewhat hyped, and rather haphazard. Moreover, many of the allegedly comparative studies in fact had concentrated on one country—in recent times usually Japan—with the comparison with other countries largely implicit. The actual comparative studies tended to be of two or a very small group of countries. This limitation struck the project participants as particularly serious in view of the absence of a well articulated and verified analytic framework linking institutional arrangements to technological and economic performance. In the absence of such a framework there were (and are) only weak constraints on the inclinations of analysts to draw possibly spurious causal links between differences in institutional structures that clearly are there, and differences in performance which clearly are there also. Different authors have focused on different things and made different kinds of arguments about why this feature or that was an important factor behind strong or weak performance. A broadening of a set of countries considered simultaneously seemed to us an important way to tighten these constraints by enlarging the number of 'points' that a causal theory had to 'fit'.

The way I have been putting the matter clearly signals that the orientation of this project has been to carefully describe and compare, and try to understand, rather than to theorize first and then attempt to prove or calibrate the theory. However, a comparative study like this requires, at the least, some agreement on basic terms and concepts.

There is, first of all, the concept of a national innovation system itself. Each of the terms can be interpreted in a variety of ways, and there is the question of whether, in a world where technology and business are increasingly transnational, the concept as a whole makes much sense.

Consider the term 'innovation'. In this study we, the participants, interpret the term rather broadly, to encompass the processes by which firms master and get into practice product designs and manufacturing processes that are new to them, whether or not they are new to the universe, or even to the nation. We do so for several reasons. First, the activities, and investments associated with becoming the leader in the introduction of a new product or process, and those associated with staying near the head of the pack, or catching up, are much less sharply distinguishable than commonly is presumed. Second, much of the interest in innovative capability is tied to concern about economic performance, and here it is certainly the broader concept rather than the narrower one (the determinants of being first) that matters. This means that our orientation is not limited to the behavior of firms at the world's technology forefront, or to institutions doing the most advanced scientific research, although in some countries the focus is here, but is more broadly on the factors influencing national technological capabilities.

Then there is the term 'system'. While to some the word connotes something that is consciously designed and built, this is far from the orientation here. Rather the concept here is of a set of institutions whose interactions determine the innovative performance, in the sense above, of national firms. There is no presumption that the system was, in some sense, consciously designed, or even that the set of institutions involved works together smoothly and coherently. Rather, the 'systems' concept is that of a set of institutional actors that, together, play the major role in influencing innovative performance. The broad concept of innovation that we have adopted has forced us to consider much more than simply the actors doing research and development. Indeed, a problem with the broader definition of innovation is that it provides no sharp guide to just what should be included in the innovation system, and what can be left out. More on this later.

──────── *National Innovation Systems: A Retrospective on a Study* ────────

Finally, there is the concept of 'national' system. On the one hand, the concept may be too broad. The system of institutions supporting technical innovation in one field, say pharmaceuticals, may have very little overlap with the system of institutions supporting innovations in another field, say aircraft. On the other hand, in many fields of technology, including both pharmaceuticals and aircraft, a number of the institutions are or act trans-national. Indeed, for many of the participants in this study, one of the key interests was in exploring whether, and if so in what ways, the concept of a 'national' system made any sense nowadays. National governments act as if it did. However, that presumption, and the reality, may not be aligned.

The studies in this project are unified by at least broad agreement on the definitional and conceptual issues discussed above. They also were guided by certain common understandings of the way technical advance proceeds, and the key processes and institutional actors involved, that are now widely shared among scholars of technical advance. In a way these understandings do provide a common analytic framework, not wide enough to encompass all of the variables and relationships that are likely to be important, not sharp enough to tightly guide empirical work, but broad enough and pointed enough to provide a common structure in which one can have some confidence.

In particular, our inquiry was strongly shaped by our shared understandings about the complex intertwining of science and technology that marks the modern world. In the first place, we take the position that technology at any time needs to be recognized as consisting of both a set of specific designs and practices, and a body of generic knowledge that surrounds these and provides understanding of how things work, key variables effecting performance, the nature of currently binding constraints, and promising approaches to pushing these back. In most fields of technology a considerable portion of generic understanding stems from operating and design experience with products and machines and their components, and generalizations reflecting on these. Thus, consider a mechanic's guide, or the general knowledge of potters, or steel makers.

However, over the last century science has played an increasing role in the understandings related to technology. Indeed most modern fields of technology today have associated with them formal scientific or engineering disciplines like metallurgy, computer science, and chemical engineering. These kinds of disciplines are basically about technological understanding, and reflect attempts to make that understanding more scientific. An important consequence has been that, nowadays, formal academic training in the various applied sciences and engineering disciplines has become virtually a prerequisite for understanding a technology.

The intertwining of science and technology which began to occur a

—————— *National Innovation Systems: A Retrospective on a Study* ——————

century ago led to the rise of the industrial research laboratory as the dominant locus of technological innovation, first in the chemical and electrical industries, and then more broadly. These facilities, dedicated to advancing technology, and staffed by academically trained scientists and engineers, were closely tied to individual business enterprises.

It is important to understand that not all of the activities and investments made by firms in innovating are conducted in R&D laboratories, or get counted as R&D. The extent to which they do varies from industry to industry. Where firms are small, or where firms are engaged in designing products to order for individual customers, much of innovative work may not be counted as R&D. Nonetheless, while not always counted as R&D, and while often drawing extensively on external sources like universities and government labs, in most industries the lion's share of innovative effort is made by the firms themselves.

There are several reasons. First, after technology has been around for a period of time, in order to orient innovative work fruitfully one needs detailed knowledge of its strengths and weaknesses and areas where improvements would yield high payoffs, and this knowledge tends to reside with those who use the technology, generally firms and their customers and suppliers. Second, profiting from innovation in many cases requires the coordination of R&D, production, and marketing, which tends to proceed much more effectively within an organization that itself does all of these. These arguments hold whether one defines the innovation concept narrowly, as the introduction of a product or process that is truly new, or whether one defines it broadly as we do in the study, as the introduction of something that is new to the firm. Thus, all of the country studies paid a considerable amount of attention to the activities and investments being undertaken by firms.

The other two institutional actors with which all of the country studies were concerned are universities (and scientific and technical educational structures more generally), and governments and their policies as these influence industrial innovation. University and kindred institutions play two different kinds of roles in modern industrial innovation systems. They are the place where scientists and engineers who go into industry get their formal training. And in most (but not all) countries they are the locus of a considerable amount of research in the disciplines that are associated with particular technologies. To a much greater extent than commonly realized, university research programs are not undifferentiated parts of a national innovation system broadly defined, but rather are keyed into particular technologies and particular industries. University training, and research, that supports technical innovation in farming and the food processing industries simply is very different than university teaching and research that

——————— *National Innovation Systems: A Retrospective on a Study* ———————

supports the electronic industries. Thus, a major question in this study was how the research and teaching orientation of a nation's universities reflected, or molded, the industries where technological innovation was important in the nation.

And, of course, the individual country studies looked closely at the range of government programs and policies bearing on industrial innovation. As is the case with the activities of universities, many government programs are focused specifically on particular technologies or industries, and these obviously were of central interest. However, as noted in my earlier discussion of the meaning of an 'innovation system', given the broad way we are using the term innovation, innovative performance cannot be cleanly separated from economic performance and competitiveness more broadly. Thus in many cases the examination of government policies bearing on industrial innovation had to get into things like monetary and trade policies.

In designing the study the participants faced a quandary. From the discussion above it is obvious that a very wide range of factors influence the innovative performance of a nation's industries. The desire for comparability across the studies seemed to call for a rather elaborate list of things all country studies would cover. Yet it was apparent that the most interesting feature of a country's innovation system varied significantly across countries, and we wanted to illuminate these. Limits on resources and space foreclosed doing both. Our compromise involved two strategic decisions. First, we agreed on the limited list of features all country studies were to cover, e.g. the allocation of R&D activity and the sources of its funding, the characteristics of firms and the important industries, the roles of universities, and the government policies expressly aimed to spur and mold industrial innovation. Beyond these the authors were encouraged to pick out and highlight what they thought were the most important and interesting characteristics of their country. But second, considerable effort was put into identifying the kinds of comparisons—similarities or differences—that seemed most interesting and important to make. In general these did not involve comparisons across all countries, but rather among a small group where for various reasons comparison was apt.

The overall project covered three sets of countries where we thought in-group comparisons would be most interesting. The first group consisted of six large high income countries—the US, Japan, Germany, France, Italy, and the United Kingdom. The second group consisted of four small high income countries, with a strong agricultural or resource base—Denmark, Sweden, Canada, and Australia. Finally, included in the set were five lower income countries—Korea, Taiwan, Argentina, Brazil, and Israel. While we were interested in the similarities and differences across groups, a con-

——————— *National Innovation Systems: A Retrospective on a Study* ———————

siderable amount of thought and effort went into laying out within group comparisons.

As I said at the offset, it is impossible to summarize what came out of this study; I can only give some highlights and a flavor. In the following section I highlight some of the key similarities and differences across countries, and our assessments about what lies behind the differences. Then I report our tentative judgements on what distinguishes systems where firms are strong and innovative from systems where they are not; most of us believe that this has somewhat less to do with aggressive 'technology policies' than current fashion might have one believe. Indeed, many of us believe that the current focus of discussion 'high tech' industries may exaggerate the importance to a nation of having strong national firms in those fields. An important reason is that firms in these industries increasingly are going transnational, which brings me to my next topic: what remains of national systems in a world where business and technology increasingly are transnational? I conclude by reflecting on the acrimonious aspects of national technology policies.

2. *Country Differences and What Lies Behind Them*

To compare means to identify similarities as well as differences. Certainly the broad view of technical innovation which I laid out above and which guided this study implies certain commonalities. That view applies to economies in which profit oriented firms are the principal providers of goods and services, and where central planning and control is weak. These conditions hold in all of the countries in our set, although in some a certain portion of industry is nationalized, and in some governments do try to mold the shape of industrial development in at least a few economic sectors. In all of the countries in our set, the bulk of education, including university education, is conducted in public institutions. In all, the government is presumed to have major responsibility for the funding of basic research, although there are major differences across countries regarding how much of that they do, and where basic research is mostly carried out. From one point of view, what is most striking about the country comparisons is the amount of basic similarity. Had the old Soviet Union been included in the set, or China, or Nigeria, the matter would have been different. But, as it is, the differences across our set of countries must be understood as differences of individuals of the same species.

Within our group of countries, it would appear that to a considerable extent the differences in the innovation systems reflect differences in economic and political circumstances and priorities. First of all, size and the degree of affluence matter a lot. Countries with large affluent populations can provide a market for a wide range of manufacturing industries and may engage in other activities that 'small' countries cannot pursue, at least with any chance of success, and their innovation systems will reflect this. Low income countries tend to differ from high income ones in the kinds of economic activities in which they can have comparative advantage, and in internal demand patterns, and these differences profoundly shape the nature of technical innovation that is relevant.

The threefold division of our countries into large high income industrial nations, small high income countries, and low income countries thus turned out to be a useful first cut analytic separation. By and large the economies in the first group had a significantly larger fraction of their economies in R&D intensive industry, like aerospace, electronics, and chemical products, which require large sales to be economic, than economies in the second and third groups. There are some anomalies, at the surface at least. Thus, Sweden in the second group and Israel and Korea in the third have higher R&D to GNP ratios than several of the countries in the first group. Some of the mystery disappears when Israel's ambitious military R&D is recognized, and Sweden's and Korea's strong presence in several R&D intensive industries that live largely through export. Both of the latter two countries also have strong defense programs and this also undoubtedly affected their R&D intensities. There are certain interesting similarities of countries in different groups— Japan and Korea for example. However, by and large there were strong intragroup similarities, and strong inter-group differences. Thus the US and Japan look much less different than advertised, once one brings Australia and Israel into the comparison set. And much of the US–Japan difference can be seen to reside in differences in their resource bases and defence policies.

Whether or not a country had rich natural resources or ample farming land clearly is another important variable influencing the shape of its innovation system. It turns out that all our 'small' high income countries also were well endowed in this respect. Among the large high income countries the US was far and away the best endowed here. Countries that possess resources and good farm land face a different set of opportunities and constraints than countries without these assets.

Countries that lack them must import resources and farm products, which forces their economies towards export-oriented manufacturing, and an innovation system that supports this. One sees this strikingly in the cases of Germany, Japan, and Korea. On the other hand, countries with a rich resource base can support relatively high living standards with farm products and resources and the affiliated industries providing exports to pay for imported manufactured goods. The countries that have been able to do this—Denmark, Canada, and Australia stand out in our set—have developed

——————— National Innovation Systems: A Retrospective on a Study ———————

significant publicly supported R&D programs to back these industries. So also has the United States. While effective agriculture and resource exploitation does require R&D, compared with 'high tech' industry the R&D intensity here is low.

The discussion above suggests that, to some extent at least, a nation's innovation system is shaped by factors like size and resource endowments that affect comparatively advantage at a basic level. But it also is true that a nation's innovation system tends to reflect conscious decisions to develop and sustain economic strength in certain areas, that is, it builds and shapes comparative advantage.

Some of the project members were surprised to find in how many of our countries national security concerns had been important in shaping innovation systems.

In the first place, among high income countries defense R&D accounts for the lion's share of the differences among the countries in government funding of industrial R&D, and the presence of large military programs thus explains why government industrial R&D spending in the US, and the UK and France, is so much greater than in Japan and Germany. In the second place, the industries from which the military procures tend to be R&D intensive, whether the firms are selling to the military or to civilians. The study of Japan shows clearly that the present industrial structure was largely put in place during an era when national security concerns were strong. This structure, now oriented to civilian products, is one of the reasons for Japan's high R&D intensity. It is possible that, to some extent, this argument also holds for Germany.

Interestingly, every one of the low income countries in our study has been influenced by national security concerns, or a military government, or both. Thus, much of high tech industry in Israel is largely oriented towards the military. The broad economic policies, industrial structures, and innovation systems of Korea and Taiwan were molded in good part by their felt need to have a capable military establishment. The pockets of 'high tech' atop the basically backward Brazilian and Argentine economies clearly reflect the ambitions of their military elites.

As noted, all of the countries in our set are, basically, ones in which firms are mostly expected to fend for themselves in markets that are, to a considerable extent, competitive. However, all are marked by significant pockets of government overview, funding, and protection. In our countries with big military procurement programs, the defense industries are the largest such pocket. However, in many of our countries government support and protection extends into space, electric power, telecommunications, and other areas of civilian 'high tech'. While by and large these extensions are most significant

──────── *National Innovation Systems: A Retrospective on a Study* ────────

in the big high income countries, Canada has large public programs in electric power and telecommunications, and so does Sweden.

There clearly are significant differences across the nations regarding beliefs about which kind of a role government should play in shaping industrial development. The role of military concerns clearly is a powerful variable influencing this. But a relatively active government also is associated with 'late' development, along the lines put forth by Alexander Gerschenkron (1962). Aside from the arena of national security and related areas, Britain and the US are marked by restrained government. On the other hand, all of our low income late developing countries have quite active governments. However, there certainly are exceptions to this rule. France's Etatism goes way back in history, and while Italy is a late developer except during the Fascist era her government has been weak.

The above discussion suggests that one ought to see considerable continuity in a nation's innovation system, at least to the extent that the basic national objectives and conditions have a continuity. Although this proposition clearly has only limited bearing on the countries in our set that only were formed or gained independence in recent years—Israel, Taiwan, Korea— even here one can see a certain consistency within these nation's short histories. All of these countries have experienced dramatic improvements in living standards since the 1950s, and their industrial structure has changed markedly. Their innovation systems have changed as well, but as our authors tell the story, in all of these countries today's institutional structures supporting innovation clearly show their origins in those of 30 years ago.

For countries with longer histories, the institutional continuity is striking, at least to the study authors. Thus one can see many of the same things in 1990 in France, Germany, and Japan, that were there in 1890, and this despite the enormous advances in living standards and shifts in industrial structure all have experienced, and the total defeat of the latter two nations in World War II and the stripping away of their military. Britain of 1990 continues many of the institutional characteristics of Britain in 1890, although they seemed to work better then than now.

Indeed, in this author's eyes, of the countries with long histories the one that has changed most institutionally is the US. The governmental roles in funding university research, and defense R&D, that came into place only after World War II, had little precedent prior to the War, and profoundly changed the nature of the innovation system.

3. *What is Required for Effective Innovative Performance?*

We have defined innovation broadly so that the term basically stands for what is required of firms if they are to stay competitive in industries where technological advance is important. Such industries span a large share of manufacturing, many service sectors such as air transport, telecommunications, and medical care, and important areas of agriculture and mining. Staying competitive means different things in different national contexts. For firms located in high wage countries, being competitive may require having a significantly more attractive product or a better production process than firms in low wage countries. For the latter, being competitive may not require being at the forefront. Indeed much of innovation in low income countries involves the learning of foreign technology, its diffusion, and perhaps its adaption to local circumstances of demand or production. But in either kind of country, if technological advance in the industry is significant, staying competitive requires continuing innovation.

We, the group that has produced the country studies, think we can discern several basic features that are common to effective innovative performance, and which are lacking or attenuated in countries where innovation arguably has been weak. First, the firms in the industry were highly competent in what mattered to be competitive in their lines of business. Generally this involved competence in product design and production, but usually also effective overall management, ability to assess consumer needs, links into upstream and downstream markets, etc. In most cases significant investments lay behind these firm capabilities. All this enabled firms to master the relevant technologies and other practices needed to compete and to stay up with or lead with new developments.

This observation does contain a hint of tautology, but is better regarded as confirmation of a point stressed above, that the bulk of the effort in innovation needs to be done by the firms themselves. While they may draw on outside developments, significant internal effort and skill is needed to complement and implement these. One cannot read the studies of Japan, Germany, Italy, Korea, and Taiwan, all arguably countries where firms have displayed strong performance in certain industries, without being impressed by the authors' description of the firms. On the other hand, one is impressed the other way by the authors' commentary on the weaknesses of firms in certain industries in Britain, France, Australia, Argentina, and Israel.

Being strong did not necessarily mean that firms were large. Economists long have understood that while in some industries a firm has to be large in order to be a capable innovator, in other industries this is not the case. Many of the strong Italian, Taiwanese, and Danish firms are relatively small. Nor does it mean that the firms spend heavily on formal R&D. In some fields like electronics generally it did, at least for firms in our first two groups of countries; however, in Korea and Taiwan electronics firms often were doing

——————— *National Innovation Systems: A Retrospective on a Study* ———————

well with technical efforts mostly oriented towards 'reverse engineering'. The Italian textile industry is strong on fashion and design, and are highly innovative in these respects, but little of that work is accounted as R&D. Nor does it imply that the firms were not benefiting from publicly funded R&D programs, or favored procurement status. However, as our authors describe it, the bulk of the inputs and direction for innovative activity were coming from the firms themselves.

While our concept of strong firm entails ability to compete, in all of our cases becoming strong involved actually being exposed to strong competition and being forced to compete. As Michael Porter (1990) has noted, in a number of cases the firms faced strong rivals in their own country. Thus, the Japanese auto and electronics companies compete strongly with each other, American pharmaceutical companies compete and so do Italian clothing producers. However, it is not at all clear that this generalization holds for small countries, where there may be only one or a few national firms as Ericson in Sweden and Northern Telecom in Canada. For these firms most of their competition is with foreign rivals.

Porter (1990) and Bengt-Ake Lundvall (1988) have proposed that firms in industries where a country is strong tend to have strong interactive linkages with their upstream suppliers, who also are national firms. Our studies show many cases where this proposition is verified. The supplier networks of Japanese automobile firms, and the upstream-downstream connections in Danish agricultural product processing, are good examples. The cooperation of Italian textile producers with each other and with their equipment suppliers is another. However, there are a number of examples where the proposition does not seem to hold. Pharmaceutical companies, strong in Germany and the US, do not seem generally to have any particularly strong supplier connections, international or national. In aircraft production, the producers of components and sub-components increasingly are located in countries other than that of the system designer and assembler.

A similar observation is obtained regarding the proposed importance of a demanding set of home market customers. In many cases this holds. But in small countries or for industries that from their start have been export oriented, the main customer discipline may come from foreign customers.

While 'strong firms' are the key, that only pushes the question back a stage. Under what conditions do strong firms arise? As the discussion above suggests, to some extent the answer is 'spontaneously'. However, our studies do indicate strongly that aspects of the national background in which firms operate matter greatly.

One important feature distinguishing countries that were sustaining competitive and innovative firms was education and training systems that pro-

——————— *National Innovation Systems: A Retrospective on a Study* ———————

vide these firms with a flow of people with the requisite knowledge and skills. For industries where university-trained engineers and scientists were needed, this does not simply mean that the universities provide training in these fields, but also that they consciously train their students with an eye to industry needs. The contrast here between the US and Germany on the one hand, and Britain and France on the other, is quite sharp, at least as the authors of our studies draw the picture. Indeed these studies suggest strongly that a principal reason why the former two countries surged ahead of the latter two, around the turn of the century, in the science based industries emerging then is that their university systems were much more responsive to the training needs of industry.

While strength in 'high tech' depends on the availability of university trained people, industry more generally requires a supply of literate, numerically competent people in a wide range of functions outside of R&D, who are trained to industry demands either by the firms themselves (as in Japan) or in external training systems linked to firms (as in several German and Swedish industries). Countries differed in the extent to which their public education and training systems combined with private training to provide this supply, and the differences mattered. Thus, among high income countries Germany, Japan, and Sweden came through much stronger in this respect than Britain and Australia. Among developing countries the contrast is equally sharp between Korea and Taiwan on the one hand, and Brazil on the other.

The examples of Korea and Taiwan, and the other Asian 'tigers', can be read as remarkably successful cases of education led growth. As the authors tell the story, the ability of firms in these countries to move quickly from the relatively simple products they produced in the 1950s and 1960s to the much more complex and technologically sophisticated products they produced successfully in the 1980s was made possible by the availability of a young domestic workforce that had received the schooling necessary for the new jobs. On the other hand, the cases of Argentina and Israel suggest that the availability of an educated workforce is not enough by itself. The economic incentives facing firms must be such as to compel them to mind the market and to take advantage of the presence of a skilled work force to compete effectively with their rivals.

Another factor that seems to differentiate countries where firms were effectively innovative from those where they were not is the package of fiscal, monetary, and trade policies. By and large where these combined to make exporting attractive for firms, firms have been drawn to innovate and compete. Where they have made exporting difficult or unattractive, firms have hunkered down in their home markets, and when in trouble called for protection. As I shall indicate later, in some cases at the same time as firms

——————— *National Innovation Systems: A Retrospective on a Study* ———————

were competing abroad, they were working within a rather protected home market, so the argument is not a simple one for 'free trade'. Rather, it is that export incentives matter significantly because for most countries if firms do not compete on world markets they do not compete strongly. Up until recently the US possibly was an exception to this rule. The US market was large enough to support considerable competition among domestic firms, which kept them on their toes and innovative. No other country could afford the luxury of not forcing their firms to compete on world markets: now the US cannot either.

Of course much of the current interest in national systems of innovation reflects a belief that the innovative prowess of national firms is determined to a considerable extent by government policies. Above I have identified two features of the national environment in which firms live that seem to affect their ability and incentives to innovate profoundly, and which are central responsibilities of government in all of the countries in our sample: the education of the work force and the macro-economic climate. But what of government policies and programs more directly targeted at technological advance? This is where much of the contemporary interest is focused. How effective have been these kinds of policies?

In assessing this question in the light of the 15 country systems studied in this project, one strong impression is the wide range of policies targeted at technological advance. Thus, in recent years government policies towards industrial mergers and aquisitions, inter-firm agreements and joint ventures, and allowable industry wide activities, often have been strongly influenced by beliefs about the effects of such policies on innovative performance. Many countries (and the EC) now are encouraging firms to cooperate in R&D of various sorts. Similarly, in recent years a number of governments have worked to restructure or augment financial institutions with the goal of fostering industrial innovation; thus several have tried to establish their analogue to the 'venture capital' market that exists in the US. As suggested, these policies are a very diverse lot and differ from country to country. Our case studies do provide scattered evidence on them, but, simply because they are so diverse, I cannot see any strong generalizations that can be drawn.

Of course our country study authors were primed to look at government programs directly supporting R&D, and here I think the evidence collected is more systematic. It seems useful to distinguish between government programs that largely provide funds for university research or for research in government or other laboratories not tied to particular business firms, and government programs that directly support R&D done in firms. I consider each in turn.

Scholars of innovation now understood that, in many sectors, publicly supported research at universities and in public laboratories is an important part of the sectoral innovation system. A substantial share of the funding of such institutions goes into fields directly connected with technological or industrial needs—fields like agronomy, pathology, computer science, materials science, chemical and electrical engineering.

Do our country studies support the proposition that strong research at universities or public laboratories aids a country's firms in innovation, defining that term broadly as we have? Not surprisingly, the answer seems to differ from field to field, and to be sensitive to the mechanisms in place to mold and facilitate interactions with industry. All the countries that are strong and innovative in fine chemicals and pharmaceuticals have strong university research in chemistry and the biomedical sciences. A strong agriculture, and a strong farm product processing industry, is associated in all of our cases with significant research going on relevant to these fields in national universities, or other types of public research institutions dedicated to these industries. In contrast, Argentine agriculture is surprisingly weak, despite favorable natural endowments. The author of the study of Argentina lays the blame on Argentina's failure to develop an adequate agricultural research system.

Where countries have strong electronics firms, for the most part there is some strong research in university departments of electrical engineering, and this would appear to include Japan. Government laboratories have been important sources of new electronic product designs later taken over by firms in Taiwan. On the other hand, university research does not seem of much importance to technical advance in automobiles and aerospace.

Where universities or public laboratories do seem to be helping national firms, one tends to see either direct interactions between particular firms and particular faculty members or research teams, as through consulting arrangements, or mechanisms that tie university or public laboratory programs to groups of firms. Thus in the US agricultural experimentation stations do research of relevance to farmers, and seed producers, and have close interactions with them. Various German universities have programs designed to help machinery producers. Taiwan's electronics industry is closely linked to government laboratories. In all of these cases, the relationships between the university or government labs and the industry are not appropriately described as the universities or public laboratories simply doing research of relevance to the industry in question. The connections were much broader and closer than that, involving information dissemination, and problem solving. Universities and industry were co-partners in a technological community. While not important in all industries, a strong case can be made that such technology and industry oriented public programs have made a big difference in many fields.

——————— *National Innovation Systems: A Retrospective on a Study* ———————

These programs are far less politically visible than government programs that directly support industrial R&D, and the latter also tend to involve far more money. Countries differ significantly in the extent to which the government directly funds industrial R&D. And while most of such programs tend to be concentrated on a narrow range of 'high tech' industries, programs of this sort vary significantly and have been put in place for different reasons.

I noted above that, in most of our countries, military R&D accounts for by far the largest portion of government funding of industrial R&D. Analysts have been divided as to whether military R&D and procurement has been a help, or a hinderance, to the commercial competitiveness of national industry. Of the major industrial nations, the US spends by far the largest share of industrial R&D on military projects. A strong case can be made that in the 1960s this helped the American electronics and aircraft industries to come to dominate commercial markets, but that since the late 1960s there has been little 'spillover'. Britain has the second largest of the defense R&D budgets among our set of nations, but most of the companies receiving R&D contracts have shown little capability to crack into non-military markets. The same can be said for most of the French companies. While until recently civilian commercial spillover seldom has been a central objective of military R&D, except in the sense that it was recognized that selling on civilian markets could reduce the public costs of sustaining a strong military procurement base, it is interesting to try to understand where military R&D did lend civilian market strength and where it did not.

Analysis of the US experience suggests that civilian strength is lent when military R&D programs are opening up a broad new generic technology, as contrasted with focusing virtually exclusively on procuring particular new pieces of fancy hardware wanted by the military. Increasingly the US military effort has shifted from the former, to the latter. A much smaller share of military R&D now goes into research and exploratory development than during the 1960s, and a larger share into highly specialized systems development. And the efforts of the other countries in our set who have invested significantly in military R&D—Britain, France, and Israel—have from the beginning focused largely on the latter.

Space programs and nuclear power programs have much in common with military R&D and procurement. They tend to involve the same kind of government agency leadership in determining what is done. They too tend to be concentrated on large scale systems developments. Spillover outside the field has been quite limited.

Government programs in support of company R&D in telecommunications, other civilian electronics, and aircraft may overlap the technical fields supported by military and space programs, and in some cases the support may go to the same companies. These programs also tend to involve the same blend of industrial R&D support, and protection from foreign competition. However, there are several important differences. One is that, compared with military R&D, the public funds almost invariably are much smaller. Indeed programs like Eureka, Esprit, Jessi, Fifth Generation, and Sematech, are small relative to industry funding in the targeted areas. Second, the firms themselves usually have a major say regarding the way the public monies are spent, and the projects are subject to far less detailed public management and overview than are defense projects. Third, these programs are targeted to firms and products in civilian markets, and while their home base may be protected through import restriction or preferential procurement, the hope is that the firms ultimately will be able to stand on their own.

Thus, while they involve a commitment to high R&D spending, other-wise these programs have much in common with other 'infant industry' protection programs, many of which have grown up for reasons with no particular connections with national security, or a belief in the importance of 'high tech', but simply because of the desire of a government to preserve or create a 'national' industry. Infant industry protection, subsidy, and govern-ment guidance are policies that have been around for a long long time. They mark French policy since Colbert. During the 19th century and through World War II the US was protectionist. The Japanese and Korean steel and auto industries, which were highly protected up until the 1980s, are more contemporary examples.

Do the infants ever grow up? Some do and some do not. The Japanese auto and electronics companies and the Korean Chaebol based enterprises are well known examples of presently strong firms that grew up in a protected market, but it also should be recognized that the American computer and semiconductor industries grew up with their market shielded from foreign competition and with their R&D funded to a considerable extent by the Department of Defense. After a period of such shelter and support, these firms came to dominate the world's commercial markets. Airbus may be another successful example. On the other hand, the country studies in this project give many examples of protected and subsidized industries which never have got to a stage where the firms can compete on their own. France's electronics industry is a striking example, but so also are the import-substituting industries of Argentina and Brazil.

What lies behind the differences? If I were to make a bet it is that the differences reside in two things. First, the education and training systems which in some cases did and in others did not provide the protected firms with the strong skills they needed to make it on their own. Second, at least in today's world, the extent to which economic conditions, including government policies, provide strong incentives for the firms to quickly start trying to compete on world markets, as contrasted with hunkering down in their protected enclave.

The picture of government policies supporting industrial innovation that I have been presenting highlights the diversity of such policies and programs, and their generally fragmented nature—some supporting research and other activities aimed to help industry in universities or public labs, others connected with defense or space or nuclear power, still others aimed directly at supporting or protecting certain industries or industry groups. This is the picture I draw from the country studies of this project. These studies play down the existence of active coherent industrial policies more broadly. The interpretation they present of the industrial policies of nations widely believed to have them is closer to that of modern day infant industry protection with some R&D subsidy, than to a well structured and thought through general policy.

Some readers will dispute this conclusion, arguing that the failure of the studies in this project of countries well known to have active coherent industrial policies to highlight them and their successes reflects a serious misjudgment of the authors. The authors of those studies respond by arguing that in fact government policies in their countries are highly decentralized, and by pointing, the case of Airbus an exception, to the very small fraction of industry R&D accounted for by government programs.

The skeptics rejoin that, while the policies did not involve massive public monies, they had a lot of leverage on private decisions and investments. The authors respond that government leverage has been exaggerated and that where strong policies have been executed, they as often lead to failure as to success. This clearly is the position taken by our Japanese authors on MITI. Without a more fine grained understanding of technological innovation than we now have, there is no way of resolving this debate in a way that will persuade all people.

4. *The Dispute over 'High Tech' Policies*

Above I stressed that the bulk of government R&D support, particularly support of industrial R&D, goes into 'high tech', a portion of it through programs expressly designed to lend their firms a commercial edge. Where these latter programs exist, they tend to be complemented by various forms of protection and, sometimes, export subsidy. They are motivated and justified by the argument that if an economy does not have considerable strength in 'high tech' it will be disadvantaged relative to countries that do.

But does this seem to be the case? The logic of the case and the evidence supporting it are not totally compelling.

National Innovation Systems: A Retrospective on a Study

For a firm or industry to be competitive in a high wage country certainly requires that it make effective use of skills, and technological and managerial sophistication, that are not readily available in low wage countries. The 'high tech', high R&D intensity, industries are of this sort, but there are many others as well. The definition of 'high' tech used by statistical agencies is directly tied to R&D intensity. However, we have stressed that an industry can be characterized by considerable innovation and not have a high R&D intensity. If firms are relatively small, or if there is significant design work aimed at particular customers or market niches, while considerable innovation may be going on, the firms may not report much R&D.

Further, while national programs have tended to focus on areas like semiconductors, computers, and new materials, where technical advance clearly is dramatic, much of the economic value created by these advances occurs downstream, in the industries and activities that incorporate these new products into their own processes and products—automobiles, industrial machinery, financial services, shipping. To do this effectively often involves significant innovation and creative innovation here may generate major competitive advantage, but not much in the way of large scale formal R&D may be involved. On the other hand, it can be argued that active government policies often can be more effective when aimed to help an industry take advantage of new upstream technologies than when oriented towards subsidizing major breakthroughs. A large portion of the clearly effective public programs discussed in the various country studies of this project were or are focused on bringing an industry up to world practice (this certainly characterizes many of the successful Japanese programs) or to spread knowledge about new developments (American agriculture and several of the government programs in Germany, Denmark, and Sweden).

Of course, the lure of 'high tech' to countries that know they must be highly innovative if they are to compete with lower wage countries is not based solely on statistical illusion. The discussion above acknowledges the special place of innovation in semiconductors, computers, new materials, and the like in the contemporary pattern of industrial innovation more broadly. Advances in these fields provide the building blocks, the key opportunities, for technical innovation in a wide range of downstream industries, from high speed trains to cellular telephones to commercial banking. Many observers noting this have proposed that a nation that wants its firms to be strong over the coming years in the downstream industries had better not let foreign firms control the key upstream technologies. This argument is prevalent in some newly developing countries, like Brazil, Korea, and Taiwan, as well as today's high income ones.

Another argument seems to square the circle. It is that a nation needs to

——————— *National Innovation Systems: A Retrospective on a Study* ———————

have strength in the downstream industries in order to provide a market for the key component industries. Thus, nations are supporting firms working on high definition television, and telecommunications, partly on the argument that in the absence of a home market a nation's semiconductor and computer firms will be disadvantaged. Similarly, public support of aerospace is justified partly on alleged stimulation to upstream technology.

Put more generally, the argument is that 'high tech' industries generate unusually large 'externalities', which flow to national downstream firms. This possibility is one of those modeled in what has come to be called the 'new trade theory' (see e.g. Krugman, 1987) which has developed a collection of arguments which support subsidy or protection as a means of gaining real national advantage. The fact that these industries are natural oligopolies who, in equilibrium, likely will support higher than average profits or wages, is another 'new trade theory' argument sometimes used to rationalize protection or subsidy, on the grounds that subsidy now will yield high returns later.

The authors of our country studies clearly have different, and perhaps mixed, minds about this matter. There is a certain plaintiveness expressed in the studies of the major European countries that, while doing well in some other areas, national firms are not doing well in these critical 'high tech' fields. The authors of the studies of Australia and Canada, on the other hand, seem to regard electronics envy as silly and expensive fadism.

While our country studies cannot resolve the issues, they can at least bring to attention three matters that ought to give pause to the zealots. In the first place, there does not seem to be strong empirical support for the proposition that national economies are broadly advantaged if their firms are especially strong in high tech, and disadvantaged if they are not. Thus, the United States continues to be strong (and a major net exporter) in a wide range of 'high technology' R&D intensive industries, but its economic growth has been lagging badly for nearly 20 years. Italy has very limited capacity in these industries, but its overall productivity and income levels have been growing briskly for many years. One can argue that France has had broad economic success more despite her efforts to nurture and subsidize her high technology industries than because of them. Japan is strong in DRAMS, but also in automobile production which accounts for much more employment and export value, and her efficiency in producing cars seems to have little to do with 'high tech'. And Canada, Australia, Denmark, and the United States all continue to be strongly competitive in industries based on agriculture or natural resources.

Also, as we have noted, the record of national policies expressly aimed to help high tech industries through support of industrial R&D and protection is very uneven. Indeed, the strongest positive examples occurred long ago, when the US government provided broad support for advances in electronics and aircraft, and the American edge here has not proved to be durable. Other successful cases are largely 'infant industry' cases (e.g. Japanese electronics during the 1960s and 1970s, and Korea during the early 1980s) where, as the companies became strong, the active and protective role of government diminished. Airbus may (or may not) be a contemporary success story. However, by and large the success record is not very good.

Moreover, and of crucial importance, firms and projects in the aircraft and electronics industries are rapidly becoming transnational. Partly this is because of a need to share very high up-front R&D costs, which can be met by joining with other firms. Traditional intra-national rivalries tend to make firms look for foreign partners. And this tendency, of course, is increased to the extent that governments try to keep the products of foreign firms out of domestic markets and to channel subsidy to national firms. Unless the home market is very rich and the subsidies very high, firms have strong incentives to somehow form links with other firms so that they have a chance at other markets.

Today, there probably is no other matter which so forces one to step back, and consider the contemporary meaning of a 'national innovation system'. To what extent are there really 'innovation systems', and to the extent that there are, in what ways are they defined by nation states?

5. What Remains National About Innovation Systems?

There obviously are a number of difficulties with the concept of a 'national innovation system'. In the first place, unless one defines innovation very narrowly and cuts the institutional fabric to that narrow definition, and we did neither, it is inevitable that analysis of innovation in a country sometimes would get drawn into discussion of labor markets, financial systems, monetary fiscal and trade policies, etc. One cannot draw a line neatly around those aspects of a nation's institutional structure that are concerned predominantly with innovation in a narrow sense excluding everything else, and still tell a coherent story about innovation in a broad sense. Nonetheless, most of our authors were able to tell a pretty coherent story about innovation in their country focusing largely on institutions and mechanisms that fit the narrow definition, with discussion of country institutions more broadly serving largely as a frame.

Second, the term suggests much more uniformity and connectedness within a nation than is the case. Thus, one can discuss Canadian agriculture pretty independently of Canadian telecommunications. R&D and innovation

─────── *National Innovation Systems: A Retrospective on a Study* ───────

in the American pharmaceutical industry and R&D an aircraft by American companies have little in common. And yet, one cannot read the studies of Japan, Germany, France, Korea, Argentina, and Israel, to name just a few, without coming away with the strong feeling that nationhood matters and has a persuasive influence. In all these cases, a distinctive national character pervades the firms, the educational system, the law, the politics, and the government, all of which have been shaped by a shared historical experience and culture.

I believe that most of us would square these somewhat divergent observations as follows. If one focuses narrowly on what we have defined as 'innovation systems' these tend to be sectorally specific. However, if one broadens the focus the factors that make for commonality across sections within a country, the wider set of institutions referred to above, comes into view and these largely define the factors that make for commonality across sectors within a country.

From the start of this project we recognized that borders around nations are porous, and increasingly so. Indeed, one of the questions that motivated this study was whether or not the concept of *national* innovation systems made sense anymore. I suspect that many of us come out on this as follows.

It is a safe bet that there will be increasing internationalization of these aspects of technology that are reasonably well understood scientifically. Efforts on the part of nations, and firms, to keep new understandings won in R&D privy increasingly will be futile. Among firms with the requisite scientific and technical people, the competitive edge will depend on the details of design, of production process, of firm strategy and organization, upstream-downstream connections, etc. Today, this is quite clearly the case in fields like semiconductors, aircraft, computers and automobiles. In these fields, there are no broad technological secrets possessed by individual countries or particular firms. On the other hand, strong firms have a good deal of firm specific know-how and capability.

It is also a good bet that differences across firms stamped into them by national policies, histories, and cultures, will diminish in importance. Partly that will be because the world is becoming much more unified culturally, for better or for worse. Partly it will be because firm managers and scholars of management increasingly are paying attention to how firms in other countries are organized and managed. And cross-country inter-firm connections are likely to grow in importance. Firms in industries where there are large up front R&D design and production engineering costs increasingly are forging alliances with firms in other countries, to share some of the costs, and to get over government-made market barriers. The establishment of branch plants in protected countries or regions is another mechanism. Thus, increasingly,

—————— *National Innovation Systems: A Retrospective on a Study* ——————

the attempts of national governments to define and support a national industry will be frustrated because of internationalization.

What will remain of 'national systems'? The firms that reside in the country, for one thing, but people and governments will have to get used to dealing with plants whose headquarters are abroad. The countries of Europe have been struggling with this matter for some time, and many of the Latin American countries, too. The US is now having to try to deal with this, and Japan and Korea are beginning to. As yet, no large country seems to have made its peace with the problem, however. While in most countries, resident firms will be largely national, the presence of 'foreign' firms in important industries is something that nations will have to learn to cope with better.

We noted earlier the striking continuity of a nation's basic institutions bearing on industrial innovation. A good example is national education systems, which sometimes seem never to change in their basics. While top level scientists and engineers may be highly mobile, and some high level students will continue to take training abroad, below the PhD level, by and large, countries will be stuck with their nationals who are trained at home.

The nation's system of university research and public laboratories will continue to be, largely, national, particularly the programs that are specifically keyed to advancing technology or otherwise facilitating technical progress in industry, and with built in mechanisms for interacting with industry. These programs will have to work with foreign branch firms as well as domestic ones in certain fields. But the notion that universities and public laboratories basically provide 'public goods' and that therefore there are no advantages to firms that have close formal links simply does not fit the facts in many industries.

The nation's other public infrastructure, and laws, its financial institutions, its fiscal monetary and trade policies, and its general economic ambiance, still will be a major influence on economic activity, including innovating, and these are very durable. For large high income countries at least, the lion's share of private investment will continue to be domestic, and constrained by domestic savings. And nations will continue to have their own distinctive views of the appropriate relationships between government and business.

And these will strongly influence a nation's policies bearing explicitly on science and technology. From the evidence in this study, these must be understood as an agglomeration of policies directed towards different national objectives, each with a somewhat special domain in terms of the fields and the institutions most affected, rather than as a coherent package.

All can hope that there will be a significant diminution of defense programs, but it is a safe bet that military R&D will continue to account for the lion's share of government industrial R&D spending in the US, France, Britain, and Israel. It is likely, however, that there will be little commercial 'spillover'.

Outside of defense and space, a nation's programs of R&D support will in all likelihood continue to reflect both the needs of industry and broad attitudes towards what government should be doing and how. While there will be exceptions particularly when a defense connection is argued, the United States will continue to resist programs that directly fund industrial R&D, but will use the universities as the base for a variety of programs including some directly targeted at certain technologies and industries. European countries are likely to make much more use of programs that directly support civil industrial R&D, either in individual firms, or in industry wide research organizations. And in Japan, France, and various other countries, government agencies and high tech firms will continue to be quite close.

6. The Diversity of National Systems: Do We Need Some Standards Regarding What is Fair?

At the present time nations seem to be conscious as never before of their 'innovation systems' and how they differ from those of their peers. This consciousness of differences is leading in two very different directions.

On the one hand, it is leading to attempts on the part of nations to adopt aspects of other systems that they see as lending them strength. However, the experimentation is far from systematic, and it is highly influenced by perceptions that may have little contact with reality. Thus, the US and the European countries (and the EC) have been loosening laws that restrict interfirm R&D cooperation, and establishing programs to encourage and subsidize it in some areas. If the chapter on Japan has got it right, this may be somewhat ironic in view of the argument that the role in Japan's rapid post-war growth of cooperative R&D among firms in the same line of business probably has been exaggerated, and in any case is diminishing.

The LDCs are looking, with good reason, to Korea and Taiwan for models. But, aside from their strong support of education, high levels of investment in plant and equipment, and their pressure on firms to go for exports, these two countries have quite different innovation systems. In one, Taiwan, government research laboratories have been an important source of industrial technology; in the other, Korea, apparently they have not at least until recently. Korea has encouraged the growth of large industrial conglomerates, and resisted foreign ownership; Taiwan has not especially encouraged the growth of large firms and has admitted foreign firms selectively. But

——————— *National Innovation Systems: A Retrospective on a Study* ———————

both have been successful in building innovative competitive manufacturing industry based on foreign created technologies and other low income countries are trying to learn from their experience.

While today attempts at emulation are at a peak, they are nothing new. The study of Japan shows how earlier in the century the Japanese tried to pick and choose from European and American experience, and came out with something quite different. The Americans earlier tried to adopt the German university system, and actually built a very different one.

At the same time, perceptions of differences are leading nations to declare certain aspects of their rival's systems as illegitimate. Prominent Americans have expressed the opinion that MITI support and guidance of key Japanese industries, together with the special connections between Japanese firms and their customers and their sources of finance, amount to an unfair system, involving subsidy and dumping as well as protection. Similar complaints have been lodged against Eureka and Airbus. The Europeans complain about Japan, and about US programs like the SDI claiming that such large scale government R&D support, while aimed at a military target, is sure to build commercial advantages, and that that requires response on their part. The Japanese make similar complaints, but particularly about the import barriers being imposed by other countries. Some have gone so far as to argue that presently there is a war between competing national innovation systems that only can be resolved if there are new accepted standards regarding what is fair and what is not (see e.g. Ostry, 1990). Otherwise, nations will have to adopt the norm of managed trade in high technology products.

These two aspects of the current concern about differences in national innovation systems—attempts at emulation, and expressions of hostility— are opposite sides of the same coin. They reflect a combination of beliefs that a nation's performance in 'high tech' is vital to its broader economic performance and security, real uncertainty regarding just how to achieve high performance, and lack of agreed upon criteria for judging what are legitimate and illegitimate government policies.

In my view, which may not be shared by all of my colleagues, the current brou ha ha seems somewhat hysterical. There is little more reason to get upset over inter-country differences in the government's role in the support and protection in 'high tech' than about other areas where government policies differ sharply. For one thing, governments' anguish that their economies are fated to be surely disadvantaged if they do not have a 'high tech' industry of their own probably is unwarranted. For another, beliefs that strength in high tech is due largely to promotional government policies seem grossly exaggerated.

At the same time, the studies in this project show that the institutional

——————— *National Innovation Systems: A Retrospective on a Study* ———————

structures supporting technical innovation are complex and variegated. Technology and science interact in intricate ways. Both private for profit and public institutions play roles in virtually all arenas of technological advance and the efficient division of labor is not obvious. Simple minded arguments that private enterprise is what does industrial innovation and public institutions have little useful role in it are, simple minded.

In this area it is not totally clear what one should call subsidy or protection, as contrasted with legitimate public spending or coordination or regulation.

Economists are wont to draw the line in terms of whether or not government spending or regulation or guidance can be justified by market failure arguments. If so, while public action may give advantage to a particular national industry, such support can be argued to increase economic efficiency. If not, it is considered naked subsidy or protection, and is not to be condoned. Thus, while international trade theorists long have known that a nation could enhance the well being of its own citizens *vis-à-vis* those in other countries by selected naked subsidy or protection, the argument was that, under the theory then in vogue, for nations taken as a group, this was a negative sun game.

But the problem with this line of argument here is that 'market failure' is ubiquitous in the activities associated with industrial innovation, and thus subsidy or protection or guidance could be efficiency enhancing; hence the game of active industrial policy need not be negative sum. What has come to be called 'the new trade theory' recognizes some of this, nervously. If there are large 'up front' R&D costs, or significant learning through doing or using, or major externalities in certain activities like research and training, the simple arguments that free trade is 'Pareto Optimal' (in the parlance of economists) falls apart.

Of course 'market failure' is greater in certain activities than in others. Also, government competence and incentives are more likely to lead to productive programs in certain arenas than in others. Further, it is apparent that competitive protection and subsidy among nations can get beyond any level conceivably justified on grounds of 'efficiency'. It is in the interest of all nations to reign in such tendencies.

However, it seems unlikely that simple rules—for example that government support of R&D on public sector needs and for 'basic' research is efficient and fair and direct support of industrial R&D aimed to develop products for a civilian market is both inefficient and unfair—will carry the discussion very far. This argument certainly can be used to attack Airbus. But Europeans rejoin that government help was needed to overcome the huge headstart American companies had won in large part as a spillover from

——————— *National Innovation Systems: A Retrospective on a Study* ———————

military R&D, and can be justified economically both on infant industry grounds, and as a policy to avoid the development of a one company world monopoly. And what of government support for telecommunications R&D where telecommunications is a government service? Americans are prone to argue that telecommunications should be privatized, but there surely is limited agreement on that. One can try, and with some hope of success, to open government procurement to bids from foreign firms. However, what to one eye is blockage to competition in public procurement to another is a valuable close relationship between customer and steady supplier.

Nor are there clean lines separating 'basic research' from applied. No one seems to object to government support for research on the causes of cancer (although a breakthrough here may give the firms with close contact with the research a major advantage in coming up with a proprietary product). But what about research to advance agricultural productivity? To deal improve crops growing in a particular national soil and climate? Research on superconductivity, or on surface phenomena in semiconductors, conducted in universities? Conducted in an industry cooperative research organization? In a particular firm?

The argument about whether government funding of certain kinds of R&D is appropriate and efficient or unfair subsidy of course gets intertwined with arguments about protection, and about constraints in direct foreign investments. Here countries clearly disagree regarding what they regard as appropriate. The disagreements can be discussed, and agreements negotiated. However, it does not seem to me that the question of whether or not a protected industry is 'high tech' changes the nature of the discussion, or the stakes, that much.

All this is no argument against trying to establish some norms and rules regarding government policies bearing on industrial innovation, and in certain areas aiming for uniform or at least comparable policies. However, it is an argument against one nation or another getting self righteous that its ways are efficient, fair, and quite justified, and the policies of other nations are not. And it is an argument againt the belief that agreeing on ground rules will be simple, if only the advice of economists is heeded.

And finally, it is an argument against trying to impose too much uniformity. Countries differ in their traditions, ideologies, and beliefs about appropriate roles for government, and they will guard the differences they think matter. A central reason why this project was undertaken was, by expanding the set of countries considered, and by trying to enable comparisons where these seemed most interesting, to try to tease out what features of national systems seemed systematically to enhance innovation performance, and what features seemed useless or worse. My colleagues and I like to believe that we have learned a good deal. But there still is a lot of room for informed differences of opinion.

Given that there is, it is not simply inappropriate for one group or another to argue for its preferred uniformity. While (as this project testifies) it is not easy to tease out signal from noise, potentially we all can learn from each other about what seems to be effective and what is not.

References

Dosi, G., C. Freeman, R. Nelson, G. Silverberg, and L. Soete (1988), *Technical Change and Economic Theory*, Pinter Publishers: London.

Gerschenkron, A. (1962), *Economic Development in Historical Perspectives*, Harvard University Press: Cambridge, MA.

Krugman, P. (ed.) (1987), *Strategic Trade Policy and the New International Economics*, MIT Press: Cambridge, MA.

Lundvall, B. A. (1988), 'Innovation as an Interactive Process: From User–Producer Interaction to the National System of Innovation', in Dosi, G., C. Freeman, R. Nelson, G. Silverberg, and L. Soaete, *Technical Change and Economic Theory*, Pinter Publishers: London.

Ostry, S. (1990), *Governments and Corporations in a Shrinking World*, Council on Foreign Relations Press: New York.

Porter, M. (1990), *The Competitive Advantage of Nations*, The Free Press: New York.

Name Index

The International Library of Critical Writings in Economics

The Economics of Intellectual Property
Ruth Towse and R.W. Holzhauer

Path Dependence
Paul David

The Political Economy of Development
Amitava Krishna Dutt

The Economics of Contracts
Lars A. Stole

New Developments in Exchange Rate Economics
Mark P. Taylor

The Political Economy of Monetary Union
Paul De Grauwe

New Institutional Economics
Claude Ménard

The Economics of Politics
Dennis C. Mueller

The Economics of Barter and Countertrade
Bernard Yeung and Rolf Mirus

The Economics of Sport
Andrew Zimbalist